Early Reading Assessment

Early Reading Assessment

a practitioner's handbook

Natalie Rathvon

THE GUILFORD PRESS
New York London

A Division of Guilford Publications, Inc.
72 Spring Street, New York, NY 10012
www.guilford.com

Printed in the United States of America

This book is printed on acid-free paper.

Last digit is print number: 9 8 7 6 5 4 3 2 1

Library of Congress Cataloging-in-Publication Data

Rathvon, Natalie.
Early reading assessment : a practitioner's handbook / by Natalie Rathvon.
p. cm.
Includes bibliographical references and index.
ISBN 1-57230-984-9 (hardcover)
1. Reading (Primary)–Ability testing. I. Title.
LB1525.75.R38 2004
372.48–dc22

2003017065

To Elisabeth Catherine Dennis, a future reader

About the Author

Natalie Rathvon, PhD, earned a doctorate in education from George Mason University and a doctorate in clinical psychology from George Washington University, where she is an assistant clinical professor of psychology and supervises graduate students in school-based placements. She provides consultation and staff development to a variety of schools and agencies, including the Archdiocese of Washington, DC, where she is project director for the Early Reading Initiative, and the Center City Consortium Schools, where she is director of accountability and assessment. Dr. Rathvon is the author of *Effective School Interventions: Strategies for Enhancing Achievement and Social Competence* (1999, Guilford Press) and *The Unmotivated Child: Helping Your Underachiever Become a Successful Student* (1996, Simon & Schuster).

Contents

PART I

Advances in Early Reading Assessment

Preface

In the last two decades, a converging body of research has yielded remarkable insights into the nature and determinants of reading acquisition and reading disabilities. Although in the not-so-distant past, traditional assessment and decision-making practices virtually precluded the diagnosis of reading disabilities before third grade, advances in specifying the marker variables of specific reading disability now make it possible to identify at-risk children in the early primary grades and to provide assistance before they have failed for several years. A consensus has been reached that phonological processing plays a critical role in the development of early reading skills and that phonological problems constitute the core deficit in most reading disabilities. *Phonemic awareness*—the ability to attend to and manipulate the individual components of spoken words—helps children to discover that printed letters represent sound segments of words and that regularities in sound–symbol relationships can be used to decode unfamiliar words. Numerous studies have demonstrated that measures of phonemic awareness can predict which children will have difficulty learning to read, even when they are assessed before formal reading instruction has begun. Other cognitive–linguistic abilities, such as phonological memory and rapid naming, and early literacy skills, such as letter-name and letter-sound knowledge, have also been identified as powerful predictors of early reading acquisition.

Although a voluminous body of research now documents the predictive power of phonological processing and other cognitive–linguistic abilities, the measures investigators have used to assess them vary from study to study and often have characteristics that make them impractical for examiners in nonresearch settings. Recently, however, empirically based instruments designed to screen young children for risk of reading problems and to assess reading and reading-related skills in early primary grade children have become available through commercial test publishers and other sources, such as university-affiliated statewide assessment programs. Test development has also been spurred by concerns about the low levels of reading proficiency demonstrated by American students over the past decade on the National Assessment of Educational Progress (NAEP; National Center for Education Statistics, 2000, 2002, 2003) and by the assessment mandates of federal legislation, including the No

Child Left Behind Act of 2001 and the Reading First initiative. Although the development of these measures is welcome news, the number and diversity of tests purporting to predict or assess early reading skills are creating a new set of challenges for practitioners seeking to select the most reliable, valid, and usable instruments for their own client populations.

PURPOSE

This book is intended to be a practitioner's guide to measures that have utility in the early identification of children at risk for reading problems and in the assessment of early primary grade students who are already displaying reading problems. The target group consists of children in the early primary grades, that is, kindergarten through Grade 2. The specific objectives of this book are as follows:

1. To provide an overview of critical issues in the field of early reading assessment.
2. To offer guidelines for evaluating the technical adequacy and usability of early reading measures.
3. To describe the cognitive–linguistic abilities and early literacy skills that predict reading acquisition and to identify measures assessing these abilities and skills.
4. To review measures with demonstrated or potential utility for identifying children at risk for reading failure and clarifying the nature of early reading problems.
5. To illustrate the use of these measures with actual case examples of early primary grade children.

This book is also designed as a resource guide for practitioners conducting reading assessments with early primary grade children. Most of the chapters include annotated lists of recommended print references to help practitioners locate other useful materials, and an appendix provides an annotated list of selected assessment and reading-related Web sites.

AUDIENCE

This book is written for practitioners in psychology and education and for graduate or preservice students in those fields. It should be especially useful for school administrators, assessment directors, school and clinical psychologists, reading specialists, classroom teachers, and others involved in designing early reading assessment programs or conducting reading assessments with early primary grade children.

ORGANIZATION OF THE TEXT

The text consists of an Introduction and two parts. The Introduction begins with a case example of a young poor reader. It then reviews the shift in the understanding of the proximal causes of reading problems from perceptual deficits to language processing problems, specifically deficits in phonological processing, and the delineation of a set of marker variables for reading disabilities. The Introduction also presents the criteria for test selection and the organization and format of the book. Part I includes three chapters. Chapter 1 discusses critical issues relating to early reading assessments, including early reading screenings and early reading diagnostic assessments. Chapter 2 presents guidelines for evaluating the technical adequacy and usability of early reading measures. Chapter 3 reviews 10 components with demonstrated utility in predicting reading acquisition, diagnosing reading problems, or both: (1) phonological processing, (2) rapid naming, (3) orthographic processing, (4) oral language, (5) print awareness and concept of word, (6) alphabet knowledge, (7) single word reading, (8) oral reading in context, (9) reading comprehension, and (10) written language. For each of the 10 domains, the discussion includes a description of its relationship to reading development, assessment issues related to that component, and types of tasks measuring it. One or two tables within each section list the measures assessing the component that are reviewed in this text, including single-skill measures and subtests from multiskill instruments and comprehensive assessment systems.

Part II consists of comprehensive reviews of 42 early reading measures and is divided into two chapters. Chapter 4 reviews 11 early reading assessment batteries, defined as instruments specifically designed to evaluate prereading, reading, and/or reading-related skills in early primary grade examinees and often intended for large-scale screening. Chapter 5 reviews an additional 31 instruments that measure 1 or more of the 10 components described in Chapter 3 but cover a broader age and grade range. Reviews are presented in the order in which the components are discussed in Chapter 3. Instruments measuring a single component are reviewed in the relevant section, whereas multiskill reading tests and multisubject instruments that include reading and reading-related measures for early primary grade children are reviewed in separate sections.

Following the text proper are three appendices. Appendix A lists contact information for test publishers, including citations or sources for research-based or state-sponsored measures. Appendix B presents an annotated list of selected assessment and reading-related Web sites, and Appendix C consists of a glossary of terms related to early reading assessment.

NATALIE RATHVON

Acknowledgments

I would like to express my sincere appreciation to the test authors and publishers for permission to reprint or adapt measures from the literature and tables from assessment manuals, for their assistance with technical and software questions, and for their feedback on the reviews of their instruments. Many thanks go to Chris Jennison, Senior Editor at The Guilford Press, for helping to make the preparation of this book an enjoyable process. I acknowledge with gratitude the continuing support of the Archdiocese of Washington Catholic Schools Office (especially Patricia Weitzel-O'Neill, superintendent, and Kathleen Schwartz, assistant superintendent for elementary schools), and of the Center City Consortium Schools (especially Mary Anne Stanton, executive director, and Don Tyler, director of technology). I extend special thanks to the faculties of St. Anthony and St. Francis de Sales Schools and principals Bill Eager and Matt Johnson, for hosting George Washington University graduate students in externship placements.

I also want to express my appreciation to the faculty and students of The George Washington University Department of Psychology, especially Rolf Peterson, director of the PhD clinical training program. This book would not have been possible without the support and assistance provided by The George Washington University Gelman Library staff, including Daniel Barthell, collection development librarian for the social sciences; Bill Mayer, assistant university librarian for information technology; Gale Etschmaier, assistant university librarian for public services; Quadir Amiyar and Glenn Canner of the interlibrary loan service; and Kim To of the consortium loan service.

As always, I happily acknowledge my gratitude to my husband, James, my dearest companion and collaborator.

List of Measures Reviewed

Measures marked with an asterisk are nonstandardized.

Introduction

JASON: ON THE ROAD TO READING FAILURE

In the spring of his first-grade year, Jason is already falling behind his classmates. He can identify most letter names and sounds in isolation, but he has trouble using that knowledge to read and spell, and he has only a small sight word vocabulary. His teacher notices that he is becoming inattentive and distractible, and she wonders whether he should be tested for attention problems or retained in first grade. Jason's parents notice that he is reluctant to read on his own or do his reading homework, and they wonder whether they should transfer him to a private school with smaller classes.

When I come into the classroom to observe Jason, the first graders are sorting rhyming word cards. While the other children eagerly arrange the cards in stacks on their desks, Jason looks down disconsolately at the cards scattered in front of him, but does not begin. One of the other students, noticing that I am looking in Jason's direction, leans over and whispers helpfully, "Jason doesn't like to read." Jason, overhearing the remark, nods his head vigorously in agreement, his eyes still fixed on the cards. When I meet with him later that day and ask how school is going, he acknowledges sadly, "Bad! I can't read!" At the age of 6½, Jason already views himself as a reading failure.

This true story (the child's name has been changed) has a happy ending. An early reading assessment revealed that although Jason's listening comprehension and oral expression skills were well developed, his phonological awareness skills were very delayed. He had also failed to grasp the *alphabetic principle*—the insight that spoken sounds have regular relationships to printed letters. He began receiving supplementary phonological awareness training from the school's reading specialist, and his parents worked with him diligently over the summer. By the beginning of second grade, Jason was well on his way to becoming a successful reader and had become much more enthusiastic about reading and school in general.

Only a few years ago, Jason's story might have had a very different ending. Reliance on assessment and decision-making procedures that identified children for special help on the basis of a discrepancy between cognitive ability and reading achievement made it virtually impossible for children to receive assistance until they had failed for several years. Now, with an understanding of the cognitive and linguistic markers of reading, assessment has shifted from an emphasis on IQ–achievement testing for the purpose of categorical labeling to the evaluation of reading and reading-related components for use in planning instruction and developing interventions. It is this component-based, intervention-oriented approach to early reading assessment that provides the framework for this book.

TARGET POPULATION

The focus in this book is on children in the *early primary grade range*, defined as kindergarten through second grade (ages 5 years, 0 months [5-0] through 8 years, 11 months [8-11]). The emphasis on assessment in the first 3 years of school is not meant to imply that reading assessments are not useful for older children. Rather, the selection of this grade range is based on longitudinal studies (Shaywitz, Escobar, Shaywitz, Fletcher, & Makuch, 1992; Shaywitz, Shaywitz, Fletcher, & Escobar, 1990) demonstrating that reading problems become much more resistant to treatment after third grade and on national and statewide reading initiatives that set a goal of having every child reading by third grade. Information obtained from reading assessments conducted during the early primary grades is much more likely to lead to positive changes in children's reading trajectories because prevention and intervention programs provided in those grades have the best chance of success.

CRITERIA FOR SELECTION OF MEASURES

This book does not attempt to review every available instrument that measures some aspect of early reading acquisition or reading achievement in early primary grade children. Instead, it focuses on measures that combine psychometric soundness with usability, and it describes them in sufficient detail that practitioners can evaluate their appropriateness for their own purposes, settings, and examinee populations. The measures included in this book were located by searching databases, journals, books, test catalogs, and reading-related Web sites and by contacting test authors and publishers. The four criteria for selecting measures are presented below.

Criterion 1: Designed to Assess the Reading or Reading-Related Skills of Children in Kindergarten, First Grade, or Second Grade

Only norm-referenced measures that included early primary grade children in the standardization sample or nonstandardized tests designed to assess reading or reading-related skills in early primary grade children were included. Standardized tests yielding age norms had to provide derived scores for some part of the target age range (i.e., children aged 5-0 through 8-11). Standardized tests yielding grade norms had to provide derived scores for some part of the target grade range (i.e., kindergarten through second grade). The age interval has been made broader than the grade range to include second graders who are older than their classmates because they entered school at a later age or have been retained.

Criterion 2: Potential or Demonstrated Utility in Predicting Reading Acquisition and/or Identifying Early Reading Problems

To be considered for inclusion, measures had to assess abilities or skills that have been identified by empirical studies to be predictive of or associated with reading acquisition or reading disabilities. Abilities and skills linked to risk for reading problems and/or reading disabilities include cognitive–linguistic markers, such as phonological awareness, rapid naming, and orthographic processing; oral language skills, such as listening comprehension and oral expression; and early literacy skills, such as print awareness, alphabet knowledge, single word and contextual reading, reading comprehension, and spelling. Many of the measures in this book are the products of long-term research programs by leading reading investigators who have made invaluable contributions to our understanding of the nature of reading development and reading disabilities.

Criterion 3: Adequate Psychometric Properties

Norm-referenced tests had to meet minimal standards of technical adequacy in terms of the psychometric characteristics critical to early reading measures, as presented in Chapter 2. Tests designed to provide information for educational decision making for individual students (i.e., eligibility for special services, interventions, and/or accommodations) have been held to a higher standard than measures designed for screening purposes. Criterion-referenced and nonstandardized measures had to be empirically validated, modeled on evidence-based assessment tasks, or both. Tests, like examiners, are never perfect, and all of the norm-referenced measures in this text have some technical shortcomings—in part because of the inherent difficulties in designing reliable and valid instruments for young children. In some cases, instruments that do not meet the specified criterion levels for psychometric adequacy for several or even the majority of technical characteristics have been included because they have been frequently used as predictor or criterion measures in reading research studies, are linked to empirically validated intervention programs, or are among the few currently available tests assessing a particular domain or subskill.

Criterion 4: Adequate Usability

In this text, *usability* is a general term referring to a set of factors related to examiners' ability to use tests successfully in their practice. These factors include cost, ease of administration and scoring, adaptability for use with culturally and linguistically diverse children, and linkages to intervention. Even if a test is psychometrically sound, it is unlikely to become part of practitioners' repertoires if its usability quotient is too low. For this book, the usability of each measure was evaluated in two ways: first, on the basis of information in the test manual(s) and the research literature; and second, through field testing with early primary grade children referred for reading problems or with groups of students participating in screening programs. Promotional materials and test manuals may describe an instrument as user-friendly, but a test's true usability can be discovered only by administering, scoring, and interpreting it in the context of assessments with examinees with a wide range of ability and skill levels.

TEST REVIEW ORGANIZATION AND FORMAT

Information about the measures reviewed in this text is presented in two formats. First, for each reading component described in Chapter 3, a summary of the characteristics of measures of that component–including single-skill measures and subtests from multiskill and multisubject tests–is presented in one or two tables within the relevant section. Measures that assess a variety of reading skills in a single subtest, such as Reading Basics on the *Basic Early Assessment of Reading* (Riverside, 2002), are not included in these component-specific tables. Second, comprehensive reviews of selected early reading measures are presented in Chapters 4 and 5. Chapter 4 reviews 11 early reading assessment batteries, defined as multimeasure instruments specifically designed to predict and/or evaluate reading development in early primary grade examinees. Chapter 5 includes reviews of 31 instruments that measure 1 or more of the 10 components described in Chapter 3 and target a broader age and grade range.

To help practitioners evaluate the relative merits of the measures more easily, reviews follow a standard format consisting of up to 13 components. Because of the tremendous diversity of the tests reviewed in this book, ranging from the 13-item *Test of Auditory Analysis Skills* (Rosner, 1975/1979) to the 42-test *Woodcock-Johnson III* (Woodcock, McGrew, & Mather, 2001a), the number of sections per review and the length of the reviews vary. Factors related to the number of sections and length include the scope of the test; whether it is norm-referenced, criterion-referenced, or nonstandardized; the amount of information available regarding its technical adequacy and other characteristics; the extent to which the test has been used in reading research; and its overall utility in early reading assessment. If no information is available for a particular section, it is omitted from the review. Test review sections are described below.

Overview

The first section of each review presents an overview of the measure, including the type of test (norm-referenced, criterion-referenced, or nonstandardized); administration format (individual, small-group, and/or classwide); skills measured; ages/grades for which it is designed; purposes; and test materials. If examiners must provide materials and equipment other than timing devices, audiocassette players, and writing implements, these are also listed. For a revised test, a summary of changes from the previous edition, with an emphasis on the relevance of those changes for early reading assessments, is included.

Subtests and Composites

This section describes the subtests and composites included in the instrument. For measures yielding a single score and screening batteries that do not identify separate tasks as subtests, this section is headed "Assessment Task(s)." Examples are provided for item formats and item types that may be less familiar to practitioners.

Administration

This section discusses administration procedures, including the time required; basals and ceilings, if relevant; and special administration considerations relative to early reading assessments, such as live-voice versus audiotaped delivery of phonological processing tasks. Any problems related to administration are reported here.

Scores

This section discusses scoring procedures, the types of scores yielded by the test, and any scoring issues or problems. Today's early reading measures yield a variety of derived scores, several of which may be unfamiliar to some practitioners. For that reason, Chapter 2 includes a table describing score types. For Rasch-model tests, such as the *Woodcock–Johnson III*, information on the additional score types yielded by thesc instruments is included in the reviews.

Interpretation

This section describes information presented in the manual and other supplementary test materials to assist users in interpreting the obtained results, such as descriptions of derived scores, tables for analyzing subtest and composite score differences, discussions of the relationship between score patterns and reading proficiency, and case examples.

Technical Adequacy

This section reviews five aspects of technical adequacy: (1) standardization, (2) reliability, (3) test floors, (4) item gradients, and (5) validity. Technical adequacy is evaluated in light of the standards set by the American Educational Research Association, American Psychological Association (APA), and National Council on Measurement in Education (1999) in the latest edition of *Standards for Educational and Psychological Testing* and by the APA (2000) Council of Representatives in the *Report of the Task Force on Test User Qualifications*, as well as according to specific criteria relevant to early reading assessment drawn from the testing literature. Across the 42 measures, the amount of technical data provided by test authors and publishers ranges from voluminous to none. Several early reading assessment batteries and norm-referenced tests have separate technical supplements or manuals in addition to examiner manuals, and reviews include information from both sets of manuals. A few measures, especially those intended for administration by classroom teachers or tutors, provide no information on psychometric characteristics. In these cases, any technical information available in studies using the measures or their prototypes is reported in the "Relevant Research" section below. For nonstandardized measures published in the literature, technical information from the original study is included in this section. The section on standardization is entitled "Test Development" for criterion-referenced and nonstandardized measures and "Norms" for measures with research norms. Characteristics of the norm group, including representativeness and recency, are reviewed for the entire age range covered by the test, whereas other characteristics are reviewed only for the early primary grade years as defined above.

Usability

As noted above, *usability* refers to a variety of considerations relevant to practitioner selection and use of tests. Usability factors considered in this section relate to the following areas: (1) test materials and format, including the readability of the manual or examiner guide; (2) cost; (3) time and effort required for administration, scoring, and interpretation, including the availability and utility of software scoring programs; (4) adaptability for culturally and linguistically diverse examinees; and (5) the degree to which assessment results can be linked to evidence-based interventions to address the identified deficits.

Links to Intervention

This section reviews information presented in the manual or other materials that can assist practitioners in increasing the educational relevance of the test results. Identification of at-risk children is only the first step in the effort to prevent early reading failure. Assessment must also lead to effective intervention if such children are to become successful readers. Assessment–intervention links provided in examiner manuals or other materials may include suggestions for remediation, lists of instructional resources, and citations of prevention or remediation studies in the literature. Test authors and manuals vary widely in the amount of information they provide in this area. Manuals for some of the measures included in this book provide little or no information on using test results for instructional and intervention planning. In contrast, statewide early reading screening batteries, such as the *Texas Primary Reading Inventory* (Foorman et al., 2002) and Virginia's *Phonological Awareness Literacy Screening* (Invernizzi & Meier, 2002a), are specifically designed to provide data for supplementary instruction and offer a wealth of instructional activities and resources in both print and Web-based formats. Several of the commercially published tests reviewed here, such as the *Lindamood Auditory Conceptualization Test–Revised Edition* (Lindamood & Lindamood, 1971/1979) and the *Process Assessment of the Learner: Test Battery for Reading and Writing* (Berninger, 2001), are directly linked to empirically based intervention programs.

Relevant Research

This section reviews selected published studies that provide information about the reliability and validity of the measure, especially research regarding the test's utility in identifying children at risk for reading failure or clarifying the nature of early reading problems. Several of the tests reviewed in this text are so new that no reliability and validity studies have yet been published in the research literature, whereas others have been used in numerous studies as predictor and/or criterion measures. For recently revised tests, selected research studies using the previous version of the test are included if they are relevant to early reading assessment and if the current version of the test does not differ too radically from its predecessor.

Source and Cost

This section identifies the test publisher and cost for commercially published measures, the source and cost for measures from noncommercial publishers, such as state departments of education and universities, or the citation for the original article in the case of instruments taken directly from the research literature. The five nonstandardized measures that are drawn directly from the literature are provided with minor adaptations in the reviews where they are covered, with the gracious permission of the journal publishers and/or test authors.

Test Reviews

This section lists test reviews published in the *Mental Measurement Yearbooks*, the primary reference for psychological and educational test reviews, and other assessment sources, such as test reference books, professional journals, and newsletters. For a recently revised test, reviews of the previous edition are listed if no reviews of the current version had been published at the time this book went to press. Although in some cases the latest edition of a test represents a substantial modification from the previous version, in other cases there is considerable overlap between current and earlier editions. Moreover, examining reviews of previous editions of a test is useful because authors and publishers attempt to respond to reviewers' criticisms in subsequent revisions. Test manuals often include reviewers' comments on previous editions of an instrument, along with an explanation of how problems identified by reviewers have been addressed in the latest version.

Summary

This component provides a summary of the overall utility of the measure in early reading assessment, including both technical and usability aspects.

Case Example

A case example is presented for each measure to illustrate its use in a practical context. Each case example includes a full score array or, for multisubject tests, an array of scores on reading and reading-related subtests, and an interpretation of the obtained scores, based on guidelines provided in the testing materials and my own assessment experience with early primary grade examinees. Case example formats differ somewhat, depending on the nature and scope of the measure and the scores yielded. Formats also vary in order to illustrate a variety of score presentation and report writing options. Case examples are based on actual early primary grade referrals, but identifying data and test scores have been modified to ensure confidentiality. For a few screening measures, classwide results are provided instead of or in addition to individual student results.

TEST CITATIONS, LISTINGS, AND SOURCES

To enhance readability and conserve space, test citations are provided the first time a test is discussed and, for each of the 42 measures, the first time the test name appears in the review, but not thereafter. For tests with multiple editions, a citation is given the first time each edition is mentioned, and only the name of the test is given subsequently. Tests reviewed in this text are listed alphabetically at the beginning of this book, as well as in the subject index located at the back. Contact information for test publishers and other assessment resources is given in Appendix A.

CAUTIONS

Although the field of psychological and psychoeducational testing is always in flux, with new tests and revisions of previously published instruments constantly appearing, there is probably no area in which change is occurring more rapidly than that of early reading assessment. Pressure from many directions, including federal legislation, federally sponsored reports on reading instruction and specific reading components, and national assessments detailing the dismal state of American students' reading proficiency, is accelerating the development of tests designed to identify young children at risk for reading problems. Moreover, technology is transforming assessment across numerous domains, including test development and construction; administration, scoring, and interpretation; data collection and analysis; and linkages to intervention. The end result is that early reading assessment is a moving target for authors and practitioners alike. Prior to publication, test reviews were sent to authors and/or publishers to provide an opportunity to give feedback and correct any inaccuracies, but any errors that remain are mine alone. I welcome comments, feedback, and corrections, as well as information regarding new and revised early reading measures from test authors, publishers, and practitioners for subsequent editions of this text, at rathvonn@centercityconsortium.org.

PART I

Advances in Early Reading Assessment

chapter 1

Critical Issues in Early Reading Assessment

Two and a half decades of research have documented the importance of early intervention in preventing reading failure, as well as the disastrous academic and social consequences associated with delaying assistance until children have failed in school for several years. The need to intervene in the early primary grades is underscored by the most recent results of the National Assessment of Educational Progress (NAEP). On the 2002 NAEP reading assessment, 36% of fourth graders scored at the Below Basic level in reading, indicating that they are unable to read and comprehend a simple paragraph from a grade-level text. Moreover, there are profound differences in reading achievement among racial/ethnic groups. Among African American, Hispanic, and American Indian/Alaska Native students, the respective percentages of fourth graders reading at the Below Basic level were 60%, 56%, and 49%, compared with 25% and 30% for white and Asian/Pacific Islander students (National Center for Education Statistics, 2002).

With the growing consensus regarding the cognitive–linguistic markers of reading acquisition and the development of empirically validated instruments to measure them, early identification would appear to be a relatively straightforward process. Nevertheless, many questions, controversies, and challenges remain regarding the most effective way of identifying children at risk for reading problems. This chapter focuses on seven critical issues related to early reading assessments. These issues, which are framed as questions for consideration, relate to the following areas: (1) the goals of early reading assessments; (2) the variables that should be measured, including the role of IQ tests in early reading assessments; (3) the role of teacher ratings in identifying at-risk children; (4) the most effective time(s) to screen for early reading problems; (5) the determination of at-risk status; (6) the assessment of linguistically diverse children; and (7) the interpretation and use of the results of reading screening programs.

ISSUE 1: WHAT ARE THE GOALS OF EARLY READING ASSESSMENTS?

Depending on their goals, early reading assessments can be grouped into one of two general categories: (a) early reading screenings and (b) early reading diagnostic assessments (see Table 1.1). *Early reading screening* refers to the evaluation of large groups of children with relatively brief, cost-effective measures to identify which students are at risk for reading failure and require intervention so that they do not fall behind their peers. Early reading screenings include assessments that are administered in kindergarten prior to formal reading instruction (sometimes called *preliteracy assessments*), as well as measures administered in first and second grade after formal reading instruction has begun. Some reading screening batteries are also designed for progress monitoring. *Early reading progress monitoring* refers to the repeated assessment of specific literacy skills to determine whether or not children

TABLE 1.1. Characteristics of Early Reading Screenings and Early Reading Diagnostic Assessments

Characteristics	Early reading screenings	Early reading diagnostic assessments
Goal	To identify children at risk for reading failure and monitor progress in early reading skills	To provide information about the nature and extent of reading problems for intervention planning and educational programming
Outcome	Additional instructional opportunities	Instructional interventions and/or remedial or special education programming
Examinee	All students in the population (e.g., classroom, school, district, or state)	Students identified as at risk by poor performance on screening measures and/or failure to respond to interventions
Skills measured	Reading precursors and early literacy skills	A more comprehensive set of reading-related cognitive–linguistic variables and early literacy skills; may include noncognitive and environmental variables
Time required	Relatively brief (e.g., 20–30 minutes per child)	Relatively lengthy; may include multiple test sessions over several days
Frequency	One, two, or three times a year (e.g., fall and spring)	Infrequent (e.g., every 3 years)
Examiner	Classroom teachers or trained paraprofessionals	Psychologists, special educators, reading specialists, or others with specialized assessment training
Administration format	May include group-administered as well as individually administered measures	Individually administered measures
Scores	Emphasis on a cutoff score indicating at-risk or not-at-risk status	Variety of norm comparison and proficiency-level scores
Sensitivity	Designed to identify the lowest performing children	Designed to differentiate among children across the full range of ability levels
Scoring and interpretation	Designed to be scored and interpreted by classroom teachers	Specialized training required for scoring and interpretation
Norms	Local norms (classroom, grade, district, or state) or criterion-referenced measures	National norms; may include some criterion-referenced measures

are demonstrating adequate growth, in terms of meeting either predetermined *benchmarks* (levels of reading skills necessary for success at the next stage of literacy development) or goals for individual students participating in early intervention programs. Early reading screenings thus have three major goals: (1) to identify children who are failing to make progress in acquiring crucial early literacy skills; (2) to monitor reading development to determine whether children are keeping up with grade-level expectations; and (3) to monitor the progress of individual students in prevention and intervention programs so that educational programming can be modified if needed.

Early reading diagnostic assessments are assessments designed to evaluate children's strengths and weaknesses in a variety of reading and reading-related areas and to obtain information for developing interventions. Early reading diagnostic assessments are typically administered after children have been identified as at risk for reading problems through some kind of screening process, but they may also be administered to children who have failed to respond to interventions after a specific period of time. Early reading diagnostic assessments have three major goals: (1) to determine the nature and extent of a child's reading deficits; (2) to determine the extrinsic and intrinsic factors contributing to the problems (e.g., ineffective instruction, reading-related cognitive deficits, etc.); and (3) to provide information for designing interventions to address the identified needs of the child. Table 1.1 summarizes the characteristics of these two categories of early reading assessments. In practice, however, it can be difficult to distinguish between the two types of measures. Several of the commercially published tests reviewed in this text are described as screening measures, although they have national norms; require substantial amounts of time to administer, score, and interpret; and include assessment tasks typically administered by psychologists. Some instruments include both types of measures, with one set of tasks designed for screening and another set for a more comprehensive evaluation of children who perform poorly on the screening section.

ISSUE 2: WHAT ABILITIES AND SKILLS SHOULD BE MEASURED IN EARLY READING ASSESSMENTS?

Although there are numerous instruments designed to screen for learning problems in young children, traditional screening tests have several characteristics that limit their utility in identifying children at risk for early reading failure (Bracken, 2000; Gredler, 1992, 1997). First, many of these instruments assess skills that have little predictive value for reading acquisition, such as perceptual and motor functioning. Second, they are often costly and time-consuming to administer. Third, because they assess general developmental skills rather than empirically validated reading precursors, it can be difficult to determine whether poor performance is the result of low cognitive ability, lack of literacy and language experiences, behavioral problems, or other factors (O'Connor & Jenkins, 1999). Finally, most traditional screening instruments lack *treatment validity*; that is, they provide little or no information that can be used to design interventions for addressing the deficits that have been identified (Majsterek & Ellenwood, 1990; Satz & Fletcher, 1988).

With the identification of a set of critical cognitive and linguistic markers for reading acquisition, however, a new era in screening has emerged, with the emphasis shifting from multiaptitude readiness batteries to instruments that target phonological skills and other variables predictive of reading acquisition. This text advocates a *component-based approach* to early reading assessment, in which the variables that have been empirically verified as predictors of reading acquisition constitute the core components of early reading assessments. These marker variables, along with the early literacy and language skills associated with successful reading development, form the 10 reading dimensions identified in the Preface and discussed in subsequent chapters: phonological processing, rapid naming, orthographic processing, oral language, print awareness, alphabet knowledge, single-word reading, oral reading in context, reading comprehension, and written language (including spelling). The emphasis on evidence-based reading predictors is not intended to imply that other variables are not important in understanding and remediating early reading problems. Because early reading problems are not only related to the child's characteristics but also develop and are expressed in environmental contexts, early reading assessments must take into consideration the ecological systems within which the child functions, including the classroom, school, home, and community. Other extrinsic and intrinsic factors, including instructional, familial, social, biological, and environmental variables, also have relevance for children's reading development and their ability to respond to early intervention (e.g., Torgesen, 2000; Vellutino et al., 1996). A discussion of these other components is beyond the scope of this book, however (see Fletcher, Foorman, & Boudousquie, 2002, for an assessment model that includes additional factors).

The Role of IQ Tests in Early Reading Assessments

Perhaps the greatest controversy in the debate regarding which abilities and skills should be measured in early reading assessments centers around the role of IQ tests. From the perspective of this book, the key questions regarding IQ tests are these: (1) to what extent does IQ predict children's ability to learn to read, and (2) to what extent does it predict response to remediation in poor readers? The reliance on IQ tests in diagnosing reading disabilities derives from an earlier period in learning disabilities assessment when, in the absence of a consensus on the specific cognitive and linguistic markers for reading disability, diagnosis became an exclusionary process. That is, IQ tests were administered to rule out the possibility that a child's reading problems resulted from low intelligence. This practice derived from the assumptions that the reading problems of children with average general intelligence (so-called *discrepant readers*) differ from those of children with low general intelligence (so-called *garden-variety* or *nondiscrepant readers*), arise from a different set of cognitive limitations, require different kinds of interventions, and have a different (better) prognosis (Torgesen, 2000). All of these assumptions have recently been challenged, however, with many researchers arguing that the IQ–achievement discrepancy model should be abandoned on a variety of grounds (e.g., Fletcher et al., 1998; Meyer, 2000; Sternberg & Grigorenko, 2002; Torgesen & Wagner, 1998). First, both discrepant and nondiscrepant readers exhibit phonological deficits and do not differ in terms of word-level reading skills. Second, IQ can be influenced by reading experience. Third, because it is difficult to demonstrate an IQ–achievement discrepancy in young children, reliance on the discrepancy model means that children are unlikely to be identified before third grade, when interventions are much less effective. Fourth, the discrepancy criterion has led to overidentification of children with higher ability and underidentification of children with lower ability, even though students with lower

IQs may be reading at much lower levels. Finally, the finding of an IQ–reading achievement discrepancy not only fails to specify the nature of the reading disability but also fails to yield information relevant to treatment planning.

IQ as a Predictor of Reading Skills

For beginning readers, the predictive utility of IQ depends on the reading subskill being measured. A large body of evidence indicates that when reading achievement is defined in terms of basic reading skills, including word identification and phonological decoding, neither verbal nor nonverbal IQ differentiates between poor and proficient readers at the early stages of reading acquisition. Instead, poor readers, regardless of whether or not their achievement is discrepant from their IQ, display the same kinds of deficits in phonological awareness and phonological decoding. Moreover, IQ does not predict word-level reading skills in normally developing readers (for reviews, see Fletcher et al., 1994, 1998; Lyon, 1995, 1996b; Meyer, 2000; Vellutino, Scanlon, & Lyon, 2000). When reading achievement is defined as the ability to comprehend text, however, a different picture emerges. During the initial stages of reading, decoding skills are the most powerful predictors of reading comprehension. As children progress through school, IQ, especially verbal IQ, makes a stronger contribution to individual differences in reading comprehension (Badian, 2001; Felton, 1992; Share & Stanovich, 1995; Stanovich, Cunningham, & Cramer, 1984). The relationship between IQ and reading comprehension is not surprising, given that intelligence tests typically assess the kinds of language-based skills needed for reading comprehension, such as vocabulary knowledge, verbal memory, and verbal reasoning (Vellutino et al., 2000).

IQ as a Predictor of Response to Intervention

As in prediction studies, the utility of IQ in predicting individual differences in children's response to prevention and intervention programs varies according to the reading subskill used as the criterion measure and the other variables included as predictors. When reading growth is measured in terms of word recognition and phonological decoding, IQ does not differentiate between children who are difficult to remediate and those who are readily remediated (Hatcher & Hulme, 1999; Vellutino, Scanlon, & Tanzman, 1998; Vellutino et al., 1996, 2000). For example, in a study evaluating the effectiveness of three approaches to early intervention for at-risk kindergartners (Torgesen, Wagner, Rashotte, Rose, et al., 1999), kindergarten verbal ability was a significant predictor of growth in word-level reading in the first two grades of school. Once phonological processing variables were included in the predictive equation, however, verbal ability did not contribute to intervention outcome. In contrast, when reading comprehension is the criterion, variations in verbal ability are significant predictors of children's responsiveness to remediation (Hatcher & Hulme, 1999; Torgesen, Wagner, Rashotte, Rose, et al., 1999; Vellutino et al., 1996, 1998). In the intervention study by Torgesen and his colleagues cited above, kindergarten verbal ability was a unique predictor of second-grade reading comprehension, even when phonological variables were included in the equation. IQ also becomes more important after the earliest stages of reading acquisition. In an intervention study with students in second through fifth grades (Wise, Ring, & Olson, 1999), computer-assisted phonological awareness training was equally effective for children across IQ levels in terms of improvement in phonemic awareness, but children with higher IQs made greater gains in reading decoding, word recognition, and comprehension.

IQ Tests and Component-Based Early Reading Assessment

In the component-based approach advocated in this text, cognitive ability measures play a role in early reading assessments—not as tools for excluding children from receiving services, but as tools for providing additional information for diagnosis and intervention planning. Rather than routinely administering IQ tests to children who are at risk for or are already displaying reading problems, practitioners should first assess children's strengths and weaknesses specific to the reading domain to obtain information for developing appropriate interventions. Reading-related cognitive abilities can then be evaluated to assist in determining whether basic cognitive deficits or experiential and/or instructional deficits are the major factors underlying a child's reading problems and to provide further information regarding the types, intensity, and duration of intervention needed (Vellutino et al., 1998). Cognitive ability tests can also help to differentiate between at-risk readers whose deficits are primarily confined to the word recognition module and those who display more global cognitive and language deficits. Although young poor readers with low IQs do not differ significantly from average-IQ poor readers in terms of phonological processing abilities, they show significantly more oral language deficits (Catts, Fey, Zhang, & Tomblin, 1999). Children who lack the oral language skills to compensate for deficits in phonological processing or decoding will need additional interventions to remedy their deficits in verbal knowledge in order to develop adequate reading comprehension. Because of the complexity and extent of the knowledge and skills required for comprehension, remediating oral language deficiencies is likely to be much more difficult than addressing decoding problems (Torgesen & Wagner, 1998).

ISSUE 3: WHEN SHOULD CHILDREN BE SCREENED FOR RISK OF EARLY READING PROBLEMS?

Designing effective early reading screening programs is complicated by the interaction of screening tasks with the time of year and grade at which they are administered. Because of the rapidly changing nature of children's phonological and early literacy skills, as well as the influence of instruction on those skills, a measure may be a highly effective predictor at one screening window and ineffective at another—even within the same school year (O'Connor & Jenkins, 1999; Torgesen, Wagner, & Rashotte, 1994). This is especially the case with phonological awareness skills, which develop along a continuum of complexity and interact with reading instruction (Schatschneider, Francis, Foorman, Fletcher, & Mehta, 1999). For example, segmenting words into individual phonemes (*cat* = /c/-/a/-/t/) is such a difficult task for most kindergarten children that using phoneme segmentation screening measures early in the year is likely to result in many misidentifications (Scarborough, 1998a). Moreover, screening measures are maximally effective in identifying children at greatest risk if most children achieve at least partial success on the tasks selected. If tasks are so easy or so hard that examinees score close to zero or perfect, they are of little utility in identifying children at risk or monitoring the progress of those receiving remediation.

Most of the multigrade early reading screening batteries reviewed in this text initiate screening in the kindergarten year, typically in October or November. Screening in preschool, in the summer prior to entry to kindergarten, or at the beginning of the kindergarten year is likely to reduce predictive accuracy for several reasons. First, the instability of young children's behavior increases the likelihood that poor performance on screening measures administered before children have adapted to the classroom setting may reflect problems with behavior, attention, and task motivation rather than genuine delays in early literacy development. Second, children may score poorly if they are tested too soon in their kindergarten year because they lack language and literacy experiences related to early reading acquisition. Children from low socioeconomic status (SES) and language minority families are especially likely to be overidentified in kindergarten screening programs. In contrast, vocabulary or print awareness measures administered early in the kindergarten year may *underpredict* future reading problems among children who are older than their grade peers and those who come from literacy-rich home environments, compared with children who have had fewer print experiences due to their younger age or home circumstances (Gredler, 1997; Mantzicopoulos & Morrison, 1994; O'Connor & Jenkins, 1999).

Although prediction studies have consistently demonstrated that the later screening measures are administered in the early primary grades, the better the classification accuracy is, practitioners must weigh accurate identification against the importance of early intervention. In Scarborough's (1998a) review of kindergarten studies, the investigation with the highest predictive accuracy (Hurford, Schauf, Bunce, Blaich, & Moore, 1994) administered initial assessments in the fall of first grade rather than in early kindergarten. The longer screening is delayed, however, the more entrenched reading problems become and the more likely they are to have adverse effects on cognitive and language development. Because longitudinal studies (Juel, 1988) indicate that children's level of phonemic awareness *when they enter first grade* is a key determinant of future reading development, waiting until first grade to screen for reading problems may mean that some children who are behind will never catch up with their peers.

The most effective method of ensuring that all children in need of remediation will be identified at the earliest possible point is to administer screening batteries several times during the early primary grades, beginning in kindergarten. Several of the screening instruments reviewed in this text are designed to be administered at more than one window during the school year, with more frequent assessments for students in kindergarten and Grade 1 and less frequent assessments for students in Grade 2. Although this book focuses on assessment in the first 3 years of formal schooling, an increasing number of screening batteries are expanding to include tasks that extend through Grade 3 to provide progress monitoring in compliance with Reading First legislative requirements and to build in another level of assessment for older children receiving reading interventions. By Grade 3, however, most districts already have in place a system of state-sponsored assessments.

Early Reading Screening Models

Depending on available resources and the needs of the student population, one of several early reading screening models may be selected.

Screening Model 1: Screening, Intervention, and Rescreening

In the first model, a set of screening measures assessing grade-specific prereading and/or reading skills is administered to all children in the early primary grades in the fall of the school year. Children who score below a preestablished criterion level on the screener are targeted for additional instruction. After a period of intervention, these children are rescreened on the same types of measures to evaluate their progress, and those who are continuing to experience difficulty are referred for more comprehensive assessments. This model is especially appropriate for districts serving a high proportion of children potentially at risk for reading failure, such as districts with large numbers of low SES and linguistic and ethnic minority children.

Screening Model 2: Two-Tier Screening

In the second model, a brief set of grade-specific screening measures (e.g., letter-sound naming and word identification for Grade 1) is administered to all early primary grade children in the fall. Children scoring below the criterion score on the screener take a more comprehensive set of measures assessing a variety of reading domains to obtain information for instructional planning. After a period of intervention, children are rescreened to determine whether they have met the semester and/or end-of-year benchmarks for the reading tasks relevant to their current grade placement. This is the model underlying several statewide screening programs, including those in Texas, which uses the *Texas Primary Reading Inventory* (TPRI), and Virginia, which uses the *Phonological Awareness Literacy Screening* (PALS).

Screening Model 3: Screening—Intervention—Progress Monitoring

In a third model, all children in designated grades are assessed in the fall with brief fluency-based measures of reading precursors and/or early reading skills to determine their preintervention skill levels and establish local norms. All children participate in evidence-based reading instruction as part of an early prevention program and take time-sensitive fluency-based batteries three times a year to monitor their reading progress and ensure that no students are falling behind. Children who fail to display expected developmental growth trajectories receive additional interventions and assessments. This is the model underlying the *Dynamic Indicators of Basic Early Literacy Skills* (DIBELS; Good & Kaminski, 2002b), which is used in numerous school districts across the country.

ISSUE 4: HOW SHOULD CHILDREN'S AT-RISK STATUS BE DETERMINED?

In determining which children are at risk for reading problems, two related issues are relevant: (1) the selection of norms for interpreting children's performance and (2) the development of benchmarks or cutoff scores for differentiating children who are at risk from those who are not at risk.

Selecting Norms for Interpreting Performance

Two basic types of comparisons for interpreting children's performance relative to that of their peers are available: national norms and local norms. Tests with *national norms* compare children's performance with that of a sample of examinees selected to represent the entire population of children in that age or grade range living in the United States. In contrast, tests with *local norms* compare children's performance with that of students from a specific educational setting relevant to those examinees, such as a classroom, grade, building, district, or state. Many phonological awareness and early literacy tasks, including alphabet knowledge, letter-naming fluency, phonemic segmentation, and oral reading fluency, lend themselves readily to local norming. In this text, examples of classroom and grade norming are included in the reviews of the PALS and the *Phonological Awareness Screening Test* (Adams, Foorman, Lundberg, & Beeler, 1998).

Advantages and Disadvantages of Local Norming

Compared with national norms, local norms have several advantages for evaluating performance in reading screening programs. First, they reduce the likelihood of bias in decision making because they represent a relevant comparison group. That is, the information obtained represents students who are not only in the same grade but also in the same geographical region and school and receiving the same curriculum as the child being compared. Second, locally normed measures increase the opportunity for linkages between assessment and instruction because testing can include materials to which students have been exposed in the school curriculum. Using local norms to evaluate student performance on reading screening measures is not without problems, however. Local norms can be unstable if the sample size is small, and performance levels may fluctuate from year to year, depending on the characteristics of the student population and the instructional environment. It is also important to remember that using local norms to interpret student performance does not mean that the level of local normative performance is acceptable. For example, if a kindergartner scores near the mean of her grade peers in alphabet knowledge on spring testing, but the kindergarten average in that particular school is only 3 out of 26 letters correct, that student is failing to develop a critical early literacy skill, despite the fact that that her performance is comparable to that of her peers (Habedank, 1995).

Developing Local Norms

Local norms can be developed at the classroom, grade, building, building cluster, or district level. If the student population and school resources available are relatively homogeneous, developing local norms at the district level is preferable because it yields more stable performance standards. If the district varies considerably in terms of student characteristics and instructional resources, however, establishing building-level or cluster-level norms may be more appropriate (Kaminski & Good, 1998). For classroom norms, a minimum of 7–10 students should be assessed. Sampling can be conducted by creating a random subset of 7–10 students, randomly selecting 7–10 students from a group of students judged to be average or typical, or assessing all students on group-administered measures and then selecting a subset of 7–10 students for individually administered tasks. For building-level norms, 15%–20% of students at each grade level, with a minimum of 20 students per grade, should be randomly sampled. At the district level, 100 students per grade should be randomly sampled (Habedank, 1995). Selection of norm size also depends on the scores desired. If percentile rank scores are desired, at least 100 children should be included at each grade level so that "true" percentiles can be derived. If smaller groups are used, percentiles must be smoothed via linear interpolation to determine the values at each percentile point. Because of the rapid growth of early literacy skills in young children, developing local norms for fall, winter, and spring is optimal (Shinn, 1989).

Organizing Information from Local Norming

Data from local norming can be summarized in terms of medians, means, ranges, and rank orderings. At the classroom or building level, means, medians, ranges, and standard deviations can be calculated and used for screening and monitoring student progress. For samples of 100 or more students at a grade level, percentile ranks can be calculated for use in identifying at-risk status and setting goals for expected literacy skills at various points during the year, such as fall and spring. Although it takes additional time to calculate percentile rank (PR) scores, they are easily understood by parents and teachers; are comparable across measures, grades, and time of administration; and facilitate the development of cutoff criteria to identify students in need of additional assistance. Scores from single classes can be listed and summarized in tabular form with the Table menu in Microsoft Word. This approach is especially appropriate when one is developing classroom or grade norms. For larger sets of scores involving multiple classrooms, building clusters, or an entire district, spreadsheet programs, such as Microsoft Excel, can be used to organize and summarize data.

Developing Cutoff Scores for Determining Risk Status

Once the appropriate referent group has been determined, scores indicating at-risk versus not-at-risk status must be determined. Two terms are used to refer to scores that indicate risk status: benchmarks and cutoffs. As noted earlier, the term *benchmark* refers to the minimum level of proficiency a child must achieve on a task in order to benefit from the next level of instruction. For example, a widely accepted benchmark for oral reading fluency for the end of first grade is 40 words read correctly per minute. A *cutoff score* is the score used to classify an examinee as being at risk for failure as defined by the criterion measure. Cutoff scores can be based on a theoretical rationale or on normative data. In research studies, investigators often set an arbitrary cut point after outcome data have been collected, based on the value that produces the best predictive accuracy for their particular sample.

Because the consequences of failing to identify at-risk children outweigh the consequences of overidentification, cutoff scores in screening programs are usually designed to minimize the number of false negatives (see below) so that future poor readers do not go unidentified. For example, on the screening portion for Grades 1 and 2 of the TPRI, the cutoff score is set to reduce the number of false negative errors to less then 10% in order to overidentify children who may be at risk for reading problems. Cutoffs may also be adjusted depending on the grade level, with higher cut points or cutoffs for older children because of the shorter time for intervention. On the TPRI, the criterion for risk status at the end of Grade 1 is set at a grade equivalent (GE) of 1.4 (PR = 18) on the Broad Reading cluster of the *Woodcock–Johnson Psycho-Educational Battery–Revised* (WJ-R; Woodcock & Johnson, 1989). In contrast, the criterion for risk status at the end of Grade 2 is set at a WJ-R Broad Reading GE of 2.4 (PR = 35). Reading screening programs often set cutoff scores that demarcate the lowest quartile (25%) or the lowest 20% of the distribution to eliminate most false negative errors.

Until quite recently, norm-referenced reading tests did not provide cutoff scores or an explicit discussion of possible risk associated with various levels of test performance. Instead, test performance was interpreted based on the position of the examinee's score in the normal curve, with scores falling more than 2 standard deviations below the mean (i.e., standard scores of less than 70 for tests with a mean of 100 and a standard deviation of 15) indicating extremely low or deficient performance. Although several of the instruments reviewed in this text specify a score or score range designating risk status, cut points vary from test to test. For example, on the *Process Assessment of the Learner: Test Battery for Reading and Writing* (Berninger, 2001), decile scores of 30–40 and below indicate at-risk or impaired performance, whereas on the *Phonological Abilities Test* (Muter, Hulme, & Snowling, 1997), scores below the 10th percentile indicate impaired performance.

Evaluating the predictive accuracy of commercially published early reading measures is complicated by the fact that test manuals often fail to include information about predictive validity. Even when manuals provide data from predictive validation studies, test authors typically present only correlation coefficients as evidence. Positive correlations between the scores of the standardization sample on a screening measure (or, more commonly, a relatively small group of examinees) and their scores on a subsequent reading measure provide information only regarding the strength of the relationship between predictor and criterion measures for *groups* of examinees, not about the accuracy of the predictor in correctly identifying individual children as at risk or not at risk (Satz & Fletcher, 1988). Instead, screening tests should provide evidence of *predictive validity*—that is, the degree to which a screening measure identifies children who later experience learning problems and does not identify children who do not develop subsequent learning problems, as indicated by performance on a criterion measure. The predictive validity of a test can only be evaluated by setting a cutoff score that classifies each child as either at risk or not at risk, based on performance on the predictor. Information from the results of the screening and criterion measure can then be presented in a 2 × 2 matrix indicating the results of the screening process. Table 1.2 presents possible screening results and two sets of indices for evaluating the predictive accuracy of a screener.

TABLE 1.2. Reading Screening Outcomes and Indices of Predictive Accuracy

Later reading performance (criterion)	Decision on the reading screening measure (predictor)		
	At risk	Not at risk	Indices of predictive accuracy
Poor	Valid positive (VP)	False negative (FN)	Sensitivity = $\frac{VP}{VP + FN}$
Adequate	False positive (FP)	Valid negative (VN)	Specificity = $\frac{VN}{VN + FP}$
Totals	Positive predictive value = $\frac{VP}{VP + FP}$	Negative predictive value = $\frac{VN}{VN + FN}$	Hit rate = $\frac{VP + VN}{VP + FN + VN + FP}$

Possible Screening Outcomes

The second and third columns of Table 1.2 present the four possible outcomes of a screening measure. Children who are correctly identified by the screening measure appear in the cells designated "Valid positive (VP)" and "Valid negative (VN)" in the table. The *valid positive rate* refers to the number of children who were correctly identified as being at risk and who later became poor readers. The *valid negative rate* reflects the number of children who were correctly identified as not being at risk and who did not later develop reading problems. In contrast, children who were incorrectly identified by the screening measure appear in the "False positive (FP)" and "False negative (FN)" cells in the table. The *false positive rate* refers to the number of children who were identified as being at risk by the screening measure but who did not later develop reading problems. The *false negative rate* refers to the number of children who were not identified as being at risk by the screening measure but who later became poor readers. For early intervention programs, false negatives are considered the more serious type of errors because unidentified children will fail to receive additional assistance at the earliest opportunity in their schooling. False positive errors are also of concern, however, because resources will be allocated to children who do not truly need remediation.

Indices of Predictive Accuracy

The information obtained from these four outcomes can be used to calculate a set of indices that are useful in evaluating the predictive accuracy of screening measures. The three indices in the last column of Table 1.2 represent information obtained from a *retrospective* viewpoint. That is, given children's later poor or adequate reading performance, what percentage was correctly identified originally by the screening measure? The *sensitivity index* reflects the ability of the screener to identify correctly poor readers and is calculated by comparing the number of valid positives with the number of children who later developed reading problems. The *specificity index* reflects the ability of the screener to identify correctly children who did not become poor readers and is calculated by comparing the number of valid negatives with the number of children who later became adequate readers. The *hit rate*, or overall effectiveness of the screening measure, refers to the percentage of the total group correctly identified by the screener and is calculated by comparing the number of valid positives and valid negatives with the total number of children screened. Screening measures often have high hit rates because they are able to predict children who will *not* become poor readers rather than to predict those who will develop reading problems—that is, they have high valid negative rates. Examining the other predictive indices is important, however, because the same instrument may also have a low valid positive rate and have low predictive accuracy in terms of identifying at-risk children (Gredler, 2000). For example, in a study that followed kindergarten children through third grade (Felton, 1992), a screening battery consisting of phonological awareness, phonological memory, and rapid naming measures had an overall hit rate of 80%, as measured by third-grade reading achievement. In contrast, the valid positive rate was only 31%, and the false positive rate was 69%! Because the valid negative rate was very high, however (97%), the hit rate made the screening battery appear more useful than it actually was.

The indices at the bottom of the first two columns of the table represent information obtained from a *prospective* viewpoint, that is—the accuracy of the screening measure in predicting at-risk or not-at-risk status. The *positive predictive value* reflects the proportion of valid positives among all children whom the screener identified as at risk for reading problems and is calculated by comparing the number of valid positives with the total number identified as at risk. The *negative predictive value* refers to the proportion of valid negatives among all children whom the screener identified as not at risk who later became adequate readers and is calculated by comparing the number of valid negatives with the total number identified as not at risk. Most authors (e.g., Gredler, 2000; Kingslake, 1983) have recommended that the sensitivity index, specificity index, and positive predictive value should be at least 75%. Carran and Scott (1992) have recommended that the indices should approximate 80% to conform to reliability standards for screening measures.

ISSUE 5: WHAT IS THE ROLE OF TEACHER RATINGS IN IDENTIFYING EARLY READING PROBLEMS?

Although teacher judgments have often been used to screen for early learning problems and to assess children's at-risk status for future academic problems (see Hoge & Coladarci, 1989, for a review), research has yielded conflicting results regarding their efficacy in the early identification of reading problems. In a study evaluating the concurrent and predictive value of teacher ratings (Taylor, Anselmo, Foreman, Schatschneider, & Angelopoulos, 2000), kindergarten children identified by their teachers as making unsatisfactory academic progress scored significantly lower than nonidentified children on standardized tests of word identification and spelling and on informal measures of letter-name and letter-sound knowledge. At a 1-year follow-up in spring of first grade, group differences on achievement tests were still present, and a significantly greater proportion of identified children were receiving special education or remedial assistance. In another study assessing the utility of kindergarten teachers' ratings in predicting first-grade achievement (Teisl, Mazzocco, & Myers, 2001), teachers were relatively good predictors in terms of overall accuracy and specificity (79.1% and 83.3%, respectively), but sensitivity and positive predictive indices were considerably lower (48% and 27.9%, respectively). Limbos and Geva (2001) obtained similar results in a sample of first graders with English as a second language (ESL) or English as a first language (L1) who were followed through the end of second grade. Teacher ratings and nominations had low to moderate sensitivity in identifying ESL and L1 students who were currently poor readers (77.1% and 74.3%, respectively) and poor readers 1 year later (69.2% and 73.1%, respectively), but high specificity (above 87% for both groups of students at both time periods). When the two types of teacher judgments were combined, however, sensitivity for both groups of children rose to between 85% and 100% for the two time periods.

Relatively few recent studies have compared the predictive utility of teacher ratings with children's performance on reading and reading-related tests. In a first-grade sample of predominantly ethnic minority students (Hecht & Greenfield, 2001), teacher ratings predicted individual differences in third-grade reading achievement with similar accuracy to that of the combined reading-related measures, which included tests of phonological awareness, print awareness, and receptive vocabulary.

Moreover, first-grade teacher ratings classified children into third-grade reading groups with at least 73% accuracy, comparable to classification based on reading-related test performance. Other investigations have yielded less positive results, however. In a study comparing the predictive validity of a group-administered literacy screening battery and a teacher rating scale based on the same set of predictors as in the screener (Flynn & Rahbar, 1998a), teacher ratings of kindergarten children's performance were much less accurate than the literacy battery in predicting first- and third-grade poor readers (80% vs. 64% valid positives). When test and teacher information were combined, the valid positive rate rose to 88%, but the false positive rate reached 39%. Overall, research suggests that although teachers are often highly accurate in predicting which students are *not* likely to develop reading problems, they have more difficulty identifying which children will become poor readers.

Teacher Ratings of Children's Academic, Behavior, and Social Competence

Although evidence is mixed regarding the utility of teacher ratings in predicting children's risk for reading problems, there is an increasing body of research demonstrating that teacher ratings of children's attention and behavior are key predictors of individual differences in response to prevention and intervention programs. In a prevention study (Torgesen, Wagner, Rashotte, Rose, et al., 1999) that provided children with one-to-one instruction beginning in the second semester of kindergarten and extending through Grade 2, classroom behavior ratings were among the most consistently important predictors of reading achievement, along with rapid naming and home literacy environment. Similarly, in a study comparing the efficacy of two instructional programs for children aged 8 to 10 with severe reading disabilities, the best overall predictors of long-term growth were resource room teacher ratings of attention and behavior, along with receptive language and prior reading skills.

Researchers have used a variety of measures to obtain information from teachers regarding children's academic and/or social competence, ranging from a single-item, 6-point scale indicating children's likelihood for developing future learning problems (Mantzicopolous & Morrison, 1994) to norm-referenced measures of academic competence and behavior (Hecht & Greenfield, 2001; Taylor et al., 2000). One of the instruments reviewed in this book, the *Predictive Reading Profile* (Flynn, 2001), includes a 10-item teacher rating scale assessing the same set of reading precursors represented in the test. The Report Writer for the *Woodcock–Johnson III* (Schrank & Woodcock, 2002) includes a teacher checklist with ratings of classroom behavior in six areas.

ISSUE 6: HOW SHOULD LINGUISTICALLY DIVERSE CHILDREN BE SCREENED FOR RISK OF READING PROBLEMS?

One of the most challenging issues confronting today's practitioners relates to the early identification of linguistically diverse students who may be at risk for reading problems. In the last two decades, the number of children learning English as a second language (ESL) in U.S. classrooms has increased dramatically, with Hispanics constituting the largest of the various ESL minority groups (Garcia, 2000). These children may be vulnerable to reading failure not only because of limited proficiency in English, but also because of home literacy factors that exacerbate their reading problems, such as parents who have little formal education, have little time to read to their children, and are struggling to cope with poverty and acculturation issues. Determining whether ESL students' reading problems are the result of limited English proficiency or of a specific reading disability or language disorder can be very difficult. Many practitioners lack appropriate assessment instruments and/or the foreign-language proficiency needed to evaluate ESL students in their first language (L1), especially considering the number of different languages spoken by students in many school districts. Even when it is possible to assess students in their first language, many immigrant ESL children lose their L1 proficiency over time, so that L1 norms cease to serve as valid indicators of their language and literacy development (Quiroga, Lemos-Britton, Mostafapour, Abbott, & Berninger, 2002).

In recent years, concerns about misidentifying children with language proficiency problems as having learning disabilities or mental retardation have led to the practice of delaying both assessment and intervention for several years until children have developed oral language proficiency in English. Such a practice overlooks the fact that some ESL students may be struggling in reading not because they have failed to acquire adequate English oral language skills, but because they have deficits in phonological processing and single word reading similar to those displayed by English as a first language (L1) children with reading disabilities. Failing to include ESL learners in reading screening programs deprives these children of the opportunity to participate in the kinds of early intervention programs that could prevent later reading failure (Geva, Yaghoub-Zadeh, & Schuster, 2000; Limbos & Geva, 2001).

Two lines of evidence offer support for including ESL children in early identification and intervention programs. First, cross-cultural studies of reading acquisition and reading disabilities have consistently found that neither native-language nor English-language proficiency is a significant predictor of English word recognition and decoding skills (Durgunoĝlu, Nagy, & Hancin-Bhatt, 1993; Geva & Siegel, 2000; Geva et al., 2000; Limbos & Geva, 2001). Unfortunately, teachers tend to rely primarily on oral language proficiency as an indicator of ESL children's reading performance, resulting in the misclassification of many such children. For example, in a study examining the accuracy of teacher judgments in screening for reading disabilities among ESL and L1 children, Limbos and Geva (2001) reported that relative to objective screening measures, teacher rating scales and teacher nominations were much less effective predictors of both groups' risk for reading problems. For both groups, however, children's oral proficiency in their native language is a significant predictor of reading when it is measured in terms of comprehension (Carlisle & Beeman, 2000; Geva & Ryan, 1993; Verhoeven, 2000).

Second, a growing body of research (Bruck & Genesee, 1995; Cisero & Royer, 1995; Comeau, Cormier, Grandmaison, & Lacroix, 1999; Durgunoĝlu et al., 1993; Geva & Siegel, 2000; Geva, Wade-Woolley, & Shavy, 1993, 1997; Geva et al., 2000; Margolese & Kline, 1999) indicates that the same cognitive–linguistic factors that predict reading acquisition in L1 learners—including phonological awareness, phonological memory, orthographic knowledge, and rapid naming—are also effective predictors for ESL children. Moreover, these factors show similar predictive patterns, with phonological memory predicting word recognition and reading comprehension

(Geva & Ryan, 1993; Geva & Siegel, 2000) and phonological awareness and rapid naming predicting word recognition and decoding (Geva & Siegel, 2000). Of the variables measured, the best predictors of beginning word recognition and spelling skills among ESL children are phonological awareness and rapid naming, identical to those identified as the most effective predictors for L1 children.

Measuring Early Reading Skills in ESL Children

Despite mounting evidence that phonological processing measures are reliable indicators of risk for reading disability across alphabetic languages, ESL children's performance on these tasks may be confounded to some degree with their English oral language proficiency. Some English speech sounds may not be present in a child's native language and vice versa, and ESL children are likely to be less familiar with the vocabulary and syntax of the task directions and test stimuli. For example, on a phoneme blending item that requires listening to and blending together the sounds /c/-/a/-/t/, the L1 child will have a lexical entry to consult (*cat*), whereas the ESL child may have no referent or may have it less firmly fixed in long-term memory. Reading researchers have dealt with the problem of frequency effects for phonological processing measures in a variety of ways. Some investigators (Margolese & Kline, 1999) have used English norm-referenced tests of phonological processing such as the *Test of Phonological Awareness* (Torgesen & Bryant, 1994b), whereas others (Geva et al., 2000) have adapted phoneme deletion measures such as the *Auditory Analysis Test* (AAT) so that the stimulus words and the words remaining after sound deletions include only high-frequency English words. Still others (Cisero & Royer, 1995; Comeau et al., 1999; Durgunoĝlu et al., 1993; Quiroga et al., 2002) have created foreign-language equivalents of phonological processing measures, such as the AAT. Still other researchers have attempted to control for frequency effects by substituting phonologically legal English pseudowords for real words (Bruck & Genesee, 1995) or by using pseudowords that comply with the morphological rules of a language unfamiliar to ESL and L1 children alike, such as Hebrew pseudowords for a study with South Asian, Chinese, and English students (Geva et al., 2000).

Fewer investigators have used measures of rapid automatized naming (RAN) to predict reading acquisition or risk for reading problems in ESL students, compared with phonological processing tasks. Researchers have typically administered English-language RAN measures, with some (Comeau et al., 1999) including all four RAN tasks (color, letter, object, and digit naming) and others (Geva et al., 2000; Limbos & Geva, 2001) using only the RAN-Letters task. Overall, converging evidence supports the view that ESL children's phonological awareness and rapid naming skills assessed in English are reliable, valid predictors of subsequent English word-level reading and spelling skills and that risk for reading disabilities can be determined in children who have not attained full English oral language proficiency. In addition, a growing number of studies demonstrate that ESL children identified as at risk benefit as much as L1 at-risk children from intervention programs targeting phonological awareness and decoding skills (Gunn, Biglan, Smolkowski, & Ary, 2000; Haager & Windmueller, 2001; Quiroga et al., 2002). For ESL as well as for L1 students, early identification of potential reading problems is not only possible but also imperative for preventing reading failure in a highly vulnerable population.

ISSUE 7: HOW SHOULD THE RESULTS OF EARLY READING SCREENINGS BE INTERPRETED AND USED?

A final question for consideration relates to the interpretation and use of the results of early reading screenings. That is, once reading screenings have been conducted, how should low-scoring children be treated? In the past, children who scored below the cutoffs on screening measures were usually referred immediately for further diagnostic assessment to determine whether they qualified for special education programs (i.e., whether they displayed a discrepancy between IQ and reading achievement). Now, however, there is an emerging consensus (e.g., Berninger, 1998a, 1998b; Berninger & Abbott, 1994b; Gresham, 2002; Lyon et al., 2001; Torgesen, 2000, 2002a; Vellutino et al., 1996, 1998), that diagnostic assessments should be delayed until a period of intervention has been provided. That is, diagnosis should be based on the *failure to respond to research-validated treatments* rather than on an arbitrarily specified discrepancy between cognitive ability and reading achievement. In this two-tier model, kindergarten and first-grade children who scored below the criterion on screening measures and were not classified with some other primary disability, such as mental retardation, would be eligible for early intervention programs without having to be labeled as learning disabled. Screening results would be used to help design the most effective interventions for addressing children's deficits.

During the intervention period, which could extend across the early primary grades, children's responsiveness to treatment would be frequently monitored with measures sensitive to change, such as curriculum-based oral reading fluency assessments. Children whose performance did not improve to acceptable levels (so-called *treatment nonresponders*) would receive follow-up assessments that would include measures of reading-related cognitive abilities to help determine the nature and extent of their deficits and provide information for educational programming. In other words, screening batteries would serve as a "first-cut" diagnostic strategy to help distinguish between poor readers whose reading problems are caused primarily by deficits in the cognitive–linguistic abilities underlying reading (i.e., reading-disabled children) and those whose reading problems are caused primarily by experiential and/or instructional deficits (i.e., garden-variety poor readers). Moreover, test results obtained in the second tier would be more accurate because they would be informed by the nature of each child's response to evidence-based interventions (Vellutino et al., 1996, 1998). At that point, children with severe reading difficulties who were not classified with another primary disability would be considered as learning disabled for the purposes of receiving services and accommodations.

Support for a Responsiveness to Intervention Approach to Classification

Support for the efficacy of this approach has been demonstrated by several intensive intervention studies with kindergarten and Grade 1 children (Brown & Felton, 1990; Foorman, Francis, Fletcher, Schatschneider, & Mehta, 1998; Torgesen, Wagner, & Rashotte, 1997; Torgesen, Wagner, Rashotte, Rose, et al., 1999, Vellutino et al., 1996). In a recent summary of these studies, Torgesen (2002b) reported that all of the intervention programs resulted in a significant reduction in the number of children who would have been eligible for special services. In these investigations, children were identified as at risk for reading disabilities based on assessments indicating that they fell in the lowest 12%–18% of the school population on either phonological processing skills (kindergarten) or reading skills (Grade 1). Across the five studies, early intervention was successful in reducing the percentage of at-risk children from about 18% to about 1.4%–5.4%.

Challenges Ahead

Although a classification model based on responsiveness to intervention offers a positive alternative approach to defining specific reading disability, it also raises a host of questions. What kinds of intervention programs are most effective for children with different kinds of reading problems (i.e., deficits in decoding, comprehension, and/or fluency)? What is most effective in terms of the length and intensity of interventions? How can treatment integrity be assured? What criteria should be used to document adequate versus inadequate progress? What kinds of programs are not only effective in improving reading performance but also cost-effective? (See Gresham, 2002; Lyon et al., 2001.) Moreover, as Torgesen and his colleagues have observed (Torgesen, 2002a; Torgesen & Wagner, 1998), shifting from current identification practices to an assessment–intervention model would have profound consequences for the student population served and the manner in which learning disabilities services are provided. First, the students identified for learning disabilities services would be more heterogeneous in terms of general intelligence, necessitating a more flexible approach to instructional accommodations. Second, children identified under this model would be more likely to come from low SES and ethnic and linguistic minority groups, who tend to have fewer of the kinds of preschool language and literacy experiences that support prereading and phonological awareness skills (Whitehurst & Lonigan, 1998). Finally, many of the students currently receiving reading disabilities services would no longer be eligible under this model. One group of these students would become ineligible because they would be more appropriately classified with some other primary disability, such as mental retardation or emotional disturbance. Another group would no longer be served because their absolute level of reading achievement, although lower than their intellectual ability, is not sufficiently low to warrant special services.

PRINT RESOURCES

Bradley, R., Danielson, L., & Hallahan, D. P. (Eds.). (2002). *The identification of learning disabilities: Research to practice.* Mahwah, NJ: Erlbaum.

This book is the product of a learning disabilities summit conference convened by the Office of Special Education Programs in August 2001 prior to the 2002 congressional reauthorization of the Individuals with Disabilities Education Act. Chapters cover alternative approaches to diagnosis, classification, and intervention; discrepancy models; and other critical issues in the field of learning disabilities. Also included is a series of consensus statements regarding the identification of children with learning disabilities prepared by a group of the contributors.

Neuman, S. B., & Dickinson, D. K. (Eds.). (2001). *Handbook of early literacy research.* New York: Guilford Press.

This edited collection of chapters by researchers with a variety of theoretical orientations covers a broad range of early literacy topics, including literacy development; literacy and language skills; home and community influences on reading acquisition; the impact of preschool experiences on early literacy; instructional materials and practices; and special intervention efforts. The chapter by Frank Vellutino and Donna Scanlon on the role of early identification and intervention in preventing reading impairment will be of particular interest to readers of this text.

Stanovich, K. E. (2000). *Progress in understanding reading: Scientific foundations and new frontiers.* New York: Guilford Press.

This collection of articles traces the development of the understanding of the cognitive processes associated with reading and reading disabilities by one of the most influential researchers in the field. The book is divided into seven parts, each beginning with a chapter written expressly for this volume that places the contribution in its historical and autobiographical context. Included are Stanovich's classic articles on Matthew effects in reading and the phonological core deficit model in reading disabilities.

chapter 2

Evaluating the Technical Adequacy and Usability of Early Reading Measures

When practitioners select tests for use in early reading assessments, two types of considerations are most relevant. The first set of considerations relates to the *technical adequacy* or psychometric soundness of a particular measure. Regardless of how attractively packaged, comfortably familiar, or heavily marketed a test may be, it is of no use to practitioners and the children they serve if it does not provide a reliable and valid assessment of the skills it is designed to measure. The first section of this chapter discusses five psychometric characteristics critical to early reading measures and provides recommendations for minimum levels of technical adequacy for these properties: (1) standardization, (2) reliability, (3) test floors, (4) item gradients, and (5) validity. Also included are introductions to *item response theory* (IRT) and *generalizability theory* (G theory)—approaches that are becoming increasingly important in the development and validation of psychological and educational tests.

The second set of considerations relates to the *usability* of a test—that is, the degree to which practitioners can actually use a measure in applied settings. Although technical adequacy should be the first consideration in selecting assessment tools, usability also plays a role in the selection process (Goodwin & Goodwin, 1993). The second section of this chapter discusses practical characteristics relevant to early reading measures and offers guidelines for evaluating their usability.

Evaluating the Technical Adequacy of Early Reading Measures

A comprehensive understanding of the technical adequacy of early reading measures is an essential competency for practitioners. When tests are used to identify children for risk of reading failure or to diagnose the nature and extent of early reading deficits, the validity of those assessments depends directly on the psychometric soundness of the measures. Tests with inadequate reliability and validity can lead to a misdiagnosis or the failure to identify a genuine problem and thus can result in inappropriate intervention or no intervention at all. Given the current proliferation of early reading measures, acquiring an adequate knowledge of their psychometric characteristics is a formidable challenge. Instruments purporting to have utility in early reading screenings or early reading diagnostic assessments are constantly being developed and revised by commercial test publishers, state education agencies, and researchers. Moreover, studies using these measures are continually appearing in a research literature that spans a wide variety of disciplines and encompasses numerous professional journals and other print and electronic resources. Practitioners trained more than a decade ago may also have limited familiarity with recent approaches to test construction and evaluation—notably IRT and G theory—that are providing the foundation for an increasing number of psychological and educational instruments.

Despite these challenges, practitioners have an ethical responsibility to educate themselves regarding the psychometric characteristics of the instruments they use. Because reading problems are much more amenable to treatment in the early primary grades, selecting measures that permit early, accurate identification of children at risk for reading failure is essential. The more fully an instrument meets the criteria described in this chapter, the more confidence test users can have that the obtained scores provide a reliable and valid estimate of a child's early literacy skills and yield accurate information for intervention and educational planning.

STANDARDS FOR ASSESSMENT

The American Educational Research Association (AERA), the American Psychological Association (APA), and the National Council for Measurement in Education (NCME) have jointly published standards for the development and use of psychological and educational tests since 1954. These standards offer general guidelines rather than specific criteria for various psychometric characteristics, however. For example, in its guidelines for reliability, Standard 2.1 of the latest version of the *Standards for Psychological and Educational Testing* (AERA, APA, & NCME, 1999) states: "For each total score, subscore, or combination of scores that is to be interpreted, estimates of relevant reliabilities and standard errors of measurement or test information functions should be reported" (p. 34). Although this standard stipulates that reliability estimates should be reported, it does not set criteria for minimum levels of reliability.

The National Association of School Psychologists' (NASP's) *Principles for Professional Ethics* (2000) also emphasize the importance of evaluating the psychometric soundness of instruments used by practitioners. Principle IVC2 states: "School psychologists are knowledgeable about the validity and reliability of their instruments and techniques, choosing those that have up-to-date standardization data and are applicable and appropriate for the benefit of the child" (p. 626).

Like the AERA and colleagues *Standards*, the NASP *Principles* do not provide specific criteria to assist practitioners in evaluating the adequacy of reliability or validity information or judging when norms are "up to date" and when they are so old that they are no longer "applicable and appropriate." Moreover, despite the current interest in the early identification of reading difficulties, the *Standards* fail to address several technical characteristics that are critical in early reading assessments, notably test floors and item gradients. First identified by Bracken (1987) as essential properties of measures for young children, *test floors* determine the degree to which a test can effectively differentiate among performance levels at the low end of functioning, whereas *item gradients* determine the degree to which a test is sensitive to individual differences across the entire range of functioning.

A FRAMEWORK FOR EVALUATING THE TECHNICAL ADEQUACY OF EARLY READING MEASURES

This section is designed to provide practitioners with a framework for evaluating the technical adequacy of early reading measures and with specific criterion levels for five sets of psychometric properties. It begins with a brief, practitioner-oriented introduction to IRT. Because test manuals increasingly provide development and validation information derived from IRT as well as from classical test theory (CTT) procedures, practitioners need to have a basic familiarity with its concepts so that they can evaluate the information presented. A brief introduction to G theory, an important extension of CTT, is included later under the discussion of reliability.

This section then reviews five psychometric properties relevant to the technical adequacy of early reading measures: (1) standardization, (2) reliability, (3) test floors, (4) item gradients, and (5) validity. For each psychometric property, minimal criteria and the rationale on which those criteria are based are presented. Several considerations are relevant in applying the criteria to early reading measures. First, these criteria can be most appropriately and completely applied to norm-referenced tests designed for individual diagnostic assessment. Early reading screening batteries whose primary purpose is to differentiate at-risk from not-at-risk children must be evaluated according to somewhat different standards because of their structure and purpose, and those differences are noted in the discussion of the relevant characteristics. Second, although nonstandardized measures can be very useful in identifying early reading problems and monitoring response to intervention, less information regarding their psychometric properties is generally available for review than is the case with norm-referenced instruments. Finally, even among norm-referenced instruments, test manuals vary tremendously in terms of the amount and quality of the technical information they provide. For example, the *Woodcock–Johnson III* (WJ III) provides a separate 209-page technical manual in addition to the two examiner manuals, whereas the 45-page examiner manual for the *Phonological Abilities Test* contains 7 pages of technical information.

Sources of Evaluative Criteria

Criteria for evaluating the technical adequacy of early reading measures are based on the following sources: (1) the *Standards for Educational and Psychological Testing* (AERA et al., 1999); (2) Salvia and Ysseldyke's (2001) standards for testing in applied settings; (3) Bracken's (1987, 1988, 2000), Bracken and Walker's (1997), and Alfonso and Flanagan's (Alfonso & Flanagan, 1999; Flanagan & Alfonso, 1995) standards for the psychometric properties of preschool intelligence tests; (4) Bracken, Keith, and Walker's (1994) guidelines for preschool behavioral rating scales; (5) Hammill, Brown, and Bryant's (1992) rating system for tests; (6) Reynolds's (1990) recommendations for tests used to determine ability–achievement discrepancies; and (7) my own review of the literature on early reading assessment. Table 2.1 summarizes the guidelines for evaluating the psychometric soundness of early reading measures that are discussed below and that form the basis for the test reviews in this book.

ITEM RESPONSE THEORY: THE REVOLUTION IN TEST CONSTRUCTION

Most practitioners are familiar with tests that have been constructed and evaluated using classical test theory (CTT) models and with CTT concepts such as true score, standard error of measurement, and classic item difficulty and discrimination statistics. In recent years, however, test developers have increasingly relied on a new system of measurement termed *item response theory* (IRT) in the test construction and validation process. IRT can be used to design, scale, and calibrate tests; construct test item banks; investigate potentially biased test items; maximize the amount of information provided by tests; and clarify the nature of the constructs underlying test performance. The following discussion is intended as a brief introduction to IRT for practitioners and is drawn primarily from Embretson and Hershberger (1999), Hambleton and his colleagues (Hambleton, 1996; Hambleton, Swaminathan, & Rogers, 1991; Hambleton & Zaal, 1991), and Suen (1990).

IRT is a measurement system consisting of a set of models with applications that are useful in designing, constructing, and validating psychological and educational tests. IRT models assume that performance on a given item can be explained by the latent ability of a given examinee, denoted *theta*, which is analogous to the concept of true score in CTT. Although this trait or characteristic cannot be directly observed, IRT assumes that an examinee's observed response to an item is determined by the examinee's ability level and the characteristics of the item, such as its difficulty and discrimination power. Second, IRT models assume that the relationship between an examinee's performance on an item and the ability measured by the test can be described by a mathematical function called an *item characteristic curve* (ICC).

ICCs describe models that include numerical values or parameters for both item characteristics and examinee ability. Up to three parameters can be estimated for each item (see Figure 2.1). The first parameter, the *item difficulty parameter*, called b, represents the point on the ability scale at which the probability of a correct response is 50%. In CTT, this is analogous to the *percent-correct value* (p value), the proportion of examinees who pass an item. A second parameter that can be estimated is the *item discrimination parameter*, called a, which corresponds to the slope

TABLE 2.1. Psychometric Characteristics of Early Reading Measures

Psychometric characteristics	Guidelines for evaluating the technical adequacy of early reading measures
Standardization	
Representativeness of norms	Norms should match the U.S. population on at least three important demographic variables (e.g., age, SES, gender, ethnicity, etc.). Norms for screening measures designed for local use should match the reference population in terms of gender, grade, ethnicity, school SES level, and disability status.
Subgroup size	Each subgroup should include at least 100 individuals.
Total sample size	The total sample should include at least 1,000 individuals.
Recency of norms	The date of collection of normative information should be no earlier than 12 years prior to the current date.
Norm table intervals	Norm table intervals should be no more than 6 months for children aged 7-11 and younger and no more than 1 year for children aged 8 and up. Grade-based intervals should be no more than 5 months for kindergarten through Grade 2.
Reliability	
Internal consistency reliability	Composite and total test coefficients should be at least .80 for screening measures and at least .90 for diagnostic measures. Subtest coefficients should be at least .80 if they are to be interpreted.
Test–retest reliability	Coefficients should be at least .80 for screening measures and at least .90 for diagnostic measures. Test–retest studies should include at least 50 individuals and represent the U.S. population or the relevant norm group on three or more demographic variables. The age range for test–retest studies should include the early primary grade years and span no more than 4 years or four grades. Test–retest intervals should be no more than 3 months and preferably no more than 1 month in length.
Interscorer reliability	Coefficients should be at least .80 for screening measures and at least .90 for diagnostic measures. Reliability estimates should be provided for all tasks and subtests involving subjective judgment.
Test floors	
Subtest floors	A subtest raw score of 1 should produce a standard score that is greater than 2 standard deviations below the subtest mean.
Scale, composite, and total test floors	Given a raw score of 1 on each of the subtests constituting the scale, composite, or total test score, the summed raw scores should produce a scale, composite, or total test standard score that is greater than 2 standard deviations below the scale, composite, or total test mean.
Item gradients	
Subtest item gradients	For subtests with a mean of 10 and a standard deviation of 3, the number of items between the floor and the mean should be equal to or greater than 6. For subtests with a mean of 100 and a standard deviation of 15, the number of items between the floor and the mean should be equal to or greater than 10.
Validity	
Content validity	The manual should provide two or more kinds of content validity evidence, including differential item functioning analyses.
Criterion-related validity	The manual should provide two or more kinds of criterion-related validity evidence for the early primary grade range. Screening measures should provide a theoretical rationale and empirical evidence for cutoff scores or benchmarks.
Construct validity	The manual should provide two or more kinds of construct validity evidence, including at least one group or training differentiation study.

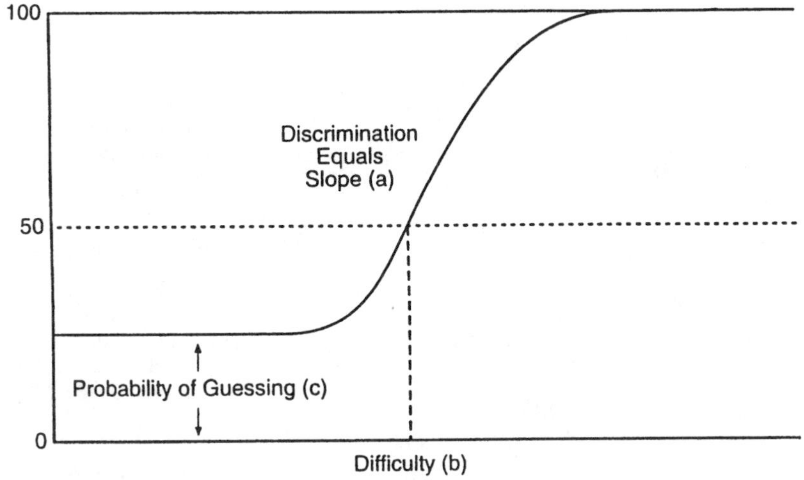

FIGURE 2.1. Item characteristic curve (ICC). From "IRT and Intelligence Testing: Past, Present, and Future" by R. M. Thorndike (p. 23), in S. E. Embretson and S. L. Hershberger (Eds.), *The New Rules of Measurement: What Every Psychologist and Educator Should Know*, 1999, Mahwah, NJ: Erlbaum. Copyright 1999 by Lawrence Erlbaum Associates. Reprinted with permission.

of the ICC at the point on the ability scale at which ability equals the difficulty parameter. For items of identical difficulty, the steeper the slope, the better the discrimination is. The CTT analogue of this parameter is the item–total score correlation (*r* value), with higher discrimination values for items that are more closely related to the construct measured by the test. The third parameter, *c*, the *pseudoguessing parameter,* is the height of the lower asymptote of the ICC and represents the probability of a correct response occurring by chance on multiple-choice test items.

IRT Models

The most popular IRT models differ primarily in the number of parameters used to describe test items. In the three-parameter model, items can vary with response to difficulty, discrimination, and the probability of being guessed correctly. In the two-parameter model, difficulty and discrimination parameters are estimated for each item, and the pseudoguessing parameter is assumed to be zero. In the one-parameter or Rasch model, a difficulty parameter is estimated for each item, but the discrimination parameter is fixed to be equivalent across items, and the effects of guessing are assumed to be zero. The Rasch model is used most frequently in psychological and educational test development because estimating item parameters and ability is greatly simplified. Rasch-model tests reviewed in this text include the WJ III and the *Woodcock Reading Mastery Tests–Revised/Normative Update* (WRMT-R/NU; Woodcock, 1987/1998).

Advantages of IRT Procedures

IRT methods have several distinct advantages over CTT procedures. First, scores on IRT-based tests are not dependent on the particular set of items administered to an examinee. In CTT, an examinee's test score is based on the total number of items correctly answered, so that the obtained score varies with each item sample. In the IRT ability estimation process, the examinee's test score incorporates information about the items but does not depend on the specific set of items administered. This can be achieved because the examinee's score is based not only on the number of items correctly answered but also on the statistical properties of the items the examinee answered correctly and incorrectly, such as their relative difficulty and discrimination power. Second, the item parameters derived from an IRT model are not dependent on the sample from which the item responses were derived. In CTT, item difficulty and item discrimination values depend on the examinee sample from which they are obtained. The higher the ability of the examinees in the sample on which the test is calibrated, the higher the values for difficulty indices derived from that sample will be. Similarly, the more heterogeneous the examinee sample is, the higher the values for discrimination indices will be. In IRT, however, the values of the item parameters are characteristics of the items themselves and are thus independent of the ability of the particular sample of examinees. Third, IRT procedures make it possible to evaluate the relative contribution of each item to the overall information provided by the test. As a result, items can be selected based on the amount of information they provide, greatly increasing the precision of measurement.

PSYCHOMETRIC PROPERTIES CRITICAL TO EARLY READING MEASURES

The following discussion describes the five psychometric properties critical to early reading measures, the minimal criteria for each property in terms of early reading assessments, and the rationale on which those criteria are based.

Standardization

Relevant psychometric considerations pertaining to standardization for early reading measures include the following: (1) representativeness of the normative sample, (2) subgroup and total sample size, (3) recency of norms, and (4) norm table age and/or grade intervals.

Representativeness of the Normative Sample

The validity of a test's norms depends on the degree to which the standardization sample represents the population with which an individual examinee's test results will be compared. For most assessment purposes, norms should be based on a large, nationally representative sample of examinees because samples from restricted geographical regions limit the degree to which users can generalize test results to their own examinee populations. As noted in Chapter 1, the general population may not be the appropriate reference group for some purposes, such as state, district, or building-level screening programs designed to identify the lowest performing children so that they can receive additional services. In these situations, local normative groups provide the most relevant comparisons.

For national samples, test authors should demonstrate that the norm group includes individuals with characteristics that are relevant to the construct being measured and approximate those of the current U.S. population. Relevant characteristics for early reading measures include age or grade; gender; geographical region; community size; community location (i.e., urban, suburban, or rural); type of school (i.e., public, private, or home); race/ethnicity; family socioeconomic status (SES), including parental education and occupation; curriculum; and disability status. To assist users in evaluating the representativeness of the norms relative to their own examinee populations, test manuals should provide tables comparing the demographic characteristics of the U.S. population to each age/grade subgroup rather than to the entire sample. Salvia and Ysseldyke (2001) suggest that the correspondence between the U.S. population and the norm group should be within about 5 percentage points for relevant characteristics.

Although family SES, curriculum, and disability status are often omitted from descriptions of standardization samples, they are especially important in evaluating the adequacy and utility of early reading measures. Because parental SES is associated with children's performance on a variety of tests, including phonological awareness measures (Bowey, 1995; Raz & Bryant, 1990), comparing a particular child's test performance with norms that do not include this information is problematic. Test authors should provide SES information in terms of parental educational attainment, parental occupational level, and/or family income data. Similarly, numerous studies (e.g., Brown & Felton, 1990; Foorman, Francis, & Fletcher, et al., 1997; Scanlon & Vellutino, 1997) have found that the type of reading instruction children receive in kindergarten and the primary grades is strongly related to the rate at which they acquire reading and spelling skills. Test authors should identify the curriculum to which students in the norm group have been exposed so that users can judge its similarity to the instruction provided to their own examinees. If students in a norm group received primarily whole language instruction, for example, examinees in a code-based reading instructional curriculum are likely to obtain higher scores on tests assessing decoding skills (Salvia & Ysseldyke, 2001). Unfortunately, test manuals almost never provide a description of instructional program characteristics, perhaps because of the diversity of instructional environments across districts and regions, as well as the time and labor involved in gathering curricular information from large numbers of classrooms.

Finally, the inclusion of students with disabilities in standardization samples is critical to the utility of test norms. Until quite recently, most test developers did not include groups of children with identified disabilities in standardization samples. Test users should review norm group descriptions to determine whether students with disabilities were included in the sampling process and, if so, in the correct proportion based on current U.S. census data. Excluding students with identified disabilities from the standardization sample results in a biased representation of test performance, with inflated means and reduced score variance. In contrast, including children with disabilities in the normative group produces more accurate estimates of test means and standard deviations and thus a more representative picture of the performance of the total school population in terms of the abilities and skills in question (Salvia & Ysseldyke, 2001).

CRITERIA FOR EVALUATING THE REPRESENTATIVENESS OF THE NORMATIVE GROUP

Criteria for evaluating the adequacy of the representativeness of standardization samples are adapted from the standards proposed by Hammill and colleagues (1992). At a minimum, the sample should represent the U.S. population on three or more demographic variables, one of which should include SES as measured by family income, parental educational level, and/or parental occupational level. For screening measures designed for use at the local level, samples should reflect important demographics in the reference population, such as the gender, grade, race/ethnicity, school SES level, and disability status of the students in the school, district, or state.

Subgroup and Total Sample Size

Adequate size for age and/or grade subgroups and for the standardization sample as a whole is essential to ensure score stability and a full range of derived scores. Adequate total sample size is needed to ensure sufficient dispersion for calculating percentile ranks and standard scores, as well as adequate representation of infrequent characteristics in the population. Test users should also review the size of the subgroups relevant to their purposes, however, because an examinee's performance is compared with that of his or her age or grade peers rather than with the performance of all the individuals in the norm group. Many tests sample unequal numbers of individuals per age or grade group, typically with fewer individuals per group at the lower and upper extremes. Moreover, because disproportionately fewer individuals in certain racial and ethnic categories may be represented in some or all age/grade subgroups, practitioners should examine both size and racial/ethnic diversity for the age and grade groups relevant to the children they plan to assess.

CRITERIA FOR EVALUATING SUBGROUP AND TOTAL SAMPLE SIZE

In accordance with the criteria set by Alfonso and Flanagan (1999), normative group size should be at least 100 individuals per age or grade subgroup and at least 1,000 individuals overall.

Recency of Norms

The relevance of the normative group is also related to the recency of those norms. Shifts in national demographic characteristics, as well as changes in curriculum and instructional methods, can exert a powerful influence on patterns of test performance. Flynn (1987, 1999) has demonstrated that performance on intelligence tests has risen over time, about 3 points per decade, so that older norms on these measures provide inflated estimates of children's level of functioning. In contrast, there is evidence (Ukrainetz & Duncan, 2000) that at least one recently revised achievement test (the *Peabody Picture Vocabulary Test–III* [PPVT-III]; Dunn & Dunn, 1997) yields substantially *lower* average standard scores compared with the previous version.

Norms for early reading measures are especially likely to become outdated rapidly because of the changes in reading instruction (e.g., from code-based to whole language methods or vice versa) that have occurred in many districts and states in recent years. Tests with outdated norms may provide spuriously inflated scores and thus fail to indicate the presence of significant skill deficits in need of remediation. Salvia and Ysseldyke (2001) have recommended a maximum of 7 years for achievement test norms. In Hammill and colleagues' (1992) evaluative system, tests with norm ages of 6 years or less are rated as "good," 7 to 16 years as "adequate," and 17 years or greater as "inadequate." Users should note that test publication dates are typically 1 or more years later than the year(s) during which normative information was collected. For example, data for the school-age sample for the WJ III, which bears a publication date of 2001, were collected from September 1996 to May 1999. Unfortunately, some manuals fail to indicate the actual year or years in which standardization data were collected, so that it is impossible to evaluate the age of the norms precisely.

CRITERIA FOR EVALUATING THE RECENCY OF NORMS

Criteria for evaluating the recency of normative data are adapted from Hammill and colleagues (1992) and Salvia and Ysseldyke (2001). The outer limit for the collection of normative data (as opposed to the publication date of the test) is set at 12 years. For instance, as of 2004 (the publication date of this book), data should have been collected no earlier than 1992.

Norm Table Age/Grade Intervals

Although norm table intervals of 1 year are typical for many tests, early reading measures should provide smaller intervals because of the rapid development of literacy skills in the primary grades. Tests designed to assess individuals over a wide age range often provide smaller intervals for younger examinees, with intervals of increasing size for older examinees. For example, the *Oral and Written Language Scales* (Carrow-Woolfolk, 1995) provide 3-month intervals for ages 3-0 through 8-11, 4-month intervals for ages 9-0 through 13-11, 6-month intervals for ages 14-0 through 18-11, and 1-year intervals for ages 19-0 through 21-11. Reynolds (1990) has recommended 2- to 6-month age intervals for tests used in ability–achievement discrepancy analyses, with intervals no greater than 6 months for children younger than 6 and no greater than 1 year for children at or above the age of 6.

CRITERIA FOR EVALUATING NORM TABLE AGE/GRADE INTERVALS

Criteria for evaluating the adequacy of norm table intervals are based on Reynolds's (1990) standards for tests intended for use in evaluating ability–achievement discrepancies, with the modification that the age at which intervals should be no greater than 6 months is extended through age 7 because of the rapid changes in reading skills in the first few years of school. Therefore, norm table intervals should be no more than 6 months for children through age 7-11 and no more than 1 year for children ages 8 and above. For tests that provide grade-based norms, intervals should be no more than 5 months in length (i.e., one school semester) across the entire early primary grade range.

GRADE VERSUS AGE NORMS

When tests yield both age and grade norms, practitioners must decide which type is more appropriate for their purposes. Although the type of norms selected does not affect age and grade equivalents, it does affect standard scores, percentile ranks, and proficiency scores, such as the WJ III Relative Proficiency Index scores. For early reading assessments, grade norms are more useful because reasons for referral are typically related to a child's performance relative to other individuals at the same grade level rather than the same age. Moreover, in the early grades, children's level of academic skill development is likely to be more closely associated with their instructional experiences than with their chronological age (Salvia & Ysseldyke, 2001).

There are several situations in which age norms should be selected, however. First, when children have been retained in grade, their scores on tests of academic proficiency may be low relative to their chronological age but within average limits for their current grade placement. Using norms that compare them with their grade peers may obscure the extent of their deficits. Thus for retained children, test users should use age norms or evaluate both sets of scores for a more comprehensive picture of examinee performance (Hessler, 1993). Second, grade-based norms may be less accurate than age-based norms for some measures because of the smoothing and extrapolation procedures needed to calculate them. Third, if examiners will be analyzing ability–achievement discrepancies, both ability and achievement tests must be scored using the same reference group. Finally, age-based norms are generally mandated when assessments are conducted to determine eligibility for special education services. Noting that the Public Law 94-142 criterion for severe discrepancy specifies that a child must fail to achieve commensurate with his or her age and ability level, Reynolds (1990) recommends that examiners evaluate ability–achievement discrepancies in terms of age-based standard scores.

Reliability

Reliability refers to the degree of consistency in the scores obtained from a test or measure. When tests are administered to identify children at risk for reading problems or to diagnose specific reading deficits, tests with adequate reliability permit users to be confident that examinees would perform comparably on equivalent sets of test items (*alternate-form* or *internal consistency reliability*), at different times (*test–retest reliability*), and with different scorers (*interscorer reliability*). As Traub and Rowley (1991) have observed, however, reliability depends not only on the characteristics of the test, such as the number and quality of the test items and the conditions under which the test is administered, but also on the characteristics of the individuals who take the test. Compared with tests for older examinees, tests for younger individuals tend to be less reliable because of young children's diverse maturational rates, behavioral and attentional fluctuations, and variations in experiential backgrounds. Test developers should provide evidence of reliability not only for the total sample but also for each age or grade subgroup and for demographic subgroups that may be vulnerable to test bias because of gender, racial, ethnic, linguistic, or disability differences. When subtest scores are to be interpreted, reliability coefficients should be presented for these scores as well as for composite scores.

Generalizing to Different Sets of Test Items

Content sampling error reflects the degree to which an examinee's scores on a test depend on the particular items included in the test. To estimate the extent to which examiners can generalize to different samples of items, test authors generally use one or both of two approaches: alternate-form reliability and internal consistency reliability.

ALTERNATE-FORM RELIABILITY

In the *alternate-form reliability* method, test authors develop two equivalent forms of a test, administer both forms to a group of examinees in a single testing session, and correlate scores from the two forms to derive a reliability coefficient. When an interval of time passes between administrations of the two forms, alternate-form reliability is an estimate of both temporal stability (time sampling error) and the consistency of responses to the two forms (content sampling error). Because these stability coefficients include two sources of errors, test authors generally subtract the error variance attributable to content sampling and report the adjusted coefficients.

If a test has two forms, test authors should report not only the correlations between the forms but also the means and standard deviations for each form at each age or grade interval. Without this information, users cannot evaluate the magnitude of differences between the two test forms. Although most tests with alternate forms have separate norm tables for each form, some provide only a single set of tables on the grounds that the correlation between the two forms is so high that separate tables would be redundant. When tables are combined, authors should present information regarding not only the size of subtest and total test correlations between the two forms but also the equivalence of test means and standard deviations for each age or grade interval.

INTERNAL CONSISTENCY RELIABILITY

Internal consistency reliability reflects the degree of consistency with which examinees perform across individual items or subsets of items in a single test administration and can be considered an estimate of alternate-form reliability. Methods of estimating internal consistency include the split-half, coefficient alpha, and Kuder–Richardson formula 20 procedures. In the *split-half reliability* method, a test is divided into two half-tests of equal length; both are administered to a group of examinees; and the correlation between the two sets of scores is calculated. Because reducing the number of items reduces the size of the reliability coefficient, the Spearman–Brown formula is used to adjust the correlation and correct for the reduction. The result is an estimate of the total test's alternate-form reliability. For tests with basal–ceiling formats, however, the standard procedure of correlating raw scores on odd versus even items can produce spuriously high coefficients by including scores from unadministered items. Test developers deal with this problem in different ways. On the PPVT-III, split-half reliability coefficients were obtained by dividing the items taken by each examinee in the standardization sample into comparable halves, using Rasch-model procedures to estimate a *W*-ability scale score for each part, and then correlating the scale scores. The Spearman–Brown formula was then applied to produce an estimate of reliability for the entire test length. In contrast, the developers of the WJ III computed split-half coefficients using odd–even test items on the grounds that basal–ceiling rules used during sampling were so stringent that the probability of failing an item below the basal or passing an item above the ceiling was extremely low.

The *coefficient alpha* technique can be used for tests that are scored pass–fail or for tests that award more than a single point for a correct response. Coefficient alpha is the average of all possible splittings of a test into two parts and is based on the variance of the total test score and the variances of the individual item scores. The higher the alpha coefficient, the more highly correlated the items are, and the more precise the measurement is. For tests with items scored pass–fail, internal consistency reliability can be estimated using the *Kuder–Richardson formula 20* procedure (KR-20), a special case of coefficient alpha based on the proportion of examinees who pass and fail each item and the variance of the test scores.

For speeded tests, such as measures of rapid naming and oral reading fluency, reliability estimates based on a single administration will be inflated. Instead, content sampling error can be estimated using alternate-form or test–retest reliability procedures. If two forms of a test have been developed, they are administered in immediate succession, and the correlation between the two forms serves as an estimate of how consistently examinees perform on comparable sets of items at different times. If a test includes only one form, test–retest procedures are used, and the resulting coefficient indicates how consistently examinees perform on the same set of items on different occasions. For speeded tests developed using IRT procedures, such as the WJ III Rapid Naming test, internal consistency reliability estimates can be calculated from Rasch-based standard errors of measurement.

STANDARD ERROR OF MEASUREMENT

The standard error of measurement (SEM) is the standard deviation of an examinee's observed scores if a test were to be repeatedly administered under identical conditions and is based on the reliability coefficient of the test. Whereas the reliability coefficient is useful for comparing the precision of measurement among different tests, the SEM is more useful for interpreting individual test results because it provides an estimate of the amount of error associated with an examinee's obtained score. The smaller the SEM, the more precise the measurement is. The SEM, along with the z score associated with the confidence level chosen, is used to construct confidence intervals for an examinee's "true" score. Whereas CTT-based procedures provide an average SEM per age and/or grade interval, IRT-based tests yield SEMs that are specific to each ability level. On IRT-model tests, SEMs are smallest when test items are most appropriate for a particular ability level and, for two- or three-parameter models, when item discriminations are high (Embretson & Reise, 2000). Test developers should report SEMs for composite and total test scores for each age and grade subgroup and for subtests, if subtest scores are to be interpreted.

CRITERIA FOR EVALUATING INTERNAL CONSISTENCY RELIABILITY

Criterion levels for internal consistency vary depending on the assessment purpose. Bracken (1987, 2000) and Salvia and Ysseldyke (2001), among others, stipulate that reliability coefficients should be at least .80 for screening purposes and .90 or above for individual diagnostic and placement purposes. In accordance with these recommendations, criterion levels for coefficient size for composite and total test scores are set at a minimum of .80 for screening measures and at a minimum of .90 for tests designed for individual diagnostic and programming purposes. If subtests are to be interpreted, internal consistency reliability coefficients of .80 are considered minimal for either type of measure, a criterion that is consistent with the standard for screening tests. When internal consistency coefficients fall below this level, subtest scores should not be interpreted (Bracken, 1987).

Generalizing to Different Testing Times

The degree to which an examinee's test performance is stable over time is usually estimated by the *test–retest* procedure. In this method, the test is administered to a group of examinees, an interval of time elapses, and the identical test is administered to the same examinees a second time, yielding a correlation called the *stability coefficient*. Determining an appropriate level of stability for a test is more difficult than setting acceptable criteria for internal consistency (Bracken, 1987). Test–retest reliability coefficients include not only measurement error but also error due to changes in examinees resulting from maturation, instruction, or other experiences, as well as error arising from the instability of the trait being measured. As a result, test–retest coefficients tend to be lower than internal consistency coefficients (McGrew, Werder, & Woodcock, 1991). Bracken and his colleagues (Bracken, 1987; Bracken & Walker, 1997) have proposed that for short test–retest intervals (2–4 weeks), stability coefficients for total test scores should approximate internal consistency coefficients, that is, they should equal or exceed .90.

In addition to trait stability, three other factors should be considered in evaluating test–retest reliability estimates: (1) the size and representativeness of the test–retest sample(s), (2) the age range of the sample(s), and (3) the length of the test–retest interval(s) (Flanagan & Alfonso, 1995). Test–retest coefficients are sometimes based on a single study with a small number of examinees drawn from a restricted geographical location. Under these conditions, users' confidence in the generalizability of the findings must also be limited. Test authors should report the size and demographic characteristics of each of the samples used to estimate stability. Ideally, test–retest studies should be conducted with various subgroups for which test stability may be of concern, such as racial/ethnic and disability groups.

Stability coefficients should be reported for all age or grade intervals for all scores that are to be interpreted (i.e., for subtest as well as composite and total test scores if subtests are to be interpreted). In practice, however, test publishers usually report test–retest reliability for subgroup intervals spanning several years or grades rather than for each age or grade grouping in the norm tables. The more closely the age or grade range of a test–retest sample matches that of the target examinee population, the more confidence test users can have in the stability estimates provided. For example, if users plan to administer a test to children in the first semester of kindergarten, stability information from a test–retest sample with an age range from 5 to 12 years is likely to be misleading. Moreover, test–retest reliability estimates derived from examinees whose ages span a wide range of years will be inflated because of age heterogeneity.

The length of the test–retest intervals reported in stability studies varies considerably among the tests reviewed in this text. The shorter the test–retest interval, the higher the stability coefficient will be, because fewer factors intervene to influence individual test performance. Given the rapid growth in literacy skills during the early primary grades, test–retest intervals of 2–4 weeks are most appropriate for early reading measures.

CRITERIA FOR EVALUATING TEST–RETEST RELIABILITY

Criteria for evaluating stability coefficient size and test–retest sample size and representativeness, age or grade range, and length of interval are adapted from the guidelines set by Bracken and his colleagues (Bracken, 1987; Bracken & Walker, 1997) and Alfonso and Flanagan (Alfonso & Flanagan, 1999; Flanagan & Alfonso, 1995). In terms of magnitude, stability coefficients for composite and total scores should be at least .80 for screening measures and at least .90 for individual diagnostic and programming measures. If subtests are to be interpreted, stability coefficients should be at least .80. In terms of size and representativeness, test–retest samples should include at least 50 examinees and should approximate the U.S. population (or the appropriate reference group) on three or more demographic variables. In terms of age or grade range, the test–retest sample should span no more than 4 years or four grades and should include the early primary grade age range of 5-0 to 8-11 years. The test–retest interval should be no more than 3 months and preferably no more than 1 month.

Generalizing to Different Scorers

Interscorer reliability reflects the amount of error in a test related to differences among scorers. For some types of tests, scoring procedures can be so highly standardized that interscorer variability is minimal. On other measures, subjective judgment is required to evaluate the accuracy and quality of responses, so that variation is likely to occur across different examiners. Reynolds (1990) has recommended that test authors report reliability estimates for all subtests that require examiners to make fine distinctions among responses. Interscorer variability can result not only from scorer differences in judging the quality of responses after a test has been administered but also from differences in recording and scoring responses during the administration process. *Examiner variance* is especially likely to occur on tasks that require quick, accurate scoring during test administration, such as oral reading fluency, pseudoword reading, and rapid naming.

Early reading tasks with live-voice presentation are also vulnerable to examiner variance because of differences in linguistic competence among test users. To achieve acceptable consistency on orally delivered tasks, such as measures of pseudoword repetition, sound blending, and memory span, examiners must not only possess satisfactory articulation but must also be capable of administering the type of items accurately. Some examiners may have difficulty pronouncing pseudowords correctly, whereas others may lack the fully developed phonemic awareness required to manipulate individual phonemes, as in phoneme blending tasks (Lindamood, 1994;

Moats & Lyons, 1996). Similarly, examiners may vary in their ability to pronounce digits, words, pseudowords, or sentences clearly and accurately and, for memory span tasks, to deliver test stimuli at the specified rate.

MINIMIZING INTERSCORER AND EXAMINER VARIANCE

To minimize error arising from interscorer and examiner variance, test manuals should provide clear, comprehensive directions for all tasks, as well as additional administration supports, depending on the scoring complexity and linguistic demands of the task. For tests of word identification and pseudoword reading or repetition, pronunciation keys for infrequent real words and all pseudowords should be provided in the record booklet as well as in the manual, and additional pronunciation guides on audiocassettes are highly desirable. For phonemic manipulation measures, such as sound blending tasks, test authors should specify time intervals for pronouncing phonemes, syllables, or word segments. Audiocassette-recorded delivery is preferred for phoneme blending, pseudoword repetition, and memory span tasks to ensure that test items are delivered consistently to all examinees. When tests provide audiocassette recordings of task stimuli, manuals should indicate the conditions (if any) under which examiners may substitute live-voice administration.

PROCEDURES FOR ESTIMATING INTERSCORER DIFFERENCES

Interscorer reliability can be estimated using a variety of methods, including Pearson product–moment correlation, comparison of means, intraclass correlation, percentage of agreement, and G theory approaches. When test scores are interval-level, the *Pearson product–moment correlation* approach is frequently used. In this method, two examiners independently score a sample of tests, the two scores for each examinee are correlated, and the resulting coefficient reflects the agreement for the relative placement of examinees in terms of total score. A large positive coefficient obtained by correlating total scores may mask sizable differences in the level of scores assigned to examinees, however. When the level of the scores is of interest, the *comparison of means* approach can be used that compares the mean ratings of two or more scorers, followed by a *t* test or analysis of variance (ANOVA) to determine whether there are significant differences among mean ratings (Goodwin & Goodwin, 1991).

When multipoint criteria are used to evaluate test responses, as on written language measures, interscorer reliability can be investigated using an *intraclass correlation,* which takes into account both the pattern and the level of agreement (Shrout & Fleiss, 1979). When measurement data are nominal or categorical, *percentage of agreement* procedures, such as simple agreement or Cohen's (1960) kappa, are often used. In the *simple* or *uncorrected agreement* approach, reliability is expressed as the number of times two or more scorers agree relative to the total number of protocols scored. This uncorrected percentage of agreement is likely to overestimate the degree of agreement, however, because there is no correction for chance agreement. In contrast, the *kappa index of agreement,* which can be used for multiple scorers and multiple categories, adjusts the proportion of agreement across scorers by removing the proportion of agreement that would be expected to occur by chance. Kappa coefficients range from –1.00 to +1.00, with a positive kappa coefficient indicating that the proportion of scorer agreement is greater than the proportion of chance agreement.

REPORTING INTERSCORER RELIABILITY

For tasks that require scorers to make subjective judgments, test manuals should include information regarding the procedures used to evaluate interscorer reliability, as well as the number of scorers, the training provided for scorers, the process by which protocols were selected, and the number and type (i.e., examinee age and/or grade) of protocols scored. Practitioners should note that the interscorer reliability coefficients reported in test manuals nearly always represent agreement among scorers who have evaluated responses on completed protocols rather than agreement among examiners who have simultaneously recorded and scored responses for the same set of examinees during test sessions. For tasks that are vulnerable to examiner variance because of complex administration and scoring procedures, test authors should provide evidence of interscorer agreement *at the time responses are being recorded* by videotaping testing sessions or audiotaping verbal responses and having several examiners score the responses independently. Correlations between the sets of scores or statistical analyses of mean score differences across examiners can be then calculated for each task or subtest.

CRITERIA FOR EVALUATING INTERSCORER RELIABILITY

Very few of the sources of evaluative criteria reviewed for this book included interscorer reliability as a separate category of reliability estimation. Bracken and colleagues (1994) set a criterion of .90 as desirable for interrater reliability for preschool behavior rating measures, whereas Reynolds (1990) recommended that interscorer reliability coefficients for tests used in discrepancy analyses should be at least .85–.90. Accordingly, for tests requiring subjective judgment in scoring and tests vulnerable to examiner variance because of complex administration and/or scoring procedures, minimum criterion levels for interscorer reliability coefficients are set at .80 for screening measures and at .90 for measures designed for diagnostic or placement purposes.

GENERALIZABILITY THEORY: A NEW APPROACH TO EVALUATING RELIABILITY

In classical test theory (CTT), multiple reliability coefficients, including test–retest, internal consistency, interscorer, and alternate-form reliability, can be estimated for each test. These reliability coefficients are rarely equal in magnitude, however, leaving test users to judge for themselves which estimate is of primary importance, given the measurement context. Moreover, CTT procedures cannot be used to evaluate the relative contributions of these sources of error simultaneously, examine the possible interactions among error sources, or estimate the overall effect of measurement error. Generalizability theory (G theory; Cronbach, Gleser, Nanda, & Rajaratnam, 1972) is an extension of CTT that was developed to overcome these problems and is increasingly being used to assess the dependability of behavioral measurements, including reading measures (e.g., Hintze, Owen, Shapiro, & Daly, 2000; Hintze & Petitte, 2001), and large-scale assessments such as statewide literacy screening programs (e.g., Foorman, Fletcher, et al., 1998). The following discussion provides a practitioner-oriented overview of G theory and is based primarily on the following sources: Goodwin and Goodwin (1991), Hoyt and Melby (1999), Shavelson and Webb (1991), and Suen (1990).

G theory refers to a conceptual framework and set of statistical methods that apply analysis of variance (ANOVA) to assessing the dependability of measurement in the behavioral sciences. In CTT, an examinee's observed test score is assumed to be a linear combination of two components: a true score and an error score. In contrast, G theory assumes that an examinee's observed test score consists of a *universe score* (the examinee's average score over the entire universe of items measuring the construct of interest), along with one or more sources of error. The goal of G theory procedures is to evaluate the extent to which generalizations may be made from the observed score to the *universe of admissible observations*, defined by the conditions of measurement or *facets* included in the generalizability study. Unlike CTT procedures, which yield only one coefficient per reliability study, the ANOVA procedures in G theory make it possible to estimate in a single study the amount of error attributable to multiple sources of errors, such as differences among raters, among items, between alternate forms, and across time.

Generalizability and Decision Studies

G theory distinguishes between two types of studies: *generalizability* (G) studies and *decision* (D) studies. The purpose of a G study is to estimate the variance associated with specific facets of measurement, such as errors across raters, items, forms, and time. A D study uses the information obtained in the G study regarding the various sources of error and their interactions to design a measure that has maximum reliability for a particular purpose. G theory also distinguishes between relative decisions and absolute decisions in the interpretation of measurements. *Relative decisions* address situations in which individual differences among examinees are important, such as on norm-referenced tests, with the meaning of a score based on its position relative to the sampling distribution on the test. *Absolute decisions* address situations in which the level of performance is important, such as on screening measures with a cutoff score indicating risk status. G theory provides a coefficient analogous to CTT reliability coefficients that also ranges from 0.0 to 1.0 and indicates the level of generalizability or dependability of scores in terms of the sources of error included in the design of the G or D study. For relative decisions, the reliability coefficient is termed the *generalizability coefficient* (G), whereas for absolute decisions, the reliability coefficient is termed the *index of dependability* (D).

Test Floors and Item Gradients

Test Floors

A *test floor* or *cellar* refers to the lowest range of standard scores that can be obtained when an examinee answers no items or only a few items correctly on a subtest or test. Tests with adequate or *low floors* include a sufficient number of easy items to differentiate effectively among examinees performing in the average, low average, and low ranges and to identify accurately very low performance in terms of the ability or skill being assessed. In contrast, tests with inadequate or *high floors* yield standard scores that overestimate examinees' level of competency on the relevant ability or skill and thus fail to indicate the presence of deficits and the need for intervention.

Subtest and total test "floor effects" are most often evident for the youngest children among the age groups covered by a test. For example, on the *Comprehensive Test of Phonological Processing* (CTOPP; Wagner, Torgesen, & Rashotte, 1999), which is designed for individuals aged 5-0 to 24-11, a raw score of 1 at ages 5-0 to 5-5 on the Elision subtest (*M* = 10, *SD* = 3) is associated with a standard score of 8, less than 1 standard deviation below the normative mean. Because of its inadequate floor, the Elision subtest is unable to distinguish children with average phonemic deletion skills from those with very poor phonemic deletion skills. In contrast, on the *Kaufman Survey of Early Academic and Language Skills* (Kaufman & Kaufman, 1993), a raw score of 1 at ages 5-0 to 5-2 on the Vocabulary subtest (*M* = 100, *SD* = 15) is associated with a standard score of 55, which falls 3 standard deviations below the normative mean. Such a test is capable of distinguishing between children with low and very low levels of vocabulary knowledge as well as between children with average and below average vocabulary skills.

Although test users should examine subtest floors for all age and grade ranges relevant to their examinee populations, evaluating composite and total test floors is even more critical because decisions about additional instruction or special education services are primarily based on scores derived from composite measures of performance rather than individual subtests (Flanagan & Alfonso, 1995). For example, a raw score of 1 on each of the subtests constituting the CTOPP Phonological Awareness composite score for ages 5-0 to 5-5 yields a standard score of 85, only 1 standard deviation below the mean of 100. Thus at the lower end of the CTOPP age range, the Phonological Awareness composite cannot distinguish between children with average and below average phonological awareness nor accurately identify children with very low levels of phonological awareness.

Test Ceilings

Although the adequacy of test floors is much more critical than that of test ceilings for the purposes of this text, a brief discussion of ceilings is in order at this point. A *test ceiling* refers to the highest range of standard scores that can be obtained when an examinee answers most or all items correctly on a subtest or test and reflects the degree to which a test is able to identify very high levels of the ability or skill being assessed. A test has an inadequate or *low ceiling* when it includes too few difficult items to distinguish between examinees with average skills and those with very well developed skills. "Ceiling effects" are not a serious threat to the utility of most of the early reading measures reviewed in this text because they are designed to identify children with deficits in reading and reading-related skills rather than to differentiate children with average skills from those with above average to excellent skills. For example, the highest standard score children ages 6-6 to 6-11 can obtain on the *Test of Phonological Awareness–Early Elementary* (TOPA-EE; Torgesen & Bryant, 1994b) is 116, compared with a test floor of 52. Because the stated purpose of the TOPA-EE is to identify children who are seriously delayed in phonological awareness rather than to discriminate among children with well developed skills, however, this is not problematic for the test.

Whereas some test authors direct users' attention to the presence of ceiling and/or floor effects for certain age or grade levels and include cautions in the manual about interpretation at those levels, others do not. Before administering any early reading measure, practitioners should review subtest, composite, and total test floors for the age and grade ranges of the population with which they plan to use the test. Criteria for evaluating test floor adequacy are presented below.

CRITERIA FOR EVALUATING TEST FLOORS

Criteria for evaluating test floors are based on Bracken's (1987, 2000) and Alfonso and Flanagan's (Alfonso & Flanagan, 1999; Flanagan & Alfonso, 1995) guidelines for intelligence tests for preschoolers. At a given age level, a subtest floor is considered adequate when a raw score of 1 is associated with a standard score greater than 2 standard deviations below the normative mean. Tests meeting this criterion are capable of differentiating the lowest 2% of examinees from the rest of the distribution in terms of the ability or skill being measured. In practical terms, this means that on a subtest with a mean of 10 and a standard deviation of 3, a raw score of 1 must yield a standard score equal to or less than 3 to meet this criterion. On a subtest with a mean of 100 and a standard deviation of 15, a raw score of 1 must yield a standard score of 69 or less. For scale, composite, and total test floors, a raw score of 1 on each of the subtests making up that scale, composite, or total test score must yield, when summed, a standard score greater than 2 standard deviations below the mean. For a scale, composite, or total test with a mean of 100 and a standard deviation of 15, the sum of the subtest raw scores comprising the scale, composite, or total test score when an examinee answers 1 item correctly per subtest must yield a standard score of 69 or less to meet this criterion.

Item Gradients

The *item gradient* of a measure refers to the steepness with which standard scores change from one raw score unit to another. The smaller the change in standard scores relative to small increments in raw score values, the more sensitive the test is to small differences in performance within and across ability levels and the more useful test results are for making diagnoses, designing interventions, and monitoring progress (Bracken, 1987; Bracken & Walker, 1997). Whereas floors determine the degree to which a test differentiates effectively among performance levels at the low end of the range of functioning, item gradients determine the extent to which a test differentiates effectively across the entire range of the ability or skill being measured (Flanagan, Mascolo, & Genshart, 2000).

Tests with adequate item gradient characteristics include a sufficient number of items that are approximately equally spaced in difficulty throughout the entire range of the test to permit differentiation among fine gradations of performance throughout all levels of functioning, from very low to very superior. When item gradients are too steep, a small increase in raw score values will produce a relatively large increase in standard scores, obscuring differences among different performance levels. For subtests with a mean of 10 and standard deviation of 3, Bracken (1987, 2000) has recommended no fewer than 3 raw score items per standard deviation of standard scores (i.e., a single item should be worth no more than one-third of a standard score deviation). This means that for a subtest with a mean of 10 and a standard deviation of 3, a 1-point raw score increase should produce a standard score increase of no more than 1 point. For a subtest with a mean of 100 and a standard deviation of 15, a 1-point raw score increase should produce a standard score increase equal to or less than 5 points. Failure to meet this criterion has been termed an *item gradient violation* (Flanagan & Alfonso, 1995).

An evaluation of item gradient characteristics should always be conducted in conjunction with an evaluation of test floors, however. A subtest may have few or no item gradient violations between the floor and the mean because the test floor is inadequate and a raw score of 1 produces a standard score that falls near or within the average range (Flanagan & Alfonso, 1995). For example, the Phonemic Word Efficiency (PWE) subtest on the *Test of Word Reading Efficiency* (Torgesen, Wagner, & Rashotte, 1999), which requires reading pseudowords as rapidly as possible, has no item gradient violations for the 6-0 to 6-5 age range. The PWE floor at that level is a standard score of 98, however, so that it is unable to differentiate children with average speeded pseudoword reading skills from those with low average skills, much less very delayed skills.

CRITERIA FOR EVALUATING ITEM GRADIENTS

Although various systems for evaluating item gradient characteristics have been developed, some are highly complex and require a substantial amount of time to apply (Flanagan & Alfonso, 1995; McGrew & Flanagan, 1998), whereas others fail to consider the problem of inadequate test floors (Athanasiou, 2000). The criterion levels presented here take into account not only the steepness of standard score increases relative to raw score increases (Bracken, 1987, 2000) but also the relationship of test floors to item gradient adequacy (Flanagan & Alfonso, 1995). Given a subtest mean of 10 and a standard deviation of 3, the number of items between the floor and the mean should be equal to or greater than 6 for a given age/grade level. This allows for a subtest floor that extends at least 2 standard deviations below the mean and includes at least 3 items per standard deviation. Similarly, given a subtest mean of 100 and a standard deviation of 15, the number of items between the floor and the mean should be equal to or greater than 10 (i.e., allowing for at least 5 items for each of 2 standard deviations below the mean).

EVALUATING TEST FLOORS AND ITEM GRADIENTS FOR NONTRADITIONAL TESTS

Three categories of tests require a different set of considerations and/or procedures in evaluating the adequacy of test floors and item gradients: (1) screening measures, (2) tests that do not yield standard scores, and (3) Rasch-model tests.

Screening Measures

In the case of screening tests designed to differentiate among examinees at a predetermined place in the distribution (i.e., around a cutoff score) rather than to differentiate among examinees across the entire range of performance, test floors and item gradients are much less important than the test's sensitivity around the criterion score. If the goal is to differentiate good readers from poor readers, an instrument does not need to be sensitive at all levels of performance (i.e., to differentiate very good readers from adequate readers or very poor readers from poor readers). Instead, it should be highly accurate at differentiating examinees around the cutoff score that indicates risk status (Tracey & Glidden-Tracey, 1999). Examiner manuals and/or technical reports should provide evidence from predictive validity studies documenting the ability of the screening measure to differentiate good readers from poor readers.

Tests Not Yielding Standard Scores

Several of the norm-referenced tests reviewed in this book yield decile, percentile ranges, quartile, or stanine scores rather than standard scores (i.e., scores with a mean of 100 and a standard deviation of 15 or 16) for some or all subtests or tasks. Some of these instruments are early reading assessment batteries that specify a range of scores indicative of at-risk status (e.g., the *Early Reading Diagnostic Assessment–Revised* [Psychological Corporation, 2002]), whereas others are supplementary measures in multiskill batteries (e.g., the Reading Speed score on the *Wechsler Individual Achievement Test–II* [Psychological Corporation, 2001a]). Because of the developmental nature of phonological and other early literacy skills, instruments measuring these skills are especially susceptible to cellar and ceiling effects at the lower and upper age ranges and may display bimodal score distributions rather than gradually increasing item gradients. For example, a test measuring letter-name knowledge is likely to show floor effects for the fall of kindergarten but ceiling effects for the fall of second grade. Test users should examine the conversion tables in the manual to evaluate the adequacy of floors for the age/grade of their examinees and to determine whether there are large gaps between the derived scores or score ranges as raw scores increase (i.e., inadequate item gradient characteristics). For tests yielding percentile or percentile range scores, a raw score of 1 should yield a percentile rank or range of 2, which is equivalent to a standard score of 70.

Rasch-Model Tests

For most instruments, evaluating the adequacy of test floors is a simple if time-consuming procedure that requires consulting the raw score–standard score conversion tables in the manual for each age or grade interval of interest. For Rasch-based tests, however, a direct inspection of raw score–standard score relationships is not possible because of the additional steps in the score conversion process. On the WRMT-R/NU, deriving standard scores from raw scores by hand requires a three-step process that is spread across three separate tables. Examiners must first convert raw scores to *W* (Rasch-ability) scores, then subtract the age or grade reference score from the *W* score to obtain a difference score, and finally convert the obtained difference score to a standard score. In the latest edition of the WJ III, score conversion tables have been omitted from the manuals, and only computer scoring is available. Examiners can obtain rough estimates of item gradient steepness for WJ III tests by comparing changes in raw scores with corresponding changes in the estimated age and grade equivalents listed in tables in the record booklets. Examiners who wish to conduct a more precise evaluation of test floors and item gradients for Rasch-model tests can use the software scoring program to generate subtest and composite standard scores for the relevant age or grade group. The steps for using software scoring programs to evaluate test floors and item gradients for Rasch-model tests are listed below. Of course, this method can also be used for non-IRT tests, but it is much less time-consuming to use the norm tables in the manual to compare raw and standard scores.

1. Enter a sample case that corresponds to an examinee of the desired age and/or grade by typing in sufficient identifying data (i.e., name, gender, grade, birth date, and testing date) to create a record. For example, to determine the test floor for an examinee aged 6-6 in the year 2004, enter the following birth and testing dates: birth date = 3/5/1998; test date = 9/5/2004.
2. Enter a raw score of 1 for all subtests.
3. Select age or grade norms.
4. Save and display or save and print the results. This will produce a display or printout with age- or grade-based standard scores corresponding to a raw score of 1 for every subtest and composite score available for that test. The adequacy of test floors can then be evaluated according to the criteria presented above.
5. If desired, the same procedure can be used to evaluate item gradients by entering 1-point raw score increments for the selected age and/or grade level. That is, using the same identifying data, enter a raw score of 2 on each subtest, select the desired norms, and save and display or print the results. Continue with this procedure by entering successive increases of 1 raw-score point until the obtained standard score is equal to the mean for that subtest.

Validity

Validity refers to the degree to which theory and empirical evidence support the proposed interpretations and uses of test scores (AERA et al., 1999). Like reliability, validity is not a property of a test per se. Instead, validity relates to the inferences that are made based on the obtained test scores. As a result, the validation of a specific instrument is not a one-time determination but an ongoing process of accumulating evidence to support the proposed interpretations and uses of test scores. Although test manuals typically provide several types of validation evidence when tests are initially published, the meaning of test scores continues to be specified through use by practitioners and researchers (Anastasi & Urbina, 1997). Moreover, validity is not an all-or-nothing situation. That is, a test may be valid for some purposes, settings, and examinees but not for others. For example, a test may be appropriate as a screening instrument to identify children whose phonological awareness skills are delayed relative to a national or local normative sample but not to specify the type or intensity of interventions required to bring their performance up to expected levels.

Traditionally, validity has been conceptualized as consisting of three separate types: content, criterion-related, and construct validity. In recent years, however, there has been a shift toward a unified theory of validity, in which construct validity is viewed as the fundamental, all-encompassing concept underlying test validation. From this perspective, content and criterion-related validity are viewed not as separate types of validity but as additional sources of evidence that contribute to an understanding of the construct measured by a test (Messick, 1989a, 1989b, 1995). Accordingly, the AERA and colleagues (1999) *Standards* refer not to *types of validity* but to *types of evidence* for validating tests, and the traditional three categories have been replaced with five types of evidence: (1) evidence based on test content, (2) evidence based on response processes, (3) evidence based on internal structure, (4) evidence based on relations to other variables, and (5) evidence based on the consequences of testing. Despite this shift in the conceptualization of validity, many publishers continue to present validation evidence in test manuals according to the traditional three-part organization. Moreover, the distinctions among the various kinds of validation procedures have utility because they provide concrete guidelines for the validation process for test developers and help clarify test purposes for users (Anastasi & Urbina, 1997; Brennan, 1998). In keeping with the goals of this text, which include increasing test users' ability to evaluate the technical adequacy of early reading instruments, the following discussion retains the traditional categories, with the addition of the term *evidence* to underscore that validity is not inherent in a test but is acquired through a continuing process of theoretical and empirical analysis.

Content Validity Evidence

Content validity refers to the degree to which a test adequately assesses the essential aspects of the domain it is designed to measure. Although test developers have traditionally relied on subjective reviews by experts to evaluate the relevance and thoroughness of content coverage, evidence of content validity based on expert judgment provides only limited support for the validity of test scores for a particular purpose (Plante & Vance, 1994). As a result, most test developers now also use some form of multivariate statistical procedures, such as factor analysis, to evaluate the content domains assessed by an instrument. These techniques are described below in the discussion of construct validity. For early reading measures, four areas of content validity evidence are most relevant: (1) a rationale for how the domain was defined; (2) evidence that the test adequately samples the domain; (3) a rationale for task format and item type selection; and (4) item analyses, including a demonstration of the lack of bias in test items.

DOMAIN DEFINITION

Test authors should present a clear definition of the domain(s) of test content represented in the instrument, including a theoretical rationale and empirical evidence. For early reading measures, relevant domains include phonological processing, rapid naming, orthographic processing, oral language, print awareness/concept of word, alphabet knowledge, single word reading, oral reading in context, reading comprehension, written language (including spelling), and the cognitive abilities and skills associated with those domains.

DOMAIN SAMPLING

Test developers should also provide evidence that the instrument adequately samples the domain(s) of interest. For example, for a test intended to assess phonological awareness, authors should present the theoretical and empirical basis for selecting particular components as testing tasks (e.g., rhyming, syllable segmentation, phoneme segmentation, sound blending, phoneme deletion, etc.). Evidence of the appropriateness and adequacy of content sampling can be demonstrated by having expert judges review tasks and items, surveying available tests to ensure that the content of the new test aligns with that of other related measures, and conducting factor analytic studies. In addition, users should review the content validity information presented in the manual to determine a test's *curricular validity*, the degree to which test objectives match local instructional objectives (Suen, 1990).

SELECTION OF TASK FORMATS AND ITEM TYPES

Researchers and test developers have used a wide variety of task formats and item types to assess reading and reading-related processes. Many of the tests reviewed in this text are based on their authors' long-term research programs on reading acquisition and reading disabilities, with subtest and item formats based on experimental tasks they have developed (e.g., Berninger, 2001; Nicolson & Fawcett, 1996; Torgesen, Wagner, & Rashotte, 1999; Wagner et al., 1999). At a minimum, test manuals should include an explicit rationale for task format and item type selection, with citations from the literature.

ITEM ANALYSIS

Content validity is also demonstrated by item analyses, which provide evidence that the items included in a test are valid for its particular purposes. In CTT methods, item analyses include studies of item discrimination, item difficulty, and differential item functioning (DIF or item bias; see below). Analyses of *item discrimination* indicate the degree to which an item is effective in discriminating between examinees with high ability (i.e., those who score high on the test as a whole) from those with low ability (those with a low total test score). The higher the item discrimination coefficient, the more effective is the item. Test developers use a variety of item discrimination indices, including the *D*-index, which expresses the difference between the proportions of high-ability and low-ability examinees answering an item correctly, and the Pearson correlation and point biserial indices, which indicate the correlation between the score on a particular item and the score on the total test. In general, item discrimination indices of .30 or higher are considered acceptable (Aiken, 2000).

Analyses of *item difficulty* are used to identify items that are too easy or too difficult and to arrange items in a hierarchical order of difficulty. The *item difficulty index* or *p value* of an item indicates the proportion of examinees that answered the item correctly and ranges from 0 for items that no examinees in the norm group answered correctly to +1.00 for items that all examinees in the norm group answered correctly. For example, a *p* value of .85 indicates that 85% of examinees in the standardization sample answered that item correctly. In general, tests that include items with a moderate range of difficulty (e.g., .15 to .85) and an average difficulty of .50 provide the most accurate assessment of individual performance levels. Selection of item difficulty levels should match the type of discrimination desired, however (Anastasi & Urbina, 1997). For screening measures, item difficulty values should match the predetermined cutoff score as closely as possible. If the test is designed to identify the lowest 25% of children, items approximating a *p* of .75 (or higher, to allow for the guessing factor) are optimal. In other words, a measure designed to identify children with severe skill deficits should consist of items that are considerably easier than average. For example, on the TOPA, which targets children with serious delays in phonological processing, the authors selected only items with moderate difficulty levels, with median difficulties ranging from .63 to .89. Test manuals should report item discrimination coefficients and item difficulty values for each age/grade interval across the entire test range. Many test developers are currently using both CTT and IRT procedures in the item selection and validation process. By examining item information functions, test developers can select items that contribute the maximum amount of information to the overall information provided by the test and thus can construct an measure that does not sacrifice brevity to discriminative accuracy.

DETECTING DIFFERENTIAL ITEM FUNCTIONING

An item is said to display *differential item functioning* (DIF) when examinees with equal ability but from different groups (e.g., males vs. females) have different probabilities of answering that item correctly. This was formerly referred to as *item bias*, but DIF is now preferred because the statistical procedures used to evaluate items for possible bias do not detect "bias" as such; rather, they indicate that an item functions differently for different groups of examinees. The following discussion provides a practitioner-oriented overview of methods for detecting DIF and is primarily drawn from Camilli and Shepard (1994), Hambleton (1996), and Holland and Wainer (1993).

Two basic approaches are used to detect DIF: (1) judgmental procedures, such as task and item reviews by curriculum experts and representatives of various demographic subgroups; and (2) statistical procedures designed to identify whether item content, format, scoring criteria, or other aspects of a test have differential effects on the performance of particular examinee groups. Although studies have demonstrated that judgmental reviews are generally ineffective in predicting which items will be more difficult for members of a particular group, most test publishers continue to use expert judges from various demographic groups in the item review process to ensure that any stereotyped and potentially offensive items are identified and removed.

Among statistical DIF methods, two types of procedures are currently recommended: (1) IRT methods and (2) nonparametric or contingency table (CT) approaches. In IRT approaches to detecting item bias, test developers compare the item characteristic curves (ICCs) of the majority or *reference* group and the minority or *focal* group for each item. If the probability of a correct response on a particular item is higher for the reference than for the focal group for examinees with the same ability level (based on total test score), the item is exhibiting DIF for the focal group. Another IRT approach compares item parameters for the reference and focal groups. DIF is present if item parameters differ between the groups, that is, if an item varies in terms of its difficulty, discriminating power, or possibility of being guessed for one group versus another. CT approaches differ from IRT approaches in that they rely on comparisons between discrete item scores and total test scores rather than on ICCs or item parameters. That is, examinees with equal ability (i.e., examinees with the same total test score) but from different subgroups are compared in terms of their chances of success on a particular item. Differences in item performance between subgroups can be tested with a variety of statistical methods to determine whether those differences are significant, indicating that the item displays DIF. Test developers often use CT rather than IRT approaches because CT methods can be used with smaller sample sizes and the computer programs for applying CT procedures are less complex than the IRT-based programs. CT methods include logistic regression, the Mantel–Haenszel approach, and the delta scores approach.

Controversy continues regarding the most optimal DIF detection procedure and the manner in which test developers should interpret the results obtained from the application of these methods. A positive DIF finding indicates that an item is functioning differently for different groups of examinees, not that the item is biased against a particular group of examinees. That judgment should be based on subsequent rational and empirical analyses to determine whether the observed differences are relevant or irrelevant to the test construct. Thus, when an item, set of items, or task has been identified as displaying DIF, test developers must attempt to determine first what the source of the unexpected difficulty is, and then whether the source is relevant to the construct being measured. Test manuals should provide evidence that flagged items were examined to determine the characteristics contributing to their greater difficulty for the focal group. Depending on the results of the follow-up investigation, items may be revised, deleted, or retained, if they are relatively few in number. Test publishers sometimes report the percentage of items that were flagged using DIF procedures to demonstrate that the vast majority of test items are unbiased.

Criterion-Related Validity Evidence

Criterion-related validity evidence refers to the effectiveness of a test in predicting an individual's performance on a criterion measure at the same time the predictor test is administered (*concurrent validity*) or at a later time (*predictive validity*) and is usually expressed statistically in the form of a Pearson correlation coefficient. Interpreting the criterion-related validity coefficients provided in test manuals can be difficult, however, because the criterion-related validity of the predictor measure (the test being validated) is directly related to the psychometric soundness of the measure with which it is compared. If the predictor test is compared with a criterion measure that has lower validity than the predictor, the predictor test will appear less valid than it actually is. Similarly, because a test's validity coefficient cannot exceed the square root of its reliability, the correlations between the two measures will be lower for criterion measures with lower reliability (Bracken, 1987; Bracken & Walker, 1997). The size of concurrent and predictive validity coefficients is also affected by differences in the way in which the predictor and criterion measures assess the test construct (Flanagan & Alfonso, 1995). Consequently, studies correlating two tests that measure some aspect of reading or reading-related processes may provide little useful information regarding the predictive utility of either instrument. Test authors should provide a rationale for selection of the criterion measures and should describe the criterion measures accurately (AERA et al., 1999). In addition, descriptions of criterion-related validity studies should specify the nature of the samples, type of analyses used for determining predictive accuracy, amount of time between administration of the two measures, and limitations of the generalizability of the validity data (Salvia & Ysseldyke, 2001).

CONCURRENT VALIDITY EVIDENCE

A new or revised instrument should show substantial relationships with previously published measures assessing the same construct. If the relationship is too high, however, the new test is likely to be redundant and to contribute little of value to the measurement of that construct. For instruments designed to identify kindergarten children at risk for reading failure, concurrent validity studies with reading achievement tests are not possible because most such children are at a preliterate level. Instead, studies documenting children's future reading performance are needed to support the proposed interpretation and uses of the test.

PREDICTIVE VALIDITY EVIDENCE

If a test purports to be effective in predicting reading, test authors should present evidence of the relationship between current test scores and later reading performance. Unfortunately, test manuals often provide little or no predictive validity evidence, even for measures specifically designed to identify children at risk for reading failure. Instead, test authors typically provide information about performance on other reading or reading-related measures administered at the same time as the predictor (i.e., concurrent validity evidence).

Construct Validity Evidence

Construct validation involves determining the degree to which the test actually measures the hypothetical construct or trait it is designed to measure. A *construct* is a theoretical, unobservable variable that is inferred from multiple sources of evidence, including test content, the relationships of test scores to other variables, and the internal structure of the test (AERA et al., 1999). In the current unified theory of validity, construct validity is viewed as the fundamental concept underlying validation because it specifies the meaning and interpretation of test scores (Messick, 1989a, 1989b, 1995). Test developers use a variety of procedures to provide construct validity evidence, including age and group differentiation studies, correlations with other measures, item- and subtest-test correlations, factor analysis, and training or intervention differentiation studies.

AGE DIFFERENTIATION

Because reading and reading-related skills are developmental in nature, scores on measures assessing those skills should increase with chronological age and level off in adulthood. Moreover, rapid growth in the early grades and more gradual growth in the later grades are characteristic of most reading subskills. Construct validity for reading measures can therefore be demonstrated by showing that mean test scores increase with chronological age, with more rapid increases at the lower age range. Test manuals may also present correlations between raw scores and age to demonstrate that age has a positive relationship to test performance.

GROUP DIFFERENTIATION

Another form of construct validity evidence consists of group differentiation or *contrasted groups* studies documenting that groups known to differ on the ability measured by the test display score differences in the expected direction. For example, children with reading disabilities would be expected to score lower than children without reading disabilities on tasks assessing phonological processing, decoding, and word identification. Test developers commonly present mean standard scores for various groups and may also use statistical procedures, such as ANOVA, to test whether the obtained differences are significant. Although the finding of observed differences among groups in predicted directions appears to lend strong support to the construct validity of a test, test users should consider several factors in evaluating this kind of evidence. First, group differentiation studies are often based on small samples, a broad range of ages, or both, which limits the generalizability of the findings to other populations and specific examinee ages. Second, the relative level of performance for the contrasted groups must be taken into consideration. Although the relevant contrasted group may score significantly lower than the reference group, its performance may still fall within the normal range, limiting the diagnostic utility of the results. Finally, demonstrating statistically significant differences between groups is not the same as demonstrating that these differences have clinical validity. That is, documenting that mean scores for a group of examinees with reading disabilities are significantly lower than those of examinees without reading disabilities (or documenting a pattern of scores consistent with theoretical expectations) is not the same as demonstrating that a particular test is capable of diagnosing reading disabilities in individual examinees.

ITEM–TOTAL TEST AND SUBTEST–TOTAL TEST CORRELATIONS

Additional evidence for construct validity can be obtained by correlating performance on individual items with total test score and performance on individual subtests with total test score. For item–total test comparisons, the higher the correlation coefficients, the more homogeneous the items are, and the greater the likelihood is that the items are measuring the same overall construct. Similarly, subtest–composite intercorrelations may be cited as evidence that the entire test is internally consistent. Correlations should be high enough to indicate that subtests are measuring related abilities and can be combined to form a composite but low enough to support the interpretation that each subtest is measuring something unique and should be designated as a separate component in the test.

FACTOR ANALYSIS

Test developers generally use two basic types of factor analysis to provide construct validity evidence. *Exploratory factor analysis* identifies the factor structure of a test by calculating the intercorrelations among all of the test items or subtests and then reducing the number of items or subtests to a smaller number of factors. The results are typically presented in a factor matrix that displays the factor loadings of each item or subtest on each factor. When test authors use orthogonal techniques (i.e., keeping the angles between factors at 90 degrees so that the factors are uncorrelated), factor loadings represent the correlations between the item or subtest and the factor and range from –1.00 to +1.00. In contrast to data-driven exploratory factor analysis, which does not assume an a priori model, *confirmatory factor analysis* (CFA) assesses the degree of correspondence between a theoretical factor structure and the observed pattern of relationships among the items and subtests. When tests are based on specific models, CFA can be used to evaluate the goodness of fit between alternative measurement models and the factor structure of the test. For example, CFA can confirm the hypothesized number of factors, the relationship between the subtests and the factors, and the relationship among the factors. Depending on the goodness of fit between the model and the obtained factor structure, test developers may modify the model to fit the data more closely.

CONVERGENT AND DISCRIMINANT VALIDITY

Test authors may also demonstrate construct validity by showing that the test correlates highly with measures with which it has a theoretically strong relationship (*convergent validity*) but fails to correlate significantly with measures with which it is expected to differ (*discriminant validity*). Thus a test that purports to measure phonological processing should correlate highly with other measures of phonological skills, such as tests of phonemic segmentation, but display lower correlations with measures of different constructs not considered an aspect of those skills, such as tests of mathematics achievement. Test developers typically evaluate convergent and discriminant validity by correlating subtest and total test scores with the subtest and total test scores from other measures measuring related constructs.

TRAINING OR INTERVENTION DIFFERENTIATION

One type of construct validity evidence that is especially important for early reading measures is derived from studies evaluating the effects of training on test performance. If a test measures a particular construct, training in the skills related to that construct should have positive effects on test performance. For example, pre- and postintervention scores on a phonological awareness test should differentiate between groups that received phonological awareness training and groups that received no training or training unrelated to phonological processing.

CRITERIA FOR EVALUATING VALIDITY EVIDENCE

Although validity is the most fundamental consideration in evaluating tests, determining acceptable criteria for validity is also the most complex (Bracken, 2000). Because validity is a property of the inferences based on test scores, not of a test itself, an instrument may be valid in one context and with one type of examinee but invalid in another context with another type of examinee. Moreover, depending on the use made of the test scores, some types of validation evidence may be more important than others (AERA et al., 1999). For example, evidence that test scores accurately predict future levels of reading proficiency is critical for measures purporting to identify children at risk for reading failure. Because of these complexities, most authors of psychometric rating systems have evaluated validity in terms of the presence or absence of various types of validity evidence, along with an overall evaluation of available data—an approach that is used in this text. Criteria for validation evidence are based on those of Alfonso and Flanagan (Alfonso & Flanagan, 1999; Flanagan &

Alfonso, 1995). In terms of early reading measures, the validation evidence presented in the test manual (and/or technical manual, if available) should include the following: (1) two or more kinds of content validity evidence, including item bias or DIF analyses; (2) two or more kinds of criterion-related validity evidence, including at least one study with examinees in the primary grade years; and (3) two or more kinds of construct validity evidence, including at least one study documenting group or training differentiation.

Because many of the tests reviewed in this text are new instruments or recent revisions of previously published tests, validation evidence beyond what is provided in the manual is often limited. This evidence will accumulate, however, as the tests are used in research and applied settings. Practitioners interested in particular tests are encouraged to search the literature frequently to locate studies evaluating the technical adequacy and utility of those measures in contexts and with examinees similar to their own. Test publishers can also help direct test users and potential users to technical reports and published studies investigating the reliability and validity of their instruments. As the current *Standards* (AERA et al., 1999) stress, validation is the joint responsibility of test developers and test users. Whereas test developers are responsible for providing a theoretical rationale and empirical evidence supporting score interpretations and applications, test users are responsible for evaluating the appropriateness of that information for their own settings, purposes, and populations.

Evaluating the Usability of Early Reading Measures

Although the psychometric soundness of a measure should always take precedence over its practical features, no test can help to identify a reading problem or provide information for remediation if it is so user-unfriendly that it never enters a practitioner's repertoire. Surveys of school psychologists (Hutton, Dubes, & Muir, 1992; Stinnett, Havey, & Oehler-Stinnett, 1994; Wilson & Reschly, 1996) have consistently reported that some of the most frequently used instruments have inadequate psychometric characteristics, indicating that factors other than technical adequacy influence selection. For busy psychologists and educators, such practical considerations as the amount of time required for administration, scoring, and interpretation; the types of scores yielded; the availability of software scoring options; and the cost of the test and supplementary materials can be of critical importance.

SOURCES OF GUIDELINES FOR USABILITY

Despite the importance of practical features in the selection and use of tests in applied settings, there has been surprisingly little discussion of this topic in the recent assessment literature. Although some authors (Alfonso & Flanagan, 1999; Bracken & Walker, 1997) have presented guidelines for evaluating the qualitative characteristics of measures, these considerations are based on the appropriateness of tests for preschool examinees rather than on their convenience for users. Table 2.2 lists seven

TABLE 2.2. Practical Characteristics of Early Reading Measures

Practical characteristics	Guidelines for evaluating the usability of early reading measures
Test construction	
Test manual	The test manual should be well organized, easy to read, and comprehensive enough to permit reliable administration, scoring, and interpretation. Tables should be easy to locate and readily interpretable. For screening measures designed for administration by classroom teachers, the language in the manual should be accessible to regular educators.
Profile/examiner booklets	Profile/examiner booklets should be well organized and easy to use. Complete test directions, including practice items and basal and ceiling rules (if relevant), should appear in booklets as well as the test manual. For tests requiring rapid scoring during administration, all items of a particular subtest should appear on a single page of the booklet. For pseudoword reading tasks, pronunciation guides should be printed in both the booklets and the manual.
Test materials	Test materials should be attractive to children and capable of engaging them in the testing tasks. Pictorial and printed test materials should be free of gender and racial/ethnic stereotyping.
Cost	The price of the test and supplementary materials, such as software scoring programs, should be commensurate with the nature and scope of the instrument. When tests are revised, users should receive some form of discount or credit for proof of purchase of the previous edition.
Administration	
Test format	Screening batteries should include as many group-administered tasks as reliability and validity considerations permit. The test manual should specify both maximum and optimal group sizes and the number of monitors for these tasks (e.g., 4–5 students optimal, 15 students maximum with 2 monitors).
Examiner qualifications	The test manual should specify the qualifications required to administer, score, and interpret the test, such as training, certification, and competencies. Any restrictions should be clearly noted. Screening measures should be capable of being administered, scored, and interpreted by classroom teachers.
Test directions	Test directions should be as explicit and clear as possible to promote consistent administration. Verbal instructions to the examinee should be presented verbatim in the test book or record booklet, preferably in contrasting color or boldface type.
Sample/teaching items	The test should include a sufficient number of sample items, teaching tasks, or trials per subtest to ensure examinee understanding of task requirements.
Technology supports for administration	For linguistically complex and difficult-to-administer tasks, such as phoneme blending and memory span tasks, test stimuli should be presented on audiocassette. The manual should specify in what (if any) situations live-voice delivery can be used for testing tasks designed to be presented on audiocassette. Training videotapes or CD-ROMs with administration, scoring, and interpretive guidelines are highly desirable, especially for large-scale screening programs and complex, multiskill batteries.
Testing time	Testing time for screening measures should be no more than 30 minutes per student. For comprehensive skill inventories or diagnostic assessments, tests should be designed to permit administration across several sessions.
Accommodations and adaptations	
Accommodations for examinees with disabilities	The test manual should indicate what (if any) accommodations and adaptations in administration, scoring, and/or interpretation may be made for examinees with various types of disabilities.
Multicultural adaptability	The test manual should indicate whether the test is appropriate for children whose primary language is not English. If the test can be used with or adapted for bilingual children and/or children with limited English proficiency, the manual should specify what adaptations are appropriate in administration, scoring, and/or interpretation.

(continued)

TABLE 2.2. *(continued)*

Practical characteristics	Guidelines for evaluating the usability of early reading measures
Scores and scoring	
Scoring procedures	The test manual should provide clear and complete scoring procedures, with examples for items involving judgment and scoring templates (as appropriate) to permit quick, accurate scoring. The manual should include examples of completed test records, including examples of obtaining basals and ceilings, if relevant.
Software scoring	Software scoring programs should be available for tests with lengthy or complex scoring procedures, preferably as part of the basic test kit. Programs should include printed or downloadable guides to assist practitioners in using the software and interpreting the results.
Scores provided	Norm-referenced tests should yield a full range of derived scores, including standard scores, normal curve equivalents, and percentiles. If age or grade equivalents are provided, appropriate cautions about their interpretation should be presented. If a limited number of derived scores are provided, the manual should include a rationale for the choice of score(s).
Interpretation	
Score interpretation	The test manual should include step-by-step procedures for interpreting test results, including whether or not subtest scores are to be interpreted. The presence of any floor and/or ceiling effects for particular ages and grades should be noted.
Norms and interpretative tables	Norm tables for various age and grade groups should be easy to locate and readily interpretable.
Difference score interpretation	If the manual indicates that differences between standard scores are to be interpreted, it should include tables specifying the amount of difference between scores required for statistical significance and clinical utility, as well as information regarding the meaning of such differences in diagnosis and intervention planning.
Software interpretive options	For software that includes interpretive comments, the test or software scoring manual should indicate the theoretical rationale and empirical evidence supporting those interpretations.
Case examples	The test manual should include case examples to illustrate score interpretation for examinees at different grade levels and with a variety of test results.
Links to intervention	
Communicating test results	The test manual and/or test kit should include suggestions and/or materials for communicating test results to parents, examinees, and other members of the testing public.
Linking test scores to intervention	The test manual should describe ways in which test results can lead to intervention, such as suggestions for remediation and descriptions of evidence-based intervention programs and curricular materials.

practical features relevant to the usability of early reading measures and guidelines for evaluating them. These guidelines are based on the following sources: (1) Alfonso and Flanagan's (1999) recommendations for evaluating the qualitative characteristics of intelligence tests for preschoolers; (2) Bracken and Walker's (1997) recommendations for desirable criteria for intelligence tests for preschoolers; (3) Goodwin and Goodwin's (1993) discussion of the usability of instruments for young children; and (4) my own experience with early reading measures. Practitioners may find that additional qualitative characteristics are relevant to their evaluation of a test's usability, depending on their particular examinee population, setting, resources, and other factors.

Score Types

One of these usability features, the types of scores provided by a test, requires further explanation. The number of derived score types available for the tests reviewed in this text varies considerably, with some instruments yielding a wide range of derived scores and others yielding only raw scores (i.e., criterion-referenced tests) or a single derived score type, such as percentiles or deciles. Because some practitioners may be unfamiliar with several of these scores, Table 2.3 describes the score types provided by the tests reviewed in this book. Rasch-based tests, such as the WJ III and the WRMT-R/NU, include several additional score types that are discussed in those reviews.

PRINT RESOURCES

American Educational Research Association, American Psychological Association, & National Council on Measurement in Education. (1999). *Standards for educational and psychological testing*. Washington, DC: AERA.

This is the sixth version of the set of standards prepared by three sponsoring organizations for evaluating psychological and educational tests. Included are sections on test construction, evaluation, and documentation; fairness in testing; testing applications; separate chapters on psychological and educational assessment; and a glossary of assessment terms.

American Psychological Association (APA). (2000). *Report of the Task Force on Test User Qualifications*. Washington, DC: Author.

Available free of charge from the APA, these guidelines describe two types of test user qualifications: (1) generic qualifications that serve as a basis for most uses of tests; and (2) specific qualifications for optimal use of tests for specific settings, including employment, education, vocational/career counseling, health care, and forensic contexts. The section on the core set of psychometric and measurement knowledge and skills important for appropriate test use is especially helpful.

Evertson, S. E., & Hershberger, S. L. (Eds.). (1999). *The new rules of measurement: What every psychologist and educator should know*. Mahwah, NJ: Erlbaum.

This edited book provides an accessible introduction to new developments in testing, including item response theory and generalizability theory. Included is a practitioner-oriented chapter by Richard Woodcock on the interpretation of test scores based on the Rasch model.

TABLE 2.3. Score Types Yielded by Early Reading Measures and Their Description

Score types	Description
Age equivalents	Age at which an examinee's raw score is the median or mean score of all scores at that age; an age equivalent of 7-8 indicates average performance for a child aged 7 years, 8 months
Decile scores	Percentile bands that divide a distribution into 10 equal parts, with each decile containing 10% of the age or grade norm group; a decile score of 1 (or 10) represents the lowest 10% of the distribution (i.e., it contains percentile ranks from 0.1 to 9.9)
Grade equivalents	Grade at which an examinee's raw score is the median or mean of all scores at that grade; a grade equivalent of 1.2 indicates average performance for a student in the first grade, second month of school
Normal curve equivalents	Normalized transformation of age- or grade-based standard scores that divides a distribution into 100 equal intervals (M = 50, SD = 21.06)
Percentile ranks	Scores ranging from 1 to 99, with each percentile rank indicating the percentage of individuals in the normative group at a given age or grade who obtained scores equal to or less than a given raw score; because percentile ranks do not form an equal-interval scale but cluster near the median of 50, small differences in performance are magnified near the center of the distribution and minimized at the extremes of the distribution
Quartile scores	Percentile bands that divide a distribution into four equal parts, with each quartile containing 25% of the age- or grade-based norm group; a quartile score of 1 represents the lowest 25% of the distribution (i.e., percentile ranks from 0.1 to 24.9)
Raw scores	Number of items answered correctly on a test; on criterion-referenced tests, raw scores are often converted to percent-correct scores for determining proficiency levels; on norm-referenced tests, raw scores can be converted to a variety of derived scores
Scaled scores	Also called *scale scores*; age- or grade-based subtest standard scores with a mean of 10 and standard deviation of 3; test publishers are increasingly using the term *standard score* instead of *scaled score* to describe this type of subtest score
Standard scores[a]	Age- or grade-based normalized scores with a mean of 100 and standard deviation of 15 (or occasionally 16)
Stanines	Short for *standard nine*; age- or grade-based standard score bands that divide a distribution into nine parts; the percentage of scores at each stanine are 4, 7, 12, 17, 20 (the fifth stanine), 17, 12, 7, and 4, respectively

[a]Technically, *standard score* is a general term referring to raw scores that have been transformed to produce a given mean and standard deviation. Here the term is used to refer to deviation IQ standard scores, which have a mean of 100 and a standard deviation of 15 or 16, depending on the test.

chapter 3

A Component-Based Approach to Early Reading Assessment

Overview

This chapter discusses 10 cognitive–linguistic and literacy-related abilities and skills that have been demonstrated to predict reading acquisition and/or to be associated with reading problems and tests measuring those components: (1) phonological processing, (2) rapid naming, (3) orthographic processing, (4) oral language, (5) print awareness and concept of word, (6) alphabet knowledge, (7) single word reading, (8) oral reading in context (including contextual reading fluency), (9) reading comprehension, and (10) written language (including spelling). For each reading component, the discussion includes a description of the relationship of the component to the reading process, assessment issues related to that component, and types of tasks measuring it. One or two tables in each section list all of the measures assessing each component that are reviewed in this text, including single-skill measures and subtests from multiskill and multisubject instruments.

Phonological Processing

Phonological processing refers to the use of phonological or sound information to process oral and written language (Torgesen & Burgess, 1998; Wagner & Torgesen, 1987). There is now a consensus that deficits in phonological processing are the primary causes of most reading disabilities and that these deficits are evident in both garden-variety poor readers (i.e., those without ability–achievement discrepancies) and poor readers with discrepancies (i.e., dyslexics) (see Share & Stanovich, 1995, and Siegel, 1998, for reviews). Three types of phonological processing skills have been identified as most critical to reading acquisition: (1) phonological awareness; (2) phonological memory; and (3) phonological naming, also termed *phonological coding in lexical access* or *rapid automatized naming* (RAN). Although some researchers (Allor, Fuchs, & Mathes, 2001; Share, 1995; Torgesen & Wagner, 1998; Torgesen, Wagner, Rashotte, Burgess, & Hecht, 1997; Wagner, Torgesen, & Rashotte, 1994) subsume naming speed under phonological processing, there is mounting evidence that RAN tasks, which measure speed of naming visual symbols, tap additional processes such as automaticity and timing and may have particular predictive significance for reading disabilities (see Wolf, 2001, for a review). For this reason, rapid naming is discussed in a separate section of this chapter.

PHONOLOGICAL AWARENESS

Phonological awareness refers to the conscious awareness of the sound structure of speech, as opposed to its meaning (Torgesen, Wagner, Rashotte, Alexander, & Conway, 1997). This awareness is what permits children to understand the *alphabetic principle*—the fact that the sounds in oral language (*phonemes*) can be represented by written letters (*graphemes*). A *phoneme* is the smallest unit of sound in a word that makes a difference to meaning (Torgesen & Wagner, 1998). For example, the word *mat* consists of three phonemes: /m/, /a/, and /t/. Changing the first phoneme to /s/ changes the word to *sat* and alters its meaning. The English language contains approximately 44 phonemes or different speech sounds, with the specific number varying from one classification system to another.

Phonological versus Phonemic Awareness

Whereas *phonological awareness* refers to a general awareness of the sound structure of oral language, *phonemic awareness* refers to the understanding that spoken words are composed of individual sounds that can be analyzed and manipulated. Although some authors do not distinguish between the two, the National Research Council distinguishes phonological awareness from phonemic awareness as follows:

> The term *phonological awareness* refers to a general appreciation of the sounds of speech as distinct from their meaning. When that insight includes an understanding that words can be divided into a sequence of phonemes, this finer-grained sensitivity is termed *phonemic awareness*. (Snow, Burns, & Griffin, 1998, p. 51)

Phonological/Phonemic Awareness and Reading

Because we humans have a natural capacity for oral language, conscious awareness of the phonological structure of words is not necessary to speak or understand spoken words. Developing phonemic awareness is a difficult task, however, because phonemes are not pronounced separately but are *coarticulated*—that is, merged in speech. Phonemic awareness is essential in reading because to understand the alphabetic principle of written English, children must understand that words are composed of sound segments.

Several lines of evidence support the conclusion that there is a causal relationship between phonemic awareness and reading. First, a voluminous body of research demonstrates that children's preschool or kindergarten performance on phonological and phonemic awareness tasks is a powerful predictor of their reading proficiency in the early grades (e.g., Bryant, MacLean, Bradley, & Crossland, 1990; Jorm & Share, 1983; Liberman & Shankweiler, 1985; Lundberg, Frost, & Petersen, 1980; Muter, Hulme, Snowling, & Taylor, 1998; Scanlon & Vellutino, 1996; Wagner et al., 1997). Among the marker variables of reading acquisition, the predictive power of phonological awareness is equaled only by letter-name and letter-sound knowledge (McBride-Chang, 1995). Second, intervention studies (see Christensen, 2000, for a review) have consistently found that training in phonological awareness has significant positive effects on reading and spelling development, especially when it is combined with systematic instruction in letter-sound correspondences.

Despite the general consensus that phonological processing problems constitute the core deficit of poor readers, whether garden-variety or reading-disabled, the precise role of phonemic awareness in reading acquisition continues to be debated. According to one hypothesis, difficulty in developing an explicit awareness of phonemes leads to the failure to master spelling-sound correspondences, which leads directly to deficits in word recognition (Bruck, 1992; Manis, Custodio, & Szeszulski, 1993; Rack, Snowling, & Olson, 1992). Another hypothesis, which is complementary rather than contradictory, emphasizes the role of underlying phonological representations of words in the *lexicon*, or mental dictionary (Elbro, 1996; Fowler, 1991; Hatcher & Hulme, 1999; Swan & Goswami, 1997). Termed the *phonological representation hypothesis,* this model proposes that performance deficits on phonological awareness tasks do not reflect lack of phonemic awareness skills per se, but rather, inaccuracies in the phonological representations of the words to be analyzed. From this perspective, phonemic awareness tasks, especially those involving phoneme manipulation, serve as an index of the extent to which an individual possesses the fully specified, segmentally structured phonological representations that are crucial to the process of creating direct mappings between orthographic and phonological representations when the individual is learning to read (Rack et al., 1992).

Assessing Phonological Awareness

Phonological awareness measures can be classified as falling into one of two broad categories, depending on the linguistic unit involved: (1) *nonphonemic tasks*, which measure global aspects of phonological awareness, such as rhyme and syllable sensitivity; and (2) *phonemic awareness tasks*, which measure the ability to attend to or manipulate individual phonemes. Descriptions and examples of the most commonly used tasks in both categories are given below, with the correct answer for each example given in parentheses.

Nonphonemic Phonological Awareness Measures

Nonphonemic phonological awareness tasks measure sensitivity to the sound structure of language at the level of rhymes, syllables, and onset–rime units. The *onset* refers to the initial consonant or consonant cluster in a syllable, whereas the *rime* consists of the vowel and following consonant(s). For example, in the word *clap*, *cl* is the onset and *ap* is the rime. Some words (e.g., *at*, *egg*) do not have onsets.

RHYME AWARENESS

Rhyme awareness tasks are generally the easiest for children and consist of rhyme recognition or production tasks.

Rhyme Recognition. The child listens to two or more words spoken by the examiner and indicates whether or not they rhyme. Some tests use a pictorial format that requires the child to demonstrate rhyme awareness by pointing to target pictures in an array of pictured words.

Example: The examiner displays a set of four pictures and says, "Look at *bed, head,* and *bee.* Point to the two that end alike or rhyme." (The child points to the pictures of *bed* and *head.*)

Rhyme Generation. The child provides one or more real words and/or pseudowords that rhyme with an orally presented target word. Target words may be presented in isolation or may occur at the end of a two-line poem.

Example: "Finish what I say with a word that rhymes: 'When day turns to night, we switch on the ________.' " (light)

SYLLABLE AWARENESS

Syllable awareness tasks require the child to indicate the number of syllables in spoken or pictured words by oral or written means, such as drawing marks, clapping, tapping, or providing the number.

Example: "Clap to show me how many syllables you hear in *motorcycle.*" (The child claps four times.)

SYLLABLE MANIPULATION

Syllable manipulation tasks require the child to manipulate individual syllables in spoken or pictured words. More difficult than syllable awareness tasks, they include deletion, substitution, and reversal tasks.

Syllable Deletion. The child listens to a multisyllable word and then deletes a specific syllable from that word. The remaining word part may or may not be a real word. Syllable deletions that involve deleting syllables from compound words are the easiest, those that involve deleting prefixes or suffixes from multisyllable words are next in difficulty, and those that involve deleting medial syllables from multisyllable words are the most difficult.

Example: "Say *quieter.*" (quieter) "Now say it again without /er/." (quiet)

Syllable Reversal. The child listens to a multisyllable word and then says it backwards.

Example: "Say *popcorn* backwards." (cornpop)

Syllable Substitution. The child listens to a multisyllable word and then substitutes a given syllable for one of the syllables.

Example: "If I say *jumping* and then change *jump* to *run,* what would the new word be?" (running)

ONSET–RIME BLENDING

Nonphonemic blending tasks require the child to listen to one-syllable words that have been separated into onsets and rimes and to pronounce the word formed when the two sounds are blended together. Puppets are sometimes used as aids in administering blending tasks with young children. The child is told that the puppet does not talk very well and so pronounces words in parts.

Example: "Put these sounds together to make a word: /b/ – /at/." (bat)

Phonemic Awareness Measures

Phonemic awareness measures can be grouped into three broad categories: (1) sound comparison tasks, (2) phoneme segmentation tasks, and (3) phoneme blending tasks (Torgesen, 1998). In addition, some phonemic awareness tasks include a fluency component.

SOUND COMPARISON

Sound comparison tasks present a set of words orally or in pictures and require the child to identify the word or picture with the same initial or final sound as the target word or picture. In another version, the child identifies a word or picture that begins or ends with a different sound than the target stimulus. Because sound comparison tasks do not involve the manipulation of individual phonemes, they are the easiest phonemic awareness tasks.

Example: "These pictures show *tie, horse, swim,* and *tack.* Mark the picture that begins like *tie.*" (The child marks the picture of the tack.)

PHONEME SEGMENTATION

Phoneme segmentation tasks require manipulating individual phonemes in spoken or pictured words by counting, naming, deleting, substituting, or reversing the sounds. The tasks below are arranged in order from easiest to most difficult.

Phoneme Counting. The child indicates the number of phonemes in spoken or pictured words by drawing marks, clapping, tapping, or providing the number.

Example: The examiner displays a picture of a sock and says, "This is a *sock.* Draw as many lines as you hear sounds in *sock.*" (The child draws three lines.)

Phoneme Naming. The child listens to a real word or pseudoword and pronounces each of the sounds in order. Credit may be given for each correct sound or only for words for which all sounds are correctly segmented. In some versions of this task, the child provides the initial, medial, or final sound in the word.

Example: "Tell me in order all the sounds in *old.*" (/o/ /l/ /d/)

Phoneme Deletion. Also called *elision* tasks, phoneme deletion tasks require the child to listen to a word and delete a specific phoneme from it. The resulting word may or may not be a real word. Deleting initial consonants is the easiest type of phoneme deletion task, and deleting phonemes within consonant clusters is the most difficult.

Example: "Say *stream.* Now say it without the /r/." (steam)

Phoneme Substitution. The child listens to a word and changes one sound or word part to form a new word. Some tasks require the child to use manipulatives, such as colored blocks or disks, to indicate sound changes.

Example (without manipulatives): "The word is *mat.* If I change /m/ to /f/, what is the new word?" (fat)

Example (with manipulatives): From a set of colored blocks, the examiner forms a row consisting of one red, one yellow, and one green block and says, "This is *man.* Use these blocks to change *man* to *map.*" (The child replaces the green block with a block of a different color.)

Phoneme Reversal. The child listens to an orally presented word and reverses the sounds. Because children who have developed some degree of reading proficiency can draw on their spelling knowledge to assist them in performing these tasks, phoneme reversal tasks assess orthographic knowledge as well as phonemic awareness, especially among older students.

Example: "Say this word backwards: *bat.*" (tab)

PHONEME BLENDING

The child listens to segments of orally presented words and blends the sounds together to form a word or pronounceable pseudoword.

Example: "Put these sounds together to make a word: /s/-/t/-/o/-/p/." (stop)

Fluency-Based Phonological Awareness Measures

Considering the crucial role of fluency in reading acquisition (Wolf, 2001), surprisingly few phonological awareness tasks with a fluency component have been developed. One of the instruments reviewed in this text, the *Dynamic Indicators of Basic Early Literacy Skills* (DIBELS), includes fluency-based phonological awareness measures. Derived from curriculum-based measurement (CBM) research, DIBELS consists of a set of 1-minute measures of foundational reading skills targeted at specific times in the early primary grades. DIBELS includes two phonological awareness fluency measures: Initial Sound Fluency, which requires rapid recognition and production of initial sounds in orally presented words, and Phoneme Segmentation Fluency, which requires rapid segmentation of orally presented three- and four-phoneme words.

Issues in Assessing Phonological Awareness

Researchers have used a wide variety of measures to measure phonological awareness, many of which were developed for specific studies. As a result, a large number of tasks with different formats, item types, and scoring procedures, all supposedly measuring the same construct, are available in the research literature. In addition, numerous phonological awareness measures are included in commercially published tests and state-sponsored early reading batteries. Among the most critical issues in the assessment of phonological awareness are (1) the lack of standardization among tasks, (2) the relative predictive utility of various tasks during different periods of reading development, and (3) examiner and scorer variance.

Lack of Standardization among Tasks

Of the 42 instruments reviewed for this text, 24 include one or more measures that are described by their authors as assessing some aspect of phonological awareness (see Table 3.1 below). Unfortunately, there is little standardization among these tasks in terms of the linguistic unit, task format, and item content variables that influence difficulty levels. For example, for phoneme deletion tasks, item difficulty for deletion of a sound in a consonant cluster is related to the position of the target phoneme and the number of phonemes within the cluster (McBride-Chang, 1995). Other factors that affect performance levels include type of presentation format (oral or pictorial), type of response format (physical [e.g., clapping or knocking], written, or oral), the use of real words versus pseudowords, and all-or-nothing versus partial-credit scoring procedures. Measures of phonological awareness also vary in terms of the scores yielded, ranging from raw scores that are compared with grade-specific benchmarks to a variety of norm-referenced derived scores.

Predictive Utility

Controversy continues as to which phonological tasks are most effective in identifying children at risk for reading failure and at which stages of reading development these tasks are effective. Both nonphonemic and phonemic awareness measures appear to be time sensitive in terms of prediction. Most kindergarten children are able to perform tasks that measure nonphonemic phonological awareness, such as rhyming and syllable segmentation, as well as phonemic tasks that do not involve explicit manipulation of individual phonemes, such as sound comparison tasks. Although some studies (e.g., Badian, 2001) have reported that kindergarten rhyme detection and syllable segmentation were both effective predictors of first-grade word reading, other researchers have found that kindergarten syllable measures are generally better predictors of later reading proficiency than are rhyme measures (Bowey & Francis, 1991; Stanovich, Cunningham, & Cramer, 1984), perhaps because many children are at ceiling for rhyme awareness at the end of kindergarten. In addition, most studies (e.g., Christensen, 2000; Duncan & Seymour, 2000; Muter et al., 1998; Sawyer, Kim, & Kipa-Wade, 2000; Vellutino & Scanlon, 1987) indicate that kindergarten rhyming tasks are relatively poor predictors of reading compared with phonemic awareness measures. Tasks assessing rhyming and onset–rime awareness may be poorer predictors of reading, not only because of ceiling effects but also because they tap a different set of abilities. In a study with a large sample of Norwegian first graders, Hoien, Lundberg, Stanovich, and Bjaalid (1995) identified three factors among a set of six phonological awareness tasks: a phoneme factor, a syllable factor, and a rhyme factor, each with differential predictive power. Although all three factors contributed independently to variance in reading, the phoneme factor was by far the most powerful predictor.

Examiner and Scorer Variance

Another set of concerns relevant to phonological awareness tasks involves examiner variance and interscorer reliability. Although any measure that uses a live-voice format for delivering oral stimuli is vulnerable to examiner variance, tasks that require examiners to pronounce individual phonemes, such as phoneme blending measures, are especially susceptible. On blending measures with live-voice delivery, examiners are likely to vary in terms of presentation rate even if test manuals specify inter-phoneme intervals, as well as in terms of other factors, such as accuracy of pronunciation and articulation. For these reasons, phonological and phonemic awareness tasks, especially those that involve blending phonemes into pseudowords or performing more complex manipulations, such as substitutions and reversals, should be presented on audiocassette.

Measures of Phonological Awareness

Many of the instruments reviewed in this text include multiple measures of phonological and phonemic awareness. In the interests of readability and space, tests with multiple tasks in this domain are presented in Table 3.1 as single entries, with subtests or tasks listed in the order of administration. Of the 24 instruments listed, only 6 provide norm-referenced scores based on national samples of U.S. children. Many of the instruments with research norms or state-validated benchmarks can be easily adapted for local norming, however.

PHONOLOGICAL MEMORY

A second area of phonological processing that has been linked to reading acquisition and reading disabilities is *phonological memory*, also termed *phonological coding in working memory*. Phonological memory is the ability to represent phonological or sound information in short-term memory (Torgesen, 1996). Verbal short-term memory tasks are considered to tap phonological processing abilities because retaining a sequence of verbal items requires representing them in working memory in terms of their phonological features. That is, if a child is asked to remember a digit string,

TABLE 3.1. Measures of Phonological Awareness

Name and date of *measure*; subtest(s)	Admin. time (minutes)	Norms/ benchmarks	Testing tasks	Comments
Auditory Analysis Test (1971)	3–5	NS; research norms for Grades K–6	Syllable and phoneme deletion	Local norming recommended; floor effects for kindergarten children
Berninger Modification of the Auditory Analysis Test (1986, 1987)	3–5	NS; kindergarten research norms; Grades K–3	Syllable and phoneme deletion; three sets of grade-specific items	Local norming recommended; administering all items reduces floor and ceiling effects
Book Buddies Early Literacy Screening (1998); Picture Sorting	3–5	NS; Grades 1 and 2	Matching pictures with the same initial sounds	Task in an early literacy battery linked to tutorial program
Catts Deletion Test (2001)	3–5	NS; kindergarten research norms	Syllable and phoneme deletion	Local norming recommended; effective predictor for both normal-language and speech- or language-impaired children
Comprehensive Test of Phonological Processing (1999); Elision, Blending Words, Blending Pseudowords, Sound Matching, Phoneme Reversal, Segmenting Words, Segmenting Pseudowords	3–5 per subtest	Norms for ages 5–6 and ages 7–24	Syllable and phoneme deletion; blending phonemes (real and pseudowords); matching initial and final consonants; phoneme reversal (pseudowords); phonemic segmentation (real words and pseudowords)	One of the few tests with multiple measures of three phonological processing abilities; yields two phonological awareness composites
Dynamic Indicators of Basic Early Literacy Skills (2002); Initial Sound Fluency, Phoneme Segmentation Fluency	2–3 per task	NS; benchmarks for Grades K and 1	Rapidly identifying pictures beginning with a target sound; rapidly segmenting spoken words into individual phonemes	CBM-type measures; has multiple forms for progress monitoring
Dyslexia Early Screening Test (1996); Phonological Discrimination, Rhyme Detection/First Letter Sound	2–4 per subtest	British norms for ages 4-6 through 6-5	Indicating whether a pair of spoken words are the same or different; recognizing rhyming words; pronouncing initial sounds in spoken words	Percentile ranges only, grouped into five risk categories; utility limited by British norms
Dyslexia Screening Test (1996); Phonemic Segmentation	2–4	British norms for ages 6-6 through 16-5	Syllable and phoneme deletion	Five percentile ranges only; utility limited by British norms
Fox in a Box (2000); Rhyme Recognition, Rhyme Generation, Syllable Clapping, Initial Consonants, Final Consonants, Blending, Segmenting	3–5 per task	CR; benchmarks for Grades K–2	Recognizing and producing rhymes; counting syllables; pronouncing initial and final sounds; blending sounds; segmenting words	Part of a comprehensive early literacy battery; test record is designed to follow the child for three grades

(continued)

TABLE 3.1. *(continued)*

Name and date of *measure*; subtest(s)	Admin. time (minutes)	Norms/ benchmarks	Testing tasks	Comments
Group Reading Assessment and Diagnostic Evaluation (2002); Sound Matching, Rhyming	15–20 per task (GA)	Norms for Grades PreK and K; optional norms for ages 4-0 through 6-11 for PreK level	Marking the one of four pictures that begins or ends with the same sound as a word pronounced by the examiner; marking the one of four pictures that rhymes with a word pronounced by the examiner	Part of a comprehensive group-administered reading battery linked to an intervention program
Illinois Test of Psycholinguistic Abilities–3 (2001); Sound Deletion	3–5	Norms for ages 5-0 through 12-11	Phoneme deletion	Floor effects for younger examinees
Lindamood Auditory Conceptualization Test (1971/1979); Category I, Category II	15–25	Recommended minimum scores for Grades K–6 and combined Grades 7–adult	Using colored blocks to represent number and sameness–difference of sounds; for Category II, sound patterns for items are linked and increase in complexity	Requires considerable practice for accurate administration; very difficult for younger and low-performing students
Phonological Abilities Test (1997); Rhyme Detection, Rhyme Production, Word Completion, Phoneme Deletion	3–5 per subtest	British norms for ages 5-0 through 7-11	Detecting rhyming pictures; producing rhymes; providing the final syllable or phoneme for pictured words; deleting initial or final sounds	Yields four percentile scores only; utility limited by British norms
Phonological Awareness Literacy Screening (2002); Group/Individual Rhyme Awareness, Group/Individual Beginning Sound Awareness, Blending, Sound-to-Letter	4–8 per task; 15–25 per GA task	CR; Virginia benchmarks for Grades K–3	Matching rhyming pictures; matching pictures with same initial sound; blending sounds; naming initial, medial, or final letters in spoken words	State-of-the-art statewide reading screening battery; Web site has numerous instructional activities
Phonological Awareness Screening Test (1998); Detecting Rhymes, Counting Syllables, Matching Initial Sounds, Counting Phonemes, Comparing Word Lengths	5–8 per task (GA)	CR; Grades K and 1	Matching rhyming pictures; counting syllables and phonemes in pictured words; matching pictures with the same initial sound; circling one of a pair of pictures representing a longer word	One of the few entirely group-administered phonological awareness measures; linked to phonological awareness curriculum; excellent for classroom norming
Phonological Awareness Test (1997); Rhyming, Segmentation, Isolation, Deletion, Substitution, Blending	3–8 per subtest	Norms for ages 5-0 through 9-11	Rhyme recognition and production; sentence, syllable, and phoneme segmentation; sound isolation; phoneme deletion; phoneme substitution with and without colored blocks	Inadequate floors for many subtests for younger examinees; useful for instructional planning

(continued)

TABLE 3.1. *(continued)*

Name and date of *measure*; subtest(s)	Admin. time (minutes)	Norms/ benchmarks	Testing tasks	Comments
Predictive Reading Profile (2001); Syllable-Sound Counting, Sound Recognition, Phonemic Segmentation	10–15 per subtest (GA)	Preliminary kindergarten norms; Grades K and 1	Counting syllables and phonemes; identifying letter sounds; phoneme deletion	One of the few entirely group-administered reading screening batteries; percentile scores only; local norming strongly recommended
Process Assessment of the Learner: Test Battery for Reading and Writing (2001); Rhyming, Syllables, Phonemes, Rimes	5–10 per subtest (GA)	Norms for Grades K–6	Rhyme detection and generation (Grade K); syllable deletion (Grades K–6); phoneme deletion (Grades K–6); rime deletion (Grades 1–6)	Decile scores only; no separate subtest scores for phonological tasks; linked to intervention program
Test of Auditory Analysis Skills (1975/1993)	3–5	Grade-level equivalences for K–3	Deleting syllables and phonemes	Limited item set; floor effects for kindergarten
Test of Language Development–Primary: 3 (1997); Word Discrimination, Phonemic Analysis	3–8	Norms for ages 4-0 through 8-11	Indicating whether a pair of spoken words are the same or different; deleting syllables	Ceiling effects for children aged 6-6 and up
Test of Phonological Awareness (1994); Initial Sound–Same, Initial Sound–Different, Ending Sound–Same, Ending Sound–Different	15–20 total (GA)	Norms for Grades K (ages 5-0 through 6-11) and 1 (ages 6-0 through 8-11)	Comparing initial (Grade K) and final sounds (Grade 1) in pictured words	Group-administered screener designed to identify very low-performing children
Texas Primary Reading Inventory (2002); Rhyming, Blending Word Parts, Blending Phonemes, Detecting Initial Sounds, Detecting Final Sounds	2–5 per task	CR; Texas benchmarks for Grades K–2	Rhyme production (Grade K); blending onset–rimes and phonemes; deleting initial and final sounds (Grades K and 1)	Part of a comprehensive state-sponsored battery with extensive Web-based resources
Woodcock–Johnson III (WJ III) *Tests of Cognitive Abilities* (2001); Incomplete Words, Sound Blending. *WJ III Tests of Achievement* (2001); Sound Awareness	3–5 per subtest	Norms for ages 2-0 through 90+ and Grades K–8	Blending sounds; identifying words with missing phonemes; generating rhyming words; deleting, substituting, and reversing syllables and phonemes	Rasch-based tests yielding proficiency as well as norm-referenced scores
Yopp–Singer Test of Phonemic Segmentation (1995)	5–10	NS; research norms for spring of kindergarten	Segmenting words into phonemes	Very difficult for many kindergarten children; all-or-nothing scoring reduces sensitivity

Note. CR, criterion-referenced measure; NS, nonstandardized measure; GA, group-administered measure. Fluency-based measures are shaded.

such as 8-3-4-2-9, the items are represented in memory by codes that utilize their acoustic or phonetic features rather than their visual or semantic features (Gathercole & Baddeley, 1993a, 1993b). Poor readers and reading-disabled children show performance deficits on a wide variety of verbal short-term memory tasks, such as digit span, sentence repetition, serial recall of unrelated words, and pseudoword repetition, whether the material is presented aurally or visually (Mann & Ditunno, 1990; Rapala & Brady, 1990; Stone & Brady, 1995; Torgesen, 1996; Vellutino, Scanlon, & Sipay, 1997). Differences between poor and proficient readers are not apparent on tasks requiring recall of nonlinguistic materials, such as drawings of abstract figures, unfamiliar faces, or visual–spatial sequences. Only when the material to be remembered consists of spoken language or nameable visual stimuli—that is, when it can be represented in a speech code—are differences observed (see Brady, 1997, and Torgesen, 1996, for reviews).

Phonological Memory and Reading

There is now abundant evidence that the phonological memory deficits displayed by reading-disabled and garden-variety poor readers are precursors rather than simply consequences of reading problems. Numerous studies (e.g., Badian, 1998; Mann & Liberman, 1984; Torgesen et al., 1994) have demonstrated that short-term verbal memory measured in preschool or kindergarten predicts reading achievement in the primary grades. There are several mechanisms by which phonological memory deficits may exert negative effects on the development of early reading skills. First, children who have difficulty holding sound segments simultaneously in working memory are likely to be slower to develop the phonological awareness skills critical to reading acquisition. Second, phonological memory deficits limit children's ability to use letter-sound knowledge efficiently in the segmentation and blending processes involved in decoding (Torgesen, 1996). Third, phonological memory deficits can interfere with children's ability to learn and retain spoken and written vocabulary (Gathercole & Baddeley, 1993a; Gathercole, Willis, Emslie, & Baddeley, 1992).

Further evidence for the linkage between phonological memory and reading comes from research demonstrating that performance on phonological memory tasks predicts responsiveness to intervention, although support for this position is mixed. In a longitudinal study that incorporated an early intervention component (Vellutino, Scanlon, & Sipay, 1997), kindergarten verbal memory tasks, including memory for words, sentences, and nonsense syllables, along with rapid naming and phoneme segmentation, not only differentiated poor and normally developing first-grade readers, but also differentiated first-grade poor readers who were difficult to remediate from those who were readily remediated. Other studies (e.g., Hatcher & Hulme, 1999; Torgesen & Davis, 1996) have not found phonological memory to be an effective predictor of remediation responsiveness, however. For example, in a study with 7-year-old poor readers (Hatcher & Hulme, 1999), a phonological memory factor comprising digit span, pseudoword repetition, and sound categorization tasks made no significant contribution to predicting responsiveness to intervention. In contrast, a phoneme manipulation factor based on phoneme blending, segmentation, and deletion tasks was a strong predictor of improvement in both reading accuracy and reading comprehension.

Assessing Phonological Memory

Two categories of tasks have been used most frequently to assess phonological memory: verbal memory span and speech repetition.

Verbal Memory Span Tasks

Verbal memory span tasks require children to repeat sequences of words, digits, or other verbal material. Although not all researchers and test authors make the distinction, short-term memory tasks should be distinguished from those that tap working memory. *Short-term memory* tasks, such as forward digit span tests, require examinees to hold a small amount of information passively in memory for a short period of time and then reproduce it in unmodified form. In contrast, *working memory* tasks, such as backward digit span tests, require the examinee to maintain information while performing some kind of operation on it. Verbal memory span tasks are considered to assess phonological memory only if they require immediate verbatim recall of item sequences without stimulus manipulation (Torgesen, 1996) and include forward word span, forward digit span, and sentence imitation tasks.

FORWARD WORD SPAN

Forward word span tasks require children to repeat increasingly long lists of unrelated words. In one version of this task, test stimuli consist of strings of rhyming and nonrhyming words. Good readers make significantly more errors on phonetically confusable word strings (i.e., rhyming strings) than on nonconfusable strings, whereas poor readers show equivalent levels of performance, indicating that they make less use of phonological information in coding (Felton & Brown, 1990; Mann & Liberman, 1984).

Example: "Repeat the following words: *went* . . . *about* . . . *put.*" (The child repeats the sequence verbatim.)

FORWARD DIGIT SPAN

Forward digit span tasks require children to listen to sequences of randomly ordered nonrepeating digits. Researchers have used two different formats: one that presents increasingly longer digit strings, with discontinuance based on specific ceiling rules; and another that presents a fixed number of sequences of each length (e.g., two sequences of two digits, two sequences of five digits, etc.), with discontinuance based on failing all the items in a block.

Example: "Repeat the following numbers: 2 . . . 5 . . . 6 . . . 3." (The child repeats the sequence verbatim.)

SENTENCE IMITATION

Sentence imitation tasks require the child to listen to sentences of increasing length and then repeat them verbatim. Sentence imitation tasks tap syntactic and semantic language skills as well as memory, especially if the sentences consist of real words and conform to standard English syntax (Torgesen, 1996). On some sentence imitation tasks, test stimuli consist of meaningful words arranged to form syntactically nonsensical sentences to reduce the influence of semantic knowledge.

Example: "Repeat this sentence: 'Houses can fly.' " (The child repeats the sentence verbatim.)

Speech Repetition Tasks

Researchers have used two types of speech repetition tasks, which differ in terms of whether real words or pseudowords are used as test stimuli, as well as in terms of task format: speech rate and pseudoword repetition tasks.

SPEECH RATE

Speech rate tasks require the child to repeat a single word, a set of word pairs, or a set of words or digits as rapidly as possibly for a specific number of times or as many times as possible in a given time period. The score is based on the average length of time required to repeat the test stimuli. Speech rate appears to reflect memory span and the ease with which phonological representations of the words to be articulated can be accessed (Hulme & Roodenrys, 1995; Muter & Snowling, 1998). Most speech rate measures involve complex equipment to administer and score items and are impractical in applied settings. Of the tests included in this book, only the *Dyslexia Early Screening Test* (DEST) includes a speech rate measure.

Example: "The word is *watermelon*. Say *watermelon* as fast as you can until I tell you to stop." (The child repeats *watermelon* as rapidly as possible 10 times.)

PSEUDOWORD REPETITION

Pseudoword repetition or *pseudoword imitation* tasks require the child to repeat orally presented pseudowords of increasing length and complexity (e.g., *ib*, *thickery*). Pseudoword repetition tasks are thought to reflect phonological memory abilities more directly than memory span tasks because they do not involve a major rehearsal component and are less subject to attentional influences. Moreover, because pseudowords are unfamiliar, children must rely on accurate phonological encoding and storage in order to produce a correct response. Although pseudoword repetition tasks use nonlexical items, performance is affected not only by phonological processing abilities but also by vocabulary knowledge. The more pseudowords resemble real words, the more easily they can be read by analogy, at least by children with some level of reading skill (Gathercole, 1995).

Example (easy item): "Repeat this word: *tull*." (tull)

Example (difficult item): "Repeat this word: *perplisteronk*." (perplisteronk)

Issues in Assessing Phonological Memory

Assessing phonological memory is complicated by the diversity of tasks and task formats, the difficulty in interpreting poor performance on memory span tests, and low reliability for many phonological memory measures. Moreover, there is considerable controversy regarding the relative diagnostic and predictive efficacy of the various types of phonological memory measures, as well as the extent to which phonological memory predicts reading independently of phonological awareness.

Diversity of Tasks and Item Formats

The lack of consensus regarding the role of phonological memory in reading acquisition is related in part to differences in the tasks and item formats used to assess it. For example, memory span tasks vary in terms of presentation rate. According to Torgesen and his colleagues (Torgesen, 1996; Torgesen & Wagner, 1998), memory span tasks designed to assess phonological memory should use presentation rates that are no slower than one item per second in order to reduce the effect of consciously applied rehearsal strategies. On tasks with slower presentation rates, performance differences may result from differences in the use of mnemonic strategies rather than verbal short-term memory differences (Torgesen & Houck, 1980). Presentation rates for the memory span tests reviewed in this text range from two digits per second for the Memory for Digits subtest on the *Comprehensive Test of Phonological Processing* (CTOPP) to one digit per second for the Forwards Digit Span subtest on the DEST and the Memory for Words test on the *Woodcock–Johnson III* (WJ III) *Tests of Cognitive Abilities* (Woodcock, McGrew, & Mather, 2001b). Presentation rates are not specified for the two memory span subtests on the *Illinois Test of Psycholinguistic Abilities–3* (ITPA-3; Hammill, Mather, & Roberts, 2001), both of which tap other language processes in addition to phonological memory.

Interpretation of Performance Deficits

Another issue in assessing phonological memory concerns the interpretation of observed deficits on memory span tasks. Deficits on memory span tasks can occur not only because of genuine phonological memory problems, but also because of a variety of general performance factors, including inattention, fatigue, anxiety, and lack of motivation. Examinees also vary in terms of their ability to use mnemonic strategies, such as *chunking* (organizing information together into meaningful groups), or *rehearsal* (repeating information as it is presented) (Torgesen, 1996; Torgesen & Wagner, 1998).

Reliability Concerns

In part because of their vulnerability to the effects of the general performance factors discussed above, phonological memory tests tend to be among the least reliable measures in multiskill batteries. For example, on the CTOPP, which consists of 10 subtests measuring phonological awareness and rapid naming as well as phonological memory, the two phonological memory subtests (Memory for Digits and Pseudoword Repetition) had the lowest stability coefficients (.74 and .68, respectively) in a test–retest study with children aged 5–7. Phonological memory tests are also vulnerable to low interscorer reliability because of examiner variance in delivering the test stimuli. Memory span and pseudoword repetition tasks should be presented on audiocassette to ensure a consistent presentation rate for sequences of stimuli and the accurate pronunciation of pseudowords. Of the eight phonological memory tests listed in Table 3.2 below, five are presented on audiocassette (the exceptions are the two subtests on the ITPA-3 and the Speech Rate subtest on the *Phonological Abilities Test*). Phonological memory tasks are also susceptible to interscorer variance. On memory span tests, children often repeat items as quickly as possible in an effort to remember the entire stimulus sequence before it fades from memory, making it difficult to record their responses accurately. Scoring pseudoword repetition tasks presents an additional challenge because examiners, like examinees, are unable to refer to lexical entries to verify response accuracy.

Diagnostic and Predictive Utility

Debate continues regarding the most accurate and effective methods for assessing phonological memory. Evidence regarding the concurrent and predictive utility of speech rate is mixed. In a study with children aged 7–9, McDougall, Hulme, Ellis, and Monk (1994) reported that speech rate, calculated by words per second on a word-triad repetition task, significantly predicted word identification, even when phonological awareness skills were controlled. Moreover, once speech rate was controlled, short-term verbal memory, as measured by a memory span for words, was not a significant predictor. Based on these findings, the authors argued that speech rate is a more effective reading predictor than memory span because it indexes the speed and efficiency with which phonological representations in long-term memory can be activated. In a follow-up study of 9-year-old children who were originally tested in preschool (Muter & Snowling, 1998), the best concurrent predictors of reading at age 9 were phoneme deletion, grammatic knowledge, and speech rate, which together explained 87% of the variance in reading accuracy. Speech rate was again a better predictor of reading than a word span test, but its predictive power was small compared with phoneme deletion. In contrast, pseudoword repetition measured at ages 5 and 6 was one the best predictors of reading at age 9, along with phoneme deletion and letter knowledge.

Other studies provide support for the greater predictive utility of pseudoword repetition tasks compared with speech rate tasks. In a study with three groups of readers (Grade 3 skilled readers, Grade 3 unskilled readers, and younger children at the same reading level as the unskilled readers), Stone and Brady (1995) compared the predictive validity of six phonological memory tasks, including three untimed memory span measures and three speeded speech production measures. Poor readers had significantly lower scores than their age peers and younger normal readers on word span, pseudoword imitation, word pair repetition, and tongue twister tasks. Compared with the speeded speech production tasks, the untimed verbal memory tasks were more strongly related to word recognition and phonemic decoding criterion measures, with pseudoword repetition the strongest individual predictor. Moreover, some investigators (Ackerman & Dykman, 1993; Rapala & Brady, 1990; Stanovich, Nathan, & Zolman, 1988) have failed to find speech rate deficits in poor readers when age and IQ are controlled.

The predictive utility of pseudoword repetition may be related to the multiple cognitive requirements of that task, which taps vocabulary, phonemic segmentation, and articulation skills, in addition to phonological storage efficiency. As noted above, pseudoword repetition performance is significantly related to vocabulary knowledge, as well as to the phonological features of the items, such as syllable length and phonological complexity (Gathercole, 1995; Gathercole & Baddeley, 1993a).

Phonological Memory as an Independent Contributor to Reading Achievement

Although phonological memory is correlated with reading skills in early primary grade children, most studies have found that it is less strongly related than other phonological processing abilities, including phonemic awareness and rapid naming (Felton & Wood, 1989; Fletcher et al., 1994; Wagner et al., 1994, 1997). Longitudinal and cross-sectional studies (Pennington, Van Orden, Kirson, & Haith, 1991; Torgesen et al., 1994; Wagner et al., 1994, 1997) have failed to demonstrate that differences in phonological memory contribute to differences in reading skills when phonological awareness skills are taken into account. In a study following children from kindergarten through fourth grade (Wagner et al., 1997), individual differences in phonological awareness exerted an independent causal influence on reading for all three time periods assessed (kindergarten to second grade, first to third grade, and second to fourth grade). In contrast, phonological memory had significant causal effects on reading acquisition in kindergarten and first grade but became a nonsignificant influence in the later grades. Moreover, in kindergarten and first grade, phonological memory skills had the weakest relationship to reading when compared with phonological awareness and rapid naming and were redundant with the skills measured by phonological awareness tasks in terms of influencing reading growth.

Based on these results, many researchers (Elbro, Nielsen, & Petersen, 1994; Hulme & Roodenrys, 1995; Stanovich et al., 1988; Swan & Goswami, 1997; Torgesen, 1996; Wagner, Torgesen, Laughon, Simmons, & Rashotte, 1993) have concluded that the deficits demonstrated by poor readers on phonological awareness and phonological memory tasks arise from a common cause–specifically, deficiencies in the quality of the underlying phonological representations. Compared with good readers, poor readers have less distinct representations of the phonological codes in long-term memory that are critical to task performance and proficient reading. Although phonological memory tasks index the quality of these representations, they are not unique predictors of the individual differences in the phonological processing skills that are most critical to early reading acquisition (Torgesen, 1996).

Measures of Phonological Memory

Numerous commercially published instruments include verbal short-term memory subtests, but few utilize formats that are compatible with research-based methods of assessing phonological memory. Table 3.2 lists the five instruments reviewed in this text that include a total of eight measures of phonological memory. The eight measures are representative of the diversity of task formats in this area and include two types of memory span tasks (words and digits); three types of speech repetition tasks (real words, pseudowords, and rhyming sequences); and two types of sentence imitation tasks (semantically correct and semantically nonsense sentences).

TABLE 3.2. Measures of Phonological Memory

Name and date of *measure*; subtest(s)	Admin. time (minutes)	Norms/ benchmarks	Testing tasks	Comments
Comprehensive Test of Phonological Processing (1999); Memory for Digits, Pseudoword Repetition	3–5 per subtest	Norms for ages 5–6 and ages 7–24	Repeating number strings; repeating pseudowords	Yields a phonological memory composite that can be compared with phonological awareness and rapid naming composites
Dyslexia Early Screening Test (1996); Forwards Digit Span, Sound Order	2–4 per subtest	British norms for ages 4-6 through 6-5	Repeating number strings; indicating which of a pair of sounds presented on audiocassette comes first	Percentile ranges only; utility limited by British norms
Illinois Test of Psycholinguistic Abilities–3 (2001); Syntactic Sentences, Rhyming Sequences	3–5 per subtest	Norms for ages 5-0 through 12-11	Repeating syntactically correct but semantically nonsensical sentences; repeating rhyming word strings	Both subtests also tap language comprehension and phonological processing
Test of Language Development–Primary: 3 (1997); Sentence Imitation	3–8	Norms for ages 4-0 through 8-11	Repeating sentences	Also measures semantic and syntax skills
Woodcock–Johnson III Tests of Cognitive Abilities (2001); Memory for Words	5–8	Norms for ages 2-0 through 90+ and Grades K–18	Repeating word strings	Also measures language comprehension

PRINT RESOURCES

Metsala, J. L., & Ehri, L. C. (Eds.). (1998). *Word recognition in beginning literacy.* Mahwah, NJ: Erlbaum.

This edited volume of contributions by leading reading researchers includes three chapters focusing on phonological processing, including discussions of definitional and assessment issues, the role of phonological processing deficits in reading disabilities, and the development of phonological processes during the earliest years of reading acquisition.

Torgesen, J. K. (1996). A model of memory from an information processing perspective: The special case of phonological memory. In G. R. Lyon & N. A. Krasnegor (Eds.), *Attention, memory, and executive function* (pp. 157–184). Baltimore: Brookes.

This chapter presents an overview of the memory processes involved in reading, based on Torgesen's long-term research program on the verbal short-term memory problems of reading-disabled children. Topics include the human memory system, methods of and issues involved in assessing phonological memory, and the relationship of phonological memory deficits to reading disabilities.

Rapid Naming

Although there is now a general consensus that phonological processing deficits are the primary cause of early reading failure (e.g., Felton & Brown, 1990, Torgesen et al., 1994; Vellutino & Scanlon, 1987), there is also a wealth of evidence that speed of naming visually presented stimuli is strongly associated with reading achievement (Badian, 1993a; Blachman, 1984; Bowers & Swanson, 1991; Denckla & Rudel, 1976a; Wolf, Bally, & Morris, 1986), and that slow naming speed is characteristic of reading-disabled children and adults (Bowers, 1995b; Kail & Hall, 1994; Meyer, Wood, Hart, & Felton, 1998a; Van Orden, Pennington, & Stone, 1990; Wolf, 1991a, 1991b). Martha Denckla and Rita Rudel (Denckla & Rudel, 1974, 1976a, 1976b; Rudel, Denckla, & Broman, 1978) were the first to establish that naming speed for familiar visual symbols, such as letters and colors, was an effective predictor of reading ability. As designed by Denckla and Rudel, the *rapid automatized naming* (RAN) procedure requires naming as rapidly as possible 50 familiar symbols in a particular category, such as 5 letters randomly repeated in 5 rows of 10 items each on a stimulus card. Figure 3.1 shows the RAN test for letters.

The original RAN procedure consisted of four separate tasks on four stimulus cards, each involving a different category of visual symbol: letters, digits, objects, and colors (see Table 3.3). All RAN tasks begin with a pretest of symbol knowledge, as demonstrated by the examinee's ability to name each of the set of items included in the task. If children make an error, as often occurs for kindergarten students, especially in the fall of the year, that task is not administered. For each RAN task, the score is the time in seconds required to name the complete array of symbols.

o	a	s	d	p	a	o	s	p	d
s	d	a	p	d	o	a	p	s	o
a	o	s	a	s	d	p	o	d	a
d	s	p	o	d	s	a	s	o	p
s	a	d	p	a	p	o	a	p	s

FIGURE 3.1. Rapid automatized naming (RAN) test for letters. From "Naming-Speed Processes, Timing, and Reading: A Conceptual Review," by M. Wolf, P. G. Bowers, and K. Biddle, 2000, *Journal of Learning Disabilities*, *33*, p. 388. Copyright 2000 by PRO-ED, Inc. Reprinted with permission.

TABLE 3.3. Description of Rapid Automatized Naming (RAN) Tasks

RAN task	Description
Rapid color naming	The examinee names a 50-item array of five randomly repeated color patches (yellow, green, black, blue, red) as rapidly as possible.
Rapid object naming	The examinee names a 50-item array of five randomly repeated line drawings (comb, key, watch, scissors, and umbrella[a]) as rapidly as possible.
Rapid letter naming	The examinee names a 50-item array of five randomly repeated high-frequency lowercase letters (*a, d, o, p, s*) as rapidly as possible.
Rapid digit naming	The examinee names a 50-item array of five randomly repeated digits (2, 4, 6, 7, 9) as rapidly as possible.

[a]In the 1974 version, five different objects (table, door, box, ball, and hat) were used because their respective number of syllables corresponds to the syllables of the color names in the rapid color naming task.

RAN TASKS AND FORMATS

Since the development of the original RAN tasks by Denckla and Rudel, several researchers have created modifications of RAN tasks and formats, especially for use with young examinees. Catts (1991, 1993) developed *Rapid Automatized Naming of Animals* (RAN:A) for use with kindergartners because he found that many young children could not consistently name letters or numbers. RAN:A consists of a single stimulus card with 24 pictures of three animals (cow, pig, horse) randomly displayed in one of three colors (red, blue, black) and randomly repeated in four rows of six items each. The child is required to give the color and name of each item (e.g., *red cow*) as rapidly as possible. Although RAN:A has been demonstrated to be an effective predictor of reading acquisition for normal children and for children with speech–language problems (Catts, Fey, Zhang, & Tomblin, 2001), it has not been incorporated into a commercially available instrument to date.

Wolf (1986) developed two versions of the *Rapid Alternating Stimulus* (RAS), which combines serial naming with set-switching requirements. The two-set RAS consists of five letters and five numbers in a fixed A-B-A-B pattern, whereas the three-set RAS alternates five letters, five numbers, and five colors in a fixed A-B-C-A-B-C pattern. Wolf has theorized that RAS more closely approximates reading because it involves both controlled and automatic attentional processes, whereas RAN involves primarily automatic attentional processes. RAS differentiates between average and impaired readers (Wolf, 1986; Semrud-Clikeman, Guy, Griffin, & Hynd, 2000) and between groups with dyslexia and attention-deficit disorder (Ackerman & Dykman, 1993); it also predicts reading performance for reading-disabled children (Berninger, Abbott, Thomson, & Raskind, 2001). An adaptation of the two-set RAS consisting of alternating words and numbers has been incorporated as a subtest in the *Process Assessment of the Learner: Test Battery for Reading and Writing* (PAL-RW; Berninger, 2001), along with several other RAN tasks.

RAN tasks should be distinguished from *confrontation naming tasks*, such as the *Boston Naming Test* (Kaplan, Goodglass, & Weintraub, 1983), which require naming single pictured objects without stringent time limitations. Most studies (Ackerman & Dykman, 1993; Badian, 1993a; Badian, Duffy, Als, & McAnulty, 1991; Felton & Brown, 1990) have found that confrontation naming does not distinguish between normal and dyslexic readers when vocabulary or IQ is controlled, indicating that automaticity of name retrieval rather than knowledge of pictured objects has predictive significance. Rapid automatized naming for letters (RAN-Letters) should also be distinguished from letter-naming fluency tasks, which are discussed in the "Alphabet Knowledge" section of this chapter. As Table 3.3 indicates, RAN-Letters consists of five high-frequency lowercase letters randomly arrayed in rows for a total of 50 items, whereas letter-naming fluency tasks, which are derived from curriculum-based measurement (CBM) research, typically include a large array (i.e., more than 100 letters) of all 26 letters displayed in mixed uppercase and lowercase form and randomly repeated. Scoring procedures for the two types of tasks also differ. The score for RAN-Letters is the number of seconds required to name all 50 stimuli in the array, whereas the score for letter-naming fluency tasks is the number of letters named correctly in 1 minute.

RAPID NAMING AND READING

The predictive utility of rapid naming varies with the RAN task, the age or grade of examinees, and reading proficiency. Although a few studies have found similar association strengths between reading and the four RAN tasks (Denckla & Rudel, 1976b; Meyer, Wood, Hart, & Felton, 1998b; Snyder & Downey, 1995), most studies have reported that rapid letter and digit naming are more effective predictors of reading skill than rapid color and object naming (e.g., Badian, 1993a; Cornwall, 1992; Torgesen et al., 1994; Wimmer, 1993; Wolf, 1991b; Wolf et al., 1986). Naming speed tasks have maximum predictive utility in the early primary grades (McBride-Chang & Manis, 1996; Meyer et al., 1998a; Torgesen, Wagner, Rashotte, Alexander, et al., 1997; Wagner et al., 1997; Walsh, Price, & Gillingham, 1988) and in samples of poor readers (Mann & Ditunno, 1990; Scarborough, 1998b). For example, Scarborough (1998b) found that Grade 2 RAN performance was a powerful predictor of Grade 8 phonemic decoding, word identification, and spelling skills for children who had been identified as having reading disabilities at Grade 2, whereas rapid naming contributed little to prediction for nondisabled readers. Similarly, in two large longitudinal samples of students (Meyer et al., 1998b), Grade 3 rapid naming was a strong predictor of reading skills in Grades 5 and 8, even when earlier word identification, IQ, and SES were controlled, but its predictive power was limited to poor readers. For average readers, phonological skills, not rapid naming, predicted future reading achievement. The diminishing predictive power of rapid naming for normally developing readers arises from the fact that proficient readers approach asymptotic performance on naming speed measures after the early primary grades. In contrast, for poor readers, who rarely develop full automaticity in naming speed, rapid naming continues to be a good predictor of later reading ability (Wolf & Bowers, 1999).

Factors Underlying the Relationship between Naming Speed and Reading

Why would a task that requires serial naming of familiar symbols be so strongly associated with reading performance? In other words, is RAN performance directly related to reading, or is it associated with reading because it is mediated by other processes that affect reading proficiency, such as verbal ability and memory? Despite the large body of evidence documenting the relationship between rapid naming and reading, there is no general consensus regarding the way in which the processes underlying naming speed affect word recognition, decoding, and other reading skills. Naming speed appears to have little association with general cognitive ability (Bowers, Steffy, & Tate, 1988; Bowers & Swanson, 1991; Spring & Davis, 1988). Nor do naming speed deficits appear to result from slow articulation rates (Ackerman & Dykman, 1993; Stanovich et al., 1988; Wagner et al., 1993; Wimmer, 1993) or from short-term memory problems (Bowers et al., 1988; Wagner et al., 1993; Wimmer, 1993). Although RAN is moderately to highly correlated with processing speed (Kail & Hall, 1994; Kail, Hall, & Caskey, 1999), it is not identical with it, as demonstrated by research indicating that rapid naming still contributes uniquely to word reading, even when processing speed and other reading predictors are controlled (Cutting & Denckla, 2001).

Currently there are different conceptualizations of the factors underlying the association between rapid naming and reading ability. Some researchers (e.g., Allor et al., 2001; Katz, 1986, 1996; Share, 1995; Torgesen & Burgess, 1998; Torgesen & Wagner, 1998) subsume naming speed under phonological processing on the grounds that rapid naming measures rate of access to phonological information (i.e., names). Torgesen, Wagner, Rashotte, Burgess, and colleagues (1997) have argued that the results of many RAN prediction studies are difficult to interpret because researchers did not take the autoregressive effects of prior reading skill into account. In other words, without controlling for earlier reading ability, these investigations cannot answer the question of whether naming speed is directly related to later reading achievement or is only indirectly related because of its association with previous reading skills. In a longitudinal study following a large sample of children from kindergarten through Grade 5, both phoneme awareness and RAN uniquely contributed to reading in Grades 2 and 3, even when prior reading skill was controlled. When autoregressive effects were controlled, however, Grade 2 phonemic awareness but not rapid naming continued to contribute to Grade 4 reading, both in the full sample and in a reading-impaired group.

THE DOUBLE-DEFICIT HYPOTHESIS

In contrast to the view of rapid naming as a component of phonological processing, Wolf and Bowers (Bowers & Wolf, 1993; Wolf, 1999; Wolf & Bowers, 1999) argue that rapid naming constitutes a second core deficit in reading disabilities. This alternative conceptualization of dyslexia, termed the *double-deficit hypothesis*, proposes that phonological deficits and the processes underlying naming speed deficits are two largely independent sources of reading dysfunction. In a recent conceptualization of this model, Wolf, Bowers, and Biddle (2000) offer two nonexclusive hypotheses for the relationship between RAN and reading. According to the first hypothesis, naming speed and reading are linked by orthographic processing. Slow naming speed, especially for letters, reflects impairment in the processes critical to the recognition and storage of orthographic patterns in printed words. Children who are slow in identifying individual letters, as reflected in RAN tasks, do not activate single letters in words close enough in time to encode letter combinations as units, thus limiting the development of orthographic knowledge and the quality of orthographic representations in long-term memory. According to the second hypothesis, naming speed deficits are one manifestation of a system of general timing deficits affecting visual, auditory, and motoric domains in addition to phonological and orthographic processing. That is, slow naming speed represents the linguistic analogue of the processing speed deficits consistently found among individuals with dyslexia in other domains.

The double-deficit hypothesis also proposes that phonological and naming speed deficits result in three distinct subtypes of impaired readers and that children with deficits in both sets of abilities will exhibit the most severe reading problems (see Table 3.4). Wolf and Bowers (1999) have hypothesized that children with naming speed deficits, and especially those with double deficits, constitute some of the treatment nonresponders encountered in phonologically based training programs (e.g., Blachman, 1994b; Byrne & Fielding-Barnsley, 1991; Lundberg, 1988; Torgesen, 2000; Torgesen, Morgan, & Davis, 1992).

Evidence for Rapid Naming as a Separate Factor in Reading Dysfunction

Several lines of evidence support the contention that naming speed deficits constitute a separate source of reading difficulties from phonological processing deficits. First, naming speed and phonologically based tasks display generally modest correlations (e.g., Blachman, 1984; Bowers, 1995b; Cornwall, 1992; Felton & Brown, 1990). Second, RAN performance contributes sizable variance to the accuracy and latency of word reading even when phonological skill and IQ are controlled (Ackerman & Dykman, 1993a; Badian, 1993a; Blachman, 1984; Bowers, 1995b; Bowers & Swanson, 1991; Cornwall, 1992; Felton & Brown, 1990; Manis, Doi, & Bhadha, 2000; McBride-Chang & Manis, 1996). Third, a growing number of studies have found evidence of the three reading subtypes proposed by the double-deficit hypothesis, including support for the contention that children with deficits in both naming speed and phonological awareness are significantly more impaired in reading than are children with a deficit in only one area (Berninger et al., 1997; Lovett, Steinbach, & Frijters, 2000; Morris et al., 1998; Wolf & Bowers, 1999). Fourth, naming speed and phonological awareness measures show different patterns of relationships with specific reading subskills. Whereas phonemic awareness is more strongly associated with real and pseudoword decoding accuracy, naming speed is more strongly associated with word-reading latency and passage reading speed (Badian, 1993a; Bowers, 1995b; Bowers & Wolf, 1993; Cornwall, 1992; Manis et al., 2000; Meyer et al., 1998b;

TABLE 3.4. Double-Deficit Hypothesis Subtypes

Subtype	Nature of deficit	Reading profile
Rate	Naming speed deficit, but intact phonological decoding	Adequate decoding, but impaired fluency and comprehension
Phonological	Phonological deficits, but intact naming speed	Impaired decoding and reading comprehension
Double deficit	Deficits in both naming speed and phonological decoding	Severe decoding and comprehension deficits

Note. From "What Time May Tell: Towards a New Conceptualization of Developmental Dyslexia" by M. Wolf, 1999, *Annals of Dyslexia, 49*, p. 13. Copyright 1999 by the International Dyslexia Association. Adapted with permission.

Scarborough, 1998b; Torgesen, Wagner, Rashotte, Burgess, et al., 1997; Wagner et al., 1997).

Finally, there is accumulating evidence (e.g., Berninger et al., 1999; Torgesen & Davis, 1996; Vellutino, Scanlon, & Lyon, 2000) that naming speed has prognostic as well as diagnostic utility. In a study following five subgroups of children with learning disabilities (Korhonen, 1991), the subgroup of children with naming speed deficits had the most unfavorable prognosis in reading. In an early intervention study, Torgesen, Wagner, Rashotte, Rose, and colleagues (1999) found that kindergarten rapid naming (a composite of color and object naming) was the most consistent unique predictor of reading growth, as measured in Grade 2 after a 2½-year intervention program. Children who showed the least progress were characterized by double deficits in phonemic awareness and rapid naming, whereas children with stronger rapid naming skills benefited most from the intervention program. Similarly, in an intervention study with first graders (Allor et al., 2001), children with lower performance on RAN measures, including RAN-Letters, RAS, and RAN-Colors, scored lower than children with stronger naming speed skills on all outcome measures, including phonemic awareness, reading fluency, word identification, and reading comprehension.

ISSUES IN ASSESSING RAPID NAMING

Among the issues relevant to the assessment of rapid naming in early primary grade examinees are (1) the variations among RAN measures, including items, formats, and scoring procedures; (2) the limited utility of RAN tasks with prereaders; and (3) discriminative utility.

Item, Format, and Scoring Variations

RAN measures in the research literature, as well as those available from commercial publishers, vary in terms of the sets of stimuli used for the four tasks. Although most use the original set of colors, the letter and digit sets vary somewhat from measure to measure. The greatest diversity is found in measures of rapid object naming. The standard RAN-Objects task consists of a set of five common objects randomly repeated to form a 50-item array (see Table 3.3). In contrast, the Rapid Naming subtest on the *Dyslexia Early Screening Test* (DEST) and its upward extension, the *Dyslexia Screening Test* (DST), consists of a set of line drawings of 20 different objects, repeated twice to form a 40-item array. The WJ III Rapid Picture Naming test consists of 120 pictured objects, some but not all of which are repeated. Moreover, the objects vary in terms of familiarity to children (e.g., ball, [spider] web, helicopter). RAN measures also differ in terms of presentation formats—that is, whether stimulus arrays are presented on a sheet of paper or card that lies flat in front of the examinee, as in the typical RAN procedure; on pages in an easel booklet that lies flat, as in the PAL-RW RAN subtests; or on pages in a standing test easel, as in the WJ III Rapid Picture Naming test.

In addition, RAN measures differ in terms of the penalties incurred, if any, for naming errors. Most measures specify that the examinee must be able to name all the symbols on practice items after error correction if the test is to be administered. On some measures (e.g., the CTOPP rapid naming subtests), testing is discontinued if the examinee makes more than a specified number of errors. On the DEST and DST RAN subtests, time is added to the score for naming errors, whereas on the PAL-RW RAN subtests, scores is based on response completion time, regardless of errors. Of the six instruments with RAN measures reviewed in this text, only the PAL-RW provides normative data for use in interpreting the number of errors.

Utility of RAN Tasks with Preliterate Children

Despite the predictive power of naming speed tasks, RAN measures involving letters and digits cannot be used with children who do not know the alphabet or their numbers. This precludes the use of RAN tasks with many young examinees because especially in the fall of the kindergarten year, many children cannot name letters or numbers, and some may not be able to name colors. Under these circumstances, poor performance may be due to deficits in letter-, number-, or color-name knowledge rather than deficits in rapid naming. Similarly, RAN tasks with words, such as the PAL-RW RAN-Words and RAN-Words & Digits tasks, cannot be administered to children who are unable to read the stimulus items.

Discriminative Validity

A critical issue in assessing rapid naming relates to the question of whether naming speed deficits are specific to reading disabilities or are characteristic of learning problems in general. Although some studies have reported that RAN differentiates between children with reading problems and children with other types of learning or attentional problems (Ackerman & Dykman, 1993; Felton, Wood, Brown, & Campbell, 1987; Semrud-Clikeman et al., 2000; Wood & Felton, 1994), most of the naming speed research has compared poor readers with normal controls rather than with children with other types of learning disorders. In a study with children aged 7–11 referred for learning problems, Waber, Wolff, Forbes, and Weiler (2000) evaluated the diagnostic utility of RAN using receiver operating characteristic (ROC) analysis, which estimates the extent to which test performance correctly assigns individual children to a group. Although RAN was highly effective in discriminating learning-impaired from normally performing children (90% hit rate), it was much less effective in differentiating learning-impaired children with reading disabilities from those without reading problems (65% hit rate). Although the vast majority of children with reading disabilities demonstrated naming speed deficits, more than half of the learning-impaired children who were adequate readers also displayed naming speed deficits. According to Waber (2001), these results indicate that slow naming speed is characteristic of children with learning problems in general rather than specific to reading impairment and that naming speed deficits reflect different underlying mechanisms in different children rather than a single process with unique implications for reading.

The hypothesis that naming speed deficits represent a separate source of reading difficulty and that children with both deficits display the most severe reading impairment has also been challenged on statistical grounds. In a recent large-scale study with first and second graders, Schatschneider, Carlson, Francis, Foorman, and Fletcher (2002) demonstrated that the greater reading impairment found in children with double deficits could in part be due to a statistical artifact produced by grouping children according to their performance on two positively correlated predictor variables. That is, because phonological awareness and naming speed are positively correlated, a subgroup with a double deficit will necessarily have lower phonological awareness scores than a subgroup with only a phonological deficit. Because children with lower phonological awareness scores are also more likely to have lower reading skills, such a finding also casts doubt on the assertion that the poorer reading performance associated with a double deficit is solely due to the additional influence of naming speed deficits.

MEASURES OF RAPID NAMING

Whether RAN measures a timing dimension, automaticity, lexical retrieval, executive function, or all of these processes, naming speed is a critical component of early reading assessments, especially for children who are already experiencing fluency problems in reading or writing (Berninger, Abbott, Billingsley, & Nagy, 2001). Including naming speed measures in screening batteries can help to identify children at risk for reading problems, especially those with minor phonological deficits who may not be identified by batteries focusing on phonological processing skills. Evidence suggests that naming speed performance is important not only as an indicator of risk for reading problems and perhaps learning problems in general, but also as a prognostic indicator. Despite the predictive utility of rapid naming and the voluminous research literature on naming speed, surprisingly few rapid naming tests are currently available from commercial test publishers, although at least two instruments are under development. At this time, the standard set of RAN tasks is available from Wake Forest University's Bowman Gray School of Medicine. In Table 3.5, each instrument that includes multiple RAN tasks is listed as a single entry for the sake of readability.

PRINT RESOURCES

Felton, R. H. (Ed.). (2001). Case studies of students with severe reading disabilities [Special issue]. *Journal of Special Education, 35*(3).

This special issue includes three case studies of children with severe reading disabilities—one with a phonological deficit, one with both phonological and naming speed deficits, and one with a naming speed deficit. The third case study is the first published case of a child with an isolated naming speed deficit and describes the use of the intervention program RAVE-O (see next entry) to remediate processing speed and fluency deficits in reading.

Wolf, M., & Bowers, P. G. (Eds.). (2001). The double-deficit hypothesis [Special issue]. *Journal of Learning Disabilities, 33*(4).

This special issue includes articles discussing the role of naming speed processes as a separate factor beyond phonological deficits in reading failure and investigating the utility of the double-deficit hypothesis in the diagnosis and prediction of reading problems. Included is an article describing the first direct application of the double-deficit hypothesis to intervention—the Retrieval, Automaticity, Vocabulary Elaboration–Orthography (RAVE-O) program developed by Maryanne Wolf and her colleagues.

TABLE 3.5. Measures of Rapid Naming

Name and date of *measure*; subtest(s)	Admin. time (minutes)	Norms/ benchmarks	Testing tasks	Comments
Comprehensive Test of Phonological Processing (1999); Rapid Color Naming, Rapid Object Naming, Rapid Letter Naming, Rapid Digit Naming	3–5 each	Norms for ages 5–24	Naming a sets of colors, objects, letters, and numbers as rapidly as possible; score is based on two trials on separate stimulus arrays per task	Yields subtest and composite rapid naming scores; one of the few RAN measures with two trials per task for greater reliability
Dyslexia Early Screening Test (1996); Rapid Naming	2–3	British norms for ages 4-6 through 6-5	Naming two identical arrays of 20 familiar objects as rapidly as possible	Percentile scores only; identical to the task on the *Dyslexia Screening Test*
Dyslexia Screening Test (1996); Rapid Naming	2–3	British norms for ages 6-6 through 16-5	Naming two identical arrays of 20 familiar objects as rapidly as possible	Percentile scores only; identical to the task on the *Dyslexia Early Screening Test*
Process Assessment of the Learner: Test Battery for Reading and Writing (2001); RAN-Letters, RAN-Words, RAN-Digits, RAN-Words & Digits	2–3 per task	Norms for Grades K–6 (RAN-Letters, RAN-Digits) and Grades 1–6 (RAN-Words, RAN-Words & Digits)	Naming sets of letters and letter groups, words, one- and two-digit numbers; and alternating words and numbers as rapidly as possible	Decile scores only; unique tasks of naming speed for letter clusters and alternating words and numbers
Test of Rapid Automatized Naming (1998); Rapid Color Naming, Rapid Number Naming, Rapid Object Naming, Rapid Letter Naming	2–3 per task	NS; research norms for Grades 1, 3, 5, and 8	Naming a series of colors, digits, objects, and letters as rapidly as possible	The standard RAN procedure; percentiles only; examiners must extrapolate percentiles for examinees in Grades 2, 4, 6, and 7
Woodcock–Johnson III Tests of Cognitive Abilities (2001); Rapid Picture Naming	3	Norms for ages 2-0 through 90+ and Grades K–18	Naming as many familiar pictured objects as possible in 2 minutes	Easel format presentation; wide variety of objects rather than five repeated objects

Note. NS, nonstandardized measure.

Orthographic Processing

A third area of language processes associated with reading acquisition and reading disabilities is referred to as *orthographic processing*. An *orthography* is a system of printed symbols for representing the speech sounds in a written language. English orthography includes uppercase and lowercase letters, numerals, and punctuation marks. Whereas phonological awareness refers to sensitivity to the speech sounds of language, *orthographic awareness* reflects familiarity with the written symbols (i.e., letters) representing those sounds, including the ability to distinguish between correct and incorrect spellings of written words (Foorman, 1994; Vellutino et al., 2000). *Orthographic processing* is a general term that refers to the use of orthographic information in processing oral or written language (Wagner & Barker, 1994). Children acquire orthographic knowledge and processing skills through repeated exposure to printed words, which enables them to develop stable visual representations of letter sequences, word parts, and whole words in long-term memory (Barker, Torgesen, & Wagner, 1992).

After the refutation of the notion of visual-perceptual deficits as the primary cause of reading disabilities (see Vellutino, 1979, for a review), researchers focused much less attention on orthographic processing than on phonological processing. Recently, however, there has been increasing interest in orthographic processing as a possible second contributor to reading ability in view of the consistent finding that phonological skills do not account for all of the variance in word recognition (Berninger, 1994; Manis et al., 2000; Roberts & Mather, 1997; Stanovich & Siegel, 1994). In contrast to the general consensus about the nature of phonological processing and its relationship to reading, however, there is much less agreement regarding the construct of orthographic processing and the degree to which it contributes (if at all) to individual differences in reading acquisition. Debate continues regarding whether phonological and orthographic processes are independent or interactive mechanisms or have multiple connections at different levels within the word recognition system (see Berninger, 1994, for a review of these issues).

ORTHOGRAPHIC PROCESSING AND READING

According to most theories of reading acquisition (Barron, 1986; Ehri, 1991, 1992; Share & Stanovich, 1995), developing accurate visual representations of letters and words in long-term memory is essential for rapid word recognition and proficient spelling. By repeatedly associating a word's correct pronunciation with its visual representation, readers develop *unitized orthographic representations*, that is, memory for spelling patterns that are larger than individual letters, as well as for individual words as whole units (i.e., "sight words"). With increasingly developed phonological reading skills and exposure to print, children acquire fully specified orthographic representations that constitute a sight word vocabulary that can be instantly and accurately recognized (Torgesen, Wagner, Rashotte, Alexander, et al., 1997). Although orthographic codes are represented in the visual system, orthographic processing appears to be unrelated to individual differences in visual ability (Stanovich, West, &

Cunningham, 1991; Vellutino, Scanlon, & Chen, 1994). A large body of evidence documents that visual processing tasks that do not involve letters, such as tasks of visual–motor functioning, shape copying, or visual memory for designs, do not differentiate between poor and proficient readers (Berninger, 1994; Hatcher & Hulme, 1999; Manis, Szeszulski, Holt, & Graves, 1988; Mann, 1993; Margolese & Kline, 1999; Vellutino, 1979; Vellutino & Scanlon, 1991; Vellutino, Scanlon, & Spearing, 1995). Instead, orthographic processing is specific to printed words.

Two sets of findings support the role of orthographic processing skills in reading acquisition. First, as noted above, orthographic processing measures contribute additional variance to the prediction of reading skills independent of that contributed by phonological processing or general cognitive ability (Aaron, Joshi, & Williams, 1999; Badian, 1993b; Barker et al., 1992; Cunningham & Stanovich, 1990, 1993; Hoover & Gough, 1990; Stanovich et al., 1991; Wagner et al., 1994). Second, although individual differences in reading experience (i.e., print exposure) account for much of the variance in orthographic skills, they do not account for all of it (Badian, 1993b; Cunningham, Perry, & Stanovich, 2001; Cunningham & Stanovich, 1991; Stanovich et al., 1991), suggesting that individual differences in the ability to encode, store, and retrieve orthographic representations may be another important factor in reading acquisition.

The contribution of orthographic processing skills to reading proficiency depends on the nature of the reading task and the age of the reader. Orthographic processing accounts for more of the variance in reading rate for connected text than for untimed single word reading (Barker et al., 1992; Cunningham & Stanovich, 1991). Moreover, the relative contribution of orthographic processing to reading skill increases with age. In a longitudinal study by Juel, Griffith, and Gough (1986), orthographic skills accounted for only 3% of the variance in word reading for first graders but accounted for 20% of the variance in reading for second graders. Similarly, in a series of longitudinal studies following cohorts of children from preschool through the elementary grades (Badian, 1995, 2000), a preschool orthographic processing task contributed an increasing proportion of variance in reading comprehension in the later grades, even with age and verbal IQ controlled.

Evidence suggests that individual differences in orthographic skills also predict response to intervention. In a study with 114 second and third graders who received one of three reading intervention programs (Foorman, Francis, Fletcher, et al., 1997), growth in word reading was predicted by children's prior levels of orthographic knowledge as measured by spelling dictation and pseudohomophone tasks (see below), as well as by initial differences in phonological processing skills. Similarly, in a study with 48 children referred at the end of first grade for reading problems (Berninger et al., 1999), an orthographic composite consisting of a whole-word coding and a letter-coding task predicted rate of growth on an inventory of taught words, as well as which children were and were not treatment responders.

Surface versus Phonological Dyslexics

The growing interest in orthographic processing has been spurred by a series of recent studies (e.g., Castles & Coltheart, 1993; Castles, Datta, Gayan, & Olson, 1999; Manis, Seidenberg, Doi, McBride-Chang, & Peterson, 1996; Siegel, Share, & Geva, 1995; Stanovich, Siegel, & Gottardo, 1997) that have distinguished between two subgroups of dyslexics according to their performance in reading irregular words versus pseudowords. According to this subtyping research, *phonological dyslexics* are more impaired in phonological coding, as demonstrated by pseudoword reading tasks, than in orthographic coding, as demonstrated by exception word reading and orthographic choice tasks. In contrast, *surface dyslexics* show the opposite pattern, with relatively less impairment in pseudoword reading and relatively more impairment in orthographic coding. Differences in spelling errors between the two groups have also been observed, consistent with their type of dyslexia (Curtin, Manis, & Seidenberg, 2001). Compared with the phonological dyslexics, the surface dyslexics do not appear to be developmentally distinctive, however; that is, their performance is similar to that of younger normal readers matched on word reading skill (Manis et al., 1996; Stanovich et al., 1997). Moreover, the proportion of surface or orthographic dyslexics is considerably smaller than that of phonological dyslexics and is less stable over time. Two hypotheses, which are complementary rather than conflicting, have been offered for these findings. Stanovich and colleagues (1997) suggest that the surface dyslexic subtype represents a group of children with mild phonological deficits that have been exacerbated by lack of exposure to reading or limited learning opportunities, whereas Curtin and colleagues (2001) propose that surface dyslexia reflects a general delay in acquiring reading skills. These views are consistent with the finding that although surface dyslexia has a small but significant genetic component, it has a much larger environmental component compared with phonological dyslexia (Castles et al., 1999).

ASSESSING ORTHOGRAPHIC PROCESSING

Given the controversy regarding the nature of the construct and its role in the reading process, it is not surprising that there is no standard set of tasks for assessing orthographic processing (see Olson, Forsberg, Wise, & Rack, 1994; Vellutino, Scanlon, & Chen, 1994; Vellutino, Scanlon, & Tanzman, 1994). Assessment tools have ranged from standardized spelling tests (Cunningham et al., 2001) to exception word reading measures (Manis, Seidenberg, & Doi, 1999) to tasks involving novel alphabets constructed from the visual features of the Roman alphabet used in English (Vellutino, Scanlon, & Chen, 1994). Although all of these tasks involve phonological coding to some extent, information about the specific letter sequences in the word to be recognized or spelled is needed to answer correctly. The tasks most commonly used to assess orthographic processing in the literature are described below. In several of the examples below, two or more possible responses are given in parentheses, and the correct choice is underlined.

Orthographic Choice

The child sees a pair of words presented on computer or on a sheet of paper that are phonologically similar but orthographically dissimilar and identifies the real word by pushing one of two buttons or circling the real word (Olson, Wise, Conners, Rack, & Fulker, 1989). The phonological similar item is a *pseudohomophone*, a phonologically correct pseudoword that sounds the same as the stimulus word. Because the stimulus pairs sound identical when decoded, phonological decoding skills cannot be the only factor in performance. Instead, the child must rely on word-specific orthographic knowledge to answer correctly. When the task is presented on a computer, latency of response as well as accuracy can be measured.

Example: "Which is a word?" (*rain*, *rane*)

Homophone Choice

The examiner reads a sentence or asks a question, and the child presses a button to select the word that is correct for the context from a pair of words presented on a computer screen. The words are *homophones*, that is, words that sound alike but have different meanings (also termed *homonyms*) (Barker et al., 1992).

Example: "Which is a number?" (*ate*, *eight*)

Lexical Verification

The examiner pronounces a word, and the child presses a button to indicate whether a word presented on a computer screen is correctly spelled. Half the words are spelled correctly and half the words are pseudohomophones (see above), so that the child's response must be based on a fully specified orthographic representation of the word's correct spelling (Torgesen, Wagner, Rashotte, Alexander, et al., 1997).

Example: "Street" (*street*, *streat*)

In a noncomputerized version of this task, the examiner reads aloud the stimulus word and uses it in a sentence, and the child circles the correct word from a triad of words printed on a page (Manis et al., 1999). The choices are minimally different and often phonologically similar so that the child must rely on an accurate, complete orthographic representation of the word in memory. This format is similar to that of some norm-referenced spelling tests.

Example: "Tight. These shoes are too tight on my feet." (*tite*, *tight*, *tait*)

Word Likeness Choice

The child is presented with a sheet of paper on which are printed pairs of pseudowords and is instructed to circle the one of the pair that looks more similar to a real word. One word of the pair consists of letter sequences and positions that are common in English orthography, whereas the other includes uncommon or "illegal" English letter sequences and positions (Manis et al., 1999).

Example: "Circle the word that looks more like a word." (*beff*, *ffeb*)

Exception Word Reading

Exception word reading requires the child to read real words that are deliberately selected to violate phonically regular letter-sound correspondence rules. The words range from common to very infrequent and difficult (Adams & Huggins, 1985).

Example (easy item): *you*

Example (difficult item): *yacht*

Whole-Word, Letter-Cluster, and Letter-Coding Tasks

Developed by Berninger and her colleagues (Berninger & Abbott, 1994a; Berninger, Yates, & Lester, 1991), these three tasks use a similar presentation format, but the target stimulus varies according to the size of the orthographic unit. In the whole-word coding task, a word is exposed for 1 second, another word is then presented, and the child must indicate whether the second word matches the target word exactly. In the letter-cluster coding task, a word is exposed, after which a group of letters is presented, and the child must indicate whether the letters appeared in the same order in the word. In the letter-coding task, a word is presented, after which a single letter is presented, and the child must indicate whether a single letter was in the target word. Originally designed for computer administration, these tasks have been adapted for presentation in a test easel format on the Receptive Coding subtest in Berninger's *Process Assessment of the Learner: Test Battery for Reading and Writing.*

Example (letter-coding task): The child first sees *must,* then sees *st,* and says, "Yes."

Title Recognition Tests

Once children have learned to read, title recognition tests (TRTs) can be used to estimate children's levels of print exposure. The *Title Recognition Test* (Cunningham & Stanovich, 1990) was adapted from the *Author Recognition Test* developed by Stanovich and his colleagues and used in studies with adult readers (e.g., Stanovich & West, 1989). This TRT consists of a list of titles of age-appropriate popular children's books and is based on the idea that children who read more widely outside of school (i.e., children with more exposure to print) will be able to identify the titles of a greater number of books. A set of fabricated book titles ("foils") is mixed among the genuine titles to reduce the effects of guessing. TRTs are considered to be indirect measures of orthographic knowledge because the child must rely on representations of orthographic segments and words stored in memory in order to answer correctly. Performance is scored by subtracting the number of foils endorsed from the number of actual titles endorsed.

Some researchers have selected TRT items to include titles of books that are not major parts of the classroom reading activities in the schools in which they are administered in order to assess out-of-school reading, whereas others have included items based on book popularity for the relevant age group. The examiner reads the list of titles or the children read the list for themselves, and the children mark each title they believe to be an actual book. Children are told not to guess because some of the titles are not from real books. TRTs can be group-administered in about 5–10 minutes or administered and scored by computer, as on Virginia's *Phonological Awareness Literacy Screening* (PALS). TRTs must be frequently updated to reflect trends in children's literature and reading choices. Moreover, with the increasing use of literature-based instruction and literature-based readers, children may identify titles correctly because they have been exposed to them in the curriculum rather than because they engage in wide out-of-school reading (Foorman, 1994).

Although TRT scores are significant predictors of word identification (Cunningham & Stanovich, 1990) and reading comprehension (Cipielewski & Stanovich, 1992) for elementary grade students (e.g., Grades 3 and up), studies with early primary grade children have yielded mixed results. In a small first-grade sample (Cunningham & Stanovich, 1993), TRT scores displayed moderate correlations with reading and spelling, whereas in a larger study with second graders (Byrne & Fielding-Barnsley, 1995), TRT scores made no contribution to the prediction of word identification and were only weakly related to reading comprehension.

Example: "Is *Green Eggs and Ham* the title of a book?"	Yes	No	Not Sure

ISSUES IN ASSESSING ORTHOGRAPHIC PROCESSING

Among the issues involved in assessing the orthographic processing skills of early primary grade children are (1) concerns about construct validity and (2) the difficulty of using orthographic tasks with prereaders.

Concerns about Construct Validity

Vellutino and his colleagues (Vellutino, Scanlon, & Chen, 1994; Vellutino, Scanlon, & Tanzman, 1994) have challenged the construct validity of the most frequently used measures of orthographic processing on several grounds. First, they contend that most of the tasks designed to assess orthographic coding actually evaluate word identification or spelling ability rather than some basic cognitive process underlying those abilities. Second, because reading involves both orthographic and phonological coding, there are no "pure" tasks of orthographic processing. Once children have learned to read, they are able to perform orthographic processing tasks by drawing on their word recognition and spelling knowledge. For example, on lexical verification tasks, children who have learned to read the correctly spelled alternative in the set of choices will respond correctly, whereas those who do not have that particular word in their lexicon may or may not be able to guess correctly. The homophone choice task, which requires holding a phrase spoken by the examiner in working memory in order to match word spellings with word meanings, taps vocabulary and memory skills as well as orthographic skills. Finally, most of the tasks are subject to guessing strategies. Their contention that the definition of orthographic coding depends to a large extent on the measure used to assess it is supported by the results of a recent study (Cunningham et al., 2001) analyzing the relationships among six different measures of orthographic processing (three letter string choice tasks, two orthographic choice tasks, and a homophone choice task). Although the orthographic measures showed a moderate degree of task convergence, correlations among the tasks were highly variable. Moreover, several of the tasks showed low levels of reliability.

Utility of Orthographic Tasks with Preliterate Children

A second issue relates to the difficulty of measuring orthographic processing ability in children with little or no reading experience. Because the vast majority of orthographic tasks require children to distinguish real words from pseudowords or correctly spelled words from misspelled words, they cannot be used with prereaders. In an effort to address this problem, Badian (1994) developed a 10-item visual matching task that included alphanumeric symbols, such as letter and digit strings, to assess early orthographic processing skills in preschool children. Preschool performance on the orthographic measure was strongly related to first-grade reading skills, even with letter knowledge controlled. A group-administered task with a similar format has been incorporated as the Visual Matching subtest in the *Predictive Reading Profile* reviewed in this text.

MEASURES OF ORTHOGRAPHIC PROCESSING

Currently, very few norm-referenced measures that are specifically labeled as orthographic processing tasks are available from commercial test publishers. Many of the tasks commonly used in research to assess orthographic processing are not practical for school- or clinic-based practitioners because they require computerized equipment for measuring the latency and accuracy of responses. Some of the measures listed in Table 3.6 are derived from orthographic processing tasks in the research literature but are not designated as "orthographic" measures (e.g., the Sight Spelling subtest on the ITPA-3). Given the increasing interest in this reading component and growing evidence of its predictive and prognostic utility, however, more measures of orthographic processing are likely to appear in the future. Moreover, tests that provide measures of both phonological and orthographic abilities, such as the ITPA-3, have the potential to assist in differentiating between subtypes of dyslexia and identifying children whose phonological coding skills are adequate but who are falling behind in the kinds of orthographic coding skills that permit accurate, rapid word recognition.

PRINT RESOURCES

Berninger, V. W. (Ed.). (1994). *The varieties of orthographic knowledge* (2 vols.): *I. Theoretical and developmental issues. II. Relationship to phonology, reading, and writing*. Dordrecht, The Netherlands: Kluwer Academic.

This two-part series brings together articles exploring the role of orthography in reading and writing from a variety of perspectives. The chapter in the first volume by Wagner and Barker on the development of orthographic processing and the chapter in the second volume by Vellutino, Scanlon, and Chen on efforts to operationalize orthographic processing and assess it separately from phonological processing have particular relevance for practitioners assessing early primary grade children.

TABLE 3.6. Measures of Orthographic Processing

Name and date of *measure*; subtest	Admin. time (minutes)	Norms/ benchmarks	Testing tasks	Comments
Exception Word Reading Test (1985)	5	NS; research norms for Grades 2–5	Irregular word reading	Quick screening measure suitable for local norming; too difficult for many second graders
Group Reading Assessment and Diagnostic Evaluation (2002); Same and Different Words	5 per task	Norms for Grade K (when combined with two other measures)	Marking the one of four words identical to a target word and marking the one of four words that differs from the other three	Multiple-choice format; does not yield a separate subtest score
Illinois Test of Psycholinguistic Abilities–3 (ITPA-3) (2001); Sight Spelling	5–8	Norms for ages 6-6 through 12-11	Irregular word and word-part spelling	When administered with ITPA-3 Sound Spelling, permits comparisons of phonemic and orthographic coding skills
Phonological Awareness Literacy Screening (PALS) (2002); Title Recognition Task	10–15 (GA)	NS; Grades 2 and 3	Selecting actual book titles from a list that includes foils	Administered and scored on the PALS Web site; useful estimate of children's level of print exposure
Predictive Reading Profile (2001); Visual Matching	10–15 (GA)	Preliminary kindergarten norms; Grades K and 1	Matching as many letter sequences and words as possible in 8 minutes	Part of a group-administered screening battery; time limits too generous
Process Assessment of the Learner: Test Battery for Reading and Writing (2001); Word Choice	3–5	Norms for Grades 1–6	Identifying as many correctly spelled words presented with two misspelled distracters in 2 minutes	Decile scores only; also assesses spelling skills
Process Assessment of the Learner: Test Battery for Reading and Writing (2001); Receptive Coding	5–8	Norms for Grades K–6	Whole-word, letter-cluster, and letter coding; 1-second exposure per target item	Decile scores only; includes sublexical measures of orthographic processing

Note. GA, group-administered measure; NS, nonstandardized measure. Measures with a speed component are shaded.

Oral Language

Although phonological processing problems constitute the core deficit in most reading disabilities, higher level oral language abilities, such as vocabulary, syntax, and morphology, are also significantly related to reading achievement (Elbro, 1996; Kamhi & Catts, 1999; Purvis & Tannock, 1997; Stanovich & Siegel, 1994). Both dyslexic and garden-variety poor readers show problems in vocabulary (Nation & Snowling, 1998b; Purvis & Tannock, 1997), syntax (Scarborough, 1990; Tunmer & Hoover, 1992; Vellutino et al., 1991), morphology (Shankweiler et al., 1995), and text-level processing (Gardill & Jitendra, 1999; Short & Ryan, 1984; Snyder & Downey, 1991). This section discusses oral language skills outside the domain of phonological processing that are associated with and/or predict reading acquisition, as well as selected measures for assessing them. Rapid naming, which also involves oral language (i.e., naming visual symbols), is discussed in a separate section. Similarly, oral language tasks that are categorized as phonological memory measures because of their heavy demands on phonological coding, such as sentence and pseudoword repetition tasks, have been discussed in the "Phonological Processing" section.

ORAL LANGUAGE COMPONENTS

There are five basic components of oral language: (1) phonology (the sound system), (2) semantics (meaning), (3) morphology (word structure), (4) syntax (sentence structure), and (5) pragmatics (usage). Within each component, language skills can be categorized as either *receptive* (involving comprehension of spoken language) or *expressive* (involving production of spoken language). Table 3.7 describes these components, along with sample tasks assessing receptive and expressive language within each domain.

Researchers, practitioners, and test publishers use a variety of terms to describe the same language component. *Phonology* tasks are also referred to as *articulation* tasks. Semantic tasks that require nonverbal or verbal responses are referred to as *receptive vocabulary* or *expressive vocabulary* tasks, respectively. *Grammar* refers to the system of rules governing the word structures (*morphology*) and word arrangements (*syntax*) of a particular language at a given time, and knowledge of grammar is measured in the context of morphosyntactic tasks. *Supralinguistics* is the term used to refer to language analytic skills above the level of semantic or syntactic knowledge, such as comprehension of figurative language, humor, and double meanings, and higher order thinking skills. Because of the multifaceted nature of oral language, many (if not most) language tests sample more than a single component and tap both receptive and expressive language skills, even within the same subtest or scale. For example, listening comprehension tests that require children to listen to a passage and answer questions assess morphosyntactic as well as semantic knowledge and include both receptive and expressive language dimensions.

TABLE 3.7. Oral Language Components, Skills Assessed, and Sample Assessment Tasks

Component	Skills assessed	Sample receptive assessment task	Sample expressive assessment task
Phonology	Ability to discriminate among and produce speech sounds	Indicating whether two spoken words are the same or different	Pronouncing the names of pictured words
Semantics	Ability to understand the meaning of words and word combinations	Pointing to the one of four pictures best representing a word spoken by the examiner	Providing a synonym for a word spoken by the examiner
Morphology	Ability to understand and use word formation patterns, including roots, prefixes, suffixes, and inflected endings	Listening to a sentence and pointing to the one of a set of pictures that best represents the morphological forms in the sentence	Providing the correct morphological form to complete a phrase spoken by the examiner
Syntax	Ability to recognize and use correct phrase and sentence structure	Marking the one of a set of pictures that best represents a sentence read by the examiner	Completing sentences presented in a cloze format
Pragmatics	Ability to use language to communicate	Detecting whether spoken sentences are logically consistent	Providing a response appropriate to the situation depicted in a short passage read by the examiner

ORAL LANGUAGE AND READING

Numerous longitudinal studies have demonstrated that oral language abilities in young children are significant predictors of later reading achievement (Aram, Ekelman, & Nation, 1984; Bishop & Adams, 1990; Scarborough & Dobrich, 1990; Stark et al., 1984). In a study that followed a large sample of children from kindergarten through Grade 2 (Catts et al., 1999), over 70% of the Grade 2 poor readers had a history of language deficits in kindergarten. Moreover, although the largest percentage of children had deficits in both phonological processing and oral language (37%), more children had deficits in oral language alone than deficits in phonological processing alone (22% vs. 14%, respectively). Not all children with early speech–language deficits go on to have reading problems, however. Instead, reading outcome is related to the type and severity of language impairment. Children with combined phonology and language (i.e., semantic–syntactic) impairments are at higher risk for reading disabilities than children whose problems are limited to phonology (Bishop & Adams, 1990; Catts, 1993; Larrivee & Catts, 1999; Lewis, Freebairn, & Taylor, 2000b).

Despite the abundant evidence that early language deficits are associated with subsequent reading disabilities, there is considerable debate as to whether oral language predicts unique variance in reading achievement apart from phonological processing. Some studies (Tunmer, 1989; Tunmer & Hoover, 1992) have found that syntactic awareness accounts for variance in decoding even after phonological awareness is partialed out. Other researchers (Mann, Cowin, & Schoenheimer, 1989;

Shankweiler et al., 1995) have speculated that the syntactic processing deficits displayed by reading-disabled children are epiphenomena of more fundamental problems in phonological processing. In other words, the difficulty displayed by reading-disabled individuals in comprehending spoken sentences is related to deficits in phonological memory rather than to deficits in language syntax. In support of this position, some research (Gottardo, Stanovich, & Siegel, 1996) indicates that oral language measures account for very little unique variance in reading achievement when phonological awareness and phonological memory are partialed out. The differences in these findings are partly related to the reading subskill used as the criterion measure. When the criterion is word-level reading, such as word identification and pseudoword decoding, oral language measures are much poorer predictors than are phonological processing measures (Larrivee & Catts, 1999; Lombardino et al., 1999; Lombardino, Riccio, Hynd, & Pinheiro, 1997; Vellutino, Scanlon, & Spearing, 1995, Vellutino, Scanlon, & Tanzman, 1998). When reading comprehension is the outcome, however, oral language tasks contribute uniquely to reading achievement in early primary grade children (Bishop & Adams, 1990; Catts, 1993; Tomblin, Zhang, Buckwalter, & Catts, 2000). In the Catts and colleagues (1999) study cited above, kindergarten oral language ability was a significant independent predictor of reading comprehension, even after phonological awareness and rapid naming were taken into account. In fact, the best predictor of reading comprehension in the battery of phonological awareness, rapid naming, and oral language measures was a grammatic composite.

The predictive power of oral language measures also varies depending on the nature of the sample, specifically, the degree to which children with a wide range of cognitive abilities are included. As Catts and colleagues (1999) have noted, children with below average IQs (i.e., below 90) have typically been excluded from reading prediction and classification studies (e.g., Purvis & Tannock, 1997; Shankweiler et al., 1995; Vellutino et al., 1991), often by using a receptive vocabulary test as a proxy for verbal ability. Because both IQ and receptive vocabulary tests assess verbal skills, such procedures result in groups of poor readers composed of children who have average to above average verbal intelligence and who therefore can be expected to demonstrate good language skills. When these poor readers are contrasted with good readers in a research investigation, it is not surprising that performance on language tests does not differentiate the two groups. For example, in a study that did not exclude children with low IQs, Vellutino and Scanlon (1987) found significant positive correlations between semantic and syntactic knowledge measured in kindergarten and reading ability measured in first and second grade. In contrast, another study (Vellutino et al., 1995) that included only participants with an IQ of 90 or above on either the *Wechsler Intelligence Scale for Children–Revised* (WISC-R) Verbal or Performance IQ and that used some of the same language measures did not find significant differences in oral language between good and poor young readers. Efforts to evaluate the contribution of early oral language skills to later reading achievement must also take into account the bidirectional relationship between oral language and reading. That is, early oral language abilities influence reading acquisition, but reading also influences subsequent language development. Because poor readers cannot access as much text as their more proficient peers, they read less and have fewer opportunities to acquire vocabulary, syntactic knowledge, and higher level language skills; these factors in turn limit future reading growth.

ISSUES IN ASSESSING ORAL LANGUAGE

Several issues are important to consider in evaluating children's oral language in the context of early reading assessments: (1) the diversity of tasks purporting to measure the same language skills; (2) possible bias and limited predictive accuracy, especially for minority children and children with limited English proficiency; (3) low reliability for some oral language tasks; and (4) the difficulty of interpreting poor performance.

Diversity of Tasks

Of the 10 components covered in this book, oral language is characterized by perhaps the greatest diversity of measurement tasks. Researchers have rarely used the same language tests in prediction or classification studies, often devising or adapting measures for their own purposes. Even tests with identical labels of "oral expression" or "listening comprehension" can vary markedly in terms of formats, item types, and content. For example, oral expression measures differ in terms of including a single task type or several task types within the same instrument (synonym providing, sentence repetition, word fluency, story retelling, etc.); provision and type of pictorial supports (black-and-white or color photographs, black-and-white line drawings, or color plates); response formats (single-word, multiword, multiple-choice, or discourse-level); and method of analyzing responses (dichotomous, analytic, or holistic scoring). Although most studies evaluating the relationships among different language tests or comparing the performance of the same group of children on several language instruments have examined receptive vocabulary measures in preschool samples (e.g., Gray, Plante, Vance, & Henrichsen, 1999; Plante & Vance, 1994, 1995), the evidence suggests that different tests can yield very different estimates of children's language capabilities.

For these reasons, practitioners are encouraged to use measures with a variety of formats and across several language components, including samples of language in natural settings, to assess the skills of children whose language deficits may be contributing to their reading problems. Assessing oral language abilities is important not only to identify the nature and extent of children's linguistic deficits but also to provide information for developing the most appropriate intervention programs. Children with poor reading skills but age-appropriate oral language skills will need interventions targeting phonological processing and word recognition, whereas children with deficits in both oral language and reading will need interventions targeting language comprehension in addition to phonological processing and decoding (Kamhi & Catts, 2002).

Possible Bias and Limited Predictive Accuracy

Compared with the other tasks typically included in reading screening programs, oral language measures are especially vulnerable to errors of overprediction and underprediction. Early primary grade children who are older than their peers or who come from literacy-rich home environments tend to perform at higher levels on oral language measures, especially vocabulary tests, and thus may fail to be identified as at risk (O'Connor & Jenkins, 1999). In contrast, oral language measures may overidentify children with limited English proficiency (LEP) and minority children whose language experiences and background differ significantly from those of mainstream-culture children. Children from diverse linguistic and cultural backgrounds may also be overidentified by oral language tests because they lack the metalinguistic knowledge needed to understand the task requirements. For example, minority children's linguistic experiences may not prepare them to perform picture-labeling tasks as required by receptive vocabulary tests (Pena & Quinn, 1997). Similarly, minority children may have limited familiarity with the standard English syntax and grammatical constructions used in test directions, compared with their age peers from the mainstream culture.

For standardized tests, the representativeness of the normative sample for the target examinee population is of critical importance for children with LEP and minority children. Although most of the tests reviewed in this book include ethnic minorities in the standardization sample in proportions designed to reflect current population demographics, including a numerically representative percentage of minority children does not ensure that valid representation has been achieved or that the test will yield valid results for all subgroups. Moreover, test manuals seldom include information regarding the language of cultural or linguistic minority groups, such as whether the African American examinees were speakers of African American English or standard English or the number of bilingual children in Hispanic samples (Wyatt & Seymour, 1999).

Low Reliability

Some types of oral language tests, such as discourse-level listening comprehension tests with live-voice delivery and oral expression measures with open-ended response formats, are especially susceptible to interexaminer and interscorer variance. Both commercially published and research measures of listening comprehension and story retelling often show inadequate levels of internal consistency, test–retest, and interrater reliability (e.g., Fletcher et al., 1994; Joshi, Williams, & Wood, 1998). Listening comprehension tests, especially those with passage-level stimuli, should be presented on audiotape to maximize administration consistency. Similarly, although test authors may attempt to improve interscorer reliability by recommending that examiners audiotape responses to oral expression measures that require verbatim recording, such as story retelling tests, accurate recording does not invariably result in reliable and valid scoring, especially when complex scoring rubrics must be applied.

Difficulty in Interpreting Poor Performance

As with written language tests, the multidimensional nature of the skills assessed by oral language tests makes interpretation of poor performance difficult. Although some research (e.g., Vellutino & Scanlon, 1987; Vellutino et al., 1996) suggests that the more linguistically complex a task is, the most effective it is as a predictor, linguistically complex measures are also more difficult to interpret. For example, poor performance on a story recall measure may be the result of poor listening comprehension, poor word retrieval skills, attention problems, poor memory, low motivation, or a combination of these factors. Children may also perform poorly on oral language tasks because of difficulty understanding the requirements of the task rather than because of deficits in the skills being measured.

ASSESSING ORAL LANGUAGE

Oral language tests fall into two broad categories: (1) *listening comprehension* or *receptive language* measures and (2) *oral expression* or *expressive language* measures. Because of the multidimensional nature of language, however, many tests include both receptive and expressive components, and some target skills that require the integration of both sets of abilities, such as story recall. Moreover, test authors vary in the manner in which they classify the same type of language tasks and the manner in which they interpret performance on those tasks. For example, on the *Wechsler Individual Achievement Test–II* (WIAT-II), the Word Fluency task, which requires naming objects in specific categories, is classified as a measure of oral language achievement and is one of four tasks on the Oral Expression subtest. In contrast, the WJ III Retrieval Fluency test, which also requires naming objects in specific categories, is classified as a measure of long-term retrieval and cognitive efficiency and is placed in the cognitive abilities battery. Similarly, the WJ III Verbal Comprehension test, a task that requires identifying pictures and providing synonyms and antonyms, is categorized as a measure of general intellectual ability, whereas the Oral Vocabulary subtest on the *Test of Language Development–Primary: 3* (Newcomer & Hammill, 1997), which requires defining words, is classified as a measure of expressive semantics. Tables 3.8 and 3.9 below include measures reviewed in this text that are designated by the test publisher as assessing primarily receptive or primarily expressive language, respectively.

Assessing Listening Comprehension

Listening comprehension refers to the ability to understand spoken language, including structured language, such as narrative or expository text read aloud, as well as unstructured natural language. Listening comprehension is critical to school success because most classroom instruction is delivered orally. Measures of listening comprehension require children to demonstrate understanding of spoken language at one or more levels, including single words, phrases, sentences, and connected discourse. Three types of listening comprehension tasks have utility in early reading assessments: (1) single-word vocabulary measures, (2) sentence comprehension measures, and (3) text-level listening comprehension measures. Until quite recently, very few standardized tests of listening comprehension were available and even fewer had adequate psychometric characteristics. As a result, many researchers have either created listening passages for a specific investigation or converted standardized reading comprehension tests or informal reading inventories to listening comprehension measures by reading the passage and questions to the child. For example, Joshi and colleagues (1998) administered the *Woodcock Reading Mastery Tests–Revised* (Woodcock, 1987) Form G Passage Comprehension test as a reading comprehension measure and the Form H Passage Comprehension test as a listening comprehension measure. Currently, several norm-referenced listening comprehension measures are available as single-skill tests or as subtests in speech–language and multisubject batteries. More and more nonstandardized measures of listening comprehension are also available in early reading assessment batteries, including many of those reviewed in this text. These measures are typically administered in kindergarten and are replaced by reading comprehension measures once children achieve text-level reading skills. Two of the standardized tests reviewed in this text—the *WJ III Tests of Achievement* (Woodcock, McGrew, & Mather, 2001b) and the WIAT-II—include separate reading comprehension and listening comprehension measures normed on the same sample. However, because the listening and reading comprehension tests in both instruments use different task formats and the item types are not equated for difficulty and length, only general comparisons between an examinee's listening and reading comprehension performance are possible.

LISTENING COMPREHENSION AS A PREDICTOR OF READING DISABILITIES

Listening comprehension has often been proposed as an alternative assessment of aptitude in ability–achievement discrepancy models of reading disabilities (Aaron, 1991; Badian, 1999; Joshi et al., 1998; Lyon, 1995; Spring & French, 1990; Stanovich, 1993). The rationale for using an oral language measure to predict reading derives from the notion that, in contrast to other poor readers, children with reading disabilities are able to understand material read to them at a higher level than they are able to comprehend when reading on their own (Rack et al., 1992). According to this model, children would be classified as reading disabled if their predicted reading comprehension scores were lower than their listening comprehension scores by a specified amount (e.g., 1.5 standard errors of prediction), whereas children who scored poorly on both sets of tasks would be classified as garden-variety poor readers. Proponents of this approach also contend that using oral language ability as the aptitude measure contributes to a more precise definition of reading disabilities by providing a more accurate assessment of children's potential achievement level if their reading problems were resolved (Schrank, Flanagan, Woodcock, & Mascolo, 2002). The WJ III software scoring program includes a discrepancy procedure option that permits users to substitute an oral language composite score for the general intellectual ability score.

Despite the intuitive appeal of this approach, research comparing the predictive utility of listening comprehension with that of intellectual ability has yielded only limited support. Although some studies (e.g., Stanovich, Cunningham, & Feeman, 1984) have found that listening comprehension is a better predictor of reading achievement than general cognitive ability, others have not, especially in samples of younger children (Joshi et al., 1998; Margolese & Kline, 1999). Moreover, there are several problems associated with the use of listening comprehension tests as predictors of reading. First, there are still very few listening comprehension measures with adequate psychometric characteristics. Second, as on IQ tests, children with limited English proficiency may score poorly on measures of listening comprehension because of difficulty in understanding test directions and low English oral language skills. Third, there is some evidence that the listening comprehension–reading comprehension discrepancy model may overidentify children as reading disabled. In a study testing the consequences of this model, Fletcher and colleagues (1994) administered comparable passages from the *Formal Reading Inventory* (Wiederholt, 1986) as listening and reading comprehension measures to a sample of children aged 7 to 9. Children were divided into five groups: (1) a low achievement group, (2) a non-reading-impaired group, and three reading-disabled groups, (3) a standard-score definition group with a discrepancy of 1.5 standard deviations between IQ and reading decoding, (4) a regression-based definition group with a discrepancy of 1.5 standard errors of prediction between actual and expected achievement based on IQ, and (5) a low achievement definition group with reading at or below the 25th percentile but without a significant IQ–reading discrepancy. When the listening comprehension–reading comprehension (LC-RC) discrepancy definition was applied, 98% of the children identified as disabled under an IQ–reading discrepancy definition were also identified as disabled. The LC-RC definition identified an additional 43% of the standard score-only and non-reading-impaired children as disabled, however, suggesting overidentification of children with this model.

Single-Word Receptive Vocabulary Measures

Single-word receptive vocabulary tests require examinees to demonstrate an understanding of single words spoken by the examiner by pointing to pictures representing the words. In the typical test format, the examiner displays a picture plate and provides a word, and the child responds by pointing to the part of the picture or the one of a set of pictures that most closely corresponds to the meaning of the word. Because receptive vocabulary tasks do not require examinees to read or to produce spoken language, they can be used with very young and preliterate children (Bishop & Adams, 1990; Purvis & Tannock, 1997; Snow, Tabors, Nicholson, & Kurland, 1995). In Scarborough's (1998a) review of 19 kindergarten prediction studies, the median correlation between kindergarten receptive vocabulary and subsequent reading achievement was .38, similar to that for verbal IQ.

Example: The examiner displays a picture plate with drawings of a television, computer, telephone, and calculator and says, "Show me *calculator*. Point to *calculator*." (The child points to the picture of the calculator.)

Sentence Comprehension Measures

Sentence comprehension measures use a sentence–picture matching procedure to assess listening comprehension skills. The examiner reads a sentence, which is accompanied by a picture, and the child indicates whether or not the picture is a good match for the sentence. In another format, the child selects the one of a set of pictures that best represents the morphosyntactic meaning of the sentence. Although all sentence comprehension tasks involve an interaction among semantics, syntax, morphology, and memory (Johnson, 1994), they are frequently designed to assess syntactic or morphological skills rather than semantic knowledge.

Example: The examiner displays a picture plate with four drawings and says, "Point to the picture that matches what I say. 'John is showing his new toy to his friend.' " (The child points to the appropriate picture.)

Text-Level Listening Comprehension Measures

Text-level listening comprehension measures assess narrative discourse processing—that is, the ability to listen to a narrative, comprehend its main ideas and details, organize them into a meaningful structure, and construct an interpretation of the story (Snyder & Downey, 1991). These measures require the child to listen to a brief passage or story read by the examiner or presented on audiotape and demonstrate knowledge of what has been heard by responding to questions and/or retelling the story. Text-level listening comprehension tests for early primary grade examinees typically begin with single sentences and proceed to passages consisting of narrative or expository material. Because the test stimuli consist of connected text, these tasks assess knowledge of syntax and morphology as well as semantics. Listening comprehension tests have several response formats, including selecting a picture that best describes a sentence read by the examiner, supplying a word at the end of a sentence, answering questions about the passage, and retelling a story. Listening comprehension tests with story retelling formats are usually classified as measures of oral expression and are discussed later.

Example: The examiner displays a picture plate with four drawings and says, "Listen. Which picture matches this sentence? 'The boy is crying because his toy is broken.' " (The child points to the appropriate picture.)

Measures of Listening Comprehension

Table 3.8 presents 16 listening comprehension measures that either are stand-alone tests or are included in instruments reviewed in this book. As noted above, measures of listening comprehension with major loadings on phonological memory are discussed in the "Phonological Processing" section. For the sake of readability and space, each instrument with more than one measure in this domain is presented in a single entry, with subtests or tasks listed in the order of administration.

Assessing Oral Expression

Oral expression refers to the ability to produce spoken language. Oral expression skills can be assessed with a variety of formats and item types, ranging from formats designed to elicit single words to open-ended formats that permit a variety of acceptable answers. Oral expression measures with relevance for early reading assessments include (1) word fluency, (2) single-word expressive vocabulary, (3) sentence completion, and (4) story retelling tasks.

Word Fluency Measures

Word fluency measures assess the ability to generate words in response to a verbal stimulus as quickly as possible. In one format, the score is based on the number of words produced within a fixed amount of time, whereas in another format, the score is based on the time required to produce a specific number of words. A few word fluency measures, especially those designed for young children, have no time limits. Although verbal fluency measures are often used to assess executive functioning and cognitive efficiency, especially in individuals with degenerative brain disorders or traumatic brain injury, they have been used much less frequently in reading diagnostic and prediction studies, with mixed results (e.g., Levin, 1990;

TABLE 3.8. Measures of Listening Comprehension

Name and date of *measure*; subtest(s)	Admin. time (minutes)	Norms/ benchmarks	Testing tasks	Comments
Basic Early Assessment of Reading (2002); Comprehension	30–40 (GA)	CR; benchmarks for Grades K–3	Circling pictures (Grade K) or marking answers (Grades 1–3) in response to questions about passages read by the examiner	Early reading battery with three comprehension assessments per grade; also measures reading comprehension in Grades 1–3
Early Reading Diagnostic Assessment–Revised (2002); Vocabulary (Task A), Listening Comprehension	5–10 per subtest	Norms for Grades K and 1	Naming pictured objects (Grades K and 1); answering questions about a passage read by the examiner (Grade 1)	Decile scores only; both subtests are derived from the *Wechsler Individual Achievement Test*
Fox in a Box (2000); Listening Comprehension	45–50 (GA)	CR; benchmarks for Grades K–2	Listening to a story read by the examiner and drawing (Grade K) or writing a summary (Grades 1 and 2)	Scored on a 3-point rating scale; also assesses written expression skills at Grades 1 and 2
Group Reading Assessment and Diagnostic Evaluation (2002); Listening Comprehension	15–25 (GA)	Norms for Grades PreK–postsecondary	Listening to a sentence read by the examiner and marking the one of four pictures that best represents what was read	Part of a comprehensive group-administered reading battery linked to grade-specific interventions
Kaufman Survey of Early Academic and Language Skills (1993); Vocabulary	5–8	Norms for ages 3-0 through 6-11	Identifying and naming pictured objects or actions	Includes an equal number of items that measure expressive language skills
Oral and Written Language Scales (1995); Listening Comprehension Scale	10–25	Norms for ages 3-0 through 21-11	Identifying pictured objects or actions	Permits comparisons of receptive and expressive language skills when the Oral Expression Scale is administered
Peabody Picture Vocabulary Test–III (1997)	10–15	Norms for ages 2-6 through 90+	Pointing to the one of four pictures representing a spoken stimulus word	When administered with the *Expressive Vocabulary Test*, permits comparisons of receptive and expressive vocabulary based on the same normative sample
Predictive Reading Profile (2001); Vocabulary, Syntax	10–20 per subtest (GA)	Preliminary kindergarten norms; Grades K and 1	Marking pictured words; marking pictures corresponding to sentences spoken by the examiner	One of the few early literacy batteries with several oral language measures; local norming strongly recommended

(continued)

TABLE 3.8. *(continued)*

Name and date of *measure*; subtest(s)	Admin. time (minutes)	Norms/ benchmarks	Testing tasks	Comments
Test of Language Development–Primary: 3 (1997); Picture Vocabulary, Grammatic Understanding	3–8 per subtest	Norms for ages 4-0 through 8-11	Identifying pictured words; identifying the one of a set of pictures that represents a spoken sentence	Part of a comprehensive oral language battery for young children
Texas Primary Reading Inventory (2002); Listening Comprehension	5–8	CR; Texas benchmarks for kindergarten	Answering questions about a story read by the examiner	Part of a statewide early reading assessment battery for Grades K–2
Wechsler Individual Achievement Test–II (2001); Listening Comprehension	10–20	Norms for ages 4-0 through 85+ and Grades PreK–16	Identifying pictures that match a spoken word or sentence; providing a word that matches a picture and an oral description	Consists of three tasks, one of which measures expressive vocabulary
Woodcock–Johnson III Tests of Achievement (2001); Understanding Directions, Oral Comprehension	5–15 per test	Norms for ages 2-0 through 90+ years and Grades K–18	Listening to oral commands and pointing to specific objects in a picture; naming pictured objects	Permits comparisons of listening and reading comprehension within the same norm-referenced instrument

Note. CR, criterion-referenced measure; GA, group-administered measure; NS, nonstandardized measure.

Neuhaus & Swank, 2002; Vellutino et al., 1995). Word fluency tasks fall into one of two general types: (a) semantic-based word fluency tasks and (b) sound-based word fluency tasks. Semantic-based word fluency tasks require the child to provide words in a particular category, such as animals, foods, furniture, and so on. Sound-based or phonological word fluency tasks require examinees to provide as many words as possible that begin with a given letter or sound. Both types of word fluency tasks tap long-term memory, semantic knowledge, and retrieval speed as well as expressive language because the child must generate lexical items based on a verbal prompt as rapidly as possible.

Example (timed semantic word fluency task): "Tell me as many different kinds of furniture as you can in 1 minute." (chair, sofa, lamp, etc.)

Example (untimed phonological word fluency task): "Say as many words as you can that begin with the letter *t*." (tin, tap, tiger, etc.)

Single-Word Expressive Vocabulary Measures

Single-word expressive vocabulary tests require examinees to provide a one-word response to a verbal stimulus and measure a variety of cognitive and language abilities, including long-term memory, semantic knowledge, and word retrieval. Single-word expressive vocabulary tests use one or both of two basic formats: (1) picture naming and (2) synonym or antonym providing. Most expressive vocabulary tests for young children include pictorial supports. Accompanying orally presented stimuli with pictures helps to focus children's attention on the task but limits the classes of words and the types of oral language skills that can be assessed.

Example (picture-naming format): The examiner displays a picture of an airplane and says, "What is this?" (airplane)

Example (synonym-providing format): The examiner displays a picture of an airplane and says, "*Jet*. Tell me another name for *jet*." (airplane)

Sentence Completion Measures

Sentence completion tasks use an oral cloze format that requires the child to listen to a sentence or short passage and provide a final word to complete the sentence or the last sentence in the passage. In order to generate a one-word response that is both meaningful and grammatically appropriate, the child must understand the vocabulary and syntactic structure of the stimulus sentence. Some sentence completion tasks are designed to place more emphasis on morphological or syntactic knowledge than on semantic knowledge by using very simple phrases (e.g., "One girl, two ________" [girls]). Others include more complex sentences that assess general verbal comprehension and memory skills as well as semantic and syntactic knowledge.

Example: "Finish this sentence. 'Maria and Susanna walked up the ________.' " (hill, road, bank, etc.)

Story Retelling Measures

Although story retelling measures are generally classified as oral expression tasks, they include both receptive and expressive language requirements (Culatta, Page, & Ellis, 1983). In the first part of the task, which taps listening comprehension, the child listens as the examiner reads a brief story that is often accompanied by a pictorial prompt. In the second step, which requires oral expression skills, the child retells the story. Some story retelling measures include a third step that requires the child to answer questions about the passage, such as the main idea, sequence of events, characters, and so on. If comprehension questions are included, they are typically presented after the retelling in order to minimize their influence on the child's ability to recall the story. Scoring may be holistic, based on an overall assessment of language proficiency, or analytic, based on the number of words, correct word sequences, number of sentences produced, or number of specific story elements recalled. Because of the current interest in authentic assessment, story retelling measures, which resemble typical classroom literacy tasks, are increasingly being included in assessment batteries for early primary grade children.

Example: The examiner reads a story to the child and says, "Now tell me everything you remember from the story." (The child retells the story.)

Measures of Oral Expression

Table 3.9 describes 25 oral expression measures that either are stand-alone tests or are included in instruments reviewed in this book. Five of the measures are fluency-based or include subtasks with fluency components. As noted above, speech articulation is not a significant predictor of later reading achievement unless children's deficits are very pronounced (Bishop & Adams, 1990; Catts, 1991, 1993; Lewis & Freebairn, 1992). For the sake of completeness, however, articulation measures in multiskill language instruments reviewed in this text have been included in the table. Each instrument with more than one oral expression measure is presented as a single entry, with subtests or tasks listed in the order of administration.

PRINT RESOURCES

Catts, H. W., & Kamhi, A. G. (Eds.). (1999). *Language and reading disabilities.* Boston: Allyn & Bacon.

This edited volume includes chapters by leading reading and language researchers on the nature of reading development, classification and causes of reading disabilities, issues in assessing reading disabilities, and strategies for remediating word-level and text comprehension reading problems. Readers of this text will be especially interested in Joe Torgesen's chapter on assessing and teaching phonemic awareness and word recognition skills.

Moats, L. C. (2000). *Speech to print: Language essentials for teachers.* Baltimore: Brookes.

Designed primarily for language arts teachers but very useful for practitioners conducting early reading assessments, this handbook provides an excellent introduction to the structure of the English language. Included are surveys of language knowledge, a chapter on language instruction, sample lesson plans, and two developmental spelling inventories with complete scoring instructions.

Print Awareness and Concept of Word

This section discusses two related early literacy skills: print awareness and concept of word.

PRINT AWARENESS AND READING

Print awareness refers to an understanding of the ways in which written language can be used. Print awareness encompasses two related sets of concepts: print functions and print conventions. *Print function awareness* refers to a general understanding of the communicative value of print (i.e., that print tells a story or gives information), whereas *print convention awareness* refers to more specific knowledge of print features and mechanics, such as the directionality of print from left to right and top to bot-

TABLE 3.9. Measures of Oral Expression

Name and date of *measure*; subtest	Admin. time (minutes)	Norms/ benchmarks	Testing task	Comments
Dynamic Indicators of Basic Early Literacy Skills (2002); Word Use Fluency	2–3	NS; benchmarks are under development; Grades K–3	Providing as many sentences in response to a target word as possible in 1 minute; scored for number of correct words	Effort to assess oral expression within a fluency-based format; local norming recommended until benchmarks are developed
Dyslexia Screening Test (1996); Verbal Fluency, Semantic Fluency	2–3 per subtest	British norms for ages 6-6 through 16-5	Providing as many words as possible beginning with the letter *s* in 1 minute; naming as many animals as possible in 1 minute	Yields five percentile ranges only; utility limited by British norms
Early Reading Diagnostic Assessment–Revised (ERDA–R) (2002); Story Retell, Vocabulary (Task B)	5–10 per subtest	Norms for Grades K and 1	Retelling a story read by the examiner (Grade K); identifying pictures and giving labels for pictured objects (Grades K and 1)	Decile scores only; Story Retell is identical to the PAL-RW subtest (see below)
Expressive Vocabulary Test (1997)	10–15	Norms for ages 2-6 through 90 years	Providing labels and synonyms for pictured objects and actions	Permits comparisons of receptive and expressive vocabulary based on the same norm group when administered with the *Peabody Picture Vocabulary Test–III*
Fox in a Box (2000); Oral Expression	5–7	CR; benchmarks for Grades K–2	Describing a picture (Grade K) or retelling a story (Grades 1 and 2)	Scored on a 3-point holistic rating scale
Illinois Test of Psycholinguistic Abilities–3 (2001); Spoken Analogies, Spoken Vocabulary, Morphological Closure, Syntactic Sentences	5–8 per subtest	Norms for ages 5-0 through 12-11	Providing verbal analogies; providing nouns when given attributes; completing a sentence or phrase; repeating semantically nonsensical but syntactically correct sentences	Permits comparisons of oral and written language skills within the same norm-referenced instrument
Kaufman Survey of Early Academic Skills (1993); Vocabulary, Articulation Survey	5–8 per subtest	Norms for ages 3-0 through 6-11	Identifying and naming pictured objects or actions; pronouncing the names of pictured objects or actions	Permits norm-referenced comparisons of receptive and expressive language skills

(continued)

TABLE 3.9. *(continued)*

Name and date of *measure*; subtest	Admin. time (minutes)	Norms/ benchmarks	Testing task	Comments
Oral and Written Language Scales (1995); Oral Expression Scale	5–25 per scale	Norms for ages 3–21	Identifying pictured objects or actions; answering questions or completing or generating sentences in response to verbal and pictorial stimuli	Permits comparisons of receptive and expressive language skills when the Listening Comprehension Scale is administered
Phonological Abilities Test (1997); Speech Rate	2–3	British norms for ages 5-0 through 7-11	Repeating the word *buttercup* 10 times as rapidly as possible	Yields four percentile score equivalents only; utility limited by British norms
Process Assessment of the Learner–Test Battery for Reading and Writing (PAL-RW) (2001); Story Retell	5–10	Kindergarten norms	Answering questions about a story and retelling it	Decile scores only; identical to the ERDA-R subtest (see above)
Test of Language Development–Primary: 3 (1997); Picture Vocabulary, Relational Vocabulary, Oral Vocabulary, Grammatic Completion, Word Articulation	3–8 per subtest	Norms for ages 4-0 through 8-11	Identifying pictured words; describing relationships between words; defining words; supplying the missing word in a sentence; pronouncing names of pictured objects	Vocabulary tests also tap semantic knowledge and verbal comprehension skills
Wechsler Individual Achievement Test–II (2001); Oral Expression	10–20	Norms for ages 4-0 through 85+ and Grades PreK-16	Repeating sentences, generating words quickly in response to a verbal prompt, retelling a story, and explaining the sequential steps in a task	Multitask subtest with one timed task; permits quartile-score comparisons between oral and written Word Fluency tasks when the Written Expression subtest is administered
Woodcock–Johnson III Tests of Achievement (2001); Story Recall, Story Recall–Delayed, Picture Vocabulary	5–15 per test	Norms for ages 2-0 through 90+ years and Grades K–18	Listening to a story and recalling story details immediately and at a later date; naming pictured objects	Permits comparisons of listening and reading comprehension within the same norm-referenced instrument

Note. CR, criterion-referenced measure; GA, group-administered measure; NS, nonstandardized measure. Measures with a fluency component are shaded.

tom; the understanding of what constitutes a letter, word, and sentence; and the meaning of punctuation marks (Vellutino et al., 1996). Both sets of print awareness concepts are generally measured in the context of reading a short illustrated book to the child. As the examiner reads the book aloud, the child is asked to indicate certain features of print, such as the front and back of the book, the direction of print, and individual letters and words. Table 3.10 lists the skill categories assessed by typical print awareness measures and a sample testing task per category.

Although numerous studies (see Scarborough, 1998a, for a review) have demonstrated that young children's performance on print awareness measures is significantly related to future reading achievement, evidence for the utility of print awareness as an independent source of reading variance is mixed. Whereas some studies (Day & Day, 1984; Johns, 1980; Stuart, 1995) have reported that print awareness measured in kindergarten or early first grade is moderately to strongly correlated with later reading performance, most recent research has found that print awareness tasks add little or no additional predictive power when measures of other early literacy skills, such as letter-name knowledge and phonemic awareness, are included (e.g., Elbro, Borstrom, & Petersen, 1998; Iversen & Tunmer, 1993). For example, in a study (Sénéchal, LeFevre, Smith-Chant, & Colton, 2001) evaluating the concurrent and longitudinal relations among a set of literacy and language skills measured in kindergarten and first grade, print awareness measured at the beginning of kindergarten was significantly related to children's current levels of vocabulary and letter-name knowledge but was not a significant predictor of Grade 1 or Grade 3 reading when phonological awareness, alphabet knowledge, and vocabulary were controlled. Moreover, when print awareness was measured at the beginning of first grade, it was unrelated to current vocabulary or phonological awareness skills. Similarly, in a study (Lonigan, Burgess, & Anthony, 2000) that followed a cohort of children from late preschool to kindergarten or first grade, measures of environmental print and print concepts had no unique predictive relation to subsequent word reading skills or other early literacy skills, such as phonological awareness and letter knowledge. Instead, environmental print and print concepts skills were predicted by phonological awareness and letter knowledge. Based on these findings, the authors suggested that print awareness skills may serve as proxy measures for other early reading skills, may reflect print exposure and other literacy experiences, or both.

Print awareness skills are also poor predictors of response to interventions. In a large-scale longitudinal study (Vellutino et al., 1996), kindergarten performance on two concepts of print tasks (a print functions task and a print conventions task) did

TABLE 3.10. Print Awareness Skills and Sample Testing Tasks

Skill assessed	Sample testing task
Book orientation	Identifying the front of a book
Print versus pictures	Indicating where the story begins by pointing to the print on the page
Print directionality	Demonstrating the left to right progression of text
Voice-word matching	Pointing to each word as the examiner reads it
Letter, word, and sentence	Indicating word boundaries by pointing to where a word begins and ends
Letter and word order	Identifying misordered letters or words
Punctuation marks	Indicating the meaning of a period

not differentiate between normal readers and intervention reading groups or between intervention groups that made good versus limited progress. In a follow-up study of three groups of at-risk children, Scanlon and Vellutino (1997) similarly found that print functions and print conventions measures administered during the first half of the kindergarten year did not differentiate among poor, average, and good readers at the end of first grade.

CONCEPT OF WORD AND READING

Concept of word is a component of print awareness that refers to the understanding of the match between spoken and written words in contextual reading. Concept of word measures assess two related skills: (1) fingerpointing skills, as demonstrated by accurate voice–word matching for a memorized text; and (2) identification of words in context, as demonstrated by identifying target words in a line of memorized text (Bear, Invernizzi, Templeton, & Johnston, 2000; Morris, 1993). Children who have not developed a stable concept of word will point to another word when they are saying something else and are especially likely to point incorrectly when they encounter two-syllable words. Like print awareness measures, concept of word tasks use a small illustrated book or a set of illustrated sentences as the test stimulus. Concept of word tasks differ from print awareness tasks in several respects, however. First, whereas print awareness tasks require the child to read only a few (if any) words, concept of word tasks require the child to read several lines of memorized text while pointing to each word, as well as several preselected words in each sentence. Although identifying target words may appear to measure word recognition rather than concept of word, beginning readers typically use sentence context to identify the words. That is, they tend to return to the beginning of the sentence and fingerpoint while reciting the words until they come to the target word (Morris, 1992a). Second, concept of word tasks may include an additional word identification component in which lists of words from the reading selection are administered before and after the task to evaluate the child's ability to acquire new sight words during contextual reading. Because some practitioners may not be familiar with concept of word measures, the administration procedures for one such task—the Concept of Word measure in the *Book Buddies Early Literacy Screening* (BBELS; Johnston, Invernizzi, & Juel, 1998)—are described in Figure 3.2.

Scoring for concept of word fingerpointing is an all-or-none situation; that is, the child must point accurately to each word in the test sentence to receive credit. The child's performance on fingerpoint reading (number of sentences correctly fingerpointed) and target word reading (number of words read correctly) is summed to yield a total concept of word score. Figure 3.3 illustrates scoring for one of the four sentences from the Concept of Word measure in the BBELS. In the figure, the numbers under the words in the sentence indicate the order in which the examiner asks the child to read the target words.

Despite the general consensus that concept of word attainment is a critical step in the reading acquisition process (Ehri & Sweet, 1991; Morris, 1992b, 1993; Roberts, 1992), researchers disagree about the order in which concept of word and other critical literacy skills are acquired and the directionality of influences among those skills. Morris (1992a, 1993) contends that concept of word attainment is part of a develop-

1. Introduce the book or poem to the child and explain that you are going to read the story together.

2. Read the title of the book and discuss the first picture.

3. Read the first sentence aloud to the child as you point to each word.

4. Have the child join you in reading the sentence as you read and point to each word.

5. Ask the child to read and fingerpoint the sentence alone. Score the pointing (2 points for accurate pointing, 0 if there are any mistakes).

6. Point to the first target word in the sentence and ask the child to identify it. Repeat this process for the second target word in the sentence. Score 1 point for each word correctly identified.

7. Repeat this procedure for each sentence in the story.

FIGURE 3.2. Administration procedures for the *Book Buddies Early Literacy Screening* (BBELS) Concept of Word measure. Adapted from *Book Buddies: Guidelines for Volunteer Tutors of Emergent and Early Readers* (p. 39) by F. R. Johnston, M. Invernizzi, and C. Juel, 1998, New York: Guilford Press. Copyright 1998 by The Guilford Press. Adapted with permission.

mental sequence of early literacy skills, in which initial consonant knowledge facilitates the concept of word in text, which in turn facilitates phoneme segmentation, which promotes word recognition. In contrast, Ehri and Sweet (1991) assert that children need rudimentary phonemic segmentation skills to be able to match print with speech during fingerpoint reading and remember individual words in a memorized text. In either case, developing a stable concept of word is a benchmark in reading development that signals the child's ability to integrate several critical literacy skills, including letter recognition, knowledge of initial sounds, initial phoneme segmentation, the ability to identify word boundaries in running text, and the relationship between spoken and written words.

Although performance on kindergarten concept of word tasks is highly correlated with overall performance on early reading measures (Invernizzi, Meier, Swank,

Sentence	Pointing	Word identification
Alvin is <u>playing</u> in the <u>sand</u>. 2 1	____ (2)	____, ____ (1 each)

FIGURE 3.3. Scoring for the BBELS Concept of Word measure. From *Book Buddies: Guidelines for Volunteer Tutors of Emergent and Early Readers* (p. 48), by F. R. Johnston, M. Invernizzi, and C. Juel, 1998, New York: Guilford Press. Copyright 1998 by Guilford Press. Adapted with permission.

& Juel, 2002b), evidence regarding its utility as an independent predictor is mixed. In an unreferred kindergarten sample, Lombardino and colleagues (1999) reported that concept of word measured at the end of kindergarten was moderately correlated with word identification, phonemic decoding, and passage comprehension at the end of first grade. Other measures in the battery, especially spelling and word recognition tasks, were better predictors of first- and second-grade reading and spelling performance, however. In contrast, Santa and Hoien (1999) found that concept of word measured in early first grade in a sample of at-risk children did not predict reading and spelling performance at the end of an 8-month reading intervention program or on a follow-up assessment at the beginning of second grade.

ISSUES IN ASSESSING PRINT AWARENESS AND CONCEPT OF WORD

Although most recently published early reading screening instruments and many early reading diagnostic batteries include print awareness or concept of word tasks, these measures vary considerably in terms of technical adequacy. Among the assessment issues considered here are breadth of coverage, reliability, and interpretive framework.

Breadth of Coverage

Print awareness tests range from very brief to extensive in their coverage of print conventions and mechanics. Of the six print awareness measures reviewed in this text, *Concepts About Print* (CAP; Clay, 1993a, 2002) has the largest number of items (24) and covers some aspects of print awareness that other measures do not (e.g., inverted words and lines of text). On the other hand, CAP omits some concepts covered by other measures (e.g., the concept of a word and a sentence). The briefest print concepts measure discussed in this book—the Print Awareness task on the *Group Reading Assessment and Diagnostic Evaluation* (Williams, 2002)—has only four items and does not yield a separate score. Most concept of word tasks are highly similar in content and task requirements and vary chiefly in terms of whether they include a pre- and posttest of word identification.

Reliability Concerns

Relative to other measures included in reading screening batteries, concept of word and print awareness tasks are typically the least reliable tasks (e.g., Foorman, Fletcher, et al., 1998; Invernizzi, Robey, & Moon, 2000). Internal consistency and stability tend to be lower than on other measures, in part because of the limited number of items on many tasks and ceiling effects beginning as early as the second semester of kindergarten. Obtaining adequate levels of interscorer reliability is also challenging because some of the required responses are gestural rather than verbal, such as on items requiring the child to indicate print directionality, fingerpoint text, and demarcate letter and word boundaries. Of the eight print awareness and concept of word measures reviewed here, estimates of interrater consistency are provided for only two—the Concept of Word task on Virginia's PALS and the Conventions subtest on the *Test of Early Reading Ability–3* (TERA-3; Reid, Hresko, & Hammill, 2001).

Interpretive Framework

The framework for interpreting children's performance on print awareness and concept of word tasks ranges from age- or grade-based norm-referenced comparisons to qualitative analysis of correct and incorrect items. Most of the currently available print awareness and concept of word measures are nonstandardized tasks in multiskill early reading assessment batteries. Of the eight print awareness and concept of word measures covered in this text, only two yield norm-based derived scores, and the American norms for one (CAP) are inadequate in terms of size, representativeness, and recency. At the time of this book's publication, the TERA-3 Conventions subtest was the only print awareness measure yielding a separate score based on recent U.S. norms. The format of the TERA-3 Conventions subtest differs from the standard print awareness task format, however. Whereas print awareness tasks typically use a small illustrated book or poem to administer items and assess several concepts using a single page, the Conventions subtest presents test stimuli in an 8½ × 11-inch spiral-bound picture book with a separate page per item. Of the two concept of word tasks reviewed in this text, only the PALS includes benchmarks for evaluating examinee performance, based on data from large samples of kindergarten and first-grade children in the Commonwealth of Virginia. Because of the diversity in reading instructional practices and curricula across and even within districts, practitioners are encouraged to develop local norms for print awareness and concept of word measures in settings in which state-validated performance standards are not available.

MEASURES OF PRINT AWARENESS AND CONCEPT OF WORD

Table 3.11 describes the eight measures of print awareness and concept of word reviewed in this text. Because of the variability of content coverage, information regarding the number of items for each measure is included.

PRINT RESOURCES

Southern California Comprehensive Assistance Center. (2002). *Taking a reading: A teacher's guide to reading assessment.* Los Angeles: Reading Success Network, Los Angeles County Office of Education.

This spiral-bound handbook includes 20 informal reading assessments for children in kindergarten through sixth grade in a wide variety of reading domains. Among the measures is a 25-item *Concepts About Print* test modeled after Clay's test of the same name. Materials include a 1-page overview of the test, a list of the print awareness content standards for California students, and a recording sheet with examiner prompts for each item.

TABLE 3.11. Measures of Print Awareness and Concept of Word

Name and date of *measure*; subtest(s)	Admin. time (minutes)	Norms/ benchmarks	Testing task	Comments
Book Buddies Early Literacy Screening (1998); Concept of Word	10–15	NS; Grades K–2	Fingerpointing and word identification in a memorized poem (8 pointing items, 8 word items); a reproducible booklet is used	Task in an early literacy battery linked to a tutorial program; most useful for kindergarten students
Early Reading Diagnostic Assessment–Revised (2002); Concept of Print	5	NS; Grades K and 1	7-item print awareness checklist; assessment is based on observations made during the Letter Recognition and Reading Comprehension subtests	Part of a norm-referenced Grades K–3 early reading assessment battery; the checklist yields only raw scores
Fox in a Box (2000); Concepts of Print	10	CR; kindergarten benchmarks	5-item questionnaire assessing print concepts and conventions; a book in the test kit is used	Part of a Grades K–2 early literacy assessment battery
Group Reading Assessment and Diagnostic Evaluation (2002); Print Awareness	5–8 (GA)	Norms for kindergarten	Marking the one of four pictures that best represents a sentence read by the examiner (4 items)	Multiple-choice format; one of a three-task subtest; does not yield a separate score
Observation Survey (1993a, 2002); Concepts About Print	10–15	New Zealand norms for ages 5–7 and 6-0 through 7-3; U.S. norms for Grade 1	24-item questionnaire assessing print awareness and conventions; one of several small illustrated books is used	Part of the assessment battery used in the Reading Recovery program; local norming strongly recommended
Phonological Awareness Literacy Screening (2002); Concept of Word	10–15	Virginia benchmarks for Grades K and 1	Fingerpointing and word identification in a memorized poem; includes identifying words in the poem before and after the task (4 pointing items, 4 word identification items, 10-item pre- and posttest word list)	8-step procedure that includes pre- and posttest word recognition measures
Test of Early Reading Ability–3 (2001); Conventions	10–15	Norms for ages 3-6 through 8-6	21-item subtest assessing print conventions and concepts; a spiral-bound test booklet is used to present items	One of very few print conventions measures with recent national norms; inadequate floors below age 5-9
Texas Primary Reading Inventory (2002); Book and Print Awareness	5–10	CR; middle- and end-of-year kindergarten	5-item print concepts questionnaire; an illustrated book provided by the examiner is used; scores are recorded but not used in cutoff determinations	Warm-up activity for a statewide early reading assessment battery

Note. CR, criterion-referenced measure; NS, nonstandardized measure; GA, group-administered measure.

Alphabet Knowledge

Alphabet knowledge includes the knowledge of letter names, the knowledge of letter sounds, and the ability to access this information quickly and automatically. Letter-name and letter-sound tasks are also referred to as measures of *graphophonemic knowledge,* a general term that includes knowledge of both letter names and sound-symbol correspondences. A wide range of tasks tap graphophonemic knowledge, including spelling, phonological awareness, rapid automatized naming (RAN) for letters, and decoding measures. This section describes measures that involve identifying the names or sounds of printed letters and/or writing letter names or sounds in isolation. Also discussed in this section are fluency-based measures of alphabet knowledge, that is, tasks that assess speed of naming letters or sounds. Letter-naming tasks that require children to name a small, randomly repeated subset of letters as rapidly as possible (i.e., RAN-Letters) are described in the "Rapid Naming" section.

LETTER-NAME KNOWLEDGE

Letter-name knowledge measured in kindergarten is the one of the best predictors of future reading and spelling achievement (Badian, 1995; Ehri & Sweet, 1991; Muter et al., 1998; O'Connor & Jenkins, 1999; Scanlon & Vellutino, 1996, 1997; Share, Jorm, Maclean, & Matthews, 1984). In Scarborough's (1998a) review of kindergarten prediction studies, single measures of letter-name knowledge were nearly as effective in predicting subsequent reading skills as multiskill readiness batteries (median *r*s = .53 vs. .56, respectively). Similarly, in a study using 25 predictor tasks, including measures of print knowledge, phonological awareness, language, memory, conceptual development, and executive functioning (Scanlon & Vellutino, 1996), letter-name knowledge was the best single predictor of Grade 1 reading outcomes in terms of word identification, phonemic decoding, and teacher ratings of reading progress. Kindergarten letter-name knowledge is a significant predictor of reading achievement not only in the early primary grades but also throughout elementary school (Muehl & Di Nello, 1976) and even into the middle and high school grades (Badian, 1988; Stevenson & Newman, 1986).

Letter-Name Knowledge and Reading Acquisition

Why is skill in naming alphabet letters such a powerful predictor of future reading achievement? First, letter-name knowledge may be an indirect measure of another causal factor, such as an early literacy-rich environment that provides children with many experiences with books and print (Adams, 1990; Scanlon & Vellutino, 1997). Second, letter-name knowledge helps children to connect printed words with spoken language. Only when children have developed the insight that written word forms are related to the sounds rather than the meaning of language can they learn the specific correspondences between letters and phonemes (Treiman & Rodriguez, 1999; Treiman, Tincoff, & Richmond-Welty, 1996). Third, knowledge of letter names facilitates letter-sound knowledge, especially for sounds that occur in the name of the letter, such as *b*, which contains the sound /bi/ as in *beat* (Treiman, Tincoff, Rodriguez, Mouzaki, & Francis, 1998).

Despite its predictive power, letter-name knowledge does not appear to have a direct causal influence on word reading skills. Rather, it plays a causal role in the acquisition of phonemic awareness, in part because the concrete referent of the letter makes it easier for children to distinguish and represent the abstract entity of the phoneme in memory (Hohn & Ehri, 1983; Stahl & Murray, 1994). Phonemic awareness, in turn, exerts a causal influence on decoding (Johnston, 1998; Wagner et al., 1994). This may account for the finding that teaching children to name alphabet letters is ineffective in improving their reading skills (Ball & Blachman, 1991; Fugate, 1997).

Letter-name knowledge not only predicts reading acquisition but may also serve as an indicator of the intensity of remediation required to prevent reading failure among at-risk children. In a kindergarten intervention study (Lennon & Slesinski, 1999), performance on a letter-naming task predicted children's relative position on all posttreatment measures, including letter-sound knowledge, phonemic segmentation, decoding, word identification, and print concepts for both midpoint (10-week) and final (20-week) assessments, with one exception: Low-scoring students who received 20 weeks of the intervention program improved their relative position among all the participants. These intriguing results suggest that it may be possible to use initial scores on letter-naming tasks to identify a "dosage" level of reading intervention from less intensive to more intensive to address individual student needs while using resources most efficiently.

Letter-Naming Fluency

Like letter-name knowledge, letter-naming fluency is associated with reading achievement and is a powerful predictor of later reading proficiency (Blachman, 1984; Daly, Wright, Kelly, & Martens, 1997; Speer & Lamb, 1976; Stanovich, Feeman, & Cunningham, 1983; Torgesen, Wagner, Simmons, & Laughon, 1990; Walsh et al., 1988). Several hypotheses have been offered to explain the utility of letter-naming speed in predicting current and future reading skills. Wolf and her colleagues (e.g., Wolf & Bowers, 1999; Wolf et al., 2000) have proposed that deficits in letter-naming fluency are related to a general deficit in naming speed for familiar visual symbols that differentiates between good and poor readers (see the "Rapid Naming" section, above). Other researchers (e.g., Adams, 1990; Ehri, 1998) suggest that letter-naming fluency serves as an index of the degree to which letter identities have been learned. Children who can recognize letters and letter patterns quickly and automatically can devote more attention to decoding and storing words in memory, thus building the large sight word vocabulary essential for fluent reading. Third, letter-naming fluency may predict reading because, like letter-name knowledge, it mediates children's ability to learn and remember letter sounds and to master the *alphabetic principle,* the understanding that printed words map to spoken sounds. Training children in letter-naming fluency does not significantly improve their reading skills, however (Fugate, 1997), similar to the negative results observed in letter-name training studies.

Letter-naming fluency may have its greatest predictive value during the early stages of reading acquisition. In a longitudinal study (Walsh et al., 1988) following children from kindergarten through second grade at two different schools, kindergarten letter-naming speed, as measured by reaction time for 10 letters presented in discrete trials on a computer, was highly correlated with first-grade reading achievement (*rs* = .89 and .80), but not with second-grade reading skills (*rs* = –.13 and –.06). Moreover, kindergarten letter-naming fluency was significantly related to first-grade reading even when letter-naming accuracy and object-naming speed were controlled, supporting the hypothesis that letter-naming fluency is uniquely related to reading ability.

LETTER-SOUND KNOWLEDGE

Although many researchers and practitioners have assumed that children learn letter names and sounds by rote memorization, Treiman and her colleagues (e.g., Treiman, Sotak, & Bowman, 2001; Treiman et al., 1998) have demonstrated that children use their knowledge of letter names to learn letter sounds. Moreover, letter sounds vary in their level of difficulty, which is related to whether the letter sound occurs in the name of the letter, in what position the sound occurs, and the order of letters within the alphabet. Children learn sounds more easily when the sound of the letter is in the *onset* (initial position) of the letter's name, such as *v* and *k*, whereas knowledge of letter sounds develops more slowly for letters such as *l* and *f*, in which the letter sound occurs in the final position. Children have the greatest difficulty with the few letter sounds that have no association with their letter names, such as the /h/ sound in *h*. The order of alphabet letters is also correlated with the development of both letter-sound and letter-name knowledge, with letters at the beginning of the alphabet learned earlier, probably because of repetition and informal alphabet learning experiences (McBride-Chang, 1999).

Compared with letter-name knowledge, far fewer studies have evaluated the utility of letter-sound knowledge in predicting reading acquisition. Letter-sound knowledge measured at the beginning of kindergarten is a significant predictor of end-of-year word identification, pseudoword reading, and spelling (Byrne & Field-Barnsley, 1993). There is some evidence to indicate that kindergarten letter-sound naming has predictive power throughout the primary grade years. In a longitudinal study that followed children from kindergarten through Grade 4 (Badian, McAnulty, Duffy, & Als, 1990), letter-sound knowledge and rapid digit naming were the best predictors of Grade 4 reading group membership (good readers, average readers, mild dyslexics, or dyslexics). Even when differences in letter-name knowledge were controlled, normal readers still scored significantly higher in letter-sound knowledge than the dyslexic groups, indicating that letter-sound knowledge reflects reading-related abilities that only partly overlap with knowledge of letter names.

Letter-Sound Knowledge and Reading Acquisition

Letter-sound knowledge develops later than letter-name knowledge and appears to tap a different but related ability (McBride-Chang, 1999; Worden & Boettcher, 1990), with the two skills showing only moderate correlations in kindergarten and first grade (McBride-Chang, 1999; Wagner et al., 1994). Whereas mapping letter names to their visual symbols is a relatively simple task for children who have learned to use words to name things, acquiring letter-sound knowledge is more challenging because it requires isolating individual phonemes. In addition, different factors affect children's performance on the two types of alphabet knowledge tasks. Whereas knowledge of a letter's sound is related to whether the sound is in the letter name and in what position, letter-name knowledge is not mediated by these factors. In contrast, whether or not a letter is in a child's first name influences the child's knowledge of letter names but has little impact on the child's letter-sound knowledge (Treiman & Broderick, 1998). Letter-sound knowledge also requires a higher level of phonological awareness skills than does letter naming (Treiman et al., 1998). In addition, the two skills show differential predictive effects: Letter-name knowledge is predicted by previous letter-name knowledge but not by letter-sound knowledge, whereas letter-sound knowledge is predicted by previous letter-name and letter-sound knowledge (McBride-Chang, 1999).

Letter-Sound Fluency

Although in theory letter-sound fluency should be a better predictor of reading than letter-naming fluency because it reflects a greater depth of grapheme–phoneme knowledge and automaticity, research has yielded little support for this hypothesis to date. In a sample of first graders, Daly and colleagues (1997) examined the predictive value of 11 curriculum-based measures (CBM) of early academic skills, including two letter-sound fluency tasks (a letter-sound production task and a letter-sound selection task). Performance on the letter-sound production task but not the letter-sound selection task displayed moderate concurrent and predictive validity with Broad Reading scores on the *Woodcock–Johnson Psycho-Educational Battery–Revised* (WJ-R) and on CBM oral reading fluency for passages and word lists. Test–retest reliability coefficients for both letter-sound fluency measures fell below acceptable levels, however (.65 and .42, respectively). In a study comparing the relative predictive power of letter-naming and letter-sound fluency measures (Stage, Sheppard, Davidson, & Browning, 2001), both kindergarten letter-naming and letter-sound fluency predicted first-grade reading growth, as measured by CBM oral reading fluency, but only letter-naming fluency contributed unique variance. The researchers speculated that floor effects for the letter-sound fluency task may have contributed to the failure of that measure to serve as an independent predictor.

ISSUES IN ASSESSING ALPHABET KNOWLEDGE

Issues relevant to assessing letter-name and letter-sound knowledge in early primary grade children include (1) task format variations and (2) differences in content coverage, that is, the number of letter names or letter sounds sampled across measures.

Task Format Variations

Measures of alphabet knowledge use one of four basic task formats (see Table 3.12). As the table indicates, response demands vary considerably across the four formats, ranging from nonverbal (pointing) to verbal (singing or saying letter names or sounds) to written (producing letters from dictation or in sequential order). Two of the measures reviewed in this text—the Letter Knowledge subtest on the *Phonological Abilities Test* and the Letter Identification test on the *Woodcock Reading Mastery Tests–Revised/Normative Update* (WRMT-R/NU)—permit the child to provide either the letter name or the sound, which confounds letter-name with letter-sound knowledge. Of the four formats, the identification or recall method is the most common

TABLE 3.12. Formats for Assessing Alphabet Knowledge

Task format	Testing task
Recitation	Saying the alphabet or singing the alphabet song
Recognition	Pointing to a target letter in an array matching the name or sound pronounced by the examiner
Identification	Providing the name or sound of isolated letters or letters presented in a random array
Production	Writing letters or sounds dictated in random order or writing the entire alphabet in correct sequence

for both letter-name and letter-sound tasks. Byrne and Fielding-Barnsley (1991, 1993) assert that a recognition procedure in which the child is required to pick out the target letter representing a sound spoken by the examiner on a card with several letters (i.e., "Which of these letters makes the sound /b/?") is a more sensitive measure than the standard recall method, which requires the child to indicate the sound of an isolated letter (i.e., "What is the sound of this letter?"). Although none of the letter-sound measures reviewed in this text use this format to assess a complete set of letter sounds, early items on the WIAT-II Word Reading subtest assess sounds for single letters and consonant blends or digraphs with a recognition format.

Another variation among alphabet knowledge measures is whether they present letter items in uppercase, lowercase, or both. Because children learn uppercase letter names earlier than lowercase letter names (Worden & Boettcher, 1990), letter-naming measures that use uppercase letters may show ceiling effects as early as the fall of first grade (e.g., Wagner et al., 1994). As a result, test authors often use lowercase letters to assess letter-name knowledge and uppercase letters to assess letter-sound knowledge. Type styles also vary across measures. Although most alphabet knowledge measures present letters in printed type, a few, such as the TERA-3 and the WRMT-R/NU, present items in a variety of type styles, including cursive forms that are unlikely to be familiar to most young examinees. Assessing alphabet knowledge with different type styles produces unreliable results because it confounds alphabet knowledge with type style familiarity.

Letter-naming fluency measures use one of two task formats: a *discrete-trial* or a *continuous-list* format. In the discrete-trial procedure, one letter is presented at a time on a computer, and the score is the average letter-naming time across the set of letters presented. In the continuous-list procedure, the child names a series of letters randomly displayed on a sheet of paper, and the score is the number of letters named correctly in a fixed amount of time (usually 1 minute) or the amount of time needed to name the entire array. Correlations between reading ability and letter-naming fluency for the discrete-trial procedure have been generally nonsignificant or considerably lower than for the continuous-list procedure (Stanovich, 1981; Stanovich, Cunningham, & West, 1981; Stanovich et al., 1983). Moreover, measures with a discrete-trial format are impractical for most examiners because of the need for computer-based presentation and performance analysis.

Differences in Content Coverage

Alphabet knowledge measures also vary in terms of the number of letter names or sounds they sample. Nonstandardized or criterion-referenced alphabet knowledge tests typically assess letter-name and letter-sound knowledge for all or most of the 26 letters. In contrast, most norm-referenced instruments include only a subset of letters (see Table 3.13 below). Among the norm-referenced letter-naming tests reviewed in this text, sample sizes range from a low of 8 letters for the *Kaufman Survey of Early Academic and Language Skills* to all 26 letters for the *Early Reading Diagnostic Assessment–Revised* (ERDA-R) and the WIAT-II. Sampling only a subset of letter names or sounds not only reduces reliability, because children have fewer opportunities to demonstrate their alphabet knowledge, but also provides less information for instructional planning or progress monitoring. Measures of letter-sound knowledge also vary in the number of sounds they assess. Some measures sample short vowel sounds only, others sample both long and short vowels, and still others sample only "hard" consonant sounds. Some early literacy batteries do not sample the sounds for *q* and *x*, because these letters do not have an identifiable sound when they occur in isolation. One of the measures reviewed in this text—the *Phonological Awareness Test* (Robertson & Salter, 1997)—samples the full range of single letter sounds, digraphs, diphthongs, and blends.

MEASURES OF ALPHABET KNOWLEDGE

Examiners can easily produce letter-name and letter-sound measures by writing the alphabet letters in random order on a sheet of paper, which can be laminated for durability over frequent administrations. As noted above, letter-name knowledge should be assessed with lowercase letters, which are less familiar to young children, whereas letter-sound knowledge can be assessed with uppercase letters. Assessing alphabet knowledge with arrays of letters displayed on single sheets rather with individual flashcards reduces testing time considerably. Given that letter-naming fluency has been described as the single best predictor of reading acquisition (Adams, 1990), it is surprising that only one speeded measure sampling all 26 letters (randomly repeated on a page) has been developed—the Letter Naming Fluency task on the DIBELS. Although several recently published norm-referenced instruments include RAN-type letter naming measures, no norm-referenced measures of letter-naming fluency are currently available. Similarly, no criterion-referenced or norm-referenced letter-sound fluency measures could be located. Table 3.13 describes the 26 alphabet knowledge measures reviewed in this text, three of which are fluency-based. To assist practitioners in evaluating content coverage and task format, entries indicate how many letters/sounds are sampled for both letter-name and letter-sound knowledge tasks, as well as whether uppercase and/or lowercase test items are used.

PRINT RESOURCES

Treiman, R. (2000). The foundations of literacy. *Current Directions in Psychological Science, 9*, 89–92.

This brief, readable article by a leading researcher in the acquisition of alphabet knowledge provides an excellent summary of the role of letter-name and letter-sound knowledge in learning to read and spell.

TABLE 3.13. Measures of Alphabet Knowledge and Letter-Naming Fluency

Name and date of *measure*; subtest(s)	Admin. time (minutes)	Norms/ benchmarks	Testing task	Comments
Book Buddies Early Literacy Screening (1998); Letter Identification	3–5	NS; Grades K–2	Identifying 26 uppercase and 26 lowercase letters, randomly presented	Part of a screening and progress monitoring battery designed for tutors
Book Buddies Early Literacy Screening (1998); Letter Production	8–15	NS; Grades K–2	Writing 26 uppercase and 26 lowercase letters, randomly dictated, or writing letters as the examiner sings the alphabet song with the child	One of the few measures to require written production of both uppercase and lowercase letters; also samples written language skills
Consortium on Reading Excellence Phonics Survey (1999); Alphabet Skills area	10–25	NS; Grades K–8	Consists of five subtests: identifying 26 randomly arrayed uppercase and 26 lowercase letters, 23 consonant sounds, 5 long vowel sounds, and 5 short vowel sounds	Assesses a complete set of letter names and basic letter sounds; very useful for instructional planning and progress monitoring
Dynamic Indicators of Basic Early Literacy Skills (2002); Letter Naming Fluency	2–3	NS; benchmarks are under development; Grades K and 1	Naming as many uppercase and lowercase letters randomly arrayed on a page as possible in 1 minute	Local norming recommended until benchmark development is completed
Dyslexia Early Screening Test (1996); Letter Naming	1–2	British norms for ages 4-6 through 6-5	Identifying 10 lowercase letters	Letters are printed on three cards rather than a single sheet; limited letter name sample
Early Reading Diagnostic Assessment–Revised (2002); Letter Recognition	3–5	Norms for Grades K and 1	Recognizing a target letter in a lowercase letter array (3 items) and naming 26 randomly presented lowercase letters	Decile scores only
Fox in a Box (2000); Alphabet Recognition	5–10	CR; kindergarten benchmarks	Naming 26 randomly presented uppercase letters, giving the name and sound of 26 randomly presented lowercase letters, and recognizing the 5 vowels	Letter names and sounds are assessed together for lowercase letter forms
Fox in a Box (2000); Alphabet Writing	5–10 (GA)	CR; kindergarten benchmarks	Writing 10 letters in both uppercase and lowercase form, dictated in random order	Also measures written expression skills
Group Reading Assessment and Diagnostic Evaluation (2002); Letter Recognition	10–12 (GA)	Norms for kindergarten (when combined with two other measures)	Marking the one of five uppercase and lowercase letters named by the examiner (11 items)	Multiple-choice format; does not yield a separate score

(continued)

TABLE 3.13. *(continued)*

Name and date of *measure*; subtest(s)	Admin. time (minutes)	Norms/ benchmarks	Testing task	Comments
Group Reading Assessment and Diagnostic Evaluation (2002); Phoneme–Grapheme Correspondence	15–18 (GA)	Norms for kindergarten	Marking the one of four lowercase letters matching the first or last sound in a word pronounced by the examiner (16 items)	Stanine scores; multiple-choice format
Kaufman Survey of Early Academic and Language Skills (1993); Numbers, Letters, and Words	5–8	Norms for ages 5-0 through 6-11	Pointing to or naming/reading numbers, letters, and words; 4 letter recognition and 4 letter naming items; also includes 13 word items and 19 number items	Very limited sampling of letter knowledge; inadequate floors below age 5-9
Phonological Abilities Test (1997); Letter Knowledge	3–5	British norms for ages 5-0 through 7-11	Giving the name or sound of 26 randomly ordered lowercase letters presented individually on flashcards	Five percentile scores only; utility limited by British norms
Phonological Awareness Literacy Screening (2002); Alphabet Recognition	2–3	CR; Virginia benchmarks for Grades K–3	Naming 26 randomly arrayed lowercase alphabet letters	Part of a statewide early reading assessment battery
Phonological Awareness Literacy Screening (2002); Letter Sounds	2–3	Virginia benchmarks for Grades K–3	Giving the sounds of 26 uppercase letters and digraphs (omitting *m*, *q*, and *x*, and including *ch*, *sh*, and *th*)	Only short vowel sounds are scored
Phonological Awareness Test (1997); Graphemes	10–15	Norms for ages 5-0 through 9-11	Naming letter sounds in seven categories: 20 consonants, 10 short and long vowels, 10 consonant blends, 10 digraphs, 5 *r*-controlled vowels, 5 vowel digraphs, and 5 diphthongs (lowercase format)	Yields a total score and a separate score per category; inadequate floors below age 6-0
Predictive Reading Profile (2001); Alphabet–Word	10–15 (GA)	Preliminary kindergarten norms	Circling one of three lowercase letters named by the examiner (10 items); also includes 20 word recognition items	Part of a group-administered early literacy battery; local norming recommended
Predictive Reading Profile (2001); Sound Recognition	10–15 (GA)	Preliminary kindergarten norms	Circling one of three lowercase letters corresponding to the sound pronounced by the examiner (10 items); also includes 10 sound matching and 10 sound isolation items	Part of a group-administered early literacy battery; local norming recommended

(continued)

TABLE 3.13. *(continued)*

Name and date of *measure*; subtest(s)	Admin. time (minutes)	Norms/ benchmarks	Testing task	Comments
Process Assessment of the Learner: Test Battery for Reading and Writing (PAL-RW) (2001); Alphabet Writing	3–7	Norms for Grades K–6	Printing as many lowercase letters as possible in sequence from memory in 15 seconds	Decile scores only; identical to the WIAT-II subtest of the same name (see below); also measures written expression skills
Test of Early Reading Ability–3 (2001); Alphabet	5–10	Norms for ages 3-6 through 8-6	Identifying or naming uppercase and lowercase letters and sounds, identifying or reading words, and identifying the number of syllables or phonemes in words (12 letter-name, 1 letter-sound, 5 segmentation, and 11 word items)	Letters and words are printed in a variety of fonts; limited sampling of letter-name knowledge
Texas Primary Reading Inventory (2002); Graphophonemic Knowledge	2–3	CR; Texas benchmarks for Grades K and 1	Identifying names and sounds for 10 uppercase and lowercase letters; only letter sounds are scored	Screening task on state-sponsored early reading assessment
Texas Primary Reading Inventory (2002); Letter Name Identification	2–3	CR; Texas benchmarks for kindergarten	Identifying 26 uppercase and 26 lowercase letters randomly arrayed on a card	Inventory task on state-sponsored early reading assessment
Wechsler Individual Achievement Test–II (WIAT-II) (2001); Word Reading	5–15	Norms for ages 4-0 through 85+ and Grades PreK–16	Matching lowercase letters (3 items); identifying 26 lowercase letters; identifying letter sounds and consonant blends (6 items); also includes 4 rhyming, 5 sound matching, 3 blending, and 84 word reading items	Also assesses phonological awareness and word reading skills; no separate alphabet knowledge score
Wechsler Individual Achievement Test–II (WIAT-II) (2001); Alphabet Writing	3–7	Norms for Grades PreK–2	Printing as many lowercase letters as possible in sequence from memory in 15 seconds	Decile scores only for Grades PreK and K; identical to the PAL-RW subtest of the same name (see above); also measures written expression skills

(continued)

TABLE 3.13. *(continued)*

Name and date of *measure*; subtest(s)	Admin. time (minutes)	Norms/ benchmarks	Testing task	Comments
Woodcock Reading Mastery Tests–Revised/Normative Update (1987/1998); Letter Identification	3–5	Norms for ages 5-0 through 75+ and Grades K–16	Identifying by name or sound 27 uppercase and 24 lowercase letters presented in a variety of printed and cursive type styles	Confounds letter-name with letter-sound knowledge and type style familiarity
Woodcock Reading Mastery Tests–Revised/Normative Update (1987/1998); Supplementary Letter Checklist	3–5	NS; Grades K–16	Identifying 27 uppercase letters, 29 lowercase letters, 5 digraphs, and 2 diphthongs; examiners may assess letter-name or letter-sound knowledge or both, except for digraphs and diphthongs, which must be identified by sound; 4 letters are presented in two type styles	Available for Form G only; items are presented in the sans serif type style commonly used in primary grade reading materials
Woodcock–Johnson III Tests of Achievement (2001); Letter–Word Identification	5–10	Norms for ages 2-0 through 90+ and Grades K–18	Identifying 6 uppercase and lowercase letters by matching or pointing; naming 3 uppercase and 4 lowercase letters; also includes 63 word recognition or word reading items	Rasch-model test that provides criterion-referenced as well as norm-referenced scores; limited sample of letter-name knowledge

Note. CR, criterion-referenced measure; NS, nonstandardized measure; GA, group-administered measure. Fluency-based measures are shaded.

Single Word Reading

This section discusses measures of *single word reading*, also called measures of *word identification*, *word recognition*, or *decoding*. In the discussion below, single word reading is divided into two sections: (1) single word reading (i.e., reading isolated real words) and (2) pseudoword reading. Although there is substantial evidence (e.g., Manis et al., 1999, 2000; Torgesen, Rashotte, & Alexander, 2001) that reading fluency involves additional processes beyond those that underlie word recognition, single word reading measures with a speeded component are discussed here rather than in the "Oral Reading in Context" section.

SINGLE WORD READING

Measures of single (real) word reading require the child to identify isolated words presented on a list, on a card, or on pages in a testing easel. Reading lists of isolated words provides a purer measure of the ability to use phonemic and structural analysis to decode words than does reading textual material because children cannot use pictorial and context clues in support of word identification. Traditional word reading measures are untimed, however, so that readers can use both sight word knowledge and phonemic decoding skills in the word identification process (Torgesen, 1998). Assessing word recognition skills is a complicated proposition because readers can identify words in several different ways (Ehri, 1998):

1. *Decoding* (or *phonological recoding*): Identifying the individual phonemes in words and blending them together.
2. *Decoding by spelling patterns*: Identifying and blending familiar letter combinations (e.g., *dis*, *ing*).
3. *Sight word reading*: Recognizing words as whole units.
4. *Reading by analogy*: Recognizing how the spelling of a word is similar to that of a known word.
5. *Using context clues*: Using previous text and pictorial clues to guess a word's identity.

In the beginning stages of reading, children rely primarily on letter-by-letter decoding–that is, sounding out individual letters and blending them together to form a pronounceable word. Initially, they perform these operations slowly and laboriously, but with experience they begin to process letters in larger units or *spelling patterns*, which increases decoding speed. Repeated exposure to printed words permits children to store words in long-term memory as whole orthographic units or *sight words*. These sight words do not require phonological recoding but can be recognized quickly and automatically as integrated visual representations (Torgesen, 1999).

Word Recognition and Reading Proficiency

Word recognition skills are the major determinant of reading proficiency in the early grades (Juel, 1988; Stanovich, 1991) and contribute a substantial amount of variance to reading ability in adulthood (Cunningham & Stanovich, 1997). Without accurate, fluent word recognition, comprehension is impaired because so much attention must be allocated to the decoding process (Share, 1995). In the primary grades, decoding skills account for most of the variance in comprehension, but they continue to serve as strong predictors of future reading performance throughout the school years. In the Connecticut Longitudinal Study, based on an epidemiological sample of 407 children (Shaywitz, Escobar, Shaywitz, Fletcher, & Makuch, 1992; Shaywitz, Fletcher, & Escobar, 1990), the correlation between Grade 1 decoding and Grade 9 comprehension was .52.

Numerous studies (e.g., Fletcher et al., 1994; Lyon, 1996a, 1996b; Shankweiler et al., 1999; Share, 1995; Share & Stanovich, 1995) have confirmed that the core deficits characterizing both dyslexic and garden-variety poor readers are at the word-reading level and that these deficits tend to persist and to become compounded with other learning problems throughout the school years. Children with poor decoding skills read less than good decoders do, so that by the end of first grade, good readers have seen twice as many words in running text as poor readers. In the *Matthew effect* documented by Stanovich (1986), a vicious cycle develops in which children without good word recognition skills begin to dislike reading, read less than good readers both in and out of school, and fail to develop the vocabulary and other cognitive and linguistic skills promoted by wide reading. In Juel's (1988) study of 54 children who were followed from first through fourth grade, the probability that a child in the bottom quartile in reading comprehension at the end of first grade would still be a poor reader at the end of fourth grade was 88%.

Assessing Single Word Reading

Four types of single word reading measures with utility for early reading assessments are described below: (1) norm-referenced word identification tests, (2) exception word reading tests, (3) nonstandardized graded word lists, and (4) single word reading fluency measures. Although norm-referenced reading tests are the most commonly administered type of measure in early reading assessments, an assessment of children's word recognition skills should never be based on a single norm-referenced test. Assessments should include measures of both real word and pseudoword reading, as well as graded word lists that provide an estimate of the child's instructional reading level.

Norm-Referenced Word Identification Tests

Norm-referenced single word reading tests, usually called *word recognition, word identification,* or *decoding tests,* evaluate children's ability to read isolated words relative to that of their age and/or grade peers. Most of the tests in this category consist of lists of words presented on cards or test easels and arranged in order of increasing difficulty. On these measures, the child is required only to pronounce the word, not define it, so that, strictly speaking, the task is one of decoding or word identification rather than word recognition. Word selection is based on frequency of occurrence in texts and reading curricula, with very high frequency items placed at the beginning of the list and items decreasing in frequency as the list progresses. As noted above, some recently published word identification tests include items that measure subword skills, such as letter identification or sound matching, to improve diagnostic accuracy for younger examinees.

Example (easy item): "Point to the word that begins like *cat.*" (*cow, fat, sit*)

Example (difficult item): *sabotage*

Exception Word Reading Tests

Exception words, also called *irregular words* or *sight words,* are words that do not conform to regular sound–symbol correspondences. To respond correctly, the child must rely on word-specific knowledge in long-term memory, because the words cannot be entirely decoded on the basis of spelling–sound conversion rules. Because exception words require orthographic knowledge for correct pronunciation, performance on exception word reading tests is also considered to be a good index of orthographic processing. As noted earlier, some researchers (e.g., Castles &

Coltheart, 1993; Castles et al., 1999) have proposed that comparisons between exception word reading and pseudoword reading can distinguish between dyslexic subgroups: Individuals with phonological dyslexia show more impairment in pseudoword reading, whereas those with surface dyslexia show more impairment in exception word reading. The ITPA-3 is the only currently available norm-referenced instrument that includes separate measures of exception word and pseudoword reading for making these types of comparisons.

Example (easy item): *come*

Example (difficult item): *yacht*

Nonstandardized Graded Word Lists

Nonstandardized word lists appear in a variety of instruments, including reading inventories and reading screening batteries. *Reading inventories* are nonstandardized instruments consisting of a series of reading passages that usually range from preprimer (i.e., beginning of Grade 1) through Grade 6 or Grade 8 in difficulty level. Although reading inventories are primarily intended to measure contextual reading accuracy and comprehension, many include graded word lists to provide an estimate of children's reading level as a starting point for administering the passages. Several of the early reading screening batteries reviewed in this text are based on a reading inventory format and include graded word lists for determining whether students have met grade-specific benchmarks and/or identifying the reading passage on which students should be tested for oral reading accuracy, comprehension, and/or fluency.

Example (preprimer words): = *he, in*

Example (Grade 2 words): = *knew, remember*

Single Word Reading Fluency Measures

Despite the fact that slow, laborious reading is one of the key characteristics of reading disabilities, few test developers have incorporated fluency-based single word reading tasks into norm- or criterion-referenced instruments, compared with contextual reading fluency measures. This book reviews two norm-referenced measures of speeded single word reading–the *Test of Word Reading Efficiency*, which includes separate subtests for speeded real word and pseudoword reading, and the One Minute Reading subtest on the DST.

Example: "Read these words as quickly as you can." (*go, sit, then, walk, table, come* . . .)

Issues in Assessing Single Word Reading

Although numerous measures of single word reading are available from commercial test publishers, they vary considerably in terms of their psychometric characteristics and technical adequacy, including (1) item coverage at each grade level, (2) proportion of exception words, and (3) degree of content validity.

Breadth of Grade-Level Coverage

The vast majority of norm-referenced tests of single word reading have too few items at each grade level for reliable measurement, especially at the younger age ranges (Olson et al., 1994). Although inadequate item coverage limits the ability of most norm-referenced measures to make fine discriminations among levels of reading proficiency in examinees of all ages, it is especially problematic for early primary grade children, who may be able to read only a few (if any) words. To address this problem, some test authors include items that assess sublexical skills, such as letter identification, sound matching, rhyming, and blending. For example, of the 131 items on the Word Reading subtest on the WIAT-II, 47 assess subword rather than word reading skills.

Proportion of Exception Words

Another factor that can affect children's level of performance on single word reading measures is the proportion of regular versus irregular or exception words. As noted earlier, *exception words* are real words with irregular spelling patterns, such as silent letters (*comb*) or unusual orthographic structures (*rough*). Although standardized word identification tests generally attempt to include a balance of regular and exception words, very few test manuals provide specific information regarding this aspect of test content. A test containing primarily regular words will benefit children with good phonological skills, whereas a test consisting primarily of irregular words may yield results that reflect print exposure rather than phonemic decoding ability (Rack et al., 1992). This text reviews two measures of single word reading that consist entirely of irregular words—the Sight Decoding subtest on the norm-referenced ITPA-3 and the nonstandardized *Exception Word Reading Test*, which is taken from the research literature and is the model for the ITPA-3 subtest. The criterion-referenced *Fox in a Box* (FOX; CTB/McGraw-Hill, 2000a), an early literacy battery for kindergarten through Grade 2, includes separate tasks of exception word and regular word reading so that examiners can compare children's sight word and phonemic decoding skills.

Content Validity

A third issue relating to single word reading tests is that of *content validity*, the degree to which a test includes a representative sample of current national reading curricula. Research comparing various standardized word identification tests (Bell, Lentz, & Graden, 1992; Good & Salvia, 1988; Martens, Steele, Massie, & Diskin, 1995; Shapiro & Derr, 1987; Slate, 1996; Webster & Braswell, 1991) has consistently documented that these tests differ significantly in terms of their overlap with commercially available reading programs, so that scores vary as a function of the curriculum in which students are instructed and the assessment instrument. Even among widely used tests with generally good psychometric properties, the overlap in content is surprisingly small. In a study (Hultquist & Metzke, 1993) comparing word identification measures from the WJ-R, *Kaufman Test of Educational Achievement* (Kaufman & Kaufman, 1985b), *Peabody Individual Achievement Test–Revised* (Markwardt, 1989), and *Diagnostic Achievement Battery–Second Edition* (Newcomer, 1990), only 4 of the 219 reading words on the four tests appeared on more than one instrument, and of those shared words, none appeared on more than two tests. Given the variability in test content, it is not surprising that different word

TABLE 3.14. Test Floors, Item Statistics, and Scores Obtained by a First Grader on Four Standardized Word Identification Tests

Name and date of *test*; subtest	Obtained standard score[a]	Test floor[b] for age 6-6	Total number of test items	Number of items answered correctly	Number of items shared with other tests
Illinois Test of Psycholinguistic Abilities–3 (2001); Sight Decoding	6 (75)	5 (80)	25	3	4
Wechsler Individual Achievement Test–II (2001); Word Reading	81	59	131	37[c]	7
Woodcock Reading Mastery Tests–Revised/Normative Update (1987/1998); Word Identification	66	44	106	11	8
Woodcock–Johnson III Tests of Achievement, Form A (2001); Letter–Word Identification	98	48	76	19[c]	4

[a]Standard scores are based on age norms. For subtests that yield standard scores with a mean of 10 and a standard deviation of 3, the corresponding standard score with a mean of 100 and standard deviation of 15 has been added for comparison purposes in the first two columns.
[b]A *test floor* is defined as the standard score corresponding to a raw score of 1. On the Rasch-based *Woodcock–Johnson III* Letter–Word Identification test, the test floor was calculated by entering a raw score of 1 in the software scoring program for a child aged 6-6 in January of Grade 1.
[c]The number correct for these tests includes items below the basal.

identification tests do not always produce similar levels of performance in the same individuals (Slate, 1996; Wickes & Slate, 1999).

POOR OR PROFICIENT READER? THE CASE OF TIM

Table 3.14 displays the results obtained by Tim, a first-grade student aged 6-6, on four word identification tests, along with selected psychometric characteristics for each test. The tests are listed alphabetically, which is the order in which they were administered. Depending on the test, Tim may be classified as a reader with average, below average, or very low reading proficiency. The differences among his obtained standard scores, which cover a 33-point range, are especially striking in view of the fact that all of the tests were normed within 3 years of each other and, with the exception of ITPA-3 Sight Decoding, are designed to include a balance of regular and irregular words. Item overlap is minimal across the four instruments. Of the 278 words on the four tests, only 11 words occur on more than one instrument, and of those 11 words, only 1 (*because*) appears on more than two tests.

Measures of Single Word Reading

Table 3.15 describes single word reading measures that use real words as test stimuli, whereas Table 3.16 describes pseudoword reading measures. Measures that include both real word and pseudoword items are listed in both tables. Because of the importance of item coverage in evaluating the adequacy of single-word-reading tests, the number and type of items are listed for each measure.

TABLE 3.15. Measures of Single Word Reading

Name and date of *measure*; subtest	Admin. time (minutes)	Norms/ benchmarks	Testing task	Comments
Book Buddies Early Literacy Screening (1998); Word List Reading	5–10	NS; Grades 1 and 2	Reading preprimer, primer, and Grade 1 word lists (20 items each)	Word identification measure linked to tutorial program
Consortium on Reading Excellence Phonics Survey (1999); Reading and Decoding Skills	10–20	NS; Grades K–8	Reading real words and pseudowords with specific phonics features (48 real words, 56 pseudowords)	Permits comparisons of sight word and phonemic word reading for the same spelling patterns
Dyslexia Screening Test (1996); One Minute Reading	2–3	British norms for ages 6-6 through 16-5	Reading as many words as possible in 1 minute (60-word list for primary grade children, 120-word list for older children)	Yields five percentile ranges only; utility limited by British norms
Early Reading Diagnostic Assessment–Revised (2002); Word Reading	5–8	Norms for Grades 1–3	Reading words (42 items)	Yields decile scores only; includes the first 42 word items from the WIAT–II Word Reading subtest (see below)
Exception Word Reading Test (1985)	5–8	NS; research norms for Grades 2–5	Reading sight words (45- and 50-word lists)	Very difficult for most second graders; also measures orthographic processing
Fox in a Box (2000); Decoding Words	5–15	CR; benchmarks for Grades K–2	Reading phonically regular words (72 real words, 42 pseudowords)	Permits comparisons of real word and pseudoword reading skills for the same spelling patterns
Fox in a Box (2000); Sight Words	5–15	CR; benchmarks for Grades K–2	Reading sight words (72 real words, 42 pseudowords)	Lists are divided into basic and advanced sight words for estimating independent reading level
Group Reading Assessment and Diagnostic Evaluation (2002); Word Meaning	10–12 (GA)	Norms for Grades 1 and 2	Silently reading a word and marking the one of four pictures best representing the meaning of the word (27 items)	Multiple-choice format; also measures reading vocabulary
Group Reading Assessment and Diagnostic Evaluation (2002); Word Reading	10–15 (GA)	Norms for Grades K–3	Marking the one of four or five words corresponding to a word pronounced by the examiner (10–30 items)	Multiple-choice format; optional task for kindergarten; list length varies by grade
Illinois Test of Psycholinguistic Abilities–3 (2001); Sight Decoding	5–8	Norms for ages 5-0 through 12-11	Reading irregular words (25 items)	Unique norm-referenced measure composed entirely of exception words
Kaufman Survey of Early Academic and Language Skills (1993); Numbers, Letters, and Words	5–10	Norms for ages 5-0 through 6-11	Pointing to or naming/reading numbers, letters, and words (13 word items); also includes 8 letter and 19 number items	Limited sampling of word recognition and word reading skills

(continued)

TABLE 3.15. *(continued)*

Name and date of *measure*; subtest	Admin. time (minutes)	Norms/ benchmarks	Testing task	Comments
Phonological Awareness Literacy Screening (2002); Word Recognition in Isolation	5–15	CR; Virginia benchmarks for Grades 1–3	Reading preprimer through Grade 3 word lists (20 items each)	Part of statewide early reading assessment battery for Grades K–3
Predictive Reading Profile (2001); Alphabet-Word	10–15 (GA)	Preliminary kindergarten norms; Grades K and 1	Circling the one of three letters or words named by the examiner (10 letters, 20 words)	Task on one of very few entirely group-administered reading screening measures; local norming recommended
Standardized Reading Inventory–2 (1999); Words in Isolation Checklist	5–10	NS; ages 6-0 through 14-6	Reading 20-item word lists from preprimer through Grade 8; words are drawn from the passages in the test	Used to determine entry level for passage reading
Test of Early Reading Ability–3 (2001); Alphabet	5–10	Norms for ages 3-6 through 8-6	Identifying or naming uppercase and lowercase letters and sounds, identifying or reading words, and identifying the number of syllables or phonemes in words (12 letter-name, 1 letter-sound, 5 segmentation, and 11 word items)	Assesses a variety of alphabet knowledge and word reading skills
Test of Word Reading Efficiency (1999); Sight Word Efficiency	5	Norms for ages 6-0 through 24-11 and Grades 1–12	Reading as many words as possible in 45 seconds (104 items)	Includes two forms; floor effects for first and second grade
Texas Primary Reading Inventory (2002); Word List Reading	5–10	CR; Texas benchmarks for Grades 1 and 2	Reading 15-item word lists	Serves as a placement test for passage reading in a statewide assessment battery
Texas Primary Reading Inventory (2002); Word Reading	1–2	CR; Texas benchmarks for Grades 1 and 2	Reading 8-item word lists	Screening measure on a state-sponsored early literacy battery
Wechsler Individual Achievement Test–II (WIAT-II) (2001); Word Reading	5–15	Norms for ages 4-0 through 85+ and Grades PreK–16	Reading from an 84-item word list; also includes 47 subword items	Also assesses alphabet knowledge and subword reading skills in early primary grade examinees
Woodcock Reading Mastery Tests–Revised/Normative Update (1987/1998); Word Identification	5–10	Norms for ages 5-0 through 75+ and Grades K–16	Reading words (106 items)	Rasch-model test that permits comparisons of real word and pseudoword reading in the same norm-referenced instrument
Woodcock–Johnson III Tests of Achievement (2001); Letter–Word Identification	5–10	Norms for ages 2-0 through 90+ and Grades K–18	Identifying and naming/reading letters and words (6 letter recognition, 7 letter-name, 2 word recognition, and 61 word items)	Rasch-model test that provides proficiency-level as well as norm-referenced scores

Note. CR, criterion-referenced measure; GA, group-administered measure; NS, nonstandardized measure. Fluency-based measures are shaded.

PSEUDOWORD READING

Pseudowords, sometimes also called *nonsense words* or *nonwords*, are pronounceable combinations of letters that conform to English spelling rules but that either are not real English words or occur with very low frequency. In this text, the term *pseudoword* is used rather than *nonsense word* or *nonword* because the latter two terms do not differentiate between pronounceable and nonpronounceable letter groups or combinations of nonalphabetic symbols, such as visual marks and digits. Tasks of pseudoword reading, also termed *phonemic decoding*, *phonological (de)coding*, or *word attack*, require the child to recall the phoneme associated with each grapheme and blend the separate sounds together to form a pronounceable unit. Because pseudowords have no lexical entry, pseudoword reading provides a relatively pure assessment of children' ability to apply grapheme–phoneme knowledge in decoding. Although pseudowords can be read by analogy to real words, especially by older children who have developed some reading proficiency, phonemic segmentation skills and knowledge of spelling–sound correspondence rules are still necessary to achieve a correct pronunciation. For example, to read the pseudoword *dake*, the reader must segment it into the onset *d* and the rime *ake* before it can be read by analogy to *cake* (Siegel, 1998).

Pseudoword Reading as a Predictor of Word Identification and Reading Disabilities

Pseudoword reading is a complex skill that requires many of the same cognitive and linguistic abilities that underlie the identification process for real words. Although pseudoword reading may appear to be a "pure" measure of phonological coding ability, phonological skills account for less than half of the variance in pseudoword decoding. Pseudoword reading shares significant variance with spelling and word identification, as well as with semantic and syntactic knowledge. Compared with other reading subskills, such as vocabulary and verbal memory, pseudoword decoding is the best single predictor of word identification for both poor and normal readers. In a large sample of children who were administered a comprehensive battery of predictors (Vellutino, Scanlon, & Tanzman, 1994), pseudoword decoding accounted for 73% of the variance in word identification for younger readers (Grades 2 and 3) and 62% of the variance for older readers (Grades 6 and 7). Pseudoword reading continues to serve as a powerful predictor of children's reading status during the elementary grades. In Juel's (1988) longitudinal study cited above, of the 24 children who remained poor readers from first through fourth grade, only 2 had average pseudoword decoding skills at the end of fourth grade. By the end of fourth grade, most of the poor readers still could not decode all of the one-syllable pseudowords on the test (e.g., *buf*)—the level achieved by good readers at the beginning of second grade.

Difficulty in pseudoword reading is also the single most reliable indicator of reading disabilities (Castles & Coltheart, 1993; Manis et al., 1993; Rack et al., 1992) and is characteristic of discrepant readers (i.e., children with IQ–reading achievement discrepancies) and garden-variety poor readers alike (Felton & Wood, 1992; Stanovich & Siegel, 1994). In a sample of children aged 7 through 14, Siegel and Ryan (1988) reported striking differences between normally achieving and reading-disabled children's pseudoword reading performance. By age 9, normal readers were able to read even the most difficult pseudowords (up to 3 syllables), whereas reading-disabled children were very slow to develop pseudoword reading skills. Even by age 14, many reading-disabled children were performing no better than 7-year-old normal readers.

Because pseudoword items are by definition unfamiliar, children cannot use rote memory for sight words to obtain adequate scores. As a result, pseudoword tests may reveal reading deficits that are not evident on traditional word identification tests. Analysis of pseudoword reading errors can also provide useful information for diagnosis and treatment planning. Reading-disabled individuals are especially deficient in remembering letter details in the middle of words (Ehri & Saltmarsh, 1995). This suggests that they plateau at what has been termed the stage of *phonetic cue reading*, that is, the stage of reading development in which children rely primarily on initial and/or final consonants to identify words rather than fully analyzing sound–symbol correspondences (Ehri, 1992). In other words, the word attack skills of reading-disabled individuals are not sufficiently analytic. This deficit can be more easily diagnosed by pseudoword reading tasks than by sight word vocabulary measures that permit children with good visual memories to perform at adequate levels, especially in the early primary grades.

Assessing Pseudoword Reading

Three types of pseudoword reading measures that have relevance for early reading assessments are described below: (1) norm-referenced pseudoword reading tests, (2) nonstandardized pseudoword reading measures, and (3) pseudoword reading fluency measures.

Norm-Referenced Pseudoword Reading Measures

Seven of the norm-referenced multiskill batteries reviewed for this text include measures of pseudoword reading. Most test authors attempt to sample a broad range of letter–sound correspondences or to assess certain phonics features at specific levels of development. Three of these batteries (the ITPA-3, WIAT-II, and *WJ III Tests of Achievement*) include separate measures of real word and pseudoword decoding to facilitate comparisons of sight word reading and phonemic decoding ability.

Example (easy item): *dit*

Example (difficult item): *proquebly*

Nonstandardized Pseudoword Reading Measures

Two of the nonstandardized instruments reviewed in this text—the *Consortium On Reading Excellence Phonics Survey* and the *Fox in a Box* early literacy battery—include lists of real words and pseudowords that sample the same decoding conventions to permit comparisons of children's sight word and phonemic word reading ability. Examinees who can read the real word but not the pseudoword item with the same phonics features are likely to be relying excessively on memory-based rather than analytic word reading strategies. In the examples below, real word and pseudoword items assess final *e* marker words.

Example (real word item): *cape*

Example (pseudoword item): *lape*

Pseudoword Reading Fluency Measures

There are two basic categories of pseudoword reading fluency measures: norm-referenced tests and curriculum-based measures (CBMs). Norm-referenced pseudoword reading tests require the child to read lists of increasingly complex pseudowords under time pressure. The only currently available norm-referenced measure of speeded single pseudoword reading is the *Test of Word Reading Efficiency* Phonemic Word Efficiency subtest, which requires the examinee to read as many items as possible in 45 seconds from a list of increasingly complex pseudowords. This type of pseudoword reading fluency measure is especially subject to floor effects at the lower age and grade ranges because beginning readers are just developing letter-sound knowledge and have difficulty rapidly applying letter-sound conversion rules to read unfamiliar words. A CBM-type pseudoword reading fluency task is included as one of the measures in the DIBELS screening and progress monitoring battery developed by Roland Good and his associates at the University of Oregon. The DIBELS Nonsense Word Fluency measure, which is available in multiple alternate forms, consists of a set of 80 two- and three-phoneme pseudowords of approximately the same difficulty arrayed on a page. The child may pronounce the letter-sound correspondences in correct sequence or read the words as whole units, and the score is the number of correct sounds produced in 1 minute.

Example (increasingly complex pseudoword fluency items): "Read these words as quickly as you can." (*ig, reb, scane, tebreg, narsuitical . . .*)

Example (one-syllable pseudoword fluency items): "Read or say the sounds in these words as quickly as possible." (*fep, ig, tet, lod, ril . . .*)

Issues in Assessing Pseudoword Reading

Although all pseudoword reading tests may appear to provide the same "pure" measure of children's ability to apply letter-sound relationships in decoding, performance on pseudoword measures is significantly influenced by several factors, including the nature of the items, the adequacy of test floors, and the degree of interexaminer and interscorer variance.

Differences among Pseudoword Items

Numerous studies (e.g., Rack et al., 1992; Siegel, 1998; Treiman, Goswami, & Bruck, 1990) have reported that the ability of pseudoword measures to distinguish between normally achieving and reading-disabled examinees varies according to the characteristics of the items. Many researchers and test authors have created pseudowords by replacing one of the sounds in a real word (e.g., changing the /p/ in *pat* to /n/ to produce *nat*). When pseudoword items are visually similar to real words (*nat, wust*), however, they can be read by analogy, which reduces the demands on phonological processing skills. As a result, pseudoword measures consisting primarily of nonword items that visually resemble real words are less likely to differentiate between phonologically skilled and unskilled readers. To avoid confounding differences in print exposure with differences in phonological ability, some test authors (e.g., Wagner et al., 1999) have created pseudoword items by randomly combining phonemes to form a pronounceable word (e.g., *tastanz*). The ability of pseudoword measures to detect phonological coding deficits is also related to the length and phonological complexity of the items. In a study manipulating the complexity of pseudoword test items (Snowling, 1981), individuals with dyslexia performed more poorly than average readers on difficult pseudowords (*molsmit, brigbert*) but not on easy ones (*blem, tig*).

Floor Effects

Performance levels on pseudoword reading measures are also related to the adequacy of subtest floors. Because beginning readers have limited decoding skills, creating items that can differentiate among children with average, low, and very low levels of pseudoword decoding ability is very difficult. Consequently, pseudoword reading measures are even more vulnerable to floor effects for young examinees than are traditional word identification tests. The vast majority of the pseudoword measures reviewed in this book have inadequate floors for their lower age/grade ranges, and some have inadequate floors throughout the entire primary grade range. For example, for a child aged 6-0 to 6-3, a raw score of 1 on the Pseudoword Decoding subtest of the WIAT-II yields a standard score of 91, which is in the average range. To improve diagnostic accuracy for beginning readers, some pseudoword reading measures, such as the WJ III Word Attack test, begin with subword items, including letter-sound recognition and production items.

Interrater Reliability Concerns

Finally, pseudoword tests are highly susceptible to interexaminer and interscorer inconsistency. Many pseudowords, especially those with more than one syllable, have more than one alternative pronunciation. For example, when pseudowords are derived from words with irregular spellings (*sugar, answer*), the resulting pseudowords (*sugan, inswer*) have both regular (/su-gan/, /in-swer/) and exception (/shu-gan/, /in-zer/) pronunciations (Stanovich & Siegel, 1994). When children mumble (as they often do when they are unsure of the correct answer on pseudoword tests), it can be very difficult to determine whether they are responding correctly, especially when there are several acceptable pronunciations. Reliable scoring is even more challenging on speeded measures of pseudoword reading.

Measures of Pseudoword Reading

Table 3.16 presents summary characteristics for the 12 pseudoword reading measures reviewed in this book. As in Table 3.15, the number and type of items (real word, pseudoword, and sublexical items) are provided for each measure. Despite the technical problems described above, a pseudoword reading measure is an essential component of any early reading diagnostic assessment. Assessing pseudoword reading ability in early primary grade children suspected of having reading problems is especially important because young poor readers are often able to memorize a small sight word vocabulary and obtain a score in the average range on norm-referenced

TABLE 3.16. Measures of Pseudoword Reading

Name and date of *measure*; subtest	Admin. time (minutes)	Norms/ benchmarks	Testing task	Comments
Consortium on Reading Excellence Phonics Survey (1999); Reading and Decoding Skills	10–20	NS; Grades K–8	Reading words and pseudowords with specific phonics features (48 real words, 56 pseudowords)	Permits comparisons of sight word and phonemic word reading for the same spelling patterns
Dynamic Indicators of Basic Early Literacy Skills (2002); Nonsense Word Fluency	5–15	NS; benchmarks for winter of Grade 1; Grades 1 and 2	Reading pseudowords as rapidly as possible for 1 minute (80 items); the score is the number of correct letter sounds per minute	Curriculum-based measure; multiple forms permit repeated administrations for progress monitoring
Early Reading Diagnostic Assessment–Revised (2002); Pseudoword Decoding	5–10	Norms for Grades 1–3	Reading pseudowords (40 items)	Yields decile scores only; includes the first 40 items from the PAL-RW and WIAT-II list (see below)
Fox in a Box (2000); Decoding Words	5–15	CR; benchmarks for Grades K–2	Reading regular words and pseudowords (72 real words, 42 pseudowords)	Permits comparisons of skills in real word and pseudoword reading for the same spelling patterns
Fox in a Box (2000); Sight Words	5–15	CR; benchmarks for Grades K–2	Reading irregular words (72 real words, 42 pseudowords)	Lists are divided into basic and advanced sight words for estimating independent reading level
Illinois Test of Psycholinguistic Abilities–3 (2001); Sound Decoding	5–10	Norms for ages 5-0 through 12-11	Reading pseudowords (25 items); items represent the names of fictitious animals and are accompanied by drawings	Permits comparisons of exception word and pseudoword reading within the same norm-referenced measure
Phonological Awareness Test (1997); Decoding	5–10	Norms for ages 5-0 through 9-11	Reading pseudowords in eight categories: 10 VC words, 10 CVC words, 10 consonant digraphs, 10 consonant blends, 10 vowel digraphs, 10 *r*-controlled vowels, 10 CVCe words, and 10 diphthongs	Yields a total score and separate derived scores for each category; floor effects for younger examinees on many tasks; useful for instructional planning
Process Assessment of the Learner: Test Battery for Reading and Writing (PAL-RW) (2001); Pseudoword Decoding	5–10	Norms for Grades 1–6	Reading pseudowords (55 items)	Decile scores only; identical to the WIAT-II subtest of the same name (see below)

(continued)

TABLE 3.16. *(continued)*

Name and date of *measure*; subtest	Admin. time (minutes)	Norms/ benchmarks	Testing task	Comments
Test of Word Reading Efficiency (1999); Phonemic Word Efficiency	5	Norms for ages 6-0 through 24-11 and Grades 1–12	Reading as many pseudowords as possible in 45 seconds (63 items)	Includes two forms; floor effects for early primary grade children
Wechsler Individual Achievement Test–II (WIAT–II) (2001); Pseudoword Decoding	5–10	Norms for ages 6-0 through 85+ and Grades 1–16	Reading pseudowords (55 items)	Permits comparisons of real word and pseudoword reading in the same norm-referenced measure; identical to the PAL-RW subtest of the same name
Woodcock Reading Mastery Tests–Revised/Normative Update (1987/1998); Word Attack	5–10	Norms for ages 5-0 through 75+ and Grades K–16	Reading pseudowords (45 items)	Rasch-model test that provides proficiency-level and norm-referenced scores
Woodcock–Johnson III Tests of Achievement (2001); Word Attack	5–10	Norms for ages 2-0 through 90+ and Grades K–18	Naming letter sounds and reading pseudowords (2 letter-sound items, 30 pseudoword items)	Rasch-model test that permits real word and pseudoword reading comparisons in the same instrument

Note. CR, criterion-referenced measure; NS, nonstandardized measure; GA, group-administered measure; VC, vowel–consonant; CVC, consonant–vowel–consonant; CVCe, consonant–vowel–consonant–silent *e*. Fluency-based measures are shaded.

word identification tests, despite the fact that they are failing to develop adequate levels of phonemic awareness and grapheme–phoneme conversion skills. Because inadequate floors are endemic to this type of measure, examinees who have difficulty performing pseudoword reading tasks should receive follow-up assessments of letter-sound knowledge, phonemic segmentation, and sound blending, regardless of the level of their derived score.

PRINT RESOURCES

Metsala, J. L., & Ehri, L. C. (Eds.). (1998). *Word identification in beginning literacy.* Mahwah, NJ: Erlbaum.

The outgrowth of a conference sponsored by the National Reading Research Center, this edited volume focuses on issues related to the acquisition of word reading ability, including the cognitive processes of beginning readers, the development of phonological skills in reading-disabled individuals, and instructional strategies and programs for addressing reading problems.

Oral Reading in Context

This section discusses oral reading in context, including contextual reading accuracy and contextual reading fluency. Speeded measures of isolated word reading have been discussed in the "Single Word Reading" section.

CONTEXTUAL READING ACCURACY

Tests of contextual reading accuracy require children to read connected text aloud under untimed conditions. Most of the contextual reading accuracy tests reviewed in this text are nonstandardized measures designed to provide information about children's functional reading levels for use in selecting instructional materials or passages for fluency and/or comprehension assessments. As a result, contextual reading accuracy is usually evaluated at the same time as reading fluency and/or comprehension by having the child read graded passages aloud and then answer questions about what has been read. Depending on the structure and purpose of the assessment instrument, a single grade-specific passage may be administered or multiple graded passages may be given until the child reaches a ceiling in the case of norm-referenced measures or a frustration level in the case of nonstandardized measures.

Most measures of contextual reading accuracy require the examiner to take some form of *running record* in addition to simply counting the number of deviations from print. To take a running record, the examiner notes the types of errors (e.g., misread words, omissions, insertions, etc.) on a photocopy of the text or on a copy of the passage in the record booklet while the child is reading. Although error analyses derived from running records can provide useful information for diagnosis and treatment planning, the process of taking a running record can also contribute to lower interscorer reliability because of the greater demands on examiner recording skill, especially for the more complex systems.

The Role of Contextual Reading Skills in Word Recognition

The ability to use context in word recognition promotes reading acquisition because it permits beginning readers to supplement their rudimentary sound–symbol knowledge with context clues to decode unfamiliar words (Tunmer & Hoover, 1992). The question of whether the use of context differentiates between skilled and unskilled readers has been hotly debated. Whole language advocates (Goodman, 1986; Smith, 1975, 1979) have proposed the *context use hypothesis* as an explanation for individual differences in reading ability, arguing that skilled readers rely less on an analysis of the visual information in individual words and more on context in the word recognition process. Contrary to this view, however, most recent research (e.g., Nation & Snowling, 1998a; Nicolson, 1991; Share & Stanovich, 1995) indicates that poor readers attempt to use context clues to identify unfamiliar words *more* frequently than skilled readers in an effort to compensate for their limited decoding skills. Moreover, context is not helpful in word identification for most of the words children encounter in text. Although function words (i.e., prepositions, conjunctions, auxiliary verbs, pronouns) can be guessed with about 40% accuracy, content words (i.e., nouns, verbs, adjectives, adverbs) that carry the greatest meaning can be guessed with only about 10% accuracy (Gough, 1996).

There is also some evidence that measures of oral reading in context are better predictors of comprehension than are measures of single word reading. In a study with 10-year-old children that evaluated the relationships among a set of tests of reading accuracy, comprehension, and listening comprehension (Nation & Snowling, 1997), contextual reading accuracy was the best predictor of comprehension, better than either single word reading or pseudoword reading.

Assessing Contextual Reading Accuracy

Until quite recently, the reading measures in most multisubject batteries were confined to single word reading tests and, occasionally, single pseudoword reading tests. With the emphasis on authentic assessment and literature-based reading instruction, however, more assessment batteries, especially those designed for young children, are including measures that require examinees to read connected text. Oral reading in context is an important component of early reading assessments because it provides a much closer approximation of school and home reading experiences than does single word reading. Some of the instruments reviewed in this text provide separate measures of isolated word reading and oral reading in context (see Table 3.18 below) for comparing children's strengths and weaknesses across reading formats.

Most tests of contextual reading accuracy are modeled on informal reading inventories, which classify children's performance into one of three levels of reading competence according to preestablished standards. Table 3.17 presents functional reading level standards for the contextual reading accuracy tests reviewed in this text. Although a frustration level of less than 90% accuracy is generally agreed upon, different test authors set slightly different standards for instructional and independent proficiency levels.

There are two basic categories of contextual reading accuracy tests, based on their interpretive framework: (1) norm-referenced measures and (2) nonstandardized or criterion-referenced measures.

TABLE 3.17. Functional Reading Level Standards for Contextual Reading Accuracy

Reading level	Percent accuracy	Description
Frustration	Below 90%	Level of text at which the material is so difficult that reading is slow and laborious; comprehension is poor to negligible
Instructional	90% to 97%; often set at 85% for preprimer material	Level of text at which students can read competently with outside assistance and benefit most from instruction; comprehension is adequate to good, although students need help with certain concepts and vocabulary
Independent	95% to 98% or greater	Level of text at which students can read easily and without help; comprehension is excellent

Norm-Referenced Measures of Contextual Reading Accuracy

Several norm-referenced measures of contextual reading accuracy are currently available for early primary grade examinees. Very few of these measures provide standard scores with a mean of 100 and standard deviation of 15, however; instead, they provide percentile or decile scores, which preclude discrepancy analyses based on standard score comparisons. The only contextual reading tests with norms for early primary grade examinees that offer a full set of derived scores are the *Gray Oral Reading Tests–4* (GORT-4) and the *Standardized Reading Inventory–2*.

Nonstandardized Measures of Contextual Reading Accuracy

Most of the nonstandardized early reading assessment batteries reviewed in this text include measures of contextual reading accuracy in the form of graded passages. Performance is evaluated according to guidelines for informal reading inventories (see Table 3.17) and/or statewide or test-specific benchmarks.

Issues in Assessing Contextual Reading Accuracy

Among the issues involved in assessing contextual reading accuracy in the early primary grades are (1) the use of illustrations or pictorial clues in test materials, (2) the type(s) of text used as test stimuli, (3) the unit of measurement, and (4) content validity.

Use of Illustrations

Most of the contextual reading measures reviewed for this book require children to read sentences or passages with few or no illustrations in order to reduce or eliminate the facilitative effect of pictorial clues. In contrast, *Fox in a Box*, an early literacy battery designed for administration by classroom teachers, assesses contextual reading accuracy using a set of children's trade books included in the test kit. Although this type of testing format is high in ecological validity and attractiveness to children, examinees may obtain somewhat higher scores than on unillustrated reading accuracy measures because they have the opportunity to use pictorial clues to help identify words.

Type(s) of Text

Until quite recently, most contextual reading accuracy tests for young examinees used narrative rather than expository material as test stimuli. Today, many of the new early reading assessment batteries and revisions of previously published multisubject instruments include both narrative and expository text. The use of expository as well as narrative material derives from efforts to assess students' skills in developing the academic vocabulary needed for adequate comprehension in the content areas, beginning in Grade 3. Surprisingly, no empirical studies evaluating the effects of different types of text on the performance of early primary grade students in terms of accuracy, fluency, or comprehension could be located. The majority of the nonstandardized reading accuracy measures and norm-referenced tests reviewed in this text include both types of material (see Table 3.18 below).

TABLE 3.18. Measures of Contextual Reading Accuracy

Name and date of *measure*; subtest	Admin. time (minutes)	Norms/ benchmarks	Testing task	Comments
Book Buddies Early Literacy Screening (1998); Word Identification in Stories	5–8	NS; Grades 1 and 2	Reading preprimer-level stories; narrative material only	Contextual word identification measure linked to tutorial program
Early Reading Diagnostic Assessment–Revised (2002); Reading Sentences Aloud	5–10	Norms for Grades 1–3	Reading sentences; only target words are scored; narrative and expository material	Yields decile scores only; one of two tasks on the Reading Comprehension subtest
Fox in a Box (2000); Reading Accuracy	5–7	CR; benchmarks for Grades 1 and 2	Reading from children's trade books; narrative material only	Early literacy battery with separate assessments of reading accuracy and fluency
Gray Oral Reading Tests–4 (2001); Accuracy	15–45	Norms for ages 6-0 through 13-11	Reading graded passages; scored for accuracy, fluency (rate + accuracy), and comprehension; narrative and expository material	Yields separate scores for rate, accuracy, and fluency; floor effects for younger examinees
Phonological Awareness Literacy Screening (2002); Oral Reading in Context	5–15	CR; Virginia benchmarks for Grades 1–3	Reading from preprimer through Grade 3 passages; expository material only	Results used to estimate functional reading level; also used for evaluating fluency and comprehension
Standardized Reading Inventory–2 (1999); Word Reading Accuracy	15–30	Norms for ages 6-0 through 14-6	Reading graded passages; narrative material only	Also yields reading levels (frustration, instructional, independent)
Texas Primary Reading Inventory (2002); Reading Accuracy	5–7	CR; Texas benchmarks for Grades 1 and 2	Reading graded passages; narrative and expository material	Results used to estimate functional reading level; also used for evaluating fluency and comprehension
Wechsler Individual Achievement Test–II (2001); Target Words	10–15	Norms for ages 6-0 through 85+ and Grades 1–12	Reading sentences; only target words are scored; narrative and expository material	Contributes to the overall score on the Reading Comprehension subtest; permits norm-referenced comparisons of contextual and single word reading

Note. CR, criterion-referenced measure; NS, nonstandardized measure. Measures that use the same passages to evaluate reading accuracy and reading fluency are shaded.

Unit of Measurement

On the majority of reading accuracy tests, paragraphs or passages serve as the unit of measurement; however, several recently published or revised tests with measures for early primary grade examinees assess reading accuracy using a *target word* format. On these tasks, which are embedded in reading comprehension subtests, children read connected text in the form of single sentences, but reading accuracy is evaluated only for specific words. Measures that include both target word and single word reading, such as the Reading Comprehension subtests on the *Early Reading Diagnostic Assessment–Revised* and the WIAT-II, can provide useful information regarding whether children's word reading ability in the presence of context cues is commensurate with their ability to read isolated words.

Content Validity

The content validity of all contextual reading measures, including measures of accuracy, fluency, and comprehension, depends in large part on whether the test sentences or passages consist of material that is at the grade (difficulty) level indicated. Although a few test authors use material from children's literature, most draw passages from previously used basal reading series or create reading passages specifically for the particular instrument. After development, the passages are typically analyzed with one or more *readability formulae* to determine the difficulty level of the text. Numerous readability formulae are available (e.g., Chall & Dale, 1995; Fry, 1977; Harris & Sipay, 1985), based on such variables as density of difficult words, vocabulary, and syllable and sentence length. These formulae were originally designed for hand calculation, but an increasing number are available in software programs (e.g., the Flesch–Kincaid formula in Microsoft Office 2000) or online (e.g., Lexile Framework, 2000). Because readability estimates of the reading passages in a test can vary considerably, depending on the formula used (Brown, Hammill, & Wiederholt, 1995; Good & Kaminski, 2002a; Newcomer, 1999), test authors should present information regarding readability levels from more than one formula.

Measures of Contextual Reading Accuracy

Table 3.18 describes the eight measures of contextual reading accuracy reviewed in this book, including the type of text used as test stimuli. On the GORT-4 and the two statewide early reading batteries (Virginia's PALS and the *Texas Primary Reading Inventory*), oral reading fluency and accuracy are assessed using the same set of passages.

CONTEXTUAL READING FLUENCY

Until quite recently, reading fluency was not a major focus of either reading instruction or reading assessment. Several factors have contributed to the growing interest in the fluency aspects of reading. First, research (e.g., Lyon, 1996b; Wolf, 2001; Young & Bowers, 1995) documents that reading fluency is a critical component of reading proficiency and that slow and dysfluent reading is a hallmark of reading disabilities. Second, greater attention is being focused on fluency because intervention research has consistently demonstrated that training in phonemic awareness and phonics improves word recognition and decoding skills but produces limited (if any) gains in fluency (Blachman, 1997; Foorman, Francis, Fletcher, Schatschneider, & Mehta, 1998; Foorman, Francis, Shaywitz, Shaywitz, & Fletcher, 1997; Kame'enui, Simmons, Good, & Harm, 2001; Scanlon & Vellutino, 1996; Torgesen, Wagner, & Rashotte, 1997; Torgesen, Alexander, et al., 2001). Third, the growing body of naming speed research provides a theoretical basis for interventions that target processing speed and fluency problems (Wolf & Katzir-Cohen, 2001). Finally, there is increasing support for the view that oral reading fluency assessments provide a reliable and valid method for identifying children at risk for reading problems and monitoring their progress in intervention programs (Fuchs, Fuchs, Hosp, & Jenkins, 2001; Hintze, Shapiro, Conte, & Basile, 1997; Kaminski & Good, 1998).

Compared with word recognition, reading fluency as a construct does not have the same degree of consensus in terms of definitions, theoretical and empirical basis, assessment formats, and performance standards (Kame'enui & Simmons, 2001). Some definitions of reading fluency emphasize the automatic aspects of reading. For example, Meyer and Felton (1999) define reading fluency as the "ability to read connected text rapidly, smoothly, effortlessly, and automatically with little conscious attention to the mechanics of reading, such as decoding" (p. 284). Other definitions, including that adopted by the National Assessment of Educational Progress (NAEP), emphasize the expressive aspects of fluency and define reading fluency as "ease or 'naturalness' of reading" (National Center for Education Statistics, 1995, p. 1). This view of reading fluency emphasizes not only accurate and rapid reading but also reading in phrases and with expression appropriate to the text. The definition used in this book is based on the definition of reading fluency used in CBM research (e.g., Fuchs et al., 2001; Shinn, Good, Knutson, Tilly, & Collins, 1992), that is, *rate and accuracy in oral reading*, with *rate* defined as words per minute and *accuracy* defined as number of correctly read words. As Torgesen, Rashotte, and Alexander (2001) have observed, this definition is not only capable of empirical validation but is consistent with conceptualizations of dyslexia that emphasize the role of word-level reading problems in the disorder. In addition, rate and accuracy can be more reliably assessed than the prosodic aspects of reading (the rhythmic and tonal features of spoken language), which are difficult to quantify (Dowhower, 1991).

Reading Fluency and Reading Development

Proficient readers are able to read rapidly because they process words as *orthographic units*, that is, as integrated visual representations (Ehri, 1998). Although word recognition skill contributes to fluency, naming speed is also strongly related to the rate of reading text during the elementary grades, even after phonemic word recognition and phonological skill are controlled (Bowers, 1995a). There is now abundant evidence that children with deficits in both phonemic awareness and naming speed are the poorest readers and perform especially poorly on measures of timed reading (Bowers, 1995a; Bowers & Wolf, 1993; Cornwall, 1992; Young & Bowers, 1995). Rapid, accurate word recognition is essential to reading comprehension because it frees the reader to focus attention on the meaning of what is being read rather than on decoding (Nathan & Stanovich, 1991). The more that cognitive resources, such as attention and memory, must be focused on word recognition, the less they are available for comprehension. Thus it is not surprising that reading fluency correlates strongly with comprehension throughout the elementary grades (Fuchs, Fuchs, & Maxwell, 1988; Markell & Deno, 1997). As children progress through school, the importance of reading fluency increases, as the skill requirement shifts from *learning to read* to *reading to learn* (Chall, 1983). The critical role fluency plays in comprehension is underscored by studies reporting that training students to read words or phrases rapidly results in improved comprehension (Levy, Abello, & Lysynchuk, 1997; Tan & Nicholson, 1997).

Developing an adequate level of fluency is critical to children's future reading development, attitudes toward reading, and overall educational progress. When reading is slow and laborious, it becomes a task to be avoided rather than an enjoyable pursuit. As one low-achieving fourth grader reported in Juel's (1988) classic study following children from first through fourth grade, "I'd rather clean the mold around the bathtub than read!" (p. 442). Because poor readers spend significantly less time reading than skilled readers (Allington, 1983; Biemiller, 1977–1978; Juel et al., 1986), they lose opportunities to develop the vocabulary, verbal reasoning, and other cognitive and language skills promoted by wide reading. As noted earlier in this chapter, the consequence is the *Matthew effect* or the "rich get richer" reading phenomenon described by Stanovich (1986), in which good readers become ever more proficient in reading and language skills, whereas poor readers suffer from increasing negative effects in terms of vocabulary, comprehension, and overall cognitive development.

Assessing Contextual Reading Fluency

Four types of contextual reading fluency measures are currently available for assessing early primary grade examinees: (1) norm-referenced contextual reading fluency tests, (2) nonstandardized contextual reading fluency measures, (3) CBMs of contextual reading fluency, and (4) contextual pseudoword reading fluency measures.

Norm-Referenced Contextual Reading Fluency Measures

Until quite recently, the GORT (Gray & Robinson, 1963, 1967; Wiederholt & Bryant, 1986, 1992, 2001) was virtually the only instrument with measures of oral reading fluency (reading rate and fluency [defined as rate plus accuracy]) standardized on a sample of American school-age children. Of the 11 instruments reviewed in this book that include contextual reading fluency measures, 4 are norm-referenced. Of these, only the WJ III Reading Fluency test yields standard scores with a mean of 100 (*SD* = 15). The GORT-4 Rate and Fluency subtests yield standard scores with a mean of 10 (*SD* = 3), whereas the WIAT-II Reading Comprehension subtest provides a Reading Speed quartile score and a Reading Rate descriptive category based on a comparison of the Reading Speed and Reading Comprehension quartile scores. On the ERDA-R, which is derived from the WIAT–II, reading fluency can be assessed using the passages on the Reading Comprehension subtest, but the data are used only for qualitative analyses.

Nonstandardized Contextual Reading Fluency Measures

As a result of the growing interest in fluency as a critical component of reading proficiency and indicator of risk for reading problems, many of the nonstandardized early reading assessment batteries reviewed in this text include contextual reading fluency measures, usually beginning in Grade 1. Performance may be interpreted qualitatively or according to data from statewide or research samples. Metrics vary widely, ranging from words read correctly per minute to rating scales that incorporate aspects of speed, accuracy, and expression.

Curriculum-Based Measures of Contextual Reading Fluency

Curriculum-based procedures have frequently been used to assess oral reading fluency. A large body of research (see Allinder, Fuchs, & Fuchs, 1998, for a review) demonstrates that CBM oral reading is strongly correlated with overall reading competence and is a sensitive measure of the effectiveness of reading interventions and curricular programs, as well as of individual student progress. Because beginning readers cannot process text, traditional CBM measures are generally not useful until the second half of first grade (Fuchs & Fuchs, 1999). This book reviews two CBM-type measures—the DIBELS, which assesses subword fluency processes as well as oral reading fluency for connected text, and general CBM procedures that use the child's own instructional materials or a set of generic grade-level materials.

Contextual Pseudoword Reading Fluency Measures

One of the instruments reviewed in this text, the *Dyslexia Screening Test*, includes a unique contextual reading fluency measure that requires examinees to read a passage consisting of both real words and pseudowords. The subtest is scored for number of words read in 3 minutes, with more points awarded for accurate reading of pseudowords than for real words. Unfortunately, the utility of this measure is limited by several technical and usability factors, including the fact that only British norms are available for interpreting performance, a complex scoring system, and the restriction of derived scores to five sets of percentile ranks.

Issues in Assessing Contextual Reading Fluency

Because contextual reading fluency measures use connected text to assess student performance, the issues noted above for contextual reading accuracy measures also apply to fluency instruments. Additional considerations for fluency measures include (1) floor effects for poor and beginning readers, (2) difficulty achieving adequate levels of interscorer reliability, (3) the relative utility of silent versus oral reading fluency, (4) the most appropriate level of text difficulty, and (5) lack of agreement regarding performance standards and the most appropriate method for determining a fluency score.

Floor Effects

Because beginning readers can process little or no connected text, contextual reading fluency tests are subject to floor effects at the lower age ranges. For example, on the WJ III, a first grader aged 6-6 who answers one item correctly on the Reading Fluency test earns a standard score of 86 compared with his or her age peers. As a result, reading fluency measures are generally unable to differentiate very low performing children from children with milder fluency deficits. To address this problem, Roland Good and his colleagues at the University of Oregon have developed the DIBELS, a set of fluency-based measures that assess sublexical components of word recognition, including initial sound recognition, phonemic segmentation, and letter naming. With DIBELS, examiners can assess young children's developing fluency in the alphabetic and phonological components of reading for use in screening and progress monitoring. Moreover, the DIBELS Phoneme Segmentation Fluency measure awards credit for partially segmenting a word, which reduces floor effects and increases its sensitivity to small changes in performance. Although all of the DIBELS measures use a fluency metric, such as number of initial sounds produced in 1 minute, they are discussed in this text under the relevant domains (including "Phonological Processing," "Alphabet Knowledge," and "Oral Language") rather than in this section.

Interexaminer and Interscorer Variance

Another problem common to reading fluency measures is interexaminer and interscorer inconsistency. Accurately recording children's performance on oral reading fluency measures can be challenging, even for experienced examiners. Some test authors recommend audiotaping examinee performance for later scoring, a practice that enhances scoring reliability but increases scoring time and may affect children's performance by making them feel self-conscious. Studies of CBM in oral reading invariably report very high levels of interscorer consistency (e.g., Fuchs & Deno, 1992; Hintze, Shapiro, & Lutz, 1994; Hintze et al., 1997); however, because these results are typically based on scoring by researchers or trained research assistants, it is not clear whether school- or clinic-based practitioners or classroom teachers would achieve similar consistency levels. Most norm-referenced reading fluency tests also report high levels of interscorer reliability, but these estimates provide little useful information because they are nearly always based on completed protocols rather than on simultaneous independent scoring by two or more examiners during actual or audiotaped testing sessions.

Oral versus Silent Reading Formats

There is surprisingly little research regarding the relative utility of silent versus oral reading formats in assessing reading fluency for school-age children. The only contextual reading fluency measure with a silent reading format reviewed in this text is the WJ III Reading Fluency test. This measure requires examinees to read short sentences aloud and indicate whether the sentence is true or not by circling *yes* or *no* (e.g., "An owl is a bird . . . . Y N"). Two other standardized tests reviewed in this text–the WIAT-II and the ERDA-R, which is derived from the WIAT-II–permit either silent or oral reading for the passages used to assess comprehension and generate a fluency score based on the amount of time required to read all of the stories administered. Despite the fact that silent reading is the norm for older readers, the reliability and validity of fluency assessments based on silent reading formats are questionable for early primary grade children. Poor readers tend to skim the passages rather than attempting to decode each word, resulting in spuriously high reading rates and the possibility of failing to identify children with fluency problems. Moreover, because reading is done silently, examiners are unable to conduct error analyses for diagnostic and intervention planning purposes.

Level of Text Difficulty

Very few empirical studies have been conducted to determine the level of difficulty at which fluency should be evaluated–that is, frustration, instructional, or independent. Most researchers and test authors assess reading fluency with materials at a child's instructional level, based on the child's current grade placement or score on graded word lists. The early literacy battery *Fox in a Box* provides different sets of passages for assessing accuracy and fluency; fluency passages are set at a readability level one semester lower than accuracy passages to help examiners determine the level of text a child can read independently.

Differences in Performance Standards and Methods for Calculating Fluency Scores

There is also a lack of consensus among researchers and test authors regarding oral reading fluency performance standards that indicate adequate levels of proficiency. In other words, how fluent should children be at specific grade levels to be making satisfactory reading progress? As Table 3.19 below reveals, fluency norms and recommended reading rates vary considerably from study to study and test to test. For example, the *Basic Early Assessment of Reading* (BEAR) suggests an end of Grade 1 goal of 80 words read per minute (WPM), whereas the goals set by DIBELS and *Fox in a Box* are half that rate—40 words read correctly per minute (WCPM). On the *Texas Primary Reading Inventory* (TPRI), a score of 40 WCPM or less at the end of Grade 1 indicates a need for additional instruction rather than satisfactory achievement. For the end of Grade 2, the range of recommended or normative reading rates is even greater, from a low of 60 WCPM for *Fox in a Box* to a high of 98 WCPM for Shapiro's (1989) research norms. Still other early reading assessment batteries, such as Virginia's PALS, evaluate oral reading fluency using a 3-point scale derived from the NAEP standards (National Center for Education Statistics, 1995), as well as evaluating WPM.

The variation in performance standards across normative samples and reading instruments is complicated by the fact that different authors use different methods for calculating oral reading fluency. Most oral reading fluency measures use the following formula to calculate rate: number of words read correctly (total number of words read minus errors), multiplied by 60, and divided by the number of seconds required to read the passage. For example, if a child reads correctly 80 of 100 words in a passage in 80 seconds, the oral reading fluency rate is 60 words correct per minute ([100 – 20 = 80] × 60/80 = 4,800/80 = 60 WCPM). On CBM oral reading probes, reading rate is calculated according to the number of words read correctly in the first minute, that is, the number of words read in 60 seconds minus the number of errors. Some of the measures reviewed in this text do not subtract errors from total number of words, however, resulting in a reading rate metric based entirely on speed, that is, words read per minute (WPM) rather than WCPM. The diversity in performance standards and methods of calculating reading rate is evident in Table 3.19, which presents Grade 1 and Grade 2 fluency norms for three research samples and benchmarks on guidelines for five early reading assessment batteries.

Measures of Contextual Reading Fluency

Beginning in first grade, early reading assessments should include measures of fluency as well as accuracy in order to identify children who read accurately but slowly. Although young dysfluent readers will have difficulty keeping up with the pace of classroom instruction, they are unlikely to be identified using traditional standardized tests of reading accuracy (Berninger, Abbott, Billingsley, et al., 2001). Assessing reading fluency in addition to reading accuracy yields critical information not only for diagnosis of risk status, but also for intervention planning. As Kame'enui and colleagues (2001) have observed, a first grader who reads 65 words with 5 errors in 4 minutes on a grade-level passage is a very different reader from a first grader who

TABLE 3.19. Oral Reading Fluency Norms for Three Research Samples and Benchmarks or Guidelines for Five Early Reading Assessment Batteries

Name and date of sample/*measure*	End of Grade 1	End of Grade 2
Basic Early Assessment of Reading (BEAR) (2002); Oral Reading Fluency Assessment[a]	80 WPM	90 WPM
CBM oral reading fluency norms (Hasbrouck & Tindal, 1992)[d]	Not assessed	94 WCPM
CBM oral reading fluency norms (Marston & Magnusson, 1985)[c]	71 WCPM	82 WCPM
CBM oral reading fluency norms (Shapiro, 1989)[b]	69 WCPM	98 WCPM
Dynamic Indicators of Basic Skills (DIBELS) (2002); Oral Reading Fluency	40 WCPM	90 WCPM
Fox in a Box (2000), Reading Fluency	40 WCPM	60 WCPM
Phonological Awareness Litreacy Screening (PALS) (2002), Oral Reading Fluency Assessment	WPM[e]	WPM[e]
Texas Primary Reading Inventory (2002), Reading Fluency	60 WCPM	90 WCPM

Note. WCPM, words read correctly per minute; WPM, words read per minute.
[a]Reading rates on the BEAR are described as general guidelines rather than benchmarks.
[b]Norms date not reported; n = 2,720 students in Grades 1–6.
[c]Norms collected in 1983–1984, n = 8,160 students in Grades 1–6.
[d]Norms collected in 1981–1990; n = 7,000 to 9,000 students in Grades 2–5.
[e]Benchmarks under development.

reads 65 words with 5 errors in 1 minute. Despite their identical levels of reading accuracy, their performances represent very different levels of reading proficiency and have different implications for classroom performance, diagnosis, and remediation. I recommend calculating WCPM using standard CBM procedures with a specified prompt time rather than calculating WPM to avoid the possible underidentification of children with fluency problems. Table 3.20 summarizes the characteristics of the 11 reading fluency measures reviewed in this book. Each instrument with more than one fluency measure is presented in the table as a single entry in the interests of readability and space.

PRINT RESOURCES

Rathvon, N. (1999). *Effective school interventions: Strategies for enhancing academic achievement and social competence*. New York: Guilford Press.

This handbook of empirically based classroom interventions includes step-by-step procedures for conducting CBM in oral reading, as well as sets of research norms for interpreting the results. Reading interventions target fluency, vocabulary, and comprehension.

Wolf, M. (Ed.). (2001). *Dyslexia, fluency, and the brain*. Timonium, MD: York Press.

This edited book includes contributions by leading researchers in the United States and around the world organized according to three basic questions: (1) What are the nature and extent of time-related deficits in dyslexia; (2) What are the sources of time-related deficits; and (3) What interventions are effective in addressing fluency problems in reading?

TABLE 3.20. Measures of Contextual Reading Fluency

Name and date of *measure*; subtest	Admin. time (minutes)	Norms/ benchmarks	Testing task	Comments
Basic Early Assessment of Reading (2002); Oral Reading Fluency Assessment	3–20	CR; Grades K–3	Reading isolated letters aloud (kindergarten, untimed); reading graded passages aloud (Grades 1–3, timed)	Includes a retelling component; reading rate is based on WPM, not WCPM; retelling and oral expression are scored on a 4-point scale
Curriculum-based measurement (CBM) in oral reading	5–10	NS; Grades 1– 2	Reading aloud passages drawn from the curriculum or graded materials for 1 minute	Performance is evaluated based on the median score of three oral reading probes; excellent for local norming
Dynamic Indicators of Basic Early Literacy Skills (2002); Oral Reading Fluency	5–15	NS; benchmarks for Grades 1–3	Reading graded passages aloud for 1 minute	Procedures identical with CBM oral reading probes; passages are drawn from end-of-year material
Dyslexia Screening Test (1996); Nonsense Passage Reading	5	British norms for ages 6-6 through 16-5	Reading aloud a passage consisting of real words and pseudowords	Yields only five percentile ranks; complex scoring system
Early Reading Diagnostic Assessment–Revised (2002); Reading Rate	5–10	NS; Grades 1–3	Supplemental score based on the time required for silent or oral passage reading on the Reading Comprehension subtest	Yields data for qualitative analysis only
Fox in a Box (2000); Reading Fluency, Reading Expression	5-7	CR; benchmarks for Grades 1 and 2	Reading graded passages aloud; reading expression is scored on a 3-point scale	Fluency assessments use material that is set at one semester below that for accuracy assessments
Gray Oral Reading Tests–4 (2001); Rate, Fluency (Rate + Accuracy)	15–45	Norms for ages 6-0 through 13-11	Reading graded passages aloud; rate and accuracy are scored on a 6-point scale and then summed to yield a fluency score	Permits comparisons of reading fluency and comprehension in the same norm-referenced instrument; floor effects for younger examinees
Phonological Awareness Literacy Screening (2002); Reading Fluency, Reading Rate	5–15	CR; Virginia benchmarks for Grades 1–3 (optional)	Reading graded passages aloud; reading fluency is rated on a 3-point holistic scale	Reading rate score reflects only speed (WPM), not speed plus accuracy (WCPM)
Texas Primary Reading Inventory (2002); Reading Fluency	5–7	CR; Texas benchmarks for Grades 1 and 2	Reading graded passages aloud; scored for the same selection as the Reading Accuracy task	Fluency is defined as WCPM

(continued)

TABLE 3.20. *(continued)*

Name and date of *measure*; subtest	Admin. time (minutes)	Norms/ benchmarks	Testing task	Comments
Wechsler Individual Achievement Test–II (2001); Reading Speed, Reading Rate	10–20	Norms for ages 6-0 through 85+ and Grades 1–12	Supplemental scores based on reading time for Reading Comprehension (RC) subtest passages (Reading Speed [RS]) and the relationship between RS and RC quartile scores (Reading Rate); examinees may read silently or aloud	Quartile scores only; Reading Rate is plotted on a graph on the record form comparing speed with comprehension
Woodcock–Johnson III Tests of Achievement (2001); Reading Fluency	4–5	Norms for 2-0 through 90+ and Grades K–18	Silently reading sentences, deciding whether they are true, and circling *Y* or *N* (3-minute time limit)	Measures reading comprehension as well as fluency; floor effects for young examinees

Note. CR, criterion-referenced measure; NS, nonstandardized measure.

Reading Comprehension

Comprehension, the ability to derive meaning from text, is the ultimate goal of reading, and good reading comprehension is the most critical element in school learning (Cornoldi & Oakhill, 1996). According to Gough's "simple view of reading" (Gough, 1996; Hoover & Gough, 1990), reading comprehension is the product of two component skills: (1) recognizing words on the page and (2) understanding the words once they have been recognized. That is, reading (R) equals the product of decoding (D) and linguistic comprehension (C), or $R = D \times C$. From this perspective, impairment in reading comprehension can arise from deficits in either or both of the component skills. Children will be unable to understand the meaning of a text if they cannot identify most of the words. Similarly, children with a limited knowledge of the subject of the text or the meanings of many of the words will have poor comprehension even if they are able to decode the words accurately.

In contrast to the voluminous research focusing on the development of decoding and word recognition skills, much less attention has been focused on reading comprehension, including its development, the nature and causes of comprehension problems, and ways of measuring it (Snow, 2002). Assessment of comprehension and comprehension-related skills is critical, however, because some types of future poor readers—notably, garden-variety poor readers and children with language disorders—will need special assistance to develop the oral language skills that underlie adequate reading comprehension (Torgesen & Wagner, 1998). Because beginning readers cannot read connected text, early reading screening batteries and multisubject achievement tests often substitute measures of listening comprehension for reading comprehension tests at the kindergarten level.

DETERMINANTS OF READING COMPREHENSION

For beginning readers, measures of word identification and phonemic decoding are the best predictors of reading comprehension, better than IQ or verbal ability (Foorman, Francis, Fletcher, et al., 1997; Gough & Tunmer, 1986; Stanovich, 1991; Vellutino et al., 1991). In first grade, decoding ability accounts for about 80% of the variance in reading comprehension (Foorman, Francis, Fletcher, et al., 1997). Thus, for early primary grade children, deficiencies in decoding skills are the primary constraint on reading comprehension (Badian, 2001; Olson et al., 1994; Shankweiler et al., 1999). Slow, inaccurate word recognition limits reading comprehension in two ways. First, failure to identify the individual words in text reduces comprehension for the material. Second, if decoding is slow and laborious, children will have trouble recalling what they have read and will have few cognitive resources left for comprehension.

As children move through the elementary grades, cognitive and linguistic abilities have an increasing impact on reading comprehension compared with decoding because word recognition becomes more automatic and text demands increase for semantic, syntactic, and other language-based skills (Hoover & Gough, 1990; Torgesen, Wagner, Rashotte, et al., 1997). For example, Joshi and colleagues (1998) found that correlations between reading comprehension and listening comprehension for a sample of children in Grades 3 through 6 ranged from .61 to .75, with listening comprehension serving as a better predictor of reading comprehension among older than among younger children. For children with reading problems, however, the predictive power of decoding remains high throughout the elementary grades because of the constraints it places on comprehension. In a study that included children with a wide range of reading proficiencies in Grades 2–3 and Grades 6–7 (Vellutino, Scanlon, & Tanzman, 1994), listening comprehension was the best predictor of reading comprehension for all analyses with the exception of the younger poor readers. For these children, word identification was still the best predictor of reading comprehension.

Because most texts for beginning readers use simple, high-frequency words, children with poor phonemic decoding skills may be able to maintain adequate reading comprehension skills through the end of second grade by memorizing a small sight word vocabulary. These children are at risk for future reading comprehension problems, however, because of their overreliance on memory-based reading strategies and limited ability to decode unfamiliar words (see Juel et al., 1986). With the introduction of more diverse vocabulary beginning in Grade 3, children with poor decoding skills begin to show declines in reading comprehension when compared with better decoders. In a cross-sectional study with second- and third-grade children (Freebody & Byrne, 1988), children who were more proficient in exception word reading (an index of sight word recognition) but weaker in pseudoword decoding were better comprehenders in second grade than those who were stronger in decoding and weaker in exception word reading. For third-grade students, however, the pattern was reversed: Whereas better decoders were much more proficient in reading comprehension, the children who had displayed better initial levels of sight word recognition had lost ground in comprehension. This pattern was replicated in a longitudinal follow-up study (Byrne, Freebody, & Gates, 1992) examining changes in reading skills for two groups of children with discrepancies between their decoding and comprehension skills. Children who were initially relatively weak in pseudoword decoding and relatively strong in sight word recognition were also initially better comprehenders than children who were stronger in decoding and weaker in sight word recognition. By third grade, however, their relative standing had reversed: The early better decoders were now the better comprehenders, and the early poorer decoders had lost ground in comprehension.

Decoding continues to contribute to comprehension throughout the elementary grades and into the high school years. In an analysis (Foorman, Francis, Shaywitz, et al., 1997) of the relation between decoding and comprehension in the Connecticut Longitudinal Study (Shaywitz et al., 1990, 1992), Grade 1 and 2 decoding skills accounted for between 25% and 36% of the variability in Grade 9 comprehension—a surprisingly large amount, considering that comprehension involves a wide range of processes that extend beyond word recognition.

IQ and Reading Comprehension

Although intelligence test scores are not reliable predictors of word-level reading skills, including word recognition and decoding (Fletcher et al., 1994; Foorman, Francis, Fletcher, et al., 1997; Stanovich & Siegel, 1994; Vellutino et al., 2000), IQ, especially verbal IQ, is strongly associated with reading comprehension in the later primary and elementary grade years. This is not surprising, given that reading comprehension involves the kinds of oral language abilities that are typically assessed in IQ tests, such as vocabulary knowledge, general information, and verbal reasoning. In other words, verbal IQ may predict reading comprehension because it serves as a proxy for oral language comprehension. In a study with Dutch children (de Jong & van der Leij, 2002), verbal IQ had substantial effects on reading comprehension from second to fifth grade, even when prior reading skills were taken into account, with the amount increasing across the grades. Similarly, in a longitudinal study evaluating reading growth from second to fourth and third to fifth grade (Torgesen, Wagner, Rashotte, Burgess, et al., 1997), the influence of verbal ability, as measured by the Vocabulary subtest on the *Stanford–Binet Intelligence Test* (Thorndike, Hagen, & Sattler, 1986), increased across the elementary grades. Whereas Grade 2 vocabulary explained 24% of the variance in Grade 4 reading comprehension, Grade 3 vocabulary explained 43% of the variance in Grade 5 reading comprehension.

The same pattern of relationships found between IQ and specific reading skills also applies in the prediction of treatment response. Although verbal IQ does not predict growth in decoding skills (Foorman, Francis, Fletcher, et al., 1997; Stanovich & Siegel, 1994, Vellutino et al., 2000), it is a significant unique predictor of response to reading interventions when growth is evaluated using reading comprehension criterion measures. In a large intervention study of 7-year-olds with a wide range of IQs, Hatcher and Hulme (1999) evaluated the relative efficacy of various predictors of responsiveness to remedial reading instruction as measured by growth in decoding and reading comprehension skills. Although IQ was not a significant predictor of how well children responded to remedial teaching in terms of decoding, individual differences in verbal IQ were predictive of responsiveness to remedial instruction in terms of gains in reading comprehension. Similarly, in a longitudinal intervention study comparing the effectiveness of three instructional approaches for preventing reading disabilities in young children with phonological skill deficits (Torgesen, Wagner, Rashotte, Rose, et al., 1999), the best predictors of growth in reading comprehension were rapid naming, behavior ratings, and either verbal ability, as estimated by the Listening Comprehension test on the WJ-R, or SES.

READING SUBTYPES WITH COMPREHENSION DEFICITS

In the early primary grades, decoding and comprehension skills are highly correlated, so that the vast majority of children with good decoding skills also have good comprehension skills and poor decoders are also poor comprehenders. Nevertheless, deficits can occur in one component relatively independently of the other, giving rise to different forms of comprehension problems. Research (e.g., Aaron et al., 1999; Kamhi & Catts, 2002; Stothard & Hulme, 1996) has consistently identified a subset of children with reading problems whose decoding and reading comprehension skills are discrepant. Table 3.21 presents three reading subtypes that all display reading comprehension problems but for different reasons.

Individuals with *hyperlexia*, who are sometimes termed "word callers," display advanced decoding skills but have difficulty understanding what they have read because of pronounced cognitive, social, and language deficiencies (Aram, 1997; Aram & Healy, 1988; Nation, 1999). In its extreme form, hyperlexia is associated with developmental disabilities, such as autism, schizophrenia, and mental retardation. Individuals with *dyslexia*, who have average to advanced listening comprehension skills, nevertheless exhibit problems in reading comprehension because they are such slow and inaccurate decoders that they cannot understand what they read. *Garden-variety poor readers* are impaired in both word recognition and listening comprehension abilities. These children do not have specific reading impairments but general language comprehension problems arising from poor verbal/semantic skills (Stothard & Hulme, 1996). Thus, although all three subtypes exhibit reading comprehension problems, those problems have different causes and require different forms of intervention.

Although there is very little research on the incidence of hyperlexia, practitioners, including myself, occasionally encounter children who can read rapidly and accurately but are unable to demonstrate an understanding of what they have read. For the vast majority of these children, their comprehension difficulties do not reflect a deficit confined to reading but a generalized limitation in oral language comprehension (see Stothard & Hulme, 1996). In a large study of early elementary grade children, including many with reading problems, Shankweiler and colleagues (1999) examined patterns of decoding and reading comprehension. As expected, reading comprehension was highly correlated with real word and pseudoword reading (.89 and .91, respectively), whereas listening comprehension was only moderately corre-

TABLE 3.21. Reading Subtypes with Poor Reading Comprehension Skills

Reading subtype	Decoding skills	Listening comprehension skills	Reading comprehension skills
Hyperlexics	Advanced	Poor	Poor
Dyslexics	Poor	Average to superior	Poor
Garden-variety poor readers	Poor	Poor	Poor

lated with reading comprehension (.58). Very few children (9%) displayed better reading comprehension than would be expected from their decoding skills, and even fewer children (5%) showed the opposite pattern (i.e., the "word caller" pattern).

Attention-Deficit/Hyperactivity Disorder and Comprehension Deficits

Researchers and practitioners alike have speculated that children with attention-deficit/hyperactivity disorder (ADHD) may be especially likely to have poor reading comprehension because of deficits in working memory, executive functioning, and other reading-related cognitive skills that interfere with their ability to attend to what they are reading and monitor their own understanding. Surprisingly few studies have evaluated comprehension skills for children with ADHD, however, and at this point there is little evidence that ADHD is a major predictor of either word reading or reading comprehension (Shaywitz, Fletcher, & Shaywitz, 1994; Wood & Felton, 1994). In a study with the children from the Connecticut Longitudinal Study, Shaywitz and colleagues (1994) reported that attention measures failed to explain significant variance in word recognition once phonological measures had been considered. Attention measures did account for a small but significant amount of variance (1.5%) in silent reading comprehension beyond what was explained by language variables. Some research suggests that the extent to which children with ADHD exhibit comprehension problems depends on the type of measure used to assess comprehension. In a study (Purvis & Tannick, 1997) with four groups of children aged 7 to 11 (ADHD-only, ADHD and reading disabilities, reading disabilities, and normal controls), comprehension measured in terms of number of story units recalled did not differentiate among the groups. Nevertheless, children with ADHD, regardless of their reading status, displayed significantly more errors in their verbal productions than did children with reading disabilities and normal controls.

ASSESSING READING COMPREHENSION

Most of the reading comprehension measures in norm-referenced multisubject achievement tests and multiskill reading tests are inappropriate for early primary grade children because the passages begin at too high a level. There are five different types of reading comprehension measures with utility for early primary grade examinees: (1) word comprehension measures, (2) passage comprehension measures, (3) story retelling measures, (4) cloze-procedure measures, and (5) curriculum-based measures of oral reading. Some instruments evaluate reading comprehension and reading accuracy (and often reading rate as well) using the same set of passages. That is, the child reads a passage aloud while the examiner records deviations from print and reading rate, after which the child responds to a set of comprehension questions about what has been read.

Word Comprehension Measures

Also called *reading vocabulary tests*, word comprehension measures assess reading comprehension at the single word level. Word comprehension tests typically include three types of tasks: synonyms, antonyms, and analogies. These tasks assess a combination of skills, including word retrieval, lexical knowledge, and verbal reasoning, especially for word analogy tasks. Comparing children's performance on passage comprehension tests with their performance on word comprehension tests can provide useful information for diagnosis and instructional planning. Early primary grade children with weak decoding skills often perform more poorly on word comprehension measures than on passage comprehension measures because of the absence of pictorial and context clues.

Example (analogy item): "*Fish* is to *swim* as *bird* is to . . . " (*fly*)

Passage Comprehension Measures

The most common format for assessing reading comprehension is *passage reading*, which requires the child to read a passage silently or aloud and answer one or more questions. Performance on passage comprehension tests is influenced by a variety of language and verbal reasoning skills, including lexical, semantic, and syntactic knowledge. Passage comprehension measures vary along several dimensions, including whether the child is permitted access to the previously read passage while answering the comprehension questions, whether the child or the examiner reads the questions, whether the response format is multiple-choice or open-ended, and whether the child responds orally or by marking an answer. Each type of passage comprehension test measures a somewhat different set of skills. For example, tests on which the child is not permitted to review the passage while answering the questions have a large verbal memory component. Performance levels on passage comprehension tests are also influenced by the degree to which questions are *passage-independent*, that is, the extent to which children can correctly infer the answers without having read or understood the text. When questions are passage-independent, reading comprehension for connected text is confounded with word recognition skills and background knowledge.

Story Retelling Measures

When used to assess reading comprehension rather than listening comprehension, story retelling measures require children to retell in their own words a story they have just read without access to the previously read material. Most tests for early primary grade examinees use oral rather than written response formats in order to avoid confounding reading comprehension problems with written language deficits. On the other hand, performance on story retelling tasks with oral response formats may confound reading problems with language deficits because children with expressive language problems may be able to understand the meaning of a story without being able to retell it proficiently (Gunning, 1998). Scoring may be holistic, based on overall comprehension competence, or analytic, based on the quantity and quality of recall for specific story elements. Because of the degree of subjective judgment involved in scoring, story retelling measures tend to be less reliable than other kinds of reading comprehension measures.

Cloze-Procedure Measures

In the *cloze procedure*, certain words are deleted from a reading passage, and the child is required to provide appropriate words for each deletion, usually orally. Deleted words may be key words, or they may be randomly selected (e.g., every seventh word in the passage). In the *modified cloze procedure,* also known as the *maze procedure,* the child chooses from among several options, so that the task becomes a multiple-choice format. The Passage Comprehension tests on the WJ III and WRMT-R/NU use a variation of the modified cloze procedure, in which a single key word is deleted in a sentence or a short passage. Items for beginning readers are often accompanied by pictures. Cloze-procedure formats are based on the assumption that examinees will not be able to provide the correct word unless they have understood the meaning of the sentence or passage and tap lexical knowledge, word retrieval, and knowledge of syntax and text structures in addition to reading comprehension skills. Most tests that use cloze procedures do not have time restrictions. As Joshi (1995) has observed, however, under untimed conditions, children are sometimes able to figure out the correct answer on cloze-procedure tests from pictorial or context clues, even if they cannot read all the words.

Example (accompanied by a picture of a boat in a lake): "*The boat is sailing on the* ________." (*lake, pond*)

Curriculum-Based Measurement (CBM) of Reading Comprehension

Although curriculum-based measurement (CBM) in reading is primarily used to assess reading fluency, the standard procedures include an option for evaluating comprehension. Step-by-step procedures for evaluating comprehension using CBM-type procedures are provided elsewhere (Rathvon, 1999; Shinn, 1989). Interpretation is criterion-referenced and based on informal reading inventory guidelines, with 80% accuracy for the five to eight questions typically asked indicating instructional level. The comprehension option in CBM oral reading can serve as a quick screener for determining whether a child can understand the text in which he or she is currently placed. Examiners should note that although CBM comprehension assessments are high in content validity because they are based on a child's classroom curriculum, they have several disadvantages. First, they are likely to yield relatively unreliable results because the questions are nonstandardized; that is, examiners must create the questions for each reading selection. Second, although research (Fuchs et al., 1988; Hintze et al., 1997; Kranzler, Brownell, & Miller, 1998) indicates that CBM oral reading rate is significantly correlated with performance on formal and informal reading comprehension criterion measures, no studies have been conducted comparing performance levels for the same set of examinees on comprehension assessments based on CBM-type procedures with performance on norm-referenced comprehension tests. Third, CBM in oral reading is not generally useful until the second semester of first grade because beginning readers are so limited in the degree to which they can access connected text.

ISSUES IN ASSESSING READING COMPREHENSION

The current available reading comprehension instruments have been criticized by practitioners and researchers alike on a variety of grounds, including failure to represent the complexity of the comprehension process; lack of a standardized assessment strategy; inadequate levels of reliability and validity; and confounding comprehension with vocabulary, background knowledge, word reading, and other skills (Murphy, 1998; Snow, 2002). Assessing reading comprehension in early primary grade examinees is further complicated by the fact that beginning readers have minimal contextual reading skills. This section reviews two major issues in assessing reading comprehension performance in early primary grade children: floor effects and variations in test formats.

Floor Effects

Because beginning readers have limited word and text reading skills, the vast majority of the norm-referenced reading comprehension tests reviewed in this book show floor effects at the lower age and grade ranges. As a result of variations in test floors, different measures can produce very different representations of reading comprehension skills in the same examinee (see Table 3.22 below). In an effort to improve sensitivity to individual differences in the comprehension skills of younger and less proficient readers, the latest editions of several multisubject batteries, including the WJ III and the WIAT-II, have increased the number of easy and sublexical items at the beginning of their reading comprehension measures. For example, early items may require examinees to match rebuses and pictures, single words and pictures, and phrases and pictures.

Variations in Test Formats

Perhaps no other domain of reading encompasses such a wide range of test formats. Among the features that vary among reading comprehension tests for early primary grade examinees are (1) level of measurement (word, sentence, or passage); (2) text type (narrative or expository); (3) reading format (silent or aloud); (4) response format (oral or written; multiple-choice, single-word, or open-ended); (5) time constraints (untimed or time limits per item); (6) types of skills assessed (main idea, sequence, cause and effect, etc.); and (7) types of questions (literal, inferential, or lexical). The discussion below focuses on issues relative to three of these feature and format variations.

Types of Comprehension Skills Assessed

There is no general consensus on the types of reading comprehension skills that should be measured, especially for young readers whose ability to read connected text is in the rudimentary stages (see Snow, 2002). Although some test manuals provide information about the types of skills measured and the number of items measuring each one (e.g., matching pictures with words, recognizing details, drawing conclusions, identifying the main idea, etc.), others include only a general discussion of the skills assessed. Examiners should consult the manual or, if necessary, review the test items, to determine whether the skills sampled by the test match those being taught in the classroom and whether content coverage is adequate.

Silent versus Oral Reading Formats

By necessity, group-administered standardized reading comprehension tests use a silent reading format, in which examinees respond to questions by marking one of several choices or, on open-ended formats, by giving some kind of written answer. Some test authors (e.g., Brown et al., 1995) have argued that silent reading formats are also more appropriate for assessing comprehension on individually administered tests because mature readers usually read silently and because silent reading reduces or eliminates performance anxiety factors. Although silent and oral reading rates are highly correlated in elementary grade children (Barker et al., 1992), there is virtually no research comparing comprehension levels obtained on silent versus oral reading measures for early primary grade children. On the one hand, silent reading tests may provide more accurate assessments of beginning readers' comprehension abilities because children may focus on reading accurately rather than comprehending the meaning of the text when reading aloud. On the other hand, silent reading formats make it impossible to determine whether examinees have actually read the stimulus material, are answering randomly, or are guessing based on their ability to decode a few key words and make inferences from pictorial and context clues.

Multiple-Choice versus Constructed Responses

Most of the reading comprehension tests reviewed in this text use a constructed response format that requires a single word or extended verbal production, rather than a multiple-choice response format that requires selecting the correct response from a set of choices. Tests with a multiple-choice format, such as the GORT-4, measure recognition rather than recall or construction of meaning. Although they tend to be more reliable than constructed-response tests, they also yield less information for diagnosis and instructional planning and are subject to guessing (Gunning, 1998).

THE CASE OF JACQUELINE: POOR, LOW AVERAGE, OR AVERAGE COMPREHENDER?

Given the diversity of formats and psychometric characteristics, it is not surprising that research comparing norm-referenced reading comprehension tests has consistently found that different tests yield significantly different scores for the same set of examinees (e.g., McCabe, Margolis, & Barenbaum, 2001; Slate, 1996; Wickes & Slate, 1999). For example, in a study with African American students aged 6–16 referred for a psychological evaluation or reevaluation (Wickes & Slate, 1999), reading comprehension subtests on the *Wechsler Individual Achievement Test* (Psychological Corporation, 1992b) and *Woodcock Reading Mastery Tests–Revised* were only moderately correlated (r = .42). Moreover, the reading comprehension subtests shared much less variance than did the basic reading subtests (18% vs. 38%, respectively).

Even when tests use similar formats, significant performance differences can occur. Table 3.22 displays the standard scores obtained by Jacqueline, a second grader aged 8-1, on four norm-referenced reading comprehension tests. All of the tests use a contextual reading format, all require the examinee to respond orally to comprehension questions, and all were normed within 3 years of each other. The tests were administered in alphabetical order over a 2-week period. Depending on

TABLE 3.22. Test Formats, Scoring Systems, and Scores Obtained by a Second Grader on Four Standardized Reading Comprehension Tests

Name and date of *test*; subtest	Test format	Scoring	Obtained standard score[a]	Test floor for age 8-1[b]
Gray Oral Reading Tests–4, Form A (2001); Comprehension	Timed oral passage reading; examiner-read multiple-choice questions	Dichotomous	5 (75)	2 (60)
Standardized Reading Inventory–2, Form A (1999); Passage Comprehension	Oral and silent passage reading; examiner-read open-ended questions	Dichotomous	8 (90)	3 (65)
Wechsler Individual Achievement Test–II (2001); Reading Comprehension	Oral sentence reading and silent or oral passage reading; passages are timed beginning with the Grade 3 start point; examiner-read open-ended questions	Scored 0/2 or on a 3-point scale	82[c]	49
Woodcock–Johnson III Tests of Achievement, Form A (2001); Passage Comprehension	Silent or oral reading of modified cloze items; no item consists of more than three sentences	Dichotomous	81[c]	29

[a]Standard scores are based on age norms. For subtests that yield standard scores with a mean of 10 and standard deviation of 3, the corresponding standard score with a mean of 100 and standard deviation of 15 has been added for comparison purposes in the last two columns.
[b]A *test floor* is defined as the standard score corresponding to a raw score of 1. On the Rasch-based *Woodcock–Johnson III* Passage Comprehension test, the test floor was calculated by entering a raw score of 1 in the software scoring program for a child aged 8-1 in January of Grade 2.
[c]The number correct for these tests includes items below the basal.

the measure, Jacqueline's reading comprehension skills are rated from poor to the low end of the average range (standard scores = 75–90).

MEASURES OF READING COMPREHENSION

Table 3.23 describes 18 reading comprehension measures, ranging from group-administered tests requiring written responses to individually administered measures with open-ended oral response formats. Because floors on norm-referenced tests are inadequate at the lower age ranges and because comprehension measures on nonstandardized reading screening instruments tend to be brief, children who score poorly on reading comprehension measures should receive additional assessments of decoding (real words and pseudowords) and language skills, including listening comprehension, for the purposes of differential diagnosis and intervention planning. For children who can comprehend text when they listen but not when they read it for themselves, deficits in decoding and word recognition are likely to be the major factors contributing to their poor reading comprehension. Children with poor performance on both listening and reading comprehension tests are more likely to have generalized language problems that will require additional interventions to help them improve their weak verbal and semantic skills.

TABLE 3.23. Measures of Reading Comprehension

Name and date of *measure*; subtest	Admin. time (minutes)	Norms/ benchmarks	Testing task	Comments
Basic Early Assessment of Reading (2002); Comprehension	30–40 (GA)	CR; Grades 1–3	Answering multiple-choice questions in response to examiner directions and after silently reading passages	Part of an early literacy battery with three sets of comprehension assessments (screening, diagnostic, and summative)
Curriculum-based measurement (CBM) in oral reading; comprehension option	3–5 per passage	CR (e.g., 80% accuracy)	Answering orally presented questions after reading a passage from classroom curricular materials aloud	Quick comprehension screener; examiner must develop comprehension questions
Early Reading Diagnostic Assessment–Revised (2002); Reading Comprehension	5–15	Norms for Grades 1–3	Reading sentences aloud and passages silently or aloud and answering examiner-read questions; reading passages may be timed; early items require matching pictures with words	Decile scores only; yields separate scores for target words in sentences and passage reading; derived from the WIAT-II (see below)
Fox in a Box (2000); Reading Comprehension	5–10	CR; benchmarks for Grades 1 and 2	Answering questions after reading a story aloud and retelling it; single score based on a 3-point rating scale for prediction, story retelling, and comprehension skills	Part of an early literacy battery that follows the child through the first three grades
Gray Oral Reading Tests–4 (2001); Comprehension	10–45	Norms for ages 6-0 through 18-11	Timed passage reading, followed by answering examiner-read multiple-choice questions	Modeled on informal reading inventories; floor effects throughout most of the early primary grade range
Group Reading Assessment and Diagnostic Evaluation (2002); Sentence Comprehension	15–18 (GA)	Norms for Grades 1–postsecondary	Silently reading a sentence with a missing word and marking the one of four or five words best representing the meaning of that word	Multiple-choice format; modified cloze procedure
Group Reading Assessment and Diagnostic Evaluation (2002); Passage Comprehension	20–30 (GA)	Norms for Grades 1–postsecondary	Silently reading passages and answering multiple-choice questions	Format similar to traditional group-administered standardized reading tests
Phonological Awareness Literacy Screening (2002); Comprehension	3–5 per passage	NS; Grades 1–3	Marking answers to multiple-choice questions after reading a passage aloud	Part of a statewide early reading assessment battery; no benchmarks to date

(continued)

TABLE 3.23. *(continued)*

Name and date of *measure*; subtest	Admin. time (minutes)	Norms/ benchmarks	Testing task	Comments
Process Assessment of the Learner: Test Battery for Reading and Writing (2001); Story Retell	5–10	Norms for kindergarten	Answering questions about a story and retelling it	Decile scores only
Process Assessment of the Learner: Test Battery for Reading and Writing (2001); Sentence Sense	3–4	Norms for Grades K–6	Silently reading sets of sentences and identifying the one sentence that makes sense; the score is the number of correct responses on items completed in 2 minutes	Decile scores only; also measures syntactic and semantic knowledge
Standardized Reading Inventory–2 (1999); Passage Comprehension	10–30	Norms for ages 6-0 through 14-6	Answering examiner-read questions after reading passages aloud and then silently	Modeled after an informal reading inventory; floor effects for younger examinees
Standardized Reading Inventory–2 (1999); Predictive Comprehension	2–5 per passage	Raw scores only; ages 6-0 through 14-6	From a set of examiner-read sentences, selecting the sentence that would come next in a passage after orally reading and then silently rereading the passage	Supplemental measure on a norm-referenced battery; very time-consuming; limited utility, especially for younger examinees
Texas Primary Reading Inventory (2002); Reading Comprehension	5–10	CR; Texas benchmarks for Grades 1 and 2	Answering examiner-read questions after reading a story aloud	Provides separate scores for explicit versus implicit questions
Wechsler Individual Achievement Test–II (WIAT-II) (2001); Reading Comprehension	5–15	Norms for ages 6-0 through 85+ and Grades 1–16	Reading sentences aloud and passages silently or aloud and answering examiner-read questions; passage reading may be timed; early items require matching words with pictures	Also yields three supplemental quartile scores (reading comprehension, target word, and reading speed); very time-consuming to hand-score
Woodcock Reading Mastery Tests–Revised/Normative Update (1987/1998); Passage Comprehension	5–20	Norms for ages 5-0 through 75+ and Grades K–16	Silently reading sentences or short paragraphs and supplying a missing word	Rasch-based test yielding relative proficiency scores as well as norm-referenced scores; very time-consuming to hand-score

(continued)

TABLE 3.23. *(continued)*

Name and date of *measure*; subtest	Admin. time (minutes)	Norms/ benchmarks	Testing task	Comments
Woodcock Reading Mastery Tests–Revised/Normative Update (1987/1998); Word Comprehension	5–15	Norms for ages 5-0 through 75+ and Grades K–16	Reading stimulus words aloud and providing antonyms, synonyms, and analogies	Permits comparisons of single word and passage comprehension within the same norm-referenced measure
Woodcock–Johnson III Tests of Achievement (2001); Passage Comprehension	5–20	Norms for ages 2-0 through 90+ and Grades K–18	Silently reading sentences or short passages and supplying a key missing word; early items require matching rebuses with pictures and words with pictures	Permits comparisons of connected text and single word comprehension within the same norm-referenced instrument
Woodcock–Johnson III Tests of Achievement (2001); Reading Vocabulary	5–15	Norms for ages 2-0 through 90+ and Grades K–18	Reading stimulus words aloud and providing antonyms, synonyms, and analogies	Floor effects for young examinees; when administered with the Oral Comprehension test, permits norm-referenced comparisons of reading and oral vocabulary

Note. CR, criterion-referenced measure; GA, group-administered measure; NS, nonstandardized measure. Shaded measures have a fluency component.

PRINT RESOURCES

Cornoldi, C., & Oakhill, J. (Eds.). (1996). *Reading comprehension difficulties: Processes and intervention.* Mahwah, NJ: Erlbaum.

This edited volume focuses on research contributions to the understanding of reading comprehension problems. Written from a variety of perspectives, the chapters cover five general areas: (1) the factors producing comprehension difficulties, (2) characteristics of children with poor comprehension, (3) specific aspects of reading comprehension problems, (4) reading comprehension problems related to developmental brain pathology and deafness, and (5) the educational implications of research on reading comprehension problems.

Snow, C. E. (2002). *Reading for understanding: Toward a research and development program in reading comprehension.* Retrieved from http://www.rand.org/publications.

Prepared for the Office of Educational Research and Improvement in the U.S. Department of Education, this report by the RAND Corporation's Reading Study Group proposes a research agenda for improving assessment, instruction, and teacher preparation in reading comprehension. The report reviews the present state of research in the field of reading comprehension, offers a new definition of reading comprehension, critiques currently available assessment measures, and proposes new research and assessment strategies.

Written Language

Despite the fact that reading and writing are related language processes, research in written language has lagged far behind that in reading. Unlike the domain of reading, written language lacks a generally agreed upon theoretical model, which has contributed to difficulty in achieving a consensus on an operational definition of written language disorders and a standard set of assessment strategies (Hooper, 2002). It has been especially challenging to develop reliable and valid measures of written expression for early primary grade examinees, whose limited proficiency in handwriting and spelling severely constrains the amount of writing they can produce (Graham, Berninger, Abbott, Abbott, & Whitaker, 1997). As a result, measures of written language have often been omitted from reading acquisition, diagnostic, and intervention studies.

Recently, however, there has been growing interest in the assessment of children's early written language based on an accumulating body of research (e.g., Berninger, Abbott, Abbott, Graham, & Richards, 2002; Mann, 1993; Moats, 1995; Torgesen & Davis, 1996) demonstrating that written language measures, especially spelling measures, can shed light on children's acquisition of reading skills. Moreover, writing instruction has become an area of concern, with longitudinal studies by the National Assessment of Educational Progress (National Center for Educational Statistics, 2003) documenting that only 23% of fourth graders have writing skills at or above the proficient level and indicating no significant positive trends in writing scores across recent national assessments. These findings have prompted the development of empirically based written language tests for early primary grade children, as well as the inclusion of spelling and written expression measures in many early reading and multisubject assessment batteries. The latter measures tap a wide range of skills, ranging from lower level abilities, such as writing alphabet letters, to higher level abilities, such as composing connected text in response to a prompt. Table 3.24 describes the components of written language relevant to assessments of early primary grade examinees, including the types of skills measured and sample assessment tasks. In this section, spelling and written expression measures are discussed separately because of spelling's unique contribution to early reading assessment.

TABLE 3.24. Components of Written Language

Component	Skills assessed	Sample assessment task
Grammar/ linguistics	Ability to use correct syntax, vocabulary, and sentence structure	Combining two sentences to form one correct sentence
Conventions	Ability to apply the rules of punctuation, capitalization, and spelling	Detecting spelling errors in sentences
Content	Ability to communicate meaningfully	Writing a sentence using a set of target words
Writing fluency	Automaticity of writing	Writing as many words as possible in 3 minutes, provided with a sentence starter
Handwriting/ copying	Ability to form legible letters, words, numbers, and sentences	Evaluating handwriting legibility based on the production of specific letters, sentences, or writing samples

SPELLING

Learning to spell is closely related to the process of learning to read. Although spelling requires more information in memory for accurate performance than does reading, both processes rely on knowledge of sound–symbol relationships and word-specific spellings. Not surprisingly, spelling and word reading ability are strongly correlated in the early primary grades (Foorman & Francis, 1994; Richgels, 1995; Stage & Wagner, 1992). For example, Foorman, Francis, Novy, and Liberman (1991) found that performance in either reading or spelling significantly predicted growth in the development of the other skill during first grade. The reciprocal relationship between spelling and reading acquisition is underscored by intervention studies demonstrating that spelling instruction in kindergarten or first grade that involves training in phonemic segmentation and representing phonemes with letters improves reading performance (Ehri, 1989; Uhry & Shepherd, 1997).

Individuals with reading disabilities almost invariably have spelling problems (Cornwall, 1992; Lyons, 1995; Moats, 1994). Moreover, spelling deficiencies tend to persist, even after reading problems have been remediated (Bruck, 1990, 1992; Moats, 1995). Although misordering errors (*traet* for *treat*), reversal errors (*bog* for *dog*), and so-called nonphonetic errors (*dop* for *drop*) were once thought to be primary diagnostic indicators of dyslexia, research lends little support to the hypothesis that the spelling errors of individuals with dyslexia are qualitatively different or less phonetically accurate than those of younger normal readers. Rather, individuals with reading disablilities continue to make errors that correspond to the errors made by normal readers at an earlier developmental stage and reflect their difficulty analyzing words into phonemic segments and establishing accurate orthographic representations in long-term memory (Bruck, 1988; Sawyer et al., 2000; Treiman, 1997).

Stages of Spelling

Beginning with the pioneering work of Read (1971, 1986), numerous researchers (e.g., Bear et al., 2000; Ehri, 2000; Frith, 1985; Henderson, 1990; Templeton & Bear, 1992) have demonstrated that young children's efforts to spell, called *invented spelling,* follow a predictable developmental sequence and exhibit regularities that reveal their emerging understanding of the phonological structure of words. Although the number of stages and their labels vary from one theorist to another, the nature of the progression described is similar, moving from random scribbles and letter strings to partial discovery of the alphabetic principle to increasingly accurate orthographic representations. At each stage, children rely on different kinds of phonological and orthographic knowledge, which is reflected in developmentally common spelling errors. The developmental scheme in Table 3.25 is drawn primarily from Henderson (1990) and from Bear and colleagues (2000).

Invented Spelling and Reading

Measures of invented spelling serve as powerful predictors of reading acquisition because they provide a window into young children's developing phonological and orthographic processing skills (Stage & Wagner, 1992; Tangel & Blachman, 1992, 1995). Such information is especially useful in evaluating the early literacy skills of kindergartners and first-semester first graders, whose decoding ability is so limited

TABLE 3.25. Stages of Spelling Development

Stage	Description	Sample of typical error	Grade range
Emergent	Scribbles, random letters, or letter-like forms; little or no understanding of the alphabetic principle	MX (*skip*)	Prekindergarten–middle of Grade 1
Letter name	Partial representation of letter sounds with letter names; incomplete knowledge of sound–symbol correspondences, especially vowels	skp (*skip*)	Kindergarten–middle of Grade 2
Within word pattern	Use of short vowels and long vowel markers in single-syllable words	trane (*train*)	Grade 1–middle of Grade 4
Syllables and affixes	Understanding of the structure of multisyllabic words and letter sequences; errors often occur at syllable junctures	wadded (*waded*)	Grades 3–8
Derivational relations	Understanding that words with common meanings and derivations have similar spelling patterns	consentration (*concentration*)	Grades 5–12

that they can read few or no words. Numerous studies have demonstrated that invented spelling measures administered in kindergarten and early first grade are strong predictors of growth in phonological awareness (Torgesen & Davis, 1996) and reading proficiency (Mann, 1993; Mann & Ditunno, 1990; Mann, Tobin, & Wilson, 1987; Morris & Perney, 1984; Santa & Hoien, 1999). In fact, some research has suggested that invented spelling measures may be more effective predictors of reading ability than phonological awareness tasks. In a study by Mann (1993), an invented spelling task administered at the end of kindergarten was a better predictor of first-grade reading than a phoneme segmentation task. Similarly, McBride-Chang (1998) reported that kindergarten performance on a five-item invented spelling measure was more strongly related to reading and spelling achievement than performance on three phonological awareness measures or on verbal and nonverbal IQ tests. Moreover, invented spelling contributed unique variance to the prediction of both real word and pseudoword decoding, even when performance on the phonological awareness tasks was controlled.

Assessing Spelling

Four types of spelling measures with utility in early reading assessments are described below: (1) norm-referenced spelling tests, (2) developmental spelling inventories, (3) pseudoword spelling measures, and (4) spelling fluency measures.

Norm-Referenced Spelling Measures

Traditional standardized spelling achievement tests evaluate children's performance relative to age- or grade-level expectations. All of the tests in this category reviewed in this text use production formats (vs. recognition formats) that require the child to generate spellings of dictated letters and words. The ITPA-3 and *WJ III Tests of Achievement* include separate measures of sight words and phonically regular pseudowords to permit norm-referenced comparisons of orthographic and phonological coding skills. Scoring is all-or-nothing (i.e., correct or incorrect).

Example: "*when*. When did Sarah go to school? *when*."

Developmental Spelling Inventories

For children who are in the early stages of learning to spell, tests with scoring systems that are sensitive to changes in spelling developmental level are more useful than traditional spelling achievement tests (Moats, 1995). Developmental spelling inventories consist of lists of words that are selected to reflect a hierarchical progression of spelling features, such as initial and final consonants, digraphs, short vowels, and other spelling patterns typically mastered in the early grades. These inventories have a variety of scoring systems, ranging from holistic rating scales based on the child's approximation of a particular developmental stage for each item to scoring that awards credit not only for correct items but also for phonetically acceptable substitutions (e.g., substituting *f* for the *v* in *van*) and for the presence or absence of spelling features representing a specific developmental stage (e.g., the consonant digraph *sh* in *fish*). This type of scoring is not only sensitive to small changes in spelling performance as the result of development or intervention but also permits assessment results to be linked directly to intervention. If children correctly represent a feature (e.g., a silent vowel marker) in all or most of the words sampling that feature, they are considered to have mastered it. If children consistently misspell words assessing knowledge of a feature that should be mastered at that grade level, they need additional instruction in that skill. Figure 3.4 illustrates this type of scoring, using a stimulus word from the developmental spelling inventory on the BBELS.

Pseudoword Spelling Measures

Poor readers are distinguished from normal readers not only on measures of pseudoword reading but also on measures that require them to spell pseudowords. Even when disabled readers are at the same reading level as younger nondisabled readers, they perform significantly lower on pseudoword spelling tasks (Manis et al., 1988; Siegel & Ryan, 1988; Stanovich & Siegel, 1994). Some researchers (Manis et al., 1988; Stage & Wagner, 1992; Torgesen & Davis, 1996) have used pseudoword spelling tasks to obtain information about young children's developing orthographic and phonological skills. Like pseudoword reading tasks, pseudoword spelling measures reduce the likelihood that children will give correct answers based on memorization of sight words rather than understanding of phoneme–grapheme relationships. In a

Test word	Child's response	First sound	Final sound	Vowel sound	Blends and digraphs	Silent vowel marker	Total points awarded
van	VN	1	1	0	—	—	2

FIGURE 3.4. Scoring for a word from the BBELS developmental spelling inventory. From *Book Buddies: Guidelines for Volunteer Tutors of Emergent and Early Readers* (p. 37) by F. R. Johnston, M. Invernizzi, and C. Juel, 1998, New York: Guilford Press. Copyright 1998 by Guilford Press. Adapted with permission.

kindergarten intervention study, Torgesen and Davis (1996) reported that a five-item pseudoword spelling measure was the best predictor of growth in phonemic segmenting and blending skills in a battery that included measures of verbal ability, letter and sound knowledge, rapid naming, and phonological awareness. Two of the tests reviewed in this text–the ITPA-3 and the *WJ III Tests of Achievement*–include pseudoword spelling measures.

Example (easy item): *ap*

Example (difficult item): *crinningly*

Spelling Fluency Measures

Measures of spelling fluency, which require children to write as many dictated words as possible in a prescribed period of time, tap writing ability and automaticity in addition to orthographic knowledge. Interestingly, although curriculum-based measurement (CBM) of spelling fluency is an established method for identifying children in need of spelling remediation and for monitoring spelling progress (e.g., Allinder et al., 1998; Fuchs, Fuchs, Hamlett, Walz, & Germann, 1993; Shinn, 1989), no studies using spelling fluency measures in reading diagnostic, prediction, or intervention studies could be located. The typical CBM spelling procedure requires the child to spell words taken from the classroom curriculum that are dictated at a rate of one word per 7 seconds for 2 minutes and are scored based on number of correct letter sequences and/or number of correct words (see Rathvon, 1999, for a complete description of administration and scoring procedures for CBM in spelling). Of the 14 instruments with spelling measures reviewed in this book, only the DST includes a spelling fluency subtest. Given the importance of automaticity to the reading and writing processes, it is likely that additional spelling fluency assessments will be developed and validated in the future.

Issues in Assessing Spelling

In addition to their use of all-or-nothing scoring systems, traditional norm-referenced spelling tests have several characteristics that limit their utility in early reading assessments, including (1) limited content sampling, (2) response formats that lack ecological validity, and (3) lack of a standardized system for analyzing errors.

Inadequate Content Sampling

Most standardized tests include too few items at each grade level to provide a large enough sample of major word types and patterns, especially for younger children (Bailet, 2001; Moats, 1995). Tests with a limited number of lower level items are unable to identify very poor spellers (i.e., they have inadequate floors) or to detect small changes in skills resulting from development, classroom instruction, or intervention programs (i.e., they have inadequate item gradients). Because beginning readers have limited spelling skills, spelling tests are subject to floor effects at the lower age and grade ranges. To address this problem, test developers are beginning to include prelexical items on measures designed to assess the developing skills of young children. For example, the Spelling test on the *WJ III Tests of Achievement* includes prelexical items, such as connecting dots, tracing letters, and writing single letters, in addition to spelling entire words. Moreover, norm-referenced spelling tests display little item overlap, even for high frequency words (Hultquist & Metzke, 1993; see also Table 3.26 below).

Artificial Response Formats

Another problem limiting the utility of many norm-referenced spelling tests in assessing early primary grade examinees is the use of multiple-choice recognition formats that require examinees to select the one word in a set of words that is spelled correctly. This type of format not only does not require the child to generate spellings for any words but also is subject to guessing and provides no information for instructional planning. On tests designed for large-scale administration, however, this type of response format is the most efficient option in terms of administration and scoring.

Variability in Error Analysis Systems

A third limitation of traditional norm-referenced spelling tests is the lack of a generally accepted framework for analyzing error patterns. Although many norm-referenced spelling tests offer some kind of optional error analysis in addition to yielding derived scores based on the number of correct responses, very few provide data from the standardization sample or research studies for use in interpreting the results of those analyses. Moreover, many spelling errors fit more than one category, making it difficult to link assessment results to specific remediation strategies (Moats, 1995).

DIFFERENT SPELLING TESTS, DIFFERENT SCORES: THE CASE OF ANDREW

Because of the limited number of items, lack of item overlap, and variations in format, different norm-referenced spelling tests can yield different estimates of spelling proficiency in the same examinee. Table 3.26 presents raw scores and age-based standard scores on four standardized spelling tests for Andrew, a second grader aged 7-5 who was tested in January of the school year, along with selected psychometric features for each test. Although all four tests have similar norming dates, use similar formats, and are scored dichotomously, they yielded markedly different results (SSs = 84–102). Item overlap is negligible–between 2 and 7 shared items, with the WIAT-II sharing the most items with the other instruments. Of a total of 187 items on the four tests, only 2 letters and 5 words appear on more than one instrument, and none of the 7 shared items appear on all four tests. It is also noteworthy that although three of the four standard scores fall in the average range, indicating average spelling proficiency relative to age expectations, Andrew scored very poorly on a developmental spelling inventory in a nonstandardized early reading assessment battery (17 of 48 possible points), and he was struggling in both reading and spelling in the classroom.

TABLE 3.26. Test Floors, Item Statistics, and Scores Obtained by a Second Grader on Four Standardized Spelling Tests

Name and date of *test*; subtest	Obtained standard score[a]	Test floor for age 7-5[b]	Total number of items and item types	Number of items answered correctly	Number of items shared with other tests
Illinois Test of Psycholinguistic Abilities–3 (2001); Sight Spelling	9 (95)	5 (75)	25 items (writing one to four omitted letters in irregular words)	6	2
Test of Written Spelling–4, Form A (1999)	84	77	50 items (spelling words)	6	2
Wechsler Individual Achievement Test–II (2001); Spelling	102	59	53 items (writing first and last name, 11 letters/letter blends, and 41 words)	19[c]	7
Woodcock–Johnson III Tests of Achievement, Form A (2001); Spelling	101	4	59 items (drawing and tracing lines and letters [6 items], copying letters [1 item], writing letters [7 items], and writing words [45 items])	21[c]	4

[a]Standard scores are based on age norms. For subtests that yield standard scores with a mean of 10 and standard deviation of 3, the corresponding standard score with a mean of 100 and standard deviation of 15 has been added for comparison purposes in the first two columns.
[b]A *test floor* is defined as the standard score corresponding to a raw score of 1. On the Rasch-based *Woodcock–Johnson III* Spelling test, the test floor was calculated by entering a raw score of 1 in the software scoring program for a child aged 7-5 in January of Grade 2.
[c]The number correct for these tests includes items below the basal.

Measures of Spelling

Table 3.27 summarizes 16 spelling measures, ranging from a group-administered, multiple-choice format spelling assessment to a norm-referenced spelling fluency measure. To ensure a comprehensive assessment of spelling skills, practitioners should administer both norm-referenced and criterion-referenced measures, such as a standardized spelling test to determine the child's level of proficiency compared with age or grade peers and a developmental spelling inventory to provide instructional information. Spelling assessments should also include several samples of classroom writing to generate additional information for error analysis and intervention planning.

WRITTEN EXPRESSION

Children with poor reading skills also tend to become poor writers, with the correlations between writing and reading increasing across the elementary grades. In Juel's (1988) longitudinal study following 54 children from first through fourth grade, 68% of the poor readers were also poor writers, whereas only 14% of the good readers were poor writers. Early writing skills show less stability than early reading abilities, however. In the same study, the correlation between writing skills measured at the

TABLE 3.27. Measures of Spelling

Name and date of *measure*; subtest	Admin. time (minutes)	Norms/ benchmarks	Testing task	Comments
Basic Early Assessment of Reading (2002); Language Arts	30–40 (GA)	CR; Grades K–3	Answering multiple-choice questions in response to examiner directions and after silently reading passages	Also assesses penmanship and letter knowledge in Grade K and syntax, grammar, and usage in Grades 1–3
Book Buddies Early Literacy Screening (1998); Spelling	5–8	NS; Grades 1 and 2	Writing 10 words; scored for each logically represented letter, with a bonus point for correct words	Developmental spelling measure linked to evidence-based tutoring program
Consortium on Reading Excellence Phonics Survey (1999); Spelling	5–10	NS; Grades K–8	Writing initial and final consonants of 10 one-syllable words; writing 10 CVC and CVCe words	Useful for instructional planning
Dyslexia Screening Test (1996); Two Minute Spelling	3	British norms for ages 6-6 through 16-6	Writing as many dictated words as possible in 2 minutes	Unique spelling fluency measure; utility limited by British norms
Fox in a Box (2000); Spelling	10–45	CR; benchmarks for Grades K–2	Writing 10–15 initial or final consonants or medial vowels (Grade K); writing 10–60 words (Grades 1 and 2)	Part of a comprehensive early literacy assessment designed to follow the child from Grade K through the end of Grade 2
Illinois Test of Psycholinguistic Abilities–3 (2001); Sight Spelling	5–10	Norms for ages 6-6 through 12-11	Writing omitted parts of irregularly spelled words	Also measures orthographic processing
Illinois Test of Psycholinguistic Abilities–3 (2001); Sound Spelling	5–10	Norms for ages 6-6 through 12-11	Writing omitted parts of phonically regular pseudowords or entire pseudowords	Permits comparisons of regular and exception word spelling within the same norm-referenced instrument
Phonological Awareness Literacy Screening (2002); Spelling	10–30 (GA)	CR; Virginia benchmarks for Grades K–3	Writing 5–25 words; scored according to spelling features correctly represented and word correctness	Developmental spelling measure with grade-specific phonics features; very useful for instructional planning
Phonological Awareness Screening Test (1998); Representing Phonemes with Letters	10–15 (GA)	NS; Grades K and 1	Writing 5 pictured words; items are scored for phonetically acceptable or correct letters	Part of a group-administered classroom screening battery; linked to an evidence-based phonological awareness curriculum

(continued)

TABLE 3.27. *(continued)*

Name and date of *measure*; subtest	Admin. time (minutes)	Norms/ benchmarks	Testing task	Comments
Phonological Awareness Test (1997); Invented Spelling	5–7	NS; ages 5–8	Writing 14 words; scored for spelling stage and mastery of specific sounds	No reliability or validity data; vague scoring guidelines
Process Assessment of the Learner: Test Battery for Reading and Writing (2001); Word Choice	3–5	Norms for Grades 1–6	Circling the one correctly spelled word from a set of three; the score is the number of correct responses on items completed in 2 minutes	Also measures orthographic coding
Test of Written Spelling–4 (1999)	10–15 (GA)	Norms for ages 6-0 through 18-11	Writing dictated words	Two forms for pre- and posttesting; inadequate test floors for early primary grade examinees
Texas Primary Reading Inventory (2002); Spelling Patterns	15–30 (GA)	CR; Texas benchmarks for Grade 2	Writing dictated words sampling four sets of spelling patterns (20 words total)	Part of a statewide early literacy screening battery for Grades K–2
Wechsler Individual Achievement Test–II (2001); Spelling	5–10	Norms for ages 6-0 through 85+ and Grades K–16	Writing dictated words; early items involve writing letters and letter blends	Inadequate floors below age 6-8
Woodcock–Johnson III Tests of Achievement (2001); Spelling	5–10	Norms for ages 2-0 through 90+ and Grades K–18	Writing dictated words; early items involve drawing and tracing lines, tracing letters, and writing letters	Excellent floors, even for early primary grade children
Woodcock–Johnson III Tests of Achievement (2001); Spelling of Sounds	5–10	Norms for ages 2-0 through 90+ and Grades K–18	Writing dictated letters to represent single sounds; writing pseudowords presented on audiocassette	Also assesses orthographic coding

Note. CR, criterion-referenced measure; NS, nonstandardized measure; GA, group-administered measure; CVC, consonant-vowel-consonant; CVCe, consonant-vowel-consonant-silent *e*. Measures with a fluency component are shaded.

end of first grade and at the end of fourth grade was .38, considerably lower than the correlation of .88 obtained for reading. In their decade-long research program on writing acquisition and writing disabilities at the University of Washington, Berninger and her colleagues (e.g., Berninger, Stage, Smith, & Hildebrand, 2001; Berninger et al., 2002) have examined the developmental precursors of writing in normal and clinical samples. According to Berninger, writing assessment measures should be selected depending on the child's developmental level in writing acquisition and the component skill of interest (e.g., handwriting, spelling, or composition). In an unreferred sample of early primary grade children (Berninger et al., 1992), pseudoword reading and visual–motor integration were the best predictors of spelling performance, whereas rapid production of alphabet letters, rapid coding of orthographic information, and speed of sequential finger movements were the best predictors of handwriting and composition skills. All three of the writing predictor tasks are included in Berninger's PAL-RW, and the alphabet production task is included in the WIAT-II Written Expression subtest.

Assessing Written Expression

Five general types of written expression measures with utility in the assessment of early primary grade examinees are described below: (1) writing mechanics tasks, (2) compositional tasks, (3) written language proficiency tasks, (4) writing fluency tasks, and (5) handwriting and copying tasks.

Writing Mechanics Measures

Most written expression measures, including those for early primary grade examinees, assess one or more kinds of writing conventions, such as spelling, punctuation, and capitalization. These tests include comprehensive measures of writing mechanics, such as the Written Expression Scale on the *Oral and Written Language Scales* (OWLS), as well as measures that assess specific conventions, such as the Editing test and the Punctuation and Capitalization test on the WJ III. Also included in this category are sentence sequencing tasks, which assess reading comprehension and verbal reasoning as well as understanding of sentence structure. Responses may be in oral or written form.

Example: "This says, 'The dog is in there yard.' Tell me what needs correcting." (The child indicates that *there* should be spelled *their*.)

Compositional Measures

Compositional measures of written expression require children to generate words or text in response to a prompt. Because young children have such limited writing proficiency, compositional tasks are especially vulnerable to floor effects. These tasks vary considerably in the amount of writing required, from a single word to an extended writing sample. For example, the Written Vocabulary subtest on the ITPA-3 requires supplying a noun to match a target adjective, whereas the Writing Development task on the *Fox in a Box* early literacy battery requires retelling a story read by the examiner.

Example: "Write a word that goes with these words." (The child sees *A little* _______ and writes an appropriate noun in the blank.)

Written Language Proficiency Measures

Comprehensive tests of written language, such as the Written Expression Scale on the OWLS, use both direct and indirect methods to assess a wide range of writing skills, including knowledge of writing conventions and the ability to apply those conventions to various writing tasks. For early primary grade children, the writing skills typically assessed include letter formation, letter and word spacing, copying words and sentences, and generating words and sentences in response to an oral, pictorial, or written prompt. Some of these tests sample such a wide variety of skills that interpreting the results can be problematic. I have found that first and second graders with severe reading and spelling deficits can sometimes obtain average or above average scores on written language proficiency measures because most items assess print awareness and writing vocabulary and provide few (if any) penalties for spelling errors.

Example: "Write one sentence using these words: *can girl this.*" (*This girl can run* . . . [other meaningful responses].)

Writing Fluency Measures

Measures of writing fluency require children to respond to a variety of copying and written language requirements and tap a broad range of skills, including word knowledge, written expression, reading and spelling skills, visual–motor control, and the capacity to sustain attention and effort. CBM of writing fluency, which requires writing for 3 minutes as rapidly as possible in response to a topic sentence or story starter, has been used in numerous studies to assess children's writing development and monitor the effects of writing interventions (e.g., Allinder et al., 1998; Shinn, 1989; Tindal & Hasbrouck, 1991). Performance on CBM in writing is scored based on the number of words written, number of words spelled correctly, and/or number of correct word sequences (see Rathvon, 1999). Although CBM in writing has been demonstrated to correlate significantly with both standardized written expression tests and teacher ratings of written expression (Marston, 1989; Parker, Tindal, & Hasbrouck, 1991; Shinn, 1989) and to differentiate learning-disabled students from nondisabled controls (Watkinson & Lee, 1992), it has limited utility for early primary grade children because of floor effects.

Writing fluency tasks for early primary grade examinees consist of three types: (1) measures of alphabet writing fluency, (2) measures of word writing fluency, and (3) measures of sentence writing fluency. For children with very limited writing skills, speeded alphabet writing tasks provide information about automaticity in retrieving and accurately producing alphabet letters, which is essential to the successful acquisition of higher level spelling and writing skills. As noted earlier, two of the tests reviewed in this book—the PAL-RW and the WIAT-II—share an identical measure of alphabet writing fluency developed by Virginia Berninger and her colleagues at the University of Washington. Measures of word fluency require the child to write as many words in a specific category as rapidly as possible. The WIAT-II includes a word writing fluency subtest that assesses vocabulary as well as writing speed and rate of lexical access. Sentence writing fluency tasks involve generating short, simple sentences as rapidly as possible based on a given set of words and a pictorial prompt. Because sentence fluency tasks require a higher level of compositional skills, they tend to exhibit floor effects throughout much of the early primary grade range.

Example (word fluency task): "Write as many words as you can think of for different animals. Don't worry about spelling but be sure I can read what you have written. Ready? Go!" (The child lists as many animals as possible in 1 minute.)

Handwriting and Copying Measures

Although handwriting has received little attention from reading researchers until quite recently, it is a critical skill in written language acquisition. If children do not develop automaticity in handwriting, higher level written expression skills may be negatively affected because working memory must be allocated to letter formation rather than to planning, composing, and editing (Berninger & Graham, 1998). Copying speed is significantly related to both reading and spelling achievement in primary grade children (Bear, 1991). In addition, children with spelling disabilities who also display handwriting deficits have more severe spelling problems than children without handwriting problems (Berninger et al., 1998). Two of the multisubject tests reviewed in this text include one or more measures of handwriting, all of which are based on evaluations of writing samples obtained from classroom assignments or other measures in the instrument. The alphabet production task on the PAL-RW is also a measure of handwriting because it is scored based on the correctness of letter formation as well as letters completed within the time limits. The DST includes a measure of copying fluency.

Issues in Assessing Written Expression

As noted earlier, unlike reading, writing lacks a generally agreed-upon theory of development. This situation has contributed to the tremendous variation among written expression instruments in terms of content, format, item types, and scoring systems. With such diversity, it is not surprising that standardized tests of written expression can yield significantly different results for the same individual (see Brown, Giandenoto, & Bolen, 2000). Moreover, written expression tests have been roundly criticized for their lack of an adequate theoretical base, poor technical quality, and questionable relationship to classroom writing experiences (Cole, Muenz, Ouchi, Kaufman, & Kaufman, 1997; Hooper et al., 1994; Muenz, Ouchi, & Cole, 1999). Issues in assessing written expression in early primary grade examinees that are discussed here include (1) variations in format and scoring, (2) questionable content validity, (3) reliability concerns, and (4) inadequate test floors.

Variations in Format and Scoring

Tests of written expression can be characterized as using one or both of two formats: indirect or direct. Tests with *indirect* or *contrived* formats are primarily designed to evaluate knowledge of writing conventions and use structured tasks that require the examinee to respond to specific writing situations, such as copying letters, completing a phrase, combining sentences, or detecting punctuation errors. In contrast, tests with *direct* or *spontaneous* formats are designed to elicit a representative sample of written expression skills by having the examinee generate text in response to a verbal, pictorial, and/or written prompt. Scoring systems for written expression performance also vary but can be categorized as one of three basic types: holistic, analytic, or a combination of both. *Holistic scoring systems* evaluate the overall quality of a written product by applying a *rubric*—a set of guidelines describing the standards for each of several points arrayed on a rating scale. For example, the early literacy battery *Fox in a Box* uses rubrics to assign children's writing samples to one of six levels of writing development. *Analytic scoring systems* evaluate written products according to a specific set of writing elements, such as organization, vocabulary, writing mechanics, and theme development, each of which is evaluated on a scale that assigns points to different levels of performance. For example, the OWLS Written Expression Scale is scored by applying one or more rules based on three writing skill categories to each response. Unlike holistic scoring procedures, which provide only a single rating per writing sample, analytic scoring yields information about each category or element assessed for use in identifying writing deficits and developing interventions.

Questionable Content Validity

Because of the lack of a complete model of writing development, a major issue in assessing written expression is *content validity*, that is, the match between what is evaluated on a test and what children are taught in the classroom (Hooper, 2002; Hooper et al., 1994). An inspection of Table 3.28 below reveals the diversity in the content of tasks included in written expression measures for early primary grade children, ranging from orally identifying errors in written passages (the Editing test on the *WJ III Tests of Achievement*) to writing as many words as possible that fall in a particular category (the Word Fluency task on the WIAT-II Written Expression subtest). The challenge of developing instruments with adequate content representativeness and relevance is complicated by the tremendous variability of writing instruction in schools. Although many districts and states have shifted toward an integrated approach to reading and writing instruction and an emphasis on the writing process as well as the product, vast differences remain in how written language is taught in the classroom, the time when specific writing skills are taught, and the frequency with which students engage in writing experiences. Practitioners are encouraged to review test manuals and protocols to evaluate the degree to which writing measures assess what is being taught in an examinee's curriculum.

Low Reliability

Low reliability has also plagued written expression tests, including low levels of internal consistency, stability, and interrater reliability (Hooper et al., 1994). Because even the most fully specified analytic scoring systems involve some degree of subjective judgment, written expression tests are highly vulnerable to interscorer inconsistency. Multisubject instruments with otherwise excellent psychometric characteristics often report interscorer reliability coefficients for written expression subtests that fall below acceptable levels. In other cases, the interscorer reliabilities reported in test manuals are spuriously inflated because they are based on highly heterogeneous samples that span the entire age range of the test.

Inadequate Test Floors

Because of the difficulty in creating items suitable for assessing young children with rudimentary writing skills, written expression instruments are subject to floor effects. The vast majority of the norm-referenced measures of written expression reviewed in this text have inadequate subtest floors at the lower age and grade ranges, and some have inadequate floors throughout the entire early primary grade range. Writing fluency tests, which tap automaticity as well as written expression skills, are especially likely to have inadequate floors. For example, on the WJ III Writing Fluency test, which requires writing as many sentences as possible in 7 minutes in response to sets of three words accompanied by picture prompts, a child in the third month of first grade who answers one item correctly obtains a grade-based standard score of 88 (low average range).

Measures of Written Expression

Written expression measures, especially compositional tasks, can be among the most time-consuming tests to administer, score, and interpret in an early reading assessment. Because of the diversity among writing assessments, an evaluation of children's writing proficiency should never be based on the results of a single instrument. Moreover, although norm-referenced tests can be useful for screening purposes, examiners should conduct informal evaluations of writing performance across a variety of components, such as handwriting, conventions, and fluency, and should use a variety of assessment formats, such as copying, dictation, and open-ended formats, in order to provide information for instructional activities. Table 3.28 describes the 21 measures of written expression reviewed in this text.

PRINT RESOURCES

Bain, A. M., Bailet, L. L., & Moats, L. C. (Eds.). (2001). *Written language disorders: Theory into practice* (2nd ed.). Austin, TX: PRO-ED.

This book reviews current research and theory of written language development and disorders and offers evidence-based guidelines for writing instruction and remediation of writing problems. Chapters address writing development from early childhood into the adult years, as well as spelling, handwriting, and written expression disorders. One chapter includes reviews of norm-referenced written language tests for children, adolescents, and adults.

Hooper, S. R. (Ed.). (2002). The language of written language [Special issue]. *Journal of Learning Disabilities, 35*(1).

This special issue includes five articles focusing on written language development and writing disorders. The articles address definitional and diagnostic issues, assessment strategies, neurodevelopmental components of the writing system, brain–behavior linkages, and teacher training in reading and writing instruction.

Moats, L. C. (1995). *Spelling: Development, disability, and instruction.* Baltimore: York Press.

Written by the one of the leading authorities on spelling, this book presents a comprehensive overview of the domain of spelling, including spelling development, differences between children with normally developing spelling and spelling disabilities, and effective spelling instruction. Included is a very useful chapter on spelling assessment, with guidelines for analysis of spelling errors and remediation.

TABLE 3.28. Measures of Written Expression

Name and date of *measure*; subtest	Admin. time (minutes)	Norms/ benchmarks	Testing task	Comments
Basic Early Assessment of Reading (2002); Language Arts	30–40 (GA)	CR; Grades K–3	Answering multiple-choice questions in response to examiner directions and after silently reading passages	Part of an early literacy battery that includes three types of language arts assessments; also measures spelling skills
Book Buddies Early Literacy Screening (1998); Alphabet Production	5–10	NS; Grades K–2	Writing 26 uppercase and 26 lowercase letters, randomly dictated, or writing letters as the examiner sings the alphabet song with the child	One of very few measures to require production of both uppercase and lowercase letters; also measures written expression skills
Dyslexia Screening Test (1996); One Minute Writing	3–5	British norms for ages 6-6 through 16-6	Copying as many words from a writing passage as possible in 1 minute	Unique measure of copying fluency; utility limited by British norms
Fox in a Box (2000); Writing Development	45–50 (GA)	CR; benchmarks for Grades K–2	Drawing (Grade K) or writing (Grades 1 and 2) about a story read by the examiner; scored on a 6-point scale	Group-administered task on Grades K–2 early literacy battery; also evaluated on a Writing Expression scale (see below)
Fox in a Box (2000); Writing Expression	45–50 (GA)	CR; benchmarks for Grades K–2	Writing about a story read by the examiner; scored for vocabulary, transitions, organization, and details; scored on a 3-point scale	Vague scoring guidelines; score obtained using the Writing Development sample (see above)
Illinois Test of Psycholinguistic Abilities–3 (2001); Sentence Sequencing	5–10	Norms for ages 6-6 through 12-11	Ordering three to five sentences into a sequence to form a coherent paragraph	Measures reading comprehension and semantics as well as syntax; inadequate floors throughout the early primary grade range
Illinois Test of Psycholinguistic Abilities–3 (2001); Written Vocabulary	5–10	Norms for ages 6-6 through 12-11	Writing a noun associated with a stimulus adjective	Measures reading comprehension, written vocabulary, and semantics; inadequate floors below age 8-3
Oral and Written Language Scales (1995); Written Expression Scale	15 –25 (GA)	Norms for ages 5-0 through 21-11	Writing in response to a variety of verbal, print, or pictorial stimuli	Measures conventions, linguistics, and content; inadequate floors for age-based norms below 5-9
Predictive Reading Profile (2001); Story Writing	10–20 (GA)	Preliminary kindergarten norms; Grades K and 1	Writing a story about a favorite animal; scored on a 10-point holistic scale	Optional task on a group-administered screening battery; no reliability or validity data

(continued)

TABLE 3.28. *(continued)*

Name and date of *measure*; subtest	Admin. time (minutes)	Norms/ benchmarks	Testing task	Comments
Process Assessment of the Learner: Test Battery for Reading and Writing (PAL-RW) (2001); Alphabet Writing	3–5	Norms for Grades PreK–2	Printing an ordered set of alphabet letters as rapidly as possible in 15 seconds	Decile scores only; identical to the WIAT-II task of the same name (see below); also measures handwriting and alphabet knowledge
Process Assessment of the Learner: Test Battery for Reading and Writing (PAL-RW) (2001); Copying	2–3	Norms for Grades K–6	Copying as many letters in a sentence as possible in 20 seconds (Grade K); copying as many letters in a paragraph as possible in 90 seconds (Grades 1–6)	Decile scores only; unique measure of lower level writing skills in a norm-referenced battery
Process Assessment of the Learner: Test Battery for Reading and Writing (PAL-RW) (2001); Finger Sense	10–15	Norms for Grades K–6	Performing five finger function tasks using each hand; some tasks are speeded	Assesses finger function related to written output; very challenging to administer and score reliably
Wechsler Individual Achievement Test–II (WIAT-II) (2001); Alphabet Writing	1–3	Norms for ages 4-0 through 6-11 and Grades PreK–2	Printing an ordered set of alphabet letters as rapidly as possible; score based on letters completed in 15 seconds; combined with Written Expression subtest items for Grades 1 and 2	Decile scores only for Grades PreK through K (supplemental score); identical to the PAL-RW task (see above); also measures handwriting and alphabet knowledge
Wechsler Individual Achievement Test–II (WIAT-II) (2001); Written Expression	3–18 per task	Norms for ages 6-0 through 85+ and Grades 1–16	Set of grade-specific timed tasks: Alphabet Writing (Grades PreK–2; rapidly printing letters); Word Fluency (Grades 1–16; writing as many words as possible in a category in 60 seconds); Sentences (Grades 1–6; combining sentences) (Grades 7–16; generating sentences); Paragraph (Grades 3–6, writing a paragraph [10-minute time limit]); Essay (Grades 7–16; writing a persuasive essay [15-minute time limit])	No separate task scores; decile scores only for Alphabet Writing in Grades PreK and K
Woodcock–Johnson III Tests of Achievement (2001); Editing	5–10	Norms for ages 2-0 through 90+ and Grades K–18	Orally identifying and correcting errors in punctuation, usage, capitalization, and spelling in short written passages	Inadequate floors for younger examinees

(continued)

TABLE 3.28. *(continued)*

Name and date of *measure*; subtest	Admin. time (minutes)	Norms/ benchmarks	Testing task	Comments
Woodcock–Johnson III Tests of Achievement (2001); Handwriting Elements Checklist	3–5	Norms for ages 2-0 through 90+ and Grades K–18	Informal evaluation of six elements of handwriting quality; located in the test record	Rates handwriting samples from the Writing Samples test (see below) or classroom samples
Woodcock–Johnson III Tests of Achievement (2001); Handwriting Legibility Scale	5–8	Norms for ages 2-0 through 90+ and Grades K–18	Evaluation of handwriting legibility; rated on a 100-point scale in 10-point increments; located in the examiner manual	Rates handwriting samples from the Writing Samples test or other sources; one of the few norm-referenced handwriting measures
Woodcock–Johnson III Tests of Achievement (2001); Editing	5–10	Norms for ages 2-0 through 90+ and Grades K–18	Orally identifying and correcting errors in punctuation, usage, capitalization, and spelling in short written passages	Inadequate floors for younger examinees
Woodcock–Johnson III Tests of Achievement (2001); Punctuation and Capitalization	5–10	Norms for ages 2-0 through 90+ and Grades K–18	Producing examples of correct punctuation and capitalization; early items require uppercase and lowercase letter production	Inadequate floors for younger examinees
Woodcock–Johnson III Tests of Achievement (2001); Writing Evaluation Scale	10–15	Norms for ages 2-0 through 90+ and Grades K–18	Analytic scoring method for assessing nine components of writing competence; located in the examiner manual	Based on one or more extended writing samples; designed to assess and monitor writing over time
Woodcock–Johnson III Tests of Achievement (2001); Writing Fluency	8–10	Norms for ages 2-0 through 90+ and Grades K–18	Rapidly writing simple sentences that relate to a picture and include a set of 3 words; 7-minute time limit	Permits comparisons of timed and untimed writing ability when administered with the Writing Samples test
Woodcock–Johnson III Tests of Achievement (2001); Writing Samples	10–20	Norms for ages 2-0 through 90+ and Grades K–18	Writing words and sentences in response to a variety of demands	The set of items administered is adjusted if examinees score near the extremes of the prescribed item block

Note. CR, criterion-referenced measure; NS, nonstandardized measure; GA, group-administered measure. Fluency-based measures are shaded.

PART II

Early Reading Measures

chapter 4

Early Reading Assessment Batteries

This chapter reviews 11 early reading assessment batteries. Although they vary considerably in format and content, all include multiple measures designed to assess the prereading and reading-related skills of early primary grade children. The *Group Reading Assessment and Diagnostic Evaluation* (GRADE) extends from prekindergarten through postsecondary levels but is included here because it more closely resembles these measures in structure and purpose than the multiskill reading tests reviewed in Chapter 5. All of the most recently published batteries target the five skills identified as essential by the National Reading Panel (2000)–phonemic awareness, phonics, fluency, vocabulary, and comprehension–and are designed to align with the testing mandates of the No Child Left Behind Act of 2001. Potential users should note that state-sponsored assessment batteries are typically modified each year, based on teacher feedback and continuing reliability and validity studies. Practitioners interested in these instruments are encouraged to contact state departments of education and/or university-based sources for the most up-to-date information. Table 4.1 presents summary characteristics for the 11 instruments.

BASIC EARLY ASSESSMENT OF READING

Overview

The *Basic Early Assessment of Reading* (BEAR; Riverside, 2002) is a battery of criterion-referenced tests designed to measure proficiency in reading, language arts, and oral reading fluency for students in kindergarten through Grade 3. Performance is evaluated according to grade-specific benchmarks based on nationwide standards for reading and language arts and teacher judgments. Designed for large-scale testing, the BEAR includes four components: (1) a screening measure, (2) an optional diagnostic assessment, (3) an end-of-year assessment, and (4) an oral reading fluency measure. Because all of the measures, with the exception of

TABLE 4.1. Summary Characteristics for 11 Early Reading Assessment Batteries

Name and date of measure	Admin. format	Admin. time	Norms/ benchmarks	Skills assessed	Comments
Basic Early Reading Assessment (2002)	Classwide and individual	30–40 minutes per subtest; 90 minutes for screener	CR; Grades K–3	Basic reading skills; listening/reading comprehension; language arts; letter recognition fluency; passage reading fluency	Set of group-administered screening, diagnostic, and end-of-year assessments; includes an individually administered oral reading fluency component
Book Buddies Early Literacy Screening (1998)	Individual	30–40 minutes	NS; Grades 1 and 2	Alphabet knowledge; letter-sound awareness; spelling; concept of word; word recognition	User-friendly screening and progress monitoring battery; linked to tutoring program
Dynamic Indicators of Basic Early Literacy Skills (2002)	Individual	3 minutes per task; 10–20 minutes per child	NS; benchmarks for four tasks to date; Grades K–3	1-minute fluency-based measures: phonemic awareness; pseudoword reading; letter naming; oral reading; story retelling; word usage	CBM-type progress monitoring measures; all materials are free and downloadable from the DIBELS Web site
Early Reading Diagnostic Assessment–Revised (2002)	Individual	15–20 minutes for screener; 45–60 minutes for battery	Norms for Grades K–3	Concept of print; story retell; letter recognition; phonological awareness; pseudoword decoding; rapid automatized naming; word recognition; vocabulary; reading accuracy, comprehension, and rate (rate is optional)	Includes screener and diagnostic tasks at each grade level; percentile range scores only
Fox in a Box (2000)	Individual, small-group, and classwide	1¾ hours–2 hours	CR; benchmarks for Grades K–2	Concepts of print; phonemic awareness; alphabet recognition and writing; decoding; spelling; oral and written expression; listening comprehension; reading accuracy, fluency, and comprehension	Comprehensive early literacy assessment designed to follow children through the early primary grades; no screener tasks
Group Reading Assessment and Diagnostic Evaluation (2002)	Classwide	45–90 minutes	Norms for Grades PreK–postsecondary	Prereading; reading readiness; phonological awareness; vocabulary; reading comprehension; listening comprehension	Similar format to group-administered standardized tests

(continued)

TABLE 4.1. *(continued)*

Name and date of measure	Admin. format	Admin. time	Norms/ benchmarks	Skills assessed	Comments
Phonological Awareness Literacy Screening (2002)	Individual, small-group, and classwide	20 minutes for group tests; 30 minutes for individual tests	CR; benchmarks for Grades K–3	Phonological awareness; alphabet knowledge; spelling; concept of word; word recognition; reading accuracy, fluency, and comprehension	State-of-the-art, user-friendly three-tier set of assessments; serves as the Virginia early reading instrument
Phonological Awareness Screening Test (1998)	Small-group	20–30 minutes	NS; Grades K and 1	Rhyme detection; syllable counting; phoneme counting; initial sound matching; word length comparison; spelling	Brief, group-administered set of screening tasks; linked to classroom curriculum
Predictive Reading Profile (2001)	Classwide	2–2½ hours	Preliminary kindergarten norms; Grades K and 1	Visual discrimination; letter–word recognition; syllable–sound counting; sound recognition; phonemic segmentation; story writing; syntax; vocabulary	Group-administered battery with an optional teacher rating scale; local norming recommended
Test of Early Reading Ability–3 (2001)	Individual	15–30 minutes	Norms for ages 3-6 through 8-6	Alphabet knowledge; print conventions; print comprehension	Includes one of the few norm-referenced measures of print conventions
Texas Primary Reading Inventory (2002)	Individual and classwide	5–7 minutes for screens; 20–25 minutes for inventory tasks	CR; benchmarks for Grades K–2	Print awareness; letter-sound knowledge; phonemic awareness; word recognition; spelling; reading accuracy, fluency, and comprehension	State-of-the-art battery with screener and inventory tasks; serves as the Texas early reading assessment battery

Note. CR, criterion-referenced measure; NS, nonstandardized measure; CBM, curriculum-based measurement. Fluency-based batteries are shaded. For most measures, the skills assessed vary by grade.

the oral reading fluency assessment, require written responses, they can be administered in a small-group or classwide format. The purposes of the BEAR, which are linked to the four components, include (1) assessing reading and language arts skills at the beginning of the year, (2) evaluating strengths and weaknesses in reading and language arts, (3) assessing progress in reading and language arts, and (4) monitoring oral reading fluency development. Assessment kits for Grades K–1 and for Grades 2–3 are packaged separately. Each kit includes 25 Initial-Skills Analysis student booklets per grade, two grade-specific Initial-Skills Analysis administration and scoring guides, three Specific-Skill Analysis blackline masters covering two grades, one Specific-Skill Analysis administration and scoring guide, 26 Oral Reading Fluency Assessment cards, one Oral Reading Fluency Assessment administration and scoring guide, three sets of 25 Summative Assessment student booklets per grade, two grade-specific Summative Assessment administration guides, two grade-specific Summative Assessment scoring guides, and the scoring and reporting software, all packed in a storage box.

Components and Subtests

Components

At each grade level, the BEAR consists of four sets of assessments: (1) an Initial-Skills Analysis, (2) a Specific-Skill Analysis, (3) a Summative Assessment, and (4) an Oral Reading Fluency Assessment. Each of the first three components includes three subtests: Reading Basics, Language Arts, and Comprehension. The subtest format closely resembles that of group-administered standardized tests, with students responding to all tasks by marking or writing in booklets. The Initial-Skills Analysis and Summative Assessment components are packaged in separate booklets per subtest for each grade, whereas the Specific-Skill Analysis is reproduced from blackline masters for each subtest, with Grades K–1 and Grades 2–3 combined in each of the three subtests.

Subtests

Across the first three components, the BEAR subtests cover similar content areas. Unlike the skill-specific subtests or tasks in the other early reading assessment batteries reviewed in this chapter, the BEAR subtests sample a variety of skill areas, called *standards*, within each of the three content domains (see Table 4.2). Subtests include primarily multiple-choice questions, whereas the Summative Assessment also includes open-ended questions. There are no composite scores.

Oral Reading Fluency Assessment

The fourth BEAR component, the Oral Reading Fluency Assessment, must be individually administered. At the kindergarten level, assessment materials consist of four

TABLE 4.2. Description of the BEAR Subtests

Subtest	Description
Reading Basics	The child responds to questions assessing a variety of basic reading skills, including concepts and conventions of print (Grades K and 1), phonological/phonemic awareness (Grades K and 1), decoding (phonics/word recognition and structural analysis), and vocabulary and concept development.
Comprehension	The child responds to questions assessing reading and listening comprehension. Both narrative and informational passages are included. Only listening comprehension is measured in kindergarten.
Language Arts	The child responds to questions assessing knowledge of penmanship and letter knowledge (Grade K only), sentence structure and construction, grammar, usage, spelling, punctuation, and capitalization (Grades K–3).

letter recognition cards and, for children who can read connected text, four passages (two narrative and two informational). Letter recognition cards present 10 mixed uppercase and lowercase letters per card. For Grades 1–3, six reading passages are provided at each grade level (three narrative and three informational). After the child reads a selection, the examiner asks the child to retell the information without referring to the passage.

Administration

The Initial-Skills Analysis, Specific-Skill Analysis, and Summative Assessment are designed to be administered to classroom groups, although the manual indicates that the Specific-Skill Analysis subtests may also be administered to individuals or small groups if not all students need this type of diagnostic assessment. Administration windows for the BEAR vary by component (see Table 4.3). The Initial-Skills Analysis, which serves as a quick screener, is administered at the beginning of the year or whenever a child enters the school system. The Specific-Skill Analysis, a optional diagnostic measure assessing more specific skills in the three content areas, may be administered in its entirety or in part, depending on the child's results on the Initial-Skills Analysis or teacher judgment. The Summative Assessment, a comprehensive measure of children's progress in developing grade-appropriate skills, is administered in its entirely at the end of the school year. The Oral Reading Fluency Assessment can be administered up to three times a year to monitor reading fluency development.

For the first three assessments, subtests can be given in any order, with times ranging from about 30 to 40 minutes. Although the subtests do not have strict time limits in the sense that group-administered standardized tests do, examiners are instructed to collect student booklets on the Summative Assessment after allowing a total of 50 minutes per subtest, even if children are not finished. Administration procedures are clearly spelled out, with the complete examiner script for each subtest highlighted in the guides. For the Specific-Skill Analysis, examiners may administer the test for the grade level below a child's actual placement, if desired, but no guidelines are provided to indicate which children should be tested out of level. Nor are guidelines provided to indicate which students should receive follow-up diagnostic testing after the Initial-Skills Analysis. Presumably, all children who score in the lower

TABLE 4.3. Components, Administration Windows, and Administration Times for the BEAR

	Administration window			
Component	Beginning of year	Middle of year	End of year	Time required
Initial-Skills Analysis	×			100–120 minutes[a]
Specific-Skill Analysis[b]	×			35–40 minutes per content area[a]
Summative Assessment			×	30–40 minutes per content area[a]
Oral Reading Fluency Assessment	×	×	×	10–20 minutes

[a]Times for these components are based on a group administration format.
[b]The Specific-Skill Analysis may be administered at any time during the year when more in-depth information is desired.

of the two instructional levels on one or more of the Initial-Skills Analysis subtests should take the associated Specific-Skills Analysis subtest(s), but this is not explicitly stated.

The Oral Reading Fluency Assessment is administered using a set of laminated cards and record forms reproduced from the administration and scoring guide. The manual suggests tape recording as an option for examiners. Given that kindergarten assessments are untimed and the letter recognition sample is small (10 letters total), kindergarten letter recognition fluency assessments provide limited information about either letter-name knowledge or letter-naming fluency. Timing oral reading is optional for Grade 1 but required for Grades 2 and 3. On passage reading tasks, examiners are permitted to pronounce proper nouns for students, but the guide does not specify whether subsequent mispronunciations are counted as errors. In contrast to the procedures used in most oral reading fluency measures, the examiner does not provide any words if the child pauses or struggles. Instead, the examiner is instructed to permit "adequate time" and then encourage the child to move on. In the absence of specific guidelines for prompting, reading rates obtained on the BEAR are vulnerable to examiner variance and are likely to be lower than those obtained on other measures.

Scores

The BEAR yields only raw scores and can be scored by hand or with the local scoring and reporting software. On the Initial-Skills Analysis and Specific-Skill Analysis, scoring is dichotomous for both multiple-choice and open-ended questions, whereas on the Summative Assessment, open-ended questions are scored on a 2-, 3-, or 4-point scale. Because there are only three alternatives for multiple-choice questions, which far outnumber open-ended questions, guessing is a factor in student performance. Scoring procedures are clearly spelled out in the guides, which include answer keys, scoring rubrics for open-ended questions, samples of completed record forms, samples of student responses to open-ended questions, and reproducible charts for recording student and classwide results. Raw scores are converted to percent correct and, for the Initial-Skills Analysis and the Summative Assessment, to instructional levels. Examiners can hand-score tests or, for the first three components, enter responses for multiple-choice items directly into the software scoring program. Hand scoring is a lengthy process that involves three record forms and up to five separate steps.

For reading passages on the Oral Reading Fluency Assessment, five types of errors are recorded: (1) mispronunciations, (2) omissions, (3) insertions, (4) substitutions, and (5) reversals. Instead of using a separate mark per error type, the examiner places a slash mark over any missed word, a system that reduces interexaminer variability but also reduces the amount of information available for error analysis. Letter recognition is scored on 3-point scales for accuracy and oral reading skills, whereas passage reading is scored on 3-point scales for accuracy, retelling, and oral reading skills, using rubrics in the guide. The guide includes samples of completed letter recognition and passage reading record forms. The passage reading example is for a Grade 2 student who earned the highest rating in the retelling category. Examples of less proficient retellings should also be included for comparison purposes.

The manual presents two options for calculating words per minute: one in which the child reads the entire passage and another in which the examiner stops the child after 1 minute. The administration and scoring guide includes reproducible record forms for all fluency tasks, with passage-specific formulae to facilitate calculating reading rate, and the software scoring program calculates reading rate automatically when the examiner enters the number of seconds required to read the passage. Users should note that on the BEAR, reading rate is defined as *words read per minute* (WPM), not as *words read correctly per minute* (WCPM), as on most oral reading fluency measures. According to the publisher, reading rate, accuracy, and oral reading skills (defined as appropriate word grouping, interpretation of punctuation marks, and use of appropriate expression) are measured separately to permit comparisons of children's competencies in these areas. The BEAR uses two different score types to assess the three skills, however—a WPM metric for rate versus a 3-point rating scale for accuracy and oral retelling. I have found that some children with poor decoding skills can obtain a satisfactory reading rate by guessing rapidly at unfamiliar words and moving quickly through the text. Moreover, although the record forms printed in the guide indicate the percent correct scores for each accuracy rating (e.g., 85% to 94% = 2 points), the report derived from the software scoring program displays only the point value.

Interpretation

Performance on the BEAR is interpreted in terms of proficiency categories, termed *instructional levels*. Scores are converted to percent correct and compared with cut scores for two proficiency categories for the Initial-Skills Analysis (Emerging and Limited) and three proficiency categories for the Summative Assessment (Developed, Developing, and Not Developed), using the student record form. The technical manual and an appendix in the scoring guides for the first three components provide definitions for instructional levels by grade for each of the three subtests, with separate standards for listening and reading comprehension. The technical manual also includes tables indicating the percent correct ranges that correspond to each instructional level. Instructional levels reflect combined performance (i.e., total test score) on the three subtests for the Initial-Skills Analysis, whereas on the Summative Assessment, separate instructional levels are provided for each subtest. Raw score ranges for the instructional levels vary by grade, with higher expectations as the grades increase. For example, on the Initial-Skills Analysis, the Emerging category for kindergarten includes scores from 52% to 100% correct, whereas Emerging for Grade 3 includes scores from 70% to 100% correct. The Oral Reading Fluency Assessment guide includes a table with suggested reading rates by grade level, derived from Rasinski and Padak (2001). Because reading rate is based on WPM rather than WCPM, rate guidelines are higher than those in other evaluative systems, especially for Grade 1.

Technical Adequacy

Information in this section was obtained from the guides and from the technical manual.

Test Development

In the initial research study, which was designed to evaluate the technical quality of the items prior to the development of the final form, two forms of the Initial-Skills Analysis were administered to approximately 10,000 students in 82 districts in 34 states at each of the four grade levels in the fall of 2000. In the spring of 2001, two forms of the Summative Assessment were administered in each grade, with approximately 10,000 students in 150 districts in 28 states participating. In the school year 2001–2002, a research study with 37 schools in 19 states was conducted, in which participating schools agreed to administer the entire assessment system to all students in each K–3 class. The Initial-Skills Analysis was administered in the fall (*ns* = 1,241 to 1,364), the Specific-Skill Analysis in the winter (*ns* = 754 to 1,247), and the Summative Assessment in the spring (*ns* = 932 to 1,223). Schools also administered the Oral Reading Fluency Assessment three times (fall, winter, and spring) to six randomly selected students per class or per grade (*ns* = 45 to 318). The manual lists schools participating in each of the two research studies by name, city, and state and indicates that they demonstrated a variety of demographic characteristics relative to size, SES, and geographical location, but no information is provided regarding the number or proportion of students by any demographic variable or even by state.

Reliability Evidence

Reliabilities (presumably coefficient alphas, but unspecified as to type) range from .83 to .88 for the Initial-Skills Analysis across the four grades. Reliabilities are lower for the Specific-Skill Analysis subtests (.68 to .92), which have fewer items except at Level 1 (i.e., Grade 1). Only 3 of the 12 coefficients are at acceptable levels, with Level 1 Comprehension in the .90s and Level K Language Arts and Level 1 Reading Basics in the .80s. Eight coefficients are in the .70s, with Level K Comprehension falling in the .60s. Summative Assessment reliabilities range from .71 to .89, with half of the values falling below criterion levels, including Level K Comprehension, Level 1 Language Arts, and Reading Basics across all four levels. For the Oral Reading Fluency Assessment, means and standard deviations are reported by letter recognition card and passage for accuracy, oral reading skills, and retelling (3-point scales), and by passage for average reading rates in seconds for Levels 2 and 3. No reliability estimates of any kind are provided for the Oral Reading Fluency Assessment. Test–retest reliabilities for the Initial-Skills Analysis were obtained during the research study cited above, with study participants randomly selecting five students to take the test a second time individually or in a small-group setting (approximately 4-week intervals; *ns* = 50 to 80). Correlations between large-group and individual or small-group settings fell below acceptable levels at all four levels (*rs* = .70 to .77). The publisher suggests that the longer interval may have contributed to the low values. Because means and standard deviations are not reported for the two sets of testings, it is not possible to determine the effect of practice and/or format on score levels. No evidence of interscorer reliability is presented for any of the components or subtests. Because fluency-based tasks and holistic scales are highly vulnerable to interexaminer inconsistency, conducting studies to evaluate interrater reliability for the Oral Reading Fluency Assessment should be a priority, especially given the absence of a standardized prompt procedure.

Validity Evidence

CONTENT VALIDITY EVIDENCE

Items were developed to match nationwide content standards in reading and language arts and to achieve grade-level appropriateness, fairness, usability, clarity, and relevancy. For items requiring scorer judgment, student sample responses for an item were presented and scored until a lead scorer and trainee scorers achieved a level of agreement of 80% or higher. All of the Oral Reading Fluency Assessment passages were written specifically for the BEAR to avoid the effects of prior exposure on performance. For this assessment, kindergarten passage reading difficulty was evaluated using two graded word list sources: the *EDL Core Vocabularies in Reading, Mathematics, Science, and Social Studies* (Taylor et al., 1989) and the *Children's Writer's Word Book* (Mogliner, 1992). For Levels 1 through 3, passage difficulty was assessed using the Dale–Chall, Fry, and Spache readability formulae as applied through the Readability Master 2000 software (Rodrigues & Stieglitz, 1997). As evidence that the passages are of appropriate difficulty, the technical manual reports mean words per minute for Level 2 and Level 3 passages in the final research study. Values for the four passages approximate the reading rates suggested in the manuals for Grades 2 and 3, but because mean words per minute are not provided for Level 1 passages, there is no support for the Grade 1 80 WPM rate.

Item difficulty was evaluated using both classical and item response theory (IRT) procedures. Panels of educators reviewed items for bias and sensitivity issues, and problematic test questions and/or directions were revised or eliminated. For the final forms of the BEAR, items with point biserial correlations of .25 or greater were given priority in item selection. Overall test difficulty was targeted for an average p value of about .55 to .60, with items with values of .35 to .90 given primary consideration. Differential item functioning (DIF) analyses were conducted, including the Mantel–Haenszel procedure. The cut scores used to classify students into the various proficiency categories for the Initial-Skills Analysis and Summative Assessments were based on teacher judgments obtained in the fall of 2001, with over 50 teacher judgments collected at each grade level. Prior to score setting, teachers participated in exercises designed to familiarize them with proficiency descriptions and test items.

CRITERION-RELATED VALIDITY EVIDENCE

For Levels K and 1 (ns = 202 to 562), correlations between different content areas within the Specific-Skill Analysis and Summative Assessment were generally low to moderate (.26 to .68), with Language Arts displaying the strongest relationship with Reading Basics and Comprehension. For Levels 2 and 3 (ns = 367 to 508), correlations were moderate to high (.50 to .78), with higher correlations between Reading Basics and Comprehension than between those areas and Language Arts, as predicted. Correlations between fall Initial-Skills Analysis scores and winter Specific-Skill Analysis and spring Summative Assessment scores ranged from .38 to .61 at Levels K and 1 and from .55 to .75 at Levels 2 and 3. No studies examining the concurrent or predictive relationship of the BEAR to other measures of reading, language, or academic achievement are presented.

CONSTRUCT VALIDITY EVIDENCE

No additional evidence of construct validity is presented.

Usability

Considering the amount and quality of the materials and information provided, the BEAR is a bargain. Administration and scoring guides for all four components are clear, comprehensive, and easy to use. Student booklets have attractive full-color covers, with the exception of the Specific-Skill Analysis booklets, which are reproduced from blackline masters in the guide. Examiners administering the Specific-Skill Analysis must create up to three separate booklets per child, one for each subtest. This involves photocopying from 6 to 22 pages per subtest, not including the student information sheets, and from 23 to 52 pages if all three subtests are administered. The publisher is urged to offer consumable booklets for this component as an option for purchasers. Other materials also need streamlining. The Oral Reading Fluency Assessment uses 26 separate laminated cards, which should be placed in a single spiral-bound and tabbed test book. There is no information in any of the materials about accommodations or suggestions for assessing children from diverse linguistic or cultural backgrounds, a surprising omission in a battery designed for large-scale use. Each BEAR kit includes scoring and reporting software that manages student test data for the four assessments; permits entry and reporting of teacher comments; and produces reports for administrators, teachers, and parents. Other options include disaggregating assessment data, running queries on user-defined fields, and rerostering student data. An Individual Student Profile provides a two-page report displaying performance on all assessments for one school year. Examiners can enter individual item responses directly from test booklets for multiple-choice items and previously scored open-ended items or enter previously computed raw scores. With so many options, the program is quite complex and requires an investment of time to master, especially in terms of setting up and managing files. A 42-page downloadable user's guide is embedded in the program.

Links to Intervention

Although the Specific-Skill Analysis is intended to yield diagnostic information for designing interventions, none of the guides provide any information about linking results to instruction.

Source and Cost

Each BEAR kit, which includes a copy of the software scoring and data management program and the Oral Reading Fluency Assessment for Grades K–3, is available for \$257.25 from Riverside Publishing. Test components may also be purchased separately. The BEAR software runs on Microsoft Windows only and costs \$79.00 if purchased separately. The 74-page spiral-bound technical manual retails for \$25.25. Also available is a classroom edition of a computer-administered version for the Initial-Skills Analysis, Specific-Skill Analysis, and Summative Assessment for \$199.00. The program produces a complete set of reports similar to the noncomputerized BEAR reports when the results for the Oral Reading Fluency Assessment are entered. Network editions are also available.

Summary

The *Basic Early Assessment of Reading* (BEAR) is a comprehensive early reading battery for kindergarten through Grade 3 that includes group-administered screening, diagnostic, and outcome assessments and an individually administered oral reading fluency assessment. Designed for large-scale screening and progress monitoring, the BEAR is attractive, is easy to administer, and yields an impressive amount of information for a relatively small outlay. Despite its assets, the BEAR has several limitations in terms of usability and technical adequacy. Although the group administration format is a great time saver, scoring the open-ended responses and matching student responses to content standards for the diagnostic and outcome assessments are lengthy processes. Moreover, for the diagnostic component, examiners must photocopy up to three subtests per child, which is very time-consuming, especially at the kindergarten level. Reliability is at criterion levels across all four grade levels only for the initial screening component, and no reliability estimates of any kind are provided for the oral reading fluency component. In addition, because the reading rate metric does not take errors into account and lacks a standardized prompt procedure, the oral reading fluency assessment may underidentify children with automaticity problems. For screening, diagnostic, and outcome assessments, score types are limited to percent correct and two or three broad proficiency categories, the latter of which are based on teacher judgment and vary considerably across content areas and grades. Translating the results of the BEAR into instructional interventions is also more complicated than the same process for batteries composed of single-skill measures because BEAR subtests cover several content areas per domain. Studies documenting the BEAR's relationship to validated measures of reading and its utility in predicting reading acquisition should be top priorities.

Case Example

Name of student: Margee P.
Age: 7 years, 0 months
Grade: First grade
Date of assessment: May

Reason for referral: Margee was referred by her first-grade teacher for an early reading assessment. Although Margee received extra reading assistance at home and at school this year, her teacher and parents are concerned that her skills may not meet grade-level expectations. She has been slow to learn and remember sight words, and her oral reading is halting and labored. The Summative Assessment and Oral Reading Fluency Assessment components of the *Basic Early Reading Assessment* (BEAR) were administered to assess her end-of-year skills and provide information for summer remediation.

Assessment results and interpretation: The BEAR is a comprehensive literacy assessment system that measures basic reading skills, language arts, comprehension, and oral reading fluency for students in kindergarten through Grade 3. Margee's Summative Assessment report from the BEAR software scoring program is reproduced in Figure 4.1.

For the Summative Assessment, student performance is evaluated against end-of-year benchmarks for the child's grade and yields three instructional levels, *Devel-*

bear — Basic Early Assessment of Reading™ — BEAR™

Margee P.
Summative Assessment Report

Student: P., Margee Grade: 1
Class: Ms. Jones Level: 1
School: Riverside Elementary School Date of Birth: 05/18/1995
District: Riverside Sample District Age: 7.0

SKILL	Total Number of Points Possible	Number of Points Earned	Percent of Points Earned
Reading Basics	35	25	71%
Comprehension	38	18	47%
Language Arts	32	25	78%
Total Score	105	68	64%

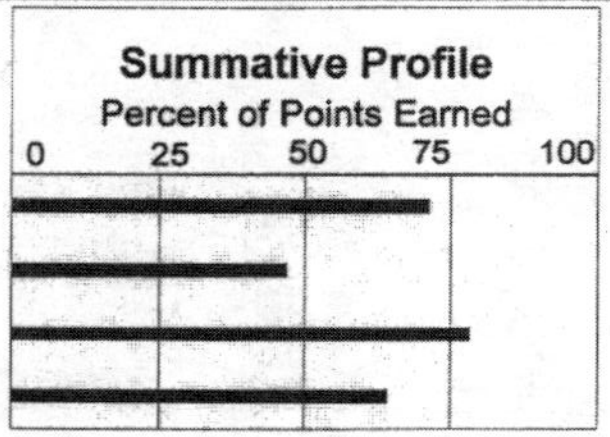

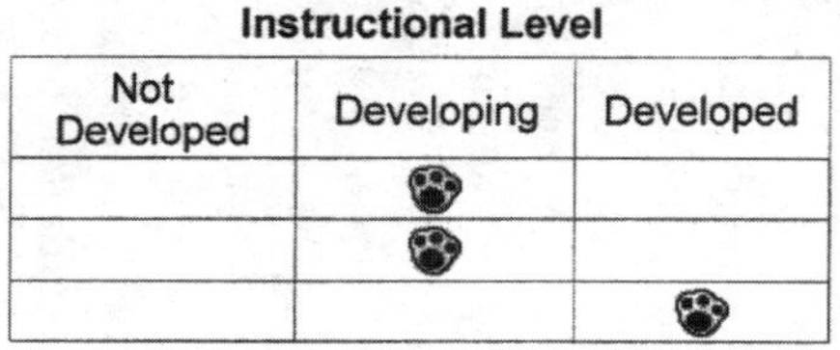

Summative Profile
(Percent of Points Earned: 0 – 25 – 50 – 75 – 100)

SKILL	Total Number of Items	Total Number of Points Possible	Number of Points Earned	Percent of Points Earned
Reading Basics				
Concepts and Conventions of Print	4	4	4	100 %
Phonological / Phonemic Awareness	9	9	8	88 %
Decoding - Phonics/Word Recognition	6	6	6	100 %
Decoding - Structural Analysis	6	8	3	37 %
Vocabulary and Concept Development	5	8	4	50 %
Total	**30**	**35**	**25**	**71 %**
Comprehension				
Reading Comprehension / Literary Respons				
Constructing Literal Understanding	17	19	8	42 %
Constructing Analytic Understanding	5	5	4	80 %
Listening Comprehension				
Constructing Literal Understanding	9	9	1	11 %
Constructing Analytic Understanding	5	5	5	100 %
Total	**36**	**38**	**18**	**47 %**
Language Arts				
Sentence Structure and Construction	4	6	1	16 %
Grammar and Usage	4	4	3	75 %
Punctuation and Capitalization	8	8	8	100 %
Spelling	14	14	13	92 %
Total	**30**	**32**	**25**	**78 %**

Instructional Level

	Not Developed	Developing	Developed
Reading Basics		●	
Comprehension		●	
Language Arts			●

Teacher Comments

Reading Basics: Test Date: 05/31/2002
Margee tended to become restless and inattentive as testing progressed.

Comprehension: Test Date: 05/18/2002

Language Arts: Test Date: 05/13/2002

FIGURE 4.1. Summative Assessment Report for Margee, generated by the BEAR scoring and reporting software. Copyright 2002 by The Riverside Publishing Company. The report form is reprinted with permission.

oped, *Developing*, and *Not Developed*, indicating consistent, inconsistent, or limited understanding of basic reading, comprehension, and language arts skills appropriate for the end of that grade. In Language Arts, Margee's performance is rated as *Developed* (78% correct), but her skills vary considerably in this domain. Her knowledge of spelling, punctuation and capitalization, and grammar and usage is grade-appropriate, but she was able to answer only one of four items assessing the understanding of sentence structure. In contrast, Margee's performance in Reading Basics and Comprehension does not meet end-of-first-grade expectations and varies considerably from skill to skill (*Developing*–71% and 47%, respectively). On the Reading Basics subtest, her phonics, word recognition, and print awareness skills are very well developed. Her phonological/phonemic awareness skills–that is, her ability to attend to and manipulate individual sounds in language–are also strong for her grade. Margee had more difficulty with items assessing vocabulary and concept development and with items requiring her to recognize sight words, identify word parts, and combine letter patterns to form words. On the Comprehension subtest, which measures both reading and listening comprehension, her ability to understand material read to her is much less well developed than her ability to understand material she reads herself.

The BEAR Oral Reading Fluency Assessment requires the child to read a grade-level passage aloud. Student performance is evaluated in terms of retelling, accuracy, oral reading skills, and reading rate. Retelling, accuracy, and oral reading skills are each rated on a 3-point scale. Reading rate is evaluated in terms of number of words read per minute (WPM) and compared with end-of-year expectations. Margee's performance in oral reading is described below.

Oral Reading Fluency	Rating/Score	Descriptive Category
Retelling	1	Incomplete Retelling
Accuracy	1	Not Fluent
Oral Reading Skills	1	Not Fluent
Reading Rate	81 WPM	Adequate

On the narrative passage presented, Margee read 81 WPM. Although her reading rate meets the suggested criterion for the end of first grade (80 WPM), her reading accuracy was poor. On the 104-word passage, she made 17 errors (84% accuracy = *not fluent*). When she encountered an unfamiliar word, she tended to substitute a word that suited the context of the story rather than taking time to decode it. Her oral reading skills, that is, her ability to read smoothly, in phrases, and with expression, were also limited. She read word by word, rather than in phrases, and ignored punctuation marks in her effort to read as rapidly as possible. She also had difficulty retelling the story as a coherent whole after she had read it aloud.

BOOK BUDDIES EARLY LITERACY SCREENING

Overview

The Book Buddies Early Literacy Screening (BBELS; Johnston, Invernizzi, & Juel, 1998) is an individually administered, nonstandardized set of measures designed to assess the early reading skills of first- and second-grade students and older poor readers. Developed by a team of reading researchers at the University of Virginia as a pre- and posttutoring assessment for Book Buddies, the first large-scale program to provide individual tutoring for children at risk for reading failure (Invernizzi, Rosemary, Juel,

& Richards, 1997), it can also be used for individual or classwide screening. The BBELS includes measures of alphabet knowledge, letter-sound awareness, and word recognition and shares many items with the *Phonological Awareness Literacy Screening* (PALS; Invernizzi & Meier, 2002a) and the *Early Reading Screening Inventory* (ERSI; Morris, 1992b). Its purposes are (1) to evaluate children's beginning reading skills and (2) to provide information for helping tutors select appropriate instructional materials and activities. It can be administered up to three times a year: as an initial assessment prior to intervention, as a progress monitoring assessment during the intervention period, and as an end-of-year evaluation. Examiner materials consist of an assessment summary sheet, assessment recording form, spelling assessment form, word identification list form, and two story assessment forms. Student materials include an alphabet naming sheet, pictures for sound awareness picture sorting, a word list sheet, and three stories for measuring concept of word and oral reading accuracy. All of the assessment materials are reproducible and contained in the handbook that describes the Book Buddies tutoring model. Examiners must provide paper for the Letter Production task and books above the preprimer level. There is a misprint on page 45 on the Assessment Summary Sheet: The Letter-Sound Knowledge total should be 62, not 78.

Assessment Tasks

The BBELS includes seven tasks in three categories of early literacy skills: alphabet knowledge, letter-sound knowledge, and word recognition (see Table 4.4).

TABLE 4.4. Description of the BBELS Assessment Tasks by Domain

Domain	Task	Description
Alphabet Knowledge	Letter Identification	The child identifies random arrays of 26 uppercase letters and 26 lowercase letters.
	Letter Production	The child writes the letters of the alphabet dictated by the examiner in random order or writes them as the examiner sings the alphabet song with the child.
Letter-Sound Knowledge	Picture Sorting	The child sorts pictures by beginning sound by placing a set of 12 pictures under 1 of 3 target pictures with the same initial consonant sound (/s/, /m/, and /b/).
	Spelling	The child writes as many letters as possible for 10 one-syllable words.
Word Recognition	Word List Reading	The child reads words from 20-item preprimer, primer, and/or first-grade lists.
	Concept of Word	After the examiner reads a brief story (*Sandcastle*) aloud and points to each word, the child reads the story again with the examiner. The child then reads and points to each word. The child also reads two words in each of the four sentences.
	Word Identification in Stories	The child reads the story *Sam* aloud. If the child can read 25 of the 30 words, the child reads the next story (*My Huge Dog Max*). If the child can read 62 of the 72 words in that story, the child reads a primer-level story (not provided).

Administration

All of the BBELS tasks are untimed, and the total assessment takes about 30–40 minutes. On Word List Reading, progressively more difficult lists are administered until the child can read fewer than 10 words per list. If the child reads fewer than 5 words on the lowest level list, the Concept of Word task is administered. If the child knows 5 or more words, the first story (*Sam*) is presented. The handbook presents step-by-step administration procedures that are attractively formatted and easy to follow.

Scores

The BBELS is nonstandardized and yields only raw scores. Items are scored 1 or 0 on all tasks except for Concept of Word and Spelling. On Concept of Word, 2 points are awarded for each sentence in which the child points to all the words correctly, and 1 point is awarded for each word the child correctly identifies. On Spelling, 1 point is awarded for each logically represented letter (e.g., *f* for *v* in *van*), with 1 bonus point per word for perfect spelling. On Letter Identification, pauses of more than 3 seconds in naming a letter are counted as errors. Reversals are scored as correct for Letter Production and Spelling. On Word Identification in Stories, 1 point is awarded for each word read correctly. If the child pauses more than 5 seconds, the examiner provides the word and counts it as an error.

Interpretation

Assessment results are evaluated in terms of two types of readers: (1) *emergent readers*, defined as children who have incomplete alphabet knowledge, lack an awareness of sounds in words, have inaccurate fingerpointing, and can identify less than 10 words on the preprimer list; and (2) *early readers*, defined as children who know the alphabet, can spell many sounds in words, and can read 15 or more words on the preprimer list and some on the primer list. Materials and activities in the handbook target one of these two types of readers.

Technical Adequacy

No information about technical adequacy is presented in the handbook, but the task formats and item types have been extensively field-tested and validated in studies of the PALS and ERSI (e.g., Invernizzi et al., 1997; Lombardino et al., 1999; Perney, Morris, & Carter, 1997; Santa & Hoien, 1999). Information from several of these studies is included in "Relevant Research," below.

Usability

The BBELS is very inexpensive, is easy to use, is readily adaptable to local norming, and yields a wealth of information for instructional planning. Administration, scoring, and interpretation procedures are described in clear and concise language, making the battery accessible to examiners with a wide range of backgrounds. Companion training videos illustrate the Book Buddies tutoring approach but do not include information about the assessment.

Links to Intervention

The BBELS is specifically designed to yield information for instructional planning in a one-to-one tutoring program for at-risk first and second graders. The handbook presents a three-step process for interpreting assessment results. First, the examiner compares the child's assessment results with criteria for emergent and early readers to select the appropriate level of lesson plans, as described above. Second, the examiner compares test results with a set of criteria for determining the child's reading level to select appropriate books. For example, if the child can read *Sam* and 5 to 9 of the 20 words on the preprimer list, the child is considered an Emergent Reader Level 2 and is ready for book levels 3 through 7 (preprimers 1 and 2). Third, the results of the Letter Identification, Letter Production, Picture Sorting, and Spelling tasks are analyzed for use in planning word study activities.

Detailed lesson plans for emergent and early readers are presented in Chapters 4 and 5, respectively, of the handbook. For the emergent reader, the lesson plan includes four parts: (1) rereading familiar material (10–15 minutes), (2) word study and phonics (10–12 minutes), (3) writing for sounds (5–10 minutes), and (4) reading new material (10–15 minutes). For the early reader, the lesson plan includes three main parts: (1) reading for fluency (5–10 minutes), (2) reading and writing (20–30 minutes), and (3) word study and phonics (5–10 minutes). When time permits, rereading familiar material or additional writing can be added (5 minutes). To assist tutors in selecting appropriate books, the authors provide a table that cross-references coding systems for Reading Recovery levels, Ready Readers stages (Modern Curriculum Press), and basal reader grade levels. Appendices contain an extensive set of reproducible forms, including alphabet cards and sound charts, a sample permission letter for tutoring, a list of books by authors organized by Reading Recovery levels, a leveled list of books by phonics features, and a list of publishers offering series books. Available by separate purchase are two training videos demonstrating each component of tutoring sessions with emergent readers, one for the first day of tutoring and the second for the middle of the year.

Relevant Research

In an evaluation of the effectiveness of the Book Buddies tutoring program with 358 first and second graders using four measures adapted from the ERSI (Alphabet Knowledge, Concept of Word, Phoneme–Grapheme Knowledge, and Word Recognition), Invernizzi and colleagues (1997) found that only Word Recognition predicted the number of tutoring sessions. In a validity study of the ERSI with 105 first graders, Perney and colleagues (1997) reported a coefficient alpha for total test of .85. September first-grade scores on ERSI Alphabet Knowledge, Concept of Word, Phoneme Awareness, and Word Recognition predicted end-of-first-grade reading performance, as measured by basal reading passages ($r = .70$), word recognition ($r = .67$), and spelling ($r = .67$). In a sample of 149 kindergarten students, Lombardino and colleagues (1999) reported an ERSI split-half reliability of .95. End-of-kindergarten ERSI total scores were moderately correlated with end-of-first-grade scores on the *Woodcock Reading Mastery Tests–Revised* Word Identification, Word Attack, and Passage Comprehension tests ($rs = .65$, .57, and .73, respectively). Of the four ERSI measures, Phoneme Awareness and Word Recognition were the best predictors.

Source and Cost

The BBELS is included in Chapter 3 of *Book Buddies: Guidelines for Volunteer Tutors of Emergent and Early Readers* by F. R. Johnston, M. Invernizzi, and C. Juel (1998), available from Guilford Press for $23.00. The two training videos, approximately 45 minutes in length and designed for use by tutoring program coordinators, cost $40.00 each.

Summary

The *Book Buddies Early Literacy Screening* (BBELS) is a practitioner-friendly set of individually administered, nonstandardized early reading tasks linked to a one-to-one tutoring program for at-risk readers. Developed for community-based tutoring programs, the BBELS is also useful for individual and classwide screening, has documented utility in predicting reading acquisition and responsiveness to intervention, and lends itself readily to classwide norming. Because all of the materials are reproducible, the only cost to examiners is the purchase of the handbook, which also contains guidelines, lesson plans, and suggested activities for an empirically based tutoring program for at-risk early primary grade children. I often cite the handbook in the recommendations section of early reading assessment reports as a resource for parents for working with their children at home or sharing with tutors.

Case Example

Name of student: Lavinia C.
Age: 6 years, 2 months
Grade: First grade
Date of assessment: January

Reason for referral: Lavinia was referred for an early reading assessment by her first-grade teacher. Lavinia's family is originally from South America, and although she was born in the United States, her parents speak very little English. She had trouble learning her letters in kindergarten and continues to struggle in acquiring early reading skills. She is scheduled to begin receiving services from an after-school tutoring program, and information on her current level of reading skills is needed to plan tutoring activities.

Assessment results and interpretation: The *Book Buddies Early Literacy Screening* (BBELS) measures a wide range of early literacy skills, including letter-name and letter-sound knowledge, single word reading, passage reading, and spelling. Lavinia's scores and the total points per task are reported below.

Domain/Task	Raw Score	Reading Level
Alphabet Knowledge		
Letter Identification–Uppercase	26/26	–
Letter Identification–Lowercase	26/26	–
Letter Production–Uppercase	26/26	–
Letter Production–Lowercase	26/26	–

(continued)

Letter-Sound Knowledge		
Picture Sorting	12/12	–
Spelling	32/50	–
Word Identification in Lists		
Preprimer list (early first grade)	20/20	Independent
Primer list (middle first grade)	10/20	Frustration
First-grade list (late first grade)	5/20	Frustration
Word Identification in Stories		
Preprimer 2 story	30/30	Independent
Preprimer 3 story	46/72	Frustration

Lavinia's overall performance can be described as that of a "late emergent reader." She was able to name and write all 26 uppercase and lowercase letters when they were randomly presented, but her letter naming and production speed were quite slow. She was also able to sort pictures according to three initial consonant sounds. The Spelling task requires children to write 10 one-syllable words, with one point awarded for each logically represented letter and a bonus point for correct spelling. Lavinia was able to spell most consonant–vowel–consonant words, such as *van*. She has not mastered consonant blends, vowel teams, and words with long vowels (e.g., *pum* for *plum*, *tet* for *treat*, *skat* for *skate*). She was able to read all of the words on the preprimer list; however, her performance fell to the frustration level for primer and first-grade lists (i.e., less than 15/20 words correct). On the first preprimer story, she was able to read all of the words correctly, but her reading speed was very slow. She made numerous errors on the more difficult preprimer 3 story (frustration level). Her current instructional level in reading is rated at a preprimer or early first-grade level.

DYNAMIC INDICATORS OF BASIC EARLY LITERACY SKILLS

Overview

The *Dynamic Indicators of Basic Early Literacy Skills* (DIBELS; Good & Kaminski, 2002) is a set of brief, individually administered fluency-based measures for monitoring the development of prereading and reading skills for children from preschool through third grade. Created as a downward extension of curriculum-based measurement (CBM) oral reading for preschool and kindergarten students, DIBELS has gone through several editions and now extends through third grade. The sixth edition includes 1-minute fluency-based measures of phonemic awareness, letter naming, pseudoword reading, oral reading, story retelling, and word usage. Retell Fluency and Word Use Fluency, which assess passage comprehension and expressive vocabulary, respectively, have been added in this version to align DIBELS more closely with the core components identified in the National Reading Panel (2000) report. The purposes of DIBELS include (1) identifying children at risk for early reading failure, (2) monitoring children's progress in acquiring early literacy skills, and (3) evaluating the effectiveness of reading interventions. DIBELS includes two types of assessments: (1) benchmark assessments, designed to be administered to all students three times a year; and (2) progress monitoring measures, designed to be administered more frequently to students receiving interventions. Benchmark assessment materials consist of scoring booklets, which contain student response forms designed to be photocopied back-to-back and saddle-stapled and examiner scoring and recording forms, and a set of reusable student materials. Progress monitoring materials consist of examiner forms and 20 alternate forms of student materials per measure. Additional materials include an administration and scoring guide that covers both types of assessments. All of the materials are formatted for 8½- × 11-inch sheets of paper, reproducible, and downloadable free of charge from the DIBELS Web site (http://dibels.uoregon.edu). Examiners must provide a colored pen for the Retell Fluency and Word Use Fluency tasks and a clipboard.

Assessment Tasks

Seven DIBELS measures are currently available, including the CBM-type oral reading fluency probes. Table 4.5 displays the measures and administration windows. Preschool DIBELS measures are included in the table for the sake of completeness. Table 4.6 describes the DIBELS measures by domain. The terms for the domains are those used by the authors.

Administration

All of the DIBELS measures must be individually administered and require about 3–4 minutes each. To administer each task, the examiner places the student copy of the probe in front of the child and the examiner probe on the clipboard so that the child cannot see what is being recorded. Administering the full set of benchmark tasks takes about 10–20 minutes, depending on the screening window, and a single examiner can screen a classroom of 25 children in approximately 1½ hours. For progress monitoring purposes, the authors recommend administering the grade-specific progress monitoring measures twice weekly for at least a month, so that teachers can evaluate the effects of instruction and make modifications as needed. Examiner materials for benchmark and progress monitoring measures include a shortened form of task directions. One or two teaching items are provided for all measures except for Oral

TABLE 4.5. DIBELS Measures by Grade and Administration Window

<table>
<tr><th colspan="3">Preschool</th><th colspan="3">Kindergarten</th><th colspan="3">Grade 1</th><th colspan="3">Grade 2</th><th colspan="3">Grade 3</th></tr>
<tr><th>Beg.</th><th>Mid.</th><th>End</th><th>Beg.</th><th>Mid.</th><th>End</th><th>Beg.</th><th>Mid.</th><th>End</th><th>Beg.</th><th>Mid.</th><th>End</th><th>Beg.</th><th>Mid.</th><th>End</th></tr>
<tr><td colspan="5">Initial Sound Fluency</td><td colspan="10"></td></tr>
<tr><td colspan="3"></td><td colspan="4">Letter Naming Fluency</td><td colspan="8"></td></tr>
<tr><td colspan="4"></td><td colspan="5">Phoneme Segmentation Fluency</td><td colspan="6"></td></tr>
<tr><td colspan="4"></td><td colspan="6">Nonsense Word Fluency</td><td colspan="5"></td></tr>
<tr><td colspan="7"></td><td colspan="8">Oral Reading Fluency</td></tr>
<tr><td colspan="7"></td><td colspan="8">Retell Fluency</td></tr>
<tr><td colspan="15">Word Use Fluency</td></tr>
</table>

Note. Retell Fluency and Word Use Fluency are optional at all administration windows.

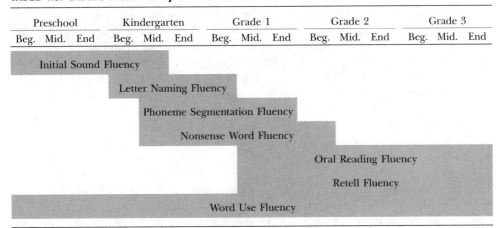

TABLE 4.6. Description of the DIBELS Measures by Domain

Domain	Measure	Description
Phonological Awareness	Initial Sound Fluency	The examiner asks the child to identify the one of four pictures that begins with a target sound. The child is also required to produce the beginning sound of an orally presented word that matches one of the pictures. The score is the number of onsets correct per minute for the set of four picture probes, obtained by multiplying the number of correct responses by 60 and dividing that number by the number of seconds required to complete the task.
	Phoneme Segmentation Fluency	The child segments three- and four-phoneme words spoken by the examiner into individual phonemes. Credit is given for each sound segment, and the score is the number of correct sound segments per minute.
Alphabetic Principle	Letter Naming Fluency	The child names uppercase and lowercase letters randomly arrayed on a page. The score is the number of letters correctly named in 1 minute.
	Nonsense Word Fluency	The child pronounces two- and three-phoneme pseudowords presented on a sheet of paper. The child may pronounce the individual sounds or read the whole word. The score is the number of correct letter sounds per minute.
Fluency with Connected Text	Oral Reading Fluency	The child reads a grade-level passage aloud for 1 minute. The score is the number of words read correctly per minute. For benchmark assessments, the score is the median of the score on three passages. Both narrative and informational passages are included.
Comprehension	Retell Fluency	After reading a grade-level passage, the child retells what has been read. The score is the total number of relevant words produced by the child in 1 minute.
Vocabulary	Word Use Fluency	The child uses a word provided by the examiner in a sentence. The examiner provides words and the child produces sentences for 1 minute. The score is the total number of words in correct utterances in 1 minute.

Note. Optional tasks are shaded.

Reading Fluency (ORF). The revised ORF directions include a retell prompt: "When I say 'stop,' I may ask you to tell me about what you have read, so do your best reading." Retell Fluency (RF) is administered after ORF if the child can read 10 or more words correctly on the first passage. Discontinue rules are provided for each task. Some of the words on the kindergarten and Grade 1 Word Use Fluency (WUF) measures are not nouns and do not lend themselves easily to sentence building, especially for young children (e.g., *which, else, meant*).

Reliable administration of the DIBELS tasks–especially Initial Sound Fluency (ISF), Phoneme Segmentation Fluency (PSF), and WUF–takes practice because examiners must deliver the test stimuli at a steady pace while recording children's rapid and sometimes less than intelligible responses. For example, for the first three ISF items per page, the examiner pronounces the names of the pictures, identifies the target sound, starts the stopwatch, and stops the stopwatch as soon as the child responds. If the child does not respond in 5 seconds, the examiner scores the question as 0 and presents the next question. For the fourth item, the examiner asks the child to point to a picture beginning with a target sound. Results depend not only on the child's sound knowledge and response rate but also on the speed with which the examiner manages the materials and proceeds through the four pages. The administration and scoring guide includes a useful assessment integrity checklist for each measure.

Scores

All of the DIBELS measures use a fluency metric for scoring (e.g., the number of correct initial sounds produced in 1 minute or number of words read correctly per minute [WCPM]. Although the guide includes scoring examples for each task, scoring procedures for many tasks are complex and require considerable study and practice before they can be rapidly and accurately applied during test administration. I strongly recommend several practice sessions per measure with an experienced colleague to observe and provide corrective feedback, especially for ISF, RF, and WUF. On ISF, children may respond with the first sound or the first several sounds of the stimulus word, provided that they omit the final sound. On Letter Naming Fluency (LNF), PSF, Nonsense Word Fluency (NWF), and ORF, if the child delays longer than 3 seconds on a letter, sound, or word, the examiner records an error and provides the letter, sound, or word. On WUF, pauses of 5 seconds are counted as errors. For LNF, inaccuracies and omissions are also scored as errors. Because in some fonts, uppercase *I* and lowercase *l* are difficult to distinguish, responses of either "I" or "L" are scored as correct for those letters. Scoring for PSF is liberal. Additional sounds are not counted as errors if they are separated from the other sounds in the word. Credit is awarded for elongations (e.g., *rrreeesssttt* = 4/4 points), as well as for each correct sound segment, even if the word is not segmented to the phoneme level (e.g., *tr . . . ick* = 2/4 points). Pronunciation guides are provided to facilitate scoring for ISF, PSF, and NWF. For ORF, inaccuracies, omissions, and substitutions but not insertions are scored as errors. To score RF and WRF, the examiner counts the number of words the child produces by moving a colored pen through a row of numbers on the record sheet. For RF, only words that demonstrate an understanding of the passage receive credit. Minor repetitions, redundancies, and inaccuracies are scored as correct, but rote repetitions and stories from the child's experience are counted as errors. For WUF, examinee utterances (phrases, expressions, or sentences) must reflect an understanding of the meaning of the word for any words to be scored as correct.

Interpretation

DIBELS was originally designed for local norming, with fall, winter, and spring administration of grade-specific tasks to establish cutoff scores indicating risk for reading failure. When local norms are developed, the authors suggest three risk categories: below the 20th percentile (PR) = at risk; 20th to 40th PR = some risk; and above the 40th PR = low risk. Over the last several years, DIBELS has evolved into a benchmark-based system for evaluating group as well as individual performance in early literacy skills and predicting performance on high-stakes tests (see Table 4.7). Longitudinal studies (Good, Simmons, & Kame'enui, 2001) indicate that students who

TABLE 4.7. Timelines, Benchmark Goals, and Risk Indicators for DIBELS Measures

Measure	Benchmark goal	Risk indicator
Initial Sound Fluency	25–35 initial sounds correct per minute by winter of kindergarten	<10 initial sounds correct per minute in winter of kindergarten
Phoneme Segmentation Fluency	35–45 phonemes correct per minute by spring of kindergarten/fall of Grade 1	<10 phonemes correct per minute in spring of kindergarten/fall of Grade 1
Nonsense Word Fluency	50 letter sounds correct per minute by winter of Grade 1	<30 letter sounds correct per minute by winter of Grade 1
Oral Reading Fluency	≥40 words correct per minute by spring of Grade 1	<10 words correct per minute in spring of Grade 1
	≥90 words correct per minute by spring of Grade 2	<50 words correct per minute in spring of Grade 2
	≥110 words correct per minute by spring of Grade 3	<70 words correct per minute in spring of Grade 3

Note. Benchmarks and risk indicators have not been set for Letter Naming Fluency, Retell Fluency, and Word Use Fluency.

achieve a DIBELS benchmark at the specified time period are very likely to achieve the following benchmark, whereas students whose performance falls below a DIBELS benchmark goal are at high risk for subsequent reading difficulties. The anchor for the system is the benchmark for end-of-first-grade ORF, which is set at 40 WCPM. No benchmarks have been established for LNF or for the two new measures (RF and WRF). According to the administration and scoring guide, when children who are reading at or above 40 WCPM have RF scores of 25% or less compared with their ORF scores, this suggests possible comprehension problems. A technical report available on the DIBELS Web site (Good, Wallin, Simmons, Kame'enui, & Kaminski, 2002) presents descriptive statistics for each measure by grade and administration window for the 2001–2002 school year, based on all students entered into the data system (between 185 and 706 schools and a median of about 50 students per school per window).

Several case examples interpreting children's performance on the DIBELS are available in the DIBELS literature (e.g., Good & Kaminski, 1996; Kaminski & Good, 1998). Good and Kaminski (1996) present a case example for a kindergarten student illustrating the application of the DIBELS problem-solving model using PSF and Onset Recognition Fluency (OnRF, an earlier version of ISF). The Web site includes a video clip with an end-of-first-grade reader who is reading above the 40 WCPM benchmark.

Technical Adequacy

The technical information for DIBELS reviewed below is taken from a series of articles by the authors and their colleagues, materials on the DIBELS Web site, and technical reports (Good & Kaminski, 2002b; Good et al., 2002). Many of the reliability and validity coefficients are drawn from a report by Good and colleagues (in preparation, cited in Good et al., 2002) that does not specify sample sizes and/or administration windows for all of the studies discussed.

Test Development

DIBELS was originally developed as a downward extension of CBM oral reading probes for children with limited or no textual reading skills and consisted of fluency-based tasks measuring reading precursors, such as phonemic awareness. Later editions, which incorporated CBM oral reading probes and expanded the grade range, targeted three reading domains, termed the "Big Ideas" of early literacy: phonological awareness, the alphabetic principle, and fluency with connected text. The two new tasks in the sixth edition are an effort to measure the two other domains identified by the National Reading Panel (2000)–vocabulary and comprehension. The authors emphasize that DIBELS is not intended as a comprehensive or diagnostic reading assessment battery but as a set of quick, efficient indicators of children's progress in early literacy skills for early identification and intervention purposes. Measures were designed to meet 11 criteria, including brevity, ease of administration, sensitivity to growth and to the effects of intervention, availability in multiple forms, and the use of production-type responses (Kaminski & Good, 1998). Initial benchmarks were developed by the Early Childhood Research Institute on Measuring Growth and Development at the University of Oregon, and efforts are continuing to establish validated national benchmarks for each measure. As noted above, the anchor for the system of benchmark goals was set at 40 or more WCPM on CBM oral reading on grade-level material at the end of first grade, based on research (Good, Simmons, & Smith, 1998) demonstrating that this level of performance is associated with a trajectory of reading progress with an adequate slope of improvement. Procedures for establishing benchmark goals for the other measures using a series of linked, short-term longitudinal studies are described in a recent study by Good and colleagues (2001). For example, 56 kindergarten children who took PSF in the spring were followed through the spring of first grade. Three categories of PSF performance were identified, based on the desired outcome of a Grade 1 ORF performance of at least 40 WCPM. Of children scoring 35 or more segments correct per minute (SCPM) on PSF at the end of kindergarten, 92% achieved the Grade 1 ORF goal. In contrast, Grade 1 ORF goals were attained by only 35% of children scoring between 10 and 35 SCPM and by only 11% of children scoring below 10 SCPM. Similar procedures were used to establish benchmarks and risk indicators for the other DIBELS measures.

Reliability Evidence

DIBELS measures vary considerably in reliability, with ISF/OnRF the least reliable and LNF and ORF the most reliable across the administration windows. Alternate-form reliability for OnRF was .72 in January of kindergarten (Good et al., in preparation). In a study with 38 kindergarten and 40 first-grade students (Kaminski & Good, 1996), 1-week alternate-form reliability for LNF was .93 for point estimates (performance on a single probe) and .99 for level estimates (average across all probes in a data collection period) for 18 kindergartners and .83 and .95 for point and level estimates for 20 first graders. In a more recent study (Good et al., in preparation), LNF had a 1-month alternate-form reliability of .88 in kindergarten. In the Kaminski and Good (1996) study cited above, 2-week alternate-form reliability for PSF was .88 for point estimates and .99 for level estimates for kindergartners and .83 and .95 for point and level estimates, respectively, for first graders. Coefficients were slightly lower in a later study (Good et al., in preparation), with a 1-month alternate-form reliability coefficient of .79 for PSF in May of kindergarten and a 1-month alternate-form reliability of .83 for NWF in January of first grade.

Much of the ORF reliability and validity evidence cited in materials on the DIBELS Web site is based on research with the *Test of Reading Fluency* (TORF; Children's Educational Services, 1987), an earlier version of DIBELS ORF. Moreover, many of the studies date from the 1980s and include samples of children beyond the early primary grade years. Alternate-form reliability of different reading passages drawn from the same level of the TORF ranged from .89 to .94 (Tindal, Marston, & Deno, 1983). In a more recent study (Good et al., in preparation), alternate-form reliability for the DIBELS ORF passages was .94, whereas median alternate-form reliability for the TORF passages was .95. Test–retest reliability estimates of .92 to .97 are reported for the TORF for elementary students (Tindal et al., 1983). TORF passages correlate highly (.92 to .96) with the current DIBELS ORF passages (Good et al., in preparation). No evidence of interrater reliability for any of the measures is presented in the articles cited above or on the Web site. Given the complexity of administration and scoring procedures for many tasks and the vulnerability of fluency-based measures to examiner variance, studies evaluating interexaminer and interscorer consistency for each measure at each grade level are essential.

Test Floors and Item Gradients

Because of the rapid development of the early literacy skills assessed by DIBELS measures, many tasks display floor effects at one or more administration windows. For example, children typically display floor effects on PSF in the fall and winter of kindergarten. Similarly, ORF is difficult for many first graders in the winter of the school year because they can access so little connected text, much less under time pressure. I have also found that kindergarten and first-semester first-grade students often respond so slowly and hesitatingly on PSF and NWF that they produce very few, if any, correct segments in the 1-minute period.

Validity Evidence

CONTENT VALIDITY EVIDENCE

The authors present a rationale for the development of the DIBELS measures in several articles (e.g., Good et al., 2001; Kaminski & Good, 1996, 1998) and in materials available on the DIBELS Web site and the Institute for the Development of Educational Achievement (IDEA) Web site (http://idea.uoregon.edu). Some of the ISF items use animal names that may be unfamiliar to children or that may be confused with other animals whose names begin with different sounds (e.g., *rooster* [chicken], *cub* [bear]). Although the examiner names each picture, I have found that children sometimes miss these items because they are attending to the picture rather than the target sound. Passages for the DIBELS ORF were developed and revised as a group to achieve approximate equivalence across benchmark and progress monitoring assessments. Nine formulae, including the Dale–Chall, Flesch, Frye, and Spache indices, were used to estimate passage readability. Because readabilities for the same passages varied dramatically across the different formulae, the authors selected the Spache index to set the target readability level per grade, based on a study with second graders indicating that it explained the largest amount of variance in oral reading fluency. According to the authors, target Spache readabilities were set at the end of the grade or the beginning of the next grade. For example, target Spache readabilities for Grade 1 were set at 2.0, 2.1, 2.2, or 2.3. Grade 3 target readabilities are only slightly higher than those for Grade 2, however (Grade 3 = 2.8, 2.9, 3.0, or 3.1 vs. Grade 2 = 2.4, 2.5, 2,6 or 2.7). After passages were arranged in order of increasing readability, they were assigned to benchmark assessments so that each incorporates a passage from the easier, middle, and harder third of relative readabilities. The remaining passages were assigned to progress monitoring assessments in a similar manner (Good & Kaminski, 2002a). No information is provided to indicate how the stimulus words for WUF were selected.

CRITERION-RELATED VALIDITY EVIDENCE

Of the DIBELS tasks, LNF and ORF are most strongly correlated with other measures of reading proficiency. In a sample of 36 kindergartners (Kaminski & Good, 1996), PSF and LNF were highly correlated with the *Metropolitan Readiness Tests* (Nurss & McGauvran, 1986) (.88 and .73, respectively) and with teacher ratings of reading competence (.90 and .71, respectively). For 37 to 39 first graders, LNF was highly correlated with the *Stanford Diagnostic Reading Test* (Karlsen, Madden, & Gardner, 1985) and moderately correlated with teacher ratings (.77 and .47, respectively), but PSF was not significantly related to any of the criterion measures. In the study by Good and colleagues (in preparation) cited above, the concurrent criterion-related validity of OnRF in January of kindergarten was low to moderate with other DIBELS measures and standardized reading tests (.48 with PSF and .36 with the Readiness cluster on the *Woodcock–Johnson Psycho-Educational Battery–Revised* [WJ-R]). Kindergarten LNF was strongly associated with children's current reading proficiency, as measured by the WJ-R Total Reading cluster (r = .70). Concurrent criterion validity of PSF was .54 with the WJ-R Readiness cluster in spring of kindergarten. NWF displayed low to moderate correlations with the WJ-R Readiness cluster in January and February of Grade 1 (.36 and .59, respectively). Concurrent validity estimates of .52 to .91 for ORF reported on the Web site are based on a summary of eight studies from the 1980s with the TORF (Good & Jefferson, 1998). According to the DIBELS administration and scoring guide (Good & Kaminski, 2002a), Retell Fluency correlates about .59 with measures of oral reading fluency.

Predictive validity coefficients for DIBELS measures range from moderate to high, with LNF, NWF, and ORF the best predictors of future reading achievement. In the Good and colleagues (in preparation) study cited above, kindergarten OnRF displayed only modest correlations with first-grade WJ-R Total Reading cluster scores (.36), but kindergarten LNF was a strong predictor of spring of first grade ORF and WJ-R Total Reading cluster scores (.65 and .71, respectively). Spring of kindergarten PSF was also an effective predictor of winter of first grade NWF and spring of first grade ORF and WJ-R Total Reading (.62, .62, and 68, respectively). NWF measured in January of Grade 1 was strongly predictive of ORF in May of Grade 1 (.82), ORF in May of Grade 2 (.60), and WJ-R Total Reading in May of Grade 2 (.66). In a study that followed four cohorts of students from kindergarten through Grade 3 (*ns* = 302 to 378; Good et al., 2001), correlations between earlier and later DIBELS measures ranged from .34 to .82, with the lowest correlations for OnRF and PSF and the highest for NWF and ORF. More than 90% of students who reached the earlier benchmark goal attained the subsequent benchmark goal, with the exception of spring of kindergarten PSF, for which only 55% of children attained the subsequent goal. Moreover, 96% of the children who met the Grade 3 ORF benchmark goal met or exceeded grade-level performance standards on the high-stakes Oregon Statewide Assessment.

CONSTRUCT VALIDITY EVIDENCE

Evidence of the construct validity of DIBELS measures is presented in an ongoing series of studies and Web-based technical reports by the authors and their colleagues at the University of Oregon (e.g., Good et al., in preparation; Good & Jefferson, 1998; Kaminski & Good, 1998). Scores on DIBELS measures increase across the school year and across grades, indicating the developmental nature of the skills assessed and the sensitivity of the tasks to performance changes over time, with several exceptions. From spring of kindergarten to fall of Grade 1, each measure shows a decrease in median performance of 3–7 points. Because the identical tasks are used at both windows, the authors attribute this decline to summer regression or Grade 1 literacy skill improvement resulting from early reading intervention programs. Scores also remain flat from spring of Grade 1 to fall of Grade 2 and decline from spring of Grade 2 to fall of Grade 3. Lack of growth at these points may arise from increases in the difficulty of the measurement material as well as the effects of summer regression.

Usability

DIBELS measures are brief to administer, require only the cost of reproduction, and can be repeated frequently to monitor progress and evaluate intervention effectiveness. The materials, which consist entirely of 8½- × 11-inch sheets of paper, are very cumbersome, however, with 20 separate pages per grade for the progress monitoring measures alone. Laminating the student stimulus materials and binding them into test books are highly recommended to facilitate administration and help preserve the probes. Over the years, the materials have become more attractive and professional in appearance, especially the ISF pictures. The current administration and scoring guide, which brings together directions for all tasks into a single publication, is also an improvement over previous versions, although achieving consistency in administration and scoring continues to be challenging for many tasks. The Web site presents video clips demonstrating how to administer most of the tasks, as well as implementation and instructional examples. Training is offered through the Web site and through Project Central, sponsored by the Florida Department of Education and the University of South Florida (http://sss.usf.edu/cbm). The DIBELS authors encourage school districts to include all children in DIBELS assessments for whom reading in English is an instructional goal, including children who are eligible for special education placements and English-language learners.

Links to Intervention

As with CBM oral reading, DIBELS is linked to a five-step problem-solving model (Kaminski & Good, 1998) designed to provide information for educational decision making. In the Problem Identification stage, the critical issue is whether the child's skills are sufficiently discrepant from expected levels to warrant intervention. The authors recommend that children whose scores fall below designated cutoff scores receive multiple DIBELS probes over a 5- to 10-day period during the Problem Validation stage to obtain more reliable skill estimates and assess the current slope of skill acquisition. In the Exploring Solutions phase, the child's progress is monitored to determine whether interventions are effective in improving early literacy skills. In the Evaluating Solutions phase, the child's performance is again compared with local norms or benchmarks to determine whether interventions have been successful in reducing the discrepancy between observed and expected skills. Finally, in the Problem Solution stage, the child's performance is evaluated to determine whether it is now commensurate with expectations so that interventions may be discontinued. Kaminski and Good (1998) include a brief discussion of remedial strategies, with general guidelines for early literacy intervention options ranging from least to most intensive/intrusive. A case example for a kindergarten child is presented to illustrate the use of graphing in evaluating intervention effectiveness.

DIBELS is linked to Project Optimize, an intervention program developed as part of a grant from the U.S. Department of Education Office of Special Education. Designed for at-risk kindergarten children, the 126-lesson program consists of two 15-minute components delivered in daily 30-minute lessons. Originally available on the University of Oregon's IDEA Web site (see above), the program is now published by Scott, Foresman. The Big Ideas in Beginning Reading Web site (http://reading.uoregon.edu) provides additional information about DIBELS-related assessment and instruction, including video clips showing teachers delivering instruction related to one or more of the five reading domains.

Relevant Research

Several studies (e.g., Gunn, Biglan, Smolkowski, & Ary, 2000; Haagar & Windmueller, 2001) have investigated the utility of DIBELS measures in identifying English-language learners at risk for reading problems and monitoring their progress in early intervention programs. In an intervention study with 256 students in kindergarten through Grade 3 (158 Hispanic, 98 non-Hispanic), Gunn and colleagues (2000) used DIBELS LNF, ISF, and PSF measures and CBM English-language oral reading probes (ORF) to identify children at risk of reading problems and evaluate intervention effectiveness. ORF measured in the fall of children's first year in the study was a strong predictor of WJ-R Passage Comprehension measured in the spring of the third year and explained more of the variance than did WJ-R Letter–Word Identification and Word Attack.

Elliott, Lee, and Tollefson (2001) evaluated the predictive utility of a set of early literacy measures modified from the DIBELS with 75 kindergarten students who were tested every 2 weeks during the last 9 weeks of the school year. The modified DIBELS battery (DIBELS–M) consisted of two tasks that were virtually identical to DIBELS LNF and PSF, a letter-sound naming task, and an initial phoneme isolation task. With general ability controlled, the four DIBELS-M measures accounted for 41% of the variance in WJ-R Skills cluster scores. Across all analyses, LNF was the best single predictor of WJ-R Broad Reading and Skills cluster scores and teacher ratings of reading achievement.

A validation study available on the Web site suggests that the DIBELS benchmark goals may be set too high. Hintze, Ryan, and Stoner (2002) evaluated the concurrent validity and diagnostic accuracy of DIBELS INF, PSF, and LNF in a sample of 85 children tested in the winter of kindergarten, using the *Comprehensive Test of Pho-*

nological Processing (CTOPP) as the criterion measure. ISF and PSF displayed low correlations with CTOPP rapid naming measures and moderate correlations with CTOPP phonological awareness and memory measures, whereas LNF correlated moderately with CTOPP subtests and composites for all three domains. When DIBELS measures were evaluated for accuracy in diagnosing reading problems, defined as a standard score of less than 85 on the CTOPP Phonological Awareness and Phonological Memory composites, DIBELS cut scores for ISF and PSF (less than 25 onsets per minute and less than 35 phonemes per minute, respectively) correctly classified only about one-third to one-half of participants, with very high false positive rates. Using lower cut scores derived from Receiver Operator Characteristic (ROC) curve analyses (15 onsets per minute for ISF and 25 letters per minute for LNF) yielded adequate levels of sensitivity and specificity, but the PSF continued to yield very high false positive rates across a wide range of cut scores. The authors concluded that the current DIBELS benchmarks may be too high and may overidentify children as having phonological awareness deficits.

Source and Cost

DIBELS materials, including the administration and scoring guide, are available for free download from the DIBELS Web site to users who obtain a password and log on to the site. Users may make unlimited copies of the materials and probes but are asked to copy them without modification, except as agreed upon by the DIBELS development and research team. The DIBELS Data System, a data entry and reporting service, is available for $1.00 per student per year. Data system users can enter scores via a Web browser and generate a variety of class and school reports, including descriptive statistics by grade for performance on benchmark measures. The intervention program, published by Scott, Foresman (http://scottforesman.com) under the name *Early Reading Intervention*, costs $999.00. Single forms of LNF, PSF, and NWF, along with abbreviated administration and scoring directions, are reproduced in *Taking a Reading: A Teacher's Guide to Reading Assessment* (Southern California Comprehensive Assistance Center, 2002). A print version of DIBELS is also available from Sopris West Educational Services. Classroom sets for kindergarten through Grade 3 are $59.00 each, and an implementation video demonstrating the administration process is available for $79.00.

Summary

The *Dynamic Indicators of Basic Early Literacy Skills* (DIBELS) is a set of individually administered fluency-based measures designed for rapid, efficient assessment of children's early literacy skills as they progress from preschool through third grade. A downward extension of CBM oral reading, DIBELS shares the assets and liabilities of that measurement system. DIBELS measures can be administered quickly and frequently to assess growth, but the tasks are restricted to those with production-type responses and yield only quantitative data with limited utility for diagnosing strengths and weaknesses or designing interventions. Technical adequacy varies considerably from measure to measure and across grades. No estimates of interscorer reliability are available for any of the tasks, a major concern in view of the complexity of administration and scoring procedures. Preliminary evidence indicates that DIBELS is measuring the same construct as other phonological processing measures, but additional studies comparing DIBELS with validated measures of phonemic awareness, oral reading, and the other skills assessed in the battery are needed. Moreover, although the authors' longitudinal studies indicate that DIBELS measures predict performance on subsequent DIBELS tasks and high-stakes assessments, other researchers have reported that the current cut scores on some DIBELS measures overidentify children as being at risk for early reading problems. More than any of the other early reading assessment batteries reviewed in this text, DIBELS is a work in progress. Thanks to its Web-based format and to the generosity of its authors and the University of Oregon, practitioners may follow the development of this innovative assessment easily and without expense.

Case Example

Name of student: Damian W.
Age: 5 years, 8 months
Grade: Kindergarten
Date of assessment: February

Reason for referral: Damian was referred for an early reading assessment by his kindergarten teacher. Compared with his classmates, Damian is making limited progress in developing phonological awareness and phonics skills. He is able to identify most letter names and some letter sounds in isolation, but his naming speed is quite slow, and he has trouble using letter-sound knowledge to read and spell simple words, even with many opportunities to practice.

Assessment results and interpretation: The *Dynamic Indicators of Early Literacy Skills* (DIBELS) is a set of 1-minute measures designed to assess prereading and early reading skills. In the winter of kindergarten, five DIBELS tasks are administered. For some tasks, student performance can be compared with *benchmarks*, expected levels of performance for a particular time in the school year. Children who score below the benchmark goal on a task need additional instruction in those skills and may be at risk for future reading problems. Damian's DIBELS scores are reported below.

Dibels Measure	Score	Benchmark Goal	Risk Indicator
Initial Sound Fluency	5.8 initial sounds correct per minute	25–35 initial sounds correct per minute by the middle of kindergarten	<10 initial sounds correct per minute by the winter of kindergarten
Letter Naming Fluency	19 letters correct per minute	Not established	Not established
Phoneme Segmentation Fluency	20 phonemes correct per minute	35 or more phonemes correct per minute by the spring of kindergarten/fall of Grade 1	<10 phonemes correct per minute by the spring of kindergarten/fall of Grade 1
Nonsense Word Fluency	11 letter sounds correct per minute	50 letter sounds correct per minute by the winter of Grade 1	<30 letter sounds correct per minute by the winter of Grade 1
Word Use Fluency	21 words correct per minute	Not established	Not established

Initial Sound Fluency requires the child to identify or produce the initial sounds in pictured words named by the examiner. Damian was able to identify the initial sound of 10 of the 16 pictures, but he responded very slowly. His score is about half of what is expected for kindergarten children at this time in the school year. **Letter**

Naming Fluency requires the child to name as many randomly arrayed uppercase and lowercase letters as possible in 1 minute. Damian's Letter Naming Fluency is quite limited at this point. He was unable to identify several letters (*b*, *m*, *n*, and *u*), which slowed his naming speed considerably. **Phoneme Segmentation Fluency** requires the child to pronounce the individual *phonemes* (sounds) in a series of words spoken by the examiner. For example, the examiner says, "sat," and the child responds, "/s/ /a/ /t/." The score is the number of correct phonemes produced in 1 minute. Damian had difficulty understanding the nature of this task. He was able to provide initial sounds for 10 words but could not segment any of the words beyond the beginning sound. His score suggests that he may not meet the benchmark goal for this task without additional interventions.

Nonsense Word Fluency requires the child to read as many phonically regular pseudowords (e.g., *tob*) as possible in 1 minute. The child may pronounce the words sound by sound or as whole words, and the score is the number of letter sounds produced in 1 minute. Although Damian made a good effort on this task, he tried to pronounce each word sound by sound and was able to produce only 11 sounds correctly in 1 minute. He confused the sounds for *b* and *d* several times and was unable to provide correct vowel sounds for any of the words presented (e.g., /a/ = /uh/). **Word Use Fluency** requires the child to use a target word in a sentence. The examiner provides words and the child produces sentences for 1 minute, and the score is the number of words produced in 1 minute that accurately reflect the meaning of the target words. Damian's sentences tended to be short and unelaborated. He responded, "I don't know that," to several of the words presented (*coach*, *which*, and *meant*).

EARLY READING DIAGNOSTIC ASSESSMENT—REVISED

Overview

The *Early Reading Diagnostic Assessment–Revised* (ERDA-R; Psychological Corporation, 2002) is an individually administered norm-referenced battery of tests assessing the early reading and reading-related skills of students in kindergarten through third grade. Designed for administration by classroom teachers, the ERDA-R measures print awareness, phonological awareness, phonics, vocabulary, listening and reading comprehension, and in Grades 2 and 3, rapid naming. Like the previous version of the test (ERDA; Psychological Corporation, 2000), the ERDA-R consists almost entirely of subtests drawn from previously published instruments, including the *Wechsler Individual Achievement Test* (WIAT; Psychological Corporation, 1992b), *Wechsler Individual Achievement Test–II* (WIAT-II), and *Process Assessment of the Learner: Test Battery for Reading and Writing* (PAL-RW). Changes to this version include (1) an expanded norm group for the WIAT-II-derived subtests; (2) reorganization of the subtests into screening, diagnostic, and optional measures; (3) a separate technical manual; (4) tabbed stimulus books with subtests presented in the order of administration on the record form; (5) percentile range rather than decile range scores; and (6) modifications to examiner manuals, record forms, and parent reports. The content of the stimulus books is identical with that of the first version. The ERDA-R is intended to be used for the following purposes: (1) as a norm-referenced assessment of children's reading achievement levels, (2) as a diagnostic assessment of children's reading progress, (3) as a source of information to classroom teachers for instructional planning, and (4) as a way of linking assessment results to empirically validated interventions. The ERDA-R is packaged as four test kits, one per grade level. Each kit includes a spiral-bound administration manual that covers all four grades, a technical manual, an easel-format stimulus booklet (Grades K–1 or 2–3), 25 grade-specific student record forms, 25 grade-specific parent reports, a word reading card and pseudoword pronunciation guide audiotape (Grades 1–3), and 30 "Thumbs Up" stickers, all packed in a flip-top storage box.

Subtests and Composites

Subtests

Across the four grade levels, the ERDA-R includes 17 subtests, organized into screener, diagnostic, and optional measures for each grade. Target Words, a sentence-reading task, is embedded in the Reading Comprehension subtest but yields a separate score and is treated in the materials as a subtest. Table 4.8 displays the ERDA-R subtests by domain and grade across the four grade levels. Kindergarten children who score in the Emerging category (i.e., percentile range [PR] = 0–29) on either Letter Recognition or Story Retell take Vocabulary and the three kindergarten-level Phonological Awareness subtests. Grade 1 children who score in the Below Basic category (PR = 0–29) on either Word Reading or Pseudoword Decoding take Letter Recognition, Concept of Print (Part A), Listening Comprehension, and the

TABLE 4.8. Subtests on the ERDA-R by Domain and Grade

Domain	Kindergarten	Grade 1	Grade 2	Grade 3
Concepts of Print	**Concept of Print, Part A** Concept of Print, Part B	**Concept of Print, Part A** Concept of Print, Part B		
Phonological Awareness	Rhyming Phonemes Syllables	Phonemes Rimes Syllables	Phonemes Rimes Syllables	Phonemes Rimes Syllables
Letter Identification	**Letter Recognition**	Letter Recognition **Pseudoword Decoding**	Pseudoword Decoding	Pseudoword Decoding
Listening Comprehension	**Story Retell**	Listening Comprehension	Listening Comprehension	Listening Comprehension
Vocabulary	Vocabulary[a]	Vocabulary	**Vocabulary**	**Vocabulary**
Reading Comprehension	Reading Comprehension[b]	Reading Comprehension	**Reading Comprehension**	**Reading Comprehension**
Oral Reading in Context	Target Words	Target Words	**Target Words**	**Target Words**
Word Recognition		**Word Reading**	Word Reading	Word Reading
Rapid Automatized Naming			RAN-Digits RAN-Letters RAN-Words RAN-Words & Digits	RAN-Digits RAN-Letters RAN-Words RAN-Words & Digits
Total time	45 minutes	60 minutes	60 minutes	60 minutes

Note. Screening subtests are given in boldface, diagnostic subtests are given in plain type, and optional subtests are shaded.
[a]Vocabulary is designated as both a diagnostic and an optional subtest at the kindergarten level.
[b]Reading Comprehension is administered only to kindergarten students with perfect scores on both Letter Recognition and Story Retell.

three Grade 1 phonological awareness subtests. Children in Grades 2 and 3 who score Below Basic on Vocabulary, Reading Comprehension, or Target Words take Listening Comprehension and three phonological awareness subtests for second and third graders. Vocabulary is assigned to both the diagnostic and the optional category at the kindergarten level, but no rationale is offered for this decision.

Table 4.9 describes the 17 subtests, beginning with the kindergarten measures. As the table indicates, 9 of the subtests are derived from the PAL-RW, 5 from the WIAT-II, and 2 from the WIAT. (Concept of Print is the only task not derived from one of these three.) As noted above, the Target Words score is based on the successful reading of specific words in sentences embedded in the Reading Comprehension subtest but is treated as a subtest in the test materials and therefore in this review.

Composite

A Phonological Awareness composite is obtained by summing differentially weighted raw scores for the Rhyming, Syllables, and Phonemes subtests for kindergarten students and differentially weighted raw scores for the Syllables, Phonemes, and Rimes subtests for students in Grades 1–3. There are no other composites.

Administration

All of the subtests must be individually administered. According to the manual, the ERDA-R screener can be administered in about 15–20 minutes, and the entire battery in about 45 minutes across all grade levels. I have found that administering the entire test for students in Grades 1–3 takes about 60 minutes, which is the time specified in the previous manual. Grade-specific start and stop points are provided for all tasks other than the RAN subtests, which are administered in their entirety. An audiotape provides correct pronunciations for Pseudoword Decoding items. If a child does not achieve 100% accuracy on the RAN sample items, that particular subtest is not administered. Syllables for Grades 1–3 has a reverse rule: If children miss the first two items on Task B, the examiner administers both Task A and Task B, but only Task B items are scored. Responses to Reading Comprehension and Story Retell must be recorded verbatim. Children may read the passages aloud or silently, and Reading Comprehension passages can be timed to obtain a reading rate score. Although the results are intended for qualitative analysis only, the reliability and validity of rate scores based on silent reading are questionable for early primary grade children, especially struggling readers who often appear to be skimming the passages rather than attempting to read them word by word. Practice items should be provided for the Vocabulary subtest, especially for the expressive vocabulary section. I have found that children often have trouble understanding the task requirements (i.e., providing a single word to match the picture and a verbal prompt).

Scores

Scoring is dichotomous for most subtests. The manual includes comprehensive, easy-to-follow scoring examples for subtests requiring examiner judgment. The three subtests at each grade level making up the Phonological Awareness composite have grade-specific differential weights. For example, at the kindergarten level the Phonemes raw score is multiplied by 1.5, whereas for Grades 1–3 it is multiplied by 1.0.

TABLE 4.9. Description of the ERDA-R Subtests

Subtest	Description
Letter Recognition[c]	For early items, the child names or points to a previously shown target lowercase letter in a letter array. For later items, the child names the lowercase alphabet letters.
Concept of Print	The examiner completes a seven-item checklist based on the child's demonstration of print concepts, such as directionality and punctuation. Part A of the checklist is completed after Letter Recognition, and Part B is completed after Reading Comprehension.
Story Retell[b]	The child listens to a story read by the examiner, responds to questions about the story, and then retells it.
Phonological Awareness: Rhyming[b]	For Task A, the examiner pronounces a set of three words, and the child identifies the one word that does not rhyme with the other two. For Task B, the child says as many real words as possible that rhyme with a target word pronounced by the examiner.
Phonological Awareness: Syllables[b]	The child repeats a polysyllabic word pronounced by the examiner and then says the syllable remaining when a target syllable is omitted.
Phonological Awareness: Phonemes[b]	For Task A, the examiner pronounces a monosyllabic word (e.g., "pill"), asks the child to repeat it, and pronounces it again with a target phoneme omitted (e.g., "ill"). The child repeats the second word and then pronounces the omitted phoneme (e.g., "ill"/p/"). For Tasks B and C, the child repeats a monosyllabic or polysyllabic word spoken by the examiner and then pronounces the phonemes that remain when a target phoneme is omitted (e.g., "sun . . . un"). Kindergarten children take only Tasks A and B.
Phonological Awareness: Rimes[b]	The child repeats a word pronounced by the examiner with a target rime omitted. For example, the examiner says, "Say *like* without /ike/," and the child responds, "/l/."
Reading Comprehension[c]	The child matches written words with pictures, reads passages silently or aloud, and responds to questions orally or by performing some action. Passages include narrative, informational, and functional material. Passage reading can be timed to yield a reading rate score.
Target Words[c]	The child reads sentences aloud, and target words in the sentences are scored for reading accuracy.
Vocabulary[c]	For Task A (receptive language items), the child points to the one of four pictures that best represents a word spoken by the examiner. For Task B (expressive language items), the child provides the appropriate word when presented with pictorial and verbal clues.
Listening Comprehension[a]	While looking at a stimulus picture, the child listens to a short passage read by the examiner and then answers questions about it.
Word Reading[c]	The child reads aloud rows of words printed on a card.
Pseudoword Decoding[c]	The child reads aloud rows of pseudowords printed on a card.
RAN-Digits[b]	For Item 1, the child names a random array of six single digits as rapidly as possible. For Item 2, the child names a random array of two-digit numerals as rapidly as possible. The score is the number of seconds required to name both arrays.
RAN-Letters[b]	For Item 1, the child names a series of 10 randomly arrayed single letters as rapidly as possible. For Item 2, the child names a series of randomly arrayed two-letter groups as rapidly as possible. The score is the number of seconds required to name both arrays.
RAN-Words[b]	The child names a series of eight randomly arrayed words as rapidly as possible. The score is the number of seconds required to name the entire array.
RAN-Words & Digits[b]	The child names a series of randomly arrayed alternating words and digits (the same stimuli as in the two previous tasks) as rapidly as possible. The score is the number of seconds required to name the entire array.

[a]Subtest derived from the WIAT.
[b]Subtest derived from the PAL-RW.
[c]Subtest derived from the WIAT-II.

No rationale is provided for the weighting system or for the differential weights across levels. On the RAN subtests, incorrect and omitted responses are noted; unlike the PAL-RW, however, the ERDA-R does not provide normative data for error totals. The Reading Comprehension subtest yields two scores: Target Words, which is scored dichotomously, and Reading Comprehension, scored on a 2- or 3-point scale. The manual recommends audiotaping examinee responses to Story Retell, which is scored on a 2- or 3-point scale and requires more scoring judgment than the other subtests. The seven-item Concept of Print checklist provides only qualitative information. The record form provides room for a description of Concept of Print skills but allows no space for recording performance on specific items, whereas the parent form reproduces Part B of the checklist but provides no space for reporting Part A performance or any qualitative information.

Raw scores are converted to 1 of 20 percentile ranges (0–4 to 95–99 PRs), with fall and spring norms for most subtests, although there are several exceptions. Norms are not provided for Reading Comprehension or Target Words at the kindergarten level, Listening Comprehension has only fall norms, and the PAL-RW-derived subtests have identical percentile range scores for fall and spring for Grades 1–3. Because of the rapid growth of phonological and orthographic skills in the early primary grades, semester norms should be provided for all measures and at all grade levels. Record booklets reproduce the "look-up" (norms) tables in the manual for converting raw scores to percentile ranges, and the student profile page indicates percentile ranges by descriptive category, so that the examiner does not have to consult the manual to determine whether screener scores are low enough to warrant administering the diagnostic subtests.

Interpretation

For interpreting ERDA-R results, percentile range scores are grouped in three broad skill categories: Below Basic, termed *Emerging* at the kindergarten level (PRs = 0–29); Basic (PRs = 30–69); and Proficient (PRs = 70–99). The manual designates Emerging/Below Basic scores as representing at-risk status but suggests providing interventions for any student scoring below the 40th percentile, based on the recommendation of the analysis of early reading instruments by the University of Oregon Assessment Committee (Kame'enui, 2002). No rationale is presented for the use of percentile ranges rather than standard scores, and no other derived scores are provided. No information is provided for interpreting reading rate, even in terms of qualitative data, and there is no space on the record form to note it. The manual presents a skills analysis for six reading domains that includes descriptions of the skills measured by each subtest; item and/or passage types for Story Retell, Listening Comprehension, and Reading Comprehension; and a review of the scientific evidence documenting the relationship of the domains and assessment tasks to reading acquisition and reading disabilities. The chapter on interpretation includes detailed case studies for each grade to illustrate how to use test results to develop intervention plans. Each case example includes a narrative describing the child's performance, a copy of the student profile, and a sample intervention plan, as well as additional recommendations for instructional activities. The kindergarten example includes the screener subtests and two optional subtests, the examples for Grades 1 and 2 include both screener and diagnostic tasks, and the Grade 3 example includes screener and diagnostic measures and two of the optional subtests. Neither the Grade 2 nor the Grade 3 example includes RAN subtests. Because examiners may be less familiar with RAN tasks than with the other measures, at least one of these examples should include a discussion of RAN subtest performance and its implications for reading acquisition.

Technical Adequacy

Standardization

The ERDA-R normative group is a subset of the standardization samples for the WIAT (for the six Listening Comprehension items only), WIAT-II, and PAL-RW. The WIAT, published in 1992, was normed on a sample of students who were selected to be representative of the 1988 U.S. population, whereas WIAT-II and PAL-RW standardization data were collected during the 1999–2000 school year to reflect 1998 U.S. Census figures. Sample sizes were 1,057 students in first through third grade for the WIAT, 1,200 students in kindergarten through third grade for the WIAT-II, and 519 students in kindergarten through third grade for the PAL-RW. Samples for each instrument were stratified by grade for gender, race/ethnicity, geographic region, and parental education. The manual reports sample characteristics for each of the contributing instruments for the grades relevant to the ERDA-R compared with 1998 census data. Because samples did not exclude students receiving school-based special services, between 8% and 10% of the norm groups consisted of children with various exceptionalities. Samples are close approximations of the 1998 U.S. school population, with a few exceptions. The WIAT sample slightly overrepresents whites and parents with a 12th-grade education and slightly underrepresents African American and Hispanic examinees and parents with college and graduate school educational levels. Across the four grades, the PAL-RW sample slightly overrepresents males, whites, the South region, and parents with 13–15 years of education and slightly underrepresents African Americans, Hispanics, the North Central and Northeast regions, and parents with a 12th-grade education. Norm group sizes are between 335 and 386 for the WIAT, 300 per grade for the WIAT-II, and between 120 and 142 for the PAL-RW. Because both fall and spring norms are provided for kindergarten PAL-RW-derived tasks, this means that derived scores are based on as few as 60 students per interval, which is below acceptable levels.

Reliability Evidence

Combined fall and spring coefficient alphas for Letter Recognition, Phonemes, Pseudoword Decoding, Story Retell, and Word Reading exceed .90 at all grades in which those measures are administered. Reliabilities for Reading Comprehension and Target Words range from .86 to .90, whereas Rimes coefficients are in the .80s for Grades K–2 but fall to .76 for Grade 3. Values for Syllables are in the .80s for kindergarten and Grade 1 but fall below acceptable levels for the older grades (.73 for Grade 2 and .66 for Grade 3), probably because of ceiling effects. Kindergarten Rhyming falls below acceptable levels (.69), and Vocabulary coefficients fall below acceptable levels at all grades (.64 to .70). Coefficients for Listening Comprehension, which has only six items, are in the .40s. Phonological Awareness composite reliability ranges from .82 to .87 across the four grades, lower than the criterion level for composite scores. Split-half reliability estimates reported for the 10 subtests with more than 10 items and the composite are slightly higher, with Phonological Awareness composite reliabilities in the .90s across all grade levels and coefficients for Letter Recognition, Phonemes, Pseudoword Decoding, and Word Reading exceeding .90 across all grades in which they are administered. Rimes coefficients are in the .80s, whereas Syllables reliability is in the .80s for kindergarten and Grade 1 but falls in the .70s for Grades 2 and 3. Kindergarten Rhyming values are again below criterion level (.70). Values for Reading Comprehension are in the .90s for Grades 1 and 2 and in the .80s for Grade 3. Target Words values are in the .90s for Grades 1 and 2 and slightly below the criterion for Grade 3 (.79). Vocabulary split-half values are below acceptable levels across all four grades (.68 to .75).

Test–retest reliability coefficients (intervals of 7–30 days) for samples (*ns* = 114 to 204) drawn from students in Grades K–3 of the WIAT-II norm group were above .90 for Letter Recognition, Pseudoword Decoding, Reading Comprehension, Target Words, and Word Reading and in the .80s for Vocabulary. Because reliability coefficients are aggregated across grade levels, however, it is not possible to determine subtest stability for examinees in a particular grade. No stability estimates are presented for the other 11 subtests. Interscorer agreement for Reading Comprehension based on responses from 600 students in Grades 1–3 (200 students per grade) for at least two unidentified independent scorers ranged between .97 and .98. For Story Retell, the correlation between pairs of scores for 199 kindergarten protocols scored by at least two unidentified independent scorers was .96. Because of the susceptibility of phoneme manipulation, rapid naming, and print awareness tasks to examiner variance, interscorer reliability estimates based on simultaneous scoring of the same set of examinees during test sessions should be provided for those subtests. No reliability data of any kind are provided for the four RAN subtests or for the Concept of Print checklist, which is designed to yield only qualitative information.

Test Floors and Item Gradients

Many subtests have inadequate floors at one or more grade levels, with adequate floors across all subtests only for Grade 3. For kindergarten, floor effects are evident on Phonemes and Syllables for both fall and spring and to a lesser extent on Story Retell for fall. A raw score of 1 on Phonemes in the fall of kindergarten yields a percentile range of 40–49, indicating how difficult the task is for children at that grade level. For Grade 1, floor effects are evident on Rimes, Syllables, and Pseudoword Decoding for both fall and spring and Listening Comprehension (fall norms only). For Grade 2, floors are inadequate for fall and spring Pseudoword Decoding. Ceiling effects on Letter Recognition are evident beginning in the spring of kindergarten. Ceiling effects are also evident on Target Words, beginning in the fall of Grade 1, and on Word Reading for fall and spring of Grade 3. Item gradients are inadequate on subtests with floor effects, especially Pseudoword Decoding, and on subtests with insufficient ceilings, such as Letter Recognition and Target Words after Grade 1.

Validity Evidence

CONTENT VALIDITY EVIDENCE

As noted above, 16 of the 17 subtests (excluding Concept of Print) on the ERDA-R are derived from the WIAT, WIAT-II, or PAL-RW. Subtests were designed to represent a composite of the typical reading curriculum in the United States and to reflect the research findings of Virginia Berninger, author of the PAL-RW, and other investigators represented in the National Reading Panel's (2000) report. Experts reviewed items for content coverage prior to national tryout studies, and potentially biased items were identified and replaced. WIAT-II pilot testing was conducted during the spring semester of 1997 with approximately 100 children in each of Grades K–3, followed in the fall of 1997 with a national tryout with 460 students in each of the four grades. Two national tryouts of the PAL-RW were conducted, the first in the spring of 1998 and the second in spring of 1999, with a total of 378 students in Grades K–3. Based on data from pilot and tryout testing, items were analyzed using both conventional and IRT procedures, but no specific information regarding item difficulty or other item characteristics is presented. Potential item bias was assessed by a panel of experienced reviewers and by means of IRT analyses, after which the final item selection was made, based on item statistical properties and curriculum representativeness. The manual does not provide specific information regarding the results of DIF analyses, nor does it present mean score comparisons for various demographic subgroups. No theoretical rationale or empirical evidence is presented for the placement of subtests into screener, diagnostic, and optional categories; the differential weighting of phonological awareness subtests within and across grades; or the single set of norms for the subtests noted above.

CRITERION-RELATED VALIDITY EVIDENCE

The manual presents correlations between the six ERDA-R subtests derived from the WIAT-II and eight WIAT-II reading and language subtests for samples ranging from 600 to 1,200 (grades unspecified), excluding correlations between the ERDA-R subtests and the corresponding WIAT-II subtests from which they were drawn. Correlations were generally moderate to high (.12 to .78), although Letter Recognition was only weakly correlated with most of the WIAT-II subtests (.12 to .47), probably because of its lack of discriminative power after the first semester of kindergarten. In samples of students in Grades K–2 (*ns* = 21 to 42), the six WIAT-II-derived ERDA-R subtests displayed generally moderate correlations (.26 to .64) with the *Peabody Picture Vocabulary Test–III*, with the highest correlations for Pseudoword Decoding and the lowest for Letter Recognition. For samples of students ranging from 29 to 39 (grades unspecified), correlations between the same ERDA-R subtests, excluding Letter Recognition, and reading, language, and/or spelling subtests on the *Stanford Achievement Tests–Ninth Edition* (SAT-9; Harcourt Educational Measurement, 1996) and the *Metropolitan Achievement Tests–Eighth Edition* (Harcourt Educational Measurement, 1999) were highly variable (.09 to .88), with the strongest correlations for Word Reading, Target Words, and Reading Comprehension.

The ERDA-R displays moderate to high correlations with teacher ratings of classroom reading performance. For small samples (*ns* = 23 to 28, grades unspecified), the Reading/Language Arts subscale of the *Academic Competence Evaluation Scales* (DiPerna & Elliott, 2000) was strongly correlated with ERDA-R Word Reading, Vocabulary, Reading Comprehension, Target Words, and Pseudoword Decoding (.63 to .80). Teacher-assigned reading and spelling grades were less strongly related to the same five ERDA-R subtests for a sample of students of unspecified grades (*ns* = 30 to 35; *rs* = .12 to .56). No criterion-related validity data are presented for Listening Comprehension, Story Retell, or Concept of Print; nor are data presented to document the relationship of the PAL-RW-derived subtests to reading or academic achievement measures other than the WIAT-II (see below).

CONSTRUCT VALIDITY EVIDENCE

Subtest intercorrelations reported separately by grade for the WIAT-II and PAL-RW samples generally show the expected pattern of relationships, although Letter Recognition for Grade 1 is only weakly correlated with the other subtests, reflecting the ceiling effects for that measure at that level. For samples ranging from 27 to 57 students (grades unspecified), correlations between seven PAL-RW-derived subtests (excluding Rhyming) and the Phonological Awareness composite and five WIAT-II-derived subtests were highly variable (–.17 to .68), lending only mixed support to the assertion that the PAL-RW-derived tasks are measuring the phonological and orthographic processing skills underlying the reading-related WIAT-II subtests. For the most part, RAN tests were weakly correlated with WIAT-II subtests. Of the 20 correlations between RAN and WIAT-II subtests, 14 were in the low range (i.e., below .40). Correlations were also lower for Vocabulary (.05 to .43), which taps lexical rather than phonological or orthographic skills.

As evidence of the diagnostic utility of the ERDA-R, the manual presents studies comparing the performance of a group of individuals in gifted programs and six clinical groups (individuals with mental retardation, learning disabilities in reading, learning disabilities in writing, attention-deficit/hyperactivity disorder [ADHD], comorbid ADHD and learning disabilities, and speech and/or language impairment) with matched controls on Word Reading, Vocabulary, Reading Comprehension, Target Words, and Pseudoword Decoding. Although the six clinical groups scored significantly lower than controls on most of the subtests, excluding Vocabulary, mean differences are reported in terms of *z* scores rather than percentile ranges or standard scores. As a result, practitioners cannot determine whether the differences have diagnostic utility or whether the clinical groups scored in the at-risk range. No group differentiation studies are presented to document the diagnostic validity of the PAL-RW-derived subtests, nor is any predictive validity evidence reported.

Usability

Considerable attention has been paid to making the ERDA-R as user-friendly as possible. Materials are color-coded by level and are attractive to examiners and children alike. The stimulus booklets contain complete administration and correct-response information so that examiners do not need to consult the manual during testing and are now tabbed to facilitate locating subtests. The word reading card is laminated for durability and printed on both front and back to reduce the number of materials examiners must manage. The examiner manual is well organized and readable, but introductory tables describing the subtests, three-tier organization, and the specific percentile ranges associated with the three proficiency categories would be helpful. Record forms include an "instruction bar" for each subtest summarizing materials needed, time limits, recording and scoring procedures, and discontinue rules. Training materials are under development.

Links to Intervention

A double-sided parent report includes a grade-specific description of test content, a score profile, tips for helping children become successful readers, and two Web-based resources. The front of the record form has a "Targeted Intervention Plan" chart that provides space for noting qualitative information and observations, as well as an instructional intervention plan for each of the five domains identified by the National Reading Panel. In addition to the intervention suggestions for the case examples provided in the manual, Chapter 4 of the manual reviews information on empirically based reading interventions, organized according to preventive and remedial instructional purposes. The section on preventive instructional strategies consists of a useful summary of the findings of the National Reading Panel in the areas of alphabetics, fluency, and comprehension, whereas the section on remedial interventions describes strategies included in Berninger's (1998a) *Process Assessment of the Learner: Guides for Intervention–Reading and Writing* for the same three areas. The chapter concludes with lists of intervention resources for phoneme awareness, phonics, fluency, and comprehension. Although the list is entitled "Intervention Resources," the citations refer to articles in the research literature rather than to instructional programs or activity books.

Relevant Research

No research studies using the ERDA or ERDA-R could be located. Selected research studies using the PAL-RW and WIAT-II, from which most of the ERDA-R subtests are derived, are discussed in the reviews of those tests in Chapter 5.

Source and Cost

Each ERDA-R test kit is available from The Psychological Corporation for $195.00. The ERDA-II has been released as of fall 2003 and is available for the same price. The new edition includes enhanced measures of fluency and vocabulary, with Web-based reporting software as an option.

Summary

The *Early Reading Diagnostic Assessment–Revised* (ERDA-R) is the second version of an individually administered norm-referenced set of subtests drawn from the PAL-RW, WIAT, and WIAT-II and designed to assess early literacy skills for children in kindergarten through third grade. Now organized as a three-tier battery to align with the screening and diagnostic assessment requirements of the Reading First mandate, the ERDA-R is one of the very few comprehensive early literacy batteries comprised of measures normed on a large, representative sample of American children, including children receiving special education services. Efforts have made in this edition to make the test as attractive and user-friendly as possible, and case examples in the manual are more detailed and intervention-oriented than those for many other screening instruments. Technical adequacy varies considerably across subtests, however. Coefficient alpha values for the composite score and numerous subtests are lower than desirable, and internal consistency estimates are lacking for 5 of the 17 subtests. Stability and interrater reliability estimates are available for fewer than half of the subtests, including some of the measures most vulnerable to examiner variance and interscorer inconsistency. Adequate floors are not reached across all subtests until Grade 3, limiting the ERDA-R's ability to identify low-performing children. Although previous research on the utility of the PAL-RW-derived tasks in predicting reading and writing acquisition has been encouraging, additional studies are needed to assess the relationship of the ERDA-R to other reading measures and to evaluate its efficacy in identifying at-risk children and specifying the nature of their reading deficits.

Case Example

Name of student: Carrie M.
Age: 6 years, 4 months
Grade: First grade
Date of assessment: October

Reason for referral: Carrie was referred for an early reading assessment by her first-grade teacher. Although she has learned most of her letters, she has been slow to learn letter sounds, and she does not appear to understand how to apply that knowledge to reading and spelling. In addition, she has difficulty remembering sight words from lesson to lesson and comprehending textual material.

Assessment results and interpretation: The *Early Reading Diagnostic Assessment–Revised* (ERDA-R) measures reading and reading-related skills in early primary grade children. At each grade level, tasks are organized into screening, diagnostic, and optional measures. The ERDA-R tasks provide grade-based percentile range scores that correspond to reading proficiency categories. Percentile range scores of 0 to 29 indicate that students are at risk of failing to meet grade-level expectations for reading, percentile range scores from 30 to 69 represent basic skill development, and percentile range scores from 70 to 99 represent proficient skill development. First graders who score below the 30th percentile (Below Basic) on Word Reading and Pseudoword Decoding take the diagnostic tasks to determine the nature of their skill deficits. Carrie's scores on the ERDA-R are given below.

Skills Assessed/ Subtest/*Composite*	Raw Score	Percentile Range	Descriptive Category
Concept of Print			
Observation Checklists	6/7	Qualitative information only	
Phonological Awareness			
Composite (weighted score)	24/90	15–19	Below Basic
Phonemes	6/30	20–24	Below Basic
Rimes	3/10	35–39	Basic
Syllables	3/10	15–19	Below Basic
Phonics			
Letter Recognition	27/29	0–4	Below Basic
Pseudoword Decoding	1/40	10–14	Below Basic
Fluency			
Word Reading	2/42	5-9	Below Basic
Target Words	3/25	20–24	Below Basic
Vocabulary			
Vocabulary	7/20	20–24	Below Basic
Comprehension			
Listening Comprehension	1/6	10–14	Below Basic
Reading Comprehension	13/44	20–24	Below Basic

Carrie's scores on the Screener subtests (Word Reading and Pseudoword Decoding) fall in the *Below Basic* category of achievement. She was able to read only two of the sight words presented and only one of the pseudowords (phonically regular nonwords), indicating that her sight word vocabulary and ability to apply letter-sound correspondences in reading are very limited. Although she made a good effort to decode the pseudowords, her responses reflect an incomplete knowledge of letter sounds, especially short vowels (e.g., /hud/ for *heb*). She sometimes pronounced the individual sounds in the pseudowords correctly but then made an error when she attempted to blend them together. For example, she correctly articulated the three sounds in *pon* but then pronounced it as *plob*. As a result of her *Below Basic* performance on these two measures, the Diagnostic subtests (Letter Recognition, Listening Comprehension, Phonemes, Rimes, and Syllables) were administered. The optional subtests (Reading Comprehension, Target Words, and Vocabulary) were also given to obtain more information for intervention planning.

On the Concept of Word checklist, Carrie demonstrated an understanding of letter and print directionality, voice-to-word matching, and several other print awareness skills, but it was not possible to evaluate her understanding of punctuation because she could read so few words in connected text. In contrast, her overall phonological awareness skills fall below grade-level expectations (percentile range = 15–19, *Below Basic*). She was able to perform some sound deletion tasks at the syllable, phoneme, and rime level (e.g., "Say *like* without *ike*") but not consistently. Even after several examples, she did not appear to understand the nature of the tasks and often simply repeated the stimulus word. On the Letter Recognition subtest, she was able to recognize target letters in a set of three and to name 25 of 26 letters (except *g*, which she named *j*), but her performance falls in the *Below Basic* range because most first graders can name all the letters in the fall of the year. On the Vocabulary subtest, which measures receptive and expressive language, she was able to match the name of an object or concept with its picture for 5 of the 10 items, but she had much more trouble generating the names of pictured objects (2/10 items), and her overall performance thus falls again in the *Below Basic* category.

Carrie's comprehension for what she hears and reads is rated as *Below Basic*. On the Listening Comprehension subtest, she was able to answer only one of the questions correctly. She had difficulty sustaining attention during the longer stories and attempted to answer while the examiner was still reading. On the Reading Comprehension subtest, which required her to read sentences and passages and answer questions about what she had read, her performance is rated as *Below Basic*. She was able to match pictures to words and answer questions by using pictorial clues for several items, but she was able to read only a few words in the sentences and only three of the target words. On the two reading passages, which she chose to read silently, her reading speed, as indicated by her own report of when she finished reading, was quite rapid, but she appeared to be skimming the material rather than trying to read each word, especially on the second and longer passage. Moreover, she was unable to answer any questions on the second passage correctly.

FOX IN A BOX: AN ADVENTURE IN LITERACY

Overview

Fox in a Box: An Adventure in Literacy (FOX; CTB/McGraw-Hill, 2000a) is a criterion-referenced early literacy assessment system designed to measure children's reading development in kindergarten through second grade. Based on end-of-year benchmarks written in 1996 by reading researchers Marilyn Adams and Jerry Treadway and subsequently adapted as the end-of-year accomplishments in the National Research

Council's *Preventing Reading Difficulties in Young Children* (Snow, Burns, & Griffin, 1998), FOX assesses four sets of literacy skills: (1) phonemic awareness, (2) phonics, (3) reading and oral expression, and (4) listening and writing. End-of-semester benchmarks are set for each task so that when the assessments are administered in early fall and early spring, the results can then be used for instructional planning. Assessment results are recorded in a literacy progress record that travels with the child through the early primary grades. The purposes of FOX are (1) to monitor literacy development for children in kindergarten through Grade 2 and (2) to provide information for instructional planning. The assessment kit includes 25 literacy progress records, 25 student folders, a chart with task benchmarks, a chart with guidelines for a shorter administration form, a spiral-bound booklet of teacher task cards, a spiral-bound booklet of child assessment cards, 12 leveled readers, a teacher's guide, a training video, and a fox puppet, all packed in a flip-top storage box. The examiner must provide paper for the kindergarten Alphabet Writing task.

Assessment Tasks

The FOX consists of a set of fall and spring assessment tasks, termed "activities," in each of four skill areas or "strands" for kindergarten through Grade 2 (Levels 1–6). Activities are designed to replicate authentic classroom experiences as much as possible. Table 4.10 displays the assessment tasks and administration times for the six levels by domain and grade. Table 4.11 describes the 16 tasks. In several cases, one activity yields scores in two or three skill areas.

Administration

The FOX is designed to be administered over a 2- to 3-week period in early fall (October–November) and again in early spring (March–April). Alphabet Writing, Spelling, and Listening Comprehension/Writing Development can be administered to small groups or an entire class, but the other tasks must be administered individually. Each individual assessment task takes about 5–7 minutes, for a total of about 35 minutes. The group tasks take an additional 80 minutes to administer, for a total testing time ranging from 1 hour and 40 minutes per child for fall of kindergarten to about 2 hours per child for Grade 2. The latest version of the FOX includes guidelines for a short form at each of the six levels, with approximately one-third fewer items. Children who score below benchmarks on the short form should take all grade-level activities, however. Complete administration directions are included in the Literacy Progress Record so that examiners do not need to refer to the guide during administration. Administration and scoring rubrics for spelling, reading comprehension, reading expression, reading accuracy, reading fluency, and listening and writing tasks are provided on a set of spiral-bound prompt cards. The fox puppet is used to model the phonemic awareness tasks and help focus children's attention. Although the puppet is attractive, it is large and unwieldy, and I have found it more distracting than helpful during the administration process. The leveled children's literature texts used to assess reading accuracy and comprehension are very engaging. Reading fluency assessments are administered with laminated cards that contain only the text from the leveled readers to avoid distracting the child with illustrations or page turning. For listening and writing tasks, the examiner reads a story from a separate reader (fall of kindergarten) or from passages printed on the task cards (spring of kindergarten

TABLE 4.10. ***Fox in a Box*** **Assessment Tasks by Skill Area and Level/Grade**

Skill area/ Assessment task	Level 1 (end of Grade K)	Level 2 (end of Grade K)	Level 3 (middle of Grade 1)	Level 4 (end of Grade 1)	Level 5 (middle of Grade 2)	Level 6 (end of Grade 2)
Phonemic Awareness						
Rhyme Recognition	×					
Rhyme Generation	×					
Syllable Clapping	×					
Initial Consonants	×					
Final Consonants		×				
Blending		×				
Segmenting		×				
Phonics						
Alphabet Recognition	×	×				
Alphabet Writing	×	×				
Spelling	×	×	×	×	×	×
Decoding		×	×	×	×	×
Reading and Oral Expression						
Sight Words		×	×	×	×	×
Concepts of Print	×					
Emergent Reading		×				
Reading Accuracy			×	×	×	×
Reading Comprehension			×	×	×	×
Oral Expression	×	×	×	×	×	×
Reading Rate				×	×	×
Reading Expression				×	×	×
Listening and Writing						
Listening Comprehension	×	×	×	×	×	×
Writing Expression				×	×	×
Writing Development	×	×	×	×	×	×
Total time	100 minutes	105 minutes	115 minutes	102 minutes	122 minutes	122 minutes

Note. Shaded tasks can be administered to groups. Kindergarten students who achieve Level 2 benchmarks on the phonemic awareness tasks and Alphabet Recognition in the fall also take Decoding and Sight Words. First and second graders who perform below Level 3 benchmarks in Spelling and/or Decoding take the phonemic awareness tasks, Alphabet Recognition, and Alphabet Writing.

through Grade 2), and children draw or write on pages reproduced from blackline masters in the teacher's guide.

Scores

The FOX yields only raw scores. Scoring is dichotomous for phonemic awareness, phonics, and sight word tasks. On the Spelling task, letter reversals are noted but are not counted as errors. Examiners can conduct additional error analyses on decoding tasks to evaluate the child's mastery of 24 decoding conventions. Spelling skills can also be analyzed on a classwide basis using a class record sheet, which lists 20 spelling conventions. In scoring contextual reading fluency, six types of errors are noted: (1) misreadings, (2) substitutions, (3) omissions, (4) insertions, (5) ignored punctuation, and (6) examiner help after a pause of 2 or 3 seconds for Reading Accuracy and 3 seconds for Reading Fluency. Several of the scoring guide-

TABLE 4.11. Description of the Fox in a Box Assessment Tasks

Task	Description
Rhyme Recognition	The child indicates whether two words pronounced by the examiner rhyme.
Rhyme Generation	The examiner reads a two-line poem, and the child provides a final rhyming word for the last line (e.g., the examiner reads, "I really like . . . to ride my ________," and the child says, "bike").
Syllable Clapping	The child claps to indicate the number of syllables in words spoken by the examiner. The words range from one to four syllables in length.
Initial Consonants	The child pronounces the first sound in a series of one-syllable words spoken by the examiner.
Final Consonants	The child pronounces the final sound in a series of one-syllable words spoken by the examiner.
Blending	The examiner pronounces the individual phonemes in a series of words with three or four phonemes, and the child blends the sounds together to form a word.
Segmenting	The examiner pronounces a series of three- and four-phoneme words, and the child segments the words into individual phonemes.
Alphabet Recognition	The child names a random array of uppercase letters and gives the names and sounds of a random array of lowercase letters. For spring of kindergarten, the child also names the vowels in the lowercase letter array.
Alphabet Writing	The child writes letters in both uppercase and lowercase form that are dictated by the examiner.
Spelling	For kindergarten, the child writes initial, final, and medial vowels in a series of one-syllable words on a spelling sheet (e.g., the child sees *-un* and writes *f*). For Grades 1 and 2, the child writes a series of words dictated by the examiner.
Decoding	The child reads aloud a series of words printed on a card. Items include both phonically regular real words and pseudowords.
Sight Words	The child reads aloud a series of sight words printed on a card. The items are divided into basic sight words and advanced sight words.
Concepts of Print	This activity yields two scores. For *Concepts of Print*, the examiner assesses the child's knowledge of print concepts and conventions using a leveled reader to obtain a mastery (five out of five skills assessed) or nonmastery score. For *Oral Expression*, the child describes a picture in the book and retells the story, and the examiner rates the child's production on a 3-point scale.
Emergent Reading	This activity yields two scores and involves one of two procedures, depending on the child's skill level. In the interactive procedure of *Emergent Reading*, the examiner reads a book to the child and then reads it again, asking the child to read or point out nine words. In the independent procedure, the examiner and child take turns reading pages in a different book. The examiner also rates the child's *Reading Expression* skills on a 3-point scale.
Reading Accuracy and Comprehension	This activity requires the child to read from a book or card and yields three scores. The *Reading Accuracy* score is based on the percent of words read correctly. The child answers prediction and comprehension questions about the passage and retells the story, and the examiner rates performance on each of the three tasks on a 3-point scale and obtains an overall rating, also on a 3-point scale, for the *Reading Comprehension* score. All of the passages are narrative. The examiner also rates the child's *Oral Expression* skills on a 3-point scale.
Reading Fluency	This activity yields two scores. The child reads a passage printed on a card, and the *Reading Rate* score is the number of words read correctly in 1 minute. The examiner also rates the child's *Reading Expression* skills on a 3-point scale.
Listening and Writing	This activity yields three scores. The child listens to a story read by the examiner and draws (kindergarten) or writes (Grades 1 and 2) a summary of the story. The child's production is rated on a 3-point scale for *Listening Comprehension* and for *Writing Expression* and on a 6-point scale for *Writing Development*.

lines are ambiguous or questionable. Counting ignored punctuation as an error in oral reading assessments is highly unusual, and no rationale for this decision is given in the teacher's guide or the other test materials. For Reading Accuracy, the directions in the Literacy Progress Record indicate to the child that no help will be given with unfamiliar words ("If you come to a word you don't know, do what you would do if you were reading all by yourself," p. 24). In contrast, the directions printed on the teacher task cards list teacher assistance as an error and state, "Wait two or three seconds before giving help," implying that the examiner supplies an unfamiliar word after a pause.

Scoring for reading comprehension, reading expression, listening comprehension, and oral expression tasks is based on a 3-point rating scale (low, medium, high). The Literacy Progress Record reproduces the reading accuracy and fluency passages for use in marking errors but provides very little space for recording responses to reading comprehension questions and no space for recording responses to any of the oral expression tasks, including story retelling. The record booklet also lists rubrics for scoring the listening and writing tasks but does not provide any scoring examples. The teacher's guide includes scoring examples for two levels, one reflecting the performance of a child in the second half of kindergarten who meets most of the benchmarks and the other reflecting the performance of a first-semester second grader whose literacy development is one level below the benchmarks.

Interpretation

The FOX is criterion-referenced, with performance interpreted in terms of fall and spring benchmarks for each assessment task. An appendix in the teacher's guide lists end-of-year benchmarks by domain for kindergarten through Grade 2. On the FOX, these guidelines have been translated into midyear and end-of-year benchmarks, represented by the mastery scores for each assessment task. Reading accuracy benchmarks are set at 90% or higher, and benchmarks for reading comprehension, reading expression, listening comprehension, and oral expression are set at medium or high performance levels on a 3-point scale. Results of the Sight Words task can be interpreted in terms of independent reading level as well as benchmarks. The basic sight words are high frequency, irregularly spelled words that are intended to be taught if the child has not mastered them. The advanced sight words, which were selected for their misleading letter-sound relationships, decrease in frequency from the beginning to the end of the list. According to the authors, the point on the list at which the child begins to make errors is an index of the depth of the child's sight vocabulary and the level of text he or she can be expected to read independently. Reading fluency assessments use texts that are one level below the child's reading accuracy level because they are intended to help teachers determine the text level at which a child can read independently.

Technical Adequacy

Two technical reports are available from the publisher: a 9-page paper, *Why Fox in a Box?* (CTB/McGraw-Hill, 2000b), which reviews the empirical basis for the battery, and a comprehensive technical reference (*Technical Report 1*; CTB/McGraw-Hill, 2001). Information in the following sections is drawn from these two reports and the teacher's guide. According to the publisher, large-scale studies of task reliability and benchmark validity are currently underway. Separate reliability and validity data are not available for the short form.

Test Development

Preview editions of the FOX were pilot-tested in kindergarten, Grade 1, and Grade 2 classrooms across the United States to provide information for enhancing usability and ensuring administration and scoring accuracy. No specific information is provided regarding the number or characteristics of the students in these investigations, which primarily focused on usability considerations. Based on the results of the pilot studies, design revisions and additions were made, including the development of a training video. Test bias was examined by content validity analyses, internal reviews by four CTB staff members, and reviews by educational professionals in the community representing various ethnic groups. In fall and spring of 2000, the FOX was administered by more than 140 teachers to a total of 2,957 students in public and private schools, with grade-level sample sizes for fall and spring testing tasks ranging from 416 to 551. Students were drawn from 21 states and the District of Columbia in the North, South, and West regions of the country. Fall and spring sample characteristics are presented by grade for age, ethnicity, gender, region, SES, and school type (public vs. private), but because the tables do not include U.S. census data for comparative purposes, it is difficult to evaluate sample representativeness.

Reliability Evidence

Internal consistency reliability coefficients are reported for each grade for fall and spring measures, with the exception of most of the reading fluency tasks and several tasks scored on holistic rating scales or using error rates. Kindergarten fall and spring coefficient alphas range from .61 to .95 for phonemic awareness tasks, with Rhyme Recognition, Rhyme Generation, and Syllable Clapping falling below the .80 criterion level, which is not surprising, given that they include only six to eight items each. Kindergarten fall and spring coefficients for phonics tasks are all at or above .80 (*r*s = .84 to .98), whereas alphas for fall Concepts of Print and Oral Expression are well below criterion levels (.61 and .54, respectively). Kindergarten spring coefficient alphas for reading and oral expression tasks range from .75 to .98, with only Interactive Emergent Reading falling below the acceptable level. For Grade 1, fall and spring coefficient alphas for all the tasks evaluated are in the .90s, with the exception of Reading Comprehension (fall = .72; spring = .82), and Writing (spring = .66). For Grade 2, fall and spring coefficient alphas are in the .90s for phonics and sight word tasks. Coefficients are in the .80s for spring of Grade 2 Reading Comprehension and Reading Rate but fall below criterion levels for spring Reading Expression and fall Reading Comprehension (.78 and .60, respectively). Coefficients for Listening and Writing are below acceptable levels for both measurement periods (.74 to .77). No test–retest reliability estimates are reported for any tasks at any grade level.

Interrater reliability was evaluated for Listening Comprehension, Writing Development, and Writing Expression (number of test protocols = 64–260) in the fall and spring standardization samples by comparing teacher ratings with ratings by professional CTB raters (number unspecified). Intraclass correlations ranged from .44 for spring Writing Expression to .91 for fall Writing Expression, with only fall Writing Expression and spring Writing Development above the .80 criterion level. The difference in reliability between fall and spring Writing Expression is striking, but no explanation is provided for the disparity. Moreover, because interrater reliability estimates are aggregated across levels and grades, interrater consistency for specific tasks at specific administration windows cannot be determined. Evidence of interexaminer consistency based on independent scoring of children's responses during actual or videotaped test sessions would be desirable, especially for the numerous tasks requiring subjective judgment and the tasks most vulnerable to examiner variance, such as reading fluency and interactive reading.

Validity Evidence

CONTENT VALIDITY EVIDENCE

Domain and task content were selected based on a comprehensive curriculum review and consultations with education experts to ensure a match between test and current instructional content. Interviews with teachers and teacher responses to questionnaires during usability studies provided additional information regarding the appropriateness of the benchmarks, ease of administration, and appropriateness of the content for the specific grade. The technical report provides a readable overview of the empirical basis for each strand, with citations from the research literature. Item difficulties are reported by grade and level for each item of each assessment task and are generally in the acceptable range for level-specific items. Mastery scores were set so that approximately 75% to 80% of examinees would reach each benchmark in order to identify children having the greatest difficulty acquiring early literacy skills. The technical report includes tables listing the percentage of students in fall and spring samples who mastered each task by grade. Obtained mastery rates fall below criterion levels at each grade level for a sizable number of tasks, especially Spelling, Decoding, and Sight Words. The publisher attributes these lower mastery scores to increasing expectations for early primary grade children arising from the literacy standards recommended by the National Reading Panel, which have not yet been fully reflected in curricular changes. Three groups of individuals reviewed the materials for possible bias, including the developers, four staff members, and educational professionals in the community representing various ethnic groups.

CRITERION-RELATED VALIDITY EVIDENCE

Concurrent validity was examined by correlating FOX task scores with Reading and Language scores on the *TerraNova Complete Battery* (*TerraNova*; CTB/McGraw-Hill, 1997), administered in the spring 2000 research study. For kindergarten, correlations with *TerraNova* Reading and Language composites were in the low to moderate range (.17 to .54), with the highest correlations for Segmenting and Sight Words. For Grades 1 and 2, correlations with *TerraNova* Reading, Language, Vocabulary, Word Analysis, and Spelling (Grade 2 only) were highly variable (–.14 to .69), with the highest correlations for Spelling, Decoding, and Sight Words. Correlations between FOX reading tasks and *TerraNova* Reading were surprisingly low for both grades (Grade 1 = –.14 to .37; Grade 2 = .15 to –.35). (Note that Reading Accuracy scores, which reflect number of errors, are expected to yield negative correlations with other scores.) No predictive validity evidence is presented.

CONSTRUCT VALIDITY EVIDENCE

Mean raw scores for assessment tasks reported by grade and for each grade by level display increases from fall to spring and across grades, as expected. Task intercorrelations presented for fall and spring for each grade generally conform to the expected pattern in terms of direction and size. In a concordance study with a sample of children who took both the FOX and the *TerraNova* (*n*s = 28 to 183), students who achieved mastery on FOX tasks obtained higher *TerraNova* scale scores than the nonmastery group on 12 of 15 kindergarten tasks, 7 of 8 Grade 1 tasks, and all 8 of the Grade 2 tasks. Differences were not tested for significance, however.

Usability

The FOX is one of the most attractive early literacy batteries reviewed in this text, but it is quite time-consuming to administer and score, especially for children in Grades 1 and 2. Using the puppet as described in the manual and demonstrated on the training video increases administration time further. Moreover, if the assessment is given in the classroom, as the guide directs, the charming but bulky puppet may distract other children who are not being evaluated. The training video includes demonstrations of each assessment activity, including a practice session for administering Reading Accuracy. Because some examiners may have limited experience in conducting fluency assessments, an opportunity to practice Reading Fluency would also be helpful. There is no information in any of the materials about accommodations or suggestions for assessing children from diverse linguistic or cultural backgrounds. The teacher's guide includes a reproducible parent/guardian letter describing the assessment. It also invites the parent/guardian to volunteer time in the classroom during the assessment, however, which raises issues regarding students' privacy and test validity. The leveled readers, which consist of children's trade books, are delightful and very appealing to children. Available by separate purchase is a software program with the capability of reporting, aggregating, and storing student scores across the three grades. An online management and reporting system is under development. *Letting the Fox Out of the Box*—a CD-ROM for Windows or Macintosh applications, available free of charge with school or district purchase of the FOX test kit—contains an excellent and very comprehensive set of staff development materials, including speaker notes, a training module with videos and slides, handouts, PowerPoint presentations and overheads for a variety of training formats, and additional resources, including the technical report.

Links to Intervention

The FOX is designed to guide instruction by providing teachers with information about children's literacy development relative to grade-level expectations for the end of each semester of the school year. The teacher's guide includes a section on "Connecting Assessment to Instruction," which advises teachers to work in grade-level teams to pool scores of children in each grade, arrange them from highest to lowest on each skill, and collaborate to develop strategies to assist children with particular skill problems. The guide does not offer any specific instructional recommendations or describe any resources for children who perform poorly in any of the domains assessed, however. The scoring and reporting software provides suggestions for parent-child literacy activities as part of the home report. Available by separate purchase from the publisher is *Adventures in Literacy: Classroom and Home Activities for Early Readers* (CTB/McGraw-Hill, 2002), a handbook of reproducible activities covering the four FOX domains and matched to each FOX benchmark. The handbook, which has a three-hole punch format, includes a wealth of materials for the classroom and home activities, as well as other resource materials (e.g., picture and letter cards, word lists).

Source and Cost

The FOX test kit is available for $315.00 from CTB/McGraw Hill. A Grade 3 extension is now included as of fall 2003. The management and reporting software is priced at $74.95, and the activities handbook is available for $24.95.

Summary

Fox in a Box: An Adventure in Literacy (FOX) is a comprehensive, empirically based early literacy battery that is attractive, examiner-friendly, and more classroom-oriented than many of its competitors. The emphasis on authentic assessment techniques and materials is both positive and negative, however. Some of the activities are very time-consuming, and administration and scoring guidelines for many tasks are imprecise. Internal reliability estimates fall below criterion levels for some measures, with values lowest for kindergarten tasks and lacking for some measures at some grades. No stability estimates for any of the tasks are available, and interrater reliability estimates are aggregated across levels for three measures and absent for the rest. A commendable effort to translate the findings of reading research into an assessment that yields instructionally relevant information, the FOX also offers a variety of staff development and intervention options. Additional studies demonstrating the FOX's relationship to other early reading measures and its utility in predicting future reading proficiency are needed.

Case Example

Name of student: Leonard V.
Age: 5 years, 5 months
Grade: Kindergarten
Date of assessment: October

Reason for assessment: Leonard took *Fox in a Box* in the fall of kindergarten as part of the early reading screening program in his school. His performance is described below.

Assessment results and interpretation: *Fox in a Box: An Adventure in Literacy* is an early literacy assessment system that measures a wide range of prereading and reading skills, including phonemic awareness, phonics, reading and oral expression, and listening and writing. Student performance is evaluated against grade-level fall and spring *benchmarks,* which are levels of literacy development that children should reach by specific times in the early primary grade years. Leonard's scores on the tasks, called *activities,* and benchmarks for midyear kindergarten performance (Level 1) are presented below.

Skill Area	Activity	Obtained Score	Level 1 Benchmark
Phonemic Awareness	Rhyme Recognition	6/6	5/6
	Rhyme Generation	4/6	4/6
	Syllable Clapping	2/6	4/6
	Initial Consonants	4/8	6/8
Phonics	Alphabet Recognition–Uppercase	15/26	18/26
	Alphabet Recognition–Lowercase	16/26	18/26
	Alphabet Sounds	3/26	13/26
	Alphabet Writing	8/20	12/20
	Spelling–Initial Consonant	0/5	4/5
	Spelling–Final Consonant	0/5	2/5
Reading and Oral Expression	Concepts of Print	5/5	5/5
	Oral Expression	3/3	3/3
Listening and Writing	Listening Comprehension	Medium	Medium–high
	Writing Development	Level 1	Level 1

Leonard has mastered two of the four phonemic awareness activities for fall of kindergarten. On Syllable Clapping, he was able to segment one- and two-syllable words, but he missed most of the longer words. On Initial Consonants, he had difficulty isolating initial sounds for several items and confused *p* and *b* on one item. He did not achieve the benchmarks on any of the phonics activities, although his performance approached mastery level for Alphabet Recognition. He was able to identify only 3 of 26 letter sounds correctly and to write only 8 of 20 dictated letters. He did not appear to understand the distinction between uppercase and lowercase letters, even after the demonstration, and he reversed lowercase *b*. He also did not appear to understand the Spelling task, which requires the child to write initial or final consonants for one-syllable words, and simply copied the adjacent letter in the blank (e.g., for *nap*, he wrote *aap*). Even with additional demonstrations and assistance in pronouncing the missing sounds, he was unable to answer any items correctly.

In contrast to his weak phonics skills, Leonard's print awareness and oral expression skills are well developed for his grade placement. He understands a variety of print concepts, including page sequencing and word boundaries, and he was able to identify the characters and describe the actions in a story. His listening comprehension skills are also developing satisfactorily for his grade placement. He listened attentively to a story read to him and demonstrated a basic literal understanding of story events. When he was asked to write in his own words what the story was about, however, he protested, "I don't know how to do that." With much encouragement, he produced a string of random letters. Although this type of writing is rated at the Level 1 benchmark for fall of kindergarten, it offers further evidence that he has not yet grasped the *alphabetic principle*–the fact that letters map to specific sounds. He wrote the same five letters (*a, e, i, l,* and *m*) randomly repeated in a 12-letter string, which he read aloud as, "He went to class and everybody teased him."

GROUP READING ASSESSMENT AND DIAGNOSTIC EVALUATION

Overview

The *Group Reading Assessment and Diagnostic Evaluation* (GRADE; Williams, 2002) is a group-administered norm-referenced reading battery for individuals from prekindergarten through adult. The GRADE assesses five reading components: (1) prereading (visual skills and conceptual knowledge); (2) reading readiness (phonemic awareness, letter recognition, sound–symbol matching, and print awareness); (3) vocabulary (recognition and understanding of print vocabulary); (4) comprehension (sentences and passages); and (5) oral language. Designed for large-scale assessment, the GRADE provides two parallel forms and fall and spring norms for 11 levels from prekindergarten through high school, with fall norms for postsecondary students. Scores are linked psychometrically across levels with growth scale values for monitoring the progress of individuals or groups of students. Applications of the GRADE include (1) obtaining information for placement and instructional planning, (2) analyzing reading strengths and weaknesses for classroom groups or individual students, (3) testing students whose reading ability is significantly above or below their grade placement, (4) monitoring growth in reading skills, and (5) facilitating research. Classroom sets for Levels P (prekindergarten) through 3 include 30 consumable student booklets, an administration manual, and a spiral-bound scoring and interpretation manual. For Levels 4 and up, materials include 30 reusable student booklets, 30 answer sheets, hand-scoring templates, an administration manual, and a spiral-bound scoring and interpretation manual. Student booklets, answer sheets, and scoring templates are form specific, whereas manuals cover both forms by level, except for Levels P and K, which have one manual per form.

Subtests and Composites

Subtests

Across the 11 levels, the GRADE includes 16 subtests that measure five prereading and reading components. Listening Comprehension is the only subtest included at all levels but is optional for Levels 1 through A (adult). Table 4.12 lists subtests by component and level for the entire grade range of the test. All of the subtests are untimed. Time guidelines suggested in the manuals are indicated in the table.

For all items on all subtests, students respond by marking an × or filling in a circle (i.e., multiple-choice format). Students mark their responses in record booklets for Levels P through 3 and on separate answer sheets for Levels 4 and up. Circles are provided for each response choice across all levels, but at Levels P and K students mark an answer by putting an × directly over their response choice, and at Level 1 they do so by drawing an × over the appropriate circle. No rationale for this marking system is provided, and the Level 1 system may confuse some children. Table 4.13 describes the 16 GRADE subtests, beginning with Level P.

Composites

GRADE subtests can be combined to form a variety of composite scores at each level, as shown in Table 4.14.

Administration

At all levels, the GRADE can be administered in its entirety in a classwide format. Administration procedures are clearly spelled out in the manuals, with the examiner script highlighted for readability. Approximate testing times for early primary grade students range from about 115 minutes for Level P to about 65 minutes for Level 3.

TABLE 4.12. GRADE Subtests by Component and Level

Component	Subtest	Level P	Level K	Level 1	Level 2	Level 3	Levels 4–A
Pre-Reading	Picture Matching	×					
	Picture Differences	×					
	Verbal Concepts	×					
	Picture Categories	×					
Reading Readiness	Sound Matching	×	×				
	Rhyming	×	×				
	Print Awareness		×				
	Letter Recognition		×				
	Same & Different Words		×				
	Phoneme–Grapheme Correspondence		×				
Vocabulary	Word Reading		× (shaded)	×	×	×	
	Word Meaning			×	×		
	Vocabulary					×	×
Comprehension	Sentence Comprehension			×	×	×	×
	Passage Comprehension			×	×	×	×
Oral Language	Listening Comprehension	×	×	× (shaded)	× (shaded)	× (shaded)	× (shaded)
Total time		115 minutes	100 minutes	85 minutes	85 minutes	65 minutes	45–60 minutes

Note. Shaded tests are optional for that level.

The test's author recommends four testing sessions for Levels P–K and two sessions for Levels 1–3. At the lower grade ranges, levels cover more than one grade and should be selected on the basis of children's estimated reading skills as well as chronological grade placement. For example, Level 1 is recommended for students entering first grade who are emergent readers but also for second graders who are considered to be at risk or to have special needs. The GRADE also permits out-of-level testing for students whose reading skills appear to be more than two grades below or above their grade enrollment. The GRADE offers three options for progress monitoring: (1) Rasch-derived growth scale values (GSVs) for monitoring progress across grades and test levels, (2) fall and spring testing using the two parallel forms, and (3) testing using the two forms to evaluate intervention effectiveness as often as every 2 or 3 months. Levels P and K and Levels 1 thorough A are linked psychometrically with GSVs. GSVs for Levels P and K are centered at 100, whereas GSVs for Levels 1 through A are centered at 500.

Scores

Scoring options include templates for hand scoring, scannable answer sheets (Levels 4 through A only), and on-site scoring and reporting software. Scoring rules and procedures are clear and comprehensive, but hand scoring is a long, tedious process, espe-

TABLE 4.13. Description of the GRADE Subtests

Subtest	Description
Picture Matching	The child marks the one of four pictures that is the same as a picture in a box.
Picture Differences	The child marks the one of four pictures that is different from the others.
Verbal Concepts	The child marks the one of four pictures that best corresponds to a sentence read by the examiner.
Picture Categories	The child marks the one of four pictures that does not belong with the other three.
Sound Matching	This subtest includes two tasks. In *Begins With,* the child marks the one of four pictures that begins with the same sound as a word pronounced by the examiner. In *Ends With,* the child marks the one of four pictures that ends with the same sound as a word pronounced by the examiner.
Rhyming	The child marks the one of four pictures that rhymes with a word pronounced by the examiner.
Print Awareness	The child marks the one of four pictures that best represents a sentence read by the examiner. For example, the examiner reads, "Find the box with a capital letter in it," and the child marks the box containing a capital letter.
Letter Recognition	The child marks the one of five letters named by the examiner.
Same & Different Words	This subtest includes two tasks. For *Same Words,* the child marks the one of four words that is the same as the word in a box. For *Different Words,* the child marks the one of four words that is different from the other three.
Phoneme–Grapheme Correspondence	This subtest includes two tasks. In the first task, the child marks the one of four letters that corresponds to the first sound in a word pronounced by the examiner. In the second task, the child marks the one of four letters that corresponds to the last sound in a word pronounced by the examiner.
Word Reading	The child marks the one of four or five words that corresponds to a target word pronounced and then read in a sentence by the examiner.
Word Meaning	The child silently reads a target word and marks the one of four pictures that best conveys the meaning of the word.
Vocabulary	The child silently reads a phrase or short sentence in which one of the words is printed in bold type and marks the one of four or five words that best represents the meaning of that word.
Sentence Comprehension	The child silently reads a sentence with a missing word and marks the one of four or five words that best completes the sentence.
Passage Comprehension	The child silently reads one or more paragraphs and answers three, four, or five multiple-choice questions about the passage. Both narrative and informational passages are included.
Listening Comprehension	The child listens to a sentence read by the examiner and marks the one of four pictures that best represents what was read.

TABLE 4.14. GRADE Subtests and Composites by Level

Level	Composite	Subtests
Level P	Total Test	All subtests
Levels P and K	Phonological Awareness	Rhyming Sound Matching
Level P	Visual Skills	Picture Matching Picture Differences
	Concepts	Verbal Concepts Picture Categories
Level K	Total Test	All subtests except Word Reading
	Early Literacy Skills	Print Awareness Letter Recognition Same & Different Words
Levels 1 and 2	Vocabulary	Word Reading Word Meaning
Level 3	Vocabulary	Word Reading Vocabulary
Levels 1–A	Total Test	All subtests except Listening Comprehension
Levels 1–A	Comprehension	Sentence Comprehension Passage Comprehension

cially if examiners complete the diagnostic analyses for each subtest. On the Sound Matching diagnostic analysis worksheet in the scoring and interpretive manual for Level K (p. 24), the correct picture on the first item is circled, but the digraph *wh* rather than the single consonant *w* should be underlined in the stimulus and target words (i.e., *what/whale*, not *what/whale*). Scores can be converted to fall and spring grade norms for Levels K through H (high school), with a single set of fall norms for postsecondary students. Optional age norms are available for Level P in 6-month intervals from 4-0 through 6-11. Normative data for out-of-level testing are available in the software scoring program and the out-of-level norms supplement. For Levels 1 through A, composite and total test raw scores can be converted to grade-based standard scores (M = 100, SD = 15), percentile ranks, grade equivalents, normal curve equivalents (NCEs), and stanines (and, for total test, to growth scale values). At Levels P and K, the full range of norm-referenced scores is available only for the Total Test composite. Only stanines are provided for Listening Comprehension and the other three composites, which are designated as "subtests" in the norms tables and elsewhere in the manual. If a child scores below an NCE of 1 or in the ninth stanine, the GRADE's author recommends administering a lower or higher level of the test to obtain a more accurate estimate of reading skills and a more useful analysis of reading strengths and weaknesses.

Interpretation

GRADE results are interpreted primarily in terms of stanines and subtest diagnostic analyses. Scores in the first or second stanine (the lowest 11%) indicate reading weaknesses, whereas scores in the eighth or ninth stanine (the highest 11%) indicate reading strengths. The author recommends that students scoring in the first through third stanine on Listening Comprehension, which is a very easy task across all levels, should be referred for a comprehensive oral language assessment. The GRADE provides two types of diagnostic analysis per subtest: (1) analysis based on item *p* values and (2) analysis based on item type (e.g., long and short vowel items in Rhyming). *P* values for all items are listed on the diagnostic analysis worksheets for comparing individual and/or group item performance with national item performance (i.e., local vs. national *p* values). To analyze by item type, the examiner counts the number of correct responses by item type for each student and then records this information on the Class Score Summary. Individual Score Summary sheets provide room for recording correct responses by item type but not for conducting *p*-value analyses.

Scoring and interpretative manuals at each level use a fictional examinee and his or her classmates to illustrate procedures for group and individual scoring and interpretation, with examples of completed diagnostic analysis worksheets for all subtests. The case examples include a completed Individual Score Summary with teacher comments and a brief discussion of the child's performance and a completed Class Score Summary, which is not discussed. The explanations of derived scores are generally clear and comprehensive, but the discussion of GSVs does not define all the terms (e.g., Rasch model, *W*-ability scale); instead, it refers the reader to the separate technical manual, which may not be available to all teachers. Manuals also include suggestions for comparing performance across subtests (e.g., Listening Comprehension vs. Passage Comprehension). The readable and well-organized technical manual discusses the meaning of subtest performance, suggests subtest score comparisons, and provides recommendations for follow-up assessments and instructional activities. Although some of the same information is included in the examiner manuals, the version in the technical manual is more comprehensive. The technical manual also includes suggestions for conducting two additional sets of error analyses for Word Reading, the first based on regular–irregular word comparisons and the second based on distractor selection, using Moat's (1999) and Ehri's (1995) research on reading and spelling acquisition. For interventions, examiners are referred to the GRADE Resource Libraries on CD-ROM (see "Links to Intervention," below) and other AGS products.

Technical Adequacy

Standardization

The standardization sample, conducted in 2000 at 134 sites, included 16,408 students in the spring and 17,204 students in the fall. Because some levels span more than one grade, oversampling was used at certain levels. That is, Level P was administered in the spring and fall to both preschool and kindergarten students, Level K was administered to kindergarten and Grade 1 students in the spring and fall, and Level 1 was administered to kindergarten students in the spring who demonstrated some reading ability. Similar oversampling was used for Vocabulary and Word Reading to develop norms for Grade 2 students and for the out-of-level norms. Grade sizes by level and form range from 320 to 1,373 across the entire grade range and from 401 to 1,135 for kindergarten through Grade 3, with the smallest size for Grade 3. Fall and spring sample characteristics are reported for gender, geographic region, community type (urban, suburban, or rural), and race/ethnicity, with characteristics compared with

U.S. 1998 census data. Because only gender is reported by grade, it is not possible to determine sample representativeness at specific grade levels for the other characteristics. Overall, the South region is slightly overrepresented in both fall and spring samples, and the West region is slightly underrepresented in the fall sample. Figures for race/ethnicity presented for the total sample and in narrative rather than tabular form closely match U.S. 1998 population data, but no information on race/ethnicity specific to level, administration window, or grade is provided. Children receiving special education services were included in the sample if they were mainstreamed for at least part of the school day. A comparison of standardization sites with 1997–1998 U.S. population data by five free-lunch categories indicates that sites with very high percentages of students receiving free lunch were somewhat overrepresented, whereas sites with low percentages of students receiving free lunch were somewhat underrepresented.

Reliability Evidence

Subtest alpha and split-half coefficients for Levels P through 3 range from .50 to .98, with somewhat lower coefficients for subtests taken by students in a grade above or below the designated level. For Level P, subtest reliabilities range from .74 to .98, with 40 of the 64 reliabilities in the .90s and 21 in the .80s. For kindergartners taking Level P, Concepts falls below the criterion level for fall and spring (both .74), and Listening Comprehension is at .78 for fall. For Level K, subtest reliabilities range from .66 to .96, with 29 of the 80 coefficients in the .90s and 40 in the .80s. For both preschool and kindergarten children, coefficients are generally lowest for Listening Comprehension and Word Reading (optional at this level), with some values falling in the .70s or below. For Level 1, administered to both kindergarten and first-grade students, subtest reliabilities range from .50 to .96, with 27 of the 60 values in the .90s and 20 in the .80s. For Listening Comprehension, 6 of 12 coefficients fall in the .70s. For kindergartners, coefficients for Passage Comprehension, which is beyond the abilities of most students at that level, are in the .50s and .60s. Reliabilities for the Vocabulary composite are in the .90s across both grades, whereas values for the Comprehension composite are in the .70s for fall of kindergarten students and in the .80s for spring of kindergarten students. For Level 2, subtest reliabilities, except for Listening Comprehension, range from .87 to .96, with 21 of the 40 values at or above .90. Coefficients for Listening Comprehension, which is optional at Level 1 and above, range from .51 to .81, with 7 of 8 values falling below the criterion level. Subtest reliabilities for Level 3, except for Listening Comprehension, range from .82 to .95, with 17 of 40 coefficients at or above .90. Level 3 Listening Comprehension reliabilities are well below acceptable levels (.40 to .70). Across Levels P through 3, Total Test composite reliabilities are above .90, with the exception of the alpha coefficient for kindergarten students taking Level K in the spring (.89).

Alternate-form reliability coefficients for Total Test for Levels P through 3 (*ns* = 27 to 69; mean intervals = 14 to 32.2 days) are at .90 or above, with the exception of Level K (.88). Test–retest reliabilities (*ns* = 40 to 72; mean intervals = 10.4 to 30.0 days) reported by level and grade-enrollment group range from .83 to .96. Although most levels show minor practice effects, gains of nearly 5 or 6 points were evident for Form A of Level K and Level 2, respectively. Stability estimates are not provided for Form A of Level 1 or Form B of Levels K, 2, and 3. Three kinds of form equivalency evidence are presented: (1) standard errors of measurement for each pair of forms by level and grade enrollment group; (2) raw score means and standard deviations by level, form, and grade enrollment group; and (3) the number of items by each item type per form by level. The forms yield very similar results, with raw score mean differences of fewer than 5 points across Levels P through 3. No interscorer reliability estimates are provided. Scoring is objective, but the lengthy and complex hand-scoring process is highly vulnerable to errors, especially for the diagnostic analyses.

Test Floors and Item Gradients

In general, floors are ample for subtests other than those designated as optional. For example, Word Reading, which is optional at Level K and is very difficult for most kindergarten children, shows floor effects for both fall and spring assessments. Ceiling and item gradient violations are evident on Listening Comprehension across most levels, with ceiling effects occurring as early as the fall of kindergarten. In fall and spring of kindergarten, a child who answers every item correctly earns a stanine score of 8, whereas a child who misses 1 item receives a stanine score of 5.

Validity Evidence

CONTENT VALIDITY EVIDENCE

Items were developed to provide a broad sampling of empirically based reading tasks measuring the five components of the test. A national tryout of the GRADE was conducted in 1999 with over 20,893 students in preschool through 12th grade at 99 sites nationwide. Items were analyzed for difficulty and discrimination using classical and Rasch techniques, but no specific information on these analyses is presented in the technical manual. Although *p* values are reported by item on the diagnostic analysis worksheets, the technical manual should provide tables with median difficulties by subtest for each level. Feedback from teachers based on 777 surveys returned during national tryouts was also used in developing items and materials for the standardization and final versions. Examiner directions and items were reviewed for potential bias or culturally specific content by a review panel, followed by DIF analyses by gender and race/ethnicity (whites vs. African Americans and whites vs. Hispanics). Flagged items were modified or deleted, but no specific information is provided regarding the number or percentage removed. After items that did not meet selection criteria for difficulty, discrimination, internal consistency, model fit, or lack of bias were deleted, the remaining items were assigned to levels and divided into two parallel forms, for a total of 2,290 items for the 16 subtests. The technical manual includes a useful chapter reviewing the structure and content of the test, with a detailed discussion of each subtest in terms of the skills measured, format and item types, and interpretation of the results.

CRITERION-RELATED VALIDITY EVIDENCE

Four concurrent validity studies are reported, two of which involve early primary grade children. For 68 first graders and 51 second graders tested in the spring, GRADE Total Test standard scores were highly correlated with *California Achievement Tests–Fifth Edition* (CAT-5; CTB/McGraw-Hill, 1992) Total Reading scale scores (.82 and .87, respectively). Correlations between fall GRADE Total Test and *Gates–MacGinitie Reading Tests* (Riverside, 2000) total scores for 92 first and second graders and 76 third graders were also high (.90 and .86, respectively). In a predictive validity study with 232 students in Grades 2, 4, and 6, fall GRADE Total Test standard scores were strong predictors of spring *TerraNova* Reading scale scores (.76, .77, and .86, respectively). No evidence is presented to support the concurrent or predictive validity of the diagnostic analyses.

CONSTRUCT VALIDITY EVIDENCE

Construct validity evidence consists of a discussion of the theoretical basis of the GRADE, convergent and divergent validity studies, developmental score progression across GRADE levels and grades, and studies with special populations. For early primary grade examinees, the GRADE correlates highly with group-administered standardized achievement and reading tests, as noted above. Convergent–divergent validity evidence derives from two studies with middle grade students. In a sample of 30 fifth graders, GRADE Vocabulary, Comprehension, and Total Test scores were highly correlated with Reading Recognition, Reading Comprehension, and Total Test scores on the *Peabody Individual Achievement Test–Revised* (PIAT-R; Markwardt, 1989) (*r*s = .68 to .80), whereas GRADE Comprehension and PIAT–R General Information were only moderately correlated (.47). In a study with 117 seventh and eighth graders, the same GRADE tests were highly correlated with *Iowa Tests of Basic Skills* (Hoover, Hieronymus, Frisbie, & Dunbar, 1996) Reading, Language Arts, and Math Concepts and Problems subtests, all of which require reading ability (. 63 to .83), whereas correlations with Math Computation were generally moderate (.53 to .67). Growth curves for Vocabulary *W* ability scores for Levels 1 through A and Total Test *W* ability scores for Levels P and K and Levels 1 through A displayed by grade enrollment group show consistent increases across the 11 levels, with the greatest increases in the early primary years, as expected. Diagnostic validity was evaluated by comparing the performance of two clinical groups (students identified as dyslexic and students with learning disabilities in reading) with that of matched controls from the standardization sample. Differences between clinical and control groups were significant across both clinical groups and for four grade enrollment groups within each sample. Students with dyslexia in Grades 1 through 3 scored approximately 18 points lower than controls (SS = 84.2 vs. 102.5, respectively), whereas students with reading disabilities at the same grade levels scored approximately 15 points lower than controls (SS = 80.2 vs. 95.4, respectively).

Usability

GRADE test materials are attractive, formatted for readability, and color-coded by levels. Examiner manuals, including a technical manual written for practitioners as well as psychometricians, earn high usability ratings for clarity, comprehensiveness, and linkages between assessment results and interventions. At Levels P and K, separate administration manuals are provided for each form, with examiner directions for each subtest on the left page and student pages reproduced on the right, which greatly facilitates administration. As noted above, hand scoring is very time-consuming, especially if examiners complete all of the diagnostic analyses. For example, at Level K, examiners must complete 11 diagnostic analysis worksheets per form for the group analyses before they can complete the Class Score Summary sheet. At Level 1, completing the Class Score Summary sheet for a class of 25 students requires 725 separate calculations for the norm-referenced scores alone! There is no mention of accommodations in any of the manuals, other than to recommend out-of-level testing for children with limited English. Listening Comprehension, which samples idiomatic expressions and nonliteral language, will be difficult for children with limited English proficiency.

The software scoring and reporting program produces group and individual score summaries, group and individual diagnostic analyses, group and individual reading progress reports, and reports for parents and students, using fall and spring on-level and out-of-level normative data. Other options include importing and exporting data files, batch and ad hoc reporting, and scanning capabilities. Given the complex and time-consuming nature of hand scoring and its vulnerability to scorer variance, the software should be included in each grade-level and specialist kit.

Links to Intervention

The GRADE is intended to be used in a four-step process linking reading assessment to instruction: (1) assessment of baseline skills with one test form, (2) analysis of student strengths and weaknesses with the diagnostic analysis worksheets, (3) intervention with activities from a CD-ROM Resource Library series and a reading workbook series, and (4) reassessment with the parallel form to measure progress. The CD-ROM Resource Library for each level includes teaching suggestions, student worksheets, and a reading booklist with more than 500 titles for each level, all reproducible. Lists are organized according to various comprehension categories by level. The activities are attractively formatted, are teacher-friendly, and use materials available in most classrooms. The *Building Reading Success Workbook* series for prekindergarten through postsecondary grades targets four skill areas: vocabulary, reading comprehension, phonics, and decoding.

Source and Cost

The GRADE is available from AGS Publishing in sets by level or across levels in combination sets, with packaging suitable for classrooms or reading specialists. Single-form classroom sets are $122.95 per level, which includes materials for testing 30 students. Classroom sets with both forms are $209.95 for Levels P and K and $189.95 for Levels 1–3. The Elementary Resource Specialist set (Levels P–6) is $899.95, which includes materials for 10 students per level for both Forms A and B, hand-scoring templates, 10 administration manuals, 8 scoring and interpretation manuals, and 6 packs of answer sheets. Available by separate purchase are the CD-ROM Resource Libraries for $99.95 per level and software scoring program for $299.95 for the single-user version (Windows only). A multiuser edition is also available (pricing on request). A separate technical manual is available for $49.95. The *Building Reading Success Workbook* series retails for $9.95 per student workbook and $6.95 per teacher guide.

Test Reviews

Fugate, M. H. (2003). Review of the Group Reading Assessment and Diagnostic Evaluation. In B. S. Plake, J. C. Impara, & R. A. Spies (Eds.), *The fifteenth mental measurements yearbook* (pp. 425–429). Lincoln, NE: Buros Institute of Mental Measurements.

Waterman, B. B. (2003). Review of the Group Reading Assessment and Diagnostic Evaluation. In B. S. Plake, J. C. Impara, & R. A. Spies (Eds.), *The fifteenth mental measurements yearbook* (pp. 429–431). Lincoln, NE: Buros Institute of Mental Measurements.

Summary

The *Group Reading Assessment and Diagnostic Evaluation* (GRADE) is a group-administered norm-referenced reading battery for individuals from prekindergarten through postsecondary levels that resembles a traditional standardized test in structure and format. The GRADE has numerous assets, including local scoring capacity, child-friendly test booklets, multiple packaging options, and exceptionally well-written examiner and technical materials. The GRADE is also one of the very few commercially published norm-referenced reading measures directly linked to grade-specific intervention materials. Limitations include those common to group-administered tests, including lack of direct assessments of phoneme awareness, fluency, oral expression, rapid naming, and invented spelling. Moreover, no routing or screener tests are identified, and letter-name and letter-sound recognition are tested only at the kindergarten level and then only for a small sample of letters and letter sounds. The GRADE is an effective predictor of current and future performance on reading measures on group-administered standardized achievement tests and differentiates between groups of children identified with reading problems and controls; however, there is no empirical support for the time-consuming diagnostic analyses, on either a group or an individual level. Future studies should evaluate the utility of the GRADE in identifying individual children at risk for reading problems, diagnosing specific strengths and weaknesses, and monitoring intervention effectiveness, especially in comparison with the standardized achievement tests already in place in most districts after Grade 3.

Case Example

Name of student: Ari G.
Age: 5 years, 4 months
Grade: Kindergarten
Date of assessment: October

Reason for assessment: Ari took Level K, Form A, of the *Group Reading Assessment and Diagnostic Evaluation* (GRADE) as part of the early literacy assessment program in his school. Ari's teacher notes that he has trouble keeping up with classroom instruction, often requires directions to be repeated, and has been slow to develop reading readiness and phonics skills.

Assessment results and interpretation: The GRADE is a group-administered reading battery that measures a variety of prereading and reading skills. GRADE tasks consist of multiple-choice items, and children mark their responses in a student booklet. At the kindergarten level, the GRADE measures phonological awareness, early literacy skills, listening comprehension, and word recognition. Ari's individual score summary report from the GRADE software scoring program is reproduced below (see Figure 4.2). Stanine scores of 1, 2, or 3 indicate below average performance; stanine scores of 4, 5, or 6 indicate average performance; and stanine scores of 7, 8, or 9 indicate above average performance. In addition, children who obtain a stanine score of 1, 2, or 3 on Listening Comprehension may be at risk for oral language problems. Average scores for a student in the fall of kindergarten are as follows: stanine = 4 to 6, percentile (%ile) = 50, grade equivalent (GE) = K.2, standard score (SS) = 100, normal curve equivalent (NCE) = 50.

Ari's overall prereading and reading skills are rated as below average for his

GRADE **Individual Score Summary - Ari G** **Washington District**

Group Reading Assessment and Diagnostic Evaluation **On-Level** **Fall Norms** **Level K, Form A**

Subtest	Raw Score	Sum	Stanine	%ile	GE	SS	NCE	Descriptor	GSV
Sound Matching	6								
Rhyming	6								
Phonological Awareness		12	4					Average	
Print Awareness	4								
Letter Recognition	8								
Same and Different Words	3								
Early Literacy Skills		15	3					Weakness	
Phoneme-Grapheme Correspondence		9	4					Average	
Listening Comprehension		15	4					Average	
TOTAL TEST		51	3	12	<P.2	83	26	Weakness	28
Word Reading	0		1					Weakness	

Birth Date: 6/17/1997
Test Date: 10/21/2002
Grade: K
Teacher/Examiner: Martin Smith
Class/Group: Kindergarten One
School: Cedar Lane School

Diagnostic Analysis Summary

	NC	NP	%
Sound Matching			
Begins with	0	6	0%
End with	0	6	0%
Rhyming			
Short vowel	0	11	0%
Long vowel	0	3	0%
Print Awareness			
Word	0	1	0%
Letter	0	1	0%
Sentence	0	1	0%
Capital letter	0	1	0%
Letter Recognition			
lower case	0	2	0%
UPPER CASE	0	2	0%
Mix	0	7	0%
Same and Different Words			
Same words	0	5	0%
Different words	0	4	0%
Phoneme-Grapheme Correspondence			
Initial	0	8	0%
Final	0	8	0%
Listening Comprehension			
Grammar	0	3	0%
Inference	0	3	0%
Vocabulary	0	12	0%
Word Reading			
Decodable	0	4	0%
Sight, or irregular	0	6	0%

NC = Number Correct NP = Number Possible

Description of Results

A stanine score converts a raw score (total number correct) to a single-digit number between 1 and 9, which makes test performance easier to understand. If the stanine score is 1, 2, or 3, the test performance is considered below average or reflects a weak performance on the specific set of tasks or subtests. If the stanine score is 4, 5, or 6, the test performance is considered average. If the stanine score is 7, 8, or 9, the test performance is considered above average and reflects strong performance. Looking at stanine scores helps readily identify reading strengths and/or needs.

The **Phonological Awareness** tasks measure awareness of the sound structure of language as demonstrated by the ability to listen for and discriminate sounds in words. These tasks are an indicator of reading readiness. Ari's average performance on the Phonological Awareness tasks indicates a sensitivity to the sound structure of language and good sound discrimination skills. It is an overall prediction of future success in learning letter-sound relationships.

The **Early Literacy Skills** tasks measure the recognition of print elements, letters, and same and different printed words. These skills are a measure of reading readiness. Ari's weak performance on the Early Literacy Skills tasks indicates an inability to recognize common elements of print material, an inability to associate letter names with the actual symbols, and the need for further one-on-one assessment of recognizing the parts of print material (e.g., "Point to the first word on this page.")

Phoneme-Grapheme Correspondence measures both the ability to recognize the phoneme or sound at the beginning or end of a word and also the ability to match a symbol to that sound. Ari's average performance on the Phoneme-Grapheme Correspondence tasks indicates an ability to associate sounds with letters.

Listening Comprehension measures linguistic understanding without printed cues. Ari's average performance indicates oral language skills commensurate with the development level represented for Level K.

The **Total Test** raw score can be converted to multiple normative or derived scores for overall reading skill assessment. Ari's weak Total Test performance suggests that assistance is needed to improve pre-reading skills.

Word Reading measures the ability to decode phonetically regular words and to recognize common sight words. Ari's weak performance on the Word Reading subtest indicates a lack of knowledge of the phonics rules and/or an overdependence on the rules.

Stanine Chart

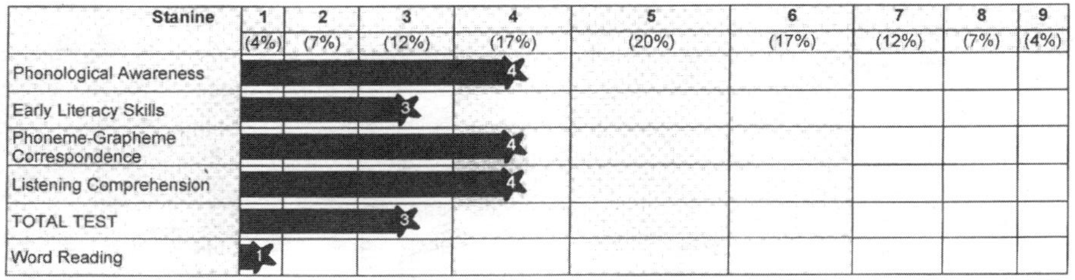

Stanine
1 (4%)
2 (7%)
3 (12%)
4 (17%)
5 (20%)
6 (17%)
7 (12%)
8 (7%)
9 (4%)
Phonological Awareness
4
Early Literacy Skills
3
Phoneme-Grapheme Correspondence
4
Listening Comprehension
4
TOTAL TEST
3
Word Reading
1

 CONFIDENTIAL 10/14/2003 - 09:59 AM

FIGURE 4.2. Individual Score Summary for Ari, generated by the GRADE scoring and reporting software. Copyright 2001 by American Guidance Service, Inc. The report form is reprinted with permission.

grade (standard score = 83, PR = 12). His phonological awareness skills, as measured by tasks requiring him to match beginning and ending sounds and identify rhyming words, are average (stanine = 4). His understanding of phoneme-grapheme relationships, as measured by a task requiring him to mark the letter of the sound at the beginning or end of a word spoken by the examiner, is also average (stanine = 4). On the Listening Comprehension subtest, which measures language understanding without reading, he scored in the average range (stanine = 4). His early literacy skills, including print awareness, letter recognition, and visual discrimination, are somewhat less well developed (stanine = 3, below average); however, his performance varied depending on the domain assessed. He was able to answer all of the print awareness items correctly, but he had more difficulty with tasks requiring him to identify letters and recognize words as alike or different. On the optional Word Reading subtest, which requires selecting a target word from a list of four choices, he was unable to answer any items correctly (stanine = 1, well below average).

PHONOLOGICAL AWARENESS LITERACY SCREENING

Overview

The *Phonological Awareness Literacy Screening* (PALS; Invernizzi & Meier, 2002a) is a set of criterion-referenced early reading assessment batteries designed for large-scale screening and progress monitoring for children in kindergarten through third grade. Developed through a grant from the Virginia State Department of Education to the Curry School of Education at the University of Virginia, the PALS serves as the state-provided assessment tool for Virginia's Early Intervention Reading Initiative (EIRI) and is used by most school districts in the state. Many of the tasks and items are similar to those on the *Book Buddies Early Literacy Screening* (BBELS) and the *Early Reading Screening Inventory* (ERSI). Initially targeted at students in kindergarten and Grade 1, PALS has been extended upwards to include Grade 3 and downwards to include prekindergarten (PALS Pre-K; Invernizzi, Sullivan, & Meier, 2002). This review discusses two versions of PALS: PALS-K for kindergarten students (Invernizzi, Meier, Swank, & Juel, 2002a) and PALS 1–3 for first- through third-grade students (Invernizzi & Meier, 2002a). The purposes of PALS are (1) to identify children who are behind their peers in their acquisition of fundamental literacy skills and (2) to provide specific information about children's early literacy skills for instructional planning. Materials for PALS-K include an administration and scoring guide; a spiral-bound student packet containing alphabet recognition and letter sound sheets, concept of word materials (picture sheet, word list, and booklet), word lists, an individual rhyme awareness booklet, and beginning sound awareness pictures and headers; 25 group rhyme and beginning sound picture booklets; 25 spelling sheets; 25 student summary sheets; a class summary sheet; and a technical reference. PALS 1–3 includes an administration and scoring guide; a teacher packet with spelling words and sentences and reproducible running records and comprehension questions for each reading passage; a spiral-bound student packet containing word lists, oral reading passages, alphabet recognition and letter sound cards, word lists, a concept of word booklet, a readiness booklet, and three preprimer reading booklets; 25 spelling sheets; 25 student summary sheets; a class summary sheet; and a technical reference.

Assessment Tasks

Table 4.15 describes the PALS-K and PALS 1–3 tasks by domain and grade. PALS-K consists of five core tasks and one supplementary task. PALS 1–3 uses a three-tier approach to screening, in which the first tier or "entry level" is a routing set of two or three measures that provides an estimate of general reading skill, called the "summed score" (Word Recognition, Spelling, and Letter Sounds for Grade 1; Word Recognition and Spelling for Grades 2 and 3). The summed score on the entry-level tasks is used to determine which students receive extra instruction and follow-up diagnostic testing with other PALS tasks. Children in Grades 1 through 3 also take Level A Oral Reading in Context, with the passage level based on the highest grade-level word list on which a student can read at least 15 words. Grade 1 students who score below the summed score benchmark on the entry-level tasks take three Level B

TABLE 4.15. PALS Assessment Tasks and Administration Times by Domain and Grade

Domain	Kindergarten	Grade 1	Grade 2	Grade 3
Phonological Awareness	**Group Rhyme Awareness*** **Group Beginning Sound Awareness*** **Individual Rhyme Awareness** **Individual Beginning Sound Awareness**	Blending Sound-to-Letter	Blending Sound-to-Letter	Blending Sound-to-Letter
Alphabet Knowledge	**Alphabet Recognition**	Alphabet Recognition	Alphabet Recognition	Alphabet Recognition
Letter-Sound Knowledge	**Letter Sounds** **Spelling***	**Letter Sounds** **Spelling***	**Spelling***	**Spelling***
Word Recognition	Preprimer–Grade 1 lists (optional)	**Word Recognition in Isolation** (fall = preprimer list; spring = Grade 1 list)	**Word Recognition in Isolation** (fall = Grade 1 list; spring = Grade 2 list)	**Word Recognition in Isolation** (fall = Grade 2 list; spring = Grade 3 list)
Concept of Word	Concept of Word	Concept of Word	Concept of Word	Concept of Word
Oral Reading in Context		Passage based on Word Recognition score	Passage based on Word Recognition score	Passage based on Word Recognition score
Oral Reading Fluency		Fluency scale Words per minute	Fluency scale Words per minute	Fluency scale Words per minute
Print Exposure			Title Recognition Task (spring)	Title Recognition Task (spring)
Total time	20–40 minutes	10–60 minutes	10–60 minutes	10–60 minutes

Note. Core tasks included in the summed score to calculate fall and spring benchmarks are given in boldface. Tasks marked with an asterisk can be group-administered.

alphabetics tasks (Alphabet Recognition, Letter Sounds, and Concept of Word). Grade 2 and 3 students who are unable to read at least 15 words on the preprimer word list also take Level B tasks. Students who fail to meet Level B summed score benchmarks for their grade take two Level C phonemic awareness tasks (Blending and Sound-to-Letter). In Virginia, students in Grades 1 and 2 who obtain a "high-pass" benchmark at certain screening windows are exempt from assessments during future screening windows. For example, first graders who achieve a score of 18/20 correct on the spring Grade 2 word list and 98% or greater accuracy and a fluency rating of 3 on the spring Grade 2 passage are exempt from later screening.

Table 4.16 describes the PALS tasks, beginning with the kindergarten measures. At both levels, phonological awareness tasks are identical for fall and spring, whereas literacy tasks (Spelling, word lists, Concept of Word, and reading passages) vary from fall to spring.

Administration

In Virginia, PALS is administered during 2-week fall and spring screening windows, with spring designated as the primary window. Fall screening dates for kindergarten are later than those for Grades 1–3 (6 weeks vs. 2 weeks from the first day of school) to permit children to adjust to the classroom environment. All of the tasks are untimed and are administered individually, with several exceptions. At the kindergarten level, Group Rhyme Awareness, Group Beginning Sound Awareness, and Spelling may be administered in groups of five or fewer students. In Grades 1–3, Spelling may be administered in a classwide format. Administering the entire battery takes about 10–60 minutes at both levels, depending on the skill level of the child and/or group, with another 15 minutes for PALS 1–3 if the supplementary Level B and Level C tasks are administered. Concept of Word involves an eight-step administration procedure (see Table 4.21) and can be very time-consuming.

Scores

The PALS is criterion-referenced and yields only raw scores. For most tasks, scoring is dichotomous. For Concept of Word, children earn 1 point for each sentence in which they point correctly to all words, 1 point for each correctly read target word, and 1 point for each correct response on a pretest and posttest list of words in the poem. For PALS-K Spelling, 1 point is awarded for each phonetically acceptable or correct letter, with a bonus point for perfect spelling. For PALS 1–3 Spelling, 1 point is awarded for each correctly spelled phonics feature (e.g., *ch* [consonant digraph] in *chop*), with a bonus point for each correctly spelled word. For both PALS versions, static letter reversals (i.e., letters written backwards) are not counted as errors and do not disqualify words from receiving bonus points. Kinetic reversals (i.e., errors of order, such as *net* for *ten*) receive credit for correct representation of phonics features but are not eligible for bonus points.

For Oral Reading in Context, four types of errors are recorded: (1) substitutions, (2) insertions, (3) omissions, and (4) examiner-supplied words after a 5-second pause. The number of errors is compared to passage-specific criteria to determine percent accuracy and functional reading level (frustration, instructional, or independent). The PALS Web site (http://pals.virginia.edu) calculates overall reading level based

TABLE 4.16. Description of PALS-K and PALS 1–3 Tasks

Task	Description
Group Rhyme Awareness	From a set of four pictures named by the examiner, the child circles the one of three pictures that rhymes with the stimulus picture. Students who score below the benchmark on this task take Individual Rhyme Awareness, and that score is used in calculating the summed score.
Individual Rhyme Awareness	From a set of four pictures named by the examiner, the child points to the one of three pictures that rhymes with the stimulus picture.
Group Beginning Sound Awareness	From a set of four pictures named by the examiner, the child circles the one of three pictures that begins with the same sound as the stimulus picture. Students who score below criterion on this task take Individual Sound Awareness, and that score is used in calculating the summed score.
Individual Beginning Sound Awareness	Using a set of 10 cut-out pictures identified by the examiner, the child places each picture under one of four target pictures with the same initial sound.
Alphabet Recognition	The child names a randomly arrayed set of 26 lowercase letters.
Letter Sounds	With *M* as a practice item, the child pronounces the sound of 23 uppercase letters (not including *Q* and *X*) and 3 consonant digraphs (*Ch*, *Sh*, and *Th*).
Spelling	The child spells a set of words dictated by the examiner. Sets range from 5 words for kindergarten to 24 words for Grade 3.
Word Recognition in Isolation	The child reads preprimer, primer, first-grade, second-grade, and/or third-grade 20-item word lists.
Concept of Word	After the examiner administers a pretest list of words in a nursery rhyme, the examiner teaches the rhyme to the child. The examiner then reads and fingerpoints the poem, followed by choral and echo reading with the child. The child then reads and fingerpoints the poem and reads two words in each of the four sentences. The examiner then administers the same list of words.
Oral Reading in Context	The child reads informational passages ranging from primer to third-grade level, based on the highest level list on which the child can read 15 or more words correctly. Students reading fewer than 15 words on the primer list read from one of five preprimer booklets. While the child reads the passage aloud, the examiner takes a running record of errors and, beginning with primer-level passages, records the time required to read the selection. Multiple-choice comprehension questions are also optional. For primer and first-grade passages, the examiner reads the questions and answer choices aloud to students, whereas for second- and third-grade passages, students read and answer the questions independently.
Blending	The examiner pronounces individual sounds, and the child blends them together to form words.
Sound-to-Letter	The child names initial, final, or medial letters in words pronounced by the examiner. Two points are awarded for the correct letter and 1 point for the correct sound or a word that begins with the same sound.
Title Recognition Task	This task is administered in the spring semester using the PALS Web site. The child reads a list of titles and presses a button to indicate whether it is a real book title or a nonsense book title.

on the Word Recognition in Isolation and Oral Reading in Context scores. Reading rate, defined as words per minute (WPM) rather than as words read correctly per minute (WCPM), is recorded, beginning with primer-level passages. As noted earlier, I recommend calculating WCPM rather than WPM as a more precise and accurate reflection of children's oral reading proficiency. The prosodic aspects of reading fluency are scored on a 3-point scale. The Title Recognition Task, administered in the spring to second and third graders, is administered and scored online.

Interpretation

At each level, raw scores on the core tasks are added to obtain the summed score (see Table 4.16). Performance on each task and for the summed score is interpreted in terms of fall and spring benchmarks established for Virginia students. Benchmarks for word list reading are set at 15 out of 20 words correct, whereas passage reading benchmarks are set at 90% accuracy, with a lower benchmark for preprimer passages (85%). Primer passages represent middle-of-first-grade material, whereas first-, second-, and third-grade passages represent end-of-year text. Benchmarks are not provided for the Title Recognition Task or for the optional comprehension questions. According to the authors, the Title Recognition Task is designed to provide feedback to teachers about children's level of print exposure compared with their grade peers, whereas establishing comprehension benchmarks is difficult because of the numerous factors contributing to successful understanding of textual material. Administration and scoring guides at each level include a classwide case study to illustrate how to translate PALS results into instructional activities, with a sample lesson plan and schoolwide plan for providing additional instruction to identified students. Task scores for the classroom group are not provided, however, and there are no case examples for individual students.

Technical Adequacy

Information on technical adequacy is drawn from materials on the PALS Web site, administration and scoring guides, and a series of annual technical references and reports (Invernizzi & Meier, 2002b; Invernizzi, Meier, Swank, & Juel, 2002b; Invernizzi, Robey, & Moon, 2000).

Test Development

PALS has been used in large statewide samples of Virginia students since the fall of 1997. The current PALS version, which was developed in response to the expansion of the EIRI from a K–1 to a K–3 initiative, was initially pilot-tested in spring 2000, with large-scale pilot studies conducted in spring and fall 2001. Overall, pilot studies included data from 8,910 students in Grades K–3. The fifth cohort (2001–2002) included 65,036 kindergarten students and 207,194 students in Grades 1–3. The technical references for school year 2002–2003 report cohort characteristics by grade for gender, four categories of free-lunch status, race, and ethnicity. Summed score criteria and benchmarks were theoretically and empirically determined; sources included 9 years of research on similar tasks with at-risk readers in the Book Buddies Tutorial Program (Invernizzi et al., 1997), statewide data from the first four cohorts of Virginia's EIRI, and data from pilot and research studies conducted between 2000 and 2002 with approximately 4,000 kindergarten students and 8,000 students in Grades 1–3 in Virginia. For the PALS-K, data from the statewide sample were used to calculate quartiles for the summed score, with the summed score criterion representing the highest number in the bottom quartile. Benchmarks for Alphabet Recognition and Letter Sounds were established by subtracting 1 standard deviation from the mean score for students achieving above the lowest quartile and making additional adjustments based on modal data for each task. Benchmarks for Concept for Word and Spelling were based on score distributions and correlations with other core tasks in pilot studies, previous reading research, and consultation with the advisory board. For the PALS 1–3 entry-level tasks, the upper number in the benchmark range represents an adjusted mean for students achieving at expected levels. The lower number in the range was obtained by subtracting 0.5 or 1 standard deviation from the mean and making other adjustments based on task-specific modal data. The sum of the lower benchmark numbers for the core tasks equals the entry-level summed score benchmark for each grade. Benchmark ranges for the other tasks are based on theoretical expectations and statistical analyses with normative data. Benchmarks and criteria are reevaluated each year based on an analysis of the statewide results and ongoing pilot studies. Beginning in fall 2002, panels of reading experts conducted a formal standard-setting process to provide additional verification of benchmarks.

Reliability Evidence

For the PALS-K, Cronbach alpha reliabilities for subtasks, based on statewide samples for fall screenings from 1998 through 2001 and spring 2002 screening, are reported by total sample, gender, SES, ethnicity, and region. Coefficients range from .79 to .89, with only one value (fall 1998 in one region) falling below the .80 criterion level. Alpha coefficients for Group Rhyme Awareness and Beginning Sound Awareness based on pilot studies from the fall of 2001 (ns = 1,855 and 1,862) were .87 and .83, respectively. Coefficients for spelling lists from fall 2001 pilot studies (ns = 847 and 1,980) were above .90. For Concept of Word, pretest word list alpha coefficients ranged from .76 (n = 162) to .90 (n = 402), whereas posttest word list coefficients ranged from .81 (n = 161) to .93 (n = 421), based on spring and fall 2001 pilot studies with kindergarten and first-grade students. For the PALS 1–3, alpha reliabilities for entry-level tasks, based on statewide samples for 1998–1999 and 1999–2000 and reported by grade, gender, SES, and ethnicity, ranged from .66 to .88, with a mean coefficient of .81 for all segments of the sample. For Word Recognition in Isolation, alpha coefficients for each of the first three word lists for a statewide subsample in the fall of 2001 with over 4,300 students were .92 or above. For Spelling, alpha reliabilities for fall and spring 2001 pilot samples (ns = 267 to 463) ranged from .86 to .92.

Interrater reliabilities are consistently high across tasks for both levels. For the PALS-K, interrater reliability studies were conducted in the fall of 1997 and spring of 1999 (ns = 45 to 154), with one individual administering the tasks while another observed and scored the tasks simultaneously and independently. Both individuals received the same training provided to teachers using PALS (i.e., reading the manual and viewing the training video). Correlations between raters were high across the seven tasks (.96 to .99). For the PALS 1–3, the same procedures were used to evaluate interrater reliability in the fall of 2000 (*ns* = 36 to 375), with correlations ranging from .94 to .99 across the eight tasks. No stability estimates are available for any of the tasks at either level.

Validity Evidence

CONTENT VALIDITY EVIDENCE

Tasks and items were developed and modified during 5 years of research in large statewide samples, with scores from more than 280,000 kindergarten students and more than 291,400 students in Grades 1–3 between 1997 and 2001. The technical references for each level present a clear and comprehensive rationale for task format and item selection, including citations from the research literature. Phonological awareness items were selected to be of moderate difficulty, to demonstrate strong predictive relationships to reading outcomes, and to be suitable for group assessment. The literacy screening tasks are similar to or identical with items in the ERSI and the BBELS that have been used with thousands of early primary grade children in more than 25 sites across the United States. Word lists were first derived from a random sample from a word database created from three of the most frequently used basal readers in Virginia, and then supplemented by words from grade-level lists in such resources as the *EDL Core Vocabularies in Reading, Mathematics, Science, and Social Studies* (EDL, 1997) and the *100 Most Frequent Words in Books for Beginning Readers* (Bodrova, Leong, & Semenov, 1999). Spelling words were selected from a pool of words used in previous research in the Virginia Spelling Studies (e.g., Henderson, 1990; Invernizzi, 1992) to elicit responses to particular speech sounds and phonics features.

Preprimer passages were written by PALS staff, whereas PALS 1–3 passages were adapted from basal reading passages in reading series published before 1990 to address concerns about relaxing of vocabulary control after 1990 and to control for practice effects. As evidence of passage readability levels, the technical reference for the PALS 1–3 provides a table with print, word, sentence, language, text, and literary features across the four preprimer texts. Primer through Grade 3 passages were subjected to six readability formulae, with agreement among three of the six formulae used to establish readability levels. Title Recognition Task titles are derived from annual surveys of Virginia children conducted by Joan Kindig, director of the Virginia Center for Children's Books at the University of Virginia, and are revised each year. PALS content and materials were reviewed for possible bias or stereotyping and for technical adequacy by four external reviewers, an advisory panel of Virginia educators, and an external measurement professional

CRITERION-RELATED VALIDITY EVIDENCE

For a sample of 137 kindergartners, PALS-K end-of-year summed scores for spring of 1997 were highly correlated (.72) with the Total Reading scaled score on the *Stanford Achievement Tests–Ninth Edition* (SAT-9; Harcourt Educational Measurement, 1996). PALS summed scores were also strongly correlated with scaled scores on three SAT-9 reading subtests (Sounds and Letters, $r = .79$; Word Reading, $r = .74$; and Sentence Reading, $r = .58$). The PALS 1–3 displays moderate to high correlations with other reading inventories, standardized reading tests, and high-stakes assessments. For 65 first graders, correlations between spring of 2001 instructional reading levels on the PALS 1–3 and the *Qualitative Reading Inventory–II* (QRI-II; Leslie & Caldwell, 1995) were high (.73), as were correlations between PALS entry-level summed scores and QRI-II oral reading scores for 146 first graders (.73). In addition, for a spring 2000 pilot study with 679 students in Grades 1–3, PALS and QRI-II word lists were highly correlated (.73 to .90). For 197 students in Grades 1–3, correlations between instructional and independent reading levels on the *Developmental Reading Assessment* (Beaver, 1997) and spring 2001 PALS summed scores were .82 and .81, respectively. For 195 first graders, *California Achievement Tests–Fifth Edition* (CAT-5) Total Reading, Word Analysis, and Spelling scaled scores were strongly correlated with PALS 1–3 summed scores and Spelling (*r*s = .66 to .75), with the highest correlation between CAT-5 Total Reading and the PALS summed score. Correlations between PALS spring summed scores and SAT-9 Total Reading scaled scores for 174 first graders and 50 second graders who were receiving interventions were moderate to high (.67 and .57, respectively). In a sample of 283 Grade 3 students, PALS Spelling and summed scores were moderately correlated (.51 to .57) with Total Reading and Word Analysis scores on Virginia's Standards of Learning (SOL) assessment, which is given to all third graders in the state

PALS scores are moderate to strong predictors of future performance on PALS tasks and other reading measures. For 1998–1999, fall PALS-K summed scores for 74 students, none of whom received supplementary instruction, were highly correlated with spring SAT-9 Total Reading scaled scores (.70). For 2000–2001, fall of kindergarten summed scores were moderately correlated with spring PALS-K scores (.56), as well as with first-grade PALS 1–3 entry-level scores from fall and spring (*r*s = .67 and .53, respectively). For fall 2000, PALS-K summed scores explained 30% to 45% of the variance in PALS-K and PALS 1–3 summed scores in the next three screening windows (spring of kindergarten, fall of Grade 1, and spring of Grade 1).

For 739 first graders and 766 second graders, fall 2000 PALS 1–3 summed scores predicted 53% and 34% of the variance in SAT-9 scores. First- and second-grade fall PALS summed scores also predicted approximately 50% and 25%, respectively, of the variance in spring SAT-9 Reading Comprehension. For a sample of 277 third graders, fall PALS summed scores predicted 36% of the variability in spring SOL Total Reading scores. In an analysis of data from the entire statewide sample, PALS spring 2001 scores were also significant predictors of PALS scores the following fall. For first graders and second graders, 71% and 79%, respectively, of the variance in fall summed scores could be predicted from their Word Recognition and Spelling scores the previous spring.

CONSTRUCT VALIDITY EVIDENCE

Construct validity evidence includes a rationale for the theoretical model underlying the PALS, principal components analyses, discriminant analyses, DIF analyses, and intercorrelations among tasks. Results of principal components analyses each year have yielded a single factor for each level of the assessment and for each level of tasks (i.e., entry level, alphabetics, and phonemic awareness), indicating that PALS is measuring a unitary trait. Discriminant analyses, based on the PALS subtasks included in the entry-level summed score, are conducted each year on the statewide data to determine the degree to which PALS task scores differentiate between students who are identified as needing additional services, based on their summed score, and those who are not identified. Since PALS was first administered, discriminant analyses at both levels have correctly classified 94% to 97% of students as Identified or Not Identified, based on their subtask scores.

As further evidence of diagnostic validity, the Mantel–Haenszel procedure was used to compare DIF on PALS-K core tasks and PALS 1–3 entry-level tasks for groups defined as Identified and Not Identified for additional EIRI instruction, based on their PALS summed score. Because PALS is designed to identify children in need of additional interventions, items on each task should function differently for the two groups. From each of the last mandatory screening windows (fall 2000, fall 2001, and spring 2002), the obtained statistic was significant for each PALS subtask. For PALS 1–3 task scores from fall 1998 through spring 2000 and entry-level task scores for first through third graders in 2000–2001, the statistic was also highly significant for all tasks for fall and spring at all grade levels.

Intercorrelations between PALS-K summed scores and Alphabet Recognition, Letter Sounds, Spelling, and Concept of Word have been consistently high (e.g., .84 to .91 for fall of 2001). Summed scores are also strongly correlated (*r*s = .61 to .76) with Group and Individual Beginning Sound Awareness and the preprimer and primer word lists. Lower correlations (.46 and .57, respectively) are consistently obtained between Group and Individual Rhyme Awareness and the summed score. For the PALS 1–3, medium-high to high intercorrelations are consistently obtained at all grade levels between Spelling and Word Recognition and the entry-level summed score, with moderate to high correlations between Concept of Word and other Level B tasks and the entry-level summed score. Level C tasks, word list reading, and passage reading display generally moderate correlations with the summed score, whereas Blending is only weakly correlated with the summed score.

Usability

After several revisions incorporating feedback from Virginia teachers, the PALS now earns high usability ratings in terms of ease of administration, scoring, and interpretation. The PALS is also the most cost-effective early reading assessment battery reviewed in this text—$80.00 for a class of 25 students. Teacher and student materials are attractive and conveniently packaged, with spiral-bound test booklets tabbed by task. Administration videotapes for each level that include step-by-step instructions for each task are available, although a considerable amount of time is devoted to familiarizing Virginia teachers with the Web-based score entry and reporting process. In the Virginia screening program, all children in the designated grades, including those with identified disabilities and students with English as a second language, take the PALS unless their Individualized Education Programs (IEPs) exempt them from participation or they obtain high-pass scores. The Web site permits direct score entry and report generation for Virginia teachers free of charge and for outside users for a fee. Reports include a student summary report suitable for parent–teacher conferences, a class report identifying students scoring below benchmarks and grouping students for reading and spelling instruction, a score history report displaying students' scores from previous PALS screenings, and a year-end summary report. The Web site also has rerostering capability and can form fall class grouping for teachers with results from the previous spring testing.

Links to Intervention

For Virginia schools, additional resources for students scoring below benchmarks are available through the Virginia Department of Education's EIRI. Administration and scoring guides include a sample parent letter for sharing results. An instructional strategies videotape for PALS-K with a sample lesson and suggestions for interventions is also available. The PALS Web site includes an activities link with more than 100 instructional activities, grouped by grade level and skill category, as well as sample lesson plans for intervention. Other links include reading-related Web sites and a "parent corner" with suggestions for children at emergent, beginning, and instructional reader stages.

Relevant Research

Research on the reliability and validity of PALS tasks and benchmarks is presented in annual technical references and reports. Studies of the ERSI and BBELS, which share many tasks and items with the PALS, have been discussed in the review of the BBELS.

Source and Cost

PALS is available without cost to participating Virginia public schools. Private schools, out-of-state schools, and individual users may purchase PALS materials from the University of Virginia bookstore. The price of the PALS-K or PALS 1–3 is $80.00 per teacher set and $55.00 for the administration set, which includes one of each fall and spring screening item and a technical reference. Assessment training videos and instructional strategies for each level of the assessment are available for $15.00 each. Out-of-state or private schools that do not participate in Virginia's EIRI may register at the PALS office and rent space on the University of Virginia server for $5.00 per student, which includes use of the PALS database for 1 year (covering fall and spring administrations), access to reports, and support from the PALS staff.

Summary

The *Phonological Awareness Literacy Screening* (PALS), the statewide reading assessment for Virginia, is an individually administered, criterion-referenced battery of measures for children in kindergarten through third grade. An outstanding example of the new generation of evidence-based reading screening instruments, the PALS also receives high usability ratings and yields a wealth of instructionally relevant information. For a large-scale, teacher-administered battery, its technical quality is unsurpassed, with regular reviews and modifications to ensure the most accurate and valid measurement. Despite its general excellence, the current version of the PALS is not without its limitations. No measures of vocabulary or listening comprehension are included, and reading comprehension benchmarks have not yet been developed to assist users in comparing children's performance to grade-level expectations. The method for calculating reading rate does not take oral reading errors into account and thus may result in the underidentification of children with fluency problems. Because the PALS is continually being refined, potential users are encouraged to contact the PALS office for information on the most recent version of the assessment.

Group Case Example

Description of group: First-grade class (n = 25)
Date of assessment: October

Reason for assessment: Ms. J. administered the *Phonological Awareness Literacy Screening* (PALS) to her first-grade students as part of the districtwide early reading screening program.

Group assessment results and interpretation: Below are the PALS results for Ms. J.'s class. The results are ranked by the summed score criterion, from highest to lowest. Class means and medians are presented for each task and for the summed score criterion.

	PALS task (benchmark/total points)					
Student name	Spelling (9/44 points)	Word Recognition in Isolation, preprimer word list (10/20 points)	Letter Sounds (20/26 points)	Summed Score (39/90 points)	Alphabet Recognition (24/26 points)	Oral Reading in Context, preprimer passage (85% accuracy = <10 errors/64 words)
Elisabeth	44	20	26	90	26	0/Independent
Paul	29	20	25	74	26	0/Independent
Christina	25	20	26	71	26	2/Instructional
Luis	23	19	26	68	26	2/Instructional
Phyllis	27	16	24	67	26	3/Instructional
Jamaal	21	20	25	66	26	1/Independent
Miguel	21	18	26	65	26	4/Instructional
Carly	21	19	25	65	26	5/Instructional
Latisha	21	15	24	60	26	4/Instructional
Jose	15	20	25	60	26	3/Instructional
Joseph	17	20	22	59	26	7/Instructional
DeQuan	20	18	20	58	26	1/Independent
Michael	19	14	23	56	25	5/Instructional
Mark	16	15	24	55	26	4/Instructional
Jennifer	16	15	24	55	26	3/Instructional
Lorraine	15	14	23	52	25	9/Instructional
Lynne	15	13	23	51	26	9/Instructional
Sally	14	19	18*	51	25	8/Instructional
Martin	15	14	22	51	24	8/Instructional
James	13	13	22	48	23*	10/Frustration
Juan	14	12	19*	45	23*	14/Frustration
Hannah	13	14	15*	42	22*	13/Frustration
Tomas*	11	10	17*	38*	21*	15/Frustration
Lawrence*	12	9*	17*	38*	21*	26/Frustration
Emma*	7*	9*	11*	27*	18*	30/Frustration
Grade mean	18.20	15.84	21.26	54.32	24.68	7.12/Instructional
Grade median	16	14	23	56	25	5/Instructional

Note. The summed score fall criterion for Grade 1 is 39 points out of a possible 90, based on the summed scores for Spelling, the preprimer word list, and Letter Sounds. Students in the shaded area scored in the lowest quartile (lowest 25%) of the classwide distribution, based on the summed score. Scores marked with an asterisk indicate performance below fall benchmarks. Each student whose name is asterisked scored below the summed score criterion. Reading levels are as follows: independent, 98% accuracy or greater; instructional, 85%–97% accuracy; frustration, less than 85% accuracy.

Ms. J.'s 25 first graders vary widely in their current levels of phonological awareness and early literacy skills (summed score range = 27–90 points). One child has achieved a perfect score on all tasks, whereas three children have scored below the summed score criterion for fall of Grade 1. Most of the students have achieved the fall benchmarks for spelling and word recognition, but nearly 25% of the children are performing below grade-level expectations in terms of letter-name and letter-sound knowledge. As indicated by scores on the preprimer oral reading passage, children's oral reading skills are also quite diverse. Most students are reading at an instructional level in preprimer material (85% to 97% accuracy) or higher, but more than 20% are reading at a frustration level (less than 85% accuracy).

PHONOLOGICAL AWARENESS SCREENING TEST

Overview

The *Phonological Awareness Screening Test* (PAST; Adams, Foorman, Lundberg, & Beeler, 1998) is a group-administered nonstandardized set of measures designed to identify kindergartners and first graders with low levels of phonological processing skills. It is included in *Phonemic Awareness in Young Children: A Classroom Curriculum* (Adams et al., 1998), a kindergarten and first-grade curricular program that was developed with support from the National Institute of Child Health and Human Development. In the curriculum handbook, the authors do not give the assessment a title, but it is referred to as the *Phonological Awareness Screening Test* in a collection of assessments published by the Consortium on Reading Excellence (CORE; Honig, Diamond, & Nathan, 1999). The purposes of the PAST include (1) screening groups of children to determine their levels of phonological awareness and (2) monitoring the progress of children receiving phonological awareness instruction. According to its authors, the PAST can be repeated at 1- to 2-month intervals to monitor group progress in developing phonological awareness skills. Materials consist of six teacher demonstration pages and six student test pages, all reproducible and contained in the last chapter of the spiral-bound handbook.

Subtests

The PAST includes six subtests that assess a developmental hierarchy of phonological awareness skills and correspond to the sequence of lessons included in the curriculum. Each subtest consists of five items and is presented on a single page. For each subtest, the examiner identifies the pictorial stimuli, and children respond by marking on the student test pages, which can be stapled together to form booklets. Table 4.17 describes the subtests.

Administration

The PAST is designed for group administration, but it can also be used with individual students. For kindergarten students, the test's authors recommend groups no larger than six children and preferably two or three; for first-grade students, they recommend groups no larger than 15, with monitoring by two teachers. Administration takes about 20–30 minutes, depending on the size of the group. A teacher demonstration page with two practice examples accompanies each subtest. As with any group-administered test for early primary grade children, examiners should monitor

TABLE 4.17. Description of PAST Subtests

Subtest	Description
Detecting Rhymes	The child matches rhyming pictures by drawing lines between them.
Counting Syllables	The child indicates the number of syllables in pictured words by drawing the appropriate number of tallies on a response line.
Matching Initial Sounds	The child matches pictures that begin with the same sound by drawing lines between them.
Counting Phonemes	The child indicates the number of phonemes in pictured words by drawing the appropriate number of tallies on a response line.
Comparing Word Lengths	For five pairs of pictures, the child circles the picture that represents the word with the greater number of phonemes.
Representing Phonemes with Letters	The child represents the sounds in one-syllable pictured words by writing letters on a response line.

students carefully during testing sessions to avoid confounding phonological problems with performance deficits caused by inattention or failure to understand directions. According to the authors, instruction in phonological awareness should be provided prior to testing kindergarten students, presumably to avoid floor effects and enhance task sensitivity to individual skill differences.

Scores

Items are scored 0 or 1, for a maximum of 5 on each subtest and a maximum total score of 30. The curriculum handbook does not provide the correct answers for test items, but they are included in the CORE publication (Honig et al., 1999). The Representing Phonemes with Letters subtest can be rescored by awarding 1 point for each sound correctly represented in correct left-to-right order (maximum score = 17), which provides a finer differentiation of student performance than scoring the five items as correct or incorrect.

Interpretation

Interpretation is based on classroom norms for subtest performance. Mean scores for each subtest are calculated for the group, and the results are compared with benchmarks for both class and individual performance. If the average score of the class is less than 4 on any of the subtests, that portion of the curriculum should be retaught. Individual students who score 2 or more points below the class average on any subtest should receive additional attention to determine whether they need extra help. My own experience with the PAST suggests that several cautions in interpreting student performance are in order. First, the Counting Phonemes subtest is very difficult for kindergarten children, even in the second semester of the year, and floor effects are common. Second, because Comparing Word Lengths requires a child to choose one of two pictures per item, guessing may inflate task scores.

Third, some children who perform poorly on the two phonemic segmentation tasks (Counting Phonemes and Comparing Word Lengths) do relatively well on Representing Phonemes with Letters because they have memorized some of the items as sight words. Moreover, the five items on that subtest sample a limited number of short vowel sounds. Three of the five one-syllable words include short *o* (*mop, pot, frog*), whereas none of the words include short *a* or *i*. For this reason, I name the third picture as "pan" rather than "pot" to elicit another spelling–sound correspondence.

Technical Adequacy

The curriculum is adapted from a phonological awareness training program developed and validated in Sweden and Denmark (Lundberg, Frost, & Petersen, 1988). Although the original program included only oral language activities, the authors added a set of lessons on representing phonemes with letters because of subsequent research demonstrating that phonemic awareness training with instruction in letter-sound as well as speech-sound correspondences has more positive effects on reading and writing acquisition. The curriculum was then field-tested in 23 kindergarten classrooms in Houston over a 3-year period, with feedback from teachers incorporated in the final product. No evidence of the effectiveness of the modified curriculum or the reliability or validity of the assessment is provided in the handbook, other than a caution that subtest reliability is weak because of the limited number of items per task. Each of the subtests is preceded by a brief explanation of the rationale for the task, with citations from the phonological awareness literature. The chapter containing the PAST also includes a brief discussion of the relationship of each of the five tasks to reading acquisition.

Usability

A model of usability among early reading measures, the PAST is very inexpensive; attractive to children; and easy to administer, score, and interpret. Preparing student test booklets for an entire classroom of 25 children can be accomplished in less than 30 minutes. The PAST is especially appealing to teachers because of the specific, instructionally relevant information it yields in a short period of time and because the results can be readily shared with parents.

Links to Intervention

The PAST is linked to the phonological awareness curricular program in the same handbook, with each subtest corresponding to a chapter of activities for whole-class or small-group instruction. The lessons, in the form of interactive language games, are designed to supplement the regular reading and language arts curriculum and to be conducted for 15 minutes a day for about 8 months in kindergarten and 8 weeks in first grade. Included in the manual are step-by-step procedures for each activity, a materials list, a set of advanced language games for younger children who have completed the program or older children in special education, and blackline masters of suggested kindergarten and first-grade lesson schedules.

Relevant Research

The PAST tasks are modeled on phonological awareness measures widely used in the reading research literature. The validation study for the original curriculum is reported in the Lundberg and colleagues (1988) article. In that longitudinal study with 235 Danish preschool children, daily training in phonological awareness for 8 months had significant positive effects not only on phonological skills but also on reading and spelling measured in Grades 1 and 2, compared with controls. Training studies (Schneider, Kuespert, Roth, & Vise, 1997) that replicated the original investigation with two samples of German kindergarten children obtained similar results.

Source and Cost

As noted above, the PAST is included in *Phonemic Awareness in Young Children: A Classroom Curriculum* (Adams et al., 1998). This handbook is available from the Paul H. Brookes Publishing Company for $25.95. Permission is granted to photocopy the assessment for educational purposes.

Summary

The *Phonological Awareness Screening Test* (PAST) is a brief, nonstandardized set of phonological awareness measures for kindergarten and first-grade children. Designed for classroom administration and norming, it is one of the few empirically based phonological awareness instruments that can be entirely group-administered. Although the PAST should not be used as the sole measure to identify children at risk for reading problems, it is useful as a classroom-based component of a screening and progress monitoring program for kindergarten children and as a beginning of the year screener for first graders. It also makes an excellent, easy-to-administer addition to an individually administered early reading assessment battery. Users should bear in mind that the phonemic segmentation subtests are too difficult to be sensitive to individual differences among kindergarten children, especially in the fall semester.

Group Case Example

Description of group: Kindergarten class (n = 20)
Date of assessment: November

Reason for assessment: Mr. S. wanted to obtain information about his students' level of phonemic awareness skills for use in instructional planning and skill grouping. He is especially concerned about several children who are having persistent difficulty with prereading and phonological awareness activities.

Group assessment results and interpretation: Mr. S. administered the *Phonological Awareness Screening Test* (PAST) in groups of 5 or 6 to all the children in his classroom. Below are the results ranked by total score, from highest to lowest. Medians and means for the class as a whole are also reported.

Student name	Detecting Rhymes (5 items)	Counting Syllables (5 items)	Matching Initial Sounds (5 items)	Counting Phonemes (5 items)	Comparing Word Lengths (5 items)	Representing Letters (5 items, 17 letters)	Total score (30 items)
Renarda	5	3	5	2	5	2 (13)	22
Charles	5	0	5	2	5	2 (12)	19
Trey	5	3	5	1	3	2 (12)	19
Lakeshia	3	2	5	2	5	2 (12)	19
Tonya	5	5	3	1	3	2 (12)	19
Samuel	5	5	3	1	4	0 (5)	18
Lonnell	5	2	5	0	5	1 (6)	18
Christina	4	4	5	0	3	1 (3)	17
Alphonso	5	1	5	2	3	0 (3)	16
Michael	5	5	0	2	4	0 (0)	16
Marvin	5	5	3	1	0	0 (0)	14
Devon	5	1	3	1	4	0 (4)	14
Tiffany	5	4	1	2	1	0 (3)	13
Gerald	5	2	1	3	1	0 (4)	12
Terry	3	2	3	0	4	0 (7)	12
Jennifer	1	0	4	1	5	0 (2)	11
Isaiah	1	4	3	0	2	0 (1)	10
Miranda	0	1	0	1	4	0 (0)	7
Juan	0	1	3	1	2	0 (0)	7
Keith	0	1	1	1	1	0 (0)	4
Class mean	3.60	2.55	3.15	1.20	3.20	0.60 (4.95)	14.35
Class median	5	2.5	3.0	1.0	3.5	0 (3.50)	15.0

Mr. S.'s kindergarten class displays a wide range of phonological awareness skills at this point in the school year. Most of the students are able to perform tasks of rhyming and matching initial sounds. Many are able to segment words at the syllable level and to compare the number of individual sounds in words, but only a few are able to perform complete phonemic segmentation, which is to be expected in the fall of kindergarten. Three of the children have not developed rhyming skills, an entry-level phonological awareness competency. These and other students scoring 2 or more points below the class average on any subtest will receive individual attention and follow-up assessments to determine whether they are in need of extra assistance. Mr. S. plans to continue using the *Phonemic Awareness in Young Children* curriculum in his classroom and has scheduled another classwide PAST assessment for the end of January.

Individual Case Example

Name of student: Jorge T.
Age: 6 years, 6 months
Grade: First grade
Date of assessment: December

Reason for referral: Jorge was referred for an early reading assessment by his first-grade teacher, Mrs. V., because of concerns about his slow progress in acquiring phonological and phonics skills. Mrs. V. reports that Jorge's letter-sound knowledge is limited and that he has trouble decoding even one-syllable, phonetically regular words, despite extensive classroom instruction and practice.

Assessment results and interpretation: The *Phonological Awareness Screening Test* (PAST) consists of six phonological awareness subtests and includes teaching items for each task to ensure that children understand the nature of the required responses. Children who score 2 or more points below the class average on a subtest or in the lowest 25% of their peer group on the overall test are in need of additional training on those skills. Jorge's scores are reported below.

PAST Subtest	Score
Detecting Rhymes	3/5
Counting Syllables	2/5
Matching Initial Sounds	3/5
Counting Phonemes	3/5
Comparing Word Lengths	2/5
Representing Phonemes with Letters	0/5
Total test	13/30

On *Detecting Rhymes*, an entry-level phonological awareness task requiring the child to match pictures that rhyme, Jorge matched three of five pictures correctly. The *Counting Syllables* subtest requires the child to indicate the number of syllables in pictured words by drawing the appropriate number of tallies beside each picture. Jorge was able to pronounce each of the five words correctly but had trouble differentiating the separate syllables. On the *Matching Initial Sounds* subtest, which requires matching pictures beginning with the same sound, he had trouble distinguishing the sounds *l* and *f*. *Counting Phonemes* requires the child to draw tallies to represent each sound in pictured words. Jorge had difficulty understanding the nature of this task and appeared to be guessing on many of the items. He also had trouble on the *Comparing Word Lengths* task, which requires the child to identify which of two words (represented by pictures) has more sounds. Because he did not sound out the words aloud, it is possible that he was also guessing on this task. *Representing Phonemes with Letters* requires the child to write letters corresponding to the sounds in pictured words. The items consist of one-syllable, phonetically regular words with a variety of consonant and vowel sounds. Jorge was able to write some of the initial and final consonants but none of the vowels (e.g., *mp* for *mop*). On a testing-of-limits procedure, he continued to have trouble distinguishing and producing short vowel sounds.

Overall, Jorge's phonological awareness skills are quite delayed for his grade. Given his difficulty in identifying and manipulating individual sounds in words, it is not surprising that he is struggling with phonics. Individual or small-group phonemic awareness training should be provided, preferably daily, to supplement regular classroom instruction in letter-sound correspondences.

PREDICTIVE READING PROFILE

Overview

The *Predictive Reading Profile* (PRP; Flynn, 2001) is a group-administered screening battery designed to measure a set of kindergarten-level reading precursors for children aged 5 to 6. It consists of eight subtests assessing orthographic, phonological, semantic, and syntactic processing, as well as a teacher rating scale measuring eight skill categories linked to those processes. According to its author, the PRP is designed not only to predict reading failure that occurs in first or second grade because of phonological, orthographic, or automaticity deficits but also to predict reading failure that occurs in third grade and above because of deficits in language comprehension. Although the manual includes end-of-year norms for a sample of kindergarten children from Minnesota and Wisconsin, the PRP is primarily intended for classroom or district norming. Based on the theories of Rumelhart (1977), Chall (1983), and Frith (1985), the PRP is a modified version of the *Literacy Screening Battery* (LSB; Flynn & Rahbar, 1998a, 1998b), which Flynn and her colleagues have used in a program of research designed to predict reading failure using a group-administered instrument (see Flynn, 2000). Purposes identified in the manual include (1) identifying children at risk for reading failure and (2) identifying children's literacy instructional needs. Test materials consist of a spiral-bound examiner manual and 30 student response booklets.

Subtests, Rating Scale, and Composites

Subtests and Rating Scale

The PRP consists of six core subtests. Two optional subtests and an eight-item Teacher Rating Scale (TRS) may also be administered to provide additional information or for a second screening. The subtests and TRS are designed to assess the reading processes described in Rumelhart's (1977) reading model (see Table 4.18). Table 4.19 describes the eight subtests. For each subtest except for the optional Story Writing, the child responds to the examiner's oral instructions or to printed test stimuli by circling or marking an × on a picture in a response booklet. Phonemic Segmentation should be renamed to reflect its content, which consists entirely of sound deletion items.

Composites

Raw scores on Alphabet–Word, Sound Recognition, Visual Matching, and either Syllable–Sound Counting or Phonemic Segmentation are summed to form an Early Achievement cluster. A Language cluster is obtained by summing the raw scores for Vocabulary and Syntax. The manual states that a total battery score can be obtained,

TABLE 4.18. Reading Processes Measured by the PRP Core Subtests and TRS Categories

Reading process	PRP subtests	TRS categories
Phonological processing	Sound Recognition Syllable–Sound Counting Phonemic Segmentation	Letter Sounds Phonological Awareness Sound–Letter Knowledge
Logographic/orthographic processing	Alphabet–Word Visual Matching	Letter Names Sight Words Visual Discrimination
Semantic processing	Vocabulary	Receptive Language
Syntactic processing	Syntax	Oral Language

Note. From "From Identification to Intervention: Improving Kindergarten Screening for Risk of Reading Failure," by J. M. Flynn, 2000, in N. A. Badian (Ed.), *Prediction and Prevention of Reading Failure* (p. 140). Copyright 2000 by York Press. Adapted with permission.

TABLE 4.19. Description of the PRP Subtests

Subtest	Description
Alphabet-Word	For Part A, the child circles the one of three lowercase letters named by the examiner. For Part B, the child circles the one of three words named by the examiner.
Sound Recognition	For Part A, the child circles one of three letters corresponding to a sound pronounced by the examiner. For Part B, the child circles the one of three letters that corresponds to the initial sound in a pictured word identified by the examiner. For Part C, the child marks one of three parts of a drawing of a train to indicate the position of a sound in a series of three-phoneme words. For example, the examiner says, "The sound is /t/. Mark wherever you hear /t/ in *sat*," and the child marks the third part of the drawing.
Syllable–Sound Counting	For Part A, given a row of five circles, the child fills in one circle for each syllable in two- to four-syllable words pronounced by the examiner. For Part B, the child fills in one circle for each phoneme in two- to five-phoneme words pronounced by the examiner. This subtest is omitted if Phonemic Segmentation is administered.
Visual Matching	The child circles the one of four letter sequences or words that matches a target letter sequence or word. The score is the number of items completed on two pages in 8 minutes.
Vocabulary	The child circles the one of four pictures that best represents a word pronounced by the examiner.
Syntax	The child circles the one of three pictures that corresponds to a sentence read by the examiner.
Story Writing	The child writes a story about his or her favorite animal.
Phonemic Segmentation	The child listens to a word pronounced by the examiner, silently reconstructs that word with a syllable or phoneme deleted, and marks one of three pictures representing the reconstructed word. For example, the child sees pictures of an eye, glass, and trash. The examiner says, "The big word is *eyeglass*. Take away /glass/ and circle what's left," and the child circles the picture of the eye. This test is administered instead of Syllable–Sound Counting to kindergarten or first-grade children who have received phonological awareness instruction.
Teacher Rating Scale	The teacher uses a 10-point scale to rate the child in eight skill areas corresponding to the PRP subtests.

Note. The optional subtests and rating scale are shaded.

but no norms are provided for total score, and there is no space on the group profile form in the manual or the individual profile form in the response booklet to record it.

Administration

The PRP can be administered to individuals, small groups, or entire classrooms. For group administrations, the test's author recommends providing one adult monitor for every six to eight children tested. The subtests require 10–20 minutes each to administer in a group format. Individual administrations take a total of about 35–45 minutes. For Syllable–Sound Counting and Phonemic Segmentation, the examiner uses reproducible training cards in the manual to teach the nature of the tasks prior to administration, which takes another 5–10 minutes per subtest. The author suggests administering only one or two subtests per day, which is the manner in which the PRP was given during standardization. Pages in the student response booklets are marked with pictures at the top, but numerals rather than pictures are used to designate item rows. Because subtests have up to 26 items, kindergarten children unfamiliar with two-digit numerals (perhaps the majority of kindergarten examinees) are likely to have difficulty locating the correct set of items, especially in a group-administration format.

Items on several subtests reflect the difficulty in creating oral language test stimuli that use a written rather than a pointing or an oral response. Phonemic Segmentation items are limited to words that can be easily depicted in terms of the syllable or phoneme remaining after sound deletion (e.g., *yardstick*, with pictures of a yardstick, yard, and stick). For Syntax items, the examiner instructs the child to "circle the picture I talked about," but Items 5 and 12 consist of a single large picture rather than three separate pictures. For example, for Item 5, which portrays a teacher with four children in a classroom, the examiner reads, "The third child from the teacher knows the answer," but the directions do not indicate that the examinee is to circle the image of the third child instead of the entire picture. Stimuli for these items should be redrawn, or the directions should be modified. Three of the Syntax items (Items 3, 9, and 25) use very similar language to assess the identical construction (indirect object). Vocabulary Item 16 (*wild*) should be modified in the interests of clarity and discriminative accuracy. On that item, the four pictorial choices consist of a dog's head, a squirrel clinging to a tree (correct choice), a cow's head, and a leaping cat with a bristling tail. Not only are the four animals not presented in equivalent form (head vs. whole body, front vs. profile view, static pose vs. movement), but urban and suburban youngsters accustomed to seeing squirrels in parks and yards may not view them as "wild" animals. In fact, the manual states (p. 40) that teachers who participated in the field-testing were surprised at the number of children who selected the picture of the cat, apparently because children confused the notion of acting wild with the concept of an undomesticated animal.

Scores

Items are scored 1 or 0, using an appendix with reduced facsimiles of correctly completed pages from the record booklet. Four to six pages from the student response booklet are reproduced on a single page in the manual, which results in small, difficult-to-read pictures and print, especially for Visual Matching. Normative scores are not available for Story Writing, which is scored on a 10-point holistic scale. The manual provides between one and three examples of student responses for each value on the scale, but additional examples and more specific guidelines are needed. Scoring takes about 2–3 minutes per subtest and about 5 minutes for Story Writing, depending on the length and legibility of the child's written production. For the TRS, the teacher evaluates the child's skills in eight categories from 1 to 10. The 10-point rating system seems excessive for this purpose. For example, for the Sight Words category, the descriptor for a rating of 1 reads "recognizes own name and/or one or two words," whereas the descriptor for a rating of 10 reads "recognizes more than 10 words (*go, stop, the*)." With 10 ratings, this means that there is one point on the scale per additional sight word. Given these characteristics, it is not surprising that the TRS shows halo effects; that is, teachers tend to assign similar ratings across categories (Flynn & Rahbar, 1998a).

Raw subtest scores and cluster scores can be converted to percentiles or stanines, using a set of preliminary kindergarten norms. Scoring is complicated by the fact that stanines are provided for a single raw score rather than for raw score ranges. Although for most subtests an increase of 1 raw score point produces an increase of one stanine, in some cases examiners must interpolate. According to the test's author, estimates for first graders relative to the norm group can be obtained by adding 2 points to each score. Raw scores for subtests and the two clusters can be recorded on a reproducible group profile form in the manual and on a detachable individual profile form on the back of the student record booklet. On the individual profile form, subtest scores are classified as at risk, average, or advanced, based on the norms provided in the manual or locally derived norms. No normative scores are provided for the TRS, and there is no place to enter data from the TRS on either the group or the individual profile form.

Interpretation

The PRP's author appropriately cautions that the preliminary kindergarten norms included in the manual should be used only when the characteristics of the children being tested are similar to those of the normative group. If examiners use the norms in the manual, the author offers the following guidelines for classifying raw scores: at risk, PR ≤ 35; average, PR = 36–83; and advanced, PR ≥ 84. The manual includes a section with guidelines for developing local norms using statistics programs such as SPSS. The author also suggests creating a group profile with a computer spreadsheet (e.g., Microsoft Excel) and provides suggestions for developing cut scores for identifying risk status, such as the districtwide percentage of children enrolled in remedial and special education programs. If the district base rate for reading failure is unknown, the author suggests using a cutoff score corresponding to the lowest 35% of the distribution, citing data from the development phase of the PRP. The manual includes an example of a completed group profile for a class and a discussion of the way in which one school district uses PRP cut scores to identify children for early intervention. For interpreting locally normed scores, the author suggests assigning ratings to raw scores as follows: at risk, subtest or cluster scores below the local cut score for those measures; average, scores between at-risk and advanced cutoffs; and advanced, highest 15% of scores. No interpretative guidelines or case examples are provided for the TRS.

Technical Adequacy

Standardization

The normative group for the *Literacy Screening Battery* (LSB), the first version of the PRP, consisted of three cohorts of kindergarten children (total n = 4,872) enrolled in 26 school districts in Minnesota and Wisconsin. The cohorts are described in terms of age, gender, town versus rural residence, and SES (defined by lunch pay status). The manual states that the ethnic backgrounds of the participating districts were primarily northern European, but no specific information is provided on race or ethnicity; nor are comparison data for the U.S. school-age population presented. For the PRP, preliminary kindergarten norms are based on a sample of 366 kindergarten children from two small school districts in the Midwest, with testing conducted in March or April of the school year. Demographic characteristics for the samples from each district are reported in terms of gender, town/rural residence, lunch pay status, limited English proficiency status, special education status, mobility index, and dropout rate, but not race/ethnicity. Because of the sample's lack of representativeness, local norming is strongly recommended.

Reliability Evidence

Coefficient alphas are reported for subtests and total score for both the LSB and PRP. For the PRP, internal consistency reliabilities based on 67 examinees (grade and administration window not specified) were in the acceptable range for the total battery and the Early Achievement cluster (.94 and .92, respectively), but the Language cluster coefficient fell below the criterion level for composites (.83). Coefficients for Alphabet–Word, Sound Recognition, and Visual Matching were in the .80s, whereas Vocabulary, Syntax, and Syllable–Sound Counting coefficients fell below acceptable levels (.70 to .73). Coefficient alpha reliabilities for LSB Phonemic Segmentation, which is identical to the PRP measure of the same name, were .86 and .80 for two cohorts of children (*ns* = 100 and 194).

Group versus individual administration formats were compared for 67 kindergarten children (testing date not specified) and 66 first graders tested in the first week of school, with half of the children at each grade level taking each format. Although no significant differences were found between administration formats on any subtests for either sample, administration was in groups of 10–12 children rather than the whole-class format described in the manual. It is also not clear whether this study was conducted with the LSB or the PRP. Test–retest reliabilities for a class of kindergarten children (*n* = 18, 2-week interval) for four LSB subtests were .97 for total score, .96 for Alphabet, .85 for Syntax, .80 for Vocabulary, and .79 for Phonemic Segmentation. No evidence of interscorer reliability is provided, and no reliability estimates of any kind are presented for Story Writing or the TRS.

Test Floors and Item Gradients

Subtest and composite floors are adequate, with a subtest raw score of 1 and raw scores of 1 on the subtests making up each cluster yielding scores at or below the 1st percentile. In contrast, item gradients are inadequate for many subtests, as indicated by large gains in percentile ranks for a single raw score point. For example, for Sound Recognition, a raw score of 29 yields a percentile rank of 49, whereas a raw score of 30 yields a percentile rank of 80.

Validity Evidence

CONTENT VALIDITY EVIDENCE

LSB and PRP tasks were designed to measure kindergarten precursors of the reading processes described in Rumelhart's (1977) model and the nature of reading acquisition as presented in Chall's (1983) and Frith's (1985) theories. According to Rumelhart's model, lower level processes, including phonological, logographic/orthographic, and automaticity skills, support the development of word recognition, whereas higher level syntactic and semantic processes support reading comprehension. Children with deficits in lower level processes will experience reading failure in first or second grade, whereas children with deficits in higher level processes will experience reading failure in third grade or above when the focus is on comprehension of textual material. Measures of automaticity (e.g., rapid naming tasks) were not included in the PRP because of the group administration format. Changes from the LSB to the PRP included the addition of a core subtest (Syllable–Sound Counting, thus changing Phoneme Segmentation to optional status) and an optional subtest (Story Telling). One LSB subtest was dropped (a form copying task), and responses to Alphabet–Word and Sound Recognition tasks were adapted to use a recognition (circling) rather than written answer format. Items were also added to LSB Visual Discrimination, which was renamed Visual Matching to reflect recent research documenting the role of orthographic processes in predicting reading acquisition.

Item difficulty indices were calculated for subtest items in the field trial version of the PRP, with items between .50 and .70 retained, along with a few easy items because of the goal of identifying low- rather than high-achieving students. To improve discriminating power, items correctly answered by more than 30% of low-scoring examinees and by less than 70% of high-scoring examinees were eliminated or revised. Items that did not correlate at least moderately with total test score (.20 or higher) were also eliminated or revised. Specific information regarding item difficulty, discrimination, and item–test correlations is not reported by subtest, however. Kindergarten teachers, speech–language clinicians, and reading specialists then reviewed test stimuli and drawings for the revised subtests to eliminate ambiguous items or pictures. No evidence of sensitivity reviews or DIF analysis is presented.

CRITERION-RELATED VALIDITY EVIDENCE

For an unspecified sample, concurrent validity correlations between Syntax and Vocabulary and the *Peabody Picture Vocabulary Test–Revised* (PPVT-R) were moderate to high (.80 and .60, respectively), whereas Phonemic Segmentation, which measures a specific linguistic skill (sound deletion) rather than general language ability, was not significantly related to PPVT-R scores (r = .06). In contrast, Phonemic Segmentation correlated highly (.72) with the *Auditory Analysis Test* and moderately (.58) with the Auditory Discrimination subtest of the *Stanford Diagnostic Reading Test*. The number and grade level of examinees in the studies are not specified, nor is it clear whether the studies were conducted with the LSB or the PRP.

In a predictive validity study with 1,071 students, LSB cut scores set at the 35th percentile on either the Early Achievement or Language cluster correctly identified 80% of children who failed in Grades 1–3, 83% in Grade 4, and 89% in Grade 5, with failure defined as a total reading score at or below the 35th percentile on regional norms for district-administered standardized tests or enrollment in Title I or learning disabilities programs. In a follow-up investigation with 70 children, LSB scores correctly predicted 68% of children with reading failure as late as Grade 8. In another study comparing the predictive utility of the LSB and TRS in two kindergarten samples (*ns* = 158 and 210), a TRS cut score set at the 35th percentile correctly identified 63% to 65% of children who failed in reading in Grades 1–3, but missed 35% to 37% of children who failed. Valid positive rates for the LSB were higher (73% and 80%), and false negative rates were lower (27% and 20%). When the predictive validity of either the TRS or LSB cut score was evaluated, the valid positive rate increased (85% and 88% for the two samples) and the false negative rate decreased (12% and 15%), but the false positive rate also increased (44% and 49%). Given these results, the test's author suggests using the TRS as a tool for reporting progress to parents after intervention rather than as a screening component.

CONSTRUCT VALIDITY EVIDENCE

Construct validity evidence includes a discussion of the theoretical basis of the PRP, as well as multiple regression and factor analyses evaluating developmental changes in the component reading processes specified by the model. Results of multiple regression analyses of LSB subtests on group-administered standardized reading tests, such as the *Iowa Tests of Basic Skills*, the *Metropolitan Achievement Test* (Prescott, Balow, Hogan, & Farr, 1985), or the *Stanford Achievement Test* (Gardner, Rudman, Karlsen, & Merwin, 1982) at Grades 1–5 (*ns* = 109 to 708), were generally supportive of the model. LSB subtests assessing precursors to lower level reading processes (Sounds, Alphabet, and Phonemic Segmentation) accounted for decreasing amounts of variance in reading achievement from Grades 1–5, whereas subtests assessing higher level skills (Vocabulary and Syntax) accounted for a greater proportion of the variance in Grades 3–5. Contrary to prediction, Sounds explained very little variance in Grades 1 and 2 but a significant amount of variance in Grade 5, along with Vocabulary and Syntax. The manual states that the results were replicated with two additional cohorts, but specific results are not provided.

Usability

The PRP is inexpensive, is easy to administer and score, and can be administered in its entirety in a group setting. Although the manual is spiral-bound and tabbed, locating information can be time-consuming because the table of contents is too brief and because information on the same topic is sometimes placed in several different sections. For example, the table of contents gives no hints as to where to find scoring instructions, and users must flip through the pages to find an overview of scoring procedures at the end of a section on administration procedures and then turn to the appendices to find the answer keys for the subtests. Similarly, directions for administering the subtests are in a section near the end of the manual, whereas the "Administration Procedures" section near the front refers to organizing the classroom for group administration. The student response booklets are entirely black and white, including the cover, and are less attractive than the booklets in other early literacy batteries.

Links to Intervention

A chapter in the manual presents suggestions for instructional activities targeting the skills assessed by each of the subtests and clusters. The test's author describes a classroom-based intervention program designed for first graders scoring low on Phonemic Segmentation, as well as a variety of empirically based phonological awareness training materials for use in instructional planning. The manual also includes a section with guidelines for reporting PRP results to parents, including a sample letter informing parents that the PRP will be administered and a sample parent/caregiver score report.

Relevant Research

In a study evaluating the predictive validity of the LSB and TRS with data from 1,634 kindergarten children (Flynn & Rahbar, 1998a), teacher ratings on the TRS categories were moderately to highly correlated (.51 to .87), indicating a halo effect rather than differential appraisal of the various skill domains. Moreover, with the exception of TRS Letter Names and Letter Sounds categories, teacher ratings showed only low to moderate correlations with LSB subtests measuring similar processes. In a subsample of 210 children, TRS scores correctly predicted 64% of Grade 3 poor readers, with a false positive rate of 23%, whereas the LSB correctly predicted 80% of Grade 3 poor readers, with a false positive rate of 31%. Using a risk classification rule of either an LSB or a TRS score at or below the 35th percentile resulted in a valid positive rate of 88%, with only 12% false negatives, but the false positive rate increased to 39%.

Source and Cost

The PRP is available from LinguiSystems for $89.95.

Test Review

Mather, N. (2002). Review of the Predictive Reading Profile. *Journal of Psychoeducational Assessment, 20*, 312–316.

Summary

The *Predictive Reading Profile* (PRP) is a group-administered battery designed to measure reading precursors for kindergartners and children beginning first grade. Intended primarily for local norming, the PRP includes a set of preliminary kindergarten norms that are too lacking in representativeness to be appropriate for most practitioners' purposes. An effort to develop an empirically based group analogue to individually administered phonological awareness and early literacy skills measures, the PRP is not only one of the few instruments that can be entirely group-administered but is also one of the few commercially published reading tests that provides predictive validity evidence based on cut scores. Although predictive validity studies with the first version of the test have yielded impressive hit rates, they have also produced high false positive rates. Internal consistency reliability estimates are adequate for the Early Achievement cluster but fall below acceptable levels for the Language cluster. Stability estimates are based on a very small number of children, and there is no evidence of interrater reliability for the subjectively scored Story Writing subtest. The Teacher Rating Scale, which has undocumented reliability and displays halo effects, does not contribute significantly to the predictive power of the screening tasks. In addition, the PRP's primary administration window is later than that for any of the other reading screening batteries reviewed in this text—the end of kindergarten. As a result, interventions based on PRP screening results are unlikely to be implemented until the fall of first grade. The test's author is now recommending (J. F. Anderson, personal communication, February 10, 2003) that the window be moved to the beginning of Grade 1. Studies evaluating the relationship of the PRP to other multiskill early reading batteries are also needed.

Case Example

Name of student: Gabriel T.
Age: 5 years, 9 months
Grade: Kindergarten
Date of assessment: May

Reason for referral: Gabriel was referred for an early reading assessment by his kindergarten teacher. Gabriel's teacher reports that he is having trouble learning and using sound–symbol knowledge to decode words and has trouble remembering sight words taught in class. His teacher also notices that he has difficulty following directions and participating effectively in classroom discussions.

Assessment results and interpretation: The *Predictive Reading Profile* (PRP) measures two sets of early reading skills: alphabetic and language skills. All of the tasks except Story Writing require children to respond to items read by the examiner by marking one of three choices in a booklet. Performance on the alphabetic tasks making up the Early Achievement cluster is the best predictor of reading success in first and second grade, and performance on the language tasks making up the Language cluster is the best predictor of reading success in third grade and above. Gabriel's scores on the PRP and stanine scores expected for children in spring of kindergarten are reported below. Stanine scores range from a low of 1 to a high of 9, with stanines from 1 to 3 indicating below average or at-risk performance, stanines from 4 to 6 indicating average performance, and stanines from 7 to 9 representing advanced performance.

Cluster/subtest	Number correct/ Number of items	Stanine	Descriptive category
Early Achievement Cluster	86/106	4	Average
Alphabet–Word	23/30	2–3	Below average
Sound Recognition	27/30	6–9	Above average
Visual Matching	19/20	8–9	Above average
Phonemic Segmentation	17/26	8	Above average
Language Cluster	23/52	<1	Below average
Vocabulary	11/26	1	Below average
Syntax	12/26	<1	Below average
Story Writing	–	–	Average

Gabriel's overall alphabetic skills fall in the average range for the spring of kindergarten. His ability to isolate and recognize letter sounds (Sound Recognition) and his ability to match letter and word sequences (Visual Matching) are rated as above average. Although he also scored in the above average range on a task that required him to delete syllables from words (Phonemic Segmentation), he responded very rapidly and appeared to be guessing randomly rather than carefully studying the pictured choices. On a letter and word recognition task (Alphabet–Word), he was able to identify 9 of 10 lowercase letters but only 14 of 20 one-syllable words (stanine = 2–3, below average).

In contrast to his overall average alphabetic skills, Gabriel's oral language skills are quite delayed (stanine = <1, below average). His receptive vocabulary, as measured by his ability to identify pictured objects (Vocabulary), is rated as below average. He also scored in the below average range on a task requiring him to listen to a sentence and mark the picture best representing the sentence (Syntax). On Story

Writing, which requires the child to write a story about a favorite animal, Gabriel initially protested that he couldn't write a story and drew a picture of a dinosaur instead. Even with considerable encouragement, he continued to be very hesitant and asked the examiner how to spell each word as he began to write it. Told that the examiner could not help him with spelling, he finally wrote the following: "wat to the cat wet," which he read aloud as, "I want to go see my cat." Although his story production is rated as average for kindergarten children, it reflects the syntax and letter-sound knowledge deficits observed on other PRP tasks.

TEST OF EARLY READING ABILITY—3

Overview

The *Test of Early Reading Ability–3* (TERA-3; Reid, Hresko, & Hammill, 2001) is an individually administered, norm-referenced test of early reading skills for children aged 3-6 to 8-6. Like its predecessor, the TERA-2 (Reid, Hresko, & Hammill, 1989), the TERA-3 has two parallel forms, each of which measures three components of reading: (1) alphabet knowledge, (2) print conventions, and (3) meaning. Changes to this edition include (1) provision of separate subtest scores for the three components; (2) a new normative sample; (3) a lowered age range at the upper end (from 9-11 to 8-6); (4) new items, especially for the upper and lower age ranges; (5) the use of color for all pictorial stimuli; and (6) additional reliability and validity evidence. Items requiring the use of logos (e.g., a Jell-O label) are now standardized and provided as part of the test kit so that examiners do not have to prepare their own materials. Written from an emergent literacy perspective, the TERA-3 is one of very few instruments yielding a norm-referenced score for a print conventions measure. The authors identify five purposes for the TERA-3: (1) to identify children who are significantly below their peers in reading development and are in need of early intervention, (2) to identify children's reading strengths and weaknesses, (3) to monitor students' progress in reading intervention programs, (4) to serve as a research tool, and (5) to serve as a companion test to other assessment procedures. The test kit includes a spiral-bound examiner's manual, a spiral-bound stimulus book for each form, and a set of 25 profile/examiner record booklets for each form, all packaged in a storage box.

Subtests and Composite

Subtests

Each form of the TERA-3 consists of three subtests: Alphabet, Conventions, and Meaning, which are described in order of administration in Table 4.20.

Composite

Standard scores on the three subtests are summed to yield a composite, called a "Reading Quotient" ($M = 100$, $SD = 15$). The use of this term for the composite is inappropriate because it suggests that the TERA-3 is measuring aptitude for reading rather than acquired print-related early literacy skills. Moreover, at several points in the test manual (e.g., pp. 24 and 42), the authors also apply this term to subtest standard scores.

TABLE 4.20. Description of the TERA-3 Subtests

Subtest	Description
Alphabet	The child identifies letters, words, and sounds in words by pointing or naming and identifies the number of syllables or phonemes in printed words. Letters and words are printed in a variety of fonts.
Conventions	The child demonstrates by a pointing or oral response an understanding of print conventions, including book orientation, letter and word orientation, text directionality, uppercase and lowercase letters, punctuation, spelling, and capitalization.
Meaning	The child identifies logos; matches words with pictures; and demonstrates comprehension of relational constructs, words, sentences, and paragraphs.

Administration

Administration time for the TERA-3 ranges from 15 to 30 minutes, depending on the examinee's age and level of skill. Although the subtests are untimed, the examiner is directed to encourage a response if the child has not responded to an item within 15 seconds after presentation or repetition, and then score the item as incorrect if no response is forthcoming. Testing begins at age-specific start points, with basals and ceilings set at three consecutive correct or incorrect items, respectively. Stimuli for all subtests are presented in a spiral-bound stimulus book that lies flat in front of the child, with item-by-item directions in small print at the top of each page. The manual indicates that the examiner may sit next to or diagonally across from the child, but only abbreviated directions and prompts are provided in the record booklet, and I have found it necessary to sit next to the child in order to read the complete instructions for each item. The same spiral-bound test book is used to administer items on the Conventions subtest, which differs from the standard format for print awareness measures (i.e., a small illustrated book). The test's authors do not provide a rationale for the decision to use this type of format, and although it is more convenient for the examiner, who does not have to provide a separate book for the task, it also provides a less authentic assessment of children's understanding of books and print.

The examiner prompts in the stimulus books for items requiring two responses for credit are not uniformly provided. For most two-response items, the examiner is directed to prompt if the child gives only one answer, but on some (e.g., Conventions Item 17, Form A; Conventions Item 19, Form B), no such prompt is given. Several items should be rewritten for clarity, form equivalence, and/or grammatical correctness. On Form B, Item 12 on the Alphabet subtest asks the child to identify the first letter in *baseball bat*. Although both words begin with the same letter, a single-word item would be preferable. On Form A, Item 17 on Conventions presents a three-sentence paragraph and asks, "How many things are wrong with these sentences?" The answer given in the record booklet is two (for an omitted capital letter at the beginning of a sentence and an omitted period), but many examiners, including myself, would also add a comma to separate *too* from the end of the sentence that contains it. On Form B, the parallel item (Item 19) reads, "What is wrong with this sentence?" This item not only includes one less error for the child to find (a missing capital letter in a name) but also does not involve the same two-step process of first identifying the errors and then counting the number of errors detected. As with Item 17 on Form A, the authors do not consider the omission of a comma before the word *too* at the end of the stimulus sentence as one of the two errors to be detected.

Scores

Scoring is dichotomous for all items. The record booklet includes correct responses for each item but provides very little room for recording alternative responses or partially correct responses for later analysis. The manual contains no scoring guidelines, and although the authors state that scoring is straightforward, numerous items elicit responses that require subjective judgment to score, especially on the Meaning subtest. Subtest raw scores are converted to age-based standard scores (M = 10, SD = 3), percentiles, and age and grade equivalents. Norm group intervals are in 6-month intervals for ages 3-6 to 4-11, 3-month intervals for 5-0 to 6-11, and 6-month intervals for 7-0 to 8-6. Because referrals for reading assessments are nearly always based on children's failure to attain grade-level expectations, grade norms should also be provided. Moreover, although the authors caution users regarding age and grade equivalent scores and do not include tables of these scores for the Reading Quotient, they provide a formula for computing age equivalents for the Reading Quotient in a subsequent section, which belies the cautions offered earlier.

Interpretation

The manual includes a case example of a boy aged 6-4 (grade not specified) to demonstrate how to calculate derived scores and complete the record form. All of the child's TERA-3 scores fall in the average range, as do the scores on the three tests provided for comparative purposes, and the test's authors conclude that he does not have reading problems. It would have been more helpful to include a case example with skill deficits in one or more areas for a discussion of diagnostic issues and appropriate interventions. The authors include a section on factors contributing to low scores on the composite and subtests and the implications of these factors for school performance. A second case example for a child identified by name but not age, grade, or referral question, is provided to illustrate discrepancy analysis procedures. The manual does not include a completed protocol or table of scores for the example, and the discussion is difficult to follow. The case example displays statistically and clinically significant differences between her Alphabet and Meaning subtest scores, but no interpretation of those differences or suggestions for intervention are provided.

The authors state that minimal differences required for statistical significance and clinical utility between pairs of TERA-3 subtest scores are identical for all comparisons (3 and 5 points, respectively), but a table illustrating the comparisons would be useful. Moreover, because a single value is used to evaluate statistical significance, only differences at the .05 level can be calculated. The value for determining severe discrepancies (i.e., differences with clinical utility) is based on Reynolds's (1990) formula. Rather than calculating minimal difference scores for each subtest, the authors report a single discrepancy score for all subtest comparisons (a 5-point difference) based on the average intercorrelation among the three subtests. No rationale is given for the use of an average intercorrelation rather than subtest-specific intercorrelations in calculating minimal score differences, and intercorrelations among TERA-3 subtests vary considerably across both forms (rs = .43 to .91). The manual provides a table with difference scores needed for statistical significance (.05) and clinical usefulness for 10 intelligence tests for use in aptitude–achievement discrepancy analyses for both forms of the TERA-3. The TERA-3 Reading Quotient for the child in the second case example is compared with her Nonverbal IQ on the *Test of Nonverbal Intelligence–3* (Brown, Sherbenou, & Johnsen, 1997), yielding a difference that is statistically significant but not severely discrepant. Again, however, the difference is not interpreted, and no recommendations are offered.

Technical Adequacy

Standardization

The TERA-3 was standardized in 1999 and 2000 on 875 children in 22 states, with examinees sampled to be representative of the 2000 U.S. school-age population in terms of geographic area, gender, race, residence, ethnicity, family income, parental education, and disability status. Norm characteristics are stratified by age for geographic area, gender, race, residence, ethnicity, family income, and parental education. Demographic characteristics are generally consistent with U.S. 2000 population data, although families with incomes of $75,000 or over are slightly underrepresented and parents with a bachelor's degree are slightly overrepresented. Subgroup sizes vary markedly across the age range of the test, from a low of 160 students at age 5 to a high of 231 at age 6. Because norms are reported in intervals of 3 months for ages 5 and 6, scores for examinees at these ages are based on only about 40 and 57 children per interval, respectively, which falls below acceptable levels.

Reliability Evidence

Alternate-form reliability estimates based on an immediate administration procedure for the three subtests range from .82 to .92 across the six age groups. For the early primary grade range, coefficients are at or above .90 for Alphabet for ages 5 and 6, Conventions for age 8, and Meaning for ages 5 and 7, with the remainders of the coefficients in the .80s. Raw score means and standard deviations for the two forms differ by only a single point across all three subtests. The authors justify the use of a single normative table for the two forms on the basis of similar means and standard deviations, as well as item analyses; however, correlations between forms fall below .90 for 9 of the 18 coefficients, making this decision questionable. Alternate-form reliability estimates are not provided for the Reading Quotient. Coefficient alphas for the Reading Quotient range from .94 to .96 for the early primary grade range. Internal consistency reliabilities for Alphabet range from .88 to .92, with values in the .80s for Form B for ages 7 and 8. Coefficient alphas for Meaning are in the .90s for both forms and all ages, with the exception of age 5 (.84 for both forms). For Conventions, internal consistency reliabilities are in the .80s for both forms for ages 5–7 but below acceptable levels for both forms at age 8 (.79 and .75 for Forms A and B, respectively). Coefficient alphas for eight subgroups in the standardization sample, including three groups of examinees with exceptionalities (learning disabled, language impaired, and reading disabled), range from .91 to .99 for the three subtests and composite for both forms.

Test–retest reliability using alternate-form procedures was investigated in two separate samples, with examinees taking both forms of the test twice (2-week interval). For 30 children ages 4–6, stability estimates ranged from .94 to .98 for all the subtests and the composite, excepting Conventions (.88 and 86 for Forms A and B, respectively). In a second sample with 33 children aged 7–8, test–retest reliabilities ranged from .94 to .98, with the exception of Meaning (.88 and .86 for Forms A and B, respectively). Means and standard deviations were very similar, and practice effects were minimal. Interscorer reliability coefficients based on independent scoring of 40 completed protocols for children ages 5-0 to 7-0 by one of the test's authors and two advanced graduate students were all .99 for the subtests and composite. Because the items are dichotomously scored, interscorer agreement statistics based on completed protocols provide no information about consistency in scoring the open-ended items on the Meaning subtest or the items on the Conventions subtest that require nonverbal responses (e.g., fingerpointing text, indicating text directionality, etc.).

Test Floors and Item Gradients

Floors for the composite score are adequate throughout the early primary grade range, but floors for Alphabet and Conventions are inadequate below age 5-9. For example, a Conventions raw score of 1 for a child aged 5-0 yields a standard score of 6 (below average range). The TERA-3 also displays item gradient violations for Conventions and Meaning below age 5-6. Although the emphasis in this text is on the adequacy of floors rather than ceilings, users should note that there are ceiling effects on all subtests, beginning at age 7-6. For example, a child aged 8-0 who answers 18 of the 21 Conventions items correctly earns a standard score of 10, and the ceiling extends only to a standard score of 13 (PR = 84).

Validity Evidence

CONTENT VALIDITY EVIDENCE

As evidence of content validity, the TERA-3's authors offer a rationale based on reviews of research, curriculum materials, and existing early reading tests. They state that because they were developing a test of emergent reading, only items related to print material were included, and phonemic awareness skills were not measured because they do not directly involve print. As evidence of the appropriate assignment of items to subtests, the manual reports percentages of agreement for a panel of six experts. Mean percentages of agreement across items were 90% for Conventions, 98% for Meaning, and 99% for Alphabet. The manual does not indicate the number of items retained from the TERA-2 or the number of new items. Although the total number of items on the TERA-3 is nearly twice that of the TERA-2 (80 vs. 46 items per form), the item types are highly similar. Indeed, the very high correlations between the current and previous versions of the test (see below) indicate that although the content validity section in the manual has been rewritten, the TERA-3 measures essentially the same skills as its predecessor.

Median item discrimination coefficients fall within acceptable values across the entire age range of the test. Median item difficulties are also in the acceptable range but vary somewhat between forms for Conventions and Meaning at ages 5 and 6. For example, median item difficulty for Meaning at age 5 is .50 for Form A but .63 for Form B. Overall, item difficulty indices suggest that 5-year-old examinees may obtain lower scores if Form A is used. DIF analyses using logistic regression procedures for four dichotomous groups (males vs. females, European Americans vs. non-European Americans, African Americans vs. non-African Americans, and Hispanic Americans vs. non-Hispanic Americans) revealed that 13 of the 160 items on both forms of the TERA-3 exhibited DIF, only 1 of which had a moderate effect size. Reviews by the test's authors and two PRO-ED staff members of each flagged item indicated that item content did not appear to account for the observed differences. The manual includes an additional chapter entitled "Controlling for Test Bias" that discusses the nature of test bias and reviews the procedures used to evaluate and reduce bias during test development.

CRITERION-RELATED VALIDITY EVIDENCE

Correlations between the TERA-2 and TERA-3 range from .85 to .98, with the lowest correlations for Meaning (.85 to .86 across both forms) and the highest for the Reading Quotient (.98 across both forms). For a sample of 70 second- and third-grade children that excluded students with disabilities, correlations between the TERA-3 and reading subtests and composites on the *Stanford Achievement Tests–Ninth Edition* (SAT-9) ranged from .36 to .74. TERA-3 Reading Quotient scores correlated moderately with SAT-9 Total Reading (.57 and .52 for Forms A and B, respectively) and highly with SAT-9 Reading Comprehension (.74 for both forms). For a sample of 64 second- and third-grade students with reading disabilities or learning disabilities primarily in the area of reading, correlations with the *Woodcock Reading Mastery Tests–Revised/Normative Update* (WRMT-R/NU; Woodcock, 1987/1998) were generally moderate (.41 to .67), with the highest correlations between TERA-3 and WRMT-R/NU Reading composite scores (Form A = .64, Form B = .67). The manual also reports correlations for TERA-3 subtests and composite scores with teacher ratings of children's reading skills and classroom grades for 411 students from the normative group (ages and grades unspecified). Correlations with teacher ratings ranged from .48 to .71, with the highest correlations for ratings of reading comprehension and decoding with Meaning and Reading Quotient scores (*r*s = .68 to .71). Correlations with reading or language arts classroom grades were moderate (.45 to .62), with the highest correlations for Meaning and Reading Quotient scores (.62 across both forms).

CONSTRUCT VALIDITY EVIDENCE

TERA-3 raw scores increase over the six age groups covered by the test and are strongly related to age. Intercorrelations among the three subtests range from .43 to .66 for both forms; correlations between subtests for each form are .91 for Alphabet but fall in the .80s for the other two subtests, which is lower than desirable in terms of form equivalence. Diagnostic validity was examined by comparing mean standard scores for each age group in the standardization sample and for eight demographic subgroups, including three disability subgroups (learning-disabled, reading-disabled, and language-impaired examinees). Mean scores for all three disability groups were in the low average range, with the lowest score on the Reading Quotient for language-impaired examinees (SS = 81). Among the three subtests, Meaning scores were the lowest for all three disability subgroups (SSs = 5–7).

As evidence of discriminant validity, the authors report TERA-3 subtest and composite correlations with SAT-9 nonreading measures for the sample of 70 second and third graders described above. Correlations ranged from .31 to .77, with the highest correlations between the Reading Quotient and SAT-9 Listening Comprehension (.75 and .77 for Forms A and B, respectively). In the same sample, the

TERA-3 displayed generally low to moderate correlations (*r*s = .33 to .64) with the *Otis–Lennon School Ability Test–Seventh Edition* (Otis & Lennon, 1995). For the sample of 64 reading-disabled students described above, correlations between TERA-3 subtest and composite scores and *Wechsler Intelligence Scale for Children–III* (WISC-III; Wechsler, 1991) scores were much higher for Verbal IQ (.74 to .84) than for Performance IQ (.31 to .43), as anticipated. Correlations between TERA-3 Reading Quotient and WISC-III Full Scale IQ scores were also high, however (.77 for both forms), indicating that the TERA-3 is assessing many of the same factors as cognitive ability tests.

As evidence that the subtests measure three different components of early reading ability, the authors present results of a confirmatory factor analysis evaluating the TERA-3 three-subtest model. All three subtests display very high intercorrelations (.81 for Alphabet and Meaning, .88 for Meaning and Conventions, and .95 for Alphabet and Conventions), supporting the contention that they measure a unitary construct but providing limited support for the discriminant validity of the latter two subtests. Moreover, the manual provides little information to assist practitioners in interpreting the figure displaying the results of the factor analysis. No evidence of the utility of the TERA-3 in diagnosing strengths and weaknesses, predicting reading acquisition, or documenting the effects of reading interventions is presented.

Usability

Compared with its predecessor, the TERA-3 is much more attractive, appealing to children, and easy to administer. Space should be added to the record form for indicating the child's grade in school, as well as beside open-ended items for recording errors for further analysis. As noted above, the use of a stimulus test book to administer print convention items improves usability for the examiner but differs from the standard format.

Links to Intervention

The authors appropriately caution that the TERA-3 includes too few items to be used as the sole basis for instructional planning and recommend obtaining additional information from a variety of sources, such as authentic assessment and criterion-referenced tests. Given the authors' stated purpose of identifying children at risk for reading failure so that they can receive early assistance, guidelines and descriptions of strategies and resources for designing interventions based on TERA-3 results should be included.

Relevant Research

In an intervention study with 183 first-grade students of varying reading ability, Mathes, Torgesen, and Allor (2001) used the TERA-2 to evaluate the effectiveness of peer-assisted learning strategies (PALS) and computer-assisted phonological awareness instruction (CAI). Children were classified as high-achieving, average-achieving, or low-achieving readers, based on their performance on an oral reading probe and a phonemic awareness deletion task. Low-achieving children participating in PALS and PALS with CAI displayed significantly greater gains on the TERA-2 than controls. In contrast, average- and high-achieving participants did not demonstrate significant gains on the TERA-2 compared with the control group, perhaps because of ceiling effects.

Source and Cost

The TERA-3 is available from PRO-ED for $236.00.

Test Reviews

de Fur, S. (2003). Review of the Test of Early Reading Ability, Third Edition. In B. S. Plake, J. C. Impara, & R. A. Spies (Eds.), *The fifteenth mental measurements yearbook* (pp. 940–943). Lincoln, NE: Buros Institute of Mental Measurements.

Smith, L. F. (2003). Review of the Test of Early Reading Ability, Third Edition. In B. S. Plake, J. C. Impara, & R. A. Spies (Eds.), *The fifteenth mental measurements yearbook* (pp. 943–944). Lincoln, NE: Buros Institute of Mental Measurements.

Summary

The *Test of Early Reading Ability–Third Edition* (TERA-3) is an individually administered, norm-referenced instrument measuring alphabet knowledge, print conventions, and meaning for children aged 3-6 through 8-6. Currently, the TERA-3 is the only commercially available instrument that includes a measure of print conventions normed on a large, recent sample of American children. Although the usability of the current version has been improved, the structure and content of the test are very similar to those of previous editions. There is some evidence that the TERA-3 has utility in documenting the progress of low-performing children receiving interventions, but its diagnostic validity is limited by inadequate floors for two of the three subtests below age 5-9. No criterion-related validity data are presented for children in preschool, kindergarten, and first grade, where presumably the test would have its greatest use. Studies evaluating the concurrent and predictive utility of the TERA-3 across the early primary grade range, especially in comparison with other early reading instruments that include nonprint measures, such as phonemic awareness and rapid naming, should be a priority for future validation studies. Comparisons of the performance of normally achieving and at-risk children on the Conventions subtest with their performance on print awareness measures that employ an illustrated book format would also be useful.

Case Example

Name of student: Adrienne C.
Age: 6 years, 4 months
Grade: First grade
Date of assessment: November

Reason for referral: Adrienne was referred for an early reading assessment by her first-grade teacher. Adrienne has a positive attitude toward learning, but she is having difficulty keeping up with the pace of classroom instruction in reading and reading-related skills. Her ability to decode and spell unfamiliar words is limited, and she has trouble learning and remembering sight words. She also has trouble participating effectively in class discussions and often needs directions to be delivered individually.

Assessment results and interpretation: The *Test of Early Reading Ability, Third Edition* (TERA-3) measures three kinds of early reading skills: alphabet knowledge, print conventions, and meaning in print. Average scores for a child's Adrienne's age are as follows: subtest standard score = 10, composite standard score = 100, percentile rank = 50, grade equivalent = 1.3, age equivalent = 6-4. Adrienne's performance on the TERA-3 is described below.

Composite/subtest	Subtest Standard Score	Composite Standard Score	Percentile Rank	Age Equivalent	Grade Equivalent
Reading Quotient	—	79	8	—	—
Alphabet	9	—	37	6-1	1.0
Conventions	7	—	16	5-4	K.2
Meaning	4	—	2	5-1	K.0

Adrienne's overall reading skills are in the poor range (PR = 8) for her age, but she shows significant variability in the skills assessed. On the Alphabet subtest, which measures knowledge of letters and sounds, her performance is rated as average (PR = 37). She was able to identify letters in isolation and within words, to recognize several sight words, and to match words with pictures. On the Conventions subtest, which measures understanding of print conventions, such as book orientation and print directionality, her performance is rated as below average (PR = 16). She had trouble noticing inverted words, indicating the direction of print and the sequence of story pages, and identifying punctuation marks. On the Meaning subtest, which assesses a variety of ways in which children comprehend print, her performance is rated as very poor and falls at the 2nd percentile for her age. She was able to identify several words with accompanying pictures and recognize common food labels, but she had trouble identifying pictured animals, illustrations from fairy tales, and different kinds of printed material, such as road signs and a friendly letter. The difference between her average Alphabet score and her very poor Meaning score is both statistically and clinically significant and indicates that her alphabet knowledge is much better developed than her comprehension skills.

TEXAS PRIMARY READING INVENTORY

Overview

The *Texas Primary Reading Inventory* (TPRI; Foorman et al., 2002) is an early reading instrument designed for children in kindergarten through Grade 2. Developed in 1997 by the Texas Education Agency and revised in 1998 by the Center for Academic and Reading Skills (CARS) at the University of Texas–Houston Health Science Center and the Texas Institute for Measurement, Evaluation, and Statistics (TIMES) at the University of Houston, it is currently administered in more than 95% of Texas schools. Based on longitudinal data from studies sponsored by the

National Institute of Child Health and Human Development (NICHD), the TPRI consists of measures assessing five reading components: (1) phonemic awareness, (2) graphophonemic knowledge, (3) reading accuracy, (4) listening/reading comprehension, and (5) reading fluency. At each grade level, the TPRI consists of two parts: a screener and an inventory. The screener provides a brief assessment to identify students who are not likely to be at risk for the development of reading problems so that additional attention can be focused on children who are having trouble acquiring reading skills. The inventory is administered to all students whose scores fall below benchmarks on the screener, indicating that important reading concepts and skills are still developing. The purposes of the TPRI are (1) to identify children at risk for reading problems in the early primary grades and (2) to provide information to teachers for setting learning objectives and developing instructional plans. Each classroom kit includes a spiral-bound K–2 teacher's guide, a spiral-bound K–2 intervention activities guide, 24 grade-specific student record sheets, a classroom summary form, a magnetic board and set of magnetic lowercase alphabet letters with carrying case, a set of letter and word list task cards, a spiral-bound story booklet (Grades 1 and 2), a stopwatch, and a CD-ROM training module, all packed in a flip-top box. Two additional student record booklets at each of the other two grade levels are also included in each kit. Examiners must provide a short illustrated storybook for the kindergarten Book and Print Awareness warm-up activity, a blank sheet of white paper for the graphophonemic knowledge and word reading tasks, and (if desired) a puppet to support the administration of phoneme blending tasks.

Assessment Tasks

The TPRI includes a set of screeners (termed *screens*), which are designed for administration at the middle and end of kindergarten; the beginning, middle (optional), and end of Grade 1; and the beginning of Grade 2 (see Table 4.21). At each grade level, the screens vary, whereas the inventories are constant to permit progress monitoring up to three times a year. For each screening task, benchmarks are provided to indicate whether or not the examiner should stop screening. The listening and/or reading comprehension portion of the inventory is administered to all students, regardless of their performance on the screen. Moreover, the inventory may be given to all students, regardless of their performance on the screen, if time and resources permit. Most of the inventory measures include several tasks, each of which consists of five items. Table 4.21 displays target grades, administration windows, and components for the TPRI screens and inventories.

Kindergarten Assessment Tasks

The TPRI provides two sets of kindergarten screens, one for the middle and one for the end of the year. The graphophonemic knowledge task is identical at each testing, but the phonemic awareness task involves different sets of stimuli. Children who score below benchmarks on the two screening tasks take eight inventory tasks, following a warm-up activity: five phonemic awareness tasks, two graphophonemic knowledge tasks, and a listening comprehension task. Table 4.22 describes the kindergarten screening and inventory tasks.

TABLE 4.21. TPRI Screening and Inventory Tasks by Grade and Administration Window

Grade	Administration window	Screen	Inventory
Kindergarten	Middle and end of year	Graphophonemic Knowledge Phonemic Awareness	Book and Print Awareness (warm-up activity) Phonemic Awareness Graphophonemic Knowledge Listening Comprehension
Grade 1	Beginning of year	Graphophonemic Knowledge Word Reading Phonemic Awareness	Phonemic Awareness Graphophonemic Knowledge Word List/Passage Placement Reading Accuracy and Fluency (optional) Reading Comprehension
	Middle of year (optional) and end of year	Word Reading Phonemic Awareness	Phonemic Awareness Graphophonemic Knowledge Word List/Passage Placement Reading Accuracy and Fluency (optional) Reading Comprehension
Grade 2	Beginning of year	Word Reading	Graphophonemic Knowledge Word List/Passage Placement Reading Accuracy and Fluency Reading Comprehension
	Middle of year (optional) and end of year		Graphophonemic Knowledge Word List/Passage Placement Reading Accuracy and Fluency Reading Comprehension

TABLE 4.22. Description of TPRI Kindergarten Screening and Inventory Tasks

Task	Description
Graphophonemic Knowledge	This measure consists of one task. For *Letter Sound*, the child identifies first the letter name and then the letter sound for 10 uppercase and 10 lowercase letters. Only letter sounds are scored.
Phonemic Awareness	This measure consists of one task. For *Blending Onset–Rimes and Phonemes*, the child blends individual sounds pronounced by the examiner to form words. Examiners may use a puppet (not provided) to "say" the sounds, if desired.
Book and Print Awareness	In this warm-up activity, the child demonstrates print awareness concepts, such as text directionality and identification of letters, words, and sentences, using a storybook provided by the examiner. Correct responses are recorded, but no score is tallied.
Phonemic Awareness	This measure includes five tasks. For *Rhyming*, the child produces real or nonsense words that rhyme with sets of three words spoken by the examiner. For *Blending Word Parts*, the child blends onset–rimes pronounced by the examiner to form words. For *Blending Phonemes*, the child blends individual phonemes pronounced by the examiner to form words. For *Detecting Initial Sounds*, the child deletes initial sounds from words pronounced by the examiner, and the results form words. For *Detecting Final Sounds*, the child deletes final sounds from words pronounced by the examiner, and the results form words.
Graphophonemic Knowledge	This measure consists of two tasks. For *Letter Name Identification*, the child identifies all 26 letters of the alphabet randomly ordered and presented in both uppercase and lowercase on a task card. For *Letter to Sound Linking*, the child identifies the initial sound in a word and then points to the letter making that sound from a set of three letters.
Listening Comprehension	The child answers five comprehension questions about a story read by the examiner. Two alternative passages each are provided for mid-year and end-of-year testing.

Note. Screening tasks are shaded.

Grade 1 Assessment Tasks

The Grade 1 screen consists of three measures: a graphophonemic knowledge task, a word reading task, and a phonemic awareness task. The beginning-of-year graphophonemic knowledge task is identical to that on the kindergarten form, whereas the phonemic awareness and word reading tasks involve different sets of stimuli at the two administration windows. Children who score below benchmarks on the screen take the inventory, which includes 12 tasks: 4 phonemic awareness tasks, 5 graphophonemic knowledge tasks, a word list to determine placement in one of five reading passages, and 2 reading accuracy, fluency, and comprehension tasks, yielding 3 scores (see Table 4.23).

TABLE 4.23. Description of TPRI Grade 1 Screening and Inventory Tasks

Task	Description
Graphophonemic Knowledge	This measure consists of one task. For *Letter Sound*, the child identifies first the letter name and then the letter sound for 10 uppercase and 10 lowercase letters. Only letter sounds are scored.
Word Reading	The child reads a list of eight words.
Phonemic Awareness	This measure consists of one task. For *Blending Word Parts/Phonemes*, the child blends three to six phonemes pronounced by the examiner to form words.
Phonemic Awareness	This measure consists of four tasks. For *Blending Word Parts*, the child blends onset–rimes and phonemes pronounced by the examiner to form words. For *Blending Phonemes*, the child blends three to five phonemes pronounced by the examiner to form words. For *Detecting Initial Sounds*, the child deletes initial sounds from words pronounced by the examiner, and the results form words. For *Detecting Final Sounds*, the child deletes final sounds from words pronounced by the examiner, and the results form words.
Graphophonemic Knowledge	This measure consists of five tasks. For each task, the child uses magnetic letters on a magnetic task board to create words. For *Initial Consonant Substitution*, the child makes words based on a rime. For *Final Consonant Substitution*, the child makes words by adding a final consonant to a two-letter combination. For *Middle Vowel Substitution*, the child makes words by adding a medial vowel to an initial- and final-letter combination. For *Initial Blending Substitution*, the child makes words by adding two-letter consonant blends to a set of two-letter rimes. For *Blends in Final Position*, the child makes words by adding two-letter consonant blends to consonant–vowel onsets.
Word List/ Passage Placement	The child reads a list of 15 words. Based on the child's performance on the list, one of five stories is administered to assess reading accuracy, reading fluency (optional), and reading comprehension.
Reading Accuracy, Fluency, and Comprehension	This measure consists of two tasks, which yield two separate scores (three, if *Reading Fluency* is calculated). *Reading Accuracy* requires the child to read aloud a passage presented in the story booklet. Both narrative and expository passages are included. The number of words miscalled is used to determine a reading accuracy level (frustrational, instructional, or independent). For *Reading Comprehension*, the child answers five questions about the passage. If the child reads at the frustrational level for Stories 2, 3, or 4, the examiner moves down a level to an easier story. If the child miscalls three or more words in the first sentence or scores at the frustrational level on Story 1, the examiner administers it as a listening comprehension measure. For *Reading Fluency*, the examiner calculates the number of words read correctly per minute.

Note. Screening tasks are shaded.

Grade 2 Assessment Tasks

The Grade 2 screen consists of a word recognition task. The Grade 2 inventory consists of four graphophonemic measures; a word list to determine placement in one of five reading passages; and two reading accuracy, fluency, and comprehension tasks, yielding three scores (see Table 4.24). All of the graphophonemic tasks can be administered in a group setting.

Administration

As Table 4.21 indicates, TPRI administration windows differ in several respects from those of the other large-scale early reading assessment batteries reviewed in this text. First, kindergarten screening is delayed until the middle of the year to permit children to acclimate to the school environment. Second, no screening is provided at the end of Grade 2 because, according to the test's authors, the beginning-of-year screen has sufficiently high predictive accuracy. That is, children who fail to meet the benchmarks for the Grade 2 screen are very likely to require intensive intervention. At all three grade levels, the screens are intended to be administered individually in a single session, with all students in a classroom screened within 1–2 weeks. The inventory may be spread out over several sessions. All of the tasks except Grade 2 Graphophonemic Knowledge must be individually administered. Across the three grades, the screening portion takes 5–7 minutes at each window, and the inventory portion takes about 20 minutes. Administration procedures are clearly described in the manual, but neither the task cards nor the record booklet includes task directions. As a result, examiners must consult the manual throughout the administration process until they are thoroughly familiar with the instrument. Items on the Graphophonemic Knowledge and Word Reading tasks are presented one at a time, using a blank sheet of paper to cover the remaining items.

TABLE 4.24. Description of TPRI Grade 2 Screening and Inventory Tasks

Task	Description
Word Reading	The child reads a list of eight words.
Graphophonemic Knowledge	This measure consists of four five-item tasks assessing different spelling patterns: *CVC, CVCe, R-controlled Vowels, and Blends; Long Vowels, Digraphs, and Orthographic Patterns; Blends, Digraphs, Compounds, Past Tense, Homophones, and Orthographic Patterns; Plural, Digraphs, Blends, Consonant Doubling, Past Tense, Inflectional Endings, and Changing* y *to* i.
Word List/Passage Placement	The child reads a list of 15 words. Based on the child's performance on the list, the examiner administers one of four stories to assess reading accuracy, reading fluency, and reading comprehension.
Reading Accuracy, Fluency, and Comprehension	This measure consists of two tasks, which yield three separate scores. *Reading Accuracy* requires the child to read aloud a passage in the story booklet. Both narrative and expository passages are included. The number of words miscalled is used to determine a reading accuracy level (frustrational, instructional, or independent). If the child scores at the frustrational level on Stories 2–4, the examiner drops down a story. If the child scores at the frustrational level on Story 1, the examiner administers the Grade 1 word list to determine story placement and then administers that passage. For *Reading Comprehension*, the child answers five questions about the passage. For *Reading Fluency*, the examiner calculates the number of words read correctly per minute.

Note. The screening task is shaded.

Scores

The TPRI is criterion-referenced and yields only raw scores. Scoring is dichotomous for all tasks with the exception of Reading Accuracy. For Reading Accuracy, five types of errors are recorded: (1) mispronunciations, (2) substitutions, (3) omissions, (4) reversals, and (5) hesitations of more than 3 seconds, after which the examiner provides the correct word. Insertions, self-corrections, and repetitions are not counted as errors. Passages are reproduced in the record booklet, and words not read correctly are marked with a slash, regardless of error type. Although this simplifies scoring and enhances interrater reliability, it also reduces the amount of information available for instructional planning. The number of errors is compared to passage-specific criteria to determine percent accuracy and functional reading level (frustrational, instructional, or independent). The record booklet indicates the number of miscalled words per passage for each level so that examiners do not have to perform this calculation and includes a formula for calculating reading rate.

Interpretation

For each screening and for most inventory tasks, scores are evaluated against statewide benchmarks. For example, a score of 5 or more words read correctly on the 8-item Grade 2 screen indicates that the child is *not* at risk and that the examiner should administer only the reading passages from the inventory section. For inventory tasks, concepts are rated in terms of mastery or nonmastery ("developed" or "still developing"). Concepts are considered "developed" when the child answers 4 of 5 items correctly on a task (3 of 5 items on kindergarten Book and Print Awareness). Benchmarks for reading accuracy correspond to functional reading levels, defined as follows: (1) frustrational (less than 90% accuracy), (2) instructional (90% to 94% accuracy), and (3) independent (95% accuracy and above). The goal for reading rate at the end of Grade 1 is set at 60 WCPM, with 40 WCPM or fewer indicating the need for additional interventions. For Grade 2, the goal for end-of-year reading rate is set at 90 WCPM, with 60 WCPM or fewer indicating a need for additional help. Children reading 10 WCPM or fewer are considered nonfluent and in need of intensive assistance. No benchmarks are provided for listening comprehension or reading comprehension tasks.

Technical Adequacy

Information on technical adequacy is taken from a series of technical reports posted on the TPRI Web site (http://www.tpri.org), including the technical manual for the 1998 edition of the TPRI (Foorman et al., 2000), an executive summary for the 1998 TPRI (Foorman, Fletcher, et al., 1998), and a technical report for the 1998–1999 edition (CARS & TIMES, 2002).

Test Development

The five sets of screening measures are based on a set of reading predictors that were validated in a longitudinal study conducted in 1992–1996 in Houston, Texas, through an NICHD grant. The sample consisted of 945 children in Grades K–3 who were randomly selected from regular education programs at three elementary schools and included four ethnic groups (African Americans, Asians, Caucasians, and Hispanics) and approximately equal numbers of boys and girls. Children with severe emotional problems, uncorrected vision problems, hearing loss, acquired neurological disorders, or classification at the lowest level of English as a second language were excluded. The technical manual reports demographic characteristics for kindergarten children in terms of free-lunch status, ethnicity, and SES, and states that Grades 1 and 2 characteristics were similar. Participants were evaluated four times yearly for 1–3 years, with additional norm-referenced achievement tests administered at the end of Grades 1 and 2. Screening tasks were drawn from a broad array of instruments, including five intelligence/achievement batteries, nine measures of reading and reading-related skills, and six behavioral and environmental measures. From these instruments, the smallest subset of measures with the best predictive validity relative to reading outcomes at the end of Grade 1 and 2 was used to create the five screens. The WJ-R Basic Reading cluster for kindergarten end-of-year performance and WJ-R Broad Reading cluster for first and second graders served as criterion measures. Risk status was defined as 6 months below grade level, which represented a reading grade equivalent (GE) of 1.4 or lower (the 18th percentile [PR] for Broad Reading and the 22nd percentile for Basic Reading) for first graders and a GE of 2.4 or lower (PR = ≤ 35) for second graders. The cutpoint was set higher in Grade 2 because the prediction equations were more stable and because children have less time to be brought up to the goal of having all students reading on grade level by the end of Grade 3.

At the kindergarten level, screening cutoff scores were designed to keep false negative error rates below 10% while maintaining the lowest possible false positive error rate. In other words, the kindergarten TPRI cutoff is intended to overidentify children who may be at risk for reading difficulties. Screening windows were selected to occur at multiple points to reduce false positive errors reflecting limited exposure to English literacy-related activities for children from culturally and linguistically diverse backgrounds. For a sample of 421 students, final cut points for December produced a false positive rate of 44% and false negative rate of 5% for end of Grade 1 WJ-R Basic Reading, and those for April produced a false positive rate of 38% and false negative rate of 10%. Grade 1 and Grade 2 screens were developed in a similar manner.

Reliability Evidence

In May 1998, CARS and TIMES conducted a field study to assess the reliability and validity of the TPRI with 32 teachers, 128 kindergarten students, and 144 first graders in four elementary schools. Students took the screen and inventory portions on two separate occasions, with tasks administered by two different teachers within a 1-week interval. Classical test theory and generalizability theory approaches were used to evaluate the reliability of the screening and inventory tasks for all of the screening windows except for midyear kindergarten. For the kindergarten end-of-year assessment, median Cronbach's alpha coefficients were .92 for the screen and .87 for the inventory. Median generalizability coefficients were .76 and 70 for the screen and inventory, respectively. For the Grade 1 beginning-of-year assessment, internal consistency coefficients were .86 and .79 for the screen and inventory, respectively, whereas median generalizability coefficients were .86 and .68. Median alpha coefficients for the end-of-year Grade 1 form were .81 and .66 for the screen and inventory, respectively, with median generalizability coefficients at .77 and .81. For the

Grade 2 beginning-of-year assessment, median internal consistency coefficients were .91 and .67 for the screen and inventory, whereas median generalizability coefficients were .88 and .76.

For kindergarten measures, median test–retest coefficients were .87 and .60 for the screen and inventory, respectively, whereas beginning-of-year Grade 1 median stability coefficients were .76 and .54. Stability coefficients for the end-of-year Grade 1 screening measures were .93 for Word Reading and .51 for Blending Phonemes, with a median stability estimate of .42 for the inventory tasks. Test–retest median reliability for Grade 2 tasks was .90 for the Word Reading screening measure and .65 for the inventory tasks. Book and Print Awareness, Phonemic Awareness, and Comprehension tasks were less stable than other measures across all three levels.

Interscorer reliability for samples ranging from 6 to 62 students was evaluated using two procedures for evaluating agreement: a difficulty index (percentage of students scoring at or above the mastery criterion on both testing occasions) and the kappa index. Difficulty indices were within a few percentage points for kindergarten measures but varied considerably over the two sets of examiners for some Grade 1 and 2 screening and inventory tasks, in part because of small sample sizes and ceiling effects. Kappa coefficients for end-of-year kindergarten screening tasks ranged from .93 for Letter Name Identification to .61 for Blending Phonemes, whereas values for inventory tasks were highly variable (.13 to .84), with 2 of the 12 values at or above .80). For the beginning-of-year Grade 1 form, kappa coefficients for screening tasks ranged from 1.00 for Word Reading to .35 for Blending Phonemes, whereas kappas for the inventory tasks ranged from –.09 to .60. For the end-of-year Grade 1 form, kappa values were .69 for Word Reading and .87 for Blending Phonemes. Kappa coefficients for inventory tasks were again highly variable (0 to 1.0), with values for all but 1 of the 11 coefficients falling below .80. For the beginning-of-year Grade 2 form, the Word Reading kappa coefficient was .69, whereas inventory kappa values ranged from -0.2 to 1.0, with 9 of the 11 values falling below .80.

Based on these results, the TPRI was revised, and a statewide implementation study was conducted in 1998–1999 with a sample of over 4,500 children in 299 classrooms and 52 schools drawn from 14 school districts. The sample included four types of districts (two urban, one suburban, two small city, and nine rural districts); approximately equal numbers of boys and girls; and over 900 African American students, over 700 Hispanic students, and over 2,000 Caucasian students. Coefficient alphas for the middle and end-of-year kindergarten screens ranged from .88 to .91, whereas alphas for inventory tasks were above .90 for Letter Name Identification and end-of-year Detecting Final Sounds; in the .80s for Rhyming, Detecting Initial Sounds, and midyear Letter to Sound Linking: Letter Sound; and in the .70s for Blending Word Parts, midyear Letter to Sound Linking: Letter Identification, and end-of-year Letter to Sound Linking: Letter Sound. Alphas for the remaining tasks ranged from .43 to .69, with Book and Print Awareness and the Comprehension tasks the least reliable.

For Grade 1 measures, alpha reliabilities for the beginning and end-of-year screens were in the .80s for all of the tasks except end-of-year Blending Phonemes (.77). Coefficient alphas for inventory tasks were in the .80s for Rhyming, Detecting Initial Sounds, Detecting Final Sounds, Initial Consonant Substitution, and beginning-of-year Initial Blend Substitution and Final Blend Substitution. Alphas fell in the .70s for beginning-of-year Blending Word Parts, Final Consonant Substitution, Medial Vowel Substitution, and end-of-year Final Blend Substitution. Coefficients for Book and Print Awareness and Comprehension tasks ranged from .45 to .69. For the

Grade 2 form, the coefficient alpha for the beginning-of-year screen (Word Reading) was .85. Coefficient alphas for inventory tasks were lower than for kindergarten and first-grade tasks, with values falling at acceptable levels for only two tasks–beginning-of-year Initial Consonant Substitution (.81) and Comprehension (.82). Values for Initial Blend Substitution, beginning-of-year Final Blend Substitution, and beginning-of-year Spelling of Long Vowels were in the .70s, whereas values for the remaining tasks were in the .50s and .60s.

Alphas reported separately by ethnicity were generally similar to the overall estimates, with the highest reliability for the screens and the lowest reliability for Book and Print Awareness and most of the stories. Compared with kindergarten and Grade 1 forms, Grade 2 tasks showed more variability in reliability estimates across ethnicity and gender groups. As the test's authors observe, differences may have resulted from the small number of items per task and low sample sizes for some of the analyses, and no patterns indicating systematic bias were evident.

Validity Evidence

CONTENT VALIDITY EVIDENCE

Item development followed a five-step process. First, items were drawn from item pools known to measure the five content domains assessed by the TPRI and were evaluated using IRT methods, with selection based on difficulty and discrimination parameters. Second, IRT-derived information was used to generate new items to provide a broad range of difficulty while discriminating maximally at the designated cut points. Third, reading experts reviewed items and provided suggestions. Fourth, items were aligned with the Texas Essential Knowledge and Skills guidelines, and fifth, items were refined and placed in the TPRI. The final set of items was then field-tested with the same sample of 272 students who participated in the reliability study described above. The technical manual reports item difficulty ranges for each item on each task for four of the five screening forms (except midyear kindergarten) for the 1998–1999 TPRI. The technical manual also includes a rationale for item and format selection for each domain. IRT-based DIF analyses were conducted in the 1998–1999 implementation study described above. Gender and ethnic comparisons (whites vs. African Americans, whites vs. Hispanics) indicated an overall DIF rate of less than 5% for each analysis and no consistent pattern of bias.

For the 2001–2002 TPRI, new reading passages were created by a writer of children's stories to reflect grade-specific word-level features. A list of the word-level features used for each grade level is provided on the TPRI Web site. In second grade, expository passages were also included that conform to informational text structure. Levels of difficulty were verified using readability formulae. The new stories were tested in 1999–2000 with more than 3,000 students across Texas and then arranged to reflect student performance, with the easiest stories placed first. Word lists were then developed to predict which story is the most likely to represent a student's instructional level for passage reading.

CRITERION-RELATED VALIDITY EVIDENCE

Concurrent validity was assessed by correlating student performance on teacher-administered TPRI tasks and reading and reading-related measures administered by trained assessment individuals as part of a larger NICHD-supported study initiated in

1997. Measures varied across grades, but included letter name and sound tasks; subtests from the *Comprehensive Test of Phonological Processing*; RAN-Letters and RAN-Objects from the *Rapid Automatized Naming* procedure (Denckla & Rudel, 1976b); the PPVT-R; WJ-R Letter–Word Identification, Word Attack, and Passage Comprehension; *Gray Oral Reading Tests–3* Rate, Accuracy, and Comprehension; and *Kaufman Test of Educational Achievement* Spelling. Correlations among TPRI tasks and related criterion measures were generally statistically significant and in the expected direction, although Book and Print Awareness, Rhyming, and some of the comprehension stories were only weakly correlated with criterion measures.

As evidence of predictive validity, the technical manual presents classification accuracy tables for preliminary and final cut points for each of the five screening windows for samples ranging from 376 to 599 students. Across the three grades, false positive rates for final cut scores ranged from a high of 44% for end-of-Grade 1 WJ-R Basic Reading with the midyear kindergarten screen as the predictor to a low of 15% for end-of-Grade 2 WJ-R Broad Reading, with the beginning-of-year Grade 2 screen as the predictor. False negative rates were uniformly low (5% to 9%). Screens were also analyzed at each grade level to determine whether identifications based on the cut points differed among the four ethnic groups in the sample (African Americans, Asians, Caucasians, and Hispanics). For both kindergarten screening windows, there was a significant interaction for ethnicity, with classification of risk status more accurate for Hispanic and African American than for Caucasian students. For Grades 1 and 2, prediction equations did not yield significantly different identification rates for any of the groups.

CONSTRUCT VALIDITY EVIDENCE

Construct validity evidence presented in the technical manual includes an analysis of the relationship of the TPRI screening and inventory tasks to the reading and reading-related predictor and criterion measures described above. In general, the TPRI tasks appear to be measuring the same construct as the norm-referenced and criterion-referenced instruments from which they are derived, although no factorial analyses or theoretical models are presented. Item–total score correlations reported for each task at four of the five screening windows range widely, even within a single task at a single screening window. No other evidence of construct validity is reported.

Usability

The TPRI test materials for examiners and students alike are attractive, and record booklets are color-coded by grade and formatted for readability, although examiners must refer to the teacher's guide for task directions. Supports for examiners, many of them Web-based, are extensive and extremely well done. The CD-ROM training module included in the test kit and available on the Web site is a model for the field. Designed to guide teachers through the assessment process and provide practice on various TPRI tasks, it includes audios of teachers administering the TPRI, including the phonemic awareness items; audios of children reading stories for practice in marking errors and timing; and videos of administrations with students at each of the three grade levels, which illustrate common errors and include checklists for "rating the rater." The teacher's guide includes a list of allowable test accommodations, such as translating oral directions into the native language of students with limited English proficiency. A Spanish version of the TPRI for kindergarten and first graders is available: *El Inventario de Lectura en Espanol de Tejas* (Tejas LEE). The authors are in the process of developing the TPRI Web site to accommodate Web-based data entry and a data collection system for personal digital assistants.

Links to Intervention

The TPRI provides a wealth of high-quality resources for linking assessment results to evidence-based interventions. The Intervention Activities Guide included in each assessment kit and available on the TPRI Web site provides a set of attractively formatted, easy-to-follow instructional activities for each of the TPRI assessment domains. Also included is a guide to differentiated instruction for at-risk students, sample lessons for small-group instruction, and guidelines for vocabulary instruction. Among the many useful resources on the CD-ROM training module is a section entitled "Making Instructional Decisions," which includes a model for diagnosis, four case studies, and examples of diagnostic decision making based on TPRI results. The case studies, consisting of one kindergarten, one first-grade, and two second-grade examples, include descriptions of the students' background and classroom performance, interpretation of screening and inventory results, and instructional implications. Also available are downloadable examples of parent letters that provide information about results for the various screening windows; printable pages for setting instructional objectives and developing lesson plans; and links to the CARS Web site (http://www.cars.uth.tmc.edu) and other reading-related sites.

Relevant Research

The TPRI is based on a longitudinal NICHD-supported database of reading and reading-related skills, and reliability and validity studies are ongoing. A recent article by Fletcher, Foorman, and Boudousquie (2002) includes a readable overview of the development of the TPRI, the use of IRT-based procedures in test construction, and the process of setting cut points to maximize predictive accuracy on screening measures.

Source and Cost

The TPRI and *Tejas Lee* are free of charge to Texas schools and are available for out-of-state users at the Texas Reading Instruments Web site (http://www.txreadinginstruments.com) for $225.00 per kit, plus shipping and handing.

Summary

The *Texas Primary Reading Inventory* (TPRI) is an early reading assessment battery for students in kindergarten through Grade 2 that serves as the Texas statewide screening instrument. Developed by a leading team of researchers and based on state-of-the-art test construction practices, the TPRI combines high predictive accuracy with outstanding usability. The TPRI is a cost-effective choice for out-of-state users and earns high marks in terms of ease of administration, scoring, and interpretation; examiner supports; and links to interventions. Despite its general technical excellence, most of the currently available reliability estimates are based on small samples, and reliability falls below acceptable levels for numerous inventory tasks, especially on the Grade 2 form. Moreover, the TPRI offers fewer and later screening windows than other large-scale screening measures, with the first kindergarten screening at the midyear point, which is likely to delay the provision of interventions to some at-risk children. All-or-nothing rather than feature-specific scoring also reduces the sensitivity of the spelling tasks to individual differences and small changes in performance, and benchmarks are not yet available for listening and reading comprehension measures. Like other state-sponsored early reading instruments, the TPRI continues to undergo refinements and revisions in content, implementation, and instructional linkages based on statewide results and teacher feedback. A Grade 3 assessment is under development and will be implemented in the 2004–2005 school year.

Case Example

Name of student: Luis K.
Age: 7 years, 9 months
Grade: Second grade
Date of assessment: October

Reason for assessment: The *Texas Primary Reading Inventory* (TPRI) was administered to Luis as part of the schoolwide early reading screening program. Luis tries hard in class, but his teacher notes that he is performing far below most of his classmates on reading and reading-related tasks.

Assessment results and interpretation: The TPRI is an early reading assessment that includes measures of graphophonemic awareness; phonemic awareness; word identification; spelling; and reading accuracy, comprehension, and fluency at the second-grade level. Student performance is evaluated against fall and spring *benchmarks*, which are levels of literacy development that children should reach by specific times in the early primary grade years. At each grade, the TPRI includes a set of brief screening tasks and a set of more comprehensive inventory tasks. Children who score below benchmarks on the screener take the inventory tasks. Luis's scores on the TPRI tasks, benchmarks for beginning-of-Grade 2 performance, and descriptive ratings are presented below.

Task	Luis's Score	Benchmark	Rating
Word Reading	3/8 correct	5 or more correct	Still developing
CVC, CVC*e*, *R*-Controlled Vowels, and Blends	3/5 correct	4 or more correct	Still developing
Long Vowels, Digraphs, and Orthographic Patterns	5/5 correct	4 or more correct	Developed
Blends, Digraphs, Compounds, Past Tense, Homophones, and Orthographic Patterns	3/5 correct	4 or more correct	Still developing
Plural, Digraphs, Blends, Consonant Doubling, Past Tense, Inflectional Endings, and Changing *y* to *i*	2/5 correct	4 or more correct	Still developing
Word List/Passage Placement	6/15 correct	Placed in Story 3	
Reading Accuracy	10 errors out of 172 words (94% accuracy)	≥90% accuracy	Instructional
Reading Fluency (words read correctly per minute [WCPM])	67 WCPM	90 WCPM by the end of Grade 2	–
Reading Comprehension	3/5 correct	Qualitative information	

Note. The screening task is shaded.

On the screening section of the inventory, Luis's Word Reading score falls below benchmarks for the beginning of second grade (3/8 vs. 5/8 words correct). As a result, the inventory tasks were administered. On three of four tasks that required him to spell words containing various phonics features, Luis's performance is rated as Still Developing. He was able to spell a set of words with long vowels, digraphs, and *y* endings, but he had difficulty representing other orthographic (spelling) patterns, including *r*-controlled vowels (*from* for *farm*), consonant–vowel–consonant–silent *e* words (*glod* for *globe*), and past tense with consonant doubling (*caled* for *called*).

Luis's word recognition and textual reading skills are somewhat better developed than his spelling skills. On the Word List/Passage Placement task, which is administered to determine which of several stories the child reads, he was able to read 6 of the 15 words correctly. On the reading passage, he was able to decode 94% of the words accurately, earning a reading accuracy score in the instructional range. He tended to guess when he came to unfamiliar words, based on the first letter of the word (*angry* for *arguing*). His reading fluency rate appears to be on track for the end-of-Grade 2 benchmark (67 WCPM vs. 90 WCPM), but he was able to answer only three of five comprehension questions (two explicit, one implicit) about what he had read.

chapter 5

Measures of Reading Components

This chapter reviews 31 measures assessing the 10 components described in Chapter 3. Although they measure many of the same skills as the early literacy batteries described in Chapter 4, they are quite diverse, ranging from nonstandardized single-skill measures taken from the literature to commercially published, norm-referenced multiskill reading instruments and multisubject assessment systems. Reviews of the single-skill measures are grouped by component, and the 10 components are presented in the same order as they appear in Chapter 3. The multiskill reading measures and multisubject batteries are then reviewed.

Measures of Phonological Processing

This section reviews 12 measures of phonological processing, including 6 norm-referenced tests and 6 nonstandardized measures. Four of the measures are variations of a single measure from the literature, the *Auditory Analysis Test*, and are discussed as a group under that heading.

AUDITORY ANALYSIS TEST (FOUR VERSIONS)

Overview

The *Auditory Analysis Test* (AAT; Rosner & Simon, 1971) is a brief, nonstandardized, individually administered measure of children's ability to delete syllables and phonemes from spoken words. Sound deletion tasks are among the best predictors of reading acquisition and reading disabilities and can be used with preliterate children (e.g., Badian, 1995; Manis, Seidenberg, & Doi, 1999; Torgesen, Wagner, & Rashotte, 1994; Yopp, 1988). Although the AAT was originally designed for children in kindergarten through Grade 6, researchers have developed several downward extensions with additional items for early primary grade examinees. This review describes four versions of the AAT: (1) the original AAT; (2) the commercially published *Test of Auditory Analysis Skills* (TAAS; Rosner, 1975/1979) for children in kindergarten through Grade 3; (3) the *Berninger Modification of the AAT* (B-AAT; Berninger, 1986; Berninger, Thalberg, DeBruyn, & Smith, 1987) for children in kindergarten through Grade 2; and (4) the *Catts Deletion Test* (CDT; Catts, 1993; Catts, Fey, Zhang, & Tomblin, 2001; Swank & Catts, 1994) for kindergartners. Materials for the TAAS consist of a tear-off pad with 50 single-sheet test forms. The other AAT versions appear in the original articles and are presented with minor adaptations in Figures 5.1 through 5.3. For all four versions, the examiner must provide two or three picture plates or line drawings to demonstrate the nature of the task.

Assessment Task

For all four AAT versions, the assessment task consists of syllable deletion (e.g., "Say *cowboy* without saying *cow*") and/or phoneme deletion (e.g., "Say *gate* without /g/"). The original AAT consists of 40 words ranging in length from one to four syllables. The items are arranged in order of difficulty according to seven task categories: (1) deletion of the final syllable of a two-syllable word (1 item); (2) deletion of the initial syllable of a two-syllable word (1 item); (3) deletion of the final consonant of a one-syllable word (6 items); (4) deletion of the initial consonant of a one-syllable word (6 items); (5) deletion of the first one or two consonants of a consonant cluster (8 items); (6) deletion of a medial consonant (8 items); and (7) deletion of a medial phoneme or syllable (10 items).

The TAAS consists of 13 items, 2 from the AAT and 11 new items. Item types are organized by four grade levels as follows: kindergarten, syllable deletion (3 items); Grade 1, initial and final consonant deletion (6 items); Grade 2, deletion of the initial consonant from a consonant cluster (2 items); Grade 3, deletion of the second consonant from a consonant cluster (2 items). The B-AAT includes a total of 30 items, organized into three sets of 10 items each for kindergarten, first grade, and second grade. The tasks consist of initial and final syllable deletion at the kindergarten level, initial and final single phoneme deletion at the first-grade level, and initial and final deletion of blends and digraphs at the second-grade level. The CDT consists of 21 items, including 13 initial syllable deletions and 8 single phoneme deletions. There are several minor variations in the CDT across the articles in which it appears in terms of items, item order, error feedback procedures, and ceiling rules. The most recent version of the CDT (Catts et al., 2001) is described below.

Administration

The AAT and its adaptations take about 3–8 minutes to administer. A single examiner can test a classroom of 25 students in 60–90 minutes, depending on the version selected. The examiner pronounces the stimulus word and asks the child to repeat the word and then to say it again without a specific sound (e.g., "Say *coat* without

AUDITORY ANALYSIS TEST

Directions: Show the child the top half of a sheet of 8½- x 11-inch paper on which pictures of a cow and a boy's head have been drawn side by side. Say to the child, "Say *cowboy*." Then cover the picture of the boy and say, "Now say it again, but without *boy*." If the child's response is correct (*cow*), expose the bottom half of the sheet with drawings of a tooth and a brush, and say, "Say *toothbrush*." Then cover the picture of the tooth and say, "Now say it again, but without *tooth*." If the child fails either trial item, teach the task by repeating the procedures. After the practice items, ask the child to say each test item after deleting the portion that is in parentheses. Be sure to pronounce the sound, not the letter names to be omitted. If the child fails to respond to an item, repeat it. If there is still no response, score the item as incorrect and present the next item. Discontinue testing after four consecutive errors.

Practice items:

A. cow(boy) ____________

B. (tooth)brush ____________

1. birth(day) ____________
2. (car)pet ____________
3. bel(t) ____________
4. (m)an ____________
5. (b)lock ____________
6. to(ne) ____________
7. (s)our ____________
8. (p)ray ____________
9. stea(k) ____________
10. (l)end ____________
11. (s)mile ____________
12. plea(se) ____________
13. (g)ate ____________
14. (c)lip ____________
15. ti(me) ____________
16. (sc)old ____________
17. (b)reak ____________
18. ro(de) ____________
19. (w)ill ____________
20. (t)rail ____________
21. (sh)rug ____________
22. g(l)ow ____________
23. cr(e)ate ____________
24. (st)rain ____________
25. s(m)ell ____________
26. Es(ki)mo ____________
27. de(s)k ____________
28. Ger(ma)ny ____________
29. st(r)eam ____________
30. auto(mo)bile ____________
31. re(pro)duce ____________
32. s(m)ack ____________
33. phi(lo)sophy ____________
34. s(k)in ____________
35. lo(ca)tion ____________
36. cont(in)ent ____________
37. s(w)ing ____________
38. car(pen)ter ____________
39. c(l)utter ____________
40. off(er)ing ____________

Score: __/40

FIGURE 5.1. Auditory Analysis Test (AAT). From "The Auditory Analysis Test: An Initial Report," by J. Rosner and D. P. Simon, 1971, *Journal of Learning Disabilities*, *4*, p. 42. Copyright 1971 by PRO-ED, Inc. Adapted with permission.

BERNINGER MODIFICATION OF THE AUDITORY ANALYSIS TEST

Directions: Show the child the top half of a sheet of 8½- x 11-inch paper on which pictures of a cow and a boy's head have been drawn side by side. Say to the child, "Say *cowboy.*" Then cover the picture of the boy and say, "Now say it again, but without *boy.*" If the child's response is correct (*cow*), expose the bottom half of the sheet with drawings of a tooth and a brush, and say, "Say *toothbrush.*" If the response is correct, say, "Say it again, but without *tooth.*" If the child fails either trial item, teach the task by repeating the procedures. After the practice items, ask the child to say each test item after deleting the portion that is in parentheses. Be sure to pronounce the sound, not the letter names to be omitted. If the child fails to respond to an item, repeat it. If there is still no response, score the item as incorrect and present the next item. Discontinue testing after four consecutive errors.

Practice items:

A. cow(boy) ______________

B. (tooth)brush ______________

Kindergarten Level

1. base(ball)	______________	6. pic(nic)	______________
2. (cow)boy	______________	7. morn(ing)	______________
3. (sun)shine	______________	8. see(saw)	______________
4. (pa)per	______________	9. bun(ny)	______________
5. (cu)cumber	______________	10. farm(er)	______________

Score: __/10

First-Grade Level

1. (c)oat	______________	6. ga(me)	______________
2. (m)eat	______________	7. (m)ake	______________
3. (p)et	______________	8. wro(te)	______________
4. (b)all	______________	9. plea(se)	______________
5. (t)ake	______________	10. farm(er)	______________

Score: __/10

Second-Grade Level

1. (c)lap	______________	6. (ch)ew	______________
2. (p)lay	______________	7. tea(ch)	______________
3. s(t)ale	______________	8. s(tr)ing	______________
4. s(m)ack	______________	9. (g)row	______________
5. (sh)oes	______________	10. tra(sh)	______________

Score: __/10

FIGURE 5.2. Berninger Modification of the Auditory Analysis Test (B-AAT). From "Preventing Reading Disabilities by Assessing and Remediating Phonemic Skills," by V. W. Berninger, S. P. Thalberg, I. DeBruyn, & R. Smith, 1987, *School Psychology Review, 16,* p. 565. Copyright 1987 by the National Association of School Psychologists. Adapted with permission.

CATTS DELETION TEST

Directions: Show the child a picture of a cow and a boy's head, and ask the child, "Say *cow-boy.*" After the child responds, cover the picture of the cow and say, "Now say it again, but without the *cow.*" If the child's response is correct (*boy*), repeat the procedure with a picture of a tooth and a brush (*toothbrush*) and a picture of a cup and a cake (*cupcake*). If the child fails a practice item, provide the appropriate response. After the practice items, ask the child to say each test item after deleting the portion that is in parentheses. Discontinue testing after six consecutive errors.

Practice items:

A. (cow)boy ______________

B. (tooth)brush ______________

C. (cup)cake ______________

1. (base)ball	______________	11. (ba)by	______________
2. (hair)cut	______________	12. (per)son	______________
3. (Sun)day	______________	13. (mon)key	______________
4. (rail)road	______________	14. (f)at	______________
5. (some)time	______________	15. (s)eat	______________
6. (re)turn	______________	16. (sh)out	______________
7. (a)round	______________	17. (t)all	______________
8. (mo)tel	______________	18. (d)oor	______________
9. (al)most	______________	19. (f)ew	______________
10. (help)ful	______________	20. (sn)ail	______________
		21. (th)read	______________

Score: __/21

FIGURE 5.3. Catts Deletion Test (CDT). From "Estimating the Risk of Future Reading Difficulties in Kindergarten Children: A Research-Based Model and Its Clinical Implementation," by H. W. Catts, M. E. Fey, X. Zhang, and J. B. Tomblin, 2001, *Language, Speech, and Hearing Services in Schools*, *32*, p. 49. Copyright 2001 by the American Speech–Language–Hearing Association. Adapted with permission.

/c/"). Discontinue rules vary among the four measures. On the AAT, TAAS, and B-AAT, each of which have two syllable-deletion demonstration items, the test is discontinued if the child fails both items, and a score of 0 is assigned. The CDT provides three syllable-deletion teaching items, but there are no discontinue rules based on performance on the practice items. Testing is discontinued after two consecutive errors on the TAAS, after four consecutive errors on the AAT and B-AAT, and after six consecutive errors on the CDT.

Scores

For all AAT versions, items are scored as correct or incorrect to yield a total raw score.

TABLE 5.1. AAT Spring Mean Scores and Standard Deviations by Grade

Grade	*n*	Mean	*SD*
Kindergarten	50	3.5	3.5
Grade 1	53	17.6	8.4
Grade 2	41	19.9	9.3
Grade 3	37	25.1	8.5
Grade 4	29	25.7	7.9
Grade 5	35	28.1	7.6
Grade 6	39	29.9	6.9

Note. Total items = 40. From "The Auditory Analysis Test: An Initial Report," by J. Rosner and D. P. Simon, 1971, *Journal of Learning Disabilities, 4,* p. 42. Copyright 1971 by PRO-ED, Inc. Adapted with permission.

Interpretation

For the AAT, B-AAT, and CDT, only raw scores and research norms are available. On the 13-item TAAS, raw scores are converted to one of four grade-level equivalencies by using the chart on the record sheet. Scores of 1–3 are expected in kindergarten, 4–9 in first grade, and 10–13 in second grade, based on Rosner's clinical experience. For all of the AAT variations, local norming is recommended to develop grade-specific performance standards for interpreting the results. For comparison purposes, Tables 5.1 through 5.4 present research norms from the original article in which the measure appeared or from relevant studies with early primary grade examinees.

Technical Adequacy

The AAT and its adaptations have been used in a large number of reading prediction, diagnostic, and classification studies. Psychometric information from the original articles and selected relevant research is presented below.

Auditory Analysis Test

In the original study with 284 children in kindergarten through Grade 6 (Rosner & Simon, 1971), correlations between the AAT and the *Stanford Achievement Test* (Harcourt, Brace & World, 1964) language arts scores were significant for all grades and ranged from .53 in Grade 1 to .84 in Grade 3. Even with IQ held constant, correlations for all but Grade 6 were significant (*r*s = .40 to .69 for Grades 1–3). Item analysis supported the hierarchical categorization of item difficulty. Reliability estimates

TABLE 5.2. B-AAT Mean Score and Standard Deviation for Spring of Kindergarten

Grade	*n*	Mean	*SD*
Kindergarten	48	14.3	7.9

Note. Total items = 30. Data from Berninger (1986).

TABLE 5.3. CDT Mean Scores and Standard Deviations for Four Kindergarten Age Ranges

Age range	Mean	*SD*
5-0 to 5-5	7.58	6.20
5-6 to 5-11	8.10	6.39
6-0 to 6-5	9.47	6.35
6-6 to 6-11	9.92	6.52

Note. Total items = 21; total *n* = 604. Data from J. B. Tomblin et al. (1997) for kindergarten students tested between November and May. From "Estimating the Risk of Future Reading Difficulties in Kindergarten Children: A Research-Based Model and Its Clinical Implementation," by H. W. Catts, M. E. Fey, X. Zhang, and J. B. Tomblin, 2001, *Language, Speech, and Hearing Services in Schools*, *32*, p. 49. Copyright 2001 by the American Speech–Language–Hearing Association. Adapted with permission.

were not provided, and floor effects were evident for kindergarten children (see Table 5.1). In a more recent longitudinal study of 24 children (MacDonald & Cornwall, 1995), AAT kindergarten scores were significant predictors of reading and spelling achievement 11 years later. Even when SES and vocabulary were controlled, the AAT accounted for 25% of the variance in word identification and spelling scores. Geva, Yaghoub-Zadeh, and Schuster (2000) created a 25-item adaptation of the AAT in a study of risk factors for reading difficulties in 200 English as a second language (ESL) children and 70 children for whom English was their first language (EL1). The modified AAT consisted of 25 high-frequency words, and the words remaining after syllable or phoneme deletion were also high-frequency words. First-grade scores on the modified AAT were significant predictors of English word recognition 6 months and 1 year later for both EL1 and ESL students.

Berninger Modification of the Auditory Analysis Test

Berninger (1986) reported a test–retest stability coefficient of .81 for the B-AAT in a sample of 48 kindergarten children. Scores of 6 or less at the end of kindergarten were associated with below average word decoding skills at the end of first grade. B-AAT scores accounted for 35% to 43% of the variance in reading achievement at the end of kindergarten and for 31% to 64% of the variance at the end of first grade. In a

TABLE 5.4. TAAS Mean Score and Standard Deviation for Spring of Kindergarten

Grade	*n*	Mean	*SD*
Kindergarten	96	5.96	2.99

Note. Total items = 13. From "The Validity and Reliability of Phonemic Awareness Tests," by H. K. Yopp, 1988, *Reading Research Quarterly*, *23*, p. 168. Copyright 1988 by the International Reading Association. Adapted with permission.

longitudinal study with three cohorts of children (total *n* = 445), O'Connor and Jenkins (1999) reported that the predictive power of the B-AAT kindergarten syllable deletion items varied with the time of administration. When administered in November of kindergarten, the B-AAT served as a primary discriminator of reading disabilities at the end of Grade 1, using cutoff scores of less than 5 out of 10 correct. When administered in April of kindergarten, however, it no longer served as a primary discriminator because of ceiling effects. In a study with first, second, and third graders (*n* = 300) tested between February and May (Berninger et al., 1992), both B-AAT syllable and phonemic segmentation items were significantly related to handwriting, composition, and spelling performance (*r*s = .19 to .43). Phonemic segmentation items displayed higher correlations with all outcome measures than did syllable deletion items.

Catts Deletion Test

Several studies have documented the efficacy of the CDT in predicting reading achievement for children with speech–language impairments and normal children in the early primary grades. In a study evaluating the predictive utility of a battery of norm-referenced and experimental language measures in a sample of 56 kindergarten children with speech–language impairments (Catts, 1993), spring CDT performance was the best predictor of word identification and phonemic decoding measured in spring of first grade (*r*s = .59 and .60, respectively) and spring of second grade (.55 and .63, respectively). CDT scores were also significantly associated with spring of second grade reading rate and comprehension (.61 and .56, respectively). In a sample of 54 first graders (Swank & Catts, 1994), CDT performance measured at the beginning of the year was the most effective of four phonological awareness measures in predicting end-of-year decoding and identified good versus poor decoders with 88% accuracy. In a larger study with 604 children (Catts et al., 2001), CDT kindergarten scores significantly differentiated between good and poor readers in second grade.

Test of Auditory Analysis Skills

The commercially published TAAS has no manual, and the single-page record sheet provides no information about its technical characteristics. The back of the record sheet has a brief general discussion of the role of auditory processing skills in reading and spelling. Yopp (1988) reported a coefficient alpha of .78 for the TAAS in a sample of 96 kindergarten students tested in April and May. In a sample of 80 first graders tested in October, Foorman, Francis, Novy, and Liberman (1991) reported an internal consistency coefficient of .88. In another study with the same sample (Foorman & Liberman, 1989), good readers scored significantly higher than poor readers on the TAAS (*M* = 8.35 vs. 5.36, respectively). TAAS October scores also predicted overall performance in reading and spelling at the end of the year, although the TAAS ceiling was too low for valid estimation of reading growth for a sizable proportion of the sample. In a longitudinal study of 92 children who were followed from preschool through sixth grade (Badian, 1995), TAAS scores in February of first grade were significant predictors of spring reading vocabulary and comprehension for first through third grade and of spring spelling achievement for first through fourth grade, even after age and listening comprehension were controlled. In another study with 131 students in Grades 1 through 3, Badian (1996) reported that the TAAS was an effective discriminator of reading group membership. TAAS mean scores for both dyslexic children and garden-variety poor readers were significantly lower than those of controls for both younger (aged 6 and 7) and older (aged 8 to 10) participants.

Usability

The AAT and its modifications are quick and easy to administer, are inexpensive or free (except for the cost of reproduction for the research-based measures), and lend themselves readily to local norming. Examiners can prepare a set of drawings for the demonstration items beforehand or draw the practice items on a sheet of paper during test sessions. The AAT and its adaptations have been used more frequently than any other phonological processing measure in early identification and intervention studies with second-language learners. Some researchers have created foreign-language equivalents of the AAT and the B-AAT (e.g., Cisero & Royer, 1995; Comeau, Cormier, Grandmaison, & Lacroix, 1999; Durgunoĝlu, Nagy, & Hancin-Bhatt, 1993; Quiroga, Lemos-Britton, Mostafapour, Abbott, & Berninger, 2002), whereas others have modified the AAT to include only high-frequency English words in an effort to avoid confounding language proficiency with phonological awareness (Geva et al., 2000).

Links to Intervention

In the original article presenting the B-AAT, Berninger and colleagues (1987) cite several instructional strategies and training programs for improving phonemic skills. More recently, Berninger (1998a) has published the *Process Assessment of the Learner: Guides for Intervention–Reading and Writing*, an intervention program that includes 24 lessons of phonological awareness training focusing on syllable and phonemic segmentation. On the TAAS record sheet, Rosner states that teaching the test items will improve reading and spelling skills but presents no theoretical rationale or empirical evidence to support that assertion. He also recommends that children falling below expected performance levels receive the training described in the most recent edition of his book, *Helping Children Overcome Learning Difficulties* (Rosner, 1993). First published nearly three decades ago, the book includes reading and spelling exercises targeting language, auditory-perceptual, visual-perceptual, and decoding skills. Although the latest edition has added a chapter on learning disabilities, ADHD, and dyslexia, much of the book is devoted to visual-perceptual training, a remedial approach that has been largely abandoned in light of overwhelming evidence that language rather than visual processing deficits are central to the vast majority of reading problems (see Kavale & Forness, 2000, for a recent review).

Source and Cost

The TAAS is available from Academic Therapy Publications for $16.00. It is also reproduced in Rosner's (1993) book (see above; $19.00 from Walker & Company). The versions of the AAT, B-AAT, and CDT provided in Figures 5.1 through 5.3 are taken from the original articles, with some amplification of directions and minor changes in format.

Test Reviews

Defendorf, A. O., & Kessler, K. S. (1992). Review of the Test of Auditory Analysis Skills. In J. J. Kramer & J. C. Conoley (Eds.), *The eleventh mental measurements yearbook* (pp. 935–936). Lincoln, NE: Buros Institute of Mental Measurements.

Lindskog, R. (1992). Review of the Test of Auditory Analysis Skills. In J. J. Kramer & J. C. Conoley (Eds.), *The eleventh mental measurements yearbook* (p. 936). Lincoln, NE: Buros Institute of Mental Measurements.

Summary

The *Auditory Analysis Test* (AAT) and its three adaptations–the *Berninger Modification of the AAT* (B-AAT), *Catts Deletion Test* (CDT), and *Test of Auditory Analysis Skills* (TAAS)–are brief, individually administered, nonstandardized measures of syllable and phoneme deletion, a phonological processing skill that has been demonstrated to be a highly effective predictor of reading acquisition and reading disabilities. All are easy to administer, inexpensive, and suitable for local norming. Because they assess only one aspect of phonemic awareness, however, they should never be used as the sole screening measure in identifying children at risk for reading problems. Moreover, the sensitivity of these measures to individual differences depends in part on the time of administration and the reading curriculum because the phoneme awareness skills necessary to perform deletion tasks do not emerge until formal reading instruction has begun. Floor effects are likely to occur for kindergarten children on the AAT and TAAS at fall and spring screening windows because of the limited number of syllable deletion items. Of the four versions reviewed, the B-AAT and CDT are the most useful for screening early primary grade children, especially kindergartners and first graders, because of the larger number of easier items. Administering the entire B-AAT rather than only the grade-specific items is recommended to reduce the possibility of floor or ceiling effects.

Case Example

Name of student: Samantha R.
Age: 5 years, 8 months
Grade: Kindergarten
Date of assessment: March

Reason for referral: Samantha was referred for an early reading assessment by her kindergarten teacher. Her teacher reports that Samantha's ability to perform phonological awareness tasks, such as rhyming and sound matching, is limited at this point, and that she is having difficulty learning and remembering letter names and sounds.

Assessment results and interpretation: The *Catts Deletion Test* (CDT) assesses *phonemic awareness*, that is, the child's ability to isolate and manipulate speech sounds. Phonemic awareness is critical to learning letter-sound relationships and using that knowledge in decoding. The CDT requires the child to listen to a word, repeat it, and say it again without a specific syllable or sound. For example, the examiner says, "Say *cowboy* without *cow*," and the child responds, "Boy." No reading is required.

Samantha listened attentively to the words presented, but she was able to answer only 4 of the 21 items correctly. Her performance is considerably lower than what would be expected for a child at her grade level (about 8/21 items correct for the spring of kindergarten). She was able to delete syllables from compound words, although not consistently. She was unable to delete syllables from words in which the deleted syllable was not itself a word. For example, asked to say *almost* without /al/, she said, "moke." She was unable to perform any single phoneme deletions (e.g., "Say *fat* without /f/").

COMPREHENSIVE TEST OF PHONOLOGICAL PROCESSING

Overview

The *Comprehensive Test of Phonological Processing* (CTOPP; Wagner, Torgesen, & Rashotte, 1999) is an individually administered, norm-referenced set of measures assessing phonological processing abilities for individuals from 5 to 24 years of age. Developed with support from a grant from the National Institute of Child Health and Human Development (NICHD), the CTOPP is based on its authors' three-dimensional model of phonological processing, including phonological awareness, phonological memory, and rapid naming, and subtests are derived from experimental tasks the authors have used during more than a decade of research (e.g., Wagner & Torgesen, 1987; Wagner, Torgesen, & Rashotte, 1994). The manual identifies four uses for the CTOPP: (1) identifying individuals who are significantly below their peers in phonological abilities, especially kindergarten and first-grade children at risk for reading failure; (2) determining strengths and weaknesses among phonological processes; (3) documenting progress in phonological processing skills as the result of intervention programs; and (4) serving as a measure in phonological processing research. The CTOPP includes two versions, the first for 5- and 6-year-olds (kindergarten and Grade 1), and the second for 7- through 24-year-olds (Grade 2 through adulthood). Test materials include a spiral-bound examiner's manual, 25 profile/examiner record booklets for each of the two versions, a spiral-bound picture book, and an audiocassette, all packaged in a storage box.

Subtests and Composites

Subtests

The CTOPP is unique among phonological processing measures in providing multiple norm-referenced subtests to assess each of three phonological domains. The version for ages 5 and 6 consists of seven core subtests and one supplemental test, whereas the version for ages 7 through 24 consists of six core subtests and six supplemental tests. Table 5.5 describes the subtests in order of administration, beginning with the version for 5- and 6-year-olds.

Composites

The subtests are combined to form three core and three supplemental composites that represent the three constructs underlying the CTOPP (see Table 5.6). Segmenting Words and Phoneme Reversal are not included in any of the composites.

TABLE 5.5. Description of the CTOPP Subtests

Subtest	Description
Elision	The child listens to a word spoken by the examiner, repeats it, and then says it without a specific sound (e.g., "Say *bold* without saying /b/").
Rapid Color Naming[a]	The child names a 36-stimulus random array of blocks printed in six different colors (black, green, blue, red, brown, and yellow) as rapidly as possible. There are two trials, and the score is the total number of seconds across both trials.
Blending Words	The child listens to separate sounds presented on an audiocassette and blends the sounds together to form real words (e.g., the child hears "/n/-/o/" and says "no").
Sound Matching	From a set of four pictures identified by the examiner, the child points to the one that begins or ends with the same sound as the first picture.
Rapid Object Naming[a]	The child names a 36-stimulus array of six objects (boat, star, pencil, chair, fish, and key) as rapidly as possible. There are two trials, and the score is the total number of seconds across both trials.
Memory for Digits	The child repeats an increasingly long series of digits presented on an audiocassette at a rate of two digits per second.
Nonword Repetition	The child repeats pseudowords presented on an audiocassette. Stimulus items range in length from 3 to 15 phonemes.
Blending Nonwords[b]	The child listens to separate sounds presented on an audiocassette and blends them together to form pseudowords (e.g., the child hears "/j/-/ad/" and says, "jad").
Rapid Digit Naming	The child names a 36-stimulus array of six numbers (2, 3, 4, 5, 7, and 8) as rapidly as possible. There are two trials, and the score is the total number of seconds across both trials.
Rapid Letter Naming	The child names a 36-stimulus array of six lowercase letters (*a, c, k, n, s,* and *t*) as rapidly as possible. There are two trials, and the score is the total number of seconds across both trials.
Phoneme Reversal[b]	The child listens to a series of pseudowords presented on an audiocassette, repeats the item, and then pronounces it backwards to form a real word (e.g., the child hears "tis" and says "sit").
Segmenting Words[a]	The child listens to a word pronounced by the examiner, repeats it, and then pronounces the word one phoneme at a time (e.g., the child hears "no" and says "/n/-/o/"). Items range in length from two to nine phonemes.
Segmenting Nonwords[b]	The child listens to pseudowords presented on an audiocassette, repeats each item, and then pronounces it one phoneme at a time (e.g., the child hears "ta" and says "/t/-/a/"). Items range in length from two to eight phonemes.

[a]Supplemental tests for ages 7–24.
[b]Supplemental test for both age groups.

Administration

The CTOPP requires 20–30 minutes for the core tests and another 5–15 minutes for the supplemental tests. For each subtest, the examiner begins with the first item. Ceilings are three consecutive errors for all subtests except the rapid naming subtests, which are administered in their entirety to all examinees, and Sound Matching, which has a ceiling of four incorrect out of seven consecutive items to account for guessing. Practice items are provided for each subtest, and on many subtests, the examiner provides feedback on initial items to ensure that the examinee understands the nature of the task. Blending, memory, and pseudoword tasks are presented on audiocassette to promote a standardized administration. For rapid naming subtests, testing is discontinued if the examinee identifies more than four items incorrectly, and no score is given for that task.

Scores

Except for the rapid naming subtests, for which the score is the number of seconds required to complete the two trials, items are scored 1 for correct and 0 for incorrect, using the record booklet. Blanks should be provided on the record booklet for recording errors for later analysis on the phonological awareness and memory subtests. Raw scores can be converted to age-based percentile ranks, standard scores, and age and grade equivalents. There is an error in the conversion table on page 120 that shows Sound Matching as a core subtest for ages 7-0 through 7-11. Subtest standard scores ($M = 10$, $SD = 3$) can be summed to yield composite scores or "quotients" ($M = 100$, $SD = 15$). Norms are in 6-month increments for ages 5-0 through 7-11, in 1-year increments for ages 8-0 through 16-11, and in a single block for ages 17-0 through 24-11.

Interpretation

The test's authors present a set of useful guidelines for interpreting the three major composite scores in terms of phonological processing strengths and weaknesses and the implications of deficits in each domain for different reading skills. Interpretation focuses primarily on composites, and the authors caution that subtest findings should be interpreted only in terms of the specific skills measured. The manual includes a section on conducting discrepancy analyses with CTOPP scores and provides tables with minimal differences between CTOPP subtest and composite standard scores for statistical significance at the .05 level and for clinical utility, using Reynolds's (1990) formula for identifying severe discrepancies. A case example for a third grader, aged 8-4, illustrates how to record CTOPP scores and evaluate discrepancies. The case example displays a relatively flat profile, with average to below average subtest scores, below average to poor composite scores, and no statistically or clinically significant discrepancies. His Nonverbal IQ as measured by the *Comprehen-*

TABLE 5.6. CTOPP Subtests and Composites by Level

Composites	Subtests	
	Ages 5 and 6	Ages 7–24
Phonological Awareness	Elision Blending Words Sound Matching	Elision Blending Words
Phonological Memory	Memory for Digits Nonword Repetition	Memory for Digits Nonword Repetition
Rapid Naming	Rapid Color Naming Rapid Object Naming	Rapid Digit Naming Rapid Letter Naming
Alternate Phonological Awareness		Blending Nonwords Segmenting Nonwords
Alternate Rapid Naming		Rapid Color Naming Rapid Object Naming

sive Test of Nonverbal Intelligence (CTONI; Hammill, Pearson, & Wiederholt, 1997) is average, however, and the results are interpreted as indicating a need for further assessment and special phonological instruction. Given the emphasis in the manual on assessing first and second graders, an example of a younger child should also be included.

Technical Adequacy

Standardization

The CTOPP was normed on 1,656 individuals ranging in age from 5 through 24 and residing in 30 states. Subgroup size ranges from 77 to 155, with fewer examinees at older age intervals. Between 140 and 151 examinees were tested at each age level in the primary grade range, but because norms are in 6-month intervals for ages 5-0 through 7-11, scores are based on only about 70–78 examinees per interval for ages 5 through 7. Sample characteristics are reported in terms of race, ethnicity, gender, residence, geographical region, family income, and parent education, with characteristics stratified by six age intervals (excluding ages 18 through 24) and keyed to 1997 U.S. census data. In general, the CTOPP school-age sample closely represents the U.S. population except in terms of slightly underrepresenting Hispanics, examinees with family incomes over $75,000, and parents with less than a bachelor's degree and slightly overrepresenting examinees classified as "Other," examinees with family incomes of $35,000 to $49,999, and parents with a bachelor's degree.

Reliability Evidence

Coefficient alphas for subtests for examinees ages 5 through 8 range from .70 to .96, with reliability for Blending Words and Memory for Digits falling below .80 for half of the age groups. For the rapid naming subtests, internal consistency was estimated using alternate-form reliability procedures, but because the CTOPP has only one form, estimates are apparently based on correlations between the two test trials. Internal consistency reliability for the rapid naming subtests is in the .80s for 9 of the 16 relevant age group values but falls in the .70s for 7 values. Coefficient alphas for composites range from .81 to .96, with only the Phonological Awareness and Alternate Phonological Awareness composites in the .90s. Coefficient alphas for eight subgroups within the normative sample (students with learning disabilities, students with speech and language problems, males, females, and four racial groups) are in the .80s and .90s, with the exception of Rapid Object Naming for learning-disabled examinees (.76) and Nonword Repetition and the Phonological Memory composite for Asian Americans for the 5- and 6-year-old version of the test (.68 and .76, respectively).

Subtest stability estimates for 32 children ages 5–7 ranged from .68 to .97, with Elision, Blending Words, Sound Matching, Rapid Digit Naming, and Rapid Letter Naming at or above .80. Coefficients for Rapid Color Naming, Rapid Object Naming, and Memory for Digits were in the .70s, whereas that for Blending Nonwords was .68. For composite scores, only Phonological Memory was at an acceptable level for stability (r = .92), whereas the other two composites were in the .70s. Although presumably these children took the 5- and 6-year-old version of the test, it is not clear why examinees aged 7 were included and how many in the sample were that age.

Moreover, although reliability estimates are provided for Rapid Digit Naming and Rapid Letter Naming, these subtests are not included in the 5- and 6-year old version of the test. Test–retest reliability coefficients for 30 children aged 8 through 17 ranged from .72 to .93 for subtests and from .79 to .95 for composites. Five of the 12 subtests (Memory for Digits, Rapid Digit Naming, Rapid Color Naming, Rapid Object Naming, and Segmenting Nonwords) were at or above the criterion level of .80. Of the composites, Alternate Rapid Naming was in the .90s, whereas Phonological Awareness, Phonological Memory, and Alternate Phonological Awareness were in the .80s, and Rapid Naming was .79. Because the age group in the sample was so broad, however, evaluating score stability for 8-year-old examinees is not possible.

Interscorer reliability for 60 randomly selected completed protocols (30 for 5- and 6-year-olds and 30 for 7- to 24-year-olds) independently scored by two individuals in PRO-ED's research department ranged from .95 to .99. Because estimates were obtained after the tests had been administered, however, the correlations provide no information about interexaminer consistency during test sessions. Additional interscorer reliability estimates based on independent scoring of audiotaped examinee responses or simultaneous independent scoring of actual administrations should be provided, especially for rapid naming, pseudoword, and phoneme manipulation subtests.

Test Floors and Item Gradients

Although the CTOPP's authors state that revisions prior to national norming were conducted to ensure adequate floors and item gradients through the entire age range, floors for many subtests and two of the five composites are problematic for young examinees. For ages 5-0 through 5-11, 7 of the 8 subtests (except Memory for Digits) have inadequate floors. Floors for Sound Matching and Nonword Repetition are inadequate below age 7-0; floors for Elision and Blending Words are inadequate below age 7-6; Blending Nonwords, Phoneme Reversal, Segmenting Words, and Segmenting Nonwords have inadequate floors throughout the entire early primary grade range (i.e., below 9-0); and Segmenting Words is inadequate throughout the entire age range of the test. For composite scores, only the Phonological Memory and Alternate Rapid Naming composites have adequate floors throughout the entire test. Floors for the Rapid Naming and Phonological Awareness composites are inadequate below ages 5-6 and 6-6, respectively. A child aged 5-5 who answers one item correctly on each of the Elision, Blending Words, and Sound Matching subtests obtains a Phonological Awareness composite score of 85. The Alternate Phonological Awareness composite is inadequate for ages 7-0 through 7-11. Item gradients are inadequate for Elision and Blending Nonwords for ages 5-0 to 6-5, for Blending Words for ages 5-0 to 5-11, and for Phoneme Reversal for ages 7-0 to 7-5.

Validity Evidence

CONTENT VALIDITY EVIDENCE

The CTOPP subtests are based on a set of experimental tasks that have been developed and validated during the authors' long-term research program in reading acquisition and reading disabilities (e.g., Torgesen et al., 1994; Wagner et al., 1987, 1994). Experts in the area of phonological processing reviewed preliminary versions of the task formats and items, after which the revised CTOPP was field-tested with 603 children in kindergarten through fifth grade. After additional subtest and item analyses, the final version was administered to another sample of 164 individuals from kindergarten through college. The manual includes a useful discussion of the origins of each subtest and the relationship of subtest content to the reading process. Both conventional item analysis and item response theory (IRT) procedures were used to select items during test development. Median item difficulty coefficients are in the acceptable range with the exception of Elision for ages 5 and 6 (*r*s = .03 and .10, respectively), indicating that the subtest is so difficult that it provides little useful information for examinees at these ages. Blending Nonwords is also at the lower end of acceptability for ages 5 and 6 (both *r*s = .19). Item discrimination power is adequate across the age range. Differential item functioning (DIF) analyses for all subtests except rapid naming using the logistic regression technique were conducted for four dichotomous groups (males vs. females, European Americans vs. non-European Americans, African Americans vs. non-African Americans, and Hispanic Americans vs. non-Hispanic Americans). The authors reviewed each of the 14 items for which statistically significant comparisons were found and ultimately eliminated 25 items because of suspect content. The delta scores approach was applied to the same four dichotomous groups, yielding coefficients at or above .98 with the exception of Sound Matching (.86) for the African American–non-African American comparison. Although the manual does not discuss the implications of this result, the mean on this subtest for African Americans in the normative sample was in the average range (*M* = 10.5). As noted in Chapter 2, the delta scores approach is not recommended in DIF analyses because it is dependent on the ability levels in the sample.

CRITERION-RELATED VALIDITY EVIDENCE

The authors present concurrent validity studies for the preliminary, revised, and final versions of the CTOPP. In a sample of 603 students in kindergarten through fifth grade using the revised CTOPP, partial correlations controlling for age between CTOPP subtests and *Woodcock Reading Mastery Tests–Revised* (WRMT-R; Woodcock, 1987) Word Identification and Word Analysis ranged from .33 to .74, with the highest correlations for Elision and Blending Words. Elision and Blending Words also displayed the highest correlations with the *Test of Word Reading Efficiency* (TOWRE) Sight Word Efficiency and Phonemic Decoding Efficiency subtests in the same sample (.27 to .68, respectively). In a study using the final version of the CTOPP with 164 students from kindergarten through college, partial correlations controlling for age between core CTOPP subtests and WRMT-R Word Identification were generally moderate (.46 to .65), with the highest correlations for Elision. In a study with 73 reading-disabled examinees in kindergarten through Grade 12 (median grade = 3.5) who took the final version of the CTOPP before and after a 6-month phonological awareness training program, core CTOPP subtests were moderately to highly correlated (.41 to .75) with the *Lindamood Auditory Conceptualization Test* (LAC), with the highest correlations again for Elision. Correlations with Rate, Accuracy, and Comprehension subtests on the *Gray Oral Reading Tests–Third Edition* (GORT-3; Wiederholt & Bryant, 1992) were much more variable (.00 to .62), with the highest correlations for Rapid Digit Naming. Correlations with the Spelling subtest on the *Wide Range Achievement Test–Third Edition* (WRAT-3; Wilkinson, 1993) were generally low to moderate (.29 to .62), with the highest correlations for Elision. Correlations between the final version of the CTOPP and the TOWRE for the entire normative sample ranged from .19 to .70 for the 5- and 6-year-old version, with the strongest correlations for the Phonological Awareness composite. In contrast, for the 7- to 24-year-old version, correlations ranged from .25 to .61, with the highest correlations for the Rapid Naming composite.

Predictive validity evidence is reported for the preliminary and final CTOPP. In a longitudinal study with 216 children (Wagner et al., 1994, 1997), kindergarten Phonological Awareness composite scores on the preliminary CTOPP were highly correlated with Grade 1 decoding, as measured by a composite of WRMT-R Word Identification and Word Analysis (.71), whereas Phonological Memory and Rapid Naming were significantly but less strongly correlated with WRMT-R decoding (.42 and .66, respectively). First-grade CTOPP composite scores were also effective predictors of Grade 2 WRMT-R decoding, with high correlations for Phonological Awareness and Rapid Naming composites (.80 and .70, respectively) and a moderate correlation for Phonological Memory (.52). For the sample of 73 reading-disabled students described above who took the final version of the CTOPP after a phonological awareness intervention program, Elision, Rapid Letter Naming, and Rapid Digit Naming were the best predictors of reading achievement (*rs* = .46 to .72), whereas blending and phonological memory tasks were poor predictors (.21 to .48).

CONSTRUCT VALIDITY EVIDENCE

Construct validity evidence consists of confirmatory factor analyses, age and group differentiation studies, item validity studies, and studies of differential training effects. Confirmatory factor analyses reveal that although the Phonological Awareness and Phonological Memory composites are very highly correlated (.88 and .85) for both versions of the CTOPP, they are only moderately correlated with the Rapid Naming composite for the 5- and 6-year old version (.46 and .45, respectively) and weakly correlated for the 7- to 24-year-old version (both .38), challenging the notion of a unitary construct. Most of the CTOPP subtests are significantly related to age, with increasing mean scores that gradually level off, demonstrating the developmental nature of the tasks. Diagnostic utility was evaluated by comparing mean standard scores for eight subgroups in the normative sample (males, females, African Americans, Asian Americans, European Americans, Hispanic Americans, examinees with speech–language impairments, and examinees with language impairments). Examinees with speech–language impairments scored below average on 8 of 13 subtests and 4 of the 5 composites, with the poorest performance on Rapid Naming and Alternate Rapid Naming (standard scores [SS] = 84.2 and 83.6, respectively). Differences in some cases are only a few points below the average range, however, and none are evaluated for level of significance. Examinees with language impairments scored in the average range on all 13 subtests and only slightly below average on the Phonological Memory composite (SS = 89.6). African American examinees scored slightly below average on 6 of the 12 subtests and on the Phonological Awareness composite (SS = 89.6) but in the average range on memory and rapid naming measures. The authors contend that these differences are not the result of test bias but are consistent with research (Hecht, Burgess, Torgesen, Wagner, & Rashotte, 2000) indicating that differences in home language experiences can affect phonological awareness development.

In a second group differentiation study, mean standard scores were lower for 32 reading-disabled students in Grades 1 through 9 than for matched nondisabled controls from the normative sample. Although there were significant group differences in the predicted direction for all three composites, with the largest differences for the Phonological Awareness composite (SS = 85 vs. 100), Rapid Naming composite scores were in the average range for both groups (SS = 92 vs. 103). Moreover, the broad age range of the sample makes it impossible to determine the nature of differences for primary grade versus older examinees. Differential training effects were also evident in the study with 73 reading-disabled students who received an intervention targeting phonological awareness. Pretest to posttest gains were double for the CTOPP phonological awareness measures compared with the phonological memory or rapid naming measures, as anticipated.

Usability

The developers of the CTOPP have expended considerable effort to make this complex set of measures as attractive to children and as easy to administer as possible. The spiral-bound manual, like all the new generation of PRO-ED manuals, is a model of usability—well organized, readable, and practitioner-oriented. The use of audiocassette administration for pseudoword, phoneme manipulation, and memory tasks to promote interexaminer consistency is commendable and should become the standard for instruments assessing phonological processing skills. Administering the entire test is quite time-consuming, however, even with ceilings of only three consecutive errors. Moreover, given the large number of subtests and composites for which derived scores must be computed, a software scoring program would be a helpful addition.

Links to Intervention

After administering a "comprehensive" test of phonological processing, examiners may be taken aback to read in the manual that the CTOPP should serve as "the first step in a comprehensive evaluation of a student's problem in phonological processing" (p. 56). This caution is appropriate, however, because as with any survey-type instrument, CTOPP subtests include too few items to be used as the basis for instructional planning. This is especially true for low-performing kindergarten and first-grade children, who may answer only a few or no items correctly on some tasks. No specific suggestions for further assessments or interventions are provided for the case example noted above or for remediating deficits in any of the domains evaluated. Although this is not mentioned in the manual, Torgesen and a colleague have developed an intervention program for at-risk kindergarten students or struggling first or second graders. The program (*Phonological Awareness Training for Reading*; Torgesen & Bryant, 1994a) is available from PRO-ED and can be used by classroom teachers, tutors, or reading specialists.

Relevant Research

The authors have used versions of the CTOPP tasks in numerous diagnostic, prediction, and intervention studies as part of their ground-breaking research program. In a longitudinal study of 216 children whose phonological processing, word reading, and vocabulary skills were assessed each year from kindergarten through Grade 4 (Wagner et al., 1997), individual differences in phonological awareness predicted growth in reading for each time period, indicating that the influence of phonological awareness extends at least throughout the early elementary period. In contrast, phonological memory did not independently influence word reading growth for any time period but was redundant with phonological awareness. Rapid naming and vocabulary initially influenced word reading skills, but their influence faded with development as previous levels of word reading skills accounted for more of the variance. In a subsequent study following the same sample through Grade 5 (Torgesen, Wagner, Rashotte, Burgess, & Hecht, 1997), both phonological awareness and rapid naming were significant predictors of individual differences in reading 2 years later. When prior levels of reading skills were taken into account, however, only individual differences in phonological awareness explained variability in reading outcomes. Interestingly, phonological awareness played a more important role in explaining growth in word reading and comprehension skills for poor readers than it did for proficient readers.

A recent study (Havey, Story, & Buker, 2002) provides additional evidence that the CTOPP is significantly related to concurrent reading achievement, although the composites vary considerably in their predictive power. For a sample of 81 children, spring of kindergarten scores on the CTOPP Phonological Awareness and Rapid Naming composites were effective predictors (.65 and .49, respectively) of scores on the *Woodcock Diagnostic Reading Battery* (Woodcock, 1997) Letter–Word Identification test obtained 4–6 weeks later. The Phonological Memory composite was not significantly related to concurrent reading performance, however (.23). Research evaluating the CTOPP's ability to predict responsiveness to preventive and remedial programs has yielded mixed results. In a study evaluating the relative efficacy of three intervention programs with 135 at-risk kindergarten children (Torgesen, Wagner, Rashotte, Rose, et al., 1999), all three phonological composites contributed uniquely to the prediction of reading growth, along with SES and teacher ratings of attention and behavior. Of the three phonological abilities, rapid naming was the most consistent unique predictor, followed by phonological memory and phonological awareness. In contrast, in a study with 60 learning-disabled children aged 8 to 10 who received one of two types of instructional programs (Torgesen, Alexander, et al., 2001), none of the three phonological abilities were unique predictors of reading progress. Instead, the best predictors of long-term growth were teacher ratings of attention and behavior, receptive language scores, and prior levels of reading skills.

Source and Cost

The CTOPP is available from PRO-ED for $231.00. The *Phonological Awareness Training for Reading* program retails for $139.00 from the same publisher.

Test Reviews

Hurford, D. P. (2003). Review of the Comprehensive Test of Phonological Processing. In B. S. Plake, J. C. Impara, & R. A. Spies (Eds.), *The fifteenth mental measurements yearbook* (pp. 226–229). Lincoln, NE: Buros Institute of Mental Measurements.

Lennon, J. E., & Slesinski, C. (2001, March). Comprehensive Test of Phonological Processing (CTOPP): Cognitive-linguistic assessment of severe reading problems. *Communiqué*, pp. 38-40.

Mitchell, J. (2001). Comprehensive Test of Phonological Processing. *Assessment for Effective Intervention, 26*, 57-63.

Wright, C. R. (2003). Review of the Comprehensive Test of Phonological Processing. In B. S. Plake, J. C. Impara, & R. A. Spies (Eds.), *The fifteenth mental measurements yearbook* (pp. 229-232). Lincoln, NE: Buros Institute of Mental Measurements.

Summary

The *Comprehensive Test of Phonological Processing* (CTOPP) is an individually administered, norm-referenced test of phonological awareness, phonological memory, and rapid naming for examinees aged 5 through 24. The CTOPP is the product of an innovative research program that has made invaluable contributions to the understanding of reading acquisition and the early identification and remediation of reading problems. A large body of evidence demonstrates that CTOPP tasks are effective predictors of growth in reading for both poor and proficient readers, although their utility in predicting responsiveness to intervention is less clear. Despite the CTOPP's goal of identifying young children with phonological processing deficits, inadequate floors for most subtests for ages 5 and 6 limit its diagnostic accuracy at those ages. In addition, internal consistency and stability estimates for some of the composites are too low for educational decision-making purposes. Moreover, the effects of interexaminer variance on test performance are unclear because interrater reliability studies were conducted with completed protocols. Despite these drawbacks, the CTOPP is rapidly becoming the standard tool for assessing phonological processing abilities, and its increasing use in research studies assures that validation evidence regarding its diagnostic and predictive utility will continue to accumulate.

Case Example

Name of student: Brian F.
Age: 8 years, 0 months
Grade: Second grade
Date of assessment: January

Reason for referral: Brian was referred for an early reading assessment by his second-grade teacher because of very slow progress in reading, despite receiving individual tutoring assistance during the first semester of the year. He has a limited sight word vocabulary, his decoding and spelling skills are poor, and he attempts to use picture clues and context rather than decoding strategies to identify unfamiliar words.

Assessment results and interpretation: The *Comprehensive Test of Phonological Processing* (CTOPP) assesses three kinds of phonological processing skills: phonological awareness, phonological memory, and rapid naming. Deficits in phonological skills are the most common cause of reading disabilities. Average scores for a child Brian's age and grade are as follows: Composite Standard Score = 100, Subtest

Standard Score = 10, Percentile Rank (PR) = 50, Age Equivalent = 8-0, and Grade Equivalent = 2.5. Brian's results on the CTOPP are presented below.

Composite/Subtest	Composite Standard Score	Subtest Standard Score	Percentile Rank	Age Equivalent	Grade Equivalent
Phonological Awareness	70	–	2	–	–
Elision	–	4	2	5-3	K.2
Blending Words	–	6	9	6-6	1.4
Phonological Memory	79	–	8	–	–
Memory for Digits	–	4	2	5-0	K.0
Nonword Repetition	–	6	9	5-3	K.2
Rapid Naming	97	–	42	–	–
Rapid Letter Naming	–	10	50	9-0	4.0
Rapid Digit Naming	–	9	37	8-0	3.0
Alternate Phonological Awareness	82	–	12	–	–
Blending Nonwords	–	7	16	6-3	1.2
Segmenting Nonwords	–	7	16	<6-9	<1.7
Alternate Rapid Naming	94	–	35	–	–
Rapid Color Naming	–	13	84	10-0	5.0
Rapid Object Naming	–	9	37	7-6	2.4
Segmenting Words	–	6	9	<6-9	<1.7
Phoneme Reversal	–	5	5	5-6	K.4

Compared with that of other children his age, Brian's performance on the CTOPP varies from average to poor, depending on the skills assessed. His best performance was on rapid naming tasks, which measure the ability to retrieve sound-based information from memory efficiently. He scored in the average range on letter and digit naming tasks (PR = 42) as well as on color and object naming tasks (PR = 35), suggesting that slow retrieval speed is not a major contributor to his problems with accessing and using sounds in the decoding process. In contrast, his phonological awareness and phonological memory skills are significantly less well developed. His performance on phonological memory tasks, which require coding information phonologically for storage in memory, is rated as poor (PR = 8). Phonological memory deficits are not likely to interfere with reading familiar material but are likely to impair decoding of new words and listening and reading comprehension for more complex sentences.

Brian's poorest performance was on phonological awareness tasks, which require awareness of and access to the sound structure of oral language. His overall phonological awareness skills, as measured by tasks with real word and pseudoword (nonsense word) stimuli, fall in the poor and below average range, respectively (PRs = 2 and 12, respectively). He was able to delete syllables from compound words, but he was unable to delete single phonemes from words. For example, asked to say *mat* without saying /t/, he responded, "et." He was able to blend sounds together to form real words, although not consistently, but he was less successful in blending sounds to form pseudowords. He had particular difficulty with tasks requiring him to pronounce the individual sounds in spoken words. For example, asked to segment the word *to*, he responded, "/too/ - /wah/."

DYSLEXIA EARLY SCREENING TEST

Overview

The *Dyslexia Early Screening Test* (DEST; Nicolson & Fawcett, 1996) is an individually administered, norm-referenced set of measures designed to screen for difficulties related to dyslexia in children aged 4-6 through 6-5 years. An upward extension, the *Dyslexia Screening Test* (DST; Fawcett & Nicolson, 1996), is designed for children aged 6-6 through 16-5 (see the next review). Developed and normed in the United Kingdom, it is based on tasks in the dyslexia literature and the authors' research program (e.g., Fawcett & Nicolson, 1994; Nicolson & Fawcett, 1994). The DEST assesses five areas: (1) literacy skills, (2) phonological awareness, (3) verbal memory, (4) motor skill and balance, and (5) auditory processing. The DEST is unusual among early reading screening batteries in that it includes a measure of postural stability. This inclusion is based on the authors' cerebellar deficit hypothesis, which proposes that mild cerebellar dysfunction underlies many of the problems displayed by individuals with dyslexia (see Nicolson & Fawcett, 1999, 2001). Purposes of the DEST include (1) identifying young children at risk for reading failure so that they can receive assistance as soon as possible, (2) providing a profile of strengths and weaknesses for intervention planning, and (3) monitoring progress in the skills assessed. According to its authors (Fawcett & Nicolson, 2000), the DEST is designed to screen for learning problems of all types, including language delay and intellectual impairment, in addition to dyslexia. Materials include an examiner's manual; 50 record forms on a tear-off tablet; scoring keys; rapid naming, letter naming, digit naming, and shape copying cards; beads and threading string; balance tester and blindfold; forward digit span and sound order audiotapes; and a sample permission letter, all packed in a nylon carrying case. Examiners must provide blank paper for Shape Copying, a place-keeping card for Rapid Naming, and a basket or box for Bead Threading.

Subtests and Composite

The DEST consists of 10 subtests, which are described in Table 5.7 in order of administration. A weighted mean is calculated for subtests on which the child scores in the at-risk range to yield an overall At-Risk Quotient (ARQ).

Administration

Each subtest takes approximately 2–5 minutes to administer, and the entire test can be given in about 30 minutes. Administration procedures are clearly laid out in the manual, but because time limits, discontinue rules, and practice items are not printed on the record form, the examiner must refer to the manual during the entire administration process. On Rapid Naming, the examiner provides the name of the picture if the child pauses for more than 5 seconds, which differs from the no-prompt procedure used in the other rapid naming measures reviewed in this text. The Postural Stability subtest takes practice to administer consistently. The examiner stands behind the standing, blindfolded child; rests the pommel of a plastic "balance tester" against the child's back; and gently pushes a sliding collar along the shaft, stopping just be-

TABLE 5.7. Description of the DEST Subtests

Subtest	Description
Rapid Naming	The child names two identical arrays of 20 familiar objects as rapidly as possible. The score is the amount of time required to name the entire set. Five seconds are added to the time for each error, and 10 seconds are added if the examiner must use a card to help the child keep his or her place.
Bead Threading	While standing, the child threads a set of wooden beads on a string as rapidly as possible. The score is the number threaded in 30 seconds, minus 1 point if the child drops the string more than once.
Phonological Discrimination	The child indicates whether a pair of one-syllable words pronounced by the examiner are the same or different. Words differ in terms of the initial or final consonant.
Postural Stability	The child attempts to maintain balance while blindfolded after being gently pushed by the examiner on the back with a balance tester. There are two trials of two pushes each, twice with the child's arms at the side and twice with arms extended in front. The child's degree of stability is scored on a 7-point scale, and the score is the total number of points for the four trials.
Rhyme Detection/First Letter Sound	This subtest consists of two tasks. For *Rhyme Detection*, the child indicates whether two words spoken by the examiner rhyme. For *First Letter Sound*, the child pronounces the first sound or provides the name of the first letter in a word spoken by the examiner.
Forwards Digit Span	The child repeats an increasingly long series of digits presented on an audiocassette.
Digit Naming	The child names seven one-digit numerals presented on two cards (10-second limit per digit).
Letter Naming	The child gives the letter name or letter sound for 10 lowercase letters presented on four cards (10-second limit per letter).
Sound Order	The child listens to pairs of sounds (a squeak to represent a mouse and a quack to represent a duck) presented on audiocassette and indicates which sound was first by saying "mouse" or "duck." The interval between sounds becomes progressively smaller.
Shape Copying	The child copies seven line drawings presented on a card (time limit of 2 minutes for ages 4-6 to 4-11, 90 seconds for ages 5-0 to 5-5, and 60 seconds for ages 5-6 and up). Drawings are scored on a 4-point scale, and the score is the total points for the seven drawings.

fore it reaches the pommel, while the child tries to maintain balance. To provide a consistent amount of force, the collar should be adjusted to provide a 1.5-kg force (about 3.3 pounds). The authors state that examiners should check the calibration by pressing the balance tester down on a 5-kg kitchen scale and adjusting the washer on the collar until the correct force of 1.5 kg is measured. The examiner may push the child with three fingers with a force of 1.5 kg if the balance tester is not available. The manual should indicate whether asking examinees to shut their eyes is an acceptable alternative to the standard procedure for children who may react adversely to being blindfolded.

Scores

With the exceptions of Rapid Naming, Bead Threading, Postural Stability, and Shape Copying, items are scored dichotomously. Because the Rapid Naming test stimuli are not reproduced on the record form, the examiner must tally errors on a sheet of paper or on the short line on the record form while attempting to follow the child's responses using the test card or the picture array in the manual. Age-based percentile ranges are available at 6-month intervals for four age groups: 4-6 to 4-11, 5-0 to 5-5, 5-6 to 5-11, and 6-0 to 6-5. Percentiles ranks are grouped into five broad categories to indicate risk status: highly at risk (PRs 1–10), at risk (PRs 11–25), normal (PRs 26–75), above average (PRs 76–90), and well above average (PRs 91–100). The examiner places the scoring key for the relevant age over the record form to convert raw scores to an indicator system corresponding to the five ranges: – – (strong risk), – (at risk), 0 (normal), + (above average), and ++ (well above average). The ARQ is obtained by awarding 2 points for each double minus, 1 point for each minus, and 0 for the rest of the scores and then dividing the sum by 10.

Interpretation

On the DEST, an examinee is considered at risk for dyslexia if he or she scores in the strong-risk range on four or more subtests, scores in the strong-risk or at-risk range on seven or more subtests, or has an ARQ of 1.00 or greater. The test's authors note that the diagnostic utility of Letter Naming and Digit Naming is limited for older children, because most 6-year-olds know their letters and numbers. The record form states that scores in the at-risk range in such areas as rhyming suggest the need for remediation, presumably phonological awareness training, whereas Forwards Digit Span weaknesses suggest possible memory difficulties, and discrimination weaknesses suggest possible hearing problems. The manual includes a case example of a child aged 6-2 to demonstrate scoring procedures, interpretation of results, and possible remediation strategies. The case example's ARQ falls in the strong-risk range, and the profile is interpreted as being characteristic of phonological dyslexia. The authors offer general guidelines for remediation for the case example and refer to intervention programs described more fully in Chapter 4 of the manual.

Technical Adequacy

Standardization

The DEST was standardized in 1995 in the United Kingdom, with approximately 1,000 children involved in the tryout and norming process. Prototypes of the DEST subtests were piloted in a series of investigations evaluating children's interest in the tasks, ease of administration, and performance stability. Based on these studies, the authors dropped 2 of the original 12 measures (speed of simple reaction and measurement of muscle tone) because of low reliability and/or the need for complex equipment. Other tests were modified to improve reliability and/or ease of use, and the balance tester was developed for the Postural Stability subtest. Following these preliminary studies, norms were developed for each subtest by testing entire classes of children at selected schools in Sheffield and throughout England and Wales. The manual indicates that at least 100 children were tested at each of the four age groups, but no other details are provided regarding the characteristics of the sample.

Reliability Evidence

The authors do not provide internal consistency reliability estimates on the grounds that split-half reliability procedures are not appropriate for short tests that progress from easy to difficult. There are several ways of splitting a test, however, and coefficient alpha is an alternative procedure typically used with subtests of this type. Test–retest reliability (no interval specified) for 26 children aged 5-5 to 6-5 ranged from .63 to .88 for the 10 subtests. Coefficients for Postural Stability, Rhyme Detection, Digit Naming, Letter Naming, and Shape Copying are at or above .80. Reliabilities for Rapid Naming and Bead Threading fall in the .70s, and Phonological Discrimination, Forwards Digit Span, and Sound Order fall in the .60s. Interrater agreement for Postural Stability was .98, based on a validation study for the DEST's upward extension, the DST, in which three experimenters independently rated videotaped sessions for 14 children. Two of the experimenters were experienced in administering the test and one had only studied the manual. Interrater agreement was .98 for the experienced examiners and .94 for the inexperienced examiner and each of the experienced examiners. Evidence of interrater reliability should also be provided for Rapid Naming, Shape Copying, and the live-voice phonological subtests.

Test Floors and Item Gradients

Evaluating the adequacy of test floors and item gradients is complicated by the fact that scores are converted to risk categories by placing one of four age-specific scoring keys over the record form rather than by consulting conversion tables in the manual. Floor effects appear to be less of a problem than ceiling effects, which are evident for all of the subtests except for Rapid Naming, Bead Threading, and Shape Copying at the upper age ranges. With only five risk categories, the DEST is not sensitive to small individual differences in skill levels.

Validity Evidence

CONTENT VALIDITY EVIDENCE

As evidence of content validity, the authors present a rationale for subtest selection, based on their own studies and tasks developed by other reading researchers. Subtests were designed to assess indicators associated with three theories of the origins of dyslexia: (1) the phonological deficit theory, (2) the cerebellar impairment theory, and (3) the magnocellular pathway impairment theory. For example, Sound Order is based on Tallal's (1984) magnocellular deficit hypothesis, which suggests that children with dyslexia have difficulty discriminating between rapidly changing sounds because of impairment in the magnocellular auditory pathway. Bead Threading, Shape Copying, Rapid Naming, and Postural Stability are based on the authors' cerebellar impairment theory, which proposes that dyslexic children suffer from mild cerebellar abnormality, as demonstrated by motor and balance problems and lack of fluency on a variety of tasks (Fawcett, Nicolson, & Dean, 1996; Nicolson & Fawcett, 1999, 2001). No information is provided regarding item difficulty, discrimination, or possible bias.

CRITERION-RELATED VALIDITY EVIDENCE

The authors state that establishing concurrent validity for the DEST is not possible because there are no tests comparable to the DEST and offer no criterion-related validity evidence. However, comparisons with Badian's (1994) early literacy screening battery, which the authors acknowledge as having a "clear commonality" with the DEST, or with other norm-referenced measures assessing similar skills, such as the *Test of Phonological Awareness*, are not only possible but are essential to the validation process. The authors are currently conducting longitudinal studies with the DEST (see "Relevant Research" below) to evaluate its effectiveness in predicting reading acquisition and response to interventions.

CONSTRUCT VALIDITY EVIDENCE

Intercorrelations for 9 of the 10 subtests are reported for a sample of 910 children, whereas correlations between Shape Copying and the other subtests are reported for a sample of 25 children in the same table. Postural Stability displays negligible correlations with the other subtests (–.17 to .15), including the other three subtests based on the cerebellar impairment hypothesis. As evidence of diagnostic utility, the authors report the results of a study using the DST. In a sample of 37 children (ages unspecified), 17 of whom were diagnosed with dyslexia, the DST correctly classified 15 of the 17 children with dyslexia and all 20 of the control children. Moreover, when the two misclassified children were given further diagnostic tests, their reading and spelling had improved to the point that they were no longer classifiable as having dyslexia.

Usability

The DEST tasks are brief, varied, and engaging to children, but the test earns a low usability rating nevertheless. Considering that it was designed to be a brief, teacher-administered screening measure, the DEST requires the examiner to manage far too many stimulus materials. For example, the Letter Naming subtest uses 4 cards to present 12 items, and the Digit Naming subtest uses 3 cards for 9 items. Moreover, users must operate and calibrate the Postural Stability balance tester. Today's practitioners, like myself, may lack ready access to a kitchen scale for the calibration process, giving rise to examiner variance and exerting unknown effects on the obtained results. The manual is poorly organized, with information on test development and score interpretation scattered across several sections. Moreover, because it is not spiral-bound, it does not lie flat for easy consultation during administration.

Links to Intervention

Chapter 4 of the manual includes an annotated list of resources for assistance, including phonological awareness training programs, remedial teaching packages, articles, and books. The list is comprehensive, but all of the references are published in the United Kingdom, and American practitioners are unlikely to be familiar with any of the resources other than Reading Recovery.

Relevant Research

In a longitudinal study following the 5-year-old cohort in the norm group (n = 97, mean age = 7-9), Fawcett, Singleton, and Peer (1998) reported that a DEST ARQ of 1.0 or greater at age 5 correctly classified 75% of the children with reading–age discrepancies of 1 or more years on the Reading and Spelling tests on the *Wechsler Objective Reading Dimensions* (Psychological Corporation, 1993) administered 3 years later. Using an ARQ cutoff of 0.9 resulted in a hit rate of 90%, with a false positive rate of 12%. In an intervention study (Nicolson, Fawcett, Moss, & Nicolson, 1999) with 62 poor readers (mean age = 6-0), a DEST ARQ of 0.9 or higher identified 44% of the problem readers, defined as children with a postintervention reading–age deficit of at least 6 months and less than 6 months' growth in word reading. When the cutoff was lowered to an ARQ of 0.6 or higher, the DEST correctly classified 88% of the poor readers. With this revised cutoff, the DEST had the highest sensitivity index of all the pretests administered and was also the best discriminator between problem readers and recovered readers. Based on these studies, Fawcett and Nicolson (2000) now recommend adding a category of borderline or mild risk for children with ARQs of 0.6 to 0.8.

Source and Cost

The DEST is available from the Psychological Corporation for $124.00.

Test Reviews

Johnson, K. M. (2003). Review of the Dyslexia Early Screening Test. In B. S. Plake, J. C. Impara, & R. A. Spies (Eds.), *The fifteenth mental measurements yearbook* (pp. 338–340). Lincoln, NE: Buros Institute of Mental Measurements.

Wilkinson, W. K. (2003). Review of the Dyslexia Early Screening Test. In B. S. Plake, J. C. Impara, & R. A. Spies (Eds.), *The fifteenth mental measurements yearbook* (pp. 340–342). Lincoln, NE: Buros Institute of Mental Measurements.

Summary

The *Dyslexia Early Screening Test* (DEST) is an individually administered, norm-referenced battery for children aged 4-6 through 6-5 that assesses a variety of diagnostic indicators of dyslexia and provides an at-risk index for dyslexia. Attractive to young children, the DEST is less attractive to examiners because of the many testing materials to manage, its cumbersome scoring procedures, and the use of a single score type. Although the DEST shows promise in predicting reading problems and response to intervention, its utility for U.S. practitioners is limited by a norm group that is restricted to the United Kingdom and has unspecified demographic characteristics. There is no evidence of internal consistency, test–retest reliability is unacceptably low for half of the subtests, and interrater reliability is provided for only one subtest. Criterion-related validity evidence is also lacking. A second edition of the DEST, with additional subtests, validation data, and scoring software, is in preparation. According to the publisher, efforts are also underway to norm the DEST in the United States.

Case Example

Name of student: Tammy C.
Age: 5 years, 6 months
Grade: Kindergarten
Date of assessment: April

Reason for referral: Tammy was referred for an early reading assessment by her kindergarten teacher because she is having trouble keeping up with the pace of classroom instruction in reading and language arts. She earned one of the lowest scores on the gradewide reading screening battery administered in the fall of the year, and her letter-name and letter-sound knowledge is still quite limited.

Assessment results and interpretation: The *Dyslexia Early Screening Test* (DEST) is a set of measures assessing literacy skills, phonological awareness, verbal memory, and motor skill and balance in young children. The DEST yields percentile range (PR) scores that indicate children's degree of risk for reading problems, as follows: PRs 1–10, highly at risk; PRs 11–25, at risk; PRs 26–75, average; PRs 76–90, above average; and PRs 91–100, well above average. Children are considered at risk for dyslexia if they score in the high-risk range on four or more subtests, score in the high-risk or at-risk range on seven or more subtests, or have an overall risk score (At-Risk Quotient) of 1.00 or greater. Tammy's performance on the DEST is described below.

DEST subtest	Raw score	PR range	Descriptive Category
Rapid Naming	39 seconds	76–90	Above average
Bead Threading	5/10	26–75	Average
Phonological Discrimination	9/9	91–100	Well above average
Postural Stability	3/24	26–75	Average
Rhyme Detection/First Letter Sound	10/13	26–75	Average
Forwards Digit Span	6/14	26–75	Average
Digit Naming	7/7	91–100	Well above average
Letter Naming	7/10	11–25	At risk
Sound Order	14/16	26–75	Average
Shape Copying	11/21	26–75	Average

On the DEST, Tammy scored at age-appropriate levels on tests of rapid naming, fine motor and postural skills, and short-term verbal memory. Although her phonological awareness skills, as measured by rhyming and sound awareness tasks, are also average or above average, her performance in this domain varied considerably, depending on the skill assessed. On the Phonological Discrimination subtest, which requires the child to indicate whether two words pronounced by the examiner are the same or different, she achieved a perfect score. On the Rhyme Detection/First Letter Sound subtest, she was able to detect whether or not two words spoken by the examiner rhymed (8/8 items correct), but she had more difficulty identifying the initial sound in spoken words (2/5 items correct). She was able to identify all 7 numbers on the Digit Naming subtest (well above average), but she had to count up on her fingers to identify numbers higher than 3, indicating that her digit-naming skills are not yet automatic. She scored in the at-risk range on a task requiring her to name isolated letters. Of the 10 lowercase letters presented, she was unable to identify *w* and confused *d* and *b*. As on Digit Naming, her naming rate was quite slow, and she often looked at the examiner while giving a response as if unsure of its accuracy.

DYSLEXIA SCREENING TEST

Overview

The *Dyslexia Screening Test* (DST; Nicolson & Fawcett, 1996) is an individually administered, norm-referenced battery of measures designed to screen for dyslexia in children and adolescents aged 6-6 through 16-5 years. Based on tasks in the literature and the authors' research program (see Fawcett et al., 1998; Nicholson & Fawcett, 2001, for reviews), the DST includes measures of cognitive markers of dyslexia, such as rapid naming and phonemic segmentation, and skills affected by dyslexia, including reading, spelling, and writing fluency. The DST includes several subtests that are unique among early reading screening batteries, including spelling fluency and pseudoword passage reading tasks. Like its downward extension, the *Dyslexia Early Screening Test* (DEST), it was developed and normed in the United Kingdom and is intended for classwide screening by teachers. The purposes of the DST include (1) identifying children who are in need of more comprehensive assessments or additional assistance in reading, (2) providing information for determining the need for test accommodations, (3) helping to distinguish between dyslexia and more general learning difficulties, and (4) monitoring the progress of children receiving reading interventions. Materials include an examiner's manual; 50 record forms on a tear-off tablet; score keys; cards for the Rapid Naming, One Minute Writing, and Nonsense Passage Reading tasks; Form A and Form B reading cards and scoring transparencies; beads and threading string; a balance tester and blindfold; a backwards digit span audiotape; and a sample permission letter, all packed in a nylon carrying case. The examiner must supply a box or basket for the beads, writing paper, and a card for place keeping on the Rapid Naming subtest.

Subtests and Composite

The DST includes 11 subtests, which are described in Table 5.8 in order of administration. Three of the subtests (Rapid Naming, Bead Threading, and Postural Stability) are identical with those of the same names in the DEST. A weighted mean is calculated for 10 subtests on which the child scores in the at-risk range to yield an overall At-Risk Quotient (ARQ). Semantic Fluency is not considered an index of dyslexia and thus is not included in the calculation of the ARQ.

Administration

Each subtest takes about 2–4 minutes to administer, and the entire test can be given in about 30 minutes. Because the record form does not include time limits, discontinue rules, complete descriptions of scoring procedures, or practice items, the examiner must refer to the manual during the entire administration process. For Postural Stability, the collar on the balance tester must be calibrated to provide a 2.5-kg force (about 5½ pounds) for children younger than 11-6 or a 3-kg force (about 6 pounds) for children older than 11-6. The examiner may push the child with three fingers with the degree of appropriate force if the balance tester is not available. The manual should indicate what, if any accommodations, may be made for children who are uncomfortable with being blindfolded on the Postural Stability subtest. On One Minute Reading, the child is told to say "pass" if omitting a word, but no prompting guide-

TABLE 5.8. Description of the DST Subtests

Subtest	Description
Rapid Naming	The child names two identical arrays of 20 familiar objects on a card as rapidly as possible. The score is the amount of time required to name the entire set. Five seconds are added to the time for each error, and 10 seconds are added if the examiner must use a card to help the child keep his or her place.
Bead Threading	While standing, the child threads a set of wooden beads on a string as rapidly as possible. The score is the number threaded in 30 seconds, minus 1 point if the child drops the string more than once.
One Minute Reading	The child reads word lists aloud as rapidly as possible for 1 minute. There are two versions of the card, each with two forms: a 60-word card for examinees aged 6-6 to 8-5 and a 120-word card for examinees aged 8-6 to 16-6. The score is the number of words read correctly in 1 minute, with 1 bonus point for each second less than 60.
Postural Stability	The child attempts to maintain balance while blindfolded after being gently pushed by the examiner on the back with a balance tester. There are two trials of two pushes each, twice with the child's arms at the side and twice with arms extended in front. Degree of stability is scored on a 7-point scale, and the score is the total number of points for the four trials.
Phonemic Segmentation	The child deletes syllables and single phonemes from words pronounced by the examiner.
Two Minute Spelling	The child writes as many words dictated by the examiner as possible in 2 minutes. There are two starting points: one for examinees aged 6-6 to 9-5 and one for examinees aged 9-6 to 16-6.
Backwards Digit Span	The child repeats backwards an increasingly long series of digits presented on an audiocassette.
Nonsense Passage Reading	The child reads aloud a short passage that includes both real words and pseudowords (3-minute time limit). There are four passages, one for each of four age groups. One point is awarded for each real word correctly read, and 2 points are awarded for each pseudoword correctly read.
One Minute Writing	The child copies as many words from a writing passage printed on a card as possible in 1 minute. There are five passages, one for each of five age groups. The score is the number of words written in 1 minute, with bonus points for rapid copying and penalty points for copying errors, poor handwriting, and, for examinees aged 8-6 and up, poor punctuation.
Verbal Fluency	The child says as many words beginning with the letter *s* as possible in 1 minute. The score is 1 point for every different valid word.
Semantic Fluency	The child names as many animals as possible in 1 minute. The score is 1 point for every different valid animal.

lines are provided (e.g., telling the child to try the next word after a pause of 3 seconds). On Two Minute Spelling, the list for children aged 6-6 to 9-5 consists of only 8 words, whereas there are 28 words for examinees aged 9-6 to 16-5. I have found that early primary grade children sometimes finish writing all or nearly all of the 8 words before the 2-minute time limit has elapsed, but, unlike the reading and writing fluency subtests, no bonus points are awarded for rapid spelling. The directions for Verbal Fluency indicate that the child should say as many words as possible in 1 minute "starting with *s* (the letter *s* or the sound 'suh')." The directions should be modified to indicate that examiners should pronounce /s/ *without* adding "uh" (i.e., /s/, not /suh/) and to include only the letter sound to reduce children's reliance on memory for word spellings in responding.

Scores

Scoring is dichotomous for Phonemic Segmentation and Backwards Digit Span. Scoring procedures for several other subtests are likely to increase the influence of examiner variance on the results. Items for each form of One Minute Reading are reproduced on transparencies for marking errors with a water-soluble pen. Although this permits greater scoring precision than trying to tally errors on the line on the record form, the examiner must then transfer the error count to the record form, which provides no space for noting error types for later analysis. One Minute Writing has a five-step scoring procedure, with four types of penalties (time, copying errors, handwriting quality, and punctuation errors). Scoring procedures for Nonsense Passage Reading involve up to nine steps, with separate calculations for real and pseudoword reading, a time bonus if the child earns 15 or more points for pseudowords, and a time penalty of no more than half the earned score. Partial credit is awarded for "a close try" in pronouncing a pseudoword, but no guidelines or examples are provided to indicate what constitutes a close try. Nor are pronunciations provided for the pseudowords, which range from simple consonant–vowel–consonant items to complex five-syllable items.

Norms consist of percentile ranges at 1-year intervals for ages 6-6 to 16-5. Intervals of 6 months or smaller should be provided for early primary grade examinees. Percentile ranks have been collapsed into five risk status categories: very highly at risk (PRs 1–4), highly at risk (PRs 5–11), at risk (PRs 12–22), normal performance (PRs 23–77), and well above average performance (PRs 78–100). To score the DST, the examiner places the "cutaway" scoring key for the relevant age group over the record form to convert raw scores to a risk indicator system corresponding to the percentile ranges: --- (very highly at risk), -- (highly at risk), - (at risk), 0 (normal), and + (well above average). The ARQ is obtained by awarding 3 points for each triple minus, 2 points for each double minus, 1 point for each single minus, and 0 for the rest of the scores, and then dividing the sum by 10 (excluding Semantic Fluency).

Interpretation

Children are considered at risk for dyslexia if they score in the very-high-risk or high-risk range on four or more subtests, score in the high-risk or at-risk range on seven or more subtests, or have an ARQ of 1.00 or greater. According to the test's authors, children with language disorders or hearing problems typically score poorly on the phonological subtests, whereas children with dyslexia tend to perform poorly on the first 10 subtests but often do well on Semantic Fluency. Children with general learning difficulties show deficits on both Semantic and Verbal Fluency but often achieve average levels of performance on Postural Stability and Bead Threading. The manual includes a case example of a child aged 11-9 to demonstrate scoring procedures, interpretation of results, and possible remediation strategies. The case example's ARQ exceeds the cutoff score, with high-risk to very-high-risk scores on phonological, verbal memory, and literacy subtests and average scores on Verbal and Semantic Fluency; the profile is interpreted as being characteristic of phonological dyslexia.

Technical Adequacy

Standardization

Norms for the DST are based on data from over 1,000 children in schools in Sheffield, London, Gwent, and Kent in the United Kingdom. Prototypes of the DST subtests were piloted in a series of studies designed to evaluate ease of administration, performance stability, and children's interest in the tasks. As a result of these investigations, 3 of the original 14 tests (speed of simple reaction, measurement of muscle tone, and tone order) were omitted because of problems with reliability and testing equipment. Several other subtests were modified to improve reliability and ease of administration, and the balance tester was developed for the Postural Stability subtest. Subtest norms were then developed by testing entire classes of children at selected schools in Sheffield, London, and Wales. The manual indicates that at least 100 children were tested for age groups 6-6 to 7-5 and 7-6 to 8-5 and at 2-year intervals thereafter to permit the calculation of percentile ranks, but no other details regarding sample characteristics or sample sizes for specific age groups are provided. This suggests that at the upper age ranges, scores are based on as few as 50 children per interval, which falls well below the criterion level.

Reliability Evidence

As on the DEST, the authors assert (incorrectly) that internal consistency reliability cannot be estimated because the subtests contain too few items. In a sample of 22 children (age unspecified, 1-week interval), alternate-form reliability for One Minute Reading was .96. Test–retest reliability (approximately 1-week interval) for 34 children aged 6-6 to 12 ranged from .76 to .99 for the 11 subtests. Coefficients for One Minute Reading, Two Minute Spelling, Nonsense Passage Reading, and One Minute Writing were at or above .90, whereas coefficients for Rapid Naming, Phonemic Segmentation, Backwards Digit Span, and Verbal Fluency were between .80 and .89. Stability estimates for Bead Threading, Postural Stability, and Semantic Fluency were in the .70s, which is below acceptable levels. Moreover, given the small sample size and wide age range, these estimates provide limited information about the stability of test results for early primary grade examinees. Interrater agreement for Postural Stability, based on independent ratings of videotaped sessions for 14 children by two experienced and one inexperienced testers, was .98 for the two experienced examiners and .94 between the inexperienced tester and each of the experienced examiners. Interscorer reliability estimates should also be provided for Phonemic Segmentation and all of the timed subtests because of their vulnerability to examiner variance, and for Nonsense Passage Reading, One Minute Reading, and One Minute Writing because of the complex bonus and penalty point systems.

Test Floors and Item Gradients

A precise evaluation of test floor and item gradient characteristics is complicated by the fact that raw scores are converted directly to risk categories by placing age-specific scoring keys over the record form rather than by consulting conversion tables in the manual. Considering that the DST covers an age span of nearly 10 years and that several subtests are quite brief, it is not surprising that many subtests show both floor and ceiling effects at the extremes of the age range. Item gradients are also very steep for some subtests. For example, at ages 6-6 to 7-5, a raw score of 2 on One Minute Reading earns an at-risk rating, whereas a raw score of 3 yields an average rating.

Validity Evidence

CONTENT VALIDITY EVIDENCE

As evidence of content validity, the authors present a rationale for subtest selection, based on their own studies and tasks developed by other reading researchers. The DST is designed to include two sets of measures: (1) tests of "attainment" (real word and pseudoword reading fluency, writing fluency, and spelling fluency) and (2) diagnostic tests assessing empirically validated indicators of dyslexia. Subtests were selected for both diagnostic utility and ease of administration. According to the authors, Semantic Fluency taps a domain that is a relative strength for children with dyslexia and is included to help differentiate such children from children with general learning problems. No information is provided regarding item characteristics, including difficulty, discrimination, or possible DIF.

CRITERION-RELATED VALIDITY EVIDENCE

No criterion-related validity data are presented.

CONSTRUCT VALIDITY EVIDENCE

A table in the manual presents intercorrelations for the 11 subtests, but the overlap among the samples from which the correlations were derived is unclear. The manual states that intercorrelations for 9 unspecified subtests are based on a sample of 817 children; that another sample of 500 children was used to collect data for 3 more subtests (One Minute Writing, Verbal Fluency, and Semantic Fluency); and that a third sample of 35 children provided data for Semantic Fluency, One Minute Writing, and "the other tests." Among the diagnostic tests, Semantic Fluency and Phoneme Segmentation displayed the highest correlations with One Minute Reading (*r*s = .70 and .67, respectively), whereas Postural Stability and Bead Threading displayed the lowest correlations (*r*s = –.39 and .40, respectively). Age–subtest intercorrelations are low to moderate for the diagnostic tests and moderate to high for the attainment tests. In a study with 37 children, 17 of whom were diagnosed with dyslexia, 15 of the 17 dyslexic children obtained an ARQ of 1.0 or greater, whereas none of the 20 nondisabled controls had an ARQ higher than 0.3. Moreover, when the two misclassified children were given further diagnostic tests, their literacy skills had improved to the extent that they were no longer classifiable as having dyslexia. No evidence is presented to support the DST's assertion that it can be used to monitor the effects of reading interventions.

Usability

For a screening measure designed for classwide administration by teachers, the DST has too many individual materials for examiners to manage efficiently. Test stimuli for reading, spelling, and writing tasks should be combined in a spiral-bound booklet rather than presented on individual age-specific cards. Some of the words used in the manual (e.g., *biro* = *pen*) are likely to be unfamiliar to American practitioners. Three items on the Phonemic Segmentation subtest (*wigwam*, *marmalade*, and *igloo*) may be unfamiliar to children from diverse linguistic or cultural backgrounds. On the single-page two-sided record form, subtests are arranged in a different order from their administration order, presumably to conserve space, and there is very little room for recording responses on Verbal Fluency and Semantic Fluency or errors for future analysis on the other subtests.

Links to Intervention

The manual includes an annotated list of resources for remediation, including phonological awareness training programs, reading curricula, research articles, and books. Because all of the resources describe educational and instructional practices in the United Kingdom, they are likely to be of limited utility to American practitioners.

Relevant Research

Like its lower extension, the DEST, the DST includes several tasks based on the authors' cerebellar impairment hypothesis, which proposes that dyslexic children show deficits on measures of cerebellar functioning as well as on tests of phonological processing. In a study (Nicolson & Fawcett, 1994) with 35 dyslexic and 33 normally achieving children aged 7-7 to 16-9, the authors evaluated the diagnostic utility of an extensive battery of cognitive and motor skill tests, including computer-administered DST prototypes. Dyslexic children scored significantly lower than matched age controls on most of the tasks and significantly lower than reading-age controls on tasks of phoneme segmentation, rapid object naming, tachistoscopic word recognition, bead threading, and balance. In a subsequent study with matched groups of dyslexic and normally achieving children aged 10, 14, and 18 (total $n = 55$), Fawcett and colleagues (1996) administered a battery of 14 cerebellar functioning measures that included a version of the Postural Stability subtest. The children with dyslexia scored significantly lower than controls on all 14 tasks and significantly lower than reading-age controls on 11 tasks, including Postural Stability.

Source and Cost

The DST is available from the Psychological Corporation for $124.00.

Summary

The *Dyslexia Screening Test* (DST) is a norm-referenced set of measures designed to screen for dyslexia in children aged 6-6 through 16-5. Derived from tasks in the authors' research program, the DST has been demonstrated to discriminate between dyslexic children and normally achieving children in several small studies. The utility of the DST in screening early primary grade examinees is limited by both technical and usability problems, however. The norm group is restricted to the United Kingdom, has unspecified demographic characteristics, and consists of too few examinees for several age groups. Moreover, there is limited evidence of reliability, stability estimates fall below acceptable levels for several subtests, floor and ceiling effects are evident on most subtests, and evidence of the DST's relationship to other reading screening measures or tests of any kind is lacking. The DST also scores low in usability because of the numerous materials examiners must manage; its complex, time-consuming administration and scoring procedures; and the use of a single score type. Without a major revision and U.S. norming, including a full complement of reliability and validity studies, the DST remains an interesting research-based instrument that has yet to fulfill its promise as an effective screening tool for American children.

Case Example

Name of student: Marvin A.
Age: 6 years, 11 months
Grade: Second grade
Date of assessment: November

Reason for referral: Marvin was referred for an early reading assessment by his second-grade teacher. He has learned letter names and most single letter sounds and has a small sight word vocabulary, but he is making very slow progress in reading and spelling, despite receiving tutoring twice weekly since the beginning of the year. His teacher notes that he also has trouble understanding verbal instructions and working independently on reading and language arts tasks.

Assessment results and interpretation: The *Dyslexia Screening Test* (DST) is a set of measures assessing literacy skills and indicators of dyslexia, including reading, writing, and spelling fluency; phonological awareness; short-term verbal memory; and motor skill and balance. Performance on each measure is rated according to five risk categories: very highly at risk (percentile ranges [PRs] 1–4), highly at risk (PRs 5–11, at risk (PRs 12–22), normal (PRs 23–77), and well above average (PRs 78–100). A child is considered at risk for dyslexia if he or she scores in the very-high-risk or high-risk range on four or more subtests, in the high-risk or at-risk range on seven or more subtests, or has an overall score (called an At Risk Quotient) of 1.00 or greater. Marvin's performance on the DST is shown below.

DST Subtest	Raw Score/Total Points	At Risk Index
Rapid Naming	95 seconds	Very high risk
Bead Threading	6/12	Average
One Minute Reading	1/60	High risk
Postural Stability	8/24	Average
Phonemic Segmentation	4/12	At risk
Two Minute Spelling	4/8	At risk
Backwards Digit Span	4/14	Average
Nonsense Passage Reading	7/48	At risk
One Minute Writing	12/20	Average
Verbal Fluency	2	High risk
Semantic Fluency	11	Average

Compared with his age peers, Marvin's overall performance on the DST is rated as "at risk" (At Risk Quotient = 1.0). He scored at age-appropriate levels on tasks of eye–hand coordination, balance, and short-term memory for digits. His phonemic segmentation skills, as measured by a task requiring him to delete sounds from spoken words, are much less well developed. He was able to delete syllables from words pronounced by the examiner, but he had difficulty deleting phonemes (single sounds). For example, asked to say *boat* without the /b/ sound, he said, "/t/." Martin's writing fluency skills, as measured by a timed copying task, are average for his age. In contrast, his ability to read and spell under time pressure is limited (at-risk and high-risk range, respectively). On One Minute Reading, which required him to read single words as quickly as possible, he was able to read only one word on the list (at-risk range). On Nonsense Passage Reading, his performance fell in the high-risk range. He was able to read a few sight words and one pseudoword but missed other common sight words and phonically regular real words and pseudowords (e.g., *fig* for *feg*). Moreover, although he made a good effort, he read very slowly and laboriously, requiring nearly 2 minutes to read the five-sentence passage. On Verbal Fluency, which requires providing as many words beginning with the letter *s* as possible in 1 minute, he was able to supply only two words (high-risk range). In contrast, he achieved an average performance on Semantic Fluency, which requires naming as many animals as possible in 1 minute. The difference between his very poor performance on the sound-based verbal fluency measure and his average performance on the meaning-based fluency measure is striking and is characteristic of some children with reading problems.

LINDAMOOD AUDITORY CONCEPTUALIZATION TEST—REVISED EDITION

Overview

The *Lindamood Auditory Conceptualization Test–Revised Edition* (LAC; Lindamood & Lindamood, 1971/1979) is an individually administered, criterion-referenced test that measures the ability to discriminate speech sounds and compare the number and order of sounds in spoken words in individuals from kindergarten through adulthood. According to the authors, the ability to compare how and where spoken words differ in phonemic structure, termed the *comparator function,* is critical to the detection and self-correction of errors in decoding and spelling. First published in 1971, the current LAC version has a publication date of 1979 and has two forms. Although the words "Revised Edition" are printed on the cover of the manual, the authors make no references to what, if any changes, were made, and the publisher's catalog does not identify the test as "revised." The LAC has been used in numerous studies to predict at-risk reading status and to evaluate the effects of reading interventions (e.g., Alexander, Andersen, Heilman, Voeller, & Torgesen, 1991; Felton, 1998; Uhry & Shepherd, 1997) and is linked to a remedial program widely used in clinical and research settings (Lindamood & Lindamood, 1998). Purposes of the LAC include (1) facilitating early identification of children with auditory-conceptualization deficiencies, (2) providing information for remediation, (3) serving as a diagnostic instrument in speech pathology, and (4) serving as a research tool. Materials include a spiral-bound examiner's manual, an audiocassette administration and pronunciation guide, 24 colored blocks, two cue sheets (one in English and one in Spanish), and 50 record sheets for each form, all packed in a box.

Assessment Tasks and Composite

Assessment Tasks

The LAC consists of two levels, termed Category I and Category II. For both tasks, the child uses colored blocks to represent individual sounds or pseudoword syllables pronounced by the examiner at half-second intervals (see Table 5.9).

Composite

Raw scores from Category I Parts A and B and Category II are multiplied by weights and summed to obtain a total score. No separate scores are available for the two categories.

Administration

The examiner administers a pretest to ensure that the child understands the concepts of numbers up to 4, sameness–difference, left-to-right order, and first–last. The manual indicates that the LAC can be administered in 10 minutes, but I have found that administration, including the pretest, takes about 15–25 minutes for early primary grade children. The test's authors state that the examiner should sit beside the child to facilitate accurate recording of responses and to permit the child to use visual as well as auditory cues in responding. There are three teaching tasks for Category I and one teaching task for Category II. Demonstration items and a summary of administration procedures are printed on a cue sheet. Using a color code printed in the record form, the examiner records the block patterns made by the child for each item. Appropriate patterns for each item are presented in the manual rather than on the record sheet, so that examiners must refer to the manual during administration until they are thoroughly familiar with the test.

The LAC takes a considerable amount of time to learn to administer accurately because error corrections and feedback are specific to the type of error the child makes. I recommend that examiners new to the test conduct several practice admin-

TABLE 5.9. Description of the LAC Assessment Tasks

Assessment task	Description
Category I	This category consists of two parts. For Part A, the child uses colored blocks to represent the number and sameness–difference of sounds pronounced by the examiner. For example, the examiner says, "Show me /f/ /s/ /th/," and the child places three blocks of different colors in a row. For Part B, the child uses blocks to represent the number, sameness–difference, and order of sounds. For example, the examiner says, "Show me /k/ /t/ /k/," and the child places three blocks in a left-to-right sequence, with the first and third blocks of the same color and the second of a different color.
Category II	The child uses colored blocks to indicate the number, sameness–difference, and order of sounds that the examiner pronounces as a syllable. Once the child has represented the initial syllable pattern with a row of blocks, the child uses that row to represent a series of changes as the examiner adds, substitutes, omits, shifts, or repeats sounds. For example, the examiner says, "Show me /i/." Once the child represents the sound with a single block, the examiner extends the pattern by saying, "If that says /i/, show me /ip/," and the child adds a second block of a different color to the right of the first block.

istrations in the presence of an experienced colleague who can offer corrective feedback as needed. For Category I, the examiner provides feedback for the first error, with feedback depending on the nature of the error. If the child is able to correct the error after the feedback, credit is given for that item. Testing is discontinued after five consecutive errors. For Category II, if the child makes an error, the examiner clears the blocks and sets up a new block pattern to represent the next item on an error alternate list printed on the record sheet. If the child makes an error later, the same procedure is followed, and the examiner returns to the original list of patterns. Testing is discontinued after five errors, which do not need to be consecutive. An overview of administration procedures, pronunciations for the isolated sounds and syllable patterns on both forms of the test, and examples of error feedback are provided on an audiocassette. Unfortunately, most of the page numbers referred to on the audiocassette do not match the numbers in the manual, so that the listener must flip through the manual to find the correct page and then rewind the tape to review the instructions. The manual includes a scoring example for an examinee of unspecified age or grade and an examiner's check sheet.

Scores

Items are scored pass–fail (1 or 0), with no partial credit awarded. Scoring takes less than 5 minutes. Raw scores from Parts I-A, I-B, and II are multiplied by weights and summed to obtain a total score (maximum weighted score = 100). Using the record form or a table in the manual, the examiner compares the total score with minimum performance scores at half-year intervals for kindergarten through Grade 6 and a combined level for Grade 7 through adult.

Interpretation

According to the test's authors, the recommended minimum scores do not represent average age- or grade-level scores but minimal levels of performance that indicate a high probability of adequate or more than adequate reading and spelling achievement. Minimum scores at the lower grades were deliberately set higher than was indicated by the standardization data to aid in the early identification of children with delays in auditory conceptualization, including children whose poor decoding skills may be disguised by the effects of sight word memorization. After first grade, scores show a bimodal distribution: Most examinees demonstrate adequate performance, but nearly a third fall in the lower ranges. For Category I, approximately 80% of children can be expected to code the patterns correctly by the end of first grade. Category I errors after second grade indicate severe dysfunction, except for item 8 (given /vop/, show /vops/), which children often code incorrectly if they are not looking at the examiner. For Category II errors, the inability to represent a medial vowel change (e.g., given /vops/, show /vaps/) after second grade indicates significant risk for reading and spelling problems. Examinees at and above the seventh-grade level are expected to achieve scores of 99, that is, virtually perfect performance.

Appendix B in the manual presents an item analysis for end-of-first-grade responses, including a table indicating the percentages of examinees in three first-grade samples passing or attempting each item. Appendix C presents 13 case examples ranging from first grade through adulthood to demonstrate the meaning of LAC scores at various ranges. The case examples, four of which are of children in first through third grades, include a description of the referral problem, data from other tests, and results of the auditory-conceptual therapy program developed by the test authors.

Technical Adequacy

Standardization

The normative, reliability, and validity data presented in the manual were gathered over 30 years ago and are long overdue for updating. The standardization sample consisted of 660 students in kindergarten through Grade 12 in Monterey, California, who were tested at midyear (Calfee, Lindamood, & Lindamood, 1973). For Grades K through 6, 15 classrooms at each grade level were divided into four groups based on gender and classroom performance (male–high, male–low, female–high, female–low). One student from each group was then randomly selected from each classroom, for a total of 60 students per grade. Similar procedures were used for Grades 7 through 12, with 40 students sampled per grade level. Because recommended minimum scores are provided in half-year intervals, this means that these values are based on only 20–30 examinees per interval, which is unacceptably low. No specific information regarding the demographic characteristics of the sample is provided, other than a statement that the sample included a wide range of ethnic, economic, and social groups.

Reliability Evidence

Test–retest reliability (minimum interval = 4 weeks) using alternate forms was .96 for 52 children from Pismo Beach, California, with 4 children at each grade level from kindergarten through Grade 12. Because reliability is not reported separately by grade, the within-grade stability of the LAC remains undetermined. Moreover, this value is inflated because of the sample's age heterogeneity. No evidence of internal consistency or interscorer reliability is presented. Given the complexities of administration and scoring and the use of a live-voice format for delivery, studies of interscorer consistency should be a priority. The authors themselves (Lindamood, Bell, & Lindamood, 1992) have acknowledged that obtaining a standardized LAC administration can be problematic because examiners may be among the estimated 30% of the population with phonological processing deficits.

Test Floors and Item Gradients

In my experience, floor effects are common for low-performing children on Category II tasks. As noted above, beginning in Grade 2, performance is bimodally distributed, with the majority of examinees scoring at or near the ceiling and the rest scoring in the lower ranges.

Validity Evidence

CONTENT VALIDITY EVIDENCE

The LAC is based on its authors' clinical experience and observation rather than on a theoretical model. According to the authors, the LAC is designed to assess auditory processing of speech-sound identities and relationships separately from learned letter-sound associations. Because specific phonemes are not the critical factors in identifying dysfunction, the sounds used are a representative sample rather than a complete set of English phonemes. In Category I, the maximum number of sounds per pattern is limited to three to minimize the memory burden. For Category II, each item requires examinees to manipulate one phoneme change, with no more than four sounds per syllable. Five categories of changes are tested (addition, substitution, omission, shift, and repetition), based on analyses indicating that one or more of these changes is always involved in errors in speech, spelling, or reading. Pseudoword syllables are used to reduce the possibility that examinees can rely on memory of real word spellings to respond. The authors state that live-voice rather than audiocassette delivery permits the child to make use of the visual cues that are normally available during daily auditory activities. No theoretical or empirical evidence is presented in support of the weighting system.

CRITERION-RELATED VALIDITY EVIDENCE

For the 660 students in the Monterey sample described above, concurrent correlations between LAC total score and combined Reading and Spelling scores on the *Wide Range Achievement Test* (WRAT; Jastak & Jastak, 1978) ranged from .66 to .81. Coefficients for examinees in kindergarten through Grade 2 were also high (*r*s = 68 to .75). The predictive utility of the two LAC tasks varied with grade. For kindergarten examinees, Category I was the major contributor to predictive validity, whereas for Grades 1 through 3, both Category I and II were significant predictors of reading and spelling performance. After Grade 3, only Category II scores were significantly related to reading and spelling, due to the ceiling effects on Category I scores for older examinees. For the 52 children in the Pismo Beach sample cited above, correlations with WRAT scores ranged from .72 to .78 for both forms. Predictive validity was assessed in an unpublished study with three groups of first graders (total $n = 62$) who were being instructed in three different reading programs. September LAC scores were strong predictors (*r*s = .88 to .98) of end-of-year scores on several reading measures, including the WRAT.

CONSTRUCT VALIDITY EVIDENCE

LAC raw scores demonstrate a gradual increase from kindergarten to Grade 2, after which there is a bimodal distribution of performance that continues through Grade 12. As evidence of the discriminative power of the recommended minimum scores, the manual presents a series of graphs indicating the percentages of students in the standardization sample in each total test score range with below- and above-grade level WRAT reading and spelling performance. No information is provided to indicate how the two half-interval scores were derived for kindergarten through Grade 6 examinees. According to the authors, no significant gender differences in LAC performance were found in any of the standardization samples, and additional small samples of examinees from various language and dialect populations (location, size, and demographic characteristics unspecified) revealed no significant differences for ethnic or linguistic backgrounds. In a replication of the standardization study in two predominantly non-Caucasian schools in Oakland, California (total $n = 140$; 20 students per grade level in Grades K–6), the authors report that correlations between LAC scores and WRAT scores were similar, although both LAC and WRAT scores were slightly lower. No scores or correlations from this investigation are provided, however.

Usability

Because of the LAC's complexity, examiners must devote considerable time and effort in order to achieve reasonable levels of consistency and efficiency in administration and scoring. Directions for administration and feedback are clearly spelled out, but the manual is poorly formatted and makes for laborious reading. Mastering the specific error feedback is the most challenging aspect of administration. Because the LAC can be a frustrating experience for children with poor phonological skills, as well as for children with attentional and/or motivational problems, the examiner's ability to deliver a brisk but accurate administration is essential. As indicated above, examiner cue sheets are provided in English and Spanish. Both formal and informal Spanish verb forms are provided on the Spanish version for addressing adult or child examinees.

Links to Intervention

An appendix in the manual discusses the educational implications of LAC scores, including developmental and remedial goals. The manual cites several studies documenting the effectiveness of the authors' remedial program in improving LAC scores for low-scoring first graders. Most of the studies are unpublished, and all are 25 years or older. The LAC is associated with an intervention program, the *Lindamood Phoneme Sequencing Program for Reading, Spelling, and Speech–Third Edition* (Lindamood & Lindamood, 1998). The multisensory program is designed to bring the articulatory (oral–motor) features of each phoneme into conscious awareness so that children learn to "feel" as well as hear the identity, order, and number of sounds in words. A growing body of research demonstrates that the program has significant positive effects on reading proficiency in samples of children at risk for reading failure (McGuinness, McGuinness, & Donohue, 1995; Torgesen, Wagner, Rashotte, Rose, et al., 1999) and children with reading disabilities (Alexander et al., 1991; Torgesen, Alexander, et al., 2001).

Relevant Research

The LAC has frequently been used in reading diagnostic, prediction, and intervention studies as a measure of phonemic awareness. In a study with 312 Australian children assessed in kindergarten through second grade (Kenny & Chekaluk, 1993), LAC performance, in combination with teacher ratings, explained approximately 50% of the variance in WRMT-R Basic Skills scores. For 94 first graders who took a battery of phonological awareness and rapid naming measures (McGuinness et al., 1995), the LAC was the strongest predictor of WRMT-R Word Identification and Word Attack scores. Moreover, LAC scores contributed a significant proportion of the variance to reading achievement, even when age and verbal ability were controlled. In a subsequent intervention study with 42 children aged 5-11 to 7-9, fall LAC scores were significant discriminators of good and average readers at the end of an 8-month training program, even when fall WRMT-R scores were taken into account. Like other measures of phonemic awareness, the LAC has maximum predictive value in the early primary grades. In a sample of 39 students (McGuinness, 1997), fall

Grade 1 LAC scores predicted 35% of the variance in spring Grade 1 WRMT-R Word Identification scores but were not significant predictors of Grade 3 reading performance.

Research indicates that the LAC is not a "pure" measure of phonemic awareness but taps other cognitive and linguistic skills, especially verbal memory (McGuinness et al., 1995). Moreover, there is some evidence that LAC performance covaries with IQ. In a sample of 81 at-risk kindergarten children (Felton & Brown, 1990), LAC scores were significantly correlated with end-of-Grade 1 *Woodcock Reading Mastery Tests* (Woodcock, 1973) Word Identification and Word Attack scores, but correlations were nonsignificant when IQ was included. In a subsequent longitudinal study with 221 kindergarten children (Felton, 1992), LAC scores, along with rapid letter naming and initial sound discrimination, predicted 38% of the variance in Grade 3 *California Achievement Tests* reading scores when general ability was removed from the analysis. When IQ was included, however, the LAC again failed to predict reading outcomes.

Source and Cost

The LAC is available from PRO-ED for $101.00. Available from the same publisher is the *Lindamood Phoneme Sequencing Program for Reading, Spelling, and Speech*. The classroom version (for groups of five children or more) is $498.00, and the clinical version for individual and small-group instruction is $249.00.

Test Reviews

Bountress, N. B. (1985). Review of the Lindamood Auditory Conceptualization Test, Revised Edition. In J. V. Mitchell, Jr. (Ed.), *The ninth mental measurements yearbook* (pp. 862–863). Lincoln, NE: Buros Institute of Mental Measurements.

Cox, J. R. (1985). Review of the Lindamood Auditory Conceptualization Test, Revised Edition. In J. V. Mitchell, Jr. (Ed.), *The ninth mental measurements yearbook* (p. 863). Lincoln, NE: Buros Institute of Mental Measurements.

Zinna, D. R. (1985). Lindamood Auditory Conceptualization Test. In D. Keyser & R. Sweetland (Eds.), *Test critiques* (Vol. 4, pp. 376–381). Austin, TX: PRO-ED.

Summary

The *Lindamood Auditory Conceptualization Test–Revised Edition* (LAC) is a criterion-referenced measure of the ability to manipulate the sound segments in spoken language for examinees from kindergarten through adulthood. The LAC has a long history in research and clinical practice, has documented utility in predicting reading and response to intervention in early primary grade children, and is linked to an empirically validated intervention program. Despite its assets, the LAC has several technical and usability limitations. It requires extensive training and practice for accurate administration, and the task is so difficult for young children that it has limited utility in kindergarten screenings. Technical information in the manual is either absent or outdated, and the manual itself is very much in need of updating. There is also some question regarding what the LAC actually measures, as several studies indicate that it overlaps considerably with IQ. Nevertheless, it can serve as a very useful diagnostic indicator of early reading problems, beginning in the second semester of first grade.

In my own experience, it has in some cases provided the first indication of phonological processing deficits in children who had been identified by their teachers as performing below their peers in the classroom but who had scored in the average range on norm-referenced reading achievement tests. According to the publisher, a standardized revision is under development.

Case Example

Name of student: Andrea P.
Age: 8 years, 1 month
Grade: Second grade
Date of assessment: March

Reason for referral: Andrea was referred for an early reading assessment by her second-grade teacher because of her persistently poor performance in reading, writing, and spelling. She recently scored in the average range on a norm-referenced reading battery, and her word recognition skills appear to be adequate; however, she has difficulty distinguishing between different sounds, blending sounds, and using letter-sound conversion rules to decode unfamiliar words.

Assessment results and interpretation: The *Lindamood Auditory Conceptualization Test–Revised* (LAC) measures children's ability to discriminate among different speech sounds (*phonemes*) and to compare the number and order of sounds in spoken words. Difficulty attending to and manipulating the individual sounds in spoken language is associated with risk for reading problems. On the LAC, the child uses colored blocks to indicate the number, sameness–difference, and order of phonemes in nonsense syllables (e.g., *vop*) pronounced by the examiner. Scores on each task are weighted, based on their predictive utility, to produce a total score that is compared with grade-level expectations for minimum performance. Andrea's performance on the LAC is described below.

LAC Task	Number Correct/Total Items	Converted Score
Category I-A	8/10	8/10
Category I-B	2/6	6/18
Category II	2/12	12/72
Total	14/28	26/100

Andrea's LAC score falls considerably below the recommended minimum score for second graders in the second half of the school year (26/100 vs. 71/100). Moreover, her score falls below that expected for first-semester kindergarten students (31/100), indicating that difficulty in understanding the sound structure of language is contributing to her reading and spelling problems. She was able to represent most of the Category I-A stimulus patterns, which required her to indicate how many sounds she heard in a pattern and whether the sounds were the same or different. She had more difficulty with Category I-B items, which required her to represent the number, likeness or difference, and sequence of sounds. She was able to answer only 2 of the 12 Category II items, which require representing changes in the sequence, number, and identity of sounds in a series of 12 syllables that are linked together. She had trouble distinguishing the number of sounds, deleting initial sounds, changing initial and medial vowel sounds, and reversing sounds. For example, given the stimulus pattern /ip/, as represented by two different-colored blocks and asked to represent /op/, she added a third block of a different color to the front of the pattern, suggesting that she did not understand that the syllable had only two sounds and that only the first sound had changed.

PHONOLOGICAL ABILITIES TEST

Overview

The *Phonological Abilities Test* (PAT; Muter, Hulme, & Snowling, 1997) is an individually administered, norm-referenced test designed to assess the phonological skills that predict early reading progress in children aged 4 through 7. Based on the types of tasks used in its authors' research program (Muter, 1996, 2000; Muter & Snowling, 1998), it was developed and normed in the United Kingdom. The PAT is the only early literacy battery reviewed in this text that includes a measure of speech rate as well as the more usual measures of phonological processing, such as rhyming and sound deletion. According to the test's authors (Hulme & Roodenrys, 1995; McDougall et al., 1994), speech rate serves as an index of speed of access to phonological codes, which is a separate skill from the processes measured by phonological awareness tasks and is a better predictor of reading than traditional memory span tasks. The authors identify four purposes for the PAT: (1) screening to identify children at risk for reading difficulties, (2) assessing the nature and degree of phonological deficits in children already experiencing reading problems, (3) serving as part of a diagnostic battery for children needing more comprehensive assessments, and (4) facilitating research. Materials include an examiner's manual, 25 record forms, an easel-format stimulus booklet, and a set of letter cards.

Subtests

The PAT consists of six subtests: four phonological awareness measures, a speech rate measure, and a letter-naming task. The manual refers to Word Completion and Phoneme Deletion as two subtests, but each is divided into two tasks and yields two scores (see Table 5.10). For three of the four phonological awareness subtests (Rhyme Detection, Word Completion, and Phoneme Deletion), pictures accompany stimulus items to help sustain children's interest and reduce memory demands. No composite score is available.

Administration

Each subtest takes approximately 3–5 minutes to administer, and the entire test can be given in about 25–30 minutes. Because the record form does not include subtest directions, examiners must consult the manual throughout the administration process. The subtests may be administered in any order, but the authors do not recommend beginning with Phoneme Deletion because that is the most difficult subtest. There are no basals or ceilings, and all examinees take all items. Demonstration tasks are provided for Rhyme Detection, Word Completion, Phoneme Deletion, and Speech Rate. For Rhyme Production, the examiner gives a single example of a rhyming word for each of the stimulus words but does not provide a full demonstration of the nature of this novel task (producing a series of rhyming words under time pres-

TABLE 5.10. Description of the PAT Subtests

Subtest	Description
Rhyme Detection	The child selects the one of three pictured words that rhymes with a pictured target word.
Rhyme Production	The child provides as many real words or pseudowords as possible that rhyme with each of two stimulus words pronounced by the examiner, with a 30-second time limit per stimulus word. The score is the total number of rhyming words produced for the two stimulus items.
Word Completion–Syllables and Phonemes	This subtest consists of two tasks and yields two scores. For *Syllables*, the examiner displays a picture, pronounces the two-syllable word represented by the picture, and then pronounces the first syllable of the word; the child provides the final syllable. For Phonemes, the examiner displays a picture, pronounces the one-syllable word represented by the picture, and then pronounces the onset of the word; the child provides the final phoneme. For example, the examiner displays a picture of a mat and says, "/ma/," and the child says, "/t/."
Phoneme Deletion–Beginning and End Sounds	This subtest consists of two tasks and yields two scores. For *Beginning Sounds*, the child deletes the initial sound of a one-syllable word pronounced by the examiner, and the correct response is also a word. For *End Sounds*, the child deletes the final sound of a one-syllable word pronounced by the examiner, but the correct response is not usually a word.
Speech Rate	The child repeats a three-syllable word supplied by the examiner 10 times as rapidly as possible. The score is the average time in seconds for three trials, divided by 10, to produce a words-per-second score.
Letter Knowledge	The child provides the name or the sound for the 26 letters of the alphabet, presented in random order on flashcards.

sure). Moreover, the directions do not inform the child that both real words and pseudowords are acceptable. Given these omissions, rhyming deficits may be confounded with the failure to understand task requirements. I have found that even after hearing an example of a rhyming word, some children provide words with the same initial sound as the stimulus word rather than rhyming words. When the example includes a *series* of rhyming words, however, the same children are often able to generate enough rhyming words to earn an average score. Assessing letter knowledge with individual flashcards is much more time-consuming than with a random set of letters arrayed on a single page or card. In addition, although examiners are told to present the letters in random order, the lack of a standardized order introduces variance into the results.

For screening purposes, the PAT's authors recommend a subset of three or four subtests, with measures varying according to the age of the examinee (see Table 5.11).

TABLE 5.11. Recommended Screening Versions for the PAT by Age

	Age of examinee		
PAT subtest	5 years	6 years	7 years
Rhyme Detection	×		×
Rhyme Production		×	
Phoneme Deletion–Beginning and End Sounds	×	×	×
Letter Knowledge	×	×	×
Speech Rate			×

The screening subsets are based on the authors' predictive validity studies, described on the previous page.

Scores

Items are scored 1 for correct and 0 for incorrect. Correct responses for Word Completion and Phoneme Deletion items are provided in the stimulus book and on the record form in terms of the International Phonetic Alphabet, which may be unfamiliar to some examiners. Moreover, on the record form, the correct answers for Phoneme Deletion–End Sounds are presented with the end sound first (e.g., meat [t] [mi]), which makes for a confusing format. On Letter Knowledge, children may provide either letter names or letter sounds, but letter-name knowledge and letter-sound knowledge are not equivalent skills. Children typically master letter names well before letter sounds, especially for vowels, and the manual does not indicate whether most of the children in the norm group reported letter names or sounds. Scores for each subtest are converted into four *centile equivalents* (the 10th, 25th, 50th, and 75th percentiles), with separate tables for the two tasks on the Word Completion and Phoneme Deletion subtests. No other derived scores are provided. With only four sets of percentile ranks, many raw scores do not correspond to the values in the tables, and examiners must often interpolate to obtain derived scores. In the absence of guidelines for interpolation, the potential for interscorer inconsistency is high. Norms are in 1-year increments for ages 4-0 to 4-11 and in 6-month increments for ages 5-0 to 7-11. The manual offers conflicting advice about using the test with 4-year-olds. On page 4, the authors state that the PAT "may be used for large scale screening within the age range of the norms i.e. from 4–7 years." Elsewhere in the manual (pp. 5, 33, and 40), they state that they do not recommend using the PAT to screen 4-year-olds because of floor effects and poor long-term predictive power at that age.

Interpretation

According to the manual, scores falling below the 10th centile (percentile) on a given subtest indicate impaired performance, low scores on all six subtests indicate a general deficit in phonological skills, and a variable profile indicates specific areas of weakness that can be targeted for remediation. To illustrate scoring and interpretation, the manual presents three case studies, all of which include *Wechsler Intelligence Scale for Children–III* (WISC-III) Verbal IQ scores and scores on British reading and spelling tests. Despite the PAT's stated purpose of screening to prevent reading failure, all of the cases involve 7-year-olds who were referred because of "delayed reading development," and two cases are from the oldest age group (7-6 to 7-11 years).

Technical Adequacy

Standardization

The standardization sample for the PAT consisted of 826 children aged 4 through 7 years from the United Kingdom who were tested in 1995–1996. Testing was conducted by undergraduate and graduate psychology students supervised by the authors, rather than by credentialed examiners. Sample characteristics are reported in terms of age and geographical distribution but not in terms of gender, race, residence, ethnicity, SES, or disability status. More than half of the norm group was drawn from northern England and Scotland, and the authors acknowledge that the sample is not representative of the United Kingdom as a whole. Norm group sizes, reported by half-yearly intervals for ages 5 through 7, are over 100 for all groups, with one exception: Subgroup size for children aged 7-6 to 7-11 is only 58, which is unacceptably low. In addition, the subgroup size for 4-year-olds is only 55, which provides additional evidence that the PAT should not be used as a screening measure with children of this age.

Reliability Evidence

Internal consistency reliabilities for seven PAT subtests (except Rhyme Production and Letter Knowledge) for a sample of 60 children aged 4-7 through 7-4 ranged from a low of .67 for Speech Rate to a high of .97 for Phoneme Deletion–Beginning Sounds. For Rhyme Production, the correlation of the two stimulus words was calculated (r = .83). Coefficients for all subtests except for Speech Rate are in the acceptable range for a screening measure (i.e., .80 or above). The authors do not offer a rationale for excluding Letter Knowledge from the internal consistency analyses. Test–retest reliability for a sample of 35 children aged 4-5 to 5-8 (3-week interval) ranged from .58 to .86. Coefficients for three of the eight subtests (Rhyme Detection, Phoneme Deletion–Beginning Sounds, and Letter Knowledge) were in the acceptable range for screening measures (.80, .84, and .86, respectively), but coefficients for the other five subtests fell below the criterion level: Rhyme Production (.65), Word Completion–Syllables (.58), Word Completion–Phonemes (.71), Phoneme Deletion–End Sounds (.61), and Speech Rate (.72). Moreover, because no test–retest studies were conducted with 6- and 7-year-olds, the stability of the PAT at those ages is unknown. No evidence of interscorer reliability is reported.

Test Floors and Item Gradients

As the PAT's authors acknowledge, all of the subtests show floor and/or ceiling effects at the extremes of the age distribution, partly because of the developmental nature of the tasks but also because of the limited number of items per subtest and the restriction of derived scores to four sets of percentile ranks. For example, a child aged 5-6 to 5-11 who obtains a raw score of 1 on Rhyme Production obtains a percentile rank of 25. The same factors produce steep item gradients. For a child aged 7-0, a raw score of 6 on Word Completion–Phonemes yields a percentile rank of 10, whereas a raw score of 7 yields a percentile rank of 25.

Validity Evidence

CONTENT VALIDITY EVIDENCE

Content validity evidence consists of a rationale for subtest and format selection. Words for the four phonological awareness subtests were chosen from a list of high-frequency spoken vocabulary in 5-year-olds (Raban, 1988). Subtests were designed to provide measures of predictors of early reading acquisition identified by the test's authors (McDougall et al., 1994; Muter, 1996) and other reading researchers (e.g., Adams, 1990). No information regarding item analyses or potential item bias is provided.

CRITERION-RELATED VALIDITY EVIDENCE

Correlations of PAT subtests with the Single Word Reading test on the *British Abilities Scales* (Elliott, Murray, & Pearson, 1983) were generally moderate (*r*s = .37 to .66), with Speech Rate demonstrating the weakest association and Phoneme Deletion–Beginning Sounds the strongest. When subtest scores for the entire norm group were entered into a simultaneous regression analysis, all of the subtests except Word Completion significantly predicted concurrent word reading ability. The best predictors varied according to age, however. For 5-year-olds, the best predictors were Rhyme Detection, Phoneme Deletion–Beginning and End Sounds, and Letter Knowledge; for 6-year-olds, the best predictors were Rhyme Production, Phoneme Deletion–Beginning and End Sounds, and Letter Knowledge; and for 7-year-olds, the best predictors were Rhyme Detection, Phoneme Deletion–Beginning and End Sounds, Speech Rate, and Letter Knowledge. Across all ages, Phoneme Deletion–Beginning Sounds demonstrated the strongest relationship with current reading skills. No evidence of the PAT's ability to predict reading performance is presented.

CONSTRUCT VALIDITY EVIDENCE

Subtest intercorrelations ranged from .18 to .68, with Speech Rate displaying the lowest correlations with the other tasks. A principal components analysis of the phonological subtests yielded three factors: (1) a segmentation factor with Word Completion and Phoneme Deletion, which accounted for 50% of the variance in PAT scores; (2) a speech rate factor with Speech Rate, which accounted for 14% of the variance; and (3) a rhyming factor with Rhyme Detection and Rhyme Production, which accounted for 12% of the variance. Because the eigenvalue of the Rhyming Factor (.86) falls below the conventional value of 1, it is not clear why this factor is interpreted.

Usability

The PAT has several features that make it appealing to practitioners, including portability and brevity of administration. The pictures in the easel booklet are colorful and attractive, and children enjoy the short, varied tasks. Other aspects are less appealing to users, however. As noted above, assessing letter knowledge with individual flashcards is much more time-consuming and yields less reliable results than having children identify a random array of letters presented on a single card. The small manual, which must be used throughout administration, is not spiral-bound and does not lie flat for easy consultation. Moreover, interpolating to obtain the one of four percentile ranks that most closely matches an examinee's raw scores is a tedious and less than reliable process.

Links to Intervention

The three case studies presented in the manual include recommendations for instruction and citations of several remediation programs published in the United Kingdom. Unfortunately, American practitioners are unlikely to be familiar with or have ready access to the programs.

Relevant Research

In a study of 38 children assessed annually at ages 4, 5, and 6 on tasks similar to the PAT (Muter, Hulme, Snowling, & Taylor, 1998), the combination of letter-name knowledge and phoneme segmentation, as defined by measures of phoneme completion and phoneme deletion, accounted for 64% of the variance in first-year reading and 70% of the variance in first-year spelling. Rhyming was not a significant predictor of reading at any point, but it did predict spelling at the end of the second year of school. In a follow-up study with 34 children from the same sample (Muter & Snowling, 1998), phoneme deletion, pseudoword repetition, and letter-name knowledge measured at ages 5 and 6 were the best predictors of reading accuracy at age 9. Although speech rate measured at age 9 was moderately correlated with reading accuracy (r = .48), the measure in this study differed from the PAT subtest in that it required repeating each of eight one-syllable words 10 times rather than repeating one three-syllable word 3 times. Phonological processing measures administered at age 4 were poor long-term predictors of reading proficiency.

Source and Cost

The PAT is available from The Psychological Corporation for $124.00.

Test Review

Ward, A. M. (2003). Review of the Phonological Abilities Test. In B. S. Plake, J. C. Impara, & R. A. Spies (Eds.), *The fifteenth mental measurements yearbook* (pp. 669–671). Lincoln, NE: Buros Institute of Mental Measurements.

Summary

The *Phonological Abilities Test* (PAT) is an individually administered, norm-referenced set of phonological awareness and literacy tasks designed as a screening test for the early identification of children with reading problems and as a diagnostic test to assess children's phonological strengths and weaknesses. The PAT is attractive to children, is easy to administer, and includes the only standardized measure of speech rate among currently available early reading assessment batteries. Although the authors' research indicates that several PAT subtests are effective predictors of future reading ability, especially Phoneme Deletion and Letter Knowledge, the PAT suffers from several practical and technical problems that limit its utility even as a screening instrument. The standardization sample consists of U.K. children, whose instructional experiences are likely to differ from those of U.S. students, and sample size is insufficient for the second half of age 7. Derived scores are limited to four sets of percentile ranks, and floor and ceiling effects are evident for most subtests. Internal consistency and stability are unacceptably low for several measures, and there is no evidence of interrater reliability, an essential consideration for live-voice phonological processing tests. Additional evidence of concurrent and predictive validity is also needed.

Case Example

Name of student: Mario W.
Age: 5 years, 3 months
Grade: Kindergarten
Date of assessment: December

Reason for referral: Mario was referred for an early reading assessment by his kindergarten teacher. Compared with his classmates, Mario has been very slow to acquire phonological awareness skills, such as rhyming and matching initial sounds, and he is having difficulty keeping up with reading and language arts instruction. On a recently administered early literacy screening measure, he obtained one of the lowest overall scores in the class.

Assessment results and interpretation: The *Phonological Abilities Test* (PAT) is a set of measures designed to predict reading development in young children. In addition to measures of *phonological awareness*, that is, tasks assessing the ability to access and manipulate the sounds of language, it includes a measure of alphabet knowledge. Performance on the PAT subtests is interpreted in terms of one of four sets of percentile rank scores: 10, 25, 50, and 75. Scores falling at the 50th percentile are average. Mario's performance on the PAT is described below.

Name of PAT Subtest	Raw Score/Number of Items	Percentile Rank
Rhyme Detection	5/10	25
Rhyme Production	0	<25
Word Completion–Syllables	8/8	75
Word Completion–Phonemes	0/8	<10
Phoneme Deletion–Beginning Sounds	0/8	10
Phoneme Deletion–End Sounds	0/8	10
Speech Rate (words per second)	.85	10
Letter Knowledge	24/26	50

On the PAT, Mario scored at age-appropriate levels on tests of syllable segmentation and letter-name knowledge, but his phonological awareness skills are quite delayed for his age. His ability to detect rhymes in spoken words is inconsistent, and he was unable to produce any rhyming words in response to stimulus words on two separate trials. Instead of giving rhyming words (e.g., *mat–may*), he provided words that began with the same sound (e.g., *mat–man*). In a testing-of-limits procedure in which the examiner provided several demonstration items that included a series of rhyming words, however, he was able to provide one or two rhyming words for each of the stimulus words.

Mario was unable to perform any tasks requiring him to manipulate individual sounds (*phonemes*) in spoken words. On the Word Completion–Phonemes subtest, which requires providing the final sound to complete a word spoken by the examiner and illustrated in a picture, he did not appear to understand the nature of the task, even with several teaching examples. For example, shown a picture of a fish and given the sound /fi/, he responded, "so." On the two Phoneme Deletion subtests, which require deleting beginning or ending sounds from spoken words (e.g., "Say *seat* without /s/"), he simply repeated the first sound in the stimulus word. On the Speech Rate subtest, which requires repeating a three-syllable word as rapidly as possible 10 times over three trials, his performance falls at the 10th percentile for his age. He made a good effort on this task, but his word repetition rate was quite slow and decreased across the three trials.

PHONOLOGICAL AWARENESS TEST

Overview

The *Phonological Awareness Test* (PAT-RS; Robertson & Salter, 1997) is an individually administered, norm-referenced set of measures designed to assess phonological awareness and phonemic reading ability in children aged 5-0 through 9-11. A standardized version of the authors' criterion-referenced instrument, the *Phonological Awareness Profile* (Robertson & Salter, 1995), the PAT-RS includes measures of phonemic awareness modeled after tasks in the research literature, as well as measures of letter-sound knowledge and pseudoword decoding. The purposes of the PAT-RS include (1) diagnosing deficits in phonological awareness and (2) assessing decoding skills and knowledge of sound–symbol correspondences for use in program planning. Test materials consist of a spiral-bound examiner's manual, eight colored cubes for the Substitution subtest, spiral-bound stimulus books for the Decoding and Graphemes subtests, and 15 record forms. The examiner must provide lined paper for the Invented Spelling subtest.

Subtests and Composites

Subtests

The PAT-RS consists of eight core subtests and one optional subtest. The core subtests, which assess phonological awareness, letter-sound knowledge, and pseudoword reading, are arranged in a developmental sequence from easiest to most difficult. Each core subtest includes between two and eight tasks or categories, each of which yields a full complement of derived scores. An optional nonstandardized measure of invented spelling is also included. The authors caution that some subtests and subtest tasks (those marked with an asterisk in Table 5.12) may not be appropriate for children below the age of 6.

Composite

Raw scores on eight subtests, excepting Invented Spelling, can be summed to obtain a total test score.

Administration

The PAT-RS takes about 40 minutes to administer when all of the subtests are given. There are no basals and no ceilings. As noted above, some subtests and tasks are likely to be too difficult for 5-year-olds. The authors advise examiners to discontinue a task if it appears too difficult and to assign a score of 0 to items not administered for that task. Directions are printed on the test form so that the examiner does not need to refer to the manual during administration. One practice item is provided for each of the phonological awareness subtests. Directions for Invented Spelling are vague and are likely to contribute to unreliable results. No sentences are provided for the items, and one of the words (*hole*) is a homonym (*whole*). The examiner is instructed to dictate spelling words until "enough" items (of a total of 14) have been presented to determine the child's spelling stage and knowledge of specific sounds. The manual does not indicate why a colloquial word (*squish*) was used for Item 14.

TABLE 5.12. Description of the PAT-RS Subtests

Subtest	Description
Rhyming	This subtest includes two tasks. *Rhyme Discrimination* requires the child to indicate whether two words spoken by the examiner rhyme. *Rhyme Production* requires the child to provide a rhyming real word or pseudoword when given a stimulus word.
Segmentation	This subtest consists of three tasks. *Sentences* requires the child to clap for each word in a sentence spoken by the examiner. *Syllables* requires the child to divide a word spoken by the examiner into syllables. *Phonemes** requires the child to pronounce each phoneme in correct sequence in a word spoken by the examiner.
Isolation	This subtest includes three tasks–*Initial, Final,* and *Medial**–all of which require the child to pronounce a phoneme in a specific position in a word spoken by the examiner.
Deletion	This subtest includes two tasks. *Compounds and Syllables* requires the child to delete a root word or syllable from a word pronounced by the examiner. *Phonemes* requires the child to delete a phoneme from a word pronounced by the examiner.
Substitution	This subtest includes two tasks. *With Manipulatives* requires the child to use colored blocks to represent phoneme changes in words pronounced by the examiner. For example, the examiner sets out three different colored blocks, points to each block in turn while saying, "/f/ /u/ /n/," and asks the child to change *fun* to *run. Without Manipulatives** is administered without blocks and requires the child to repeat a word spoken by the examiner and then change one of its phonemes to form a new word. For example, the examiner says, "The word is *paint.* Change /p/ to /f/," and the child says, "faint."
Blending	This subtest includes two tasks. For *Syllables,* the child listens to separate syllables pronounced by the examiner and blends them together to form words. For *Phonemes,* the child listens to separate phonemes pronounced by the examiner and blends them together to form words.
Graphemes	This subtest includes seven tasks, all of which require the child to provide the sound of single letters and letter combinations presented in a stimulus book: *Consonants, Long and Short Vowels, Consonant Blends,** *Consonant Digraphs,** R-*Controlled Vowels,** *Vowel Digraphs,** and *Diphthongs.**
Decoding*	This subtest requires the child to pronounce pseudowords presented in a stimulus booklet for eight categories of letter-sound combinations: *Vowel-Consonant Words, Consonant-Vowel-Consonant Words, Consonant Digraphs, Consonant Blends, Vowel Digraphs,* R-*Controlled Vowels, Consonant-Vowel-Consonant-Silent* e *Words,* and *Diphthongs.*
Invented Spelling	The child is required to spell up to 14 words dictated by the examiner.

Note. Subtests and tasks marked with an asterisk may be inappropriate for children under 6 years of age.

All of the tasks are administered in a live-voice format. Audiotaped delivery for the Blending tasks would enhance interexaminer consistency. Blanks are provided on the record booklet for writing incorrect responses only for the Phonemes task on the Segmentation subtest. For all other tasks, examiners wishing to record errors for later analysis must write incorrect responses in the small space between the item, response, and score columns. Providing a blank line beside each item for all tasks would facilitate recording errors and increase the utility of assessment results for instructional planning.

Scores

The record booklet includes a pronunciation key for vowel and consonant sounds, as well as the correct response for each item. Real words that rhyme with the correct pseudoword response are also provided for Decoding items and for all Graphemes items with the exception of single consonant sounds. Scoring is dichotomous for all subtests except Invented Spelling. For Invented Spelling, performance is evaluated for mastery–nonmastery of 11 spelling features according to a table in the manual that lists the words assessing each feature. As noted above, examiners are directed to dictate only as many words as needed to determine spelling stages and letter-sound mastery, but it is not clear how all of the features can be reliably evaluated if fewer than 14 words are administered. For example, the consonant digraph /sh/ only appears in the last two words. The child's responses are classified as falling into one of four spelling stages (prerepresentational, developmental, representational, and conventional) according to another table. The table describes each stage with a single phrase and exemplar, using the word *mouse*, which is not one of the items. Examples of student productions corresponding to each stage and using the actual spelling items should be included.

Raw scores for tasks and subtests (except Invented Spelling) can be converted into age-based standard scores (M = 100, SD = 15), percentile ranks, and age equivalents. Norms are in 6-month increments throughout the entire age range of the test. Because children's acquisition of phonological awareness and decoding skills is generally evaluated in terms of grade placement rather than age, grade-based norms should also be provided. Users should note that the relationship between standard scores and percentile ranks on the PAT-RS not only differs from that commonly found on most standardized tests but also varies according to subtest, task, and examinee age. For example, an examinee aged 8-2 who obtains a raw score of 9 on the Rhyming Discrimination task obtains a standard score of 101 and a percentile rank of 11 rather than the expected 53. An examinee aged 6-2 with the identical raw score earns a standard score of 103 and a percentile rank of 33. Similarly, on the Decoding total score, a standard score of 100 is associated with a percentile rank of 43 for an examinee aged 8-2 but with a percentile rank of 64 for an examinee aged 6-2. The manual does not inform users that the distribution of raw scores is skewed or that standard scores do not correspond to the percentile ranks expected in a normal distribution (see the case example below).

Interpretation

According to the test's authors, phonological awareness and graphemes/decoding test results should be analyzed separately to determine which type of remedial instruction (or both) should be provided. Because the PAT-RS does not provide composites for the phonological awareness subtests or the decoding subtests, however, comparisons of children's proficiency on the two sets of skills must be at the subtest level, which reduces both interpretability and reliability. The authors suggest that children scoring at or below the 25th percentile on the test may need intervention, but it is not clear whether examiners should apply the suggested cutoff to the total test score, scores on individual subtests, or both. For students scoring below the 25th percentile, the authors advise analyzing performance according to the four developmental levels assessed by the phonological awareness tasks (the word, syllable, phoneme, and grapheme levels), with instruction beginning at the earliest level at which the child displays difficulty. Unfortunately, the manual does not provide specific guidelines for analyzing task and subtest performance according to the four levels, nor does the record form provide space for this type of analysis. The authors state that Invented Spelling is designed to provide diagnostic information about the child's encoding ability, but with only 14 items to evaluate 11 phonics features (or fewer, depending on how many items the examiner chooses to administer), the results of this analysis are likely to be speculative at best. Moreover, the spelling stages presented in the PAT-RS do not correspond to the stages in the most widely accepted models of spelling development (e.g., Bear, Invernizzi, Templeton, & Johnston, 2000; Henderson, 1990). No case examples are provided to illustrate scoring or interpretation.

Technical Adequacy

Standardization

The PAT-RS format and subtests are derived from the authors' criterion-referenced version of this test, the *Phonological Awareness Profile*. A pilot version of the PAT-RS was administered to an unspecified number of children in Illinois and Iowa aged 5 through 9 (the year of this pilot study is not provided). After item analyses and additional research, trained speech–language pathologists administered the PAT-RS to 1,235 children in 175 elementary schools in five states (California, Connecticut, Florida, Texas, and Wisconsin) in 1996. Sample characteristics are reported in terms of race and gender for 10 age groups, but no information is provided regarding SES or the number of children tested per state. Contrary to recommended norming practices, children with identified disabilities were excluded from the sample. Consequently, normative data cannot be used to evaluate differences between groups of examinees with various disabilities and nondisabled examinees, a serious omission for a test designed to diagnose deficits in phonological processing. The manual states that an effort was made to ensure minority representation in accordance with 1990 U.S. census figures, but no data are presented to permit users to compare sample percentages to census proportions for any of the demographic variables.

Reliability Evidence

Kuder–Richardson internal consistency reliabilities are reported at half-year age intervals for each task and subtest. Reliabilities for tasks, which contain as few as four items, vary widely and fall near or at 0 as various age groups display cellar or ceiling effects. Reliability estimates for subtests also vary considerably across age groups. For the early primary grade range, coefficients range from .72 to .93 for Rhyming, from .79 to .89 for Segmentation, from .82 to .96 for Isolation, from .65 to .89 for Deletion, from .76 to .88 for Substitution, from .60 to .89 for Blending, from .88 to .96 for Graphemes, and from .95 to .99 for Decoding. Of the 64 coefficients, 15 fall below acceptable levels (i.e., <.80). Task and subtest stability estimates are reported for small samples (*ns* = 21 to 29; unspecified test–retest intervals) at each of the 10 age intervals. As with internal consistency reliability, stability coefficients vary widely for tasks and subtests across age groups. For example, test–retest reliability for Rhyming ranges from a low of .49 for ages 8-0 to 8-5 to a high of .93 for ages 5-0 to 5-5. Stability coefficients for other subtests range from .57 to .94 for Segmentation, .41 to .91 for Isolation, .60 to .90 for Deletion, .54 to .92 for Substitution, .37 to .95 for Blending, .70 to .95 for Graphemes, and .93 to .98 for Decoding. Of the 64 test–retest reliability coefficients, 20 fall below acceptable levels, and 12 are in the .60s or below.

Moreover, because no information is provided regarding the length of the interval between administrations, the stability of the PAT-RS remains unclear. No evidence of interscorer reliability is presented for any of the subtests and tasks, and no reliability evidence of any kind is presented for Invented Spelling.

Test Floor and Item Gradients

Given the limited number of items per task and the developmental nature of phonemic awareness and decoding skills, it is not surprising that floors and item gradients are inadequate for many subtests and tasks, especially at the younger ages. Examiners testing children in the lower age ranges should review the conversion tables carefully and heed the authors' caution that some subtests and tasks are not appropriate for younger examinees. In fact, floors for all tasks, subtests, and the composite are inadequate for examinees ages 5-0 to 5-5. Floors for Segmentation and Blending are inadequate below age 5-6; floors for Isolation, Deletion, and Graphemes are inadequate below age 6-0; and floors for Substitution and Decoding are inadequate below age 7-6. Item gradients are inadequate for Isolation below age 5-6, for Deletion below age 6-0, and for Decoding throughout the entire primary grade range. Ceiling effects are also evident for numerous tasks at the upper age range.

Validity Evidence

CONTENT VALIDITY EVIDENCE

According to the manual, the PAT-RS was based on an extensive review of other tests and the phonological awareness literature, but no specific tests or studies are cited or discussed. Grapheme and decoding subtests were included to distinguish between children who have limited phonological awareness skills and have learned phonics by memorization and those who have adequate phonological awareness but have not generalized their knowledge to decoding. Pseudowords are used to assess decoding skills to reduce examinees' ability to rely on visual memory rather than knowledge of sound–symbol correspondence. Item difficulty and discrimination indices were computed at each of the 10 age intervals. To be retained, items had to show age progression in terms of increasing percentages of examinees passing at each successive age level and had to discriminate significantly between high and low scorers at each level. Raw score means and medians presented for each task by age interval are supportive of the former claim, but difficulty and discrimination statistics are not provided. The authors state that items were analyzed for racial bias, with the results supporting the inclusion of the final set of items, but they present no information regarding the procedures used or the specific outcomes of the analysis. To evaluate possible gender bias, mean raw scores for males and females were compared for each subtest and total test by age. Differences for total test were not significant at any age, whereas there were four instances of significant subtest differences, three at the .05 level and one at the .01 level. Females scored higher than males in each of the four cases, with differences ranging from less than 1 point to about 5 points.

CRITERION-RELATED VALIDITY EVIDENCE

No criterion-related validity data are presented.

CONSTRUCT VALIDITY EVIDENCE

Point biserial correlations between item and task scores and between item and subtest total scores are reported for the 10 age groups, with 99% of items demonstrating significant average correlations with total test score. Intersubtest correlations are reported across all age groups and by each age interval. For examinees in the early primary grade range, correlations are generally low to moderate, with the lowest correlations for Rhyming and the highest for Graphemes and Decoding. Diagnostic utility was evaluated by contrasting mean raw scores of children randomly selected from the standardization sample with a matched sample of children identified as at risk for reading problems (approximately 130 children at each yearly age interval). Subtest differences between groups were significant for 37 of 40 comparisons, with the exception of Decoding for the 5-0 to 5-11 group, Rhyming for the 6-0 to 6-11 group, and Isolation for the 9-0 to 9-11 group. Total test scores also significantly discriminated between groups at all five age intervals. Because the analysis reports raw scores by year rather than half-year intervals, however, examiners cannot use the norms tables to determine whether the observed raw score differences translate into clinically meaningful standard score differences. No validity evidence of any kind is presented for Invented Spelling.

Usability

The PAT-RS is inexpensive, portable, and easy to administer and score, except for the Invented Spelling subtest, which has vague scoring guidelines. A user-friendly software scoring program compatible with Windows and Macintosh is available, which provides a two-page report, including a score summary page with a full range of derived scores for each task, subtest, and total score. Four sets of scores for 37 measures are crowded onto a single page, however, making for a very small type size, and the print quality is poor. The title of one of the Grapheme and Decoding tasks is misspelled (*Dipthongs* for *Diphthongs*). The second page of the printout, which presents subtest standard score and age equivalency profiles in the form of bar graphs, is useful when examiners are sharing results with parents and teachers.

Links to Intervention

According to the test's authors, instruction should begin at the earliest of the four levels (i.e., word, syllable, phoneme, and grapheme) at which the child displays difficulty. As noted above, the manual and record form should provide guidelines and space, respectively, for analyzing test results for this purpose. The manual includes two sample IEP goals and two activities targeting each of the four levels. The PAT-RS is linked to two intervention kits by the same authors: the *Phonological Awareness Kit–Primary* for ages 5–8 and the *Phonological Awareness Kit–Intermediate* for ages 9–14. Activities in both kits are modeled after intervention strategies drawn from the research literature.

Source and Cost

The PAT-RS is available from LinguiSystems for $119.95, and the software scoring program costs an additional $69.95. Available from the same publisher are the intervention kits for $69.95 each.

Summary

The *Phonological Awareness Test* (PAT-RS) is an individually administered, norm-referenced set of measures assessing phonological awareness and decoding skills in children aged 5-0 through 9-11. One of the few currently available standardized tests with comprehensive measures of both sound–symbol knowledge and phonemic awareness, the PAT-RS ranks high in usability. The results are directly interpretable in terms of instructional planning, and the test is linked to two intervention programs modeled on empirically validated training strategies. At the same time, however, the authors' efforts to translate a criterion-referenced inventory into a standardized instrument have not been entirely successful. The PAT-RS suffers from numerous technical problems, including a norm group that is restricted to five states and does not include children with disabilities, unacceptably low internal consistency and test–retest reliability for many subtests in the early primary grade range, and undocumented interscorer consistency. Although there is some evidence that the PAT-RS discriminates between children with reading problems and normally achieving children, its relationship to other phonological awareness and decoding tests and its utility in predicting reading achievement have yet to be documented. Because of these and other psychometric shortcomings, the results should be used for designing interventions rather than for diagnostic and placement purposes.

Case Example

Name of student: Raymond J.
Age: 8 years, 2 months
Grade: Second grade
Date of assessment: February

Reason for referral: Raymond was referred for an early reading assessment by his second-grade teacher. Although he was retained in kindergarten and has been receiving small-group assistance from the reading resource teacher for more than a year, he is struggling in phonics, reading, and spelling. His decoding skills are especially weak, and he tends to guess based on pictorial and context clues rather than trying to sound out unfamiliar words.

Assessment results and interpretation: The *Phonological Awareness Test* (PAT) measures a developmental progression of phonological awareness skills, beginning with rhyming and proceeding through syllable segmentation to single sound (*phoneme*) manipulation. It also measures children's knowledge of sound–symbol relationships (*graphemes*) and their ability to use that knowledge to decode unfamiliar words, which are represented by *pseudowords* (*loe, fepe*). Average scores for an individual Raymond's age are as follows: Standard Score = 100, Percentile Rank [PR] = 50, Age Equivalent = 8-2. His performance on the PAT is described below.

Subtests/Tasks	Raw Score	Standard Score	Percentile Rank	Age Equivalent
Rhyming	18/20	91	11	6-5
Discrimination	9/10	101	36	5-10
Production	9/10	97	25	6-7

(continued)

Segmentation	18/30	81	8	6-4
Sentences	10/10	111	75	Above norms
Syllables	6/10	79	12	5-11
Phonemes	2/10	82	14	6-2
Isolation	18/30	74	4	6-2
Initial	10/10	108	69	Above norms
Final	4/10	62	3	6-2
Medial	4/10	76	8	6-5
Deletion	10/20	57	1	6-0
Compounds and Syllables	5/10	60	1	Below norms
Phonemes	5/10	68	5	6-4
Substitution	12/20	96	37	7-7
With Manipulatives	9/10	109	68	9-2
Without Manipulatives	3/10	82	12	6-9
Blending	11/20	44	2	5-5
Syllables	9/10	73	2	5-9
Phonemes	2/10	43	10	5-5
Graphemes	35/58	78	8	6-7
Consonants	20/20	105	71	Above norms
Long and Short Vowels	6/10	84	15	6-6
Consonant Blends	5/10	74	10	6-6
Consonant Digraphs	1/4	48	2	6-3
R-Controlled Vowels	1/5	81	16	6-9
Vowel Digraphs	2/5	91	33	7-3
Diphthongs	0/4	<88	<25	Below norms
Decoding	36/80	74	17	7-1
VC Words[a]	10/10	113	83	Above norms
CVC Words[b]	7/10	98	36	7-5
Consonant Digraphs	4/10	84	15	7-0
Consonant Blends	5/10	88	21	7-2
Vowel Digraphs	2/10	78	13	7-0
R-Controlled Vowels	2/10	79	11	7-0
CVCe Words[c]	4/10	90	27	7-4
Diphthongs	2/10	81	14	7-0

[a]Vowel–Consonant Words.
[b]Consonant–Vowel–Consonant Words.
[c]Consonant–Vowel–Consonant–Silent *e* Words.

On the PAT, Raymond's phonological awareness skills are highly variable, depending on the task, and range from above average to very low, compared with others his age (PRs = 1–75). He was able to perform at age-appropriate levels on rhyming tasks and on segmentation tasks at the word and syllable level, but he had great difficulty with tasks requiring him to manipulate individual phonemes, including isolating sounds in spoken words, blending sounds to form words, deleting sounds from spoken words, and substituting sounds. For example, asked to blend the sounds /m/ /i/ /l/ /k/ (*milk*), he responded, "murt." On sound isolation tasks requiring him to identify specific sounds in one-syllable words, he was able to identify initial sounds, but he missed more than half of the items requiring him to identify middle and final sounds. For example, asked to give the middle sound in *mouse*, he said, "/a/." On a task requiring him to substitute specific sounds in words (e.g., to change *map* to *mop*), he was able to answer 9 of 10 items correctly when he was able to use colored blocks to represent sound changes. In contrast, when he was required to substitute sounds without using the blocks, he was able to answer only 3 of 10 items correctly, suggesting that his short-term memory for sound information may be limited.

Raymond's understanding of letter-sound relationships, as measured by the Graphemes subtest, is in the low range for his age (PR = 8). He was able to identify all 26 consonant sounds but only three short vowel and three long vowel sounds. He was able to identify most of the two-letter consonant blends presented (/bl/), but none of the three-letter blends (/str/). His understanding of more complex phonics features, including consonant digraphs (/th/ as in *that*), *r*-controlled vowels (*ir* as in *bird*), vowel digraphs (*oa* as in *boat*), and diphthongs (*oi* as in *boy*), is also quite limited. On the Decoding subtest, which required him to use letter-sound knowledge and phonics conversion rules to pronounce phonetically regular pseudowords, his performance is in the below average range (PR = 17). As on the Graphemes tasks, he was able to decode two- and three-phoneme pseudowords (*og*, *fum*), but he was unable to decode pseudowords with more complex phonics features (*kaut* for *coan*, *trab* for *tarb*).

TEST OF PHONOLOGICAL AWARENESS

Overview

The *Test of Phonological Awareness* (TOPA; Torgesen & Bryant, 1994b) is a brief norm-referenced measure of the ability to isolate the individual phonemes in spoken words for children from kindergarten through Grade 2. One of the few phonological awareness measures specifically designed for group administration, it was developed with the support of a grant from the NICHD. The TOPA includes two versions: (1) the TOPA–Kindergarten (TOPA-K) for kindergartners aged 5-0 through 6-11, and (2) the TOPA–Early Elementary (TOPA-EE) for first and second graders aged 6-0 through 8-11. Uses of the TOPA include (1) identifying children who need additional training in phonological awareness, (2) serving as part of a screening battery for kindergarten and beginning first-grade children, and (3) facilitating research. Materials include an examiner's manual, 25 student booklets per level, and 25 profile/examiner record forms per level, all packed in a box.

Subtests and Composite

At each level, the TOPA includes two subtests, each consisting of 10 sound comparison items (see Table 5.13). Raw scores on the two subtests are summed to yield a TOPA composite score, termed a "quotient." Children record their responses in a test booklet containing black-and-white line drawings of one-syllable words that are identified by the examiner.

Administration

The TOPA can be administered by teachers or paraprofessionals to individuals, small groups, or entire classroom groups. In my experience, classwide administrations require a minimum of two examiners–one to give the directions and another to ensure that students are following the directions and working independently. The TOPA can be administered in 15–20 minutes to individuals and small groups (four to six students). Classwide administrations require approximately 30 minutes. Testing can

TABLE 5.13. Description of the TOPA Subtests by Level

TOPA level	Subtest	Description
TOPA-K	Initial Sound–Same	The child marks the one of three pictures that begins with the same sound as a target picture.
	Initial Sound–Different	The child marks the one of four pictures that begins with a different sound than the other three.
TOPA-EE	Ending Sound–Same	The child marks the one of three pictures that ends with the same sound as a target picture.
	Ending Sound–Different	The child marks the one of four pictures that ends with a different sound than the other three.

be done in one session or spread across two sessions. An optional one-page orientation on the inside cover of the student booklet can be administered to provide children with practice in marking items and to ensure that they understand the concepts of *same* and *different*. Each subtest is preceded by a set of teaching items–three for the TOPA-K and two for the TOPA-EE. Although the examiner pronounces the names of the four pictures in each row, the stimulus words vary considerably in their recognizability (e.g., *man* [represented by a picture of a man's face] vs. *take* [represented by a larger boy snatching an ice cream cone away from a protesting younger boy]. For several items, stimulus words are represented by different pictures from one subtest to the other, which may confuse some children. I have found that children often have trouble remembering the names of the pictures, even in individual administrations. The manual does not address the question of whether picture names may be repeated, under what circumstances, or how often.

Scores

Scoring is dichotomous and takes about 5 minutes. At each level, scores for the two subtests are summed, and the total raw score is converted into age-based percentile ranks and standard scores (normal curve equivalents, *W* scale scores, *T* scores, *z* scores, stanines, and quotients [$M = 100$, $SD = 15$]). The subtests do not yield separate scores. Norms are in 6-month intervals from ages 5-0 to 6-11 for the TOPA-K and in 1-year intervals for the TOPA-EE for ages 6-0 to 8-11. Given the rapid development in phonological awareness skills during the early primary grades, 6-month norm intervals should have been maintained across both versions to increase discriminative power. Grade-based norms should also be provided because children's prereading and reading-related skills are usually evaluated in terms of grade-level rather than age-level expectations.

Interpretation

According to the test's authors, scores below the 25th percentile for children tested at the beginning of the second semester of kindergarten indicate a significant delay in the development of phonological awareness. Because the TOPA-K norms were collected in the spring, the authors recommend developing local norms if the test is administered at another time during the kindergarten year. For first- and second-grade children, scores below the 15th percentile suggest the presence of phonological processing problems. The manual includes a completed record form for a kindergarten child aged 6-1 who obtained a TOPA-K quotient in the average range (SS = 101). Scores from three other tests are recorded on the form, and the authors demonstrate how to convert scores from tests yielding other score types into "TOPA equivalents" by using a table or formula in the manual. The case example's standard scores on the other tests range from 85 to 110, but the authors do not discuss the implications of these results, nor do they present a case example for a child scoring below the cutoff score.

Technical Adequacy

Standardization

The TOPA-K was standardized on 857 children from 10 states, with more than twice as many 6-year-olds as 5-year-olds. The standardization sample for the TOPA-EE is more than three times larger than that for the TOPA-K, consisting of 3,654 students in 38 states and including twice as many 7-year-olds as 6- or 8-year-olds. For both versions, normative sample characteristics are reported in terms of race, ethnicity, gender, residence (rural/urban), and geographic area, with data for race (white/nonwhite), ethnicity, geographic region, and gender stratified by TOPA level and age and compared with U.S. 1990 census data. No information is provided about disability status, SES, or the instructional experiences of the standardization sample, although the authors acknowledge that phonological awareness is "heavily influenced by factors in the child's immediate family and school environment" (p. 15). In general, the sample appears to be representative of the U.S. population, but the manual does not indicate the specific year(s) when normative data were collected. Given the changes that have occurred in reading instruction and in the school-age population since 1990, the TOPA is due for renorming.

Reliability Evidence

Internal consistency reliabilities for TOPA quotients for 100 protocols at each 1-year interval are adequate for the TOPA-K (age 5 = .90; age 6 = .91) but fall below the preferred level for composites for the TOPA-EE (age 6 = .87; age 7 = .88). TOPA-K test–retest reliability was .84 for a sample of 40 children (6-week interval) and .94 when the error associated with internal consistency was removed. TOPA-EE test–retest reliability for a sample of 69 first graders tested at the beginning of the school year (8-week interval) was below acceptable levels (.69; adjusted stability coefficient = .77). The authors suggest that the lower stability for the TOPA-EE resulted from the longer interval between testings and the impact of reading instruction on children's phonological awareness skills. No evidence of interscorer reliability is presented.

Test Floors and Item Gradients

Composite test floors for both levels are adequate except for the TOPA-K at ages 5-0 through 5-5, where a raw score of 1 yields a standard score of 73. Item gradients are adequate across both levels.

Validity Evidence

CONTENT VALIDITY EVIDENCE

The authors selected tasks of analytic phonological awareness, based on their research (Wagner et al., 1994) indicating that analytic measures in kindergarten were the most powerful predictors of first-grade reading. They also selected tasks of phonological sensitivity rather than explicit phonological awareness on the grounds that the latter are too difficult for most kindergarten children. Item types were selected on the basis of three characteristics: (1) levels of moderate difficulty (i.e., p values above .50), (2) significant predictive relationships to first-grade reading achievement, and (3) a structure adaptable to group testing. Two different item types measuring the same underlying ability were included to maintain children's interest and to prevent very low scores in the event that examinees did not understand one task type. Items were taken from a list of the 2,500 words most frequently appearing in first graders' oral language samples (Stemach & Williams, 1988). Two item tryouts (Torgesen, Morgan, & Davis, 1992) were conducted prior to standardization, and a confirmatory factor analysis was conducted to verify that the subtests were measuring the same underlying ability. No significant differences were found in the level of scores obtained on group versus individual administration for 90 kindergarten children who took both formats (r = .77, 2-week interval). The correlation is lower than desirable, however, and neither raw score nor standard score means are provided to support the equivalence of the two formats. Median item difficulties based on 100 randomly selected protocols at each 1-year interval were .63 and .78 for the TOPA-K for ages 5 and 6, respectively, and .84, 88, and .89 for the TOPA-EE for ages 6, 7, and 8, respectively. These indices indicate that the TOPA-EE is very easy for most children; in fact, the average TOPA-EE performance (i.e., SS = 100) is 17/20 items correct, even at the youngest age level. Item discrimination indices are at acceptable levels: .54 for the TOPA-K for ages 5 and 6 and .51, .45, and .47 for the TOPA-EE for ages 6, 7, and 8, respectively. No analyses of possible DIF are presented. Some stimulus words may be unfamiliar to children from nonmainstream linguistic and ethnic backgrounds (e.g., *hut*, *jack*).

CRITERION-RELATED VALIDITY EVIDENCE

For 100 children tested at the end of kindergarten, the TOPA-K correlated moderately to highly with two nonstandardized measures of phonological awareness (.47 for a segmentation task and .66 for a sound isolation task). For 90 first graders tested in November, correlations between the TOPA-EE and the same measures were .50 and .55. Correlations with WRMT-R Word Analysis and Word Identification were .66 and .60, respectively, for the same sample. The authors also cite indirect evidence for criterion-related validity derived from two studies that used tests similar in structure to the TOPA-K. In the first study with 244 kindergarten children (Wagner et al., 1994), a confirmatory factor analysis indicated that two measures similar to TOPA-K subtests should be included among the set of analytic phonological awareness measures. In the second study with 100 kindergarten children (Mann, 1993), a phoneme segmentation test identical in structure to the TOPA-K Initial Sound–Same subtest was moderately correlated (.52) with an invented spelling measure.

Evidence of predictive validity and classification accuracy is based on a study with 90 predominantly low-SES and racial minority children who took the TOPA-K in

April. TOPA-K scores were strongly correlated with end-of-first-grade WRMT-R Word Analysis scores ($r = .62$). Of the 23 children who scored in the bottom quartile on the TOPA-K, 18 also scored below the median on first-grade Word Analysis. Beginning-of-first-grade TOPA-EE scores for the same children were slightly less effective predictors of end-of-year Word Analysis scores (.55). As indirect evidence of predictive validity, the authors cite the results of two studies using measures similar to the TOPA-K Initial Sound–Same subtest. In the Mann (1993) study cited above, performance on the kindergarten phoneme segmentation measure similar to the TOPA-K was moderately correlated with first-grade word reading ($r = .58$). In the authors' kindergarten study (Wagner et al., 1994), a composite measure of analytic phonological skills that included items similar to those on the TOPA-K displayed a causal path of .75 to first-grade word reading, even after verbal ability and early reading-related knowledge were controlled.

CONSTRUCT VALIDITY EVIDENCE

As evidence of construct validity, the authors cite studies demonstrating that tasks similar to the TOPA share a considerable amount of common variance with other phonological awareness measures (Stanovich, Cunningham, & Cramer, 1984; Wagner et al., 1994). In a differential training effects study with 60 kindergarten students (Torgesen & Davis, 1996), children with higher TOPA-K scores at the beginning of a 12-week phonological awareness training program showed significantly greater growth in both analytic and synthetic awareness than children with lower TOPA-K scores. The authors also present evidence to support their contention that correct choices on TOPA items are unlikely to be related to global phonological similarity, which is a potential threat to the validity of sound comparison tasks.

Usability

The TOPA is inexpensive and exceptionally easy to administer, score, and interpret. As noted above, however, I have found that a sizable number of kindergarten children have difficulty attending to the oral directions and remembering the names of the pictures in a group administration format.

Links to Intervention

The manual cites a variety of sources for phonological awareness training activities, such as research studies and commercially available training packages, including the authors' empirically based and user-friendly *Phonological Awareness Training for Reading* (Torgesen & Bryant, 1994a). Torgesen has also coauthored a handbook, *A Basic Guide to Understanding, Assessing, and Teaching Phonological Awareness* (Torgesen & Mathes, 2000), which includes a very useful chapter on phonological awareness instruction and descriptions of 12 evidence-based training programs.

Relevant Research

Several studies have used the TOPA-K as an estimate of phonological awareness ability (e.g., Allor, Fuchs, & Mathes, 2001; Elliott, Lee, & Tollefson, 2001) and as a predictor of present or future reading achievement (Havey et al., 2002; Margolese &

Kline, 1999), with mixed results. In a study with 81 kindergarten children (Havey et al., 2002), TOPA-K scores in spring of kindergarten were significant predictors (r = .49) of *Woodcock Diagnostic Reading Battery* Letter–Word Identification scores obtained 4–6 weeks later. In the Torgesen and Davis (1996) training study cited above, the TOPA-K was a significant predictor of individual growth rates in segmenting and blending skills (rs = .38 and .51, respectively) but a less effective predictor than pseudoword spelling (rs = .48 and .63, respectively). Moreover, when pseudoword spelling and verbal ability were each combined with the TOPA, TOPA performance did not explain any unique variance in the growth of segmenting skills. Similarly, in predictive models that included pseudoword spelling, the TOPA was not a significant predictor of blending skills. More positive results were obtained in a study (Margolese & Kline, 1999) with 65 Canadian kindergarten children with diverse linguistic backgrounds who took a battery of reading predictors, including measures of phonological processing, listening comprehension, general cognitive ability, and visual–motor coordination. The TOPA-K was the best predictor of first-grade reading, as measured by WRMT-R Letter Identification (.44) and a combined score of WRMT-R Word Attack and Word Identification (.64).

Source and Cost

The TOPA is available from PRO-ED for $154.00, which includes both versions of the test. Available from the same publisher is *Phonological Awareness Training for Reading* for $139.00.

Test Reviews

Dohan, M. (1996). The Test of Phonological Awareness: A critical review. *Journal of Speech–Language Pathology and Audiology, 20*, 22–26.

Long, S. H. (1998). Review of the Test of Phonological Awareness. In J. C. Impara & B. S. Plake (Eds.), *The thirteenth mental measurements yearbook* (pp. 1049–1050). Lincoln, NE: Buros Institute of Mental Measurements.

McCauley, R. (1998). Review of the Test of Phonological Awareness. In J. C. Impara & B. S. Plake (Eds.), *The thirteenth mental measurements yearbook* (pp. 1050–1052). Lincoln, NE: Buros Institute of Mental Measurements.

Summary

The *Test of Phonological Awareness* (TOPA) is a group-administered, norm-referenced measure of the ability to identify individual sounds in spoken words for children from kindergarten through second grade. Derived from a research program that has contributed enormously to the understanding of reading acquisition and disabilities, the TOPA is a commendable effort to translate phonological awareness assessment from research into practice. Several studies have reported that the TOPA is an effective predictor of reading achievement, although evidence is stronger for the TOPA-K's than for the TOPA-EE's predictive power. The utility of the TOPA for early identification programs is limited by several factors. The TOPA-K has inadequate floors for children younger than age 5-6. On the TOPA-EE, norm group intervals are too broad; internal consistency and stability fall below acceptable levels; and the items are very easy, even for a measure designed to identify children with serious phonological processing deficits. In my own experience with the TOPA over a period of several years, very few students have scored below the suggested cutoffs for either version of the test, even among children who had been identified by their teachers as making poor progress and/or had obtained low scores on other early literacy measures. Moreover, most of the children who scored in the at-risk range exhibited generalized oral language deficits and/or developmental deficits in addition to phonological awareness deficits. Additional studies evaluating the relationship of the TOPA to other phonological processing and early literacy measures and to later reading performance would help resolve the question of whether the TOPA in its current form may underidentify students with phonological processing problems. A second edition of the test is under development.

Case Example

Name of student: Tyrone P.
Age: 5 years, 7 months
Grade: Kindergarten
Date of assessment: March

Reason for referral: Tyrone was referred for an early reading assessment by his kindergarten teacher. His teacher reports that he is having trouble learning and remembering letter names and sounds, as well as understanding the nature of phonological awareness and phonics activities. Tyrone has been receiving individual assistance from the reading resource specialist since the beginning of the second semester but continues to perform far below his classmates.

Assessment results and interpretation: The *Test of Phonological Awareness–Kindergarten* (TOPA-K) is a measure of young children's ability to isolate the individual *phonemes* or sounds in spoken words. A child's degree of phonological awareness in the early grades is a significant predictor of success in reading. Tyrone's TOPA-K scores are reported below. Average scores for a child his age are a standard score of 100 and a percentile rank of 50.

Subtest/**Composite**	Raw Score	Percentile	Standard Score
Initial Sound–Same	4/10	–	–
Initial Sound–Different	3/10	–	–
TOPA Composite	7/20	23	89

On the Initial Sound–Same subtest, which requires the child to mark which of three words begins with the same sound as a stimulus word (all represented by pictures), Tyrone answered 4 of the 10 items correctly. Although he listened attentively as the examiner pronounced the names of the pictures, he responded quite slowly and asked to have the names of one or more of the four pictures repeated for 6 items. He had more difficulty on the Initial Sound–Different subtest, which requires the child to mark which word in a group of four words (all represented by pictures) begins with a different first sound from the other three. Of the 10 items, he answered only 3 correctly. Tyrone's overall TOPA-K performance falls at the 23rd percentile for youngsters his age (low average range). For children in the second semester of kindergarten, a score below the 25th percentile indicates that they have a significant delay in the development of phonological awareness and are at risk for difficulty in learning to read.

YOPP–SINGER TEST OF PHONEME SEGMENTATION

Overview

The *Yopp–Singer Test of Phoneme Segmentation* (YST; Yopp, 1988, 1995b) is a brief nonstandardized measure of children's ability to isolate and pronounce individual phonemes in spoken words in the correct sequence. The test is designed to assess the level of phonemic awareness in kindergarten children, but it may also be administered to first graders at the beginning of the year to help identify students in need of additional phonemic awareness training or to aid in a diagnostic assessment. For the past two decades, the YST has been widely used in reading research as a predictor and criterion measure (e.g., Kame'enui, Simmons, Good, & Harn, 2001; Spector, 1992; Yopp, 1995b). The YST appears in the original articles by the author (Yopp, 1988, 1995b) and is represented with minor adaptations in Figure 5.4.

Assessment Task

The YST consists of 22 familiar words ranging in length from two to three phonemes. The examiner says each word, and the child is required to pronounce each individual sound in the correct order. For example, the examiner says, "dog," and the child responds, "/d/-/o/-/g/."

Administration

The YST must be individually administered and takes about 5–10 minutes. Three practice items are provided. Administration procedures differ from those of most other phonemic awareness measures in that the examiner provides feedback after each response rather than only on teaching items. If the child's answer is correct, the examiner tells the child, "That's right." If the child's answer is incorrect, the examiner supplies the correct answer and records the error on the blank beside the item. Each examinee begins with the first item, and there is no discontinuation rule.

Scores

Items are scored 1 or 0. The child must pronounce each sound in the word correctly and in the correct sequence to receive credit. Letter names are scored as incorrect. Although no partial credit is awarded, the test's author recommends recording and analyzing errors to distinguish between children who are developing phonemic awareness, as shown by partial segmentation on some items, and children who have little insight into the sound structure of language and simply repeat the item or give nonsense responses. In her 1995b article, the author provides guidelines for scoring certain items. Each of the phonemes in a blend must be articulated separately, so Item 7 (*grew*) has three phonemes (/g/-/r/-/ew/). Digraphs are single phonemes, so Item 5 (*she*) has two phonemes (/sh/-/ee/), and Item 15 (*three*) has three phonemes (/th/-/r/-/ee/).

YOPP–SINGER TEST OF PHONEME SEGMENTATION

Student's name ______________________________ Date ______________

Score __ (number correct) or __ (number of sounds correctly segmented)

Directions: Say: "Today we're going to play a word game. I'm going to say a word and I want you to break the word apart. You are going to tell me each sound in the word in order. For example, if I say "old," you should say "o/-/l/-/d/." (Be sure to say the sounds, not the letters, in the word.) "Let's try a few words together." Give feedback as the child progresses through the list by saying, "That's right," if the response is correct and giving the correct response yourself if the child's response is incorrect.

Practice items:
Assist the child in segmenting these items as necessary: ride (r-i-d) go (g-o) man (m-a-n).

Scoring: Circle the number of the items that the child correctly segments. Record incorrect responses on the blank line following the item. If you are using all-or-nothing scoring criteria, the child's score is the total number of items correctly segmented into individual phonemes. If you are using partial credit scoring, award one point for each sound correctly segmented (maximum score = 56).

1. dog (d-o-g) __________
2. keep (k-ee-p) __________
3. fine (f-i-ne) __________
4. no (n-o) __________
5. she (sh-e) __________
6. wave (w-a-ve) __________
7. grew (g-r-ew) __________
8. that (th-a-t) __________
9. red (r-e-d) __________
10. me (m-e) __________
11. sat (s-a-t) __________
12. lay (l-ay) __________
13. race (r-a-ce) __________
14. zoo (z-oo) __________
15. three (th-r-ee) __________
16. job (j-o-b) __________
17. in (i-n) __________
18. ice (i-ce) __________
19. at (a-t) __________
20. top (t-o-p) __________
21. by (b-y) __________
22. do (d-o) __________

FIGURE 5.4. The Yopp–Singer Test of Phoneme Segmentation. From Yopp (1995, September). A test for assessing phonemic awareness in young children. *The Reading Teacher*, *49*(1), pp. 20–29. Adapted with permission of Hallie K. Yopp and the International Reading Association.

Interpretation

The YST is nonstandardized, and only research norms are available. Yopp (1988) reported a mean raw score of 11.78 and standard deviation of 7.66 on the YST for a sample of 96 kindergarten children tested during April and May of the school year (mean age = 5-10). In her later article, Yopp (1995b) cautions that teachers should expect a wide range of scores within a classroom and describes three broad categories of performance: (1) phonemic awareness, defined as correctly segmenting all or nearly all items; (2) emerging phonemic awareness, defined as answering some items correctly; and (3) delayed phonemic awareness, defined as answering only a few items or none correctly. According to the author, children with few or no items correct are likely to experience reading and spelling problems without intervention. If local norming is used, I recommend creating norms based on partial credit for each correct sound segment per item to increase the sensitivity of the YST to individual differences and increase its effectiveness as a progress monitoring instrument.

Technical Adequacy

Reliability Evidence

In Yopp's (1988) study comparing 10 phonemic awareness tests from the research literature, the YST had an internal consistency coefficient of .95 and was the most reliable measure of simple phonemic awareness, one of the two factors identified. No other reliability evidence is reported.

Test Floors and Item Gradients

Kindergarten children and first graders with low levels of phonemic awareness often show floor effects on the YST, in part because phoneme segmentation is a difficult task for kindergartners and low-performing children and in part because of the all-or-nothing scoring criteria.

Validity Evidence

CONTENT VALIDITY EVIDENCE

Items were selected on the basis of word familiarity from Thorndike and Lorge's (1963) list of frequently occurring words. A feature analysis was also conducted to include items representing all commonly occurring places and types of articulation for consonants and all heights and locations for vowels.

CRITERION-RELATED VALIDITY EVIDENCE

In Yopp's (1988) investigation, correlations between the YST and the nine other phonemic awareness measures were generally moderate to high (r = .33 to .82), with the lowest correlation for an auditory discrimination test and the highest for another measure of phoneme segmentation. In an unpublished study with an unspecified number of children (Yopp, 1992a, reported in Yopp, 1995b), kindergarten YST scores were significantly correlated (r = .67) with scores on a measure of pseudoword reading. Predictive validity was assessed in the same study, which followed children from kindergarten through sixth grade. Correlations between second-semester kindergarten YST scores and reading and spelling subtests on the *Comprehensive Tests of Basic Skills* (CTBS; CTB/McGraw-Hill, 1973) ranged from .38 to .78, with a correlation of .74 for CTBS total score at the end of sixth grade. Even when achievement for the previous year was controlled, 16 of 25 correlations were significant, including a correlation of .47 with CTBS total score in sixth grade.

CONSTRUCT VALIDITY EVIDENCE

In the author's comparative study of 10 phoneme awareness measures (Yopp, 1988), the tests loaded on two factors, a simple and a complex phonemic awareness factor, with the YST displaying the highest loading of the 10 measures on the first factor. The YST was also the best predictor of learning rate (r = .67) as defined by the number of trials required to learn six pseudowords.

Usability

The YST is simple to administer, score, and interpret. It makes a useful addition to a kindergarten screening or diagnostic battery, especially when credit is awarded for partial segmentation of items. Recording and analyzing errors as recommended by the test's author provides additional information for use in sharing results with teachers and parents and for instructional planning.

Links to Intervention

Although the author does not provide specific recommendations for intervention in the article presenting the test (Yopp, 1995b), several of her publications focus on developing phonemic awareness in young children. An article in *The Reading Teacher*, "Developing Phonemic Awareness in Young Children" (Yopp, 1992), includes detailed descriptions of various classroom phonemic awareness activities. A later article in the same journal (Yopp, 1995a) presents a list of 44 read-aloud books that draw attention to language sounds and promote the acquisition of phonemic awareness. In addition, Yopp has coauthored a book of phonemic awareness activities for young children (*Oo-pples and Boo-noo-noos: Songs and Activities for Phonemic Awareness*; Yopp & Yopp, 1997).

Relevant Research

The YST has been used in numerous reading investigations to predict reading acquisition and evaluate the effectiveness of early reading intervention programs (e.g., Kame'enui et al., 2001; Lennon & Slesinski, 1999; Spector, 1992). In a study with 38 kindergarten students (Spector, 1992), floor effects on the YST were evident at the November testing (M = 2.68, SD = 4.75). Because most of the children obtained a score of 0 at fall testing, Spector readministered a modified version of the test, in which points were awarded for each correctly segmented sound. The correlation between the original and revised measures was .88. Spector also administered a 14-item YST, using a dynamic assessment procedure that provided corrective feedback and increasingly supportive prompts. Performance on the dynamic assessment modification of the YST was a better predictor of end-of-year word recognition and growth in phonemic awareness than the original YST, two other phonemic awareness tasks, or verbal ability as measured by the *Peabody Picture Vocabulary Test–Revised* (PPVT-R; Dunn & Dunn, 1981). In an early identification and intervention study with 117 kindergarten children (Kame'enui et al., 2001), January YST scores were highly correlated with scores on the *Dynamic Indicators of Basic Early Literacy Skills* (DIBELS) Phoneme Segmentation Fluency (PSF) task, indicating that they measure a similar construct. YST and DIBELS Onset Recognition Fluency together were significant predictors of growth in PSF assessed after 6 months of instructional interventions, but the YST did not contribute to the prediction of alphabetic principle growth as measured by the DIBELS Nonsense Word Fluency task, beyond that explained by the PSF measure.

Source and Cost

The YST is presented in its entirety as a reproducible form, including directions, in the original journal article (Yopp, 1995b). The version provided in Figure 5.4 includes slight modifications in format, as well as the addition of the correctly segmented words beside each item. It is also reprinted in several texts and resource books, including *Taking a Reading: A Teacher's Guide to Reading Assessment* (Southern California Comprehensive Assistance Center, 2002).

Summary

The *Yopp–Singer Test of Phoneme Segmentation* (YST) is a brief, individually administered, nonstandardized measure of phonemic awareness that has been shown to be an effective predictor of future reading ability in early primary grade children. It is highly reliable, is quick and easy to administer, lends itself to local norming, and makes a useful addition to a screening battery for second-semester kindergarten children or beginning first-grade children or a more comprehensive diagnostic battery for early primary grade children. Awarding partial credit for each sound correctly segmented requires slightly more scoring time but greatly increases the sensitivity of the test and its utility in monitoring the progress of children receiving instructional interventions. Potential test users should bear in mind that phonemic segmentation is too difficult for many kindergarten children, especially for those who are not receiving code-based instruction and especially in the fall semester.

Case Example

Name of student: Serena S.
Age: 5 years, 5 months
Grade: Kindergarten
Date of assessment: March

Reason for referral: Serena was referred for an early reading assessment by her kindergarten teacher because of her difficulty in performing phonological awareness tasks and developing phonics skills. Serena often does not appear to understand the nature of classroom instruction in these areas, and she is becoming increasingly inattentive and withdrawn.

Assessment results and interpretation: The *Yopp–Singer Test of Phoneme Segmentation* (YST) measures children's ability to pronounce the individual sounds (*phonemes*) in words spoken by the examiner. For example, the examiner says, "old," and the child responds, "/o/-/l/-/d/." Phonemic segmentation is highly predictive of reading acquisition in young children.

Serena was unable to fully segment any of the 22 words, even after several practice items and additional demonstrations. Her performance is considerably lower than that expected for children in the spring of kindergarten (12/22 items correct) and indicates significant delays in phonemic awareness. She was able to provide the initial sounds for 18 of the items, but she had great difficulty providing middle and ending sounds. In a testing-of-limits procedure in which the examiner stretched out the sounds in each word, she was able to pronounce the final sounds for most of the consonant–vowel–consonant items (e.g., *sat*), but she was still unable to pronounce the final sound in words ending in a vowel (e.g., *no* = "/nuh/-/aw/") or to isolate any medial vowels correctly. At times, her responses suggested that she may have been trying to spell the word in her head (e.g., *wave* = "/w/-/yuh/").

Measures of Rapid Naming

This section reviews one measure of rapid naming derived from the research literature. Norm-referenced rapid naming measures are also included in the *Comprehensive Test of Phonological Processing*, the *Dyslexia Early Screening Test*, the *Dyslexia Screening Test*, the *Process Assessment of the Learner: Test Battery for Reading and Writing*, and the *Woodcock–Johnson III*.

TEST OF RAPID AUTOMATIZED NAMING

Overview

The *Test of Rapid Automatized Naming* (T-RAN; Meyer, Wood, Hart, & Felton, 1998a) is an individually administered, nonstandardized set of measures assessing naming speed for familiar visual stimuli for children in first through eighth grade. Deficits in rapid naming are associated with reading disabilities in both children and adults, with differential rates in naming speed occurring as early as kindergarten. Originally developed by Denckla and Rudel (1974), the rapid automatized naming (RAN) procedure has been used in numerous reading prediction and diagnostic studies (e.g., Denckla & Cutting, 1999; Neuhaus, Foorman, Francis, & Carlson, 2001; Torgesen, Wagner, Rashotte, Burgess, & Hecht, 1997). This version consists of the same four testing tasks as the original RAN procedure but uses different pictorial stimuli for four of the five objects on the Rapid Object Naming task. Materials include four 11¼- × 14¼-inch cards (one per task), a three-page scoring guide, and a five-page handout that includes administration procedures, a reproducible record form, a summary of RAN research findings, and a reprint of the norms tables from an article by the authors (Meyer et al., 1998a).

Assessment Tasks and Composites

Assessment Tasks

Each T-RAN task requires the child to name 50 stimuli, consisting of 5 different items randomly repeated in 5 rows of 10 items per row. The four T-RAN tasks are described in Table 5.14 in order of administration.

TABLE 5.14. Description of the T-RAN Tasks

Task	Description
Rapid Color Naming	The child names a 50-stimuli random array of five color patches (red, yellow, blue, green, black) as rapidly as possible.
Rapid Number Naming	The child names a 50-stimuli random array of five numbers (2, 4, 6, 7, 9) as rapidly as possible.
Rapid Object Naming	The child names a 50-stimuli random array of five line drawings (key, scissors, umbrella, watch, comb) as rapidly as possible.
Rapid Letter Naming	The child names a 50-stimuli random array of five lowercase high-frequency letters (*a*, *d*, *o*, *p*, *s*) as rapidly as possible.

Composites

Two composite scores can be derived: (1) a color/object composite score based on the mean of the Rapid Color Naming and Rapid Object Naming scores (i.e., naming speed for attributes or concrete objects), and (2) a number/letter composite score based on the mean of the Rapid Letter Naming and Rapid Digit Naming scores (i.e., naming speed for orthographic symbols).

Administration

The T-RAN is individually administered and takes about 8–10 minutes for all four tasks. The cards are presented in the following order: colors, numbers, objects, and letters. For each task, the examiner points to each of the five stimuli in turn and asks the child to identify it. If the child cannot name a color (number, object or letter), that particular task is omitted. On Rapid Object Naming, the child may identify the watch as either a watch or clock but must continue to use that word throughout the task or it is counted as an error. The test's authors do not recommend a particular seating arrangement for administration, but I have found that sitting beside children during testing makes it easier to redirect them if they lose their place or skip a row. Using the record form, which reproduces the test stimuli for each task, the examiner marks correct and incorrect responses as the child proceeds through the task and also records the time required to complete the entire card. Although the examiner does not correct errors, the child may correct errors spontaneously, and the time required for spontaneous self-correction is included in the total time. No instructions are provided as to how examiners should respond if children lose their place or skip a row. The authors state that practice effects are minimal and that the T-RAN can be administered on a yearly basis.

Scores

As with all rapid naming tasks, the T-RAN can be challenging to score reliably because scoring occurs while the child is responding as rapidly as possible. For each task, the score is the number of seconds required to name the 50 stimuli on the card. The number of errors per task is also recorded, but no normative data are provided to interpret error scores. Raw scores on each of the four tasks and the two composites can be converted to 1 of 10 percentile ranks (1, 2, 5, 10, 25, 50, 75, 90, 95, and 99) for a set of research norms for Grades 1, 3, 5, and 8. Raw scores that fall between two percentile ranks must be interpolated, and percentiles must be extrapolated for examinees in Grades 2, 4, 6, and 7. For children in grades not included in the norm group, the authors suggest that examiners assume a linear increase in naming speed between two adjacent grades but also consider examinee age in assigning a percentile. Thus, for second-grade examinees, users must first extrapolate to find the percentile rank corresponding to the obtained raw score and then interpolate for grade, while also taking the age of the child into consideration. The authors use an example of a second grader with a color/object composite score of 70 to demonstrate the extrapolation process. Also provided is a score conversion table with percentile ranks for speed in terms of items named per second. To use this table, the examiner takes the reciprocal of the child's raw score in seconds on each task and then multiplies that value by 50. Because this table requires two additional sets of calculations and because naming speed is usually reported in terms of number of seconds for task completion, practitioners are likely to prefer to use the first conversion table.

Interpretation

The test's authors recommend using composite scores for both clinical and research purposes and include several cautions regarding the percentile scores in the norm tables. First, they caution that interpretation should take into account the fact that children with very low and very high IQs (standard scores below 70 and above 130 on the PPVT-R) were excluded from the normative group. Second, because of the small sample size (*n* = 160 per grade), percentile scores at either extreme of the distribution are less reliable and valid than percentile ranks from 5 to 90. Finally, their data indicate that the predictive validity of the T-RAN is limited to poor readers and that the test is not sensitive to individual differences in reading ability for good readers. Given these cautions, T-RAN scores at or below the 10th percentile are considered to be significant and indicative of retrieval/naming deficits. Children scoring in that range may have *double deficits*–that is, weaknesses in both naming speed and phonological awareness. Children scoring between the 10th and 25th percentiles are considered to be at risk and should be monitored. According to the authors, differences between color/object and number/letter composite scores are not unusual. For primary grade children, number/letter composite scores at or below the 10th percentile indicate a severe lack of automaticity with letter and number recognition and a retrieval deficit for orthographic symbols. For students in Grade 5 and above, the color/ object composite score is a more sensitive measure because of older children's greater familiar with orthographic symbols. For children at this level of schooling, color/object composite scores falling at or below the 10th percentile indicate significant naming speed deficits.

Technical Adequacy

Norms

The T-RAN norms were obtained from a normally distributed, longitudinal random sample of 160 students tested in each of Grades 1, 3, 5, and 8. The sample was stratified to ensure that reading ability was normally distributed across the grades tested. Males and females were equally included, 73% of the examinees were European American and the other 27% were African American, and all were English-speaking. As noted above, children with scores of less than 70 or greater than 130 on the PPVT-R were excluded.

Reliability Evidence

No reliability evidence is provided in the test materials or in the two articles by the authors (Meyer et al., 1998a, 1998b) discussed below.

Test Floors and Item Gradients

The T-RAN yields 10 percentile ranks rather than standard scores. In the primary grades (i.e., Grades 1 and 3 in the research norms), the T-RAN appears to have adequate floors to identify children with very slow naming speed. Item gradients also appear adequate at the primary grade levels. As its authors have observed, the T-RAN is not sensitive to small differences in performance among children with average to above average naming speed.

Validity Evidence

Included in the test materials is a one-page summary of findings from the Bowman Gray dyslexia research group regarding the predictive validity of the T-RAN. Major findings include the following: (1) Rapid naming has predictive validity at least through Grade 8, (2) rapid naming predicts sight word identification but not passage comprehension, (3) disabled, normal, and superior readers show a predictable developmental pattern in naming speed and maintain their relative positions through Grade 8; and (4) naming speed has predictive utility as early as kindergarten.

Usability

Although the T-RAN test cards are sturdy and attractive, they are so large that they warp slightly over time. Children enjoy the game-like features of the T-RAN, but the tasks can be effortful and frustrating for examinees with severe retrieval deficits, who tend to shout the names of the test stimuli in their efforts to respond quickly. Interpolating for the grades not included in the norms is a complex procedure that increases scoring time and interscorer variance. Because of the brevity of the T-RAN, local norms can be developed in a relatively short period of time.

Links to Intervention

The test's authors recommend several intervention programs targeting the reading fluency problems associated with naming speed deficits. Although they do not provide specific citations or sources for the programs, they refer practitioners to an *Annals of Dyslexia* article summarizing the literature on fluency interventions (Meyer & Felton, 1999) and to the spring 1999 edition of the International Dyslexia Association's *Perspectives*, along with the Association's Web site and telephone number.

Relevant Research

The predictive utility of the T-RAN varies according to the specific task, reader risk status, and the reading subskill used as the criterion measure. In a longitudinal study with a randomly selected normal sample of 160 children tested in each of Grades 1, 3, 5, and 8 (i.e., the norm group), Meyer and colleagues (1998a) reported that the number/letter composite score was the strongest predictor of single word reading across all four grades (*rs* = .38 to .46), as measured by the Reading cluster score on the *Woodcock–Johnson Psycho-Educational Battery* (WJ; Woodcock & Johnson, 1977), although the color/object composite was nearly as strong a predictor (*rs* = .35 to .40). T-RAN has its greatest predictive utility among poor readers. In a normally distributed random longitudinal sample of 154 children evaluated in Grades 3 through 8

(Meyer et al., 1998b), T-RAN scores did not predict the reading performance of the 122 average readers, defined as children who scored between the 10th and 90th percentiles on the WJ Reading cluster and the *Decoding Skills Test* (Richardson & DiBenedetto, 1985). In contrast, for the 15 impaired readers, defined as children scoring at or below the 10th percentile on the criterion measures, both number/letter and color/object composites were significant predictors of Grade 5 and Grade 8 word reading, accounting for between 41% and 47% of the variance. Moreover, for impaired readers, T-RAN scores were much better predictors of Grade 5 and Grade 8 word reading than either pseudoword reading, as measured by the WJ Word Attack test, or phonemic segmentation, as measured by the *Lindamood Auditory Conceptualization Test*, both of which were nonsignificant predictors. Similarly, in a longitudinal sample (Meyer et al., 1998b) of 64 poor readers in Grade 3, defined as students scoring at or below the 10th percentile in single word reading, both T-RAN composites were strong predictors of single word reading in Grades 5 and 8 even when IQ, SES, and Grade 3 reading were controlled. T-RAN composites and individual tasks accounted for between 18% and 22% of the variance in Grades 5 and 8 WJ Reading cluster scores.

Although the T-RAN is a powerful predictor of word-level reading skills, it is much less effective as a predictor of reading comprehension. In the 1998a study cited above, T-RAN scores accounted for less than 15% of the variance in reading comprehension, as measured by the Reading Comprehension subtest on the *Gates–MacGinitie Reading Test* (MacGinitie, Kamons, Kowalski, MacGinitie, & MacKay, 1978). Similarly, in the study with poor Grade 3 readers (Meyer et al., 1998b), neither T-RAN composite nor task scores were significant predictors of WJ Passage Comprehension.

Source and Cost

The T-RAN is available from Marianne S. Meyer, Section of Neuropsychology, Wake Forest University, Bowman Gray School of Medicine, Medical Center Boulevard, Winston-Salem, NC 27157-1043. The cost is $25.00 per set.

Summary

The *Test of Rapid Automatized Naming* (T-RAN) is a brief, individually administered, nonstandardized measure of naming speed for visual symbols for children in Grades 1 through 8. Currently, the T-RAN is the only available stand-alone set of test materials for the RAN procedure. A voluminous body of research, including that of the test's authors, has demonstrated the utility of naming speed in predicting reading acquisition, diagnosing reading disabilities, and predicting response to interventions, especially among children at risk for reading problems. The T-RAN makes an excellent addition to a screening battery or diagnostic assessment beginning in first grade or for local norming beginning in kindergarten. Although its usability is limited by a small research-based norm group restricted to four grades, it is easily adaptable to local norming. Practitioners developing local norms should create and adhere to a standardized set of procedures for redirecting examinees who skip a row or otherwise lose their place during a task.

Case Example

Name of student: Susan R.
Age: 6 years, 6 months
Grade: First grade
Date of testing: November

Reason for referral: Susan was referred for an early reading assessment by her first-grade teacher. Susan's performance on the first-grade reading screening battery administered in October was much lower than that of her grade mates, and her progress in reading and other academic areas has been slow. According to her teacher, she has difficulty understanding written and oral directions, has a very limited sight word vocabulary, and can read very little connected text at this point. Although she receives tutoring twice weekly, her tutor indicates that she has trouble remembering what she has been taught from one session to another.

Assessment results and interpretation: The *Test of Rapid Automatized Naming* (T-RAN) requires the child to name as rapidly as possible a small, repeated set of familiar visual symbols, including colors, numbers, objects, and letters. Slow naming speed reflects processing inefficiency and is associated with risk for reading problems. On the T-RAN, scores at or below the 10th percentile indicate weaknesses in retrieval or naming. Scores between the 10th and 25th percentile indicate some degree of risk. Susan's scores on the T-RAN are presented below.

Task/**Composite**	Time in Seconds	Errors	Percentile Rank (PR)
Colors	86	0	1
Objects	170	2	1
Colors/Objects	128	2	1
Numbers	70	0	1
Letters	76	0	2
Numbers/Letters	73	0	1

Relative to that of other first graders, Susan's T-RAN performance represents very slow naming speed on all four tasks (PRs ≤ 2). Although she made very few errors and self-corrected these, she had trouble rapidly retrieving the names of the visual symbols, whether they were attributes or concrete objects (i.e., color patches and pictures of objects) or alphanumeric (i.e., single letters and digits). She had particular difficulty naming familiar objects and often required several seconds to retrieve the name of a single symbol.

Measures of Orthographic Processing

This section reviews one measure of orthographic processing from the research literature. Additional measures of orthographic processing, although not labeled as such, are included in the *Illinois Test of Psycholinguistic Abilities–3*, the *Phonological Awareness Literacy Screening*, the *Predictive Reading Profile*, the *Process Assessment of the Learner: Test Battery for Reading and Writing*, and the *Woodcock-Johnson III*.

EXCEPTION WORD READING TEST

Overview

The *Exception Word Reading Test* (EWRT, Adams & Huggins, 1985) is an individually administered, nonstandardized measure of sight word reading for children in Grades 2 through 5. Developed as part of an effort to design a test battery for diagnosing problems with word recognition subskills in elementary grade children (Adams et al., 1980), the EWRT includes only words that violate conventional spelling patterns. Exception word reading is considered to be an index of orthographic coding because knowledge of letter–sound relationships (i.e., phonological recoding) is insufficient for complete decoding of the stimulus words. Instead, the child must have seen the words previously and have encoded the word-specific orthographic patterns in memory. The EWRT and modifications of the original test have been used in a number of research studies to measure orthographic processing (e.g., Manis et al., 1999; Manis, Doi, & Bhadha, 2000). The EWRT also served as the model for the Sight Decoding subtest on the latest version of the *Illinois Test of Psycholinguistic Abilities–3* [ITPA-3]). The entire test appears in the original journal article (Adams & Huggins, 1985) and is presented with minor adaptations in Figure 5.5.

Assessment Task

The EWRT consists of 50 words, arranged in decreasing order of frequency and chosen to reflect irregular spelling–sound correspondences (e.g., *blind, trough*). There are two versions of the test, an original 50-word version and a 45-word modification, each in a list and sentence format. The authors state that they dropped 5 of the 50 words in the modified version to reduce the time required to administer the entire assessment battery but that they prefer the longer version. In the list format, the words are presented in isolation. In the sentence format, which is designed to assess children's ability to use contextual information to supplement orthographic information, each test word appears as the last content word of a sentence.

Administration

Administration takes about 5–7 minutes for the list version and about 10–15 minutes for the sentence version, depending on the child's reading ability. For the list version, the examiner encourages the child to attempt each word. For the sentence ver-

EXCEPTION WORD READING TEST

Student's name ________________________________ Date ______________

Score __/50

Directions: Say: "I want you to read the words on this list. Try to read them the best you can. Even if you're not sure, please try to read every word." If the child fails to respond to an item, encourage a response. If there is still no response, score the item as incorrect and prompt the child to try the next word. Discontinue testing after 10 consecutive errors.

1. ocean	11. tongue	21. sword	31. rely	41. depot
2. iron	12. lose	22. anchor	32. ninth*	42. bough
3. island	13. prove	23. echo	33. react	43. bouquet
4. break	14. rhythm	24. guitar	34. recipe	44. aisle
5. busy	15. truth	25. veins	35. pint	45. ache*
6. sugar	16. stomach	26. chorus	36. deny	46. yacht
7. touch	17. blind	27. scent*	37. vague*	47. chauffeur
8. none	18. wounded	28. deaf*	38. tomb	48. ukulele
9. heights	19. calf	29. mechanic	39. drought	49. suede
10. whom	20. sweat	30. dough	40. trough	50. fiancé

FIGURE 5.5. Exception Word Reading Test (EWRT). Asterisked (*) words are omitted from the 45-word version. From "The Growth of Children's Sight Vocabulary: A Quick Test with Educational and Theoretical Implications," by M. J. Adams and A. W. F. Huggins, *Reading Research Quarterly*, *20*, p. 280. Copyright 1985 by the International Reading Association. Adapted with permission.

sion, the examiner may provide any unfamiliar words except for the target word. For both versions, testing is terminated after 10 consecutive errors.

Scores

Scoring (incorrect = 0, correct = 1) takes less than 5 minutes. The test is not standardized, although two sets of research norms are available (see below).

Interpretation

According to the authors, correct reading of isolated *sight words*, that is, words with irregular spelling–sound correspondences, indicates that those words are fully and accurately represented in children's memory. Means for two elementary grade samples, one for the 50-word version and one for the 45-word version, are presented in the article and are provided here for comparative purposes (see Tables 5.15 and 5.16). In Table 5.16, means have been derived from the proportions of correct responses reported in the article. Because of the age of the norms, the limited numbers of examinees, and the differences in score levels between the two samples, local norming is strongly recommended.

TABLE 5.15. Mean Number of Correctly Read Words and Their Differences for Good versus Poor Readers on the 50-Word Version of the EWRT

Grade	Good readers	Poor readers	Difference
2	8.27	1.25	7.02
3	14.69	4.22	10.47
4	26.92	8.31	18.61
5	35.93	19.13	16.80

Note. Children (n = 106) were tested in the first semester of the school year. Good readers were classified as those scoring within or above the 5th stanine on the reading comprehension subtests on both the *Stanford Achievement Test* and the *Gates–MacGinitie Reading Test*. Poor readers were classified as those scoring within or below the 4th stanine on both tests. From "The Growth of Children's Sight Vocabulary: A Quick Test with Educational and Theoretical Implications," by M. J. Adams and A. W. F. Huggins, 1985, *Reading Research Quarterly, 20,* p. 267. Copyright 1985 by the International Reading Association. Adapted with permission.

Technical Adequacy

Norms

The 50-word version of the EWRT was administered to 106 children in Grades 2 through 5 from a low-SES urban school district, with testing in the first half of the school year (see Table 5.15). Children who scored below 80 or above 130 on a short-form version of the *Wechsler Intelligence Scale for Children–Revised* (WISC-R; Wechsler, 1974) were excluded. The 45-word EWRT was administered at the end of the school year to 83 children from a high-SES suburban school district (see Table 5.16). Score levels for this sample were considerably higher than for the first sample, even with five fewer words, but differences between good and poor readers were significant for both samples across all four grades.

Reliability Evidence

Spearman–Brown split-half reliability, corrected for length, was .96 for the 50-item test (list format). No reliability estimates are provided for the 45-word EWRT or the sentence format for either version.

TABLE 5.16. Mean Number of Correctly Read Words and Their Differences for Good versus Poor Readers on the 45-Word Version of the EWRT

Grade	Good readers	Poor readers	Difference
2	25.65	6.30	19.35
3	28.35	10.80	17.55
4	32.85	16.65	16.20
5	37.35	25.20	12.15

Note. Children (n = 83) were tested in the last month of the school year. Good readers were classified as those scoring within or above the 6th stanine on the reading comprehension subtests on the *Stanford Achievement Test* for the current and previous year. Poor readers were classified as those scoring within or below the 5th stanine on both tests. From "The Growth of Children's Sight Vocabulary: A Quick Test with Educational and Theoretical Implications," by M. J. Adams and A. W. F. Huggins, 1985, *Reading Research Quarterly, 20,* p. 272. Copyright 1985 by the International Reading Association. Adapted with permission.

Validity Evidence

CONTENT VALIDITY EVIDENCE

Test words were selected from a set of 80 words used in pilot testing with 80 children. Only words that violated conventional grapheme–phoneme correspondences were included (e.g., *island, yacht*). Words that were extremely easy or difficult in terms of frequency and words that did not appear to be part of children's listening or speaking vocabularies were dropped. The frequency of the 50 remaining words ranges from 134.1 per million to 0.12 per million, according to Carroll, Davies, and Richman's (1971) *Word Frequency Book.*

CONCURRENT VALIDITY EVIDENCE

In a study with 106 urban children tested in the first semester of the year, EWRT raw scores for the list format were strongly correlated with mean stanine scores on the *Stanford Achievement Test* and *Gates–MacGinitie* reading comprehension subtests (.67, .80, .85 and .82 for Grades 2, 3, 4, and 5, respectively). Lower correlations for second graders may have resulted from floor effects, as the mean EWRT score for Grade 2 poor readers in that sample was 1.25 words. In a second experiment using the sentence format with the same sample, EWRT scores were similar but displayed slightly higher correlations with reading stanine scores (.86, .94, .87, and .82 for Grades 2 through 5). For a second sample of 83 suburban children tested in the last month of school, EWRT raw scores and mean reading comprehension stanine scores were highly correlated across all four grades, whether words were presented in isolation (.84, .95, .82, and .82) or in context (.84, .85, .84, and .79). Sentence and list formats again yielded a qualitatively similar performance, but children in both samples were able to read significantly more test words in the contextual format.

CONSTRUCT VALIDITY EVIDENCE

For both the 45- and 50-word versions of the EWRT, good and poor readers displayed highly significant differences in the number of correctly read words (see Tables 5.15 and 5.16). According to the test's authors, proficient readers achieve higher EWRT scores than poor readers because they read larger amounts of textual material and more complex material and thus have greater opportunities for expanding their sight word vocabulary. The authors also propose that successfully decoding a word by using letter–sound correspondence rules does not guarantee that children have stored the word as a sight word or that they comprehend its meaning. Because the EWRT consists only of irregularly spelled words, it permits a more precise identification of the point at which lexical access fails, and thus it is a more efficient and interpretable measure than traditional word identification tests that contain both regular and irregular words.

Usability

The list version of the EWRT provides a quick, easy-to-administer estimate of sight word reading proficiency and lends itself readily to local norming. The sentence format requires much more time to administer than the list format, and the task of struggling through a long series of sentences can be a frustrating experience for less skilled readers.

Links to Intervention

The EWRT's authors suggest that efforts to build vocabulary through independent reading should focus on material within the limits of children's *secure sight vocabulary* and *partial sight vocabulary*—that is, words recognized in list and sentence formats, respectively. Words that are not recognized in either format require direct instruction and guided reading if children are to add them to their lexicons. The authors also stress that instruction should focus on teaching children metacognitive strategies designed to help them attend to the meaning of new words and create mental representation of those words. Because EWRT words are not identified by grade level, it is not clear how teachers are to select appropriate instructional materials, and the authors do not provide examples of the metacognitive strategies they advocate.

Relevant Research

Exception word reading tasks have frequently been used in research studies to assess orthographic coding (e.g., Castles & Coltheart, 1993; Castles, Datta, Gayan, & Olson, 1999; Stanovich, Siegel, & Gottardo, 1997). In two studies with second graders who took a battery of tests in the spring of the year, Manis and colleagues (1999, 2000) used an expanded 70-word version of the EWRT as a measure of orthographic processing, with easier items added at the beginning. In a sample of 67 second graders (Manis et al., 1999), the modified EWRT correlated highly with two other measures of orthographic coding, including an orthographic choice task and a word likeness task (*rs* = .71 and .62, respectively), indicating that the three tasks tap a similar construct. Moreover, the modified EWRT was highly correlated with three reading measures, including the WRMT-R Word Identification and Word Attack tests and reading comprehension as assessed by an informal reading inventory (*rs* = .75, .75, and .77, respectively). In another sample of 85 second graders (Manis et al., 2000), the EWRT was again highly correlated with the two orthographic tasks (*rs* = .73 and .62, respectively) and the same set of reading measures (.90, 71, and .69, respectively).

Source and Cost

List and sentence formats for the EWRT are included in the original article (Adams & Huggins, 1985). The version provided in Figure 5.5 includes the addition of directions and slight modifications in format.

Summary

The *Exception Word Reading Test* (EWRT) is a brief, easy-to-administer, nonstandardized measure of sight word reading for children in Grades 2 through 5 that has been frequently used in prediction and diagnostic studies as a measure of orthographic processing. Unlike most standardized word identification tests, which confound the phonological and orthographic aspects of reading, the EWRT includes only irregularly spelled words and thus serves as an index of children's orthographic coding ability. It is highly reliable for so brief a measure, discriminates between poor and proficient readers, and is strongly correlated with standardized measures of single word reading, phonemic decoding, and reading comprehension. Because of floor effects, however, it is not sensitive to individual differences in sight word acquisition among poor readers, even in the second semester of Grade 2. Other limitations include the necessity of developing local norms to interpret performance and the availability of only a single form for monitoring growth in sight word vocabulary.

Case Example

Name of student: Alan T.
Age: 7 years, 8 months
Grade: Second grade
Date of assessment: May

Reason for referral: Alan was referred by his second-grade teacher because of concerns about his persistent difficulties with word identification, oral reading, and reading comprehension. Although his grades on weekly phonics and spelling tests are satisfactory, and he appears to understand ongoing classroom instruction, he reads slowly and hesitantly and obtains low scores on assignments that require him to read and follow directions independently.

Assessment results and interpretation: The *Exception Word Reading Test* (EWRT) requires the child to read a list of "sight words," that is, words with irregular letter–sound correspondences (e.g., *ocean, pint*). A large sight word vocabulary is essential for rapid, automatic word recognition and good reading comprehension. The EWRT also serves as a measure of *orthographic coding*, or knowledge of spelling patterns, because the child cannot rely on phonemic decoding skills to pronounce the words correctly. Alan made a good effort on the EWRT and attempted to decode each word, but he was able to read only 1 of the 50 items. His score is much lower than that of his classmates with average reading skills on the same measure (12 out of 50 words correct) and suggests that his difficulty acquiring an adequate sight word vocabulary is interfering with his ability to read fluently and comprehend what he reads. An analysis of his errors suggests that he was attempting to decode the words based on his understanding of phonically regular letter–sound relationships (e.g., *izland* for *island, loze* for *lose*).

Measures of Oral Language

This section reviews six measures of oral language—that is, oral language skills extending beyond the domain of phonemic awareness. All six of the measures are norm-referenced. Additional measures of oral language are included in the *Basic Early Assessment of Reading*, the *Dyslexia Screening Test*, the *Early Reading Diagnostic Assessment–Revised*, the *Phonological Abilities Test*, the *Process Assessment of the Learner: Test Battery for Reading and Writing*, the *Texas Primary Reading Inventory*, the *Wechsler Individual Achievement Test–II*, and the *Woodcock–Johnson III*.

EXPRESSIVE VOCABULARY TEST

Overview

The *Expressive Vocabulary Test* (EVT; Williams, 1997) is an individually administered, norm-referenced measure of expressive vocabulary and word retrieval for children and adults aged 2½ through 90 years. The EVT was conormed with the *Peabody Picture Vocabulary Test–III* (PPVT-III; Dunn & Dunn, 1997) to permit comparisons of receptive and expressive vocabulary within the same sample. The EVT uses a single-word response format to assess spoken vocabulary. Purposes identified by the test's author include (1) screening for expressive language problems, (2) screening preschool children in early language development, (3) measuring word retrieval, (4) understanding reading problems, (5) monitoring growth, (6) facilitating research, and (7) evaluating English language acquisition in examinees whose primary language is not English. Test materials include an examiner's manual, test easel, and 25 record forms, packaged together in notebook form.

Assessment Tasks

The EVT consists of two types of tasks: (1) labeling items (Items 1–38) and (2) synonym items (Items 39–152), both of which are depicted in color on picture plates. For the labeling items, the examiner points to a picture or part of the body and asks a question, and the child responds with a one-word answer that is a noun, verb, or adjective. For the synonym items, the examiner presents a picture and a stimulus word or words within a carrier phrase, and the child responds with a one-word answer that is a noun, verb, adjective, or adverb. Item responses yield a single overall test score.

Administration

The EVT is untimed and takes about 10–15 minutes for early primary grade examinees. Starting points are based on age. Two examples are provided for each type of item, and each entry level begins with two or three teaching items. Incorrect responses that must be prompted are marked in the record form. Basals and ceilings are set at five consecutive correct and incorrect items, respectively. If the PPVT-III is being given, it should be administered before the EVT because that was the order for the normative sample.

Scores

Items are scored dichotomously. The record form lists from 1 to 5 of the most common correct and incorrect answers, whereas the expanded list in the manual includes many more answers, up to 23 correct and 16 incorrect responses per item. If examinees give a response that is not listed, the manual instructs examiners to record it beside the word "Other" on the record form, consider the item as incorrect for establishing a basal or correct for establishing a ceiling, and then score all previously unscored items after the session by consulting the manual. Because this process can increase administration time considerably, especially at higher age levels, examiners may wish to refer to the expanded list during testing to ensure accurate administration. Raw scores are converted to standard scores (*M* = 100, *SD* = 15), percentile ranks, stanines, normal curve equivalents, and test–age equivalents. Norms are in 2-month increments for ages 2-6 through 6-11, 3-month increments for ages 7-0 through 18-11, and increments of 2 or more years for older examinees.

Interpretation

The section of the EVT manual on interpreting test results focuses primarily on the procedures for evaluating EVT and PPVT-III standard score differences for statistical and clinical significance. Score differences can be evaluated using the score comparison section of the record form or the software scoring program. The manual presents a case example of a child aged 9-2 to demonstrate how to complete the record form, obtain derived scores, and calculate and interpret score differences. The case example has an EVT score in the moderately low range (SS = 76), which differs from her average PPVT-III score (SS = 94) in terms of both statistical and clinical significance. The test's author suggests further assessment using classroom observations and the *Oral and Written Language Scales* (OWLS; see review later in this section) to evaluate receptive and expressive language skills using separate conormed scales.

Technical Adequacy

Standardization

Standardization data were collected during 1995 and 1996 for 2,725 examinees sampled to be representative of March 1994 U.S. census data and stratified by age, race/ethnicity, geographic region, parent educational level (for examinees ages 24 or less) or examinee educational level (for examinees over age 25), and six special education categories. In general, sample characteristics closely match U.S. population data at that time. The manual indicates that between 119 and 122 examinees were tested per 6-month interval for ages 5-0 through 6-11, but because norm group intervals for these ages are in 2-month increments, derived scores are based on 39–56 examinees, which is unacceptably low. Similarly, although overall group sizes for ages 7 and 8 are 167 and 160 examinees, respectively, subgroup intervals are in 3-month increments at these age levels, leaving subgroups of only about 40 children each.

Reliability Evidence

For the early primary grade range, coefficient alpha reliabilities exceed .90 for all ages. As the test's author points out, however, these values may be spuriously high because they were computed based on total test length, with Rasch procedures used to simulate responses for items not administered because of basal and ceiling rules. Split-half coefficients, derived from Rasch ability estimates and corrected for length, range from .83 to .88 for early primary grade examinees. Test–retest reliability (intervals from 8 to 203 days; mean interval = 42 days) was .84 for a randomly selected sample of 70 examinees aged 6-0 to 10-11 but fell below acceptable levels for a sample of 67 examinees aged 2-6 to 5-11 (r =. 77). The length of at least some of the test–retest intervals for both groups is much greater than what is typical or desirable for oral language measures and may have contributed to the lower reliability coefficients, especially for the younger sample. No evidence of interscorer reliability is presented. Given the amount of teaching and prompting required during test sessions, along with the numerous alternatives for correct answers, interscorer reliability estimates should be provided, based on simultaneous independent scoring of actual or audiotaped test sessions.

Test Floors and Item Gradients

EVT test floors extend down to a standard score of 40 across the entire age range of the test. Item gradients are also ample through the primary years, making the EVT sensitive to individual differences in expressive vocabulary across the entire range of functioning.

Validity Evidence

CONTENT VALIDITY EVIDENCE

The EVT's author provides a comprehensive, readable rationale for test development and for the item selection and validation process but presents no theoretical or empirical data to support the use of a single-word response format for assessing expressive language. After words were selected from eight frequency word lists, two pilot studies and a national tryout were conducted prior to standardization. Classical item analyses were used to examine items for difficulty and discrimination, but the manual does not report specific item statistics. Items were also tested for goodness of fit to the Rasch model, but, again, no specific information regarding those analyses is provided. During the national tryout, the EVT was reviewed for potentially offensive content by consultants representing a variety of demographic groups. Rasch bias analyses were conducted at the item level by gender and region and within groups for African American, Hispanic, and European American examinees, whereas the Mantel–Haenszel procedure was used to examine item bias for Native Americans because of small sample size. As the result of the analyses, five items were dropped—three because of bias, one because of poor fit to the Rasch model, and one because of problems in scoring. In addition, numerous stimulus pictures were changed according to suggestions from the bias review panel and tryout examiners. Classical and Rasch item analyses were repeated after standardization, and 10 items were deleted—one because of bias, two because of scoring problems, and three because of poor fit. The remaining four very easy items were used as the examples in the final edition.

CRITERION-RELATED VALIDITY EVIDENCE

Correlations between the EVT and the OWLS were only moderate (.47 to .60) for a sample of 41 children aged 3-0 through 5-8 but high (.76 to .86) for an older sample of 43 children aged 8-1 to 12-10. As expected, the EVT displayed stronger correlations with OWLS Oral Expression than with OWLS Listening Comprehension for both age groups. Correlations with tests of verbal ability were higher than for nonverbal ability, as predicted. For 41 examinees aged 7-11 to 14-4, correlations between the EVT and the WISC-III ranged from .56 to .72, with the highest correlation for Verbal IQ. No evidence of predictive validity is reported.

CONSTRUCT VALIDITY EVIDENCE

Mean EVT scores show steady increases throughout the age range of the test, with rapid growth in the early years and more gradual growth in later years. Correlations between the EVT and both forms of the PPVT-III range from .61 to .79 for primary grade examinees, supporting the contention that both tests measure vocabulary knowledge but that the EVT also measures a different construct. In support of the clinical utility of the EVT, standard scores for eight clinical groups, including gifted examinees and examinees with speech impairments, language delay, language impairments, mental retardation (child/adolescent and adult samples), reading disabilities, and hearing impairments, were compared with scores of matched controls from the standardization sample. As expected, children with speech impairments did not differ significantly from matched controls. Although differences between matched controls and the remaining seven clinical groups were statistically significant and in the predicted direction, scores fell in the average range for all but the groups with mental retardation and hearing impairments. Means for language-delayed children and language-impaired children fell only 8 or 9 points below that for the matched control group and within 1 standard deviation of the test mean (SS = 92.7 vs. 94.7, respectively). The mean standard score for reading-disabled examinees ($n = 60$, ages 7-11 to 14-10) was approximately 6 points lower than that of matched controls (SS = 98.8 vs. 105.2). No evidence is presented to support the EVT's proposed use as a measure of English language acquisition in second-language learners.

Usability

With a few exceptions, the EVT has a high usability quotient. The notebook format makes it portable, basal and ceiling rules are easy to remember, and the colored picture plates are attractive. Efforts have been made to depict a variety of individuals balanced across gender and race and to portray both children and adults in nonstereotyped roles. At the primary grade level, a few of the stimulus pictures are distracting and potentially confusing rather than facilitating (e.g., a mouse crawling up a book to depict *little*). At the upper age ranges, the inherent difficulty in illustrating collective nouns, abstract concepts, and items that are not nouns sometimes results in misleading pictures (e.g., Item 188 presents a saw with the stimulus phrase "tool or utensil," but "saw" is listed as an incorrect and unprompted response). The fact that more than half of the pictures for the synonym items were changed after the national tryout, based on suggestions from examiners and bias review panelists, attests to the difficulty of selecting appropriate illustrations for this type of task, especially for more complex items. The software scoring program is exceptionally easy to use and offers a variety of report options, including a score summary, score profile comparisons, score narrative, and suggested activities for building expressive language skills. If the EVT is administered within 90 days of the PPVT-III, the software scoring program permits standard score comparisons of receptive and expressive vocabulary. Users should note that the classification ratings for standard score ranges in the printout differ from common practice by collapsing the usual seven categories into five. EVT and PPVT-III standard score categories are as follows: <70, extremely low; 70–84, moderately low; 85–114, average; 115–129, moderately high; ≥130, extremely high. Because neither the software scoring manual nor the test manual provides specific information about the rating system, examiners must discover what labels match which standard scores by experimenting with the scoring program or testing a wide range of examinees.

As noted above, examiners must either conduct a two-step scoring process or consult the manual throughout administration to determine when to discontinue testing because many items have numerous alternative correct responses. The small manual does not lie flat and should be spiral-bound for easy reference to the 11-page list of responses. Listing additional correct answers on the record form would also enhance usability. Although the form provides space for at least five correct and incorrect answers per item, many items with multiple correct responses have only a single answer or one or two alternatives listed.

Links to Intervention

Although the manual does not provide intervention suggestions, the ASSIST software scoring program includes a report option with vocabulary-building exercises for five age groups: early childhood (ages 2½ through 5), lower elementary (Grades 1 through 3), upper elementary (Grades 4 and 5), middle school (Grades 6 through 8), and high school and adult. Users can select a set of exercises based on age and current grade placement or level of functioning, with five sets of equal difficulty provided for each level. The exercises make useful additions to test reports and are suitable for use by parents, teachers, and tutors.

Relevant Research

In a study evaluating the utility of four vocabulary tests in identifying specific language impairment (SLI) in preschoolers, Gray, Plante, Vance, and Henrichsen (1999) administered the EVT, the PPVT-III, the *Expressive One-Word Vocabulary Test–Revised* (Gardner, 1990), and the *Receptive One-Word Vocabulary Test* (Gardner, 1985) to 31 children aged 4 and 5 who had been diagnosed with SLI and 31 children with normal language (NL). Although EVT mean standard scores for children with SLI were significantly lower than for NL children, they fell within the average range (SS = 92 vs. 104, respectively). Moreover, the identification accuracy of the EVT fell below acceptable levels (e.g., below .80). Based on a cutoff score derived from discriminant analysis, EVT sensitivity (accuracy in correctly identifying children with SLI as having SLI) was 71%, and EVT specificity (accuracy of identifying unimpaired children as unimpaired) was 68%. EVT positive predictive power (the percentage of children who scored below the cutoff and were also identified as language impaired) was 70%, the lowest of the four vocabulary tests.

Source and Cost

The EVT test kit is available from AGS Publishing for $154.95. The EVT can be purchased with Forms A and B of the PPVT-III for $388.95. The ASSIST software program for Windows or Macintosh is available on CD-ROM for $209.95. The combination kit with the PPVT-III, EVT, and both ASSIST programs retails for $586.95.

Test Reviews

Bessai, F. (2001). Review of the Expressive Vocabulary Test. In B. S. Plake & J. C. Impara (Eds.), *The fourteenth mental measurements yearbook* (pp. 475–476). Lincoln, NE: Buros Institute of Mental Measurements.

Carlson, J. F. (2001). Review of the Expressive Vocabulary Test. *Journal of Psychoeducational Assessment, 19*, 100–105.

Wasyliw, O. E. (2001). Review of the Expressive Vocabulary Test. In B. S. Plake & J. C. Impara (Eds.), *The fourteenth mental measurements yearbook* (pp. 476–478). Lincoln, NE: Buros Institute of Mental Measurements.

Summary

The *Expressive Vocabulary Test* (EVT) is an individually administered, norm-referenced test of expressive vocabulary and word retrieval for examinees from 2½ to 90 years of age. The EVT is appealing to practitioners assessing early primary grade examinees because of its attractiveness to children, ease of administration, conorming with the widely used PPVT-III, and user-friendly software scoring program with grade-specific language activities. When administered in conjunction with the PPVT-III, it may be useful in distinguishing word retrieval problems from limited word knowledge. The EVT's psychometric properties vary in terms of adequacy, however. Although the excellent test floors permit the identification of children with very low oral language skills, subgroup size is inadequate across the early primary grade range, and there is no evidence of interscorer reliability. Additional evidence of diagnostic and predictive validity are needed, given that some research, including studies reported in the manual, indicates that the EVT is likely to underidentify children with language impairments. The utility of the EVT in understanding reading problems and assessing English acquisition in second-language learners also remains to be demonstrated. Because the EVT measures only a limited aspect of oral language, it should never be used as the only measure in assessing children's language proficiency.

Case Example

Name of student: Kenisha T.
Age: 5 years, 8 months
Grade: Kindergarten
Date of assessment: May

Reason for referral: Kenisha was referred for an early reading assessment by her kindergarten teacher, subsequent to her very poor performance on the spring administration of the gradewide early literacy battery. Kenisha is making slow progress in all academic areas. She often does not appear to understand classroom instructions, and she is becoming increasingly reluctant to participate in class. Although she has been receiving daily assistance from the educational specialist, she still can name only a few letters consistently and cannot identify any letter sounds at this point. The *Expressive Vocabulary Test* was administered to determine whether expressive language deficits are contributing to Kenisha's problems in acquiring early reading skills.

Assessment results and interpretation: The *Expressive Vocabulary Test* (EVT) is a measure of expressive vocabulary and word retrieval. The child is required to provide a one-word label for a picture or a one-word synonym for a picture and word or words presented by the examiner. Average scores for an individual Kenisha's age are as follows: Standard Score (SS) = 100, Percentile Rank (PR) = 50, Age Equivalent (AE) = 5-8.

Kenisha's performance on the EVT falls below the 1st percentile for her age (PR = 0.5), indicating that her expressive vocabulary functioning is very delayed (SS = 61, extremely low range; AE = 3-0). She was able to identify the color and number of some sets of objects, but she was unable to name many other common objects, such as the sun, a rainbow, and a leaf. She had particular difficulty understanding the nature of the synonym-providing tasks, even after several teaching examples. For example, shown a picture of a mother reading a book to a child and asked to give another word for *mother*, she said, "book." In a testing-of-limits procedure, in which the examiner pointed to the figure of the mother and asked, "Who is that?", she was able to give a correct response ("a mommy"). On a subsequent item that assessed synonyms for *father* and depicted a father feeding a baby, however, she was unable to provide a correct response (e.g., "Daddy") when the standard directions were given. Articulation problems were observed for certain initial consonants and consonant digraphs (e.g., *sicken* for *chicken*, *gup* for *cup*).

ILLINOIS TEST OF PSYCHOLINGUISTIC ABILITIES—THIRD EDITION

Overview

The *Illinois Test of Psycholinguistic Abilities–Third Edition* (ITPA-3; Hammill, Mather, & Roberts, 2001) is an individually administered, norm-referenced test battery that measures spoken and written language in children aged 5-0 through 12-11. Originally used as an experimental instrument (McCarthy & Kirk, 1961) and then published in the late 1960s (Kirk, McCarthy, & Kirk, 1968), the ITPA was one of the most frequently used child assessment measures in the 1970s. The latest version has little resemblance to its predecessor and reflects the shift in emphasis from visual to language processing deficits as the primary cause of reading disabilities. Although the ITPA-3 is still based on Osgood's model of language functioning (Osgood, 1957; Osgood & Miron, 1963), subtests assessing visual-perceptual and visual–motor domains have been replaced with measures of oral language, reading, writing, and spelling, and the age range has been shifted upward from ages 2 through 10 to ages 5 through 12. Only 2 of the original 12 subtests have been retained–Auditory Association and Grammatic Closure, now termed Spoken Analogies and Morphological Closure. Applications identified by the manual include (1) identifying children at risk for school failure; (2) determining children's linguistic processing strengths and weaknesses; (3) evaluating the success of language intervention programs; and (4) facilitating research, such as studies assessing the relationship between phonological and orthographic abilities. The test kit includes a spiral-bound examiner's manual, 25 profile/examiner record booklets, 25 student response booklets, and a Sound Deletion audiocassette, all packed in a storage box.

Subtests and Composites

Subtests

The ITPA-3 consists of 12 subtests, 6 assessing spoken language and 6 assessing written language (see Table 5.17). Written language subtests are administered only to children aged 6-6 or older. The manual and software scoring summary report describe the Sound Deletion subtest as consisting of word and syllable deletion items, but all of the items involve deletion of a single phoneme.

TABLE 5.17. Description of the ITPA-3 Subtests

Subtest	Description
Spoken Analogies	The examiner says three parts of a four-part analogy (e.g., "Birds fly; fish ________"), and the child supplies the final missing part (e.g., "swim").
Spoken Vocabulary	The examiner says a word that is an attribute of a noun (e.g., "I'm thinking of something with a roof"), and the child responds with an appropriate noun (e.g., "house").
Morphological Closure	The examiner begins a series of words (e.g., "big, bigger, ________"), and the child completes it (e.g., "biggest").
Syntactic Sentences	The examiner says a sentence that is syntactically correct but semantically nonsensical (e.g., "Red flowers are smart"), and the child repeats the sentence verbatim.
Sound Deletion	The child deletes phonemes from spoken words, which are presented on an audiocassette. All of the resulting words are real words.
Rhyming Sequences	The examiner pronounces rhyming word strings that increase in length (e.g., "noon, soon, moon"), and the child repeats them verbatim.
Sentence Sequencing	The child silently reads a series of three to five sentences and orders them in a sequence to form a coherent paragraph.
Written Vocabulary	The child silently reads a phrase with an adjective (e.g., *A broken* ________) and then writes a noun closely associated with the stimulus word (e.g., *vase*).
Sight Decoding	The child reads aloud a list of printed words with irregular spellings (e.g., *would*).
Sound Decoding	The child reads aloud phonically regular pseudowords that are presented as the names of fictitious animals (e.g., *Flant*). Line drawings of the animals accompany each of the pseudowords, which are capitalized.
Sight Spelling	The examiner reads irregularly spelled words, and the child writes the omitted part of each word. The omitted part consists of the irregular part of the word and one or more missing phonemes. For example, the examiner reads, *said*. The child sees *s__d* and writes *ai* on the blank.
Sound Spelling	The examiner reads phonically regular pseudowords, and the child writes the missing part or the entire word. For example, the examiner reads, *pim*. The child sees *p_m* and writes *i* on the blank.

Composites

The 12 subtests can be combined to form 11 composites (termed "quotients"): 3 global composites and 8 specific composites consisting of the pooled standard scores for the two subtests assessing each area (see Table 5.18).

Administration

It takes about 45–60 minutes to administer the entire ITPA-3. All subtests have a basal of three consecutive correct responses and a ceiling of three consecutive incorrect responses. Children below the age of 9 begin with the first item on all subtests. Several aspects of administration need clarification or modification. Directions are provided on the record booklet to facilitate administration, but neither the record booklet nor the manual provides guidelines for acceptable pronunciations for Sound Decoding, a pseudoword reading task. Sound Deletion is delivered on audiocassette, but the two memory span subtests (Syntactic Sentences and Rhyming Sequences) are not. Moreover, no guidelines are offered for item presentation rate, making these subtests highly vulnerable to examiner variance. Blanks should be added on the profile/examiner booklet for recording responses to Sound Deletion, Sight Decoding, and Sound Decoding for later error analysis. The examiner dictates Sight Spelling items, but neither the manual nor the record booklet includes contextual sentences, and two of the words are homophones (*two* and *know*).

Scores

Items are scored dichotomously. Raw scores can be converted to subtest standard scores (M = 10, SD = 3), composite standard score quotients (M = 100, SD = 15), percentiles, and age and grade equivalents. Norms are in 3-month increments for ages 5-

TABLE 5.18. ITPA-3 Composites and Subtests

Global composites		Specific composites	Subtests
General Language	Spoken Language	Semantics	Spoken Analogies Spoken Vocabulary
		Grammar	Morphological Closure Syntactic Sentences
		Phonology	Sound Deletion Rhyming Sequences
		Comprehension	Sentence Sequencing Written Vocabulary
	Written Language	Word Identification	Sight Decoding Sound Decoding
		Spelling	Sight Spelling Sound Spelling
		Sight-Symbol Processing	Sight Decoding Sight Spelling
		Sound-Symbol Processing	Sound Decoding Sound Spelling

0 through 10-11 and 1-year increments for ages 11-0 through 12-11. I have encountered responses on the Spoken Vocabulary subtest that appear to be acceptable but are not included in the correct answers listed in the record booklet (e.g., "a stem" = "flower"). Pronunciation guidelines should be provided for Sound Spelling, and the manual should indicate whether reversals are scored as correct or incorrect for the two spelling subtests.

Interpretation

The manual presents guidelines for interpreting composite and subtest performance, with an appropriate emphasis on composites. The authors identify four patterns of performance for the Spoken Language Quotient (SLQ) and Written Language Quotient (WLQ) and their diagnostic implications. For example, when the SLQ is 90 or above, the WLQ is 89 or below, and the difference between the two is significant, dyslexia, dysgraphia, limited instruction, and/or poor school attendance, among other factors, may be contributing to the problem. The authors also provide descriptions of performance on the eight specific composites in terms of competence in six different language areas. The manual includes tables for evaluating subtest and composite difference scores for statistically significant and severe (i.e., clinically useful) discrepancies, with "severe" defined according to Reynolds's (1990) formula. Conducting a full set of discrepancy analyses by hand is very time-consuming and is unlikely to result in a finding of clinically useful discrepancies, given the inadequate subtest floors throughout much of the test. Indeed, the case example of a child aged 12-4 used to illustrate score comparisons displays only three statistically significant differences and no clinically significant discrepancies. Scores for the case example fall in the average range for 11 of 12 subtests and 8 of 11 composites, and the profile is relatively flat. Other than determining the presence or absence of score differences, the manual provides few guidelines for interpreting the scores for the case example, not even in terms of the four SLQ–WRQ patterns.

Technical Adequacy

Standardization

The ITPA-3 was standardized during 1999 and 2000 on 2,725 examinees sampled to be representative of the U.S. school-age population in terms of geographic area, gender, race, residence, ethnicity, family income, parental education, and disability status. Sample characteristics are generally representative of the projected 2000 U.S. population, with slight underrepresentation of Midwestern examinees, slight underrepresentation of upper-SES families, and slight overrepresentation of "Other" (i.e., European American) in terms of ethnicity. Norm characteristics are stratified by age for geographic area, gender, race, residence, ethnicity, income, and parental education. Age group sizes are 100 or greater throughout the range of the test and between 173 and 203 for ages 5 through 8. Because subgroup intervals for 5- through 11-year-olds are in 3-month increments, however, this means that norms are based on only about 43–50 examinees per subgroup.

Reliability Evidence

Across all age levels, global and specific composite coefficient alphas are at or above .90 except for Phonology, which is at .90 for ages 6 and 9 but falls in the .80s across the rest of the entire age range of the test. Average coefficient alphas for subtests range from .79 to .94 across all age groups, with coefficients for Rhyming Sequences falling below acceptable levels at ages 5 and 7 (*rs* = .75 and .78). Coefficient alphas for 11 subgroups in the normative sample, including four groups of examinees with exceptionalities (gifted/talented children and children with ADHD, articulation disorder, and learning disabilities), are in the .90s across subtests and composites, with two exceptions. Rhyming Sequences values fall in the .80s for 7 of the subgroups and in the .70s for four subgroups, whereas Phonology coefficients are in the .80s for all four exceptionality subgroups.

Stability estimates for a sample of 30 children aged 6-6 to 12-6 in Austin, Texas (2-week interval) were .98 or above for the three global composites and above .90 (*rs* = .90 to .97) for the eight specific composites. Stability estimates were in the .90s for 9 of the 12 subtests, with Syntactic Sentences, Sound Deletion, and Rhyming Sequences ranging from .86 to .88. Because of the wide age range and small size of the sample, however, these results should be viewed cautiously. Interscorer reliability estimates based on independent scoring of 30 completed protocols by two staff persons in PRO-ED's research department were .95 or above. Additional evidence of interscorer consistency based on several examiners simultaneously scoring a set of protocols is needed, however, especially for Sound Decoding, Syntactic Sentences, and Rhyming Sequences.

Test Floors and Item Gradients

Floors are inadequate across the majority of subtests throughout much of the age range. Specifically, floors are inadequate for all subtests at ages 5-0 through 6-5. For ages 6-6 through 8-2, floors are inadequate for all subtests except for Spoken Analogies and Spoken Vocabulary. For ages 8-3 through 8-8, floors are inadequate for all subtests except Spoken Analogies, Spoken Vocabulary, and Written Vocabulary. For ages 8-9 through 8-11, floors are inadequate except for Spoken Analogies, Spoken Vocabulary, Written Vocabulary, Sight Decoding, and Sight Spelling. Adequate floors are not reached across all subtests until age 12, the highest level of the test! In terms of global composites, floors are inadequate for Spoken Language below age 6-0 and for Written Language below age 7-3. For example, a raw score of 1 on all written language subtests for ages 6-6 to 6-9 yields a Written Language composite of 80 (low average range). The General Language composite is inadequate below age 6-9, and the specific composites have inadequate test floors for much of the lower age range. Test floors are inadequate for Semantics below 5-9, for Word Identification and Sight–Symbol Processing below 7-3, for Comprehension below 7-6, for Spelling below 7-6, and for Sound–Symbol Processing below 8-3.

Because of inadequate subtest floors, item gradient violations are evident for many subtests at the lower age ranges. For example, there are only 3 raw score points between the floor and the mean of Spoken Analogies for ages 5-0 through 5-2. Moreover, the floor of the test at that age is a standard score of 8 (average range). As always, users should evaluate the steepness of item gradients in relationship to subtest floor adequacy.

Validity Evidence

CONTENT VALIDITY EVIDENCE

Like previous versions of the ITPA, the ITPA-3 is based on Osgood's model (Osgood, 1957; Osgood & Miron, 1963), which proposes three dimensions of language behavior: (1) levels of organization, (2) psycholinguistic processes, and (3) channels of transmission. For this version, the model has been adapted to incorporate more recent terminology and research, with subtests constructed to represent various aspects of the model. The authors present a cogent rationale for format and item selection for each of the subtests and cite similar tasks in the research literature and on previously published standardized tests. No rationale is presented for including drawings of make-believe creatures beside the stimulus items or using capital letters for the pseudoword "creature names" on Sound Decoding, however. The authors also present evidence that the psychometric and demographic characteristics of the four groups created from the normative sample based on comparisons between SLQs and WLQs are consistent with each group's theoretical rationale. For example, the group with proficient spoken language but inadequate written language included a large percentage of the children classified as having learning disabilities.

Median item difficulties fall below acceptable levels for Spoken Analogies, Morphological Closure, and Syntactic Sentences at age 5 and Syntactic Sentences and Sight Spelling for age 6, indicating that those measures are beyond the ability of most children at those ages and are unlikely to provide useful information about individual differences in language skills. Item discrimination coefficients are adequate across the entire age range. DIF analyses using the logistic regression procedure were conducted for four dichotomous groups (males vs. females, European Americans vs. non-European Americans, African Americans vs. non-African Americans, and Hispanic Americans vs. non-Hispanic Americans). Of the 40 comparisons that were statistically significant ($p < .001$), only 4 effect sizes were moderate or large (fewer than 1% of test items).

CRITERION-RELATED VALIDITY EVIDENCE

Correlations between the ITPA-3 and five tests of spoken and written language (*Woodcock–Johnson Psycho-Educational Battery–Revised* [WJ-R]; the *Comprehensive Scales of Student Abilities* [Hammill & Hresko, 1994]; the *Comprehensive Test of Phonological Processing*; and the *Test of Language Development–Intermediate: 3* [Hammill & Newcomer, 1997]) for four samples of children (*n*s = 30 to 37, age ranges between 5 and 12) are reported. Nine of the 14 correlations with the ITPA-3 General Language composite were at or above .80, and all but one of the coefficients fell at or above .75, suggesting that the five tests are measuring similar language abilities. For a sample of 35 learning-disabled children aged 6 through 12, the correlation between WJ-R Broad Reading and ITPA-3 General Language was .79. Surprisingly, ITPA-3 Written Language was more highly correlated with WJ-R Broad Reading than with WJ-R Basic Writing Skills (.81 vs..74, respectively), perhaps because several of the ITPA-3 Written Language subtests require the child to read before constructing a written response. Because all four studies included a wide age range, however, the relationship of the ITPA-3 to other language tests relative to disabled or nondisabled early primary grade examinees remains uncertain. No predictive validity studies are reported.

CONSTRUCT VALIDITY EVIDENCE

Construct validity was assessed by investigating age and group differentiation, subtest interrelationships, relationships with achievement and intelligence tests, factor analysis, and item validity. ITPA-3 mean subtest scores increase with age, indicating the developmental nature of the abilities assessed. Diagnostic validity was examined by comparing mean standard scores for the total normative sample and for four minority subgroups, three disability subgroups, and a subgroup of gifted and talented examinees. Mean scores for all three global composites were below average for the learning-disabled group, as anticipated, with the lowest score on the Written Language composite (SS = 79). Mean scores for Hispanic American and Native American subgroups also fell in the below average range, which the authors attribute to the fact that some children were bilingual. Intercorrelations of subtests and composites range from .23 to .73, with the lowest correlations for Rhyming Sequences (.23 to .35), indicating that it may be measuring a different construct.

Correlations with the WJ-R Broad Mathematics and Broad Knowledge tests for the same sample of learning-disabled children described above were moderate to high (.43 to .88). Correlations with the Geometric Sequences subtest from the *Comprehensive Test of Nonverbal Intelligence* (CTONI) for a sample of 253 children aged 6 through 12 were low to moderate (.26 to .53). It is not clear why a single CTONI subtest rather than one of the three CTONI composites was used for the analysis. Moreover, given reviewer criticisms (see Carroll, 1972) that the previous version of the ITPA measured cognitive functioning rather than psycholinguistic abilities, comparisons with WISC-III Full Scale and Verbal IQs or with WJ-R Broad Cognitive Ability scores (now WJ III General Intellectual Ability scores) would have been more useful. Confirmatory factor analyses testing the four models used to create the 11 ITPA-3 composites indicated that the test's factor structure conforms closely to the model on which it is based.

Usability

Although the ITPA-3 is attractive, portable, and reasonably priced for so comprehensive a measure, the manual does not offer much assistance to practitioners in the scoring, interpretation, and intervention planning process. The record booklet does not provide space for recording a complete score array (e.g., percentiles for composite scores; age and grade equivalents for subtest scores), and examiners must integrate information from several different sections of the manual that discuss the meaning of subtest and composite scores in order to interpret test performance. The user-friendly software scoring program greatly reduces scoring time, given the large number of composite scores to be calculated if the entire test is administered, as well as the numerous subtest and composite score comparisons that can be conducted. Report options include a 3-page score summary and a 10-page comprehensive clinical report that is unusual in providing not only derived scores and score differences evaluated for statistical and clinical significance but also summaries of the test's psychometric characteristics. Age equivalents but not grade equivalents are provided for subtests in the comprehensive report, which also includes interpretive information on subtest and composite performance taken from the manual. Because of the large number of score comparisons and possible discrepancies (24 composite score comparisons, 66 subtest comparisons), examiners must still devote a considerable amount of time and effort to evaluating which discrepancies, if any, have utility in diagnosis and treatment planning.

Links to Intervention

Neither the manual nor the software scoring program provides any suggestions for translating test results into interventions. This omission is unfortunate, considering that evaluating the effectiveness of language interventions is one of the stated purposes of the test.

Relevant Research

In a recent study with 200 children in Grades 1 through 6, Hammill, Mather, Allen, and Roberts (2002) administered 16 measures, including eight ITPA-3 subtests, to investigate the relative importance of semantic, grammatical, phonological, and rapid naming skills in predicting word identification. For younger children (mean age = 8), multiple regression analyses indicated that a phonology composite consisting of Sound Deletion, Rhyming Sequences, and a sound blending task was the best predictor of word identification ($R^2 = .42$), followed by a rapid naming composite ($R^2 = .14$). For older children (mean age = 11), a semantics composite consisting of Spoken Analogies, Spoken Vocabulary, a listening vocabulary task, a logical sentences task, and a spoken sentence construction task accounted for the most variance in word identification ($R^2 = .38$), followed by the phonology composite ($R^2 = .11$). Specificity indices for all five composites (semantics, grammar, phonology, rapid naming, and rapid marking) were above .80, but none of the sensitivity indices or positive predictive values reached the .75 criterion for the entire sample or for first- and second-grade subgroups (.54 to .70).

Source and Cost

The ITPA-3 test kit is available from PRO-ED for $164.00. The software scoring and report program costs an additional $112.00.

Test Review

Towne, R. L. (2003). Review of the Illinois Test of Psycholinguistic Abilities, Third Edition. In B. S. Plake, J. C. Impara, & R. A. Spies (Eds.), *The fifteenth mental measurements yearbook* (pp. 458–462). Lincoln, NE: Buros Institute of Mental Measurements.

Summary

The *Illinois Test of Psycholinguistic Abilities–Third Edition* (ITPA-3) is an individually administered, norm-referenced battery of oral and written language measures for children aged 5 through 12. The current version represents the third generation of one of the most widely used psychoeducational tests in the 1970s and early 1980s, and the authors have made a commendable effort to incorporate recent research on reading acquisition and reading disabilities into this revision while also increasing its usability. The ITPA-3 is one of very few tests that permit comparisons of phonological and orthographic processing in the same norm-referenced instrument. Unfortunately, inadequate subtest and composite floors throughout much of the age range diminish its utility in identifying at-risk children, evaluating language processing strengths and weaknesses, and documenting intervention effectiveness. Additional problems include unacceptably low internal consistency reliabilities for some subtests, low subgroup size across most of the age range, stability estimates based on a single small sample with a 6-year age range, and interscorer reliability estimates based only on completed protocols. Recent efforts to document the predictive utility of ITPA-3 measures have yielded mixed results, although as the test's authors observe, validation research has just begun. Studies evaluating the relationship of the ITPA-3 to current and future reading, spelling, and writing achievement in primary grade children should be a priority for investigation.

Case Example

Name of student: Kareem A.
Age: 6 years, 9 months
Grade: First grade
Date of assessment: March

Reason for referral: Kareem was referred for an early reading assessment by his first-grade teacher. Kareem is a cooperative, hard-working student, but he performs more poorly than his classmates in reading, spelling, and language arts. On the fall administration of a classwide reading screening measure, his word identification, oral reading fluency, and spelling skills were considerably lower than the class average. He has been receiving tutoring through the school-based tutoring program since October, but his progress is still slower than expected.

Assessment results and interpretation: The *Illinois Test of Psycholinguistic Abilities–Third Edition* (ITPA-3) measures different aspects of oral and written language and can be used to compare a child's various language abilities. Average scores for a child Kareem's age are as follows: Composite Standard Score = 100, Subtest Standard Score = 10, Percentile Rank (PR) = 50, Age Equivalent = 6-9, Grade Equivalent = 1.7. Kareem's performance on the ITPA-3 is described below.

ITPA-3 Subtests	Standard Score	Percentile Rank	Age Equivalent	Grade Equivalent	Rating
Spoken Subtests					
Spoken Analogies (SA)	7	16	5-0	K.0	Below average
Spoken Vocabulary (SV)	7	16	5-0	K.0	Below average
Morphological Closure (MC)	6	9	5-0	K.0	Below average
Syntactic Sentences (SS)	8	25	<5-0	<K.0	Average
Sound Deletion (SD)	8	25	6-0	1.0	Average
Rhyming Sequences (RS)	10	50	5-6	K.4	Average
Written Subtests					
Sentence Sequencing (SSq)	5	5	<5-0	<K.0	Poor
Written Vocabulary (WV)	7	16	5-3	K.2	Below average
Sight Decoding (SiD)	8	25	5-9	K.7	Average
Sound Decoding (SoD)	6	9	<5-0	<K.0	Below average
Sight Spelling (SiS)	7	16	5-6	K.4	Below average
Sound Spelling (SoS)	7	16	5-3	K.2	Below average

ITPA-3 Global and Specific Composites	Standard Score	Percentile Rank	Rating
Global Composites			
General Language (all subtests)	80	9	Below average
Spoken Language (SA + SV + MC + SS + SD + RS)	84	14	Below average
Written Language (SSq + WV + SiD + SoD + SiS + SoS)	77	6	Poor
Specific Composites			
Semantics (SA + SV)	82	12	Below average
Grammar (MC + SS)	82	12	Below average
Phonology (SD + RS)	94	35	Average
Comprehension (SSq + WV)	76	5	Poor
Word Identification (SiD + SoD)	82	12	Below average
Spelling (SiS + SoS)	82	12	Below average
Sight–Symbol Processing (SiD + SiS)	85	16	Below average
Sound–Symbol Processing (SoD + SoS)	79	8	Poor

Kareem's overall language skills, including the ability to process spoken and written verbal information, are rated as below average for his age (PR = 9). His spoken language skills, including the ability to use vocabulary and grammar proficiently, also fall in the below average range (PR = 14). His competence with speech sounds, including phonemic awareness and phonemic sequential memory, is significantly better developed than his word knowledge and understanding of grammar (PR = 35 vs. 12). In the spoken language domain, his poorest performance was on a task tapping knowledge of morphological rules (PR = 9). He missed some of the items because he did not appear to understand the nature of the task. For example, asked to complete the sentence "A tree is big, but a house is even ________", he responded, "smaller."

Compared with his spoken language skills, Kareem's written language skills are significantly less well developed (PR = 6, poor range). His comprehension of written language, including his understanding of sentence meaning and vocabulary, is poor (PR = 5). He was not able to answer any items correctly on a task requiring him to read three sentences silently and arrange them in a logical order (PR = 5). His word identification skills, including his ability to read sight words (i.e., words with irregular spellings that must be recognized "by sight") and phonically regular pseudowords (e.g., *Ab*), fall in the below average range (PR = 12). He had particular difficulty using letter-sound knowledge to decode pseudowords and was able to read only one item on that task (PR = 9). His errors suggest that he was relying on his memory of real word spellings rather than on his knowledge of sound–symbol relationships (e.g., *make* for *nuck*). His spelling skills, including the ability to spell words with regular and unusual spelling patterns, are below average (PR = 12). It should be noted that although his performance on measures of regular and irregular spelling words is rated as below average (both PRs = 16), he was able to spell only 1 word correctly on each of these tasks. His reading and spelling ability for sight words is rated as low average, whereas his reading and spelling ability for pseudowords is rated as poor (PR = 16 vs. 8).

KAUFMAN SURVEY OF EARLY ACADEMIC AND LANGUAGE SKILLS

Overview

The Kaufman Survey of Early Academic and Language Skills (K-SEALS; Kaufman & Kaufman, 1993) is an individually administered, norm-referenced test designed to measure expressive and receptive language, preacademic skills, and articulation for children aged 3-0 through 6-11. The K-SEALS is an expanded version of the language section of the Cognitive/Language Profile of the *Early Screening Profiles* (Harrison, 1990) from the same publisher. The purposes of the K-SEALS include (1) assessing speech and language in young children; (2) measuring the preacademic development of young children; (3) evaluating the effectiveness of preschool, kindergarten, or first-grade programs targeting language development and early academic skills; and (4) facilitating research. According to the test's authors, the abilities measured by the K-SEALS are more closely aligned with the curricula of intervention or enrichment programs than are the abilities measured by traditional intelligence tests. Materials include an examiner's manual, test easel, and 25 individual test records, all packed in a carrying bag.

Subtests and Composites

Subtests

The K-SEALS consists of three subtests (see Table 5.19), all of which are presented in the test easel.

Composites

Items from the K-SEALS subtests are combined to form five composites, as shown in Table 5.20.

Administration

All of the K-SEALS subtests are untimed, and administration takes about 15–25 minutes. All examinees begin with the first item for each subtest. One sample item is provided for Vocabulary, but there are no teaching items for the other subtests. Prompts are noted for certain Vocabulary items. On the Articulation Survey, if the child does not know the name of a pictured object or gives an incorrect name, the examiner pronounces the picture and asks the child to repeat it. Space is provided beside each item to record the child's response for further error analysis. For the Vocabulary and the Numbers, Letters, and Words subtests, the ceiling is five consecutive incorrect responses. Start and discontinue rules should be noted on the record booklet as well as in the manual.

TABLE 5.19. Description of the K-SEALS Subtests

Subtests	Description
Vocabulary	The child identifies by pointing or naming pictured objects or actions and points to or names objects based on verbal descriptions of their attributes. Of the 40 items, 20 assess receptive language and 20 assess expressive language.
Numbers, Letters, and Words	The child points to or names numbers, letters, or words; counts; and points or responds orally to demonstrate knowledge of number concepts and problem-solving skills.
Articulation Survey	The child pronounces the names of pictured common objects or actions.

TABLE 5.20. K-SEALS Composites

Composites		Subtests (item types)
Early Academic and Language Skills Composite		Vocabulary (all items) Numbers, Letters, and Words (all items)
Language Scales	Expressive Skills Scale	Vocabulary (expressive language items) Numbers, Letters, and Words (expressive language items)
	Receptive Skills Scale	Vocabulary (receptive language items) Numbers, Letters, and Words (receptive language items)
Early Academic Scales	Number Skills Scale (ages 5-0 to 6-11)	Numbers, Letters, and Words (number items)
	Letter and Word Skills Scale (ages 5-0 to 6-11)	Numbers, Letters, and Words (letter and word identification items)

Scores

Items are scored dichotomously. Scoring takes between 10 and 15 minutes, with another 10–15 minutes needed to complete the optional error analysis on the Articulation Survey. Scores on the Vocabulary and Numbers, Letters, and Words subtests are converted to age-based standard scores ($M = 100$, $SD = 15$), percentile ranks, normal curve equivalents, stanines, and age equivalents. Norms are presented in 3-month intervals throughout the age range of the test. Raw scores on the Articulation Survey are converted to five descriptive categories: (1) normal articulation (within 1 standard deviation above or below the mean of the normative group), (2) below average articulation (1–2 standard deviations below the mean), (3) mild articulation difficulty (2–3 standard deviations below the mean), and (4) moderate to severe articulation difficulty (more than 3 standard deviations below the mean). Examiners can also complete a 3-point rating scale for intelligibility during continuous speech and an optional error analysis of mispronunciations. The analysis consists of identifying error patterns by calculating the number of errors in initial, medial, and final consonants or consonant clusters and graphing errors in terms of the developmental age range for each sound assessed. Although the error analysis process is fairly complex, the directions in the manual are clear and comprehensive.

Interpretation

A simulated case example of a 5-year-old child is used to illustrate procedures for recording item responses, calculating derived scores, comparing standard score differences, and conducting the optional error analysis. Although the authors state that differences between the Expressive and Receptive Skills Scales must be cautiously interpreted and supplemented with additional assessment or direct observation, a large portion of the manual is devoted to analyzing subtest and scale score differences. A table in the appendix lists subtest and composite differences required for statistical significance by 6-month interval. The authors caution that only very large differences between subtest scores should be interpreted because 30% of children aged 3-0 to 5-11 in the normative group displayed statistically significant differences between Vocabulary and Numbers, Letters, and Words. Examiners are also advised not to interpret the overall composite score for children with statistically significant different scores at the .01 level for the Vocabulary and the Number, Letter, and Words subtests or the Language Scales composite for children with similar differences on the Expressive and Receptive Skills Scales.

Examiners can evaluate the clinical utility of subtest and scale discrepancies by consulting a table with "unusual" and "highly unusual" standard score differences, defined as those occurring in 15% and 5%, respectively, of the norm group. The case example displays both statistically significant and unusual or highly unusual differences for several comparisons, including significantly lower expressive versus receptive language, and is diagnosed with a developmental delay. Interpretation of the Articulation Survey is based on the descriptive category system noted above, which differs from the system typically used to describe standard scores because raw score distributions were highly skewed for all age groups in the normative sample. The average 3-year-old pronounces 70% of the words correctly, and by age 6, most children achieve perfect or near-perfect raw scores on the Articulation Survey. According to the authors, scores that fall within or below the below average category suggest some kind of articulation difficulty that warrants a comprehensive speech evaluation. The case example displays numerous errors distributed across the three vocalic intervals, and a comprehensive articulation assessment by a speech–language pathologist is recommended.

Technical Adequacy

Standardization

Standardization was conducted for the K-SEALS in 1987 and 1988 in 28 states as part of the standardization of the *Early Screening Profiles* (ESP). Of 1,190 examinees who took the K-SEALS, 1,000 children aged 3-0 to 6-11 were selected to match 1990 U.S. census estimates in terms of gender, geographic region, parental education, and race/ethnicity. The sample slightly overrepresents examinees from the North Central region of the United States. In terms of parental education, minorities with less than a high school education are underrepresented, especially Hispanics, who were then overrepresented in the two middle parental education categories to compensate. Children with identified disabilities or developmental delays were not excluded unless their disabilities prevented them from responding to test items, but there is no information regarding the percentage of examinees with specific disabilities included in the sample. An additional sample of 158 children aged 2-0 to 2-11 who took the Articulation Survey as part of the ESP standardization were included in the item error analysis with the K-SEALS sample to establish the lower age limits for that task. Because norm intervals are in 3-month increments, norms for ages 5 and 6 are based on only about 60 and 80 examinees, respectively, which is below acceptable levels.

Reliability Evidence

For examinees in the early primary grade range (i.e., ages 5 and 6), split-half reliabilities range from .91 to .95 for the overall composite. Reliability coefficients for the language scales range from .87 to .91 for Receptive Skills and from .89 to .91 for Expressive Skills. Reliability estimates for Vocabulary range from .78 to .88, with coefficients falling below acceptable levels for ages 6-6 to 6-11. Coefficients for Number, Letters, and Words are at or above .93, whereas coefficients for the Articulation Survey range from .87 to .90. Letter and Word Skills coefficients range from .91 to .96, whereas Number Skills coefficients range from .77 to .85, falling below acceptable levels for ages 6-0 to 6-5. Test–retest reliability (5- to 28-day intervals) for 81 children aged 3-0 to 6-10 ranged from .87 for Vocabulary to .94 for the overall composite. Because of the age heterogeneity of the sample, however, these estimates are likely to be somewhat inflated. In a sample of 33 children aged 5-0 to 6-10, stability coefficients for Number Skills and Letter and Word Skills were .91 and .88, respectively. No evidence of interscorer reliability is reported. Interrater reliability studies are especially needed for the Articulation Survey, preferably based on simultaneous scoring during audiotaped or actual testing sessions by independent examiners.

Test Floors and Item Gradients

Floors are adequate throughout the early primary grade range for the overall composite; both Language Scales; Vocabulary; Numbers, Letters, and Words; and Number Skills. Floors for the Letter and Word Skills Scale are inadequate until age 5-9, however. For example, a raw score of 1 at age 5-0 yields a standard score of 82 (low average). Item gradients for Vocabulary and Numbers, Letters, and Words are adequate, but gradients for Letter and Word Skills are too steep below 6-0.

Validity Evidence

CONTENT VALIDITY EVIDENCE

Most of the items for the Vocabulary and Numbers, Letters, and Words subtests were developed during 1986–1987 by two American Guidance Service item writers, with some drawn from a pool of unused items originally developed for the *Kaufman Assessment Battery for Children* (K-ABC; Kaufman & Kaufman, 1983). Based on factor analyses of the results of a national tryout in 1987, two language/academic subtests were constructed for the standardization edition. Items on the Numbers, Letters and Words subtest were balanced to include 20 number-related items and 20 reading-related items, with each set balanced to include half receptive and half expressive items. Conventional item analyses were used to select items for the subtests, and additional items were added to ensure a wider range of difficulty. Results from the national standardization were subjected to conventional and Rasch-model analyses, but no specific information on item statistics is presented. Item bias analyses using the Mantel–Haenszel procedure were also conducted to evaluate gender or race/ethnicity bias. Seven items were eliminated, three because of poor fit to the Rasch model, three items because of bias, and one because the picture was ambiguous. On Item 19 ("Show the letter *a*"), which presents an array of 6 letters, *a* is printed in the sans serif type style, which may be less familiar to young examinees than block printing.

Items were developed for the Articulation Survey by an expert in speech assessment to represent young children's sound production using an age-appropriate vocabulary. The 20 items include 22 of 24 consonant phonemes, 2 syllabic consonants, and 5 consonant clusters in the initial, medial, or final positions. The manual includes a table indicating three mastery levels (50%, 75%, and 90%) for each item for children in the standardization sample, as well as raw score means and standard deviations by 6-month age intervals.

CRITERION-RELATED VALIDITY EVIDENCE

The test's authors cite a series of unpublished and standardization studies with the K-SEALS and several intelligence and achievement tests as evidence of concurrent validity. Despite the authors' assertion that the K-SEALS is more closely aligned with the curricula of early childhood programs than are IQ tests, the K-SEALS composite is strongly correlated with scores on individually administered cognitive ability tests. In a sample of 77 children aged 3-0 to 6-9, the K-SEALS composite displayed a correlation of .81 with the composite on the *Stanford–Binet Intelligence Scale–4*. In two other samples (*n*s = 39 and 98, mean ages = 5-5 and 6-0), the K-SEALS composite was highly correlated with the K-ABC Mental Processing composite (.63 and .68, respectively) and very highly correlated with the K-ABC Achievement composite (.82 and .84, respectively). Correlations with group-administered achievement and readiness tests, including the *Metropolitan Readiness Tests–Fourth Edition* (Nurss & McGauvran, 1976) and the *Metropolitan Achievement Test*, were in the moderate range (*r*s = .48 and .55, respectively). Correlations between the K-SEALS language scales and composite and scores on other language and screening measures were moderate to high (*r*s = .59 to .73) for the PPVT-R and the *Bracken Basic Concepts Scale* (Bracken, 1984), but considerably lower (*r*s = –.20 to .41) for other developmental measures, including the *Battelle Developmental Inventory* (Newborg, Stock, Wnek, Guidubaldi, & Svinicki, 1984) and the *Developmental Indicators for the Assessment of Learning–Revised* (Mardell-Czudnowski & Goldenberg, 1990), reflecting less content overlap.

Predictive validity was assessed with two types of criterion measures: (1) standard scores on intelligence, achievement, and language tests and (2) teacher ratings and grades. For a sample of 136 children aged 3-6 to 6-4, the K-SEALS composite was a strong predictor (*r* = .80) of K-ABC Achievement composite scores 5–8 months later. Not surprisingly, the best predictor of K-ABC Reading Decoding was the Letter and Word Skills Scale (.83). Correlations with the PPVT-R in the same sample were moderate to high (.53 to .76). For 67 children aged 5-2 to 6-10, correlations between the K-SEALS and the *Stanford Achievement Test* Reading subtest administered 1 year later ranged from .44 to .62, with the highest correlation for the K-SEALS composite. In the same sample, K-SEALS scores displayed low to moderate correlations (*r*s = .36 to .57) with the *Otis–Lennon School Ability Test–Fifth Edition* (Otis & Lennon, 1982) 1 year later. In a sample of 83 children aged 3-6 to 6-4, K-SEALS scores were moderate to strong predictors (.41 to .73) of teacher ratings of reading performance 5–9 months later, with Letter and Word Skills the best predictor. K-SEALS scores were also moderately correlated (.45 to .65) with teacher-assigned grades 1 year later for 69 children aged 5-2 to 6-10, with the composite score the best predictor. No concurrent or predictive validity evidence is presented for the Articulation Survey.

CONSTRUCT VALIDITY EVIDENCE

Raw score means for subtests and composites, including the Articulation Survey, increase with age as expected. Correlations between subtests and scales are presented for the normative group by 6-month interval. For early primary grade examinees, the Vocabulary and Numbers, Letters, and Words subtests were moderately correlated (.57 to .67), whereas the Expressive and Receptive Skills Scales were very highly correlated (.83 to .88), questioning their differential validity. Correlations between the Numbers Skills and Letter and Words Skills Scales were also high (.71 to .81). No evidence in terms of mean standard scores and standard deviations is presented to support the K-SEAL's validity and lack of bias in measuring language and preacademic skills for examinees from racial and ethnic minority groups. Moreover, despite the emphasis on discrepancy analysis in the manual, presumably for the purpose of determining special education eligibility, no validity evidence regarding differential treatment effects or the K-SEAL's utility in differentiating children with developmental delays, speech–language impairments, or other disabilities from normally developing children is presented.

Usability

The K-SEALS is attractive to children, portable, relatively inexpensive, and easy and quick to administer and score, with the exception of the Articulation Survey, which may be challenging for examiners with a limited background in speech and language assessment. Scoring expressive and receptive items is complicated by the fact that the light yellow boxes for recording responses blend into the white test record, making them very difficult to distinguish.

Links to Intervention

The manual includes a four-page reproducible report for use in sharing results with parents. Several aspects of the report should be modified. First, although the authors state in the manual that percentiles, age equivalents, and descriptive categories are useful for conveying test results to parents, the focus on the report is primarily on standard scores and score differences, and some parents may have difficulty understanding the information presented. Second, although the manual indicates that only very large score differences should be interpreted, the parent report displays statistically significant comparisons for subtests, the language scales, and the Number Skills/Letter and Word Skills Scales, and suggests that these differences are useful in instructional planning. Moreover, the report fails to provide any suggestions for enhancing language and early academic skills at home.

Relevant Research

No published studies using the K-SEALS could be located for use in this text.

Source and Cost

The K-SEALS is available from AGS Publishing for $209.95.

Test Reviews

Ackerman, P. L. (1995). Review of the Kaufman Survey of Early Academic and Language Skills. In J. C. Conoley & J. C. Impara (Eds.), *The twelfth mental measurements yearbook* (pp. 536–537). Lincoln, NE: Buros Institute of Mental Measurements.

Ford, L., & Turk, K. (1995). Review of the Kaufman Survey of Early Academic and Language Skills. In J. C. Conoley & J. C. Impara (Eds.), *The twelfth mental measurements yearbook* (pp. 537–538). Lincoln, NE: Buros Institute of Mental Measurements.

Kass, C. E. (1999). The Kaufman Survey of Early Academic and Language Skills (K-SEALS). *Diagnostique, 24,* 135–144.

Summary

The *Kaufman Survey of Early Academic and Language Skills* (K-SEALS) is an individually administered, norm-referenced screening measure of language and early academic skills for children aged 3-0 to age 6-11. Although its publication date is 1993, the items and standardization data are now more than 15 years old, and the content and format are more similar to those of traditional readiness tests than to those of the new generation of screening measures assessing empirically validated reading precursors. The K-SEALS is a significant predictor of later reading achievement and teacher ratings of academic performance, but it is also strongly correlated with cognitive ability, which provides limited support for the authors' contention that the K-SEALS is a more appropriate measure than IQ tests for young children. Because of the overlap among subtests and the language scales, and inadequate floors for the Letter and Word Skills Scale, the composite score has the greatest utility. Moreover, because of the limited number of items per subtest, especially in terms of letter knowledge and word reading skills, test results should be interpreted with caution.

Case Example

Name of student: Yuri A.
Age: 5 years, 8 months
Grade: Kindergarten
Date of assessment: January

Reason for referral: Yuri was referred for an early reading assessment by his kindergarten teacher. Yuri is an eager student who loves participating in class, but he is having great difficulty acquiring early literacy skills. Despite daily instruction in alphabetic skills, he has not yet learned most of the letter names and sounds, nor has he grasped the relationship between letters and sounds. His teacher also reports that he has trouble understanding classroom instructions and often has to have directions given individually.

Assessment results and interpretation: The *Kaufman Survey of Early Academic and Language Skills* (K–SEALS) measures oral language and early academic skills for children between the ages of 3 and 6. Yuri's scores on the K–SEALS are listed below. A Standard Score (SS) of 100, Percentile Rank (PR) of 50, and Age Eequivalent (AE) of 5-8 are in the average range for a youngster his age.

Composite/Subtest	SS	PR	AE	Descriptive Category
Early Academic and Language Skills Composite	84	14	–	Below average
Vocabulary	90	25	4-11	Average
Numbers, Letters, and Words	85	16	4-8	Below average
Early Academic Scales				
Letter and Word Skills Scale	90	25	<5-0	Average
Number Skills Scale	82	12	<5-0	Below average
Language Scales				
Expressive Skills Scale	85	16	4-7	Below average
Receptive Skills Scale	88	21	4-10	Below average
Articulation Survey	–	–	–	Normal articulation

Yuri's overall language and preacademic skills fall in the below average range for his age (PR = 14). On the Vocabulary subtest, which requires identifying pictured objects or actions or identifying objects from descriptions, his performance is rated as average (PR = 25). On the Numbers, Letters, and Words subtest, which requires identifying numbers, letters, and words; counting; and solving number problems, his performance was less adequate (PR = 16, below average). On the Early Academic Scales, which include items from the Numbers, Letters, and Words subtest, his performance ranges from average to below average. Although his performance on the Letter and Word Skills Scale falls within the average range (PR = 25), it should be noted that this score is based on his recognizing or naming four uppercase letters and recognizing two words from arrays of printed words. He was unable to identify any of the lowercase letters presented. His number knowledge, as measured by the Number Skills Scale, is less well developed (PR = 12, below average). He was able to demonstrate knowledge of size concepts, such as *biggest* and *smallest,* and to count up to 5, but he had trouble counting more than five objects and recognizing one- and two-digit numerals.

The K-SEALS Language Scales assess expressive (spoken) and receptive (listening) language skills. The Expressive Skills items require the child to name pictured objects or actions; objects from descriptions; or numbers, letters, and words. The Receptive Skills items require the child to respond to verbal instructions by pointing to pictured objects or actions; identifying objects from their descriptions; or pointing to numbers, letters, and words. Yuri's receptive and expressive language skills are evenly developed and fall in the below average range (PRs = 16 and 21, respectively).

The Articulation Survey requires the child to pronounce the names of pictured objects and actions that represent a variety of sounds. Yuri's performance falls in the Normal Articulation range for his age. He had one initial consonant error (/y/ for /j/ in *jelly*) and one error for a final consonant cluster (/t/ for /sk/ in *desk*). His intelligibility during continuous speech was good.

ORAL AND WRITTEN LANGUAGE SCALES

Overview

The *Oral and Written Language Scales* (OWLS; Carrow-Woolfolk, 1995) battery is an individually administered, norm-referenced set of measures designed to assess a broad range of receptive, expressive, and written language skills for children and young adults. The OWLS consist of three conormed scales: the Listening Comprehension (LC) and Oral Expression (OE) Scales for examinees aged 3-0 to 21-11 and the Written Expression (WE) Scale for examinees aged 5-0 to 21-11. The LC Scale measures three categories of language skills: (1) lexical skills (vocabulary), (2) syntactic skills (grammatical forms), and (3) supralinguistic skills (higher order thinking). The OE Scale also assesses pragmatic skills, that is, the understanding of language in context. The WE Scale measures three areas of language functioning: (1) conventions, such as letter formation, spelling, and punctuation; (2) linguistics, such as modifiers, phrases, and verb forms; and (3) content, such as appropriate subject matter, details, and word choice. The WE Scale contains both indirect or structured tasks (copying words, writing dictated sentences, or combining sentences) and direct or open-ended tasks (retelling a story, completing a story, or interpreting a statement). The purposes of the OWLS include (1) identifying students with language-based learning disabilities, (2) assisting in intervention planning, (3) monitoring growth in language skills, and (4) facilitating research. Although the three scales were developed and normed together, they are packaged as two separate test kits–one with the LC and OE Scales and one with the WE Scale. Test materials for the LC and OE Scales consist of an examiner's manual, two easel test books, 25 record forms, and a reproducible descriptive analysis worksheet. Materials for the WE Scale include an examiner's manual, 25 record forms, 25 student response booklets, and an administration card.

Scales and Composites

Scales

For the LC and OE Scales, test stimuli consist of plates of black-and-white line drawings contained in two easel books. For the WE Scale, test stimuli are orally presented. The assessment tasks in each scale are described in Table 5.21. None of the three scales includes subtests, and each scale yields a single score.

Composites

The LC and OE Scales can be combined to create an Oral composite. When the WE Scale is also administered, the three scales can be combined to form an overall Language composite.

Administration

The two oral language scales are untimed. On the WE Scale, examinees have 30 seconds to begin writing a response, but no time limits are set for response completion. Testing time ranges from 5 to 15 minutes for the LC Scale, from 10 to 25 minutes for the OE Scale, and from 10 to 30 minutes for the WE Scale, depending on examinee age and skills. Directions are clearly spelled out in the easel books, and the laminated administration card for the WE Scale includes item-by-item directions. According to the test's author, when only the LC and OE Scales are administered, the LC Scale should be given first because it is relatively nonthreatening and because it was the first test administered to the normative sample. When all three scales are administered, the WE Scale should be given second for similar reasons. The two oral language scales must be individually administered, but the WE Scale can be administered to small groups. The author cautions that small-group administration should

TABLE 5.21. Description of the OWLS Scales

Scales	Description
Listening Comprehension	The child responds to a statement read by the examiner by pointing to the one of four pictures or saying the number of the picture that best depicts the statement.
Oral Expression	The child answers a question, completes a sentence, or generates one or more sentences in response to a verbal stimulus read by the examiner and accompanied by one or more pictures.
Written Expression	The examiner presents a verbal stimulus, and the child responds by writing in a response booklet. For some items, the response booklet includes pictures or print prompts.

only be used with children above the age of 8 and then not for assessments related to placement decisions.

Although basals are identical for the LC and OE Scales (one correct on seven consecutive items), ceiling rules differ: a score of 0 on five out of seven consecutive items on the LC Scale and a score of 0 on six out of seven on the OE Scale. According to the manual, these ceiling procedures are based on analyses conducted during test development and are designed to maximize reliability while minimizing testing time. The WE Scale has no basals and ceilings; instead, examinees take all of the items in one of four overlapping age-specific sets (ages 5 to 7, 8 to 11, 12 to 14, and 15 to 21). Out-of-level testing is permitted, based on the examinee's estimated functioning level. If the examinee's obtained Rasch ability score falls in a shaded area in the conversion table, indicating nearly perfect or extremely low raw scores, a more difficult or an easier item set should be administered.

Scores

For the LC and OE Scales, most of the items are scored 1 or 0. The LC/OE record form presents the most common correct and incorrect responses, along with an abbreviated version of the scoring rubrics and multiple-point criteria, for use in the preliminary scoring needed to establish a basal and ceiling. The test's author advises that if examiners are unable to reach a preliminary scoring decision, they should record the response verbatim and leave it unscored until after testing is completed. On the OE Scale, 17 items require verbatim recording of responses, with 12 of those items scored 0 or 1 according to a set of rubrics and 5 items scored according to multiple-point criteria. On the WE Scale, which was constructed using Rasch procedures, raw scores must be converted to Rasch ability scores prior to transformation to other derived scores. Most items are scored dichotomously, but some have multiple-point criteria and are scored for as many as 11 points. Although scoring for some of the more advanced items is quite complex, the manual provides clear and detailed scoring procedures, with examples of correct and incorrect answers for each item. Scores for all three scales can be converted to age-based standard scores (M = 100, SD = 15), percentile ranks, normal curve equivalents, stanines, and test–age equivalents. Hand scoring for the WE Scale is more complex and time-consuming than for the oral language scales because of the conversion process from raw scores to Rasch ability scores. The WE Scale also yields grade-based norms and grade equivalents. The manual does not provide a rationale for the inclusion of grade norms for the WE but not for the LC and OE Scales.

For the LC and OE Scales, examiners can conduct an analysis of language skills for use in intervention planning by transferring correct and incorrect responses from the record form onto a reproducible descriptive analysis worksheet. The analysis classifies each item by task and language category (lexical, syntactic, supralinguistic, and, for the OE Scale, pragmatic). Similarly, for the WE Scale, examiners can use one of the four descriptive analysis worksheets provided in an appendix to the manual for each of the four item sets to conduct error analyses in the three areas of language functioning (conventions, linguistics, and content). No normative data are provided for these analyses, however. Points earned in each category are converted to percentiles, based on age and item set, and examiners can use one of two sets of guidelines to evaluate whether the number of points earned per category indicates a strength, a weakness, or an average performance. Two case examples are included to demonstrate how to conduct the analysis, one for a child aged 12-3 and one for a child aged 7-1. Although the manual provides clear, explicit directions, this aspect of scoring is very time-consuming, especially for older examinees, who take more complex items. Moreover, no reliability or validity data are presented in support of the consistency or diagnostic utility of the error analyses. For the LC and OE Scales, norms are in 3-month increments for ages 3-0 through 8-11, 4-month increments for ages 9-0 through 13-11, 6-month increments for ages 14-0 through 18-11, and 1-year intervals for ages 19-0 to 21-11. Age-based norms for the WE Scale are in identical increments but begin at age 5-0. Grade-based norms for the WE Scale are available for spring of kindergarten and for fall and spring for Grades 1 through 12.

Interpretation

The LC/OE manual includes a fictitious case example aged 10-11 to illustrate scoring, descriptive category analysis, and score comparison procedures. Examiners can evaluate receptive and expressive language standard score differences for statistical significance and prevalence by consulting tables in the appendix. The case example has average LC scores and low OE scores, a difference that is statistically significant at the .15 level but not clinically significant. The WE Scale manual includes information for comparing standard score differences on the WE Scale, the oral language scales, and the overall Language composite, using a case example aged 12-3. The case example has a low average WE Scale score but an above average OE Scale score, a difference that is both statistically and clinically significant. An identical chapter in the two manuals describes the four language processes in the author's theoretical model (listening comprehension, reading comprehension, oral expression, and written expression) and presents a brief discussion of the differences and similarities among the three areas measured by the OWLS. Each manual includes an appendix of grammar and usage guidelines as a reference for terms and constructions found in the OE/LC Scales or WE Scale scoring rules, as well as a glossary of grammatical terms and standard English constructions and examples of common grammatical mistakes in oral or written expression.

Technical Adequacy

Standardization

Standardization data for the OWLS were collected for 1,795 children and young adults in 37 states between April 1992 and August 1993. The LC/OE Scales sample included 1,795 examinees aged 3 to 21, and the WE Scale included 1,373 examinees aged 5 through 21. The sample was stratified within age group to represent 1991 U.S. census data on gender, race/ethnicity, geographical region, and mother's educational level and for joint distributions of race/ethnicity with mother's educational level and region. The manual states that special education students were included, but no specific information is provided regarding numbers or percentages. The LC/OE sample is generally representative of the 1991 U.S. population of children and adolescents except for mother's educational level for the 3- to 5-year-old age group, where mothers in the two lowest groups (Grade 11 or less and high school degree) are underrepresented. Age group sizes are 125 examinees for each of the early primary grade years, but because norms for this age range are in 3-month increments, derived scores are based on only about 42 examinees, below criterion levels. The WE Scale sample is generally representative of the U.S. 1991 population, with 5-year-old males slightly overrepresented and 5-year-old females slightly underrepresented for age norms. For grade norms, males are slightly overrepresented for kindergarten and Grade 2, whereas females are slightly overrepresented at Grade 1. Interval blocks for age norms range from 115 to 126 for the early primary grade range, but because norms are in 3-month increments, derived scores are based on as few as 38 examinees. Grade norm sizes for early primary grade examinees range from a low of 109 in Grade 2 to a high of 159 in kindergarten. Because grade norms are provided for fall and spring, subgroup intervals include only 55 to about 80 examinees, which is also below criterion level.

Reliability Evidence

For the LC Scale, internal consistency estimates using Rasch procedures range from .75 to .82 for early primary grade examinees, with values falling below .80 for ages 6, 7, and 8. OE Scale internal consistency reliabilities are slightly higher, in the .80s for ages 5, 6, and 8 and at .90 for age 7. Oral composite reliability estimates are .91 for ages 5 and 7 but fall below criterion levels for composite scores for ages 6 and 8 (.89 and .87, respectively). For the WE Scale, split-half reliability coefficients are in the .80s for the early primary grade range, except for age 7 (.94). Coefficients for the Language composite range from .92 to .94. Test–retest reliability (8-week median interval) for the LC Scale for two samples that included primary grade examinees (n = 50, ages 4-0 to 5-11; and n = 54, ages 8-0 to 10-11) was .80 for the younger age group but fell below the acceptable value for the older age group (r = .73). Moreover, practice effects were evident for both samples (gains of 6.7 and 11.7 standard score points, respectively). Test–retest reliability estimates for the same two samples were slightly higher for the OE Scale (.86 and .80) and the Oral composite (.89 and .84), and practice effects were less evident (gains of 3.3 and 3.6 standard score points, respectively). Stability coefficients were .88 for the WE Scale and .90 for the Language composite for a sample of 54 examinees aged 8-0 to 10-11 (9-week median interval). The Language composite showed substantial practice effects (standard score increase = 6.5 points), but no practice effects were observed for the WE Scale. Retest intervals were longer in all these studies than usual, which may have contributed to lower stability estimates, although the manual does not address this issue. For the LC/OE Scales, interscorer reliability based on agreement among four independent raters who scored the responses of 24 examinees in each of four age groups was .99 for ages 3 to 5 and .96 for ages 6 to 8. For the WE Scale, four raters independently scored the responses of 15 randomly selected cases from each of the four item sets. Interrater agreement was .98 for the 5- to 7-year-old group and .96 for the 8- to 11-year-old group.

Test Floors and Item Gradients

Test floors and item gradients for the LC and OE Scales are ample across all age groups. For examinees aged 5-0, LC floors extend to a standard score of 45 and OE floors extend to a standard score of 50 for a raw score of 1. WE Scale floors for grade-based norms are adequate, even for kindergarten examinees, but inadequate for age-based norms below age 5-9. For example, for Item Set 1, administered to children aged 5 through 7, a raw score of 1 (Rasch ability score of 29) yields a standard score of 87 for ages 5-0 to 5-2.

Validity Evidence

CONTENT VALIDITY EVIDENCE

Item content and formats for the OWLS are based on the author's theory of language (Carrow-Woolfolk, 1988; Carrow-Woolfolk & Lynch, 1981), which posits that language consists of four semantic categories: (1) lexical semantics (meanings of single words and word combinations); (2) syntactic semantics (grammatical structures and word order); (3) pragmatic semantics (the context of language structures and their influence on the expression and interpretation of meaning); and (4) supralinguistic semantics (higher order thinking, requiring interpretation of nonliteral language and humor). Two national tryouts were conducted prior to standardization, followed by item analyses and modifications. For the WE Scale, the readability level of the oral and written instructions for each item set was also evaluated. Content and artwork were reviewed for possible bias by consultants representing the perspectives of Asians, African Americans, Hispanics, Native Americans, and women. Classical and Rasch item analyses were conducted on standardization item responses to identify items with poor discrimination, potential bias, or poor fit to the Rasch model and for the WE Scale, to identify problematic and poorly discriminating scoring rules. Four of the 115 LC items were dropped–3 because of a poor fit to the model and 1 as the result of item bias analyses using the Mantel–Haenszel procedure–leaving 111 items in the final version. For the OE Scale, 8 of the original 104 items were dropped subsequent to item and bias analyses–7 because of poor fit to the model and 1 because of bias–leaving 96 items with 104 possible score points. Three writing prompts or items were deleted from the WE Scale, and a single name-writing item was structured as two items in the final scale, leaving 39 items. Item difficulty and discrimination indices are not provided for any of the scales.

Criterion-Related Validity Evidence

The LC/OE manual reports the results of nine concurrent validity studies, five of which included examinees in the primary grade range. The oral language scales correlate moderately with other receptive and expressive language tests, including the *Test of Auditory Comprehension of Language–Revised* (Carrow-Woolfolk, 1985; n = 31 children aged 4-1 to 5-11) and the PPVT-R (n = 98 children aged 7-0 to 11-0). Correlations with the PPVT-R, which measures receptive vocabulary, were higher for the OE Scale than for the LC Scale (.76 vs. .61), contrary to expectation. Correlations with ability measures, including the K-ABC and the WISC-III, ranged from .53 to .82 for a sample of 31 children aged 4-7 through 6-11. Correlations with the WISC-III in an older sample of children (n = 34, ages 8-1 through 11-11) were high (.64 to .74). Contrary to prediction, the OE Scale displayed identical correlations (.65) with WISC-III Verbal and Performance IQs.

Three of the seven concurrent validity studies reported in the WE Scale manual included primary grade examinees. Correlations between the WE Scale and Language composite with achievement, receptive vocabulary, and cognitive ability measures were generally higher than those for the oral language scales. For 31 children aged 8-2 to 9-9, correlations with the *Kaufman Test of Educational Achievement* (K-TEA; Kaufman & Kaufman, 1985b), ranged from .82 to .88. Contrary to prediction, the WE Scale was more highly correlated with K-TEA Mathematics composite and Battery composite scores (both .88) than with K-TEA Reading composite and Spelling scores (.86 and .82, respectively). The WE Scale score and the Language composite were highly correlated (.62 and .72, respectively) with PPVT-R scores (n = 100, ages 7-0 through 11-0) and with WISC-III scores in a sample of 34 children aged 8-1 through 11-11 (.64 to .76). No studies evaluating the relationship of the WE Scale to single-subject written expression measures or written expression subtests in multisubject instruments are reported.

CONSTRUCT VALIDITY EVIDENCE

As evidence of construct validity, intercorrelations among standard scores on the three OWLS scales are reported by 11 age groups. Intercorrelations for the LC and OE Scales are moderate to high (.58 to .73) for primary grade examinees, indicating that although the two scales measure somewhat different sets of language abilities, there is considerable overlap. The WE Scale displays somewhat lower correlations with the oral language scales, from .30 to .73 for the LC Scale and from .47 to .75 for the OE Scale. Correlations between the written and oral language scales for 6-year-old examinees are markedly lower (.30 to .47) than for other age groups, which the test's author attributes to differences in writing instruction in kindergarten. Restricted range due to floor effects at this age level may also be a factor, however. For the LC/OE Scales, mean raw scores increase across the 13 age groups in the standardization sample, with rapid growth from ages 3 through 7 and more gradual increases in later years, as predicted. Mean raw score progression data are not presented for the WE Scale.

Diagnostic validity was evaluated for the two oral language scales by comparing standard scores for seven clinical groups (examinees with speech impairments, language delays, language impairments, mental retardation, reading disabilities, undifferentiated learning disabilities, and hearing impairments) with scores for matched controls from the standardization sample. Differences between clinical and control groups were in the predicted direction, with the language-delayed group scoring 13–14 points lower than matched controls on the LC Scale, OE Scale, and Oral composite and the language-impaired group scoring 20–23 points lower than controls on the same measures. Reading-disabled examinees scored significantly lower than controls on the OE Scale and the Oral composite (SSs = 87.6 and 88.9, respectively) but not on the LC Scale (SS = 92.1). The group with undifferentiated learning disabilities scored significantly lower than controls on all three measures but obtained LC Scores in the average range (mean SS = 90.7). Contrary to prediction, scores for a Chapter 1 reading group were only slightly lower than means for the normative group (SSs = 91.8 to 93.8). On the WE Scale, five clinical groups (with language impairments, mental retardation, reading disabilities, undifferentiated learning disabilities, and hearing impairments) also scored significantly lower than matched controls from the standardization sample. Scores for reading-disabled examinees were approximately 14 points lower than for controls (SS = 79.9 vs. 93.8), whereas the group with undifferentiated learning disabilities scored about 18 points lower (SS = 82.8 vs. 101.1). As with the oral language scales, WE Scale scores for the Chapter 1 group were in the average range, with the exception of the Language composite (SS = 89.5). Studies comparing the WE Scale scores of children with documented writing disabilities with those of matched controls are also needed.

Usability

The LC and OE Scales are relatively easy to administer and score, but the WE Scale requires a major investment of time to master the scoring procedures, especially if examiners conduct the descriptive analyses. Efforts have been made to achieve diversity with regard to gender and race/ethnicity for the stimulus pictures, but the use of black-and-white drawings rather than full-color pictures for the oral language scales' test books considerably reduces their attractiveness. I have found that children with attention problems often become restless during administration and miss items because they fail to examine details in the pictures carefully. Separate software scoring programs are available, one for the LC/OE Scales and one for the WE Scale. Report options include a score profile, score narrative, item response list (LC/OE), descriptive analysis (for item entry rather than raw score entry), suggested language exercises, and a glossary. In addition to the usual derived scores, the WE Scale ASSIST program also provides Rasch ability scores and grade equivalents, as well as an option for grade-based norms. Because the oral language scales do not provide grade norms, only age-based standard score comparisons can be made among the three scales. The WE Scale ASSIST program compares standard score differences for all three scales and produces a Language composite score when the test dates for the three scales are less than 6 months apart. Unfortunately, because the oral language and written language tests were designed as separate kits, examiners must purchase and run both ASSIST programs in order to obtain the full complement of score comparisons.

Links to Intervention

Both manuals provide step-by-step procedures for conducting a descriptive analysis of item responses to identify strengths and weaknesses in the language areas assessed and to provide information for intervention planning. The manuals provide very little information on additional assessments or possible interventions targeting the identified problems, however. The LC/OE software scoring program includes a report option that provides language exercises for either scale for five age groups: early childhood (ages 2½–5), lower elementary (Grades 1–3), upper elementary (Grades 4–5), middle school (Grades 6–8), and high school/adulthood. Users can select the level based either on age and current grade placement or level of functioning. The WE software program produces sets of language exercises in the areas of conventions, linguistics, and content for six grade levels: preschool–kindergarten, Grades 1–2, Grades 3–4, Grades 5–6, Grades 7–9, and Grades 10 and up.

Relevant Research

A recent study (Gillam, Crofford, Gale, & Hoffman, 2001) with four language-impaired children aged 6-11 to 7-6 found that the OWLS LC and OE Scales were sensitive to functional language changes after intervention. After receiving one of two computer-delivered language intervention programs, all four children made clinically significant gains on two of the three OWLS measures (LC, OE, or Oral composite scores).

Source and Cost

Although the oral and written scales were originally packaged as two separate test kits, they are now available as a set from AGS Publishing for $278.95 or for $476.95 with both ASSISTS. The LC/OE Scales test kit is available for $199.95, and the WE Scale test kit is available for $100.95. ASSIST scoring programs on CD-ROM for Windows and Macintosh for the LC/OE and WE Scales are $199.95 each.

Test Reviews

Bradley-Johnson, S. (1999). Oral and Written Language Scales (OWLS). *Journal of Psychoeducational Assessment, 17,* 289–294.

Carpenter, C. D. (2001). Review of the Oral and Written Language Scales: Written Expression. In B. S. Plake & J. C. Impara (Eds.), *The fourteenth mental measurements yearbook* (pp. 864–866). Lincoln, NE: Buros Institute of Mental Measurements.

Graham, S. (2001). Review of the Oral and Written Language Scales: Listening Comprehension and Oral Expression. In B. S. Plake & J. C. Impara (Eds.), *The fourteenth mental measurements yearbook* (pp. 860–864). Lincoln, NE: Buros Institute of Mental Measurements.

Malcolm, K. K. (2001). Review of the Oral and Written Language Scales: Written Expression. In B. S. Plake & J. C. Impara (Eds.), *The fourteenth mental measurements yearbook* (pp. 866–868). Lincoln, NE: Buros Institute of Mental Measurements.

Plamondon, R. (1998). Review of the Oral and Written Language Scales (OWLS). *Psychology in the Schools, 35,* 96–100.

Summary

The *Oral and Written Language Scales* (OWLS) is a set of three conormed scales designed to measure listening comprehension, oral expression, and written expression in children and young adults. Despite the author's stated purpose of creating a test with tasks similar to those children encounter in the classroom, neither the oral nor the written language scales achieve that goal for early primary grade children. The variety of formats used on the Written Expression (WE) Scale is designed to elicit different types of written production, but many of the tasks are too difficult to be sensitive to differences among younger examinees, and floors are inadequate below age 5-9. The relative lack of emphasis on spelling in the WE Scale is also misplaced, especially for early primary grade examinees. In my experience, children who are displaying severe spelling and written expression problems in the classroom can often obtain WE Scale scores in the average range. Although there is some evidence that the OWLS differentiates between learning-disabled and normally achieving children and that the oral language scales are sensitive to changes in language functioning subsequent to intervention, additional research comparing the OWLS with other oral and written language tests is needed, especially for the WE Scale. Studies comparing the diagnostic and predictive validity of the OWLS with that of similar measures in multisubject batteries would be especially useful. In addition, considering that the OWLS norms are based on 1991 U.S. population data, renorming is in order.

Case Example

Name of student: Dalonte R.
Age: 8 years, 3 months
Grade: Second grade
Date of assessment: September

Reason for referral: Dalonte was referred by his second-grade teacher because he is making very poor progress in reading and language arts. Although he presents as a bright, capable youngster, he often fails to complete classroom tasks because he has trouble reading the directions and understanding the nature of the assignment. He makes poor grades on weekly spelling tests, and his daily journal entries are characterized by many misspellings, faulty grammar, and poor sentence structure. The *Oral and Written Language Scales* were administered to evaluate his language skills relative to his age peers as part of an early reading assessment.

Assessment results and interpretation: The *Oral and Written Language Scales* (OWLS) consist of three scales assessing listening comprehension, oral expression, and written expression. The scales are conormed so that comparisons can be made among children's receptive, oral, and written language skills. The Listening Comprehension Scale measures receptive language, including comprehension of words and phrases, grammar, and higher order language, such as double meanings. The Oral Expression Scale measures expressive language, including the comprehension and use of words and phrases, grammar, higher order language, and situation-appropriate language. The Written Expression Scale measures children's ability to use written language conventions, including spelling, punctuation, and capitalization; to use written linguistic forms, such as modifiers, phrases, and verbal forms; and to communicate meaningfully in writing. Dalonte's performance on the OWLS is described below. A standard score (SS) of 100, percentile rank (PR) of 50, and an age equivalent (AE) of 8-3 are average for a student his age.

OWLS Composites/Scales	SS	PR	AE
Listening Comprehension Scale	81	10	7-0
Oral Expression Scale	82	12	6-8
Oral Composite	85	16	6-10
Written Expression Scale	82	12	6-6
Language Composite	87	19	7-7

Oral Expression Scale: Descriptive Categories of Responses

Correct Responses		Incorrect Responses	
Preferred	13	Grammatical errors	4
Acceptable	12	Semantic/Pragmatic errors (S/P)	13
No differentiation	5	Grammatical and S/P errors	1
		No response	2

Written Expression Scale: Descriptive Analysis of Responses

Skill Area	Raw Score	Percentile	Rating
Conventions	3/27	2	Below average
Linguistics	3/32	15	Below average
Content	6/23	29	Average

Dalonte's overall language skills, including receptive, expressive, and written language, are in the below average range (SS = 87, PR = 19) compared with his age peers. His overall oral language functioning, including receptive vocabulary and oral expression, is also below average (SS = 85, PR = 16). His receptive and expressive language skills are evenly developed and fall in the below average range (PRs = 10 and 12, respectively). On the Oral Expression Scale, he gave 13 preferred responses, demonstrating complete understanding of those items, and 12 acceptable responses, demonstrating inconsistent understanding of those items. Most of his errors reflected difficulty understanding the item's meaning or understanding the nature of the task rather than difficulty with using grammatically correct language.

On the Written Expression Scale, his performance is rated as below average (SS = 82, PR = 12). His skills in writing meaningful, coherent content are average for his age (PR = 29), but his ability to use correct sentence structure is less well developed (PR = 15). His poorest performance was on tasks requiring him to use correct spelling, capitalization, and punctuation (PR = 2). On several items, his spelling errors were so severe that he had to read his sentences to the examiner so that they could be scored. For example, asked to write a sentence describing a picture in which two girls are playing with a soccer ball, he wrote, *The grsu is pigu socr* (*The girls are playing soccer*).

PEABODY PICTURE VOCABULARY TEST—THIRD EDITION

Overview

The *Peabody Picture Vocabulary Test–Third Edition* (PPVT-III; Dunn & Dunn, 1997) is an individually administered, norm-referenced test of listening comprehension for individuals aged 2-6 to 90+. First published in 1959 and revised in 1981, this edition includes two parallel forms, each with 204 items grouped in 17 sets of 12 items each. Changes from the PPVT-R include the addition of 29 items per form, an extension of norms at the upper and lower age ranges, and numerous new illustrations to reflect a more contemporary appearance and more diversified gender and ethnic representation. The authors have identified two purposes for the test: (1) to serve as an achievement test of receptive vocabulary and (2) to serve as a screening test of verbal ability. The PPVT-III was conormed with the *Expressive Vocabulary Test* (EVT) to permit comparisons of receptive and expressive vocabulary within the same standardization sample. Materials for each form consist of an examiner's manual, norms booklet, easel-format picture plate book, and 25 performance records, packaged together in notebook form. A separate 95-page publication, *Technical References to the Peabody Picture Vocabulary Test–Third Edition* (PPVT-III; Williams & Wang, 1997) provides information about test development, standardization, reliability, and validity.

Assessment Task

The Form A and Form B test easels each contain 4 training items and 17 sets of plates, each of which depicts four black-and-white pictures. The examiner reads a stimulus word for each plate, and the examinee points to the picture that best represents the stimulus word.

Administration

Starting items are based on examinee age. Administration time averages about 10–15 minutes for early primary grade examinees. The basal is the lowest set of plates administered in which the child makes one or no errors, whereas the ceiling is the highest set in which the child makes eight or more errors.

Scores

Items are scored 1 or 0, using the performance record. The raw score is obtained by subtracting the total number of errors from the number of the highest ceiling item. Raw scores can be converted to standard scores (M = 100, SD = 15), percentiles, normal curve equivalents, stanines, and age equivalents (for ages 1-9 through 22 only). Norms are in 2-month intervals for ages 2-6 through 6-11, 3-month intervals for ages 7-0 through 18-11, 2-year intervals for ages 19-0 to 24-11, and increasingly large intervals through age 90+.

Interpretation

Remarkably little information is provided in either the manual or the technical references regarding the interpretation of test results. A case example of a child aged 5-3 is used to demonstrate scoring procedures, but there is no interpretation of the scores obtained, other than a comment in the test manual that "it is important to note that Sarah's score falls in the low average range" (p. 23). Moreover, neither the test manual nor the manual for the software scoring program offers any information regarding the meaning of discrepancies between PPVT-III and EVT standard scores. For assistance, users must consult the EVT manual, which includes a one-page discussion of receptive–expressive vocabulary score differences.

Technical Adequacy

Standardization

The PPVT-III was standardized during 1995 and 1996 on a sample of 2,725 examinees sampled to reflect 1994 U.S. census data and stratified by age, race/ethnicity, geographic region, educational level, and six special education categories. Sample characteristics are generally representative of the 1994 U.S. population, with slight overrepresentation for African American examinees, the North Central region, and college-educated examinees, and slight underrepresentation for Caucasian examinees, the West region, and examinees with a Grade 11 or less education. Age group sizes are 100 or greater for all age intervals but vary widely within the early primary grade range (ns = 151, 415, and 481 for ages 6, 7, and 8, respectively). Because subgroup intervals for 6-year-olds are in 2-month increments, scores for examinees of that age are based on only about 75 examinees per interval, which falls below the criterion level.

Reliability Evidence

Across the early primary grade range, coefficient alphas are .94 or above for both forms; however, the authors caution that values may be spuriously high because Rasch procedures were used to estimate responses for unadministered items. Corrected split-half coefficients are .91 and above for both forms, with the exception of examinees in the age 6-6 group (r = .86). Alternate-form reliability coefficients range from .91 to .93 for the early primary grade range. Test–retest reliability using both forms for two samples that included primary grade examinees (n = 67, ages 2-6 to 5-11; n = 70, ages 6-0 to 10-11) for intervals from 8 to 203 days ranged from .91 to .94. The authors present three kinds of evidence of form equivalency: (1) raw score means and standard deviations for 25 age intervals, (2) correlations with the EVT for 25 age intervals, and (3) number of items per content area. The forms appear to be remarkably equivalent, with raw score means within 2.6 points of each other across the primary grade range. No evidence of interscorer reliability is presented.

The technical manual reports the results of an equating study (n = 193, ages 4-5 to 16-9) designed to evaluate the equivalence of PPVT-R and PPVT-III scores. Means and standard deviations of *W* ability scores on the PPVT-R and PPVT-III were similar (104.2 vs. 110.3, respectively; r = .97). Correlations between PPVT-R and PPVT-III standard scores for three age groups were lower, however, ranging from .83 to .89 across both forms. Williams and Wang (1997) note that the equating sample answered on average 5% more items correctly on the PPVT-III but do not present comparisons of raw score means or standard score means by age group. A table for converting raw scores from one version of the test to the other (pp. 92–95) reveals the size of the raw score increases across both PPVT-III forms. For example, a raw score of 54 on the PPVT-R Form L equates to a raw score of 75 on PPVT-III Forms A and B. In the case of a child aged 7-0 to 7-2, this translates to a 15- or 14-point standard score increase, from a standard score of 68 on the PPVT-R to a standard score of 83 or 82 on PPVT-III Form A or B, respectively! Additional information regarding these increases is presented in the "Relevant Research" section below.

Test Floors and Item Gradients

Test floors are excellent across both forms for all age groups and extend down to 40 for age 5-0 examinees. Item gradients are also ample for all age groups.

Validity Evidence

CONTENT VALIDITY EVIDENCE

Items were selected from previous PPVT item pools, picture dictionaries, word frequency lists, core vocabulary lists, and other resources with relevance to important life skills and designed to cover 20 different content areas (e.g., actions, adjectives, toys). A 1994 national tryout was conducted with 908 examinees using 480 stimulus words, 242 of which were retained from the PPVT-R and 238 of which were new items. Items were analyzed for difficulty and discrimination using classical and Rasch techniques, although specific item statistics are not reported. Item bias was evaluated using Rasch scaling methods, with analysis at the item level by gender and region and at the group level for African American, Hispanic, and Caucasian examinees. As a result of the analyses, 75 items were dropped. Although the final version of the PPVT-III contains 222 words from the PPVT-R, so many modifications have been made in the picture plates that only 30 items are identical to those in the previous edition. Additional item analyses were conducted on the standardization edition using both classical and Rasch procedures, with no item deletions. The remaining 204 items in each form were reordered for difficulty and divided into the final 17 sets of 12 items each. Items within each set were reordered so that the easiest three items are first, the six hardest items are in the middle, and the next easiest three items are last to provide examinees with a greater opportunity of starting and ending a set with some success.

CRITERION-RELATED VALIDITY EVIDENCE

The PPVT-III correlates highly with cognitive ability tests and moderately with other language measures. Two of the four criterion validity studies conducted during standardization included primary grade children. For 41 examinees aged 7-11 to 14-4, correlations between the PPVT-III and the WISC-III ranged from .82 to .92, with the highest correlation for Verbal IQ, as expected. Correlations with the *Oral and Written Language Scales* (OWLS) were moderate to high for two samples of primary grade children, but the pattern of relationships varied depending on the age group. The older group (n = 43, ages 8-1 to 12-10) displayed the expected pattern, with marginally higher correlations for the Listening Comprehension (LC) Scale than for the Oral Expression (OE) Scale for both PPVT-III forms (.70 and .77 vs. .67 and .68). For the younger group (n = 41, ages 3-0 through 5-8), however, the reverse pattern was evident, with lower correlations for the LC Scale than for the OE Scale (.66 and .63 vs. .83 and .77 for PPVT-III Forms A and B, respectively). No predictive validity studies are reported.

CONSTRUCT VALIDITY EVIDENCE

The authors include a brief rationale for the validity of vocabulary knowledge as a measure of verbal ability. As noted above, correlations with WISC-III Verbal IQ were high (.91 and .92 for Forms A and B, respectively, in a primary grade sample), but both forms of the PPVT-III also displayed very high correlations with Performance IQ (.82 and .84 for Forms A and B, respectively) and Full Scale IQ (.90 for both forms). Raw scores demonstrate the predicted pattern of increases across age groups, with the most rapid increases from ages 2½ to 12, followed by a gradual increase up to age 60 and a slight decline thereafter. The technical manual includes a full chapter on research with the PPVT-R, but because only 7.4% of the test content is identical to that of the current version, this information is of limited value. Given the concerns about bias in the PPVT-R (e.g., Sharpley & Stone, 1985; Washington & Craig, 1992), standard score means and standard deviations should be reported for gender, racial, and ethnic subgroups. Diagnostic validity was assessed in a study contrasting eight clinical groups (examinees with speech impairments, language delays, language impairments, mild mental retardation [children/adolescents and adults], learning disabilities in reading, and hearing impairments, and examinees enrolled in gifted programs) with matched controls from the normative sample. Although differences between clinical and control groups were statistically significant for all eight groups in the predicted direction, standard score means for children identified with language delays and language impairments fell only about 8 points below that of matched controls and within 1 standard deviation of the mean for both forms. Similarly, mean scores for the reading-disabled group were within 5–6 points of controls and well within the average range (SSs = 104.7 and 103.1 for Forms A and B, respectively); however, because these children were presumably defined by discrepancies between cognitive ability and reading achievement, it is not clear why lower PPVT-III scores were expected. No evidence is provided to support the authors' contention that the PPVT-III can be used to measure English language proficiency for second-language learners.

Usability

The PPVT-III is a model of usability in terms of portability, brevity, and ease of administration and scoring. The tabs on the picture plates in the easel make it easy to locate the appropriate set of test items, and record forms are well organized, with a reminder of basal and ceiling rules printed at the top of each page. The authors have taken pains to balance the stimulus pictures with regard to gender and race/ethnicity and to avoid stereotypical depictions. It is not clear why the decision was made to retain black-and-white pictures, especially given that the conormed EVT uses color picture plates. The easy-to-use ASSIST scoring program converts raw scores for either form to standard scores, percentiles, stanines, normal curve equivalents, and age equivalents and also converts PPVT-R Form L or M raw scores to PPVT-III Form A or B standard scores. Report options include a score summary, score profile comparisons, a score narrative, and sets of vocabulary-building exercises for five age groups. Other options allow users to plot individual growth graphs showing changes over time in Rasch ability scores for up to five test administrations and to calculate receptive and expressive vocabulary standard score comparisons when an EVT standard score is entered within 90 days of PPVT-III administration. Users should note that, as on the EVT, the ASSIST classification system for standard score ranges differ from common practice. Instead of seven score ranges, scores are collapsed into five broad categories: extremely low (SSs < 70), moderately low (SSs = 70–84), average (SSs = 85–114), moderately high (SSs = 115–129), and extremely high (SSs ≥ 130). A Spanish language version of the PPVT-R, the *Test de Vocabulario en Imágenes Peabody* (Dunn, Lugo, Padilla, & Dunn, 1986), is available from the same publisher.

Links to Intervention

No information regarding intervention strategies is presented in either manual. The software scoring program provides sets of vocabulary-building exercises for five age groups: early childhood (ages 2½–5), lower elementary (Grades 1–3), upper elementary (Grades 4–5), middle school (Grades 6–8), and high school/adulthood. Users can select the level based either on age and current grade placement or level of functioning, and there are five sets of equal difficulty for each level.

Relevant Research

Although no reading prediction or classification studies with the PPVT-III could be located, the PPVT-R has been widely used as an estimate of verbal ability in the reading research literature (e.g., Catts, 1991; Hurford, Schauf, Bunce, Blaich, & Moore, 1994; Leather & Henry, 1994; O'Connor & Jenkins, 1999). In Scarborough's (1998a) analysis of 19 kindergarten prediction studies, the median correlation between kindergarten receptive vocabulary scores and subsequent reading scores was .38, similar to that for Verbal IQ. Several recent studies (McGuinness, 1997; McGuinness et al, 1995; O'Connor & Jenkins, 1999) have reported that kindergarten or first grade PPVT-R scores were not significant predictors of word identification or decoding. Gray and colleagues (1999) compared the diagnostic accuracy of four vocabulary tests, including the PPVT–III, in a sample of 31 children aged 4 and 5 diagnosed with Specific Language Impairment (SLI) and 31 children with no language impairment (NL). PPVT-III mean standard scores for language-impaired children were significantly lower than those for normal language children but fell within the average range (SS = 97 vs. 112, respectively). Moreover, PPVT-III identification accuracy fell below acceptable levels (e.g., below .80). Based on a cutoff score using discriminant analysis, PPVT-III sensitivity (accuracy in identifying children with SLI as having SLI) was 74%, and specificity (accuracy in identifying NL children as NL) was 71%. PPVT-III positive predictive power (the percentage of children who scored below the cutoff and were also identified as having SLI) was 73%.

Several recent studies have examined the phenomenon of score increases on the PPVT-III relative to its predecessor. In an article describing the equating study noted above, Williams (1998) reported that mean standard scores on PPVT-III Form A and B were about 8 points higher than on PPVT-R Form L (SSs = 105.3 and 104.0 vs. 96.8), with younger examinees displaying the greatest score differences. PPVT-III standard scores for children aged 4 to 6 (n = 76) were approximately 10 points higher on both forms, whereas children aged 7 to 10 (n = 54) scored about 9 points higher on both forms. Using a single PPVT-III raw score of 31 as an exemplar, Stockman (2000) demonstrated that the size of standard score differences between the two editions varied with examinee age. Within the early primary grade range, standard score differences ranged from 17 points for ages 5-2 to 5-3 to 24 points for ages 7-0 to 7-2! Although the test's authors and Williams suggest that these increases may result from additional easy items for younger children and improvements in the distractor pictures, such changes are unlikely to produce higher standard scores. Among the possible factors contributing to the increases in PPVT-III scores are the larger number of words sampled, fewer age levels sampled, and the inclusion of larger number of low-SES and minority examinees (Stockman, 2000; Ukrainetz & Duncan, 2000).

Additional evidence of score increases come from a series of studies with African American children from low-income families. Washington and Craig (1992) reported that a sample of 105 preschool and kindergarten African American children obtained a mean standard score of 80 on the PPVT-R, with scores skewed toward the low end of the normal distribution. In a later study (Washington & Craig, 1999) with another sample with similar demographic characteristics (n = 59, ages 3-11 to 4-9), African American examinees obtained a mean standard score of 91 on the PPVT-III, 11 points higher, and the performance spread resulted in a normal distribution of scores. Although these findings can be interpreted as indicating lack of bias for the PPVT-III, they also reflect the score increases documented elsewhere.

Source and Cost

The PPVT-III test kit is available from AGS Publishing for $154.95 for each form. Both kits are available as a set for $262.95. The PPVT-III ASSIST program with both Macintosh and Windows software on one CD-ROM is available for $209.95, and the technical references publication costs $39.95. A combination kit with the PPVT-III, EVT, and both ASSIST programs is available for $586.95.

Test Reviews

Bessai, F. (2001). Review of the Peabody Picture Vocabulary Test–III. In B. S. Plake & J. C. Impara (Eds.), *The fourteenth mental measurements yearbook* (pp. 908–909). Lincoln, NE: Buros Institute of Mental Measurements.

Campbell, J. (1998). Review of the Peabody Picture Vocabulary Test, Third Edition. *Journal of Psychoeducational Assessment, 16,* 334–338.

Maddux, C. D. (1998–1999). Peabody Picture Vocabulary Test, Third Edition. *Diagnostique, 24,* 221–228.

Wasyliw, O. E (2001). Review of the Peabody Picture Vocabulary Test–III. In B. S. Plake & J. C. Impara (Eds.), *The fourteenth mental measurements yearbook* (pp. 909–911). Lincoln, NE: Buros Institute of Mental Measurements.

Summary

The *Peabody Picture Vocabulary Test–Third Edition* (PPVT-III) is the latest edition of an individually administered, norm-referenced test of listening comprehension that has been widely used as a screening measure of verbal ability in reading prediction and classification research. Although the PPVT-III is a marked improvement over its predecessor in ease of administration and scoring, examiners are still left to interpret the results on their own. Users should be aware that compared with the PPVT-R, the PPVT-III is likely to yield higher standard scores—as much as 24 points for some age groups in the early primary grade range. As a result, children who have been previously identified as exhibiting delays in vocabulary development (i.e., scores falling 1.5 or 2 standard deviations below the mean) may obtain scores that are significantly higher and may result in different educational decisions. Additional validation studies should be conducted to demonstrate the utility of the current version of the test in identifying children with language problems and predicting academic achievement. Because the PPVT-III measures only one aspect of language, it should never be used as the sole measure of language proficiency and never as the sole indicator of cognitive ability.

Case Example

Name of student: Joseph H.
Age: 6 years, 8 months
Grade: First grade
Date of assessment: May

Reason for referral: Joseph was referred for an early reading assessment by his first-grade teacher because of very poor performance on the spring gradewide literacy screening measure. Joseph has had difficulty keeping up with the pace of classroom instruction, and, despite receiving tutoring twice a week after school, is falling behind his classmates in reading and spelling. The *Peabody Picture Vocabulary Test–Third Edition* (PPVT-III) and *Expressive Vocabulary Test* (EVT) were administered to evaluate whether oral language deficits may be contributing to his reading problems.

Assessment results and interpretation: The PPVT-III is an achievement test of receptive vocabulary that measures listening comprehension for spoken words. The child is required to point to one of four pictures that best illustrates a stimulus word spoken by the examiner. The EVT measures expressive vocabulary knowledge and word retrieval with two types of items, labeling and synonym. Word retrieval can be evaluated by comparing expressive and receptive vocabulary skills using score differences between the PPVT-III and the EVT. On both tests, average scores for a student of Joseph's age are as follows: Standard Score [SS] = 100, Percentile Rank [PR] = 50, Age-Equivalent [AE] = 6-8. His scores are presented below.

Name of test	SS	PR	AE
Peabody Picture Vocabulary Test–III	93	32	6-2
Expressive Vocabulary Test	108	70	7-6

Joseph's receptive vocabulary functioning, as measured by the PPVT-III, falls in the *average range* for his age (32nd percentile). His expressive vocabulary functioning, as measured by the EVT, is significantly better developed (70th percentile, *average range*), suggesting that he may be more proficient in displaying vocabulary knowledge in an expressive rather than in a receptive format. Although this difference is statistically significant at the .05 level, 25% of children in the standardization sample displayed a difference of that size between their receptive and expressive language scores.

TEST OF LANGUAGE DEVELOPMENT—PRIMARY: THIRD EDITION

Overview

The *Test of Language Development–Primary: Third Edition* (TOLD-P:3; Newcomer & Hammill, 1997) is an individually administered, norm-referenced test designed to assess the oral language competence of children aged 4-0 through 8-11. Now in its third edition, the TOLD-P:3 includes measures of linguistic features (semantic, syntax, and phonology) and linguistic systems (listening, organizing, and speaking). Changes to this version include (1) renorming; (2) the addition of two new subtests (Phonemic Analysis and Relational Vocabulary); (3) transfer of the phonological subtests from the core battery to supplemental measures; (4) the addition of a new composite (Organizing), to assess language abilities that mediate between receptive and expressive forms of communication; (5) redrawing of the stimulus pictures in color; and (6) revision of children's names in the items, to reflect the demographic characteristics of today's students. The TOLD-P:3 has four major uses: (1) to identify children with significant deficits in language proficiency, (2) to determine children's strengths and weaknesses in specific language areas, (3) to monitor progress in intervention programs, and (4) to assess language skills in research studies. The test materials consist of a spiral-bound examiner's manual, spiral-bound stimulus picture book, and 25 profile/examiner record forms, all packed in a storage box.

Subtests and Composites

Subtests

The TOLD-P:3 consists of six core subtests measuring semantics and syntax and three supplemental subtests measuring phonology. Table 5.22 describes the subtests in order of administration. Because the skills measured by the phonological subtests have been mastered by most children by age 7, the authors recommend that those subtests should not be administered to examinees older than 7-0 unless they are exhibiting problems in these areas. As Table 5.22 indicates, Phonemic Analysis requires syllable deletion rather than phoneme manipulation and should be renamed "Syllable Deletion" to reflect its content more accurately.

TABLE 5.22. Description of the TOLD–P:3 Subtests

Subtest	Description
Picture Vocabulary	The child points to the one of four pictures that best represents the meaning of a word spoken by the examiner.
Relational Vocabulary	The examiner asks a question about the relationship between two words (e.g., "How are a pencil and pencil alike?"), and the child describes the nature of the relationship (e.g., "You write with them").
Oral Vocabulary	The child defines words on a list read by the examiner.
Grammatic Understanding	The child points to the one of three pictures that best represents the meaning of a stimulus sentence spoken by the examiner.
Sentence Imitation	The examiner reads a sentence, and the child repeats the sentence verbatim. Sentences range in length from 5 to 12 words.
Grammatic Completion	The examiner reads one or more sentences, and the child supplies the missing word in the last sentence (e.g., the examiner says, "Bill is a boy and John is a boy. They are both ________." and the child says, "boys").
Word Discrimination	The child indicates whether two words pronounced by the examiner are the same or different. Different pairs consist of words that vary by one phoneme in the initial, medial, or final position (e.g., *boy* and *toy*).
Phonemic Analysis	The child repeats a two-syllable word spoken by the examiner (e.g., "something") and then pronounces the word again without a specific syllable (e.g., "thing").
Word Articulation	The examiner displays a picture (e.g., a fireman), says a sentence in which the final word is the name of the picture (e.g., "Fires are put out by the ________"), and the child pronounces the target word (e.g., "fireman").

Note. Supplemental TOLD-P:3 subtests are shaded.

Composites

Standard scores on the six core subtests can be summed to generate one global composite and five overlapping composites consisting of subtests with common linguistic systems or features (see Table 5.23). According to the TOLD-P:3's authors, the phonological subtests were excluded from the global composite score because this permits separate assessments of speech and language competence and also because they display low correlations with the core subtests.

TABLE 5.23. TOLD-P:3 Subtests and Composites

Global composite	Specific composites	Subtests
Spoken Language	Listening	Picture Vocabulary Grammatic Understanding
	Organizing	Relational Vocabulary Sentence Imitation
	Speaking	Oral Vocabulary Grammatic Completion
	Semantics	Picture Vocabulary Relational Vocabulary Oral Vocabulary
	Syntax	Grammatic Understanding Sentence Imitation Grammatic Completion

Administration

All of the TOLD-P:3 subtests are untimed, although the authors suggest that if the child has not responded within 10 seconds to the presentation or repetition of an item, the examiner should score that item as 0. Depending on examinee age and skill, administration time for the core TOLD-P:3 battery ranges from 30 to 60 minutes. The authors state that the supplemental subtests, which they estimate to take another 30 minutes, should not be given at the same time as the core subtests because children may become inattentive or fatigued. In my own experience, the testing times given in the manual are longer than those that are actually required in practice, especially for the supplemental subtests. Examinees of all ages begin with the first item on each subtest. Ceilings are uniform for the six core subtests (five consecutive incorrect responses), but all items are administered on the three supplemental subtests, except for Word Discrimination. For Word Discrimination, if the child misses three or more of the foils (i.e., items with identical pairs of words) or answers "same" to the first five nonfoil items, the subtest is discontinued and no score is given. The record booklet contains complete administration procedures and examiner prompts, along with correct responses. Sentence Imitation and Word Discrimination should be delivered on audiocassette in the interests of interexaminer consistency. The spiral-bound stimulus book is not in the usual easel format; it lies flat on the table, so that the examiner must sit beside the child to observe and record pointing responses. For Word Discrimination, examiners are directed to turn their faces slightly away while pronouncing the items to prevent children from attempting to obtain visual cues by watching their lips. For Word Articulation, the examiner uses an imitative format (e.g., "Say *baby*") to elicit the target word if the child misidentified the picture or fails to respond verbally.

I have found that children occasionally miss items on Grammatic Completion because they fail to understand the nature of the task, such as using some form of the target word in the stimulus sentence or sentences. For example, for Item 1 ("The shoes belong to the boy. Whose shoes are they? They are the ________"), one 6-year-old said, "owner's," a response that is grammatically correct but receives a score of 0. Similar kinds of errors occur on items that assess comparative or superlative adjectival forms. The manual and record booklet should provide additional guidelines for querying and scoring these types of responses.

Scores

For all subtests, items are scored dichotomously. This simplifies the scoring process but reduces the sensitivity of subtests such as Relational Vocabulary, Oral Vocabulary, and Sentence Imitation to individual differences in children's expressive language skills. For example, the only correct answer listed for the Relational Vocabulary item "a guitar and a violin" is *string instruments.* Although *musical instruments* earns a query, another response that focuses on similarity of function rather than category (e.g., "They both make music") does not. For Sentence Imitation, children are not penalized for misarticulations or dropped word endings. The decision to score as correct the omission of word endings is a change from the previous edition and was made to avoid penalizing examinees who speak in dialect or use nonstandard English. Subtest raw scores are converted to standard scores (M = 10, SD = 3), percentiles, and age equivalents. Norms are in 6-month intervals throughout the age range. Composite standard scores (M = 100, SD = 15) are called "quotients," an unfortunate term that emphasizes the use of test results for discrepancy analyses and special education decision-making. For Word Articulation items, the record form provides two pronunciation guides, one with standard dictionary symbols and the second with International Phonetic Alphabet symbols.

Interpretation

The test's authors appropriately emphasize the use of composite scores in interpretation and include a useful discussion of the utility of the composites in diagnosing language strengths and weaknesses. The manual includes a table listing minimum difference scores for composites at the .05 level of statistical significance (incorrectly labeled throughout the discussion as level of *confidence* rather than level of *significance*) and demonstrates how the TOLD-P:3 Spoken Language Quotient (SLQ) can be compared with quotients from other tests by using Anastasi's (1988) standard error of difference formula. The authors caution against diagnosing language problems based solely on a finding of statistical significance for difference scores and recommend three criteria for evaluating the clinical utility of observed differences: (1) The difference should be statistically significant (at or beyond the .05 level), (2) it should be at least 15 points, and (3) it should be in a range indicating a "pronounced problem" (i.e., one or both quotients in the below average range). The manual includes a case example of a kindergarten child aged 5-6 to demonstrate scoring, interpretation, and discrepancy analysis procedures. The case example's composite scores range from 74 to 89, with the SLQ in the low average range. Based on the child's TOLD-P:3 SLQ of 80 and *Comprehensive Test of Nonverbal Intelligence* (CTONI) IQ of 85, the authors suggest that his language deficits may be the result of "low mental ability" and recommend further assessment of language skills and supplemental language instruction. Alternative interpretations indicating that poor performance can result from experiential and/or instructional deficiencies as well as cognitive deficits should be added, especially in view of the fact that both scores fall in the below average rather than the low or "poor" range.

Technical Adequacy

Standardization

The TOLD-P:3 was standardized in the spring of 1996 on 1,000 children aged 4 to 8 who were sampled to be representative of the U.S. school-age population in terms of geographic area, gender, race, residence (rural–urban–suburban), ethnicity, family income, parental educational attainment, and disability status. Norm group characteristics, which are stratified by age for region, gender, race, ethnicity, and residence, closely match national data, except for underrepresentation of the highest SES families. Age group sizes vary considerably for early primary grade examinees, from a low of 153 for age 5 to a high of 258 for ages 7 and 8. Because conversion tables use 6-month intervals, scores for children aged 5 are based on only about 76 examinees, which falls below the criterion level.

Reliability Evidence

Internal consistency reliability estimates for subtests and composites are reported at yearly intervals for ages 4 through 8. For early primary grade examinees, subtest coefficient alphas range from .78 to .94, with all values at or above .80 for ages 5 and 6 and 14 of 18 values at or above .80 for ages 7 and 8. Composite alphas are at or above .90 across early primary grade groups except for Listening (.89 for age 8). Coefficient alphas for 10 subgroups in the standardization sample (males, females, European Americans, African Americans, Hispanics, and students diagnosed with misarticulation, ADHD, learning disabilities, delayed speech and language, and mental retardation) are above .80 for subtests and above .90 for composites. Test–retest reliability for 33 students in kindergarten, first grade, and second grade (4-month interval) ranged from a low of .77 for Word Discrimination to a high of .90 for Sentence Imitation, with only Word Discrimination falling below the .80 criterion level. Composite stability estimates ranged from .82 to .92. Because of the length of the interval and the small sample size, these values should be considered as tentative, however. Interscorer reliability was evaluated by having two individuals in PRO-ED's research department independently score 50 completed protocols randomly selected from the normative sample. Correlations of agreement were .99 for all subtests and composites. Because these values are based on completed tests, they provide no information about examiner variance for tasks requiring precise pronunciation and timing during administration, such as Word Discrimination and Sentence Imitation, or scorer variance for tasks requiring children to pronounce target words, such as Word Articulation.

Test Floors and Item Gradients

Floors for composites are adequate throughout the early primary grade range with the exception of Speaking at age 5-0 to 5-5. Subtest floors are inadequate for Picture Vocabulary, Relational Vocabulary, and Sentence Imitation below age 5-6; for Grammatic Completion below age 6-0; and for Oral Vocabulary and Phonemic Analysis below age 6-6. As noted earlier, the three supplemental phonological subtests are very easy for most children older than 7 and show ceiling effects as early as age 6. For example, a child aged 6-6 who answers every item correctly on Word Discrimination, Phonemic Analysis, and Word Discrimination earns standard scores of 13, 12, and 12, respectively (high average and average ranges). Item gradients are adequate throughout the early primary grade age range.

Validity Evidence

CONTENT VALIDITY EVIDENCE

The TOLD-P:3 subtests are based on a model that proposes two dimensions of language structure: (1) linguistic features, including semantics, syntax, and phonology; and (2) linguistic systems, including listening (receptive skills), organizing (integrating–mediating skills), and speaking (expressive skills). Content validity evidence includes a very readable exposition of the model and a rationale for the selection of subtest formats and items, including a review of changes from the previous edition. Words on the new Relational Vocabulary subtest were selected from graded lists of reading vocabulary words, with the word pairs designed to have similar reading difficulty levels. A set of word pairs was pilot-tested in a study with 50 students, with the result that 15 items were deleted because they either were too easy or did not have acceptable item validity coefficients. The new Phonemic Analysis subtest was derived from Rosner's *Test of Auditory Analysis Skills*, which includes both syllable and phoneme deletion items. The authors do not refer to the linguistic unit of deletion in their discussion and state that they included stimulus words consisting of two smaller words (i.e., compound words) because they were "interested in a child's actual knowledge of English" (p. 70). One of the items (*pocket*) does not conform to this structure, however. For Word Articulation, words requiring the child to produce a final /r/ were eliminated to avoid biasing the subtest against examinees from New England or the South. These items were replaced with items assessing /r/ in initial and medial positions.

Item discrimination coefficients are reported for the nine subtests at five yearly age intervals. Although the manual states that a value of .30 was set as the minimum level for acceptability, median coefficients for Picture Vocabulary and Grammatic Understanding fall below this criterion at age 8 (.28 and .29, respectively). Median item difficulties fall below the acceptable .15 level for Relational Vocabulary at age 5, indicating that the items are too difficult for most examinees that age. In contrast, item difficulties are in the .80s and .90s for the three phonology supplemental subsets for ages 6, 7, and 8, indicating that most children at those ages have mastered such tasks. IRT procedures were used to compare the performance of two dichotomous groups in the normative sample (males–females and whites–nonwhites). Of the 225 items, only 8 (3.5%) demonstrated possible bias at the .01 significance level. Because 4 of the 8 items are on Oral Vocabulary, however, 14% of the items on that subtest exhibit DIF. The manual does not indicate the direction of the performance differences between the two groups, which items were flagged, or whether the flagged items were reviewed to explore factors contributing to the observed differences. Comparing the performance of a larger number of demographic groups (e.g., European Americans vs. all others, African Americans vs. all others, and Hispanic Americans vs. all others) would have been preferable.

CRITERION-RELATED VALIDITY EVIDENCE

As evidence of criterion-related validity, the manual reports correlations between the TOLD-P:3 and the *Bankson Language Test–Second Edition* (Bankson, 1990) for 30 first, second, and third graders. Although correlations were moderate to high across composites and subtests, except for Word Articulation (*r*s = .50 to .97), all of the TOLD-P:3 measures were more strongly correlated with the Bankson Semantic Knowledge Scale than with the Morphological/Syntactic Rules Scale, calling the TOLD-P:3's discriminant validity into question. Additional criterion-related studies with more recent tests of language, cognitive ability, and reading are needed to clarify the nature of the skills measured by the TOLD-P:3. No predictive validity evidence is presented.

CONSTRUCT VALIDITY EVIDENCE

TOLD-P:3 subtests demonstrate an increase in raw score means across age groups, with smaller gains on the phonological subtests after age 6, as expected. The manual reports mean standard scores for the total sample, five demographic subgroups (males, females, Hispanics, African Americans, and Caucasians) and four disability subgroups (children identified with misarticulation, ADHD, learning disabilities, delayed speech–language, and mental retardation). Mean scores for all demographic groups were in the average range, whereas scores for disability groups were lower and in the expected order, with the group with mental retardation obtaining the lowest composite scores and the group with misarticulation the highest. Composite scores for the group with learning disabilities were in the low average range (SSs = 83 to 87).

Raw score intercorrelations range from .37 to .59 for the six core subtests. The three phonological subtests display much lower correlations with the six core subtests (.07 to .43), supporting their assignment to a supplemental category. Although Word Discrimination and Phonemic Analysis are moderately related (.42), they are only weakly correlated with Word Articulation (.11 and .17, respectively), which is not surprising, given that the latter measures pronunciation rather than phonological processing. Adding a third measure of phonological processing, such as a phonemic segmentation task, and providing a composite based on those three subtests, would enhance the TOLD-P:3's diagnostic utility. A factor analysis of the six core subtests yielded a single factor, supporting the combination of all subtests into the Spoken Language composite. No factor analytic results are presented to support the grouping of the nine subtests into five composites as specified by the model. To demonstrate that the three vocabulary subtests sample different levels of spoken vocabulary skills, the authors calculated the median standard frequency index (SFI) for items for each of those subtests. Low SFIs represent mature words (infrequent words), whereas high SFIs represent less mature words (frequent words). Median SFIs were in the predicted order, with Picture Vocabulary comprising the least mature words, Oral Vocabulary the most mature words, and Relational Vocabulary in between. The manual includes a chapter summarizing the research on the TOLD and TOLD-P:2. Although six of the nine subtests are virtually unchanged since the original test and the scoring procedures for Sentence Imitation have been modified only slightly, the vast majority of studies were conducted more than two decades ago, so that the findings may not apply to today's school-age children.

Usability

The TOLD-P:3's pictures are attractive, and the authors have made a concerted effort to depict the diversity of the current U.S. school population. Several modifications in test materials and scoring procedures would improve usability, however. Because the spiral-bound picture book is designed to lie flat on the table, the examiner must sit beside the child to administer subtests with a pointing response format. The more common test easel format would facilitate administration, as would placing tabs in the test book to indicate subtest divisions. The arrangement of the columns on the record form should be altered for several subtests. For Picture Vocabulary, Grammatic Understanding, Grammatic Completion, and Word Articulation, the score column is placed at the left side of the page, the item column in the middle, and the correct response column at the right side. Consequently, the examiner must first scan the item in the center as the child is responding, then consult the correct response column at the right of the form, and finally enter a 0 or 1 on the left side of the form. Placing the score and correct response columns to the right of the item column and adjacent to each other, as is the case for Phonemic Analysis, would facilitate rapid, accurate scoring. Finally, space should be provided on the front of the record booklet for entering a complete score array; the current record form only provides space for listing standard scores ("quotients") for the composites.

The software scoring program also needs to be modified in the interests of usability. The program generates a 10-page report, including a score summary and score comparisons for subtests and composites, with comparisons flagged at the .05 level. Users can also enter standard scores from other tests with a mean of 100 and standard deviation of 15 for discrepancy analyses with TOLD-P:3 scores. Score discrepancies are not evaluated for clinical utility in terms of frequency of occurrence in the norm group, however, leaving users to interpret what can be a very large number of statistically significant findings without this critical information. Moreover, the directions in the software manual do not match the program as displayed on the screen, the manual and the program provide no information to assist users in saving and locating files, and the program does not permit the user to return to a previous screen during the data entry process to edit previously entered information. As of fall 2003, according to the publisher, the program has been revised and reformatted.

Links to Intervention

The manual includes a section that describes resources for further assessment and educational programming. Suggestions for assessment include conducting interviews and gathering information with language samples. The authors provide examples of programs and strategies for transcribing and analyzing language samples, including computer-assisted programs. The discussion of language instructional approaches is briefer and less detailed. Intervention programs and references are listed rather than described, and of the five cited, four were published in the 1970s or 1980s.

Relevant Research

In addition to the research reported in the manual, two recent studies attest to the utility of the previous version of the test in predicting reading and spelling acquisition. In a study with 604 kindergarten children, Catts et al. (2001) administered a battery of reading and language predictors that included five TOLD-P:2: subtests. All five subtests (Picture Vocabulary, Oral Vocabulary, Grammatic Understanding, Sentence Imitation, and Grammatic Completion) predicted second-grade reading comprehension, as measured by the *Woodcock Reading Mastery Tests–Revised* (WRMT-R), the *Gray Oral Reading Tests–Third Edition*, and the *Diagnostic Achievement Battery–Second Edition*. Of the set of kindergarten measures, Sentence Imitation was the second best predictor of reading problems, after WRMT-R Letter Identification. In a longitudinal study with 52 preschool children aged 4 to 6 (Lewis, Freebairn, & Taylor, 2000a), syntax deficits as measured by TOLD-P:2 Grammatic Understanding, Sentence Imitation, and Grammatic Completion, along with pseudoword repetition, predicted language impairment at school age (ages 8 to 11). Reading impairment at school age was predicted by poor performance in preschool on all six TOLD-P:2 subtests, including phonology, semantics, and syntax measures. Spelling impairment was predicted by deficits on Word Discrimination and a family history of reading disorders.

Source and Cost

The TOLD-P:3 test kit is available from PRO-ED for $246.00. The software scoring program, available for Windows or Macintosh applications, costs $101.00.

Test Reviews

Bradley-Johnson, S. (1998). Review of the Test of Language Development–Primary: Third Edition. *Psychology in the Schools, 35*, 93–95.

Madle, R. A. (2001). Review of the Test of Language Development-Primary, Third Edition. In B. S. Plake & J. C. Impara (Eds.), *The fourteenth mental measurements yearbook* (pp. 1246–1248). Lincoln, NE: Buros Institute of Mental Measurements.

Stutman, G. (2001). Review of the Test of Language Development-Primary, Third Edition. In B. S. Plake & J. C. Impara (Eds.), *The fourteenth mental measurements yearbook* (pp. 1248–1250). Lincoln, NE: Buros Institute of Mental Measurements.

Summary

The *Test of Language Development–Primary: Third Edition* (TOLD-P:3) is an individually administered, norm-referenced test of children's oral language skills. Although relatively easy to administer and score, it has a number of shortcomings, including inadequate floors for several subtests at the younger ages, limited evidence of concurrent validity, and a limited sampling of phonological processing skills. Extending the range of items on Phonemic Analysis to include phoneme deletion items and adding another phonological processing subtest would increase diagnostic utility, especially for first and second graders. Research with its predecessor, the TOLD-P:2, indicates that several subtests, especially Sentence Imitation, are significant predictors of future reading and spelling. Additional validation studies should be conducted to assess the relationship of the TOLD-P:3 to current and future academic achievement and to performance on other language tests, such as the *Illinois Test of Psycholinguistic Abilities–3*, which includes several similar subtests.

Case Example

Name of student: Jenelle M.
Age: 5 years, 10 months
Grade: Kindergarten
Date of assessment: March

Reason for referral: Jenelle was referred for an early reading assessment by her kindergarten teacher because of concerns that she is failing to develop early literacy skills at an adequate rate. Her teacher reports that she often has trouble focusing on the task at hand, needs instructions to be repeated several times, and requires individual assistance to complete classroom tasks. The *Test of Language Development–Primary: Third Edition* (TOLD-P:3) was administered to evaluate her oral language skills and provide information for educational interventions.

Assessment results and interpretation: The TOLD-P:3 measures children's oral language skills in the areas of semantics (word meanings), syntax (sentence structure), listening (receptive language), organizing (relational language), and speaking (expressive language). Average scores for a child Jenelle's age are as follows: Composite Standard Score = 100, Subtest Standard Score = 10, Percentile Rank = 50, and Age Equivalent (AE) = 5-10. Her performance on the TOLD-P:3 subtests and composites is presented below.

Subtest	Standard Score	Percentile Rank	Age Equivalent	Descriptive Category
Picture Vocabulary (PV)	7	16	3-9	Below average
Relational Vocabulary (RV)	11	63	6-3	Average
Oral Vocabulary (OV)	9	37	5-3	Average
Grammatic Understanding (GU)	9	37	5-0	Average
Sentence Imitation (SI)	6	9	3-9	Below average
Grammatic Completion (GC)	7	16	4-3	Below average
Word Discrimination	9	37	5-3	Average
Phonemic Analysis	13	84	7-6	Above average
Word Articulation	10	50	6-3	Average

Composite	Standard Score	Percentile Rank	Descriptive Category
Spoken Language (PV + RV + OV + GU + SI + GC)	87	19	Below average
Listening (PV + GU)	88	21	Below average
Organizing (RV + SI)	91	27	Average
Speaking (OV + GC)	88	21	Below average
Semantics (PV + RV+ OV)	94	35	Average
Syntax (GU + SI + GC)	83	13	Below average

On the TOLD-P:3 composites, Jenelle's performance ranges from average to below average for her age. Her overall spoken language skills fall in the below average range (PR = 19). Her vocabulary knowledge and her ability to organize language information by categories are rated as average (PRs = 35 and 27, respectively), but her listening and spoken language skills are below average (both PRs = 21). Her poorest performance was on tasks requiring her to understand and produce grammatical sentences (PR = 13). The difference between her vocabulary knowledge and her syntactical skills is statistically significant but not clinically useful.

On the TOLD-P:3 subtests, her performance also ranges from average to below average. Her skills in expressing the relationships between spoken words and defining individual words are rated as average (PRs = 63 and 37, respectively). She also performed in the average range on a task requiring her to understand sentences with different syntactic structures (PR = 37). Her phonological skills, as measured by tasks of word discrimination and syllable deletion, are average to above average (PRs = 37 and 84, respectively). Her ability to articulate single words is also average for her age (PR = 50). She scored in the below average range on a task requiring her to listen to an incomplete sentence and supply the missing morphological form (PR = 16). She had difficulty providing possessive and plural forms and supplying inflected endings (e.g., *cook* for *cooked*). Her poorest performance was on a task requiring her to repeat complex sentences and tapping attention and memory as well as syntactic skills (PR = 9, below average range).

Measures of Print Awareness and Concept of Word

This section reviews one standardized measure of print awareness. Other print awareness or concept of word measures reviewed in this text can be found in the *Book Buddies Early Literacy Screening*, the *Early Reading Diagnostic Assessment–Revised*, *Fox in a Box*, the *Phonological Awareness Literacy Screening*, the *Test of Early Reading Ability–3*, and the *Texas Primary Reading Inventory*.

CONCEPTS ABOUT PRINT

Overview

Concepts About Print (CAP) is an individually administered, standardized measure of young children's understanding of the purposes and conventions of print. Developed in New Zealand by the founder of the Reading Recovery early intervention program (Clay, 1985, 1993b), it is one of six tasks in the *Observation Survey of Early Literacy Achievement–Second Edition* (*Observation Survey*; Clay, 1993a, 2002), which also includes measures of letter identification, word recognition, writing vocabulary, dictation, and oral reading. The CAP is reviewed in this text as a separate measure because it has been used in that manner in a large number of reading prediction and classification studies (e.g., Byrne, Fielding-Barnsley, Ashley, & Larsen, 1997; Iversen & Tunmer, 1993; Neuman, 1999). Changes to the CAP in this edition include (1) placement of the CAP in a separate chapter in the *Observation Survey* handbook, (2) minor reformatting of the directions and score sheet, (3) updated norms for a sample of New Zealand children, (4) replacement of the 2-year interval stanine norms with 6-month stanine intervals, and (5) the inclusion of additional data on psychometric characteristics. The purposes of the CAP are to (1) measure young children's print awareness skills, (2) provide direction for instruction, and (3) monitor process in early literacy learning. Directions and a scoring sheet are included in the author's handbook presenting the *Observation Survey* (Clay, 2002). Additional materials needed for administration include one of four 20-page paperbacks—*Sand* (Clay, 1972), *Stones* (Clay, 1979b), *Follow Me, Moon* (Clay, 2000b), or *No Shoes* (Clay, 2000c)—and two 13- × 5-cm (about 5- × 2-inch) pieces of cardboard for the letter and word concept tasks.

Assessment Tasks

The examiner asks the child a series of questions about certain features of print in a small picture book as the examiner reads the book aloud. The 24 CAP items assess a variety of print conventions and concepts, including book orientation, print directionality, reading vocabulary (e.g., *letter, word*), concepts of lowercase and uppercase letters, and the function of punctuation marks. Several items assess the child's ability to notice errors in print, including upside-down pictures and text and incorrectly ordered lines and letters.

Administration

The CAP takes about 10–15 minutes to administer. Administration procedures, including verbatim directions for each item, are provided in the handbook for the *Observation Survey*. Each child begins at Item 1, but examiners may omit Items 12, 13, and 14, which assess the understanding of page sequence, word sequence, and letter order, if the child fails Item 10, which assesses the understanding of line order. Even if Items 12 through 14 are omitted, the examiner reads the story on those pages to the child and administers the remaining items. For the letter and word concept items, the child identifies single letters and words by using the two pieces of cardboard to cover portions of the text.

Scores

Items are scored 1 for correct and 0 for incorrect, using a scoring sheet in the handbook. Item by item administration and scoring procedures are included in one section of the manual, and a "Quick Reference" for scoring standards is provided on another page. The examiner must consult the Quick Reference page to determine how to score items assessing punctuation marks. Raw scores can be converted to stanines, using one of two sets of norms, one obtained in 2000 with 796 New Zealand children and a smaller set obtained in 1990–1991 with 109 American children. In addition, a chart presents age expectations for each item, based on the age at which 50% of "average European children" pass an item, from on a 1972 study with New Zealand children. Although the test's author appropriately cautions that age expectations for performance are dependent on the curriculum and instructional practices of a particular school, no cautions are provided regarding the use of outdated norms or norms from another country.

Interpretation

Interpretation based on local norms is strongly recommended. The larger and more recent set of *Observation Survey* norms is based on New Zealand children, whose early literacy and instructional experiences are likely to differ from those of American children. According to its author, the CAP is not a "prediction device" but a tool for providing information to inform instruction. She notes that the CAP reflects changes in reading growth during the first year of formal instruction but is less useful thereafter for children making average progress. She also states that items assessing the ability to detect changes in letter or word order are particularly sensitive to changes in reading development, but no data are provided to support that contention. The handbook includes a blank summary sheet for the entire *Observation Survey* and a completed summary sheet for a child aged 6-1, who took the survey in August and answered 10 of the 24 CAP items correctly for a stanine score of 1, based on the New Zealand norms. According to the test administration date and birth date on the sheet, the child's age should be 6-3, not 6-1, although this does not alter the stanine score. The section allotted for the CAP includes a brief narrative indicating mastery of six print and letter concepts, so it is difficult to determine precisely which items the child answered correctly. Side 2 of the summary sheet is to be used to analyze the child's useful and problematic "strategic activities" (i.e., reading strategies), organized according to three print levels: text, words, and letters. The analysis completed for the same case example is difficult to follow and includes vague comments such as "Chris controls early reading behaviours" (p. 131).

Technical Adequacy

Information in this section is drawn from the current and previous versions of the handbook (Clay, 1993a, 2002).

Norms

Comparative norms are provided in the form of stanine scores for a sample of New Zealand children and a sample of children from Ohio. The New Zealand norms are based on 796 children aged 5-0 to 7-0 from 199 schools selected by the research division of the Ministry of Education. Children were drawn randomly from the 5-to-7 age group (4 examinees per school) and given the entire *Observation Survey* by 35 Reading Recovery tutors and trainers. The handbook states that the schools constituted a representative sample of schools across the country, but no other details are provided regarding sample characteristics. Results were reviewed and collated by Reading Recovery trainers at the Auckland College of Education. Stanine scores for the CAP, four other *Observation Survey* tasks, and a research-based word reading test (Duncan & McNaughton, 2001) are provided for four age group intervals: 5.00 to 5.50, 5.51 to 6.00, 6.01 to 6.50, and 6.51 to 7.00, with interval sizes ranging from 170 to 230. The norms tables include the score range, mean, standard deviation, and standard error of estimate per task. An appendix provides graphs of score distributions and box-and-whisker plots by age group for the five *Observation Survey* tasks and age group profiles with percentile ranks and stanines for the five tasks and the word reading test.

The handbook also reports norms for a 1990–1991 Ohio sample of 106 urban first graders (ages not specified), with stanine scores for fall, midyear, and spring (*ns* = 106, 73, and 109, respectively). According to the previous edition of the handbook, fall and spring scores were averaged to obtain midyear scores, but there is no mention of this in the current handbook, nor is there any other information about the characteristics of the sample. According to the CAP's author, these norms were included at the request of the North American Reading Recovery Trainers' Group, pending publication of new normative data for the United States. Practitioners who are considering using the norms in the handbook should be aware that raw score-stanine score relationships vary somewhat from the New Zealand to the Ohio sample. For example, for a child aged 6-5 tested in the fall, a raw score of 11 yields a stanine score of 1 based on the New Zealand sample but a stanine score of 3 based on the Ohio sample.

Reliability Evidence

CAP reliability evidence is reported for six studies, four of which are at least 20 years old and one of which is not listed in the references in either version of the handbook. Split-half reliability estimates were .95 and .85 for two samples (Clay, 1966, 1968) of New Zealand children (*ns* = 40 and 100, respectively). For 56 kindergarten children in Texas tested in 1978 (Day & Day, 1984), corrected split-half coefficients ranged from .84 to .88. A coefficient alpha of .78 is reported for 106 Ohio urban children tested in 1990 in the fall of first grade (Pinnell, McCarrier, & Button, 1990). Test–retest reliability for the Texas sample ranged from .73 to .89. No evidence is presented regarding alternate-form equivalency of the four versions of the picture book. Similarly, no estimates of interscorer reliability are provided, despite the considerable amount of judgment required for evaluating many of the responses and the general vulnerability of print awareness tasks to examiner variance (Johns, 1980).

Test Floors and Item Gradients

The CAP displays floor effects at the lowest age range and ceiling effects at the highest age range for both sets of norms. Item gradients are also steep at the extremes of the age range.

Validity Evidence

CONTENT VALIDITY EVIDENCE

The 2002 handbook includes a brief rationale for the content of the *Observation Survey*. According to the author, each of the five tasks assesses aspects of literacy knowledge that provide a foundation for progress in reading and writing and represent what is taught in the classroom.

CRITERION-RELATED VALIDITY EVIDENCE

Data relating to the CAP in a brief section on concurrent validity are drawn from the author's original dissertation (Clay, 1966). In that study with 100 New Zealand children aged 6-0, CAP scores were highly correlated with scores on the *Observation Survey* Word Reading task (r = .79). In a subsequent longitudinal study (Clay, 1985) with the 83 children who remained in the same school, CAP scores at age 6 were strong predictors of scores on two New Zealand standardized word reading tests administered 1 and 2 years later (*rs* = .64 to .73). The CAP was a better predictor of word reading than the *Metropolitan Readiness Tests* or the *Stanford–Binet Intelligence Scale* (*rs* = .43 to .54), but a less effective predictor than the *Observation Survey* Word Reading and Letter Identification tasks and error rate in contextual oral reading (*rs* = .77 to .86).

CONSTRUCT VALIDITY EVIDENCE

Intercorrelations among *Observation Survey* tasks and the *Duncan Word Reading Test* are reported by age group and for the entire New Zealand sample. The CAP is moderately to highly correlated with the other tasks (.56 to .75), with correlations slightly lower for the oldest age group. The handbook also reports correlations for four CAP subscores with the total CAP score for a sample of children (age and number unspecified) described only as "school entrants." Correlations between subscores and total score were high for knowledge of "how reading is carried out" (.93), concepts about print (.84), and punctuation (.68), but low for "attention to sequences of letters in words" (.33). The author states that the low correlations for the letter sequence subscore were expected because these items discriminate among older, higher scoring children, but the items constituting the subscores are not identified.

Usability

The CAP takes practice to administer quickly and smoothly, and young children, especially those with attentional problems, often have difficulty waiting while the examiner asks questions. As Hartley and Quine (1982) have observed, children may answer some items incorrectly, especially the items requiring them to notice inverted lines and pictures, because they do not fully understand the nature of the task and are not specifically directed to look at the print. Although the books *Stone* and *Sand* use a limited-color palate, the children portrayed are clearly of European origin. The two alternative books, *Follow Me, Moon* and *No Shoes*, are in full color and present more diverse-looking children. Spanish versions of the *Observation Survey* and two picture books are also available.

Links to Intervention

The *Observation Survey* procedures constitute the assessment component of Reading Recovery (Clay, 1993b)—an early intervention program that targets the lowest performing 20% of first graders and provides them with daily individual reading instruction for 30–40 minutes daily with specially trained teachers for 12–20 weeks. Although Clay and others have reported impressive gains for children receiving Reading Recovery (e.g., Askew, Fountas, Lyons, Pinnell, & Schmitt, 1998; Clay, 1985), the program has been criticized for its lack of emphasis on phonological processing skills (Iversen & Tunmer, 1993) and limited effectiveness with a sizeable proportion of at-risk readers in some studies (Center, Wheldall, Freeman, Outhred, & McNaught, 1995; Chapman, Tunmer, & Prochnow, 2001). Although the *Observation Survey* handbook includes a chapter on assisting children who are making slow reading progress, it is general rather than specific in nature and emphasizes paying attention to the strategies children use in reading rather than designing interventions based on scores on *Observation Survey* tasks. Another chapter, entitled "The Teacher and the Observations," includes a discussion of the importance of early intervention, especially the use of individual rather than group instruction for low-achieving children, and a brief review of the Reading Recovery model of intervention.

Relevant Research

Although many investigators have administered abbreviated or otherwise modified versions of the CAP in reading prediction and intervention studies, only studies using the original CAP are discussed here. Johns (1980) reported that the CAP significantly differentiated among above average, average, and below average readers in a sample of 60 first graders tested at the end of the school year. Item analyses revealed that the major differences between above average and below average readers were on items assessing letter–word and advanced print concepts, whereas items assessing book orientation and print directionality showed ceiling effects. In a longitudinal study (Day & Day, 1984) with 56 children who took the CAP three times in kindergarten and twice in first grade, the CAP was a moderate to strong predictor of reading achievement in first through fourth grade (*rs* = .45 to .87). Kindergarten CAP scores were highly correlated (.74) with Grade 4 *Iowa Tests of Basic Skills* (ITBS) scores, and Grade 1 CAP scores were significant predictors of ITBS scores in Grades 1, 3, and 4, even when mental age scores were partialed out (*rs* = .32 to .73). In a subsequent study with 60 kindergarten children, Day and Day (1991) evaluated the concurrent validity of the CAP and three other tests of metalinguistic awareness: the *Written Language Awareness Test* (Taylor & Blum, 1980), the *Test of Early Reading Ability* (Reid, Hresko & Hammill, 1981), and the *Linguistic Awareness in Reading Readiness Test* (Downing, Ayers, & Schaefer, 1983). Correlations between the CAP and the other instruments were generally in the moderate range (.53 to .65).

More recent studies evaluating the CAP's predictive utility have yielded mixed results. In a study with 118 Australian children (Tunmer, Herriman, & Nesdale, 1988), beginning-of-first-grade CAP performance was the best predictor of pseudoword decoding and reading comprehension measured at the end of second grade (*rs* = .52 and .53, respectively) for a set of six measures that included a phonemic segmentation task and the *Peabody Picture Vocabulary Test*. In a more recent study (Stuart, 1995) with 30 British children tested in the fall of their first year in school (mean age = 4-9), CAP scores significantly predicted end-of-year word recognition on the *British Ability Scales* Single Word Reading test, even with prior reading skills controlled (*r* = .49). Moreover, CAP successfully classified 22 of 30 children into above or below average reading groups. In contrast, Iversen and Tunmer (1993) reported that CAP performance measured at the end of an intervention program for 160 at-risk first graders did not contribute to the prediction of word recognition, pseudoword decoding, or reading text level measured at the end of the school year.

Source and Cost

Procedures for administering the CAP are contained in the author's book, *An Observation Survey of Early Literacy Achievement* (2nd ed.; Clay, 2002), available from Heinemann for $26.00. The *Sand* and *Stone* booklets are $7.50 each, and the alternative booklets (*Follow Me, Moon* and *No Shoes*) are $8.50 each. A copymaster book with reproducible recording forms and summary sheets for the CAP and other *Observation Survey* tasks is $10.00. A 32-page paperback, *Concepts About Print: What Have Children Learned about the Way We Print Language?* (Clay, 2000a) that describes the CAP, reproduces the directions for the first two CAP books, and includes directions for the two new books, is $13.00. A 60-minute training video (2000) that demonstrates the entire observation battery is $99.00. The Spanish version of the *Observation Survey* (*Instrumento de Observación de los Logros de la Lecto-Escritura Inicial* (Escamilla, Andrade, Basurto, Ruiz, & Clay, 1995) is $24.00, and two Spanish equivalents of *Sand* and *Stone* are $7.50 each.

Test Reviews

Goodman, Y. M. (1981). Test review: Concepts about print test. *The Reading Teacher, 34*, 445–448.

Hartley, D. N., & Quine, P. G. (1982). A critical appraisal of Marie Clay's "Concepts About Print test." *Reading, 16*, 109–112.

Summary

Concepts About Print (CAP) is an individually administered, standardized measure of print awareness for children in kindergarten and first grade. One of thc tasks in Marie Clay's *Observation Survey of Early Literacy Achievement*, the assessment tool in the Reading Recovery intervention program, it has been widely used in reading prediction, diagnostic, and intervention studies. Like most other print awareness measures, the CAP is time-consuming to administer and highly susceptible to interexaminer variance. The handbook containing the CAP is now in its second edition, but administration and scoring procedures for several items continue to need clarification. Reliability and validity evidence is limited, outdated, or both, and there is no evidence of interscorer reliability, even in the current edition. Research provides some support for CAP's utility in distinguishing poor and proficient readers and predicting reading achievement, with predictive power greatest in kindergarten and with low-performing first graders because of ceiling effects. CAP performance for American students should be interpreted based on local norms because no recent standardization samples of adequate size are available for children in the United States.

Case Example

Name of student: Marcellus B.
Age: 6 years, 6 months
Grade: First grade
Date of assessment: September

Reason for referral: Marcellus was referred for an early reading assessment by his first-grade teacher. Marcellus recently transferred to the school and is struggling to keep up with the pace of classroom instruction. He often looks confused during reading lessons, is having trouble acquiring phonics skills and sight word vocabulary, and needs constant individual attention to complete his work.

Assessment results and interpretation: *Concepts About Print* (CAP) is an assessment task that measures children's understanding of various print conventions and mechanics. The examiner reads a short picture book to the child and asks the child to point out certain features of print during the reading process. Marcellus answered 8 of the 24 CAP items correctly. His performance is considerably lower than that of the typical child in his classroom (average of 18/24 items correct). He has mastered book orientation and print directionality, but he did not understand the concept of first and last lines on a page of text. He was unable to point out changes in word and letter order, to match uppercase with lowercase letters, or to point out any words. Moreover, he has not learned the concept of a word, letter, or punctuation mark. Asked to point out one letter, he showed a period; asked to show a word, he showed two letters. He also did not understand the concept of a capital letter. Overall, his print awareness skills are quite delayed for his grade placement.

Measures of Alphabet Knowledge

No stand-alone measure of alphabet knowledge is included in this book. All of the early reading assessment batteries in Chapter 4 include measures of letter-name and/or letter-sound knowledge. In addition, alphabet knowledge measures are included in the *Consortium on Reading Excellence Phonics Survey*, the *Dyslexia Early Screening Test*, the *Phonological Abilities Test*, the *Phonological Awareness Test*, the *Predictive Reading Profile*, the *Process Assessment of the Learner: Test Battery for Reading and Writing*, the *Test of Early Reading Ability–3*, the *Wechsler Individual Achievement Test–II*, the *Woodcock Reading Mastery Tests–Revised/Normative Update*, and the *Woodcock–Johnson III*.

Measures of Single Word Reading

This section reviews one standardized measure of single word reading. Additional single word reading measures or measures with word reading items can be found in all of the early reading assessment batteries reviewed in Chapter 4 and in the following instruments: the *Consortium on Reading Excellence Phonics Survey*, the *Dyslexia Screening Test*, the *Exception Word Reading Test*, the *Illinois Test of Psycholinguistic Abilities–3*, the *Kaufman Survey of Early Academic and Language Skills*, the *Phonological Abilities Test*, the *Phonological Awareness Test*, the *Predictive Reading Profile*, the *Process Assessment of the Learner–Reading and Writing*, the *Standardized Reading Inventory–2*, the *Wechsler Individual Achievement Test–II*, the *Woodcock Reading Mastery Tests–Revised/Normative Update*, and the *Woodcock–Johnson III*.

TEST OF WORD READING EFFICIENCY

Overview

The *Test of Word Reading Efficiency* (TOWRE; Torgesen, Wagner, & Rashotte, 1999) is an individually administered, norm-referenced measure of word reading accuracy and fluency for examinees aged 6-0 through 24-11 years. Developed by a leading team of reading researchers with support from the National Institute of Child Health and Human Development, the TOWRE is the only currently available standardized test that assesses both single real word reading fluency and pseudoword reading fluency. The TOWRE has two equivalent forms for measuring both types of reading fluency. According to the test's authors, measuring both fluency and accuracy in word reading skills is important because fluency problems can occur independently of accuracy problems and because difficulties in rapid word recognition are associated with reading problems in children and adults. The uses of the TOWRE identified in the manual are (1) to monitor growth in sight word and phonemic decoding efficiency in early elementary grade children, (2) to identify children in need of additional instruction in word reading skills, (3) to serve as a test of context-free word reading in a battery for diagnosing specific reading disabilities in older children and adults, and (4) to serve as an instrument for research applications. Test materials include a spiral-bound examiner's manual, two Sight Word Efficiency subtest reading cards (Forms A and B), two Phonemic Decoding Efficiency subtest reading cards (Forms A and B), and 25 profile/examiner record booklets per form, all packed in a storage box.

Subtests and Composite

Subtests

The TOWRE consists of two subtests, each with two alternate forms (see Table 5.24). When the TOWRE is used to monitor early reading acquisition, the authors recommend administering one form at each testing to reduce practice effects. When the TOWRE is used as part of a diagnostic battery for determining eligibility for special education services, the authors recommend administering both forms and averaging scores on the two forms to improve reliability.

Composite

Standard scores from the Sight Word Efficiency and Phonemic Decoding Efficiency subtests can be summed to yield a Total Word Reading Efficiency composite.

Administration

The TOWRE can be administered in about 5 minutes if one form is used and in 8–10 minutes if both forms are used. A set of practice items is administered prior to each list. The examiner sits beside the child during testing to follow responses if words are skipped. If the child pauses for 3 seconds, the examiner prompts the child to go on to the next item. Accurate scoring, which must be done during the administration process, is very challenging, especially on the Phonemic Decoding Efficiency (PDE) subtest. In addition to the challenges involved in scoring any measure of pseudoword fluency, scoring consistency is compromised by the fact that the PDE item list is split between two pages in the record booklet, so that the examiner must turn the page while the child continues to read. Moreover, although the test's authors emphasize the most common pronunciations for consonant–vowel sequences (e.g., *bave* rhymes with *save* rather than with *have*), many PDE items have more than one acceptable pronunciation. Of the 63 PDE items, 16 on Form A and 14 on Form B have more than

TABLE 5.24. Description of the TOWRE Subtests

Subtest	Description
Sight Word Efficiency	The child reads as many real words printed on a card as possible within 45 seconds.
Phonemic Decoding Efficiency	The child reads as many pseudowords printed on a card as possible within 45 seconds.

one acceptable pronunciation, and 3 words on Form A and 1 word on Form B have six acceptable pronunciations! Acceptable pronunciation alternatives for vowels are shown in the form of real words to the right of the PDE word list on the record booklet. For multisyllable items, real word examples for acceptable vowel pronunciations are provided for each syllable. A table in the manual also provides phonetic transcriptions for pseudowords on both forms. Examiners must be thoroughly familiar with all of the acceptable pronunciations for each item, so that they can evaluate the accuracy of the responses as children rapidly read down the list. I recommend that examiners familiarize themselves with the response alternatives before an actual administration by reciting the list for each form aloud several times, with additional oral practice on items with multiple pronunciations, and that they audiotape examinee responses to verify scoring accuracy for the first three or four administrations. The use of a stopwatch or timing device with an audible signal is also recommended to avoid having to keep glancing at a timepiece.

Scores

Scoring takes less than 5 minutes. The raw score for each subtest is the total number of items read correctly in 45 seconds. Subtest and total test scores can be converted into standard scores ($M = 100$, $SD = 15$), percentile ranks, grade equivalents, and age equivalents, termed "reading efficiency ages." Age norms are in 6-month increments for ages 6-0 through 8-11 and in 1-year increments for ages 9-0 through 24-11. Grade norms are in semester increments (i.e., 5-month intervals) for Grades 1 through 3 and in 10-month increments for Grades 4 through 12.

Interpretation

Based on their longitudinal studies of children's reading growth, the TOWRE's authors state that scores falling below the 30th percentile on either subtest indicate an increased risk for reading problems and the need for intervention. The authors offer several cautions regarding interpretation. First, the grade-based standard scores are less accurate than the age-based standard scores because of smoothing and extrapolation. Although the authors do not indicate the direction or degree of those inaccuracies, the case example of an 8-year-old second grader provided in the manual serves as an illustration. If grade-based rather than age-based norms are used, the obtained standard scores would be 8–15 points higher. Specifically, the SWE standard score would increase from 88 to 103 (from the 21st to the 58th percentile [PR]), the PDE standard score would increase from 80 to 88 (from the 9th to the 21st PR), and the Total Word Reading Efficiency standard score would increase from 81 to 95 (from the 10th to the 36th PR), changing the examinee's status from at risk to not at risk (i.e., scores at or above the 30th PR) on two of the three measures.

Second, the authors point out that floor effects are evident on both subtests for children in the first semester of first grade, with grade-based scores of 0 or 1 yielding standard scores in the low average or average range. Unfortunately, floor effects extend beyond the first-grade level and apply to age norms as well (see below). Third, because of the limited range of words at early primary grade levels, first- and second-grade children may be able to earn an average SWE score through rote memorization of words, despite obtaining a poor PDE score. As a result, children in the early elementary grades who obtain low PDE scores, regardless of their SWE performance, may be at risk and should receive additional instruction in phonemic decoding. In addition, TOWRE scores for first graders may reflect accuracy rather than speed because children often run out of words they can read before the 45 seconds have elapsed and thus are likely to be highly similar to scores obtained on untimed word reading measures.

The manual includes a section on conducting discrepancy analyses with TOWRE scores and provides tables listing the minimal differences between TOWRE subtest and composite standard scores for the two forms for statistical significance and clinical utility. The authors use Reynolds's (1990) formula for identifying a severe discrepancy to calculate "truly unusual" differences between scores on TOWRE subtests, with an unusual difference defined as one expected to occur less than 5 times in 100. Included is a case example of an examinee aged 8-11 in the first semester of second grade, but it is used chiefly to demonstrate how to complete the front of the record booklet and calculate scores and score differences. All of the case example's TOWRE subtest and composite scores fall in the below average range and below the cutoff score, with no statistically significant or clinically useful differences. Scores for the *Comprehensive Test of Nonverbal Intelligence* are entered on the protocol sheet but are not discussed. The manual include a useful section entitled "What TOWRE Scores Mean," which reviews factors that can influence scores, the instructional implications of low scores, and the role of speed versus accuracy in examinee performance.

Technical Adequacy

Standardization

The TOWRE was normed in 1997 and 1998 on 1,507 individuals ranging in age from 6 to 24 years living in 30 states, with more than half of the standardization sample drawn from Grades 1 through 5. Sample characteristics are reported in terms of geographic region, gender, race, ethnicity, residence (urban vs. rural), family income, parent education, and disability status, with characteristics (except for disability status) stratified by six age intervals (excluding ages 18 through 24) and keyed to 1997 U.S. census data. The TOWRE sample appears to be generally representative of the 1997 U.S. population, except for the geographical distribution of adults, which is mostly drawn from the South. Subgroup sizes range from 77 to 155, with fewer examinees at older age intervals. Between 140 and 155 examinees were tested at each age level in the primary grade range, but because norms are in 6-month increments for ages 6 through 8 and 5-month increments for Grades 1 through 3, scores for examinees of those ages are based on only about 70–78 examinees per interval, which is below the criterion level.

Reliability Evidence

Internal consistency reliabilities using an alternate-form reliability procedure for each subtest and the total score range from .86 to .98 for 13 age intervals, with all coefficients for the early primary grade range exceeding .93. Alternate-form reliability coefficients for eight subgroups in the normative sample, including students with learning disabilities and speech–language handicaps, are also in the .90s, although reliabilities are not reported separately by age. Based on a comparison of means and standard deviations, as well as correlation coefficients for Forms A and B at 13 age intervals, the authors argue that the forms are equivalent and that a combined normative table is appropriate. Correlations between Form A and Form B are slightly higher at the lower age ranges (.93 to .97 for ages 6 to 9) than for older examinees (.86 to .95 for ages 10 to adult). Test–retest reliabilities for a sample of 72 individuals reported for three age intervals and total sample (2-week interval between Forms A and B) ranged from .82 to .96. Stability for the 6- to 9-year-old group (n = 29) ranged from .90 to .97 for both subtests and for the total test.

Interscorer differences based on independent scoring of 30 completed protocols by two staff persons in PRO-ED's research department were .99 for both subtests and total tests. These correlations provide little meaningful information about scorer consistency, however, because they are based on protocols with responses that had already been marked for accuracy. Given the threats to scoring consistency *during* administration, especially on the PDE subtest, interscorer agreement should be calculated for several examiners who simultaneously score a set of protocols for examinees at various age intervals during live administrations or audiotaped testing sessions.

Test Floors and Item Gradients

For age-based norms, floors for the SWE subtest are inadequate below 7-6. For example, a child aged 6-0 who obtains a raw score of 1 on SWE receives a standard score of 90. PDE floors are inadequate throughout the early primary grade range (i.e., below age 9-0). Practitioners should note that children aged 6-0 to 6-5 cannot obtain a PDE score that falls below the suggested cutoff (i.e., at or below the 29th percentile), even if they obtain a raw score of 0. For example, a child aged 6-0 with a PDE raw score of 1 obtains a standard score of 98. Test floors for the Total Word Reading Efficiency composite are inadequate below age 7-0. Floors for grade-based norms are also inadequate at the lower ranges of the test. A child in the second month of first grade with a raw score of 1 on SWE receives a standard score of 87; a PDE raw score of 1 for a child at the same grade level yields a standard score of 97. Floors for grade norms are not adequate until the first semester of Grade 2 for SWE and the second semester of Grade 3 for PDE, and floors for the composite are inadequate below Grade 2. Because of these floor effects, potential users should evaluate test floors and item gradients simultaneously. For example, although the SWE subtest has 12 items between the floor and the mean for the 6-0 to 6-5 age range, the floor at that level is a standard score of 90.

Validity Evidence

CONTENT VALIDITY EVIDENCE

Words on the SWE subtest were drawn primarily from *The Reading Teacher's Book of Lists* (Fry, Kress, & Fountoukidis, 1993) and decrease in frequency as the lists progress. PDE items were designed to sample a broad range of grapheme–phoneme correspondences of increasing difficulty, with word order based on data from the standardization sample whenever possible. Median item difficulties for SWE are at the low end of acceptability for age 6 (.15 for both forms), and below the acceptable lower limit for PDE for both forms (.08 and .07 for Forms A and B, respectively), indicating that the subtest is too difficult for most children at that age. Item discrimination coefficients range from .40 at the upper age limits of the test to the .70s at age 6. According to DIF analyses using logistic regression procedures for four dichotomous groups (males vs. females, European Americans vs. all others, African Americans vs. all others, and Hispanic Americans vs. all others), group membership did not significantly influence item performance for the majority of the 334 items (3% or fewer).

CRITERION-RELATED VALIDITY EVIDENCE

Correlations with other reading measures reported in the manual indicate that in the early elementary grades, skills measured by the TOWRE are virtually identical to those assessed by untimed single word reading tests. In a study with 145 first graders, correlations between end-of-first-grade scores on PDE and *Woodcock Reading Mastery Tests–Revised* (WRMT-R) Word Attack and between SWE and WRMT-R Word Identification were .85 and .89, respectively. Similarly, in a study with 125 first-, second-, and third-grade children at risk for reading failure, correlations between PDE and WRMT-R Word Attack scores ranged from .89 to .91 and from .92 to .94 for SWE and WRMT-R Word Identification. No predictive validity evidence based on longitudinal studies is reported. Instead, the authors assert that the TOWRE is a better predictor of reading fluency than are traditional untimed measures of word reading by comparing correlations between the TOWRE and WRMT-R and scores on the *Gray Oral Reading Tests–Third Edition* (GORT-3). In a sample of fourth and fifth graders with severe reading disabilities (Torgesen, Wagner, Rashotte, Burgess, et al., 1997; Wagner et al., 1997), SWE and WRMT-R Word Identification were equally strongly related to GORT-3 Accuracy and Comprehension (both .80 and .75, respectively), but SWE was more strongly related to GORT-3 Rate than was WRMT-R Word Identification (.80 vs. .73). Similarly, PDE was more strongly related than WRMT-R Word Attack to GORT-3 Accuracy (.68 vs. .46) and GORT-3 Comprehension (.62 vs. .41).

CONSTRUCT VALIDITY EVIDENCE

TOWRE means increase with age, as expected, with the largest score increase from age 6 to 7. At age 6, however, the standard deviations are larger than the means for both subtests and across forms, indicating imprecise measurement at that age. Of eight subgroups in the normative sample (males, females, European Americans, African Americans, Hispanic Americans, Asian Americans, examinees with speech/language handicaps, and examinees with learning disabilities), the learning-disabled examinees obtained the lowest subtest and total test scores, as expected (SSs = 81.9 to 85.1), but no information is provided regarding the performance of examinees with reading disabilities. Subtest and total test intercorrelations range from .77 to .96. Confirmatory factor analysis supported a two-component model of word reading efficiency, with one component involving rapid recognition of whole words and the second involving rapid phonemic decoding processes. Additional evidence of construct validity comes from a remediation study (Torgesen, Wagner, Rashotte, Rose, et al., 1999) in which a group of severely reading-disabled children (number and grade not specified) received 8 weeks of intensive one-to-one instruction. Despite large gains in GORT-3 Accuracy scores, the children showed very little growth in fluency, as measured by GORT-3 Rate scores. Although WRMT-R Word Identification and Word Attack scores reflected the improvements in accuracy observed on the GORT-3, TOWRE subtest scores showed very small differences at posttest and 1-year follow-up. According to the authors, this indicates that TOWRE was more sensitive to changes in fluency (or rather, to the lack of fluency improvement) than the WRMT-R.

Usability

The TOWRE is quick to administer, relatively inexpensive, and portable. The spiral-bound test manual earns a high usability rating for its attractive format, excellent organization, and high level of readability. Achieving scoring consistency for the TOWRE, especially for the PDE, takes time, effort, and practice. As noted above, the record booklet should be reformatted so that all of the PDE items appear on the same page.

Links to Intervention

The authors caution that the test is designed to evaluate word reading efficiency rather than to provide detailed information for instruction. As noted above, they recommend that children scoring below the 30th percentile on either subtest or on the composite score receive additional instruction targeting phonemic awareness, knowledge of grapheme–phoneme relationships, and blending, along with additional opportunities for reading and writing. The manual includes a useful section on the instructional implications of low scores on each subtest, but no specific programs or remedial strategies are cited.

Relevant Research

Several recent studies provide empirical support for the concurrent and predictive validity of the TOWRE. In a sample of 106 children in Grades 1 through 6 with reading and/or writing problems (Berninger, Abbott, Thomson, & Raskind, 2001) using a prepublication version of the TOWRE and a large number of other reading and reading-related measures, PDE and SWE performance was strongly related to contextual reading rate, as measured by the GORT-3 (*r*s = .58 and .75, respectively). SWE was also strongly related to *Woodcock Johnson Psycho-Educational Battery–Revised* (WJ-R) Word Identification (.79) and Passage Comprehension (.66), whereas PDE scores were most strongly correlated with WJ-R Word Attack and Word Identification (.60 and .57). In a further analysis of treatment outcomes with 60 severely reading-disabled children aged 8 to 10 who received 8 weeks of one-to-one instruction (see above), Torgesen, Alexander, and their colleagues (2001) reported that SWE performance measured at the end of the intervention was the best predictor of GORT-3 Rate at the end of the 2-year follow-up period. In a review of five investigations (Torgesen, Rashotte, et al., 2001)–including two remediation studies, two prevention studies, and a longitudinal study that followed 201 children from kindergarten through fifth grade–SWE was the best predictor or was tied for the best predictor of GORT-3 Rate. In contrast, PDE was a nonsignificant or very weak independent predictor of individual differences in contextual reading rate (2% of the variance or less).

Source and Cost

The TOWRE is available from PRO-ED for $123.00.

Test Reviews

Tindal, G. (2003). Review of the Test of Word Reading Efficiency. In B. S. Plake, J. C. Impara, & R. A. Spies (Eds.), *The fifteenth mental measurements yearbook* (pp. 960–963). Lincoln, NE: Buros Institute of Mental Measurements.

Vacca, J. J. (2003). Review of the Test of Word Reading Efficiency. In B. S. Plake, J. C. Impara, & R. A. Spies (Eds.), *The fifteenth mental measurements yearbook* (pp. 963–965). Lincoln, NE: Buros Institute of Mental Measurements.

Summary

The *Test of Word Reading Efficiency* (TOWRE) is an individually administered, norm-referenced measure of reading fluency for isolated real words and pseudowords for individuals ages 6 through 24. Developed by a leading team of reading researchers, the TOWRE is a moderate to strong predictor of concurrent and future reading proficiency, especially contextual reading rate. Unfortunately, its utility as a screening, progress monitoring, or diagnostic measure for early primary grade children is limited by inadequate floors for both age and grade norms at the lower ranges of the test. Moreover, scoring consistency remains uncertain because interscorer reliability estimates are based on completed protocols rather than on independent scoring of the responses of the same set of examinees during the administration process. As the test's authors acknowledge, TOWRE scores reflect accuracy rather than fluency in the early grades, and it is difficult to see what additional information it lends to a screening or diagnostic battery for children in kindergarten through second grade in its current form.

Case Example

Name of student: Andre M.
Age: 8 years, 1 month
Grade: Second grade
Date of assessment: January

Reason for referral: Andre was referred for an early reading assessment by his second-grade teacher because of problems with decoding, oral reading, and comprehension. Andre was retained in first grade and has been receiving assistance from the reading specialist, but he continues to struggle. He is able to answer comprehension questions when they are presented orally, but he has great difficulty responding to comprehension questions when he must read the text for himself. In addition, his oral reading is slow and characterized by many errors.

Assessment results and interpretation: The *Test of Word Reading Efficiency* (TOWRE) requires the child to read lists of real words and pseudowords (e.g., *taff*) as rapidly as possible. Pseudoword items are included to help differentiate children who are able to apply letter-sound knowledge in decoding words from those who may be relying excessively on memory or context. Deficits in word reading fluency are associated with reading disabilities and interfere with reading comprehension. Average scores for an individual Andre's age are as follows: Standard Score [SS] = 100, Percentile Rank [PR] = 50, Age Equivalent [AE] = 8-1, Grade Equivalent [GE] = 2.6. The scores reported below are based on the averaged scores from the administration of both forms of the TOWRE. On the TOWRE, scores below the 30th percentile on either subtest or on the total test indicate an increased risk for reading problems and a need for special interventions targeting word reading skills.

Composite/Subtest	SS	PR	AE	GE
Total Word Reading Efficiency	86	17	–	–
Sight Word Efficiency	94	35	8-0	2.6
Phonemic Decoding Efficiency	82	12	6-9	1.6

Compared with other students his age, Andre's overall fluency for single word reading is rated as below average (17th PR), but his word reading efficiency varies depending on whether he is reading real words or pseudowords. On the Sight Word Efficiency subtest, which requires the child to read as many sight words as possible in 45 seconds, he scored in the average range (35th PR). In contrast, his ability to pronounce decodable pseudowords, as measured by the Phonemic Decoding Efficiency subtest, is less well developed (12th PR, low average range). Both his overall test score and his Phonemic Decoding Efficiency score fall below the 30th percentile, indicating an increased risk for reading problems.

An inspection of Andre's errors on the Phonemic Decoding Efficiency subtest reveals his lack of automaticity for numerous letter-sound correspondences, even for words with only two or three sounds. He had trouble reading consonant–vowel sequences (e.g., *mo, na*) and often confused short vowel sounds, especially /i/ and /e/. He also does not appear to have mastered long vowel sounds, as in consonant–vowel–consonant–silent *e* combinations (e.g., *bace* for *bice*).

MEASURES OF ORAL READING IN CONTEXT

This section includes reviews of three measures of contextual oral reading, two nonstandardized and one standardized. Additional timed and untimed measures of oral reading in context are included in the *Basic Early Assessment of Reading*, the *Dynamic Indicators of Basic Early Literacy Skills*, the *Dyslexia Screening Test*, the *Early Reading Diagnostic Assessment–Revised*, the *Fox in a Box*, the *Gray Oral Reading Tests–3*, the *Phonological Awareness Literacy Screening*, the *Standardized Reading Inventory–2*, the *Texas Primary Reading Inventory*, the *Wechsler Individual Achievement Test–II*, and the *Woodcock–Johnson III*.

CURRICULUM-BASED MEASUREMENT OF ORAL READING FLUENCY

Overview

Curriculum-based measurement (CBM) is a set of individually administered, standardized procedures designed to assess basic skills in reading, mathematics, writing, and spelling. Developed by Stanley Deno and his colleagues (e.g., Deno, 1985; Fuchs & Fuchs, 1999; Shinn, 1989), CBM uses brief, repeated fluency measures derived from the instructional curriculum or comparable material. CBM oral reading procedures, called *oral reading probes*, involve counting the number of correct words while a child reads aloud for 1 minute from a passage. Because CBM oral reading probes can have many alternate forms, fluency can be measured frequently and the results displayed graphically to monitor progress. A separate review of CBM in oral reading fluency is provided here because many early reading assessment batteries and large-scale reading screening programs now include CBM-type procedures. The purposes of CBM oral reading probes include (1) early identification of children at risk for reading problems, (2) instructional planning, (3) progress monitoring, and (4) evaluation of the effectiveness of reading interventions and instructional programs. Traditionally, materials for conducting CBM in reading have been drawn from the examinee's classroom curriculum. To construct oral reading probes, the examiner first selects three passages from the book or set of materials in which the child is currently being instructed: one from the beginning, the one from the middle, and one from the end. Then the examiner photocopies two copies of each passage, one for the child to read and the other to score. Passages from preprimer- and primer-level material should be about 60 words, and passages for Grades 1 through 3 should be about 70–150 words in length. Examiners wishing to assess comprehension can prepare five to eight comprehension questions for each passage or for a selected passage. Commercially published and state-sponsored oral reading fluency measures typically provide at least one generic (i.e., curriculum-free) passage per level or grade, complete with comprehension questions.

Assessment Task

In traditional CBM-type procedures, the child reads the three selected passages in turn aloud as rapidly as possible for 1 minute. When comprehension is also assessed, the child is permitted to read the entire passage and then answers five to eight previously prepared comprehension questions for one or more of the three passages.

Administration

If passages have been taken from the child's classroom reading materials, the examiner should ask the child whether he or she has read the passages before. Although novel passages provide the most accurate assessment of reading competence, comparing the child's performance on instructed versus noninstructed material can provide useful information for planning the intensity of interventions. The examiner tells the child to read aloud as quickly and as well as possible for 1 minute and indicates that he or she will provide any words the child does not know. As the child reads, the examiner marks errors on the scoring copy of the passage. If the child pauses more than 3 seconds, the examiner provides the word. After 1 minute, the examiner tells the child to stop and places a line in the text to indicate the last word read. For comprehension assessments, the child reads the entire passage, and the examiner marks where the child is at the end of each 1-minute period. The child may look at the passage while answering the comprehension questions. For initial screenings, the examiner administers three passages from the book or set of materials in which the child is currently placed. For survey-level assessments, the examiner continues testing up or down in difficulty levels until the child's performance is commensurate with instructional placement standards (see Table 5.25 below) or is at an instructional level relative to local norms.

Scores

Each CBM oral reading probe yields up to three scores: (1) a words-read-correctly-per-minute (WCPM) score; (2) an error score; and (3) a comprehension score, if this option is used. Five kinds of fluency errors are recorded: (1) omissions, (2) substitutions, (3) mispronunciations, (4) additions, and (5) hesitations of more than 3 seconds. Repetition of words, self-corrections, and suffix deletions (e.g., omitting *ed* from *stopped*) are not counted as errors. Mispronunciations of proper nouns are counted as errors for the first occurrence but not subsequently. Comprehension questions are scored as correct or incorrect, and the percentage of questions answered correctly is the comprehension score for that probe. The WCPM score is calculated by subtracting the number of errors from the number of words read in 1 minute. If the child reads for more than 1 minute, as when comprehension questions are administered or when complete passages are used, WCPM is calculated by multiplying the total number of words read correctly by 60 and then dividing by the number of seconds needed to read the passage. The child's scores on that book or set of materials are median WCPM, median errors, and comprehension score (or median comprehension score, if questions are asked for each probe) for the three passages. Median rather than mean scores are used to control for the effects of difficulty and variability across passages. Although traditional CBM scoring procedures do not differentiate among the various kinds of errors, examiners can use more complex marking systems, so that errors can be analyzed in terms of types of decoding errors and other qualitative aspects of performance to provide information for intervention planning.

For progress monitoring, CBM scores can be displayed on a graph, with time indicated on the horizontal axis and WCPM on the vertical axis. The graph typically includes baseline performance (the results of the initial CBM), an *aim line* (the line of progress needed to reach the child's goal), and the WCPM scores obtained at each progress monitoring assessment, usually once or twice a week. The slope of the plotted data points can be evaluated to assess rate of change, either by visual inspection or statistical analysis, most commonly using the ordinary least squares regression method (Shinn, Good, & Stein, 1989).

Interpretation

CBM oral reading performance can be interpreted in terms of local (classroom, school, or district) norms or research-based norms or benchmarks. When classroom, grade, or school norms are available, the examinee's median WCPM can be compared with median scores for grade peers to determine whether a significant discrepancy exists. In Shinn's (1995, 1998) CBM-based problem-solving model, cutting scores are based on a discrepancy ratio calculated by dividing the grade peer median score by the median score of the referred student. Discrepancy ratios equal to or greater than 2.0 indicate that the child is performing at half the fluency rate (or less) of grade peers and should receive further assessment. When large numbers of students are tested, median scores can be converted to percentile ranks, and cutting scores falling below criterion levels (e.g., below the 20th percentile) can be used to determine the need for additional assessment. For interpreting the results of initial screenings, two sets of research norms are provided below. Table 5.25 displays a set of recommended WCPM rates for frustration, instructional, and mastery levels, and

TABLE 5.25. Instructional Placement Standards for Direct Reading Assessment

Grade level of materials	Reading level	Words read correctly per minute	Errors per minute	Comprehension (% correct)
1–2	Frustration	<40	>4	<80%
	Instructional	40–60	4 or fewer	80%
	Mastery	60	4 or fewer	80%
3–6	Frustration	<70	>6	<80%
	Instructional	70–100	6 or fewer	80%
	Mastery	>100	6 or fewer	80%

Note. Data from "Developing Goals and Objectives for Educational Programs [Teaching Guide]" by L. S. Fuchs and S. L. Deno, 1982, Minneapolis: U.S. Department of Education Grant. From *Academic Skills Problems: Direct Assessment and Intervention* (2nd ed.) by E. S. Shapiro, 1996, p. 116. Copyright 1996 by The Guilford Press. Adapted with permission.

Table 5.26 displays norms based on a large number of students and collected over nearly a 10-year period.

For setting instructional goals and evaluating progress, student performance can be interpreted in terms of average learning rates based on local or research norms. Table 5.27 presents estimated realistic and ambitious rates of weekly growth, based on CBM progress monitoring data collected over a 2-year period from 3,057 students, 374 of whom participated in reading assessments (Fuchs, Fuchs, Hamle, Walz, & Germann, 1993). Realistic standards reflect expected growth under typical instructional conditions. For example, with typical instruction, first graders can be expected to increase their oral reading fluency by about 2 words a week. Ambitious standards, set at 1 standard deviation above average weekly gains, may be appropriate for students who are receiving intensive interventions designed to decrease the discrepancy between their performance and that of their peers.

TABLE 5.26. Quartiles for Median Words Read Correctly Per Minute (WCPM) Averaged across Four to Eight Different School Districts

Grade	Quartile	Fall	Winter	Spring
	25	23	46	65
2	50	53	78	94
	75	82	106	124
	25	65	70	87
3	50	79	93	114
	75	107	123	142
	25	72	89	92
4	50	99	112	118
	75	125	133	143
	25	77	93	100
5	50	105	118	128
	75	126	143	151

Note. Data collected from 1981 to 1990 on 7,000–9,000 students in Grades 2–5 in five Midwestern and Western states. From "Curriculum-Based Oral Reading Fluency Norms for Students in Grades 2 Through 5" by J. E. Hasbrouck and G. Tindal, 1992, *Teaching Exceptional Children, 24*, p. 42. Copyright 1992 by the Council for Exceptional Children. Adapted with permission.

TABLE 5.27. Realistic and Ambitious Standards for Weekly Improvement in Words Read Correctly Per Minute (WCPM) across 1 Year for Primary Grade Children

	Realistic goals	Ambitious goals
Grade	WCPM	WCPM
1	2.0	3.0
2	1.5	2.0
3	1.0	1.5

Note. From "Formative Evaluation of Academic Progress: How Much Growth Can We Expect?" by L. S. Fuchs, D. Fuchs, C. L. Hamlett, L. Walz, and G. Germann, 1993, *School Psychology Review, 22,* p. 35. Copyright 1993 by the National Association of School Psychologists. Adapted with permission.

Technical Adequacy

Numerous studies have evaluated the psychometric characteristics of CBM in oral reading and its utility as a screening and progress monitoring procedure. Evidence of technical adequacy based on studies of children in the early primary grade range is summarized here rather than in a separate "Relevant Research" section.

Reliability Evidence

Surprisingly little research has examined the test–retest reliability of CBM reading with early primary grade children. Tindal, Marston, and Deno (1983) reported a test–retest reliability of .92 for 566 students in Grades 1–6 (10-week interval), but this estimate is inflated because it was computed across a broad grade span. Moreover, this degree of stability is surprising for so long a test–retest interval, considering that CBM is designed to be sensitive to small changes in fluency (Mehrens & Clarizio, 1993). In a study with 48 third graders, Hintze, Shapiro, and Lutz (1994) reported moderate to high parallel-form reliability coefficients for literature-based probes and traditional basal probes (*r*s = .56 to .96). In a larger study with 160 students from Grades 2 through 5, Hintze and Shapiro (1997) obtained similar parallel-form reliability estimates for literature-based and traditional basal series probes (.65 to .97). For trained raters, interrater reliability for CBM oral reading probes is consistently high. Percentage agreement based on independent scoring by trained raters of randomly selected audiotapes of CBM oral reading probes is typically above .90 and often at or above .98 (e.g., Bradley-Klug, Shapiro, Lutz, & DuPaul, 1998; Hintze et al., 1994; Hintze, Shapiro, Conte, & Basile, 1997; Noell, Freeland, Witt, & Gansle, 2001).

Studies using generalizability (G) theory procedures provide additional support for the reliability of CBM oral reading probes selected from both basal and literature-based reading series, although all of the investigations involved children in Grades 2 and above. In a study with 57 fourth graders, Kranzler, Brownell, and Miller (1998) reported a generalizability (G) coefficient (reflecting reliability for interindividual decisions) for number of words read correctly for six basal series reading probes of .98, and a dependability index (reflecting reliability for intraindividual decisions) of .97. In a larger study (Kranzler, Miller, & Jordan, 1999) with 326 students in Grades 2–5, G coefficients for six CBM basal probes exceeded .90 at each grade level. In a study with 160 students in Grades 2–5, Hintze, Owen, Shapiro, and Daly (2000) also reported moderate to high levels of dependability (G coefficients of about .90) for CBM probes derived from both traditional skills-based and literature-based basal reading series.

In contrast to research attesting to the generalizability of CBM reading results, some studies have found that CBM performance is significantly affected by the individual who administers the probes, by the setting in which probes are administered, and by whether probes are timed or untimed. In a sample of 26 third and fourth graders (Derr & Shapiro, 1989), teachers as testers obtained significantly higher WCPM scores on CBM probes than did psychologists. Moreover, reading group settings provided significantly higher WCPM scores than desk settings, which in turn yielded higher WCPM scores than office administrations, and timed probes resulted in significantly higher WCPM rates than untimed probes. Similar results were obtained in a larger study with 100 third and fourth graders (Derr-Minneci & Shapiro, 1992).

Test Floors and Item Gradients

Because beginning readers' ability to access text is limited, CBM oral reading probes are generally not sensitive to individual differences in oral reading skills until the second semester of first grade or even later for less proficient readers (Hartman & Fuller, 1997; Kaminski & Good, 1996). Once children are able to read connected text, CBM is very sensitive to small changes in reading rate because progress is measured in single word units.

Validity Evidence

CONTENT VALIDITY EVIDENCE

Although CBM oral reading probes have high face validity because they are drawn from the curriculum in which children are being instructed, their content validity has been criticized on the grounds that CBM involves a very limited sampling of the reading domain, namely, number of words read correctly (Mehrens & Clarizio, 1993). Concerns have also been raised that the CBM reading metric, which was developed at a time when instruction was provided in basal reading series, may no longer be valid because of the shift toward literature-based instruction and a wide variety of reading materials with uncontrolled vocabulary. Most of the studies evaluating the impact of curriculum on CBM have reported lower levels of performance on literature-based versus basal series probes and even lower levels for trade book probes. In a study with 48 third graders, half of whom were being instructed in a literature-based reading series and half in a traditional basal reading series (Hintze et al., 1994), probes drawn from the traditional basal series were more sensitive to growth than probes selected from the literature-based basal series. In fact, students on average showed declines in oral reading rate on literature-based probes, regardless of the reading series in which they were being instructed. Bradley-Klug and colleagues (1998) similarly reported that although the slope was the same for both literature-based and basal probes in a sample of 28 second graders and 30 fifth graders who were receiving instruction in a literature-based reading series, the mean level of performance was significantly lower on literature-based than on basal probes for both grade levels. In a comparison of CBM probes from literature-based basals and authentic reading material for 57 students in Grades 2 through 4 (Hintze et al., 1997), fluency rates were similar for both kinds of probes across all three grade levels, but WCPM scores were significantly higher for literature-based basal probes than for authentic trade book probes across all grades.

Studies evaluating the possibility of bias in CBM procedures have yielded mixed results. In a study evaluating possible bias for language minority students, Baker and Good (1995) administered CBM English reading probes twice weekly for 10 weeks to a sample of 76 second graders, 50 of whom were bilingual Hispanic students and 26 of whom were English-only students. English-only and bilingual students did not differ significantly in terms of mean WCPM, but bilingual students' rate of reading progress (slope) was significantly higher. Alternate-form reliability coefficients for point (point estimates correspond to one sample of behavior on 1 day) and level of performance were high for both groups (.87 and above), whereas slope reliability estimates were much lower (below .50) but did not differ significantly for the two groups. Correlations between CBM reading and criterion measures, including the *Stanford Diagnostic Reading Test* and teacher ratings of reading competence, were moderate to high and did not differ significantly for the two groups.

In contrast, in a sample of 243 low-SES students in Grades 1 through 4 (Knoff & Dean, 1994), girls and students not receiving free lunch scored significantly higher on CBM measures for winter and spring of Grade 1 than did boys and free-lunch students. Differences were no longer evident by the winter of Grade 2, however, and no gender, SES, or racial differences were observed in the other three grades assessed. In another study with 326 students in Grades 2–5, Kranzler and colleagues (1999) found that although no evidence of bias was found at Grades 2 and 3, CBM performance overestimated the reading comprehension of African American students and underestimated that of European American students at Grades 4 and 5 and overestimated the reading comprehension of girls and underestimated that of boys at Grade 5.

CRITERION-RELATED VALIDITY EVIDENCE

Performance on CBM oral reading probes is moderately to highly correlated with scores on standardized reading tests. For 91 students in Grades 1–6 (Fuchs & Deno, 1992), CBM probes from two basal reading series were highly correlated with *Woodcock Reading Mastery Tests* Passage Comprehension (.89 to .93), with no significant differences among grade levels. Most other researchers have reported moderate correlations between individually and group-administered standardized reading comprehension tests and CBM oral reading rates in primary grade samples. Shinn, Good, Knutson, Tilly, and Collins (1992) reported correlations of .57 to .60 between CBM reading and the *Stanford Diagnostic Reading Test* Reading Comprehension subtest for 114 third-grade students. In a study with 57 students in Grades 2, 3, and 4, Hintze and colleagues (1997) also obtained moderate correlations between *Degrees of Reading Power* Reading Comprehension (Koslin, Koslin, Zeno, & Ovens, 1989) and CBM probes from literature-based basals and authentic materials (mean r averaged across difficulty level = .65 and .66, respectively). Kranzler and colleagues (1998) reported a correlation of .41 between CBM reading and the Reading subtest on the *Kaufman Test of Educational Achievement* (K-TEA; Kaufman & Kaufman, 1985b) for 57 fourth graders. In a larger study with 326 students in Grades 2 through 5 (Kranzler et al.,

1999), the average correlation between CBM reading and the Reading Comprehension subtest on the *California Achievement Tests* (CTB/McGraw Hill, 1989) was .55.

A recent investigation by Good, Simmons, and Kame'enui (2001) exploring the utility of a set of fluency-based indicators for four cohorts of children from kindergarten through Grade 3 provides support for the predictive validity of CBM reading. Attainment of a benchmark goal of 40 WCPM on CBM reading in the spring of first grade was strongly correlated (r = .82) with continued progress in second grade and achievement of desired second-grade outcomes. Of the 98 students who reached the first-grade benchmark, 95 (97%) attained the Grade 2 CBM benchmark goal (90 WCPM), whereas none of the 51 students who read fewer than 10 WCPM in grade-level material reached the Grade 2 benchmark goal.

CONSTRUCT VALIDITY EVIDENCE

The construct validity of CBM in reading is supported by studies of developmental growth rates, group differentiation, and confirmatory factor analyses. Consistent with current theories of reading acquisition, CBM oral reading rates display the greatest increases in the early primary grades, with gains of about 2 words per week in Grade 1 and between 1.5 and 0.85 words per week in Grades 2 through 4. By Grades 5 and 6, growth slows to about 0.5 word per week or less, indicating that CBM reading most directly assesses the decoding and fluency skills that are important in the early stages of reading (Fuchs et al., 1993). Group differentiation studies using CBM procedures have yielded mixed results. Using discriminant function analyses for 57 second through fourth graders, Hintze and colleagues (1997) correctly classified 63% of students by reading comprehension quartile group, based on CBM reading performance on literature-based probes and 61% of students, based on CBM reading performance on authentic material probes. Single-point CBM measures of letter-sound fluency and oral reading fluency administered in the fall were not sensitive indicators of end-of-year reading status (sensitivity indices = 55.9% and 76.9%, respectively) in a study with 47 first- and second-grade poor readers (Speece & Case, 2001).

Several investigators have used confirmatory factor analyses to evaluate the validity of CBM as a measure of reading proficiency. In a study with 114 third and 124 fifth graders, Shinn and colleagues (1992) administered a variety of tasks measuring decoding and comprehension and two CBM oral reading fluency measures. For Grade 3 students, the two CBM oral reading probes correlated highly (rs = .88 and .90) with a latent construct of reading comprehension, higher than any of the other eight reading measures in the study. For third graders, a one-factor model of reading competence provided the best fit to the data; for fifth graders, a two-factor model with separate factors reflecting decoding and comprehension was validated, consistent with current reading models. Further support for the construct validity of CBM oral reading is provided by the Kranzler and colleagues (1998) study cited above, which explored the relative roles of general cognitive ability, oral reading fluency, and processing speed and efficiency in predicting reading comprehension. Six CBM basal series reading probes, the *Kaufman Brief Intelligence Test* (Kaufman & Kaufman, 1990) Matrices subtest, the K-TEA Reading subtest, and a variety of tasks measuring cognitive speed and efficiency of progressing were administered to 57 fourth graders. CBM oral reading fluency did not correlate significantly with processing speed and efficiency tasks, indicating that it measures a different construct. Contrary to expectation, however, CBM reading accounted for much less variance in reading comprehension ($R^2 = .17$) than in previous studies and less than that explained by general cognitive ability ($R^2 = .24$).

Usability

CBM oral reading probes can be quickly and inexpensively constructed using basal reading series by photocopying the relevant passages. There are several problems associated with taking probes from material in which children are being instructed, however. First, when probes are selected from material with a wide range of readability levels, as is the case with literature-based or trade books, the reading level in the selected passages may be too easy or too challenging for reliable measurement. Although most researchers conduct readability estimates to verify reading levels, this adds considerably to the time and labor required and is not a viable option for many practitioners. Second, children may earn spuriously high scores on one or more passages because they have been instructed on that material. This is especially likely to occur for the first CBM probe, which, according to the usual procedures, should be taken from the beginning of the book (Fuchs & Deno, 1994). Third, reading performance may be affected by the numerous illustrations and fewer words per page typical of today's reading texts. Whereas the pictures may facilitate performance by providing clues to unfamiliar words, they may also result in slower reading rates because children pause to look at the pictures and turn the pages. Although researchers retype passages from texts to reduce the effects of illustrations, this option also reduces the usability of CBM for practitioners. Because of these concerns, Hintze and colleagues (1997), Shapiro (1996), and I recommend using a comparable basal reading series or set of passages controlled for readability when students are being instructed in a literature-based series or are using trade books.

A growing body of evidence documents the utility of CBM English-language reading measures with second-language learners in early identification and intervention programs (e.g., Baker, Plasencia-Peinado, & Lezcano-Lytle, 1998; Gunn et al., 2000; Haager & Windmueller, 2001). For example, in a study with 76 second graders (50 bilingual and 26 English-only students; Baker & Good, 1995), CBM oral reading in English was as reliable and valid for bilingual as for English-only students and was sensitive to the reading progress of bilingual students.

Links to Intervention

CBM reading is linked to a five-step problem-solving model (Deno, 1989; Shinn, 1995) in which CBM procedures are combined with other types of information to make educational decisions, such as determining the need for additional evaluation, monitoring student progress, and assessing intervention efficacy. To evaluate the effectiveness of interventions, CBM reading is conducted once or twice weekly from the IEP goal domain. Typically, students are assessed on challenging-level material (i.e., the level of material the student is expected to reach by the goal date) rather than on current instructional material. Slopes that do not meet the aim line indicate that instructional strategies are ineffective and need to be modified. Although CBMs appear to be ideal for progress monitoring because they are sensitive to small changes in reading fluency, debate continues regarding their efficacy in the intervention process. According to a review of 18 meta-analyses on the effectiveness of interventions in special education and related services (Forness, Kavale, Blum, & Lloyd, 1997), formative evaluation (i.e., CBM) was rated as one of the most effective strategies, especially when combined with positive reinforcement of effort or achievement. On the other hand, Mehrens and Clarizio (1993) have argued that CBMs have limited utility in designing interventions because they do not provide information about the type of instructional strategies that should be used—only an indication that the current instructional program is ineffective.

Source and Cost

If CBM oral reading probes using the child's own instructional materials are administered, the only cost incurred is that for reproducing a set of pages for the examiner to mark. Complete directions for constructing, administering, and scoring oral reading probes for screening purposes can be found in Rathvon (1999) and Shapiro (1996). Generic oral reading probes for Grades 1 through 3 are downloadable free of charge from the *Dynamic Indicators of Basic Early Literacy Skills* (DIBELS) Web site (http://dibels.uoregon.edu).

Summary

Curriculum-based measurement (CBM) in oral reading is a set of individually administered, standardized procedures designed to assess contextual reading fluency by using the child's own curricular materials or generic grade-level materials. CBM oral reading probes have been demonstrated to be a reliable and valid method of assessing reading skills and evaluating the effectiveness of reading interventions and are increasingly being included in early reading screening and diagnostic batteries. Adding the comprehension option takes additional preparation, administration, and scoring time but can serve as a useful screening measure of children's ability to obtain meaning from text. Because CBMs are sensitive to changes in fluency over time, quick to administer, and have alternate forms, students can be assessed much more frequently than with traditional norm-referenced measures. Because of floor effects, however, CBM reading is not useful until the second semester of first grade, or even later with very poor readers. Examiners should note that literature-based and trade book probes may underestimate performance levels, compared with passages constructed from traditional basal reading materials or generic passages. For this reason, and because today's early reading materials vary widely in difficulty level, screening and progress monitoring for children instructed in literature-based or authentic materials should be conducted using probes from comparable basal series or from material controlled for readability.

Case Example

Name of student: Miguel G.
Age: 7 years, 10 months
Grade: First grade
Date of assessment: December

Reason for referral: Miguel was referred for a reading assessment by his first-grade teacher because of his persistent difficulties in learning to read and spell. Miguel's family emigrated from Central America several years ago, and his parents speak very little English. Miguel struggled in kindergarten, despite receiving additional support from the reading specialist and a Spanish-speaking tutor who worked with him in an after-school tutoring program. At the end of that year, he was able to communicate in English with his teacher and classmates but still did not know all of his letters. This year his teacher reports that although he tries hard in class, his sight word vocabulary is limited, and his oral reading is very slow and laborious.

Assessment results and interpretation: A curriculum-based measurement (CBM) in reading was conducted by administering oral reading probes taken from Miguel's first-grade reading book. Oral reading probes assess reading fluency (rate and accuracy) and provide information about whether a student is appropriately placed in curricular materials and is making progress at an expected rate. Oral reading probes require the student to read passages aloud as rapidly as possible for 1 minute to yield a words-read-correctly-per-minute rate. Three passages are selected, one from the beginning, one from the middle, and one from the end of the book or set of materials. The *median*, or middle score, of the three passages is a reliable measure of reading fluency and is significantly related to word identification and comprehension skills and to scores on standardized reading tests. For each passage, the examiner asks five comprehension questions to assess the student's understanding of the material that has been read, and a percent accuracy score is derived. The results of the three CBMs are reported below. Miguel indicated that he had previously read the first passage.

	CBM 1	CBM 2	CBM 3
Words read correctly per minute	30	25	19
Errors	9	6	11
Comprehension	60%	40%	40%

Miguel's median words-read-correctly-per-minute (WCPM) rate on the three samples was 25, with a median error rate of 9. This performance indicates that he is reading at a frustration level in his first-grade textbook and that lack of fluency is severely interfering with his ability to understand what he reads. To be rated at an instructional level for first grade, he would have to read 40–60 words per minute with 4 or fewer errors. It should be noted that his WCPM rate fell below expected levels for all three passages, even on the selection on which he had already been instructed. His median comprehension score was 40% (vs. 80% expected), indicating that he is failing to understand much of what he is reading.

Miguel made a good effort but read very slowly and made numerous errors, especially on the final selection. He did not attempt to sound out unfamiliar words in their entirety but guessed, based on the first letter. His errors reflect his limited understanding of short and long vowel sounds and the rules governing their pronunciation (e.g., *time* for *Tim*), as well as confusion of verb forms and syntax (e.g., *cames* for *comes*). He was able to answer some literal questions about what he had read but had trouble with inferential questions.

Measures of Reading Comprehension

No stand-alone measures of reading comprehension are included in this book. Six of the early reading assessment batteries described in Chapter 4—the *Basic Early Assessment of Reading*, the *Early Reading Diagnostic Assessment–Revised*, the *Fox in a Box*, the *Group Reading Assessment and Diagnostic Evaluation*, the *Phonological Awareness Literacy Screening*, and the *Texas Primary Reading Inventory*—include reading comprehension measures, typically beginning in first grade. In addition, reading comprehension measures are included in the *Process Assessment of the Learner: Test Battery for Reading and Writing*, the *Standardized Reading Inventory–2*, the *Test of Early Reading Ability–3*, the *Wechsler Individual Achievement Test–II*, the *Woodcock Reading Mastery Tests–Revised/Normative Update*, and the *Woodcock–Johnson III*. The Curriculum-Based Measurement of Oral Reading procedures also provide a comprehension assessment option.

Measures of Spelling and Written Language

This section reviews one stand-alone spelling test. All of the early reading assessment batteries described in Chapter 4 include written language and/or spelling measures, with the exception of the *Test of Early Reading Ability–3*. Other measures of spelling and written language are included in the *Consortium on Reading Excellence Phonics Survey*, the *Dyslexia Screening Test*, the *Illinois Test of Psycholinguistic Abilities–3*, the *Oral and Written Language Scales*, the *Phonological Awareness Test*, the *Predictive Reading Profile*, the *Process Assessment of the Learner: Test Battery for Reading and Writing*, the *Wechsler Individual Achievement Test–II*, and the *Woodcock–Johnson III*.

TEST OF WRITTEN SPELLING—FOURTH EDITION

Overview

The *Test of Written Spelling–Fourth Edition* (TWS-4; Larsen, Hammill, & Moats, 1999) is a norm-referenced test designed to assess the spelling skills of students aged 6-0 to 18-11 (Grades 1–12). The TWS-4 uses a dictated word format and has two alternative forms, each with 50 words. First published in 1976 (Larsen & Hammill, 1976), the current version contains words that are identical to those in the TWS-2 (Larsen & Hammill, 1986) and TWS-3 (Larsen & Hammill, 1994), but the predictable and unpredictable word lists have been combined into a single list and divided between two alternate forms. According to the manual, the uses of the TWS-4 include (1) identifying students whose spelling skills are severe enough to require additional direct instruction, (2) documenting improvement in spelling as a result of intervention, and (3) serving as a measure in research on language-based learning disabilities. Materials include an examiner's manual and 50 summary/response forms on a tear-off tablet, all packed in a storage box.

Assessment Task

The TWS-4 consists of a 50-word list, with one list for each form. The examiner pronounces each word, reads a sentence using the word, and repeats the word a second time. The child writes the spelling of the dictated word on the back of the summary/response form.

Administration

To administer the TWS-4, the examiner consults an appendix in the manual, which provides Form A and Form B stimulus words, including pronunciation guides and spelling sentences. The TWS-4 can be administered to groups or individuals and takes about 10–15 minutes for individual administrations and about 20–25 minutes for group administrations. Entry points are set for four grade intervals, with basals and ceilings of five consecutive correct and incorrect items, respectively. Although the need to establish basals and ceilings complicates group administration for older examinees, children in Grades 1 through 3 begin with Item 1, making group administration a viable option at those grades. The test's authors recommend administering the first 20 words to groups of students in Grade 3 or below but note that examiners will need to test some children individually until they reach a ceiling.

Scores

Items are scored 1 for correct and 0 for incorrect, using the summary/response form. No information is provided on scoring letter reversals. Raw scores can be converted to standard scores ($M = 100$, $SD = 15$), percentiles, age equivalents (called "spelling ages"), and grade equivalents. Norms are in 3-month increments for ages 6-0 through 10-11, 5-month increments for ages 11-0 through 11-11, and 1-year increments for ages 12-0 to 18-11. Only age norms are available. Because concerns about children's spelling deficits are usually related to grade-level expectations, grade norms should also be provided.

Interpretation

Interpretation of test performance is based on three score ranges: (1) standard scores of less than 90, which indicate the need for special assistance or additional assessment to determine the cause of the spelling deficits; (2) scores of 90–110, which indicate expected age-level performance; and (3) scores above 110, which indicate excellent spelling skills. A case example for a child aged 10-5 is presented to demonstrate scoring procedures, but there is no interpretation of his performance, which falls below the suggested cutoff. Nor is there any discussion of his performance relative to the other tests listed on the summary/response form, including the 9-point difference between his TWS-4 standard score and his standard score on the *Wide Range Achievement Test–3* Spelling test (Wilkinson, 1993).

Technical Adequacy

Standardization

The TWS-4 was not renormed. The normative sample consists of 4,097 students from 23 states who formed the standardization sample for the TWS-2 in 1986, and 855 new examinees tested in 1993 at three unidentified sites (total n = 4,952). Although the test's authors attempt to justify combining the two samples on the grounds that the items of the two editions are identical, the means of the two groups were not significantly different at any age interval, and the interval between the two testings was 7 years, the older and much larger norms are now more than a decade and a half old. Moreover, means and standard deviations for the two normative groups are not reported. Sample characteristics are generally representative of the 1997 U.S. school population and the projected 2000 school-age population in terms of gender, residence, race, geographic region, and ethnicity, with "Other" (Caucasian) slightly overrepresented. Data are also presented for four age ranges in terms of geographic region, gender, race, and ethnicity. Although variables for each age range approximate 1997 U.S. census data, the degree to which each subgroup represents the population cannot be determined because the groups are combined (e.g., 6–8 years). No information regarding SES or disability status is included. Examiners should note that the subgroup size for age 6 is much smaller than those for ages 7 and 8 (151, 415, and 481, respectively). Because norm table intervals for ages 6-0 through 10-11 are in 3-month increments, this means that scores for 6-year-olds are based on only about 38 examinees per interval, which is unacceptably low.

Reliability Evidence

Coefficient alphas for early primary grade examinees range from .87 to .92, with values for ages 6 and 7 falling slightly below the preferred .90 level for Form A (.87 and .89, respectively) and for age 6 on Form B (.89). Coefficient alphas reported for both forms for seven demographic subgroups are at or above .96. Alternate-form reliability estimates are above .90 except for age 6 (r = .86). Raw score means and standard deviations reported for 13 age intervals are within 1 point of each other across the two forms for all age groups and are identical within the early primary grade range, supporting the use of a combined normative table. Test–retest reliabilities for both forms for samples of students in Grades 1, 3, and 6 (ns = 14, 14, and 13, respectively) and for the combined sample (2-week interval) were all at .94 or above. Although these coefficients are high, the samples are so small that any conclusions about score stability are necessarily limited. Interscorer reliability, based on having two members of the PRO-ED research staff independently score 108 protocols of students in Grades 1 through 8, was .99, with age effects partialed out.

Test Floors and Item Gradients

Test floors are inadequate for the entire primary grade range, up until age 9-3. For example, a child aged 6-6 who obtains a TWS-4 raw score of 1 earns a standard score of 80 (low average range). Item gradients are inadequate for ages 6-0 through 7-8. At the 6-0 to 6-2 age interval, for example, there are only five items between the test floor and the mean.

Validity Evidence

CONTENT VALIDITY EVIDENCE

Content validity evidence consists of a rationale for item selection, conventional item analysis, and DIF analyses. The authors include a very readable section on spelling assessment, the English spelling system, and spelling acquisition to justify combining the predictable and unpredictable subtests into a single test with two forms. Items on the original TWS, which was published in 1976, were included if they appeared in 10 basal spelling series for Grades 1 through 8. Additional words were added to the upper and lower levels of the TWS-2, and the words for the TWS-2, TWS-3, and TWS-4 are identical. To evaluate whether the TWS-4 word lists are still instructionally relevant, words were compared with those in five basal spelling series and the *EDL Core Vocabularies in Reading, Mathematics, Science, and Social Studies* (Taylor et al., 1989), a list consisting of words from basal reading series and/or word frequency lists. Items at the high school level were drawn from the *EDL Core Vocabularies* and are more difficult than words included in spelling series. Given the shift from basal reading and spelling series to integrated language arts instruction in many school districts, additional evidence of item representativeness and relevance is needed. Median item difficulties for age 6 are low for both forms and below acceptable levels for Form B (.15 and .12 for Forms A and B, respectively), indicating that items are very difficult for this age group. Item discrimination coefficients in the early primary grade range are between .42 and .52, which is acceptable. Two DIF approaches were used to evaluate item bias: the simultaneous item bias test and the delta scores method. Although results from these analyses suggest little item bias in the TWS-4, the delta scores approach is not recommended because it is based on *p* values (proportion of examinees passing each item), which are dependent on the particular sample from which they are derived (Camilli & Shepard, 1994).

CRITERION-RELATED VALIDITY EVIDENCE

Of the three concurrent validity studies reported in the manual, one was conducted with the original single-form TWS in which TWS scores were correlated with four other spelling tests in a sample of 63 fourth graders. Correlations were high (.78 to .95), but although the manual states that the study was conducted in 1976, the publication dates cited for all of the criterion measures are later than 1976 (e.g., *Wide Range Achievement Test–Revised* [Jastak & Wilkinson, 1984]). For a sample of 50 fourth and fifth graders, correlations between the TWS-4 and spelling subtests from the *Metropolitan Achievement Test–Sixth Edition* (MAT-6; Psychological Corporation, 1992a) and the *Norm-Referenced Assessment Program for Texas* (NAPT; Texas Education Agency, 1991) ranged from .59 to .86. In the third study, correlations between teacher ratings of spelling ability for 82 students enrolled in summer school were .60 for Form A and .55 for Form B. Because the grade and ages of these students are not indicated, however, the study provides no evidence of the TWS-4's concurrent validity for early primary grade children. No concurrent validity studies with early primary grade children or predictive validity studies with examinees of any age are included.

CONSTRUCT VALIDITY EVIDENCE

TWS-4 raw scores increase with age up to about age 12 and then level off, as expected with the termination of spelling instruction as a separate subject in the middle school years. Mean TWS-4 standard scores for 104 protocols of learning-disabled students were 80 for both forms, significantly below the mean of 100 for the norm group. This study offers limited support for the diagnostic validity of the TWS-4 for early primary examinees, however, because the ages and grades of the sample are not specified. In fact, because of inadequate test floors, children younger than 6-6 cannot obtain a score lower than 81, even if they do not answer a single item correctly. In the same study with

50 fourth and fifth graders described above, TWS-4 scores were moderately correlated (mean *r*s = .55 and .53 for Forms A and B, respectively) with the reading, language, and mathematics subtests on three achievement batteries (the MAT-6, the NAPT, and the *Texas Assessment of Academic Skills* [Texas Education Agency, 1992]) and moderately correlated (.56 for both forms) with scores on the *Otis–Lennon School Ability Test*. TWS-3 posttest scores were significantly higher than pretest scores for a sample of 255 reading-disabled elementary, middle, and high school students after a 2-year phonics training program (Hutcheson, Selig, & Young, 1990). Specific score ranges are not reported, however, and as the manual notes, no control group was used.

Usability

The TWS-4 is inexpensive and portable, is easy to use and score, and lends itself to group administration in the early primary grades. The pronunciation guide and provision of stimulus sentences enhance both reliability and usability. Because most early reading batteries and many norm-referenced multisubject instruments include spelling measures, however, practitioners evaluating early primary grade examinees must consider whether purchasing a separate spelling instrument is worth the added expense, especially when comparisons of spelling scores with scores in other domains must involve a different standardization sample.

Links to Intervention

The authors caution that the TWS-4 is not intended to serve as the basis for instructional planning. The manual includes a chapter with useful suggestion for supplementary assessments of spelling and spelling-related skills but only a single sentence on intervention.

Relevant Research

Evidence for the diagnostic validity of the TWS-4 is mixed. In the training study by Hutcheson and colleagues (1990) cited above, the greatest change in TWS-3 scores occurred among elementary grade students (n = 182). Pretest and posttest scores remained in the low range (SSs = 74.4 to 78.4, respectively), however, indicating lack of efficacy of the training program, lack of sensitivity of the TWS-3 to changes in spelling performance for elementary grade children, or both. In a study with 51 children aged 7-5 to 14-8 identified with early phonology disorders (Lewis, O'Donnell, Freebairn, & Taylor, 1998), the TWS-3 significantly differentiated between children with histories of phonology and other language problems and their normally developing siblings (SS = 82.00 vs. 106.13).

Source and Cost

The TWS-4 is available from PRO-ED for $82.00.

Test Review

DeMauro, G. E. (2003). Review of the Test of Written Spelling, Fourth Edition. In B. S. Plake, J. C. Impara, & R. A. Spies (Eds.), *The fifteenth mental measurements yearbook* (pp. 965–968). Lincoln, NE: Buros Institute of Mental Measurements.

Summary

The *Test of Written Spelling–Fourth Edition* (TWS-4) is one of the very few currently available stand-alone, norm-referenced spelling measures for school-age children. Despite efforts to update the format of the test and link it to recent research on spelling development, the latest version of the test has limited utility for practitioners assessing early primary grade examinees. The greater part (79%) of the norms are almost 20 years old, the subgroup sample size for 6-year-olds falls well below criterion levels, and inadequate test floors preclude the identification of early primary grade children with very low levels of spelling proficiency. Although the dictated word format is very similar to that of spelling assessments in the classroom, the all-or-nothing scoring system makes the TWS-4 much less sensitive to individual differences and small changes in spelling proficiency as the result of instruction or intervention than developmental spelling measures that award points for correctly represented spelling features. The publishers are encouraged to consider using a developmental scoring system, to obtain an entirely new and larger standardization sample, and to include grade norms in the next revision of this instrument, which has yet to realize its potential.

Case Example

Name of student: Lawrence W.
Age: 7 years, 6 months
Grade: Second grade
Date of assessment: January

Reason for referral: Lawrence was referred for an early reading assessment by his second grade teacher because of concerns about his poor performance in reading, spelling, and language arts. Although he usually obtains passing grades on weekly spelling tests because of intensive practice with his parents and tutor, his classroom written productions, including journal entries, seatwork, and tests in other subjects, are characterized by numerous misspellings. On the fall administration of the gradewide reading screening battery, he obtained a score of 17/48 points on the developmental spelling measure, considerably lower than the grade average of 35/48. The *Test of Written Spelling–Fourth Edition* (TSW-4), Form A, was administered to evaluate his spelling skills relative to age expectations.

Assessment results and interpretation: The TWS-4, Form A requires the child to write a series of increasingly difficult single dictated words. Average scores for an individual of Lawrence's age and grade are as follows: Standard Score (SS) = 100, Percentile Rank (PR) = 50, Grade Equivalent (GE) = 2.5, Age Equivalent (AE) = 7-6. His performance on the TWS-4 is described below.

Lawrence made a good effort but was able to spell only 6 of the 16 words presented. His performance on the TWS-4 falls in the below average range for his age (SS = 83, PR = 13, AE = 6-3) and is more than 1 year delayed compared with his current grade placement (GE = 1.2 vs. 2.5). He was able to spell several consonant–vowel–consonant words (*bed*), but his knowledge of short vowel spellings is inconsistent (*mech* for *much*). He was unable to spell any words with long vowels, including consonant-vowel-consonant–silent *e* words (*sack* for *shake*). He also had difficulty representing consonant clusters (*song* for *strong*) and words that do not conform to letter–sound conversion rules (*eaht* for *eight*).

Multiskill Reading Measures

This section reviews five multiskill reading measures, including one nonstandardized skills inventory and four standardized tests sampling a variety of reading and reading-related domains. Two of the tests—the *Gray Oral Reading Tests–4* and the *Standardized Reading Inventory–2*—are primarily measures of oral reading fluency but are included here because they assess other reading subskills, including comprehension.

CONSORTIUM ON READING EXCELLENCE PHONICS SURVEY

Overview

The *Consortium on Reading Excellence* (CORE) *Phonics Survey* (Honig, Diamond, & Nathan, 1999) is an individually administered, nonstandardized battery of phonics and phonics-related measures for children in kindergarten through eighth grade. On some tasks, pseudowords are used to assess reading and spelling skills so that children must rely on letter-sound knowledge rather than memory in order to respond correctly. Assessment results are designed for use in planning instruction and instructional groupings in the primary grades. The *CORE Phonics Survey* is one of a collection of reading assessments for elementary grade children contained in the handbook *Assessing Reading: Multiple Measures for Kindergarten through Eighth Grade* (Honig et al., 1999). Materials consist of a four-page reproducible record form and a four-page reproducible set of student materials. The examiner must provide lined paper for the spelling subtests.

Subtests

The *CORE Phonics Survey* includes 16 subtests (see Table 5.28), which are grouped according to three skill areas: (1) alphabet skills, (2) word reading and decoding, and (3) spelling skills. No composite or total scores are available.

TABLE 5.28. Description of CORE Phonics Survey Skill Areas and Subtests

Skill areas	Subtests and description
Alphabet Skills	This category includes five subtests, all of which require the child to identify the names or sounds of letters randomly arrayed on a page: (1) *Letter Names–Uppercase*, (2) *Letter Names–Lowercase*, (3) *Consonant Sounds*, (4) *Long Vowel Sounds*, and (5) *Short Vowel Sounds*.
Reading and Decoding Skills	This category includes seven subtests, all of which require the child to read real words and phonetically regular pseudowords assessing a variety of orthographic patterns: (1) *Short Vowels in CVC Words*; (2) *Short Vowels, Digraphs, and* -tch *Trigraphs*; (3) *Short Vowels and Consonant Blends*; (4) *Long Vowels*; (5) *Vowel Diphthongs*; (6) R- *and* L-*Controlled Vowels*; and (7) *Multisyllabic Words*. For the first six subtests, half of the items are real words and half are pseudowords. For *Multisyllabic Words*, one-third of the items are real words and two-thirds are pseudowords.
Spelling Skills	This category includes four subtests that require the child to write single consonants or to spell words dictated by the examiner: (1) *Initial Consonants*, (2) *Final Consonants*, (3) *CVC Words*, and (4) *Long Vowel Words*.

Administration

The *CORE Phonics Survey* can be administered in 10–25 minutes, depending on the child's skill level. Most subtests are administered in their entirety, but examiners are advised to discontinue testing if the child is making numerous consecutive errors. On Consonant Sounds, testing is discontinued if the child makes three or more consecutive errors. Multisyllabic Words is administered only to examinees who can read most of the words on the Reading and Decoding Skills subtests. Moreover, the child must be able to read at least three of the eight real word items before the pseudoword items are administered.

Scores

Scoring is dichotomous and takes about 5 minutes. Only raw scores are available. The record form reproduces in reduced size the same material that appears on the student testing pages, which facilitates scoring and the recording of incorrect responses for later analysis. For the Reading and Decoding Skills subtests, pronunciation guidelines for scoring pseudowords are provided for only 5 of the 24 multisyllabic pseudowords. Moreover, although two pronunciations are designated as acceptable for each of these items, pronunciation is indicated only in terms of syllabic division (e.g., *zuride* = *zu-ride* or *zur-ide*). Pronunciation guidelines that provide vowel markings or rhyming real word segments as well as syllable divisions should be provided for all pseudoword items.

Interpretation

The *CORE Phonics Survey* is described as a "mastery test," with children expected to answer all items correctly at some point, but no grade-specific criteria are provided. The handbook states that children who miss 2 or more items on a 5-item subtest or 3 or more items on a 10-item subtest need additional direct instruction in that area. Examiners are also advised that older children who score poorly on the consonant–vowel–consonant portions of subtests may need additional assessment with phoneme segmentation measures. For the Reading and Decoding Skills subtests, performance on real word and pseudoword reading is combined for each of the seven measures. I recommend analyzing real word and pseudoword reading performance separately, as in the case example below, to permit comparisons of sight word and phonemic decoding skills. The handbook states that children can be retested every 4–6 weeks on the subtests they have not mastered to monitor their growth in phonics skills and provide information for instructional grouping.

Technical Adequacy

The handbook does not provide any information on technical adequacy.

Usability

The *CORE Phonics Survey* is inexpensive; is quick to administer and score; and provides instructionally relevant information for teachers, parents, and tutors. A Spanish version of the test, the *CORE Spanish Phonics Survey*, is included in the same handbook.

Links to Intervention

Examiners are referred to Section IV, "Decoding and Word Attack," in the CORE companion volume, the *Teaching Reading Sourcebook* (Honig, Diamond, & Gutlohn, 2000), for instructional strategies to assist low-performing children. This section of the 800-page sourcebook provides useful, clearly presented guidelines for teaching phonics and activities targeting each of the skills covered by the *CORE Phonics Survey*.

Source and Cost

As noted above, the *CORE Phonics Survey* is included in *Assessing Reading: Multiple Measures for Kindergarten through Eighth Grade* (Honig et al., 1999), a spiral-bound collection of reading measures available from Academic Therapy Publications for $32.00. The publisher grants permission to reproduce the Survey and the other measures in the book for classroom use. The 800-page *Teaching Reading Sourcebook* is available from the same publisher for $59.00. The survey and sourcebook can also be ordered from the CORE Web site (http://www.corelearn. com).

Summary

The *Consortium on Reading Excellence Phonics Survey* (*CORE Phonics Survey*) is an individually administered, nonstandardized measure of alphabet knowledge, word recognition, decoding, and spelling for primary grade children. Unlike most norm-referenced reading tests, it provides comprehensive coverage of alphabet knowledge and phonics features. It is inexpensive; can be quickly administered and scored; and yields results that are easily understood by parents, teachers, and tutors. Because it assesses decoding and spelling skills with both real word and pseudoword items, it can help identify children who are relying excessively on memory-based rather than phonemic decoding strategies. The *CORE Phonics Survey* makes an excellent supplement to norm-referenced instruments in an early reading assessment battery and is also useful in monitoring the progress of children in intervention programs.

Case Example

Name of student: Tawanda W.
Age: 7 years, 8 months
Grade: Second grade
Date of assessment: April

Reason for referral: Tawanda was referred for an early reading assessment by her teacher because of her slow progress in acquiring decoding and spelling skills. Tawanda's grades on weekly spelling tests are usually satisfactory, but she has difficulty applying letter-sound knowledge to read and spell unfamiliar words. Her teacher also reports that she has trouble reading Tawanda's entries in her writing journal because there are so many misspellings. The *Consortium on Reading Excellence (CORE) Phonics Survey* was administered to provide information for instructional planning.

Assessment results and interpretation: The *CORE Phonics Survey* assesses three categories of reading and reading-related skills: (1) alphabet skills, (2) word reading and decoding, and (3) spelling. Its results are helpful in identifying areas in which children need additional instruction. On some decoding tasks, pseudowords (e.g., *shom, clag*) rather than real words are used so that children must rely on letter-sound knowledge rather than memory in order to respond correctly. Tawanda's performance on the *CORE Phonics Survey* is described below.

Skills Assessed	Raw Scores	
Alphabet Skills		
Letter Names–Uppercase	26/26	
Letter Names–Lowercase	26/26	
Consonant Sounds	21/23	
Long Vowel Sounds	5/5	
Short Vowel Sounds	4/5	
Total	82/85	
Reading and Decoding Skills	Real words	Pseudowords
Short Vowels in CVC[a] Words	5/5	5/5
Short Vowels, Digraphs, and *-tch* Trigraphs	5/5	1/5
Short Vowels and Consonant Blends	8/10	4/10
Long Vowels	4/5	1/5
Vowel Diphthongs	3/5	0/5
R- and *L*-Controlled Vowels	5/5	1/5
Multisyllabic Words	4/8	1/16
Total by category	34/43	13/51
Total	51/94	
Spelling Skills	Real words	
Initial Consonants	5/5	
Final Consonants	5/5	
CVC[a] Words	1/5	
Long Vowel Words	0/5	
Total	11/20	

[a]CVC, Consonant-Vowel-Consonant.

Tawanda was able to identify all 26 letters and 21 of 23 consonant sounds, except /w/, which she pronounced "yuh," and /y/, which she pronounced "wuh." She was able to provide 4 of 5 short vowel sounds (except /e/, which she pronounced "uh") and all 5 long vowel sounds when the letters were presented in isolation. She had much more difficulty using letter-sound knowledge to read words, however, especially *pseudowords* (nonwords that can be decoded using letter-sound conversion rules). She was able to read 79% of the one-syllable real words but only 25% of the phonically regular pseudowords. Her errors reflect incomplete knowledge of many phonics features, including short and long vowels, consonant blends, and vowel diphthongs (e.g., *pad* for *paid*). Moreover, presented with an unfamiliar real word or a pseudoword, she tended to guess rapidly based on the first few letters rather than taking time to look carefully at all of the letters in the word (e.g., *which* for *wheck*).

Tawanda was able to write the first and last consonants for all 10 of the one-syllable spelling words. In contrast, she was able to spell only 1 of the 5 consonant–vowel–consonant (CVC) words and none of the long vowel words. She had trouble representing consonant clusters (*taine* for *train*) and both short and long vowel patterns (*sep* for *sip*, *step* for *steep*), and she sometimes appeared to be relying on visual memory rather than knowledge of letter-sound relationships (*folt* for *float*).

GRAY ORAL READING TESTS—FOURTH EDITION

Overview

The *Gray Oral Reading Tests–Fourth Edition* (GORT-4; Wiederholt & Bryant, 2001) is an individually administered, norm-referenced measure of oral reading fluency and comprehension for individuals aged 7-0 through 18-11. Like its predecessor, the GORT-3 (Wiederholt & Bryant, 1992), the GORT-4 has two parallel forms, each containing a set of increasingly difficult reading passages. Changes to this edition include (1) the addition of a new story at the beginning of each form for younger and less proficient readers; (2) a new normative sample; and (3) changes in the placement and order of some of the stories, based on the most recent normative data. In addition, the Passage score, a combination of the Rate and Accuracy scores, has been renamed the Fluency score to reflect current terminology. Purposes for the GORT-4 identified by the manual are (1) to help identify children who are performing significantly below their peers in oral reading and may need additional assistance, (2) to evaluate reading strengths and weaknesses, (3) to document student progress in regular or special education reading programs, and (4) to serve as a tool for reading research with school-age students. The test kit includes a spiral-bound examiner's manual, a spiral-bound student book with stories and comprehension questions for both forms, and 25 profile/examiner record booklets for each form, all packed in a storage box.

Assessment Tasks

Each form of the GORT-4 consists of 14 increasingly difficult stories and resembles an informal reading inventory in structure and format. The child reads the stories aloud and answers five multiple-choice comprehension questions about what has been read. The examiner reads aloud the questions and response choices to avoid confounding decoding deficits with comprehension deficits. The child's oral reading is timed, but there are no time limits for responding to the comprehension questions. Performance yields five scores: Accuracy; Rate; Fluency (Rate + Accuracy); Comprehension; and a composite score, termed the "Oral Reading Quotient," obtained by summing the standard scores for Fluency and Comprehension. Although the GORT-4 does not have separate subtests, the manual refers to the four subscores as "subtests" to differentiate these measures from the composite score.

Administration

Although the manual states (p. 3) that the GORT-4 is appropriate for examinees from ages 7-0 through 18-11, the publisher's catalog indicates that it can be administered to 6-year-olds, and the manual includes norms and psychometric information for 6-year-old examinees in the standardization sample. Given the test's technical problems at that age level (see below), I recommend that practitioners follow the guidelines in the manual and do not use it with examinees younger than 7-0. The GORT-4 takes between 15 and 45 minutes to administer, depending on the child's skill level. For each story, the examinee reads aloud a prompt in the record booklet prior to the child's reading aloud. Children in Grades 1 and 2 begin with the first story. After the child has read the passage aloud, the examiner reads aloud the questions and response choices as the child follows along in the student book. The child is not permitted to refer to the passage while answering the questions. Basals and ceilings must be computed separately for Fluency and Comprehension scores during testing to ensure that the appropriate number of passages is administered. For Fluency, the basal occurs when the Fluency score for a story is 9 or 10, and the ceiling is reached when the child obtains a Fluency score of 2 or less for a story. For Comprehension, the basal is the point at which the child correctly answers all 5 comprehension questions, and the ceiling is reached when the child misses at least 3 of 5 questions for a story or has read the last story. For two of the three scoring examples in the manual, the Comprehension ceiling is reached before the Fluency ceiling; however, examiners are not told how to deal with this contingency, which occurs frequently in my experience. Nor are directions provided for situations in which the reverse occurs (i.e., reaching a Fluency ceiling before a Comprehension ceiling) or situations in which basals for the two scores are reached during different stories. In the GORT-3 manual, examiners were directed to continue testing downward or upward until the other basal or ceiling was reached but not to administer comprehension questions or to record time and deviations from print for the additional stories. It is not clear why these directions have been omitted from the present edition.

Scores

As the child reads, the examiner uses a slash marking system to record seven categories of deviations from print (errors): (1) misidentifications, (2) pauses of 5 seconds or more, (3) decoding attempts of more than 10 seconds, (4) self-corrections, (5) additions, (6) repetitions, and (7) skipping a line. The placement of the slash corresponds to the type of error (e.g., for a repetition, the examiner places a slash after the word that is repeated). The examiner provides the word after a 5-second pause or a 10-second decoding attempt. If the examiner has to provide more than 20% of the words for any story, the comprehension questions are not administered, and a Comprehension score of 0 is awarded for that story. The time required to read each passage and the number of deviations from print per passage are converted into Rate and Accuracy scores, using a 6-point scale in the record booklet; these two values are then summed to obtain the Fluency score per story. The Comprehension score is the number of correct responses to the five questions per story. Basic scoring takes about 5 minutes, whereas the optional miscue scoring system (see below) takes considerably longer, about 15–20 minutes. Raw scores are summed for each of the four score categories and converted to standard scores (M = 10, SD = 3), percentiles, and age and grade equivalents. Standard scores for Fluency and Comprehension are then summed to obtain an Oral Reading Quotient (ORQ) (M = 100, SD = 15). Norms are in 6-month increments for ages 6-0 through 13-11 and 1-year increments for ages 14-0 through 18-11. As noted earlier, the manual states that the test is appropriate for individuals from 7-0 to 18-11, so it is unclear why the 6-year-old norms are included in the tables. Because reading problems are usually evaluated in the context of grade-level expectations of proficiency, grade norms should be provided as well as age norms.

The GORT-4 offers an optional scoring system that classifies miscues according to five categories: (1) meaning similarity, (2) function similarity, (3) graphic/phonemic similarity, (4) multiple sources, and (5) self-correction. To use the system, the examiner must analyze the child's miscues on at least two different stories to obtain a minimum of 25 miscues. A section on the record booklet provides a worksheet for recording the number and percentage of miscues for each of the five categories. Because a single miscue can fall into several different categories, scoring time is considerably increased when this option is used. The manual provides one example each of the use of the slash marking and miscue analysis systems, with two additional samples (one per form) illustrating the use of miscue analysis in an appendix.

Interpretation

Although the guidelines for evaluating differences among subtest scores have been omitted in this version of the manual, the emphasis in interpretation remains on discrepancy analysis. The manual includes guidelines for evaluating differences between two ORQs to assess intervention effectiveness and for evaluating differences between the ORQ and scores on other tests. A table lists the values needed for statistically and clinically significant differences between Form A and Form B ORQs and scores on five language tests and four intelligence tests. A case example of a fifth grader aged 10-10 is included to demonstrate how to complete identifying information, calculate scores, record and score miscues, and conduct discrepancy analyses. All but one of the case example's GORT-4 scores fall in the average range, and none of the score comparisons meets the criterion for clinically useful differences, as defined by Reynolds's (1990) formula. According to the test's authors, miscue percentages serve as an index of oral reading strengths and weaknesses and provide useful information when one is comparing performance between GORT-4 administrations and across different kinds of reading material. No empirical data are provided to support this claim; nor is any information provided regarding the mean number or types of miscues by age or grade for use in interpretation.

Technical Adequacy

Standardization

The GORT-4 was normed between fall 1999 and fall 2000 on a sample of 1,677 individuals residing in 28 states, with sampling designed to be representative of the 1997 U.S. school-age population in terms of geographic area, gender, race, residence, ethnicity, family income, parental education, and disability status. Sample characteristics are generally representative of the population, with the exception of slight overrepresentation of urban, white (race), European American (ethnicity), and female examinees, and slight underrepresentation of black (race) and African American (ethnicity) examinees. Norm characteristics are stratified by age for geographic area, gender, race, residence, ethnicity, income, and parental education. Students with disabilities who were enrolled in general classes were included, but examinees with learning disabilities are slightly underrepresented. Linear equating procedures were used to correct for differences in passage difficulty across the two forms and to permit examiners to use scores from the two forms interchangeably. Subgroup sizes for ages 7 through 9 range from 171 to 189, but there are only 87 examinees at age 6. Because norms are in 6-month increments, subgroup sizes fall below the criterion for early primary grade examinees, with scores based on only about 43 examinees per interval at the 6-year-old level.

Reliability Evidence

Coefficient alphas for the ORQ are at or above .94 for early primary grade examinees. Coefficients for Fluency and Comprehension are at or above .90 across the early primary grade range and at .87 or above for Rate and Accuracy. Coefficient alphas for six demographic subgroups and two groups of examinees with exceptionalities (ADHD and learning disabilities) in the normative sample are at or above .90 for the four subtests and the ORQ. Alternate-form reliability using an immediate administration procedure exceeded .90 for Rate, Accuracy, and Fluency for both forms for the early primary grade range, with the exception of Accuracy at age 8 (r = .88), but Comprehension reliabilities fell below acceptable levels for the same ages (rs = .71 to .77). Children ages 6 through 9 scored lower on all four subtests for Form B for one or more age intervals, with up to a 4-point difference on Fluency. Alternate-form reliability estimates are not provided for the ORQ.

Test–retest reliabilities based on administering both forms of the test twice to 49 children aged 6 to 18 (2-week interval) ranged from .85 to .95 for the four subtest scores and from .88 to .91 for the ORQ. Delayed alternate-form reliability estimates (i.e., Form A to Form B; 2-week interval) for the same sample was .95 for the ORQ and in the .90s for all of the subtests except for Comprehension (r = .78). No information is provided regarding score stability for specific ages, and these estimates should be regarded with caution due to the small size and age heterogeneity of the sample. Interscorer reliability coefficients based on independent scoring of 30 protocols by two PRO-ED research staff members ranged from .94 to .99. These coefficients were computed for completed protocols, however, and provide no information about interexaminer and interscorer variability during the administration process. Because of the vulnerability of fluency-based measures to interscorer inconsistency, estimates based on simultaneous scoring by independent examiners during test sessions or independent raters during audiotaped sessions should be included.

Test Floors and Item Gradients

Although the addition of a new story for beginning readers has improved GORT-4 subtest and composite floors compared with the GORT-3, floor effects continue to be evident across the lowest age ranges of the test. Floors for Rate for both forms are inadequate below 8-0; floors for Accuracy are inadequate below 7-6 for Form A and below 8-0 for Form B; floors for Fluency are inadequate below 7-6 for Form A and below 8-0 for Form B. Floors for Comprehension are inadequate below 8-0 for Form A and below 9-0 for Form B. Floors for the ORQ are inadequate below 6-6 for Form A and below 7-6 for Form B. Although the GORT-4 displays no item gradient violations for the primary grade range, inadequate floors prevent it from discriminating between average and poor readers at the younger ages.

Validity Evidence

CONTENT VALIDITY EVIDENCE

With the exception of the two new stories, the content of the GORT-4 is identical with that of the GORT-R (Wiederholt & Bryant, 1986), with some passages dating back to the original GORT (Gray & Robinson, 1963). The two new stories were drawn from the *Gray Oral Reading Tests–Diagnostic* (GORT–D; Bryant & Wiederholt, 1991), based on their item characteristics. As evidence of content validity, the authors provide a rationale for the format, content, and structure of the passages and comprehension questions. New to this edition is the inclusion of a table with readability indices for the 14 stories for both forms, using the Flesch–Kincaid Readability Formula (Kincaid & McDaniel, 1974). As expected, the stories gradually increase in difficulty, although there is a marked increase from Story 4 to Story 5 for both forms (average of Grade 1.6 and Grade 4.1 readability, respectively). Passages include both narrative and expository material. Comprehension questions were designed to tap four types of comprehension questions (literal, inferential, critical, and affective), with final selection based on field-testing and item discrimination and difficulty analyses. Although the content validity section has been expanded and updated, many of the references date to the 1970s and early 1980s. Given recent advances in the understanding of reading acquisition, as well as recent changes in the conceptualization of test validity, the entire validity section should be rewritten. No rationale is offered for the use of multiple-choice rather than open-ended questions for assessing comprehension.

Item discrimination coefficients are at acceptable levels across the entire age range. Median item difficulties are also in the acceptable range but show considerable variation between the two forms at some ages, with no pattern indicating which form is consistently the more difficult. DIF analyses using logistic regression techniques compared performance on all 140 comprehension items for both forms for four dichotomous groups (males vs. females, European Americans vs. non-European Americans, African Americans vs. non-African Americans, and Hispanic Americans vs. non-Hispanic Americans). Of the 560 comparisons, 9 were statistically significant, but none had moderate or large effect sizes indicating moderate or large degrees of DIF.

CRITERION-RELATED VALIDITY EVIDENCE

The manual reports median correlations between various editions of the GORT and other reading tests for eight studies, four of which included early primary grade children and two of which used the current version of the test. In a sample of 76 children aged 6 through 13, correlations between the GORT-4 and the *Gray Diagnostic Reading Tests–Second Edition* (GDRT-2; Bryant, Wiederholt, & Bryant, 2004) were moderate to high (.41 to .72), whereas correlations with the *Gray Silent Reading Tests* (Wiederholt & Blalock, 2000) for the same sample were in the moderate range (.45 to .59), suggesting that the two formats for assessing contextual reading do not tap identical skills. Across the studies cited, GORT Rate and Accuracy display high correlations with both single word and contextual reading measures, whereas Comprehension is less strongly related. No predictive validity evidence is reported.

CONSTRUCT VALIDITY EVIDENCE

As expected, GORT-4 mean subtest scores increase with age, with the largest gains in the early primary years. Subtest intercorrelations range from .39 to .85, with the lowest correlations for Comprehension. As evidence of construct validity, the authors cite studies with the GORT-R and GORT-3 from the research literature, along with validation studies for the current version of the test. Correlations with spoken and written language tests are generally in the moderate range, with Comprehension displaying lower correlations than Rate and Accuracy, as noted above. Correlations between the ORQ and four aptitude and intelligence tests averaged .69 for verbal intelligence, .40 for nonverbal intelligence, and .65 for general intelligence. GORT-4 scores were also moderately correlated with measures of rapid automatized naming

(RAN), with median correlations ranging from .48 for Comprehension to .62 for Accuracy. In support of the GORT-4's ability to differentiate among groups, the manual reports mean standard scores for four groups of examinees with exceptionalities (learning disabilities, serious emotional disturbance, ADHD, and gifted/talented placement) and five demographic subgroups from the normative sample. As anticipated, gifted/talented examinees scored in the above average range on the ORQ (SS = 116), whereas learning-disabled examinees scored in the below average range on the ORQ (SS = 82) and on three of the four subtests (except Comprehension), with the poorest performance on Fluency (SS = 6).

The manual presents three treatment studies using the GORT-R or GORT-3 with examinees with reading disabilities as evidence of the ability of the GORT-4 to detect changes in reading performance due to intervention. In an intervention study with 10 reading-disabled students in Grades 2–4 (Burns & Kondrick, 1998), GORT-R ORQs increased significantly from pretest to posttest and again at follow-up. In a study with 40 reading-disabled children aged 8–12 (Dryer, Beale, & Lambert, 1999), in which participants received treatment programs designed for their subtype of dyslexia or inconsistent with their subtype, all participants, regardless of treatment, showed significant improvement on GORT-R Accuracy and Comprehension. Similarly, in a study (Torgesen, Alexander, et al., 2001) in which 60 severely reading-disabled children aged 8–10 received one-to-one tutoring using one of two instructional programs, all participants made moderate to large gains on GORT-3 Accuracy and Comprehension, which were maintained after 1 year. Not reported in the manual is the finding in this investigation that GORT-3 Rate standard scores showed almost no change. Although children's reading rate, as measured by words per minute, more than doubled from pretest to the end of the follow-up period, GORT-3 Rate standard scores remained constant at nearly 2 standard deviations below the mean. Although these results do not support the claim that GORT-4 Rate is sensitive to small changes in student performance, they provide additional evidence that intervention programs are generally much more successful in improving reading accuracy than fluency.

Usability

The manual for the GORT-4 is a vast improvement compared with its predecessor, not only in terms of the amount of technical information provided but also in terms of readability and organization. Administration and scoring directions have been clarified considerably, but, as noted earlier, the latest manual provides no instructions for dealing with situations in which an examinee achieves Fluency and Comprehension basals or ceilings on different stories. The slash marking system takes considerable practice, and the miscue analysis even more. Few practitioners are likely to follow the authors' recommendations of taping testing performance to record the complete miscue analysis, especially in the absence of reliability and validity evidence for those analyses.

Links to Intervention

A section of the test manual entitled "Pursuing Additional Assessment and Instruction" offers guidelines for using the GORT-4 in conjunction with two other tests in the series: the *Gray Silent Reading Tests* and *Gray Diagnostic Reading Tests–2*. Also included are suggestions for additional evaluation for examinees whose ORQs are below expected levels, including assessments of the reading environment, reading rate (based on a words read per minute [WPM] rather than a words read correctly per minute [WCPM] metric), analysis of errors in classroom reading materials, and intelligence and oral language tests. Information on possible interventions based on GORT-4 results is limited to addresses and Web sites for three reading organizations.

Relevant Research

The GORT has been used extensively in reading diagnostic, prediction, and intervention research (e.g., Ackerman, Dykman, & Gardner, 1990; Catts, 1993; Catts et al., 2001; Cornwall, 1992) and has been demonstrated to be a significant predictor of reading proficiency among school-age children. In a study (Ackerman & Dykman, 1993) with 42 dyslexic readers aged 7–12 who were contrasted with two control groups (56 adequate readers with attention-deficit disorder [ADD] and 21 nondiscrepant poor readers), GORT-R Passage scores significantly differentiated among the three groups, whereas Comprehension scores significantly differentiated between children with ADD and children with dyslexia. In a study with 79 second graders (Catts, 1993), GORT-R ORQs differentiated between language-impaired and normal language children, whereas children with articulation disorders scored within the normal range, as expected (Catts, 1993). Some research suggests that children may score significantly lower on the GORT than on other standardized reading tests. In a study (Breen & Drecktrah, 1990) with 33 learning-disabled elementary and middle school children (mean age = 11-5), GORT-R ORQs were moderately to highly correlated with *Kaufman Test of Educational Achievement* (K-TEA) Reading Decoding and Reading Comprehension (*rs* = .55 and .74, respectively). Mean GORT-R ORQs were 8–10 points lower than mean K-TEA Decoding and Comprehension scores, however (SSs = 75.97 vs. 83.94 and 86.28, respectively).

Source and Cost

The GORT-4 is available from PRO-ED for $198.00.

Test Reviews

Crumpton, N. L. (2003). Review of the Gray Oral Reading Tests, Fourth Edition. In B. S. Plake, J. C. Impara, & R. A. Spies (Eds.), *The fifteenth mental measurements yearbook* (pp. 417–419). Lincoln, NE: Buros Institute of Mental Measurements.

Miller-Whitehead, M. (2003). Review of the Gray Oral Reading Tests, Fourth Edition. In B. S. Plake, J. C. Impara, & R. A. Spies (Eds.), *The fifteenth mental measurements yearbook* (pp. 419–421). Lincoln, NE: Buros Institute of Mental Measurements.

Summary

The *Gray Oral Reading Tests–Fourth Edition* (GORT-4) is a set of individually administered, norm-referenced measures that are similar in format and content to an informal reading inventory. One of the few standardized measures of contextual reading fluency for school-age children, the GORT-4 and its predecessors have been used extensively in research and practical settings. A growing body of evidence demonstrates that the GORT family of tests discriminate among reading-disabled and language-impaired groups and are effective predictors of future reading proficiency. Although the test's authors have made a commendable effort in this edition to respond to previous reviewer criticism, several usability and technical problems remain. Basal and ceiling procedures need to be clarified, and the miscue analysis system, which has no documented utility, is not worth the additional examiner time required. The addition of a new story to the beginning of each form in this edition has reduced but not eliminated floor effects, limiting the GORT-4's utility in the early identification of children at risk for reading problems. Other technical problems include test–retest reliability based on a single small sample with a 12-year age span, interscorer reliability estimates for completed protocols only, and a content validity section in need of updating. Moreover, the Comprehension score, which is based on a multiple-choice format, displays consistently lower levels of reliability and validity than the other subtests. Despite these problems, the GORT-4 makes a valuable addition to an early reading battery for children who are able to access text because it permits comparisons of proficiency levels on a variety of reading skills with a format that is more similar to actual classroom reading experiences than that of most of its norm-referenced competitors.

Case Example

Name of student: Benjamin P.
Age: 8 years, 2 months
Grade: Second grade
Date of assessment: March

Reason for referral: Benjamin was referred for an early reading assessment by his second-grade teacher. His teacher reports that Benjamin often requires individual help to complete classwork and homework because he has so much trouble reading the directions. His sight word vocabulary is limited, and he reads and writes very slowly. On the early literacy screening battery administered in the fall, he received one of the lowest scores in the class in word recognition.

Assessment results and interpretation: The *Gray Oral Reading Tests–Fourth Edition, Form A* (GORT-4) requires the child to read aloud a series of graded passages as quickly as possible and then answer multiple-choice comprehension questions about what has been read. The examiner reads the questions and response choices aloud to avoid confounding decoding deficits with comprehension deficits. Benjamin's GORT-4 scores are reported below. Average scores for a child his age are as follows: Oral Reading Quotient = 100, Subtest Standard Score (SS) = 10, Percentile Rank (PR) = 50, Grade Equivalent (GE) = 2.7, Age Equivalent (AE) = 8-2.

Composite/Subtest	Oral Reading Quotient	Subtest Standard Score	Percentile Rank	Grade Equivalent	Age Equivalent
Oral Reading Quotient	73	–	4	–	–
Rate (R)	–	5	5	<1.0	<6-0
Accuracy (A)	–	7	16	1.4	6-6
Fluency (R + A)	–	6	9	1.0	6-0
Comprehension	–	5	5	<1.0	<6-0

On the GORT-4, Benjamin's overall reading performance falls in the low range for his age (SS = 73, PR = 4). His oral reading fluency, including rate and accuracy, is rated at the beginning of first grade, more than a year and a half below his current grade placement (GE = <1.0, PR = 9). His ability to decode words accurately and his ability to read rapidly fall at the 16th and 5th percentiles, respectively. His comprehension skills are also weak and fall below a first-grade level (GE = <1.0, PR = 5).

When the examiner presented the test book containing the stories, Benjamin looked apprehensive and exclaimed, "Do I have to read this whole book?" Although he made a good effort to read the passages, he began making errors after the first story. Similarly, he had excellent comprehension for the first passage, but he had trouble answering both literal and inferential questions on the rest of the selections. When he encountered an unfamiliar word, he did not attempt to sound it out but either guessed, based on the first letter or two, or waited for the examiner to provide it. Many of his guesses did not fit the context of the passage, indicating that his decoding problems are limiting his ability to attend to the meaning of what he is reading. His poor decoding skills also interfered with his ability to read smoothly and with expression. He read in a labored, word by word manner, without pausing for punctuation, but his reading rate was still quite slow because so many of the words were unfamiliar.

PROCESS ASSESSMENT OF THE LEARNER: TEST BATTERY FOR READING AND WRITING

Overview

The *Process Assessment of the Learner: Test Battery for Reading and Writing* (PAL-RW; Berninger, 2001) is an individually administered, norm-referenced set of measures designed to assess the development of reading and writing processes in children in kindergarten through Grade 6. Based on its author's theory of functional reading and writing systems (see Berninger, 2000, for a recent review), the PAL-RW consists of subtests assessing processes and skills relevant to reading and writing acquisition, including phonological processing, orthographic processing, and rapid naming, among others. Designed as a companion to the *Wechsler Intelligence Scale for Children–III* (WISC-III; Wechsler, 1991) and the *Wechsler Individual Achievement Test–II* (WIAT-II), the PAL-RW is statistically linked to the WIAT-II and is intended to assess the processes underlying the reading and writing skills measured by the WIAT-II. The PAL-RW is unusual among psychoeducational batteries in that it is directly linked to an intervention program, the *Process Assessment of the Learner* (PAL): *Guides for Intervention–Reading and Writing* (Berninger, 1998a). Purposes of the PAL-RW include (1) screening to identify children at risk for reading and/or writing problems, (2) monitoring the progress of students in early intervention programs and students receiving prereferral interventions, and (3) diagnosing the nature of reading- or writing-related processing problems. The test kit includes an examiner's manual, two easel-format stimulus booklets, 25 record forms, 25 student response forms, a wooden stylus and plastic shield for the Finger Sense subtests, a pseudoword decoding card, and a pseudoword pronunciation guide audiocassette, all packed either in a storage box or in a nylon bag.

Subtests

The PAL-RW consists of 19 subtests, organized by grade level. Some subtests are administered to all examinees, whereas others are grade-specific or have grade-specific item sets. Table 5.29 describes all of the subtests for the sake of completeness. Alphabet Writing and Pseudoword Decoding are the same tasks as those on the WIAT-II. There are no composite scores.

Administration

The PAL-RW offers a three-tiered approach to assessment, with specific subtests designated at each grade level for screening, progress monitoring, or diagnosis. Depending on the purpose of the assessment, the examiner may select some or all subtests at the child's grade level (10 for kindergarten, 14 for Grades 1–3, and 17 for Grades 4–6). For screening children in kindergarten through second grade, the test's author recommends administering specific subtests assessing orthographic, phonological, and rapid naming skills, in combination with selected WIAT-II tests (see Table 5.30).

For diagnosing specific reading and writing disabilities, Berninger recommends a battery of measures assessing reading and writing processes, based on her theory of the functional reading and writing systems and using subtests from the PAL-RW, WIAT-II, and WISC-III. If all of the subtests for a specific grade are given, administration time is about 45 minutes for kindergarten examinees and about 60 minutes for first- and second-grade examinees. Administration procedures are clearly spelled out in the stimulus books so that the examiner does not need to consult the manual during testing. For many subtests, examiners are instructed to record additional information, such as the number of the item completed at various intervals (e.g., 30, 60, and 90 seconds), but no guidelines or normative data are provided to assist examiners in interpreting this information. Rather than basals and ceilings, most subtests other than the RAN tasks have grade-specific start and stop points, which simplifies administration. Only Pseudoword Decoding has a discontinue rule (seven consecutive incorrect items). Examiners should note that the reverse rule for Syllables printed in the test book, manual, and record booklet has been eliminated since the PAL-RW was first published. RAN subtests are only administered to children who obtain 100% accuracy on the sample items.

Like all rapid naming tasks, the RAN subtests can be difficult to score accurately if examinees respond very quickly. Moreover, using the three-component marking system (checks for correct responses, horizontal lines for incorrect responses or omissions, and vertical lines for self-corrections) takes practice and good visual–motor skills on the part of the examiner. Because phoneme manipulation tasks are susceptible to examiner variance, Phonemes and Rimes should be presented on audiotape. The Finger Sense tasks are challenging for examiner and child alike, and some administration procedures need simplification or clarification. On Succession—a timed task that requires completing five sequences per hand of successively touching each fingertip with the thumb, beginning with the little finger—children often become confused and begin touching their fingers in reverse order or randomly, but the instructions do not indicate whether the examiner should redirect them and continue timing or stop and readminister the task. I have found it impossible to record

TABLE 5.29. Description and Target Grades of the PAL-RW Subtests

Subtest	Description
Alphabet Writing	Grades K–6. The child prints lowercase letters in order from memory. The score is the number of correctly sequenced letters written at 15 seconds.
Receptive Coding	For Task A (Grades K–3), the examiner exposes a target word for 1 second and then a comparison word for up to 5 seconds (e.g., *well/wall*), and the child indicates whether the words are the same by saying "yes" or "no." For Task B (Grades K–3), the examiner exposes a target word for 1 second and then a comparison letter for up to 5 seconds (e.g., *good/f*), and the child indicates whether or not the letter appeared in the word. For Tasks C and D (Grades 4–6), there are between one and three comparison letters.
Expressive Coding	Grades 4–6. For Task A, the examiner exposes a pseudoword for 1 second (e.g., *knad*), and the child writes the word in the response booklet. For Task B, the examiner exposes a pseudoword for 1 second, and the child writes a target letter in the word (e.g., the fifth letter). For Task B, the child writes two or three letters in the word (time limit of 5 seconds per item for both tasks).
RAN-Letters	Grades K–6. For Item 1, the child names a series of 10 randomly arrayed letters as rapidly as possible. For Item 2, the child names a series of randomly arrayed two-letter groups as rapidly as possible. The score is the number of seconds required to name all the letters or letter groups.
RAN-Words	Grades 1–6. The child names a series of eight randomly arrayed words as rapidly as possible. The score is the number of seconds required to name all of the words.
RAN-Digits	Grades K–6. For Item 1, the child names a series of six randomly arrayed one-digit numbers as rapidly as possible. The score is the number of seconds required to name all of the digits. For Item 2, the child names a series of randomly arrayed two-digit numbers as rapidly as possible.
RAN-Words & Digits	Grades 1–6. The child names a series of randomly arrayed alternating words and digits as rapidly as possible. The score is the number of seconds required to name all of the stimuli.
Note-Taking Task A	Grades 4–6. The examiner reads a four-paragraph simulated science lecture while the child writes notes in the response booklet. The child is allowed to write for up to 5 minutes after the examiner has stopped reading.
Rhyming	Grade K. For Task A, the examiner pronounces a set of three words (two rhyming and one nonrhyming), and the child says the nonrhyming word (3-second limit per item). For Task B, the child says as many real words as possible that rhyme with a target word pronounced by the examiner (10-second time limit per word).
Syllables	Grades K–6. The child repeats a polysyllabic word pronounced by the examiner and then says the syllable(s) remaining when a target syllable is omitted. For Grades 4–6, the target items are pseudowords.
Phonemes	For Task A (Grades K–3), the examiner pronounces a monosyllabic word (e.g., "pill") and asks the child to repeat it. The examiner pronounces the word again with a single target phoneme omitted (e.g., "ill"), and the child repeats the second word and then says the phoneme that was omitted (e.g., "ill, /p/"). For Tasks B and C (Grades K–3), the child repeats a monosyllabic or polysyllabic word presented by the examiner and then says the phonemes remaining when a target phoneme is omitted. For Task D (Grades 4–6), the items are pseudowords.
Rimes	For Task A (Grades 1–3), the child says a word with one or more target rimes omitted. For example, the examiner says, "Say *wither* without /ith/," and the child responds "/w/ - /er/" (3-second time limit per item). For Task B (Grades 4–6), the items are pseudowords. The score is the number of correct items administered.
Word Choice	Grades 1–6. The child circles one correctly spelled word from a set of three words presented in the response booklet. The score is the number of correct responses on items completed at the end of 120 seconds.

(continued)

TABLE 5.29. *(continued)*

Subtest	Description
Pseudoword Decoding	Grades 1–6. The child reads aloud a series of pseudowords printed on both sides of a card. Testing is discontinued after seven consecutive errors.
Story Retell	Grade K. The examiner reads a story, after which the child answers three questions about the story and then retells it. Questions and most of the story-retelling items are scored on a 3-point scale; two retelling items are scored on a 2-point scale (0, 2).
Finger Sense	Grades K–6. This subtest includes five timed tasks (*Repetition*, *Succession*, *Localization*, *Recognition*, and *Fingertip Writing*) and yields seven scores. For each task, the items are performed first with the child's right hand and then with the left hand. For the first two tasks, the child performs manipulations with the fingers, and scoring is based on task completion time for each hand. For the other three tasks, the child responds to manipulations performed by the examiner on the child's fingers, and scoring is based on the number of correct responses. For example, for *Fingertip Writing*, the examiner uses a wooden stylus to draw letters and numbers on the child's hand while the child's eyes are closed, and the child must identify the letter or number.
Sentence Sense	Grades 1–6. For each item, the child silently reads three similar sentences–one correct and two with a different word that makes the sentences illogical (e.g., *The tree his* [*sic*] *many uses*). The child circles the letter of the one sentence that makes sense. The score is the number of correct responses on items completed at the end of 120 seconds.
Copying	For Task A (Grade K), the child copies a sentence that includes all the letters of the alphabet, and the score is the number of correct letters completed in 20 seconds. For Task B (Grades 1–6), the child copies a paragraph, and the score is the number of correct letters completed in 90 seconds.
Note-Taking Task B	Grades 4–6. The child reviews the notes taken during Task A and writes a paragraph summarizing this information (5-minute time limit). The paragraph is scored on a 3-point scale for each of four components (organization, development–main ideas, development–supporting ideas, and translating skills), and the component scores are summed to yield a total score.

TABLE 5.30. Recommended PAL-RW Screening Battery for Grades K–2

Process	Kindergarten measures	Grade 1 measures	Grade 2 measures
Orthographic Processing	Alphabet Writing Receptive Coding Task A WIAT–II Letter Naming[a]	Alphabet Writing Receptive Coding Tasks A and B WIAT–II Letter Naming[a]	Alphabet Writing Receptive Coding Tasks A and B
Rapid Naming (RAN)	RAN-Letters	RAN-Letters	RAN-Letters
Phonological Processing	Rhyming Syllables	Syllables Phonemes	Phonemes Rimes
Phonological Decoding		Pseudoword Decoding[b]	Pseudoword Decoding
Spelling			WIAT–II Spelling
Total time	17 minutes	19 minutes	31 minutes

Note. From *Process Assessment of the Learner: Test Battery for Reading and Writing–Administration and Scoring Manual* (p. 85) by V. W. Berninger, 2001, San Antonio, TX: Psychological Corporation. Copyright 2001 by The Psychological Corporation. Adapted with permission.

[a]Letter naming items from the WIAT-II Word Reading subtest.

[b]Pseudoword Decoding should not be administered until the fifth month of first grade.

the recommended qualitative information noted in the record booklet (recording finger order by number of any incorrect sequences) while also timing the sequences and trying to ensure that children perform the task correctly and without looking at their fingers. For Fingertip Writing, which requires children to identify letters and numbers written with a wooden stylus on their fingertips, the arrows indicating the direction in which examiners should draw the letters and numerals are provided from the examiner's perspective. As a result, examinees experience the letters and numbers as reversed. Although this is not a problem for the sample items (*t* and *x*), six of the eight test items have a specific left-to-right orientation (e.g., *5*, *c*), so that the task measures children's ability to recognize reversed letters and numbers as much as finger function skills.

Scores

Scoring is quite time-consuming, especially if examiners analyze all of the additional information that they are prompted to collect. For most subtests, items are scored 1 or 0 for the block of items administered, whereas scores for RAN subtests and two of the Finger Sense tasks are based on response completion time. On Fingertip Writing, any items to which the child responded incorrectly are readministered, and full credit is awarded if the child then answers correctly. Scoring is subjective for Alphabet Writing, Copying Tasks A and B, Note-Taking Tasks A and B, and Story Retell. The manual provides comprehensive scoring guidelines for these and other subtests and an example of a completed record form section for each subtest. For Alphabet Writing, scoring is based on the number of letters written within 15 seconds, but letters must match the letter formation guidelines to receive credit, and several of the no-credit examples are very similar to the examples that are awarded credit. The author suggests audiotaping responses to Story Retell, which requires verbatim recording and more scoring judgment than the other subtests. An audiocassette presents correct pronunciations for Pseudoword Decoding items. The pronunciation for Item 54 (*tufle*) is given correctly on the audiocassette but incorrectly in the response booklet and in the scoring example in the manual, so that examiners who do not listen to the recording are likely to score that item incorrectly. Moreover, an alternative correct pronunciation (/tew/-/ful/) should be added. Pronunciations for items and correct responses for Phonemes and Rimes pseudoword items should also be provided on audiocassette for examiner review.

Raw scores are converted to decile scores (≤10 to ≤100), corresponding to the tenth of the distribution in which the child's performance falls. Two sets of decile scores are provided for the RAN subtests: the first for completion time in seconds (Grades K–6) and the second for the number of incorrect responses (Grades 2–6 only). Fall and spring norms are provided for kindergarten examinees, whereas norms are by full year for examinees in Grades 1 through 6. Given the rapid development of phonological and orthographic skills in the early primary grades, norms should be provided at 6-month intervals, at least through Grade 3. No rationale is presented in support of the use of full-year norms for Grades 1 and up; the use of decile scores rather than standard scores; or the use of a single score type rather than a wider variety of derived scores (i.e., standard scores, percentiles, and age and grade equivalents).

Interpretation

On the PAL-RW, decile scores are classified as follows: (1) 10 and 20 = deficient (i.e., processing weaknesses); (2) 30 and 40 = at risk; (3) 50 to 80 = adequate (i.e., processing competencies); and (4) 90 and 100 = proficient (i.e., processing strengths). According to the test's author, children scoring in the deficient or at-risk range on the screening battery for their grade should receive intervention until their performance improves to the emerging–adequate (decile = 50) or adequate range. The author cautions that of the Finger Sense tasks, only Succession can be interpreted in terms of this classification system, however. The manual also presents guidelines for diagnosing dyslexia and dysgraphia. A case study of a second grader is presented to demonstrate how to link PAL-RW results with intervention suggestions. The discussion is quite brief, considering the number of tasks administered (21), and some of the terminology is likely to be confusing to practitioners unfamiliar with Berninger's language theory.

Technical Adequacy

Standardization

PAL-RW standardization data were collected during 1999 and 2000 from 868 examinees sampled to be representative of the 1998 U.S. population of students in Grades K–6. A sample of 120 children in Grades K–6 completed both the PAL-RW and the WIAT-II. Norm characteristics are stratified by grade for gender, race/ethnicity, parental education level, and geographic region. Grade sizes range from 120 to 142 for the early primary grades. The kindergarten sample consists of 120 examinees, but because both fall and spring scores are provided for kindergarten, norms are based on only 60 students, which is below acceptable levels. Between 6% and 10% of the sample consisted of children with identified learning disabilities, speech/language impairments, or ADHD, and 1.5% to 4.3% of the sample consisted of children enrolled in gifted and talented programs. Sample characteristics are compared to the U.S. population for the entire subgroup rather than for each grade, so that it is not possible to evaluate grade-specific representativeness. Moreover, because some information is presented in bar graphs, whereas other data are presented in tables, evaluating sample representativeness is difficult. Overall, males are slightly overrepresented, and females, African Americans, and examinees from the Northeast region are slightly underrepresented. Examinees from the South are overrepresented by about 15 percentage points, and those from the North Central region are underrepresented by about 8 percentage points. Parent education levels of 13 through 15 years are slightly underrepresented, and the 12-year parent education level is slightly overrepresented.

Reliability Evidence

Coefficient alphas for 11 subtests range from .52 to .98 for the early primary grades. Coefficients for Pseudoword Decoding are .98 for Grades 1 and 2. Coefficients for the phonological subtests are in the .80s or above except for Syllables at Grade 2 (r = .74). Coefficients for Word Choice are in the .80s for Grade 2 and above but fall well below acceptable levels at Grade 1 (.66), probably because the task is too difficult for most children at that level. Alphas for Story Retell are .89 for both fall and spring kindergarten administration. According to the manual, alpha coefficients were not computed for subtests with fewer than six items (e.g., the RAN subtests) or for subtests on which performance showed little variability because of expected mastery (e.g., the Finger Sense subtests). Receptive Coding coefficients fall below acceptable levels for the entire early primary grade range, with values in the .50s for kindergarten and in the .70s for Grades 1 and 2.

Test–retest stability for 14 subtests and tasks (median interval = 49 days) based on 86 students in Grades 1, 3, and 5 from the standardization sample ranged from a low of .61 for Alphabet Writing to a high of .92 for RAN-Letters and RAN-Words & Digits. Stability estimates were in the .80s for RAN-Digits, Finger Sense Succession Items 1 and 2, and Copying Task A. Values fell in the .70s for RAN-Words, Finger Sense Repetition Item 2, and Copying Task B, and in the .60s for Alphabet Writing, Sentence Sense, and Finger Sense Repetition Item 1, Localization, and Recognition. No stability data are presented for examinees in kindergarten, Grade 2, or Grade 6 or for the remaining 12 subtests. Interscorer agreement for two independent scorers for all of the standardization protocols for Alphabet Writing ranged from .64 to .85, with a median correlation of .79, perhaps reflecting the lack of clarity in the scoring procedures. For Story Retell, the correlation between pairs of scores for at least two independent raters for 199 kindergarten protocols was .96. For Copying Tasks A and B, at least two individuals independently scored all standardization protocols. Interscorer agreement for Copying Task A (Grades K–6) ranged from .26 to .82, with a median reliability of .79. The test's author suggests that the very low correlations for kindergarten protocols (.26) were the result of attenuation due to the restricted range of scores. Agreement between pairs of scores for Copying Task B also fell below the criterion level (rs = .56 to .76, median r = .66). Given the difficulties associated with live-voice administration of deletion and pseudoword tasks, interscorer reliability estimates based on independent scoring of audiotaped responses or testing sessions with the same set of examinees should be provided for Syllables, Phonemes, Rimes, and Pseudoword Decoding. Interscorer reliability estimates based on independent scoring of responses for the same set of examinees at various grade levels should also be provided for the RAN subtests and the Finger Sense tasks, some of which are very challenging to administer and score.

Test Floors and Item Gradients

Floor effects are evident for Alphabet Writing, Syllables, Phonemes, and Copying Task A for fall and spring of kindergarten and for Grade 1 Alphabet Writing. Finger Sense Localization scores tend to be bimodally distributed.

Validity Evidence

CONTENT VALIDITY EVIDENCE

Subtest content, format, and item sets were designed to match the reading and writing processes identified in the research literature, including the author's theory of the processes of the functional reading and writing system (e.g., Berninger, 2000; Berninger & Abbott, 1994a; Berninger, Stage, et al., 2000a). The manual reviews the conceptual framework of the test, with a rationale for the inclusion of each subtest. Experts in reading and writing reviewed items for content representativeness and possible bias, and potentially biased items were replaced prior to national tryouts. Two national tryouts were conducted: the first in 1998 with 518 children in Grades K–6 and the second in 1999 with 271 children in Grades K–6. The manual reports that conventional and IRT item analyses, including percent-correct statistics, item–total correlations, grade progression of mean scores, and item difficulty, were conducted, but no specific item statistics are presented. Possible item bias was assessed by experienced reviewers and by means of IRT procedures, with final item selection based on data from the standardization testing and similar item analyses. No information is provided regarding the results of DIF analyses for various demographic subgroups.

CRITERION-RELATED VALIDITY EVIDENCE

The manual reports the results of three concurrent validity studies, two of which included early primary grade examinees. Correlations for PAL-RW handwriting and fine motor subtests with the *Developmental Test of Visual–Motor Integration* (Beery, 1997) for 12 children in Grades 1 through 3 ranged from near 0 to high, with the strongest correlations for Finger Sense Repetition and Copying Task B (.62 and .68, respectively). For 120 children in kindergarten through Grade 6, correlations between 17 PAL-RW subtests and 9 WIAT-II subtests were generally in the expected direction. For example, PAL-RW subtests tapping orthographic processing (Receptive Coding, Expressive Coding, and Word Choice) and rapid naming (RAN-Letters, RAN-Digits) correlated most highly with WIAT-II Spelling (*r*s = .74 to .81). Correlations with WIAT-II Word Reading were highest for the same orthographic subtests and all four of the rapid naming subtests (–.72 to .82). For a sample of 14 children (no grade or age specified), correlations for 11 PAL-RW subtests with the *Clinical Evaluation of Language Fundamentals–Third Edition* (CELF-III; Semel, Wiig, & Secord, 1995) ranged from –.02 to .79, with correlations for the CELF-III Total Language score generally in the low range.

CONSTRUCT VALIDITY EVIDENCE

Construct validity evidence consists of subtest intercorrelations by grade, grade score progression, correlations between the PAL-RW and other psychoeducational tests, group differentiation, and summaries of studies conducted with preliminary versions of the PAL-RW. Subtest intercorrelations vary widely, even within the same processing domain. For example, correlations among the orthographic processing subtests (Receptive Coding, Word Choice, and RAN-Letters) for Grade 1 examinees were low to moderate (–.18 to .46). Mean subtest scores increase across the grades covered by the test, with large differences between kindergarten and first grade and increasingly smaller differences for each higher grade, consistent with the developmental nature of the processes measured. Standard deviations equal or exceed means for Alphabet Writing for fall and spring of kindergarten; Syllables, Phonemes, Finger Sense Fingertip Writing, and Copying Task A for fall of kindergarten; and Finger Sense Repetition Items 1 and 2 for Grade 1, indicating that children's performance on these tasks is so variable and/or so limited that it is unlikely to be reliable.

Diagnostic validity was examined by comparing mean raw scores for 15 PAL-RW subtests for a sample of students with identified learning disabilities in reading, writing, or both, and a matched sample of students in Grades 1 through 3 (*ns* per comparison = 3–23). Scores for the clinical groups were lower than those for the control group on all 15 subtests, as anticipated, with significant differences for Syllables, Rimes, Finger Sense Succession 1 and 2, and Sentence Sense. Unfortunately, because grade-specific data are not provided and raw scores were not converted to decile scores, there is no way of determining whether differences were clinically useful, that is, whether subtest scores for the clinical group fell in the deficient or at-risk category compared with controls. The manual also reports the results of numerous studies conducted by Berninger and her colleagues using preliminary versions of PAL-RW tasks, with the discussion organized according to validity evidence for the reading- and writing-related subtests. PAL-RW tasks show utility in predicting reading and writing development and monitoring response to interventions. For example, a receptive orthographic coding task and tasks of phoneme and syllable segmentation contributed uniquely to word recognition in an unreferred sample of 300 primary grade students (Berninger & Abbott, 1994a). In an early intervention study with 128 referred first graders (Stage, Abbott, Jenkins, & Berninger, 2003), a factor based on alphabet writing and word choice tasks predicted degree of response to intervention. In a study comparing pre- and postintervention performance following first grade, RAN-Letters predicted individual growth curves in word recognition (Berninger et al., 1999). Although there is a wealth of validity evidence, it is presented entirely in narrative form and is difficult to follow. A table with descriptions of the studies, including sample size and grade level(s), tasks administered, and a summary of the results, would enhance readability and users' ability to evaluate the relevance of the evidence for their own assessment purposes and populations.

Usability

Administration and scoring procedures are clearly laid out in the manual, and the record form is well organized, with a box for each subtest containing start and stop rules, a summary of recording and scoring procedures, and time limits. Several features are less user-friendly, however. The test easels are thick and unwieldy, and the rings and easel structure are not as sturdy as they should be. As a result, the pages do not turn smoothly; this makes it difficult to achieve a consistent administration of the subtests that require a 1-second exposure of stimulus items, such as Receptive Coding. The manual is packed with useful assessment and intervention information but would benefit from reorganization. For example, information on the descriptive categories and suggested cutoffs for the decile scores is located in the chapter on test development and standardization rather than in the chapters on scoring and interpretation. The Receptive Coding and RAN subtests are novel and interesting to most children, but the Syllables, Phonemes, and Rimes subtests, all of which involve sound deletion, can seem interminable to examiner and examinee alike. Syllables items are in 10-item grade-specific blocks for children in kindergarten through Grade 3, but examinees in Grades 1 through 3 go on to take 40 more deletion items (30 Phonemes items and 10 Rimes items). A software scoring program generates a two-page printout, including the score array and a list by subtest of any additional information the examiner has recorded, but it does not provide decile scores for number of RAN errors. To facilitate interpretation, the score array should be grouped by process rather than presented in order of administration. The format of the PAL-RW Scoring Assistant differs from that of most other software scoring programs and, like the test itself, requires time and effort to master, especially in the absence of any printed guidelines for users.

Links to Intervention

Chapter 4 in the test manual provides guidelines for using PAL-RW results in conjunction with the *PAL Guides for Intervention,* organized according to Berninger's three-tier approach to assessment. For each process assessed in the screening tasks, the author directs the reader to a section of the intervention kit and/or other empirically validated resources for appropriate instructional activities. For example, she recommends that children who score in the at-risk range on the phonological subtests receive instruction using the 24-lesson phonological awareness training program in the *Guides for Intervention.* For progress monitoring purposes, the test manual provides guidelines for using PAL-RW subtests, criterion-referenced measures in the appendix, and selected measures from the WIAT-II to evaluate pre- and postintervention performance in six areas: word recognition, reading comprehension, reading rate, handwriting, spelling, and written composition. For example, for students with spelling problems, examiners can use several criterion-referenced measures in the appendix to identify the specific sound–letter correspondences that should be taught and to assess skills before and after instructional modifications. The appendix also includes compositional prompts for assessing spelling and narrative and expository compositional fluency using CBM-type procedures, with criterion-referenced scores for a sample of 100 students in each of Grades 1–6. For purposes of differential diagnosis, the author presents a discussion of dyslexia and dysgraphia, as well as guidelines for using measures on the PAL-RW, WIAT-II, and WISC-III to evaluate various components of reading and writing skills. The test manual also refers the reader to the *Guides for Intervention* for a framework and forms for developing IEPs. A case study of the second grader whose results were used to demonstrate scoring in a previous chapter is presented to illustrate how to link assessment to intervention.

Relevant Research

Berninger and her colleagues have used PAL-RW-related measures and preliminary versions of the PAL-RW tasks in a decade-long program of assessment, prevention, and intervention research (see Berninger, 1998b, and Berninger, Stage, Smith, & Hildebrand, 2001, for reviews). Their research with clinical and unreferred samples of elementary grade children has demonstrated that orthographic processing and rapid naming play a role in reading and writing acquisition in addition to that of phonological processing and that different components of the reading and writing processes predict different skills. In a sample of 102 students in first through sixth grade with documented reading and/or writing problems (Berninger, Abbott, Thomson, et al., 2001), four language factors (verbal IQ, phonology, orthography, and rapid naming) were used in structural models to predict three reading factors: reading accuracy, rate, and comprehension. The orthographic factor contributed unique variance to reading accuracy and rate, whereas the phonological factor contributed unique variance to reading accuracy and comprehension. Rapid naming predicted only reading rate, and verbal IQ contributed only to reading comprehension. In other words, all four predictors were valid for screening purposes, but each factor predicted different reading subskills.

Source and Cost

The PAL-RW test kit is available from The Psychological Corporation for $273.00 in a storage box and $299.00 in a nylon carrying bag. The *Process Assessment of the Learner: Guides for Intervention–Reading and Writing* instructional manual, together with classroom materials for 10, is available for $210.00. A combination kit with the test battery and intervention program costs $420.00 packed in a storage box and $446.00 packed in a nylon bag. The software scoring program for Windows applications is $158.00. A recently released training aid in video or CD format is $50.00.

Summary

The *Process Assessment of the Learner: Test Battery for Reading and Writing* (PAL-RW) is an individually administered, norm-referenced set of measures assessing the processes underlying reading and writing skills for children from kindergarten through Grade 6. The tasks are drawn from a decade-long research program investigating reading and writing processes, and preliminary versions of the subtests have been shown to be effective predictors of reading and writing acquisition and disabilities in unreferred and clinical samples. The PAL-RW offers a variety of options for assessment, including screening, progress monitoring, and differential diagnosis, especially when used in conjunction with the WIAT-II, to which it is statistically linked. The utility of the PAL-RW for practitioners assessing early primary grade children is limited by several usability and technical factors, however. Several of the subtests, especially the Finger Sense tasks, are difficult to administer and score reliably. The PAL-RW yields only decile scores, which not only provide less precise measurements than the usual standard scores and percentile ranks but also do not lend themselves readily to score comparisons when other tests are administered. Other technical problems include inadequate kindergarten subgroup size; floor effects and inadequate reliabilities for some subtests; lack of stability evidence for kindergarten, second-grade, and sixth-grade examinees; and limited or no test–retest and/or interscorer reliability for several subtests. Developing composite scores for use in comparing phonological processing, rapid naming, and orthographic processing skills would increase reliability and facilitate both interpretation and intervention planning.

Case Example

Name of student: Cindy S.
Age: 8 years, 1 month
Grade: Second grade
Date of assessment: October

Reason for referral: Cindy was referred for an early reading assessment by her second-grade teacher. Although Cindy has received extra school-based support for 2 years, her word recognition and phonics skills are very limited, and she has difficulty completing written work independently because she cannot read the directions for many tasks. On the early literacy screening battery administered earlier this month, she obtained the poorest overall score in the entire grade.

Assessment results and interpretation: The *Process Assessment of the Learner: Test Battery for Reading and Writing* (PAL-RW) measures a variety of processes related to reading and writing development, including phonological processing, rapid naming, and orthographic processing. The PAL-RW yields decile scores, which range from 10 to 100 and describe in which tenth of the distribution a student's performance falls. On the PAL-RW, decile scores are classified as follows: 10 and 20 = deficient; 30 and 40 = at risk; 50 to 80 = adequate; and 90 and 100 = proficient. Cindy's performance on the PAL-RW is presented below.

Process	Subtest	Raw Score	Decile Score	Descriptive Category
Orthographic	Receptive Coding	28	10	Deficient
	Word Choice	3	10	Deficient
Rapid Naming	RAN-Letters	90	20	Deficient
	RAN-Words	109 sec.	10	Deficient
	RAN-Digits	120 sec.	10	Deficient
	RAN-Words & Digits	130 sec.	10	Deficient
Phonological	Syllables	5	20	Deficient
	Phonemes	12	50	Emerging-adequate
	Rimes	3	20	Deficient
Phonological Decoding	Pseudoword Decoding	3	20	Deficient
Fine Motor	Finger Sense			
	Repetition Item 1	8 sec.	40	At risk
	Repetition Item 2	5 sec.	90	Proficient
	Succession Item 1	12 sec.	60	Adequate
	Succession Item 2	15 sec.	30	At risk
	Localization	10 sec.	100	Deficient
	Recognition	8 sec.	20	Deficient
	Fingertip Writing	3	40	Deficient
Handwriting	Alphabet Writing	4	60	Adequate
	Copying Task A	11	90	Proficient
Comprehension	Sentence Sense	2	10	Deficient

On the PAL-RW, Cindy demonstrated varying degrees of competency across reading and writing domains. On orthographic tasks, which assess the ability to attend to and remember letters and words, she scored in the deficient range. She had particular difficulty with a task requiring her to remember correct spelling patterns and was able to answer correctly only 3 of 15 items presented. On rapid naming tasks, which require naming letters, digits, and/or whole words as quickly as possible, her performance was also in the deficient range, indicating lack of automaticity in accessing verbal information. On phonological processing measures, she had difficulty understanding the nature of the tasks, which require deleting specific sounds from words spoken by the examiner. After numerous demonstrations and examples, she was able to perform 5 of 10 syllable deletions, but she was able to perform very few phoneme (e.g., "Say *vet* without /et/") or rime (e.g., "Say *what* without /at/") deletions. For example, when she was asked to say *get* without /g/, she responded, "at."

On a task requiring Cindy to read phonically regular nonsense words (e.g., *heb*), she was able to decode only 3 of the 21 items administered (deficient range). Her errors reflect her limited understanding of letter–sound correspondences, including short vowel sounds (*van* for *vun*), and consonant blends (*def* for *dreep*). On fine motor tasks requiring her to perform various finger functions, her skills ranged from deficient to proficient. She had particular trouble identifying letters and symbols traced on her fingers, even with two trials. On handwriting tasks, she was able to generate enough alphabet letters in order under time pressure to earn an adequate rating for her grade, but it should be noted that this subtest is scored for the number of letters completed at the end of 15 seconds. As she continued writing, she had to recite the alphabet from the beginning several times to retrieve the letter names, especially toward the end of the alphabet. She required a total of 3 minutes and 35 seconds to complete the task, indicating lack of automaticity for letter retrieval. On a comprehension task that required her to read sets of three sentences and mark the one sentence that made sense, her performance is rated as deficient. She appeared to be answering randomly on this task and later acknowledged that she could not read most of the words in the sentences.

STANDARDIZED READING INVENTORY—SECOND EDITION

Overview

The *Standardized Reading Inventory–Second Edition* (SRI-2; Newcomer, 1999) is an individually administered, norm-referenced test of word recognition and comprehension for individuals aged 6-0 through 14-6. Modeled after an informal reading inventory, the SRI-2 consists of two forms, each containing a contextual vocabulary measure, 10 graded word recognition lists, and 10 graded reading passages ranging in difficulty from preprimer to Grade 8. The original SRI (Newcomer, 1986) was criterion-referenced but included features of standardized tests, including specific administration procedures, objective scoring criteria, guidelines for interpretation, and information on reliability and validity. Changes to this edition include (1) the introduction of national norms, (2) the addition of a vocabulary subtest and a supplemental predictive comprehension subtest, (3) changes to several comprehension questions in the interests of clarity, and (4) a streamlined layout to facilitate administration and scoring. The reading passages are identical to those in the SRI. The SRI-2 has the following purposes: (1) to identify deficiencies in reading vocabulary for groups of students, (2) to determine a student's reading levels, (3) to provide information regarding strengths and weakness in reading strategies and skills, (4) to document progress as the result of reading interventions, and (5) to serve as a research tool. Materials include a spiral-bound examiner's manual; a spiral-bound student story book containing word lists, reading passages, and comprehension questions for both forms; 25 vocabulary sheets per form; 25 examiner record booklets per form; and 50 profile/scoring booklets, all packed in a storage box.

Components, Subtests, and Composite

Components and Subtests

The SRI-2 consists of three components: (1) a test of vocabulary knowledge, (2) a series of graded word lists, and (3) a series of graded reading passages. Performance on the reading passages produces three scores, called "subtests," one of which is optional. The components and subtests are described in Table 5.31.

Composite

A composite score, termed a "Reading Quotient," is obtained by summing the standard scores for Passage Comprehension and Word Recognition Accuracy on the reading passages.

TABLE 5.31. Description of the SRI-2 Components and Subtests

Component/subtest	Description
Vocabulary in Context	The child reads short sentences silently and selects from four choices the one word closest in meaning to an underlined word.
Words in Isolation Checklists	The child reads single words aloud from 20-item grade-specific lists. One list is provided per reading passage.
Passage Comprehension	After reading a series of passages aloud and then silently, the child responds orally to examiner-delivered comprehension questions to yield a *Passage Comprehension* subtest score. All of the passages are narrative.
Word Recognition Accuracy	This subtest score is based on the child's errors in oral passage reading.
Predictive Comprehension	The child rereads a passage silently until he or she reaches an underlined word. The examiner then reads five sentences, and the child chooses the sentence that would come next in the story.

Note. The optional subtest is shaded.

Administration

There are no time limits for the SRI-2, which takes from 30 to 90 minutes, depending on the child's reading level. The Vocabulary in Context (VOC) subtest uses a silent-reading, multiple-choice format and may be administered to individuals or groups. Entry level for the reading passages is determined by administering either VOC or the Words in Isolation Checklists located in the test book. The VOC raw score is converted to a grade equivalent using a table in the manual, and the entry level for the reading passages is set at one grade level below that grade equivalent. If VOC is not administered, the examiner begins by administering the checklist two grades below the examinee's current grade level, and the entry level is the highest checklist on which the child misses three or fewer words. The SRI-2 is unusual among contextual reading tests in that the child reads each passage at least twice (once aloud and once silently) and reads it silently a third time if the optional Predictive Comprehension subtest is administered. During the first oral reading, the examiner records word recognition errors and, if desired, word recognition irregularities for later analysis (see below). Although titles are provided for the stories, the word count does not include the title, suggesting that title reading is not scored. Unlike the procedures for most oral reading measures, the examiner does not provide assistance after a specific time interval if the child pauses or struggles. The child then rereads the passage silently, after which the examiner reads the comprehension questions aloud. The child is not permitted to look at the passage when responding to the questions.

Testing is designed to establish the examinee's independent reading level (basal), instructional reading level (highest level below frustration), and frustration level (ceiling). Basals and ceilings must be established separately for the Word Recognition Accuracy (WRA) and Passage Comprehension (PC) scores during testing to ensure that the appropriate number of passages is administered. For WRA, oral reading errors are converted to a 6-point scale, on which the basal is a score of 5 (independent level), scores of 1–4 indicate instructional level, and the ceiling is a score of 0 (frustration level). For PC, the scores associated with the three levels vary by passage, based on data from the normative sample. Procedures for obtaining basals and ceilings are complex, and the manual does not provide any scoring examples. If the examinee achieves a basal in PC but not in WRA, testing continues downward until a WRA basal is reached; if the examinee reaches a ceiling in PC but not in WRA, testing continues upward until a ceiling is reached or the last story is read. In this situation, comprehension questions may be administered but are not scored. Similarly, if a basal is reached on WRA but not on PC, testing continues downward until a basal is reached, but oral reading errors are not scored. If the child reaches a ceiling in WRA but not PC, testing continues upward, but the child reads silently and WRA is not scored.

If desired, the Predictive Comprehension questions can be administered for each passage after the PC questions but only for passages between the child's independent reading level (basal) and frustration level (ceiling). After the child rereads the passage silently, the examiner reads the five choices aloud while the child follows along in the storybook. The examiner can also assess listening comprehension by reading aloud passages that are above the child's WRA and PC frustration levels and administering the PC questions. Listening comprehension scores are not normed, however, and no interpretive guidelines are provided.

Scores

Scoring takes about 10–30 minutes, depending on whether the entire test is administered and which, if any, of the optional error analyses are conducted. For WRA, the examiner records five categories of oral reading errors: (1) omissions, (2) insertions, (3) substitutions, (4) repetitions, and (5) reversals. The total number of errors per passage is converted to an accuracy score ranging from 0 to 5, and accuracy scores are summed to yield a total WRA score. Comprehension questions are scored 1 or 0. The PC score is the number correct for the passage and does not need to be converted. Raw scores for WRA and PC are summed across the levels (passages) administered and converted to age-based standard scores (M = 10, SD = 3), percentiles, and age and grade equivalents. WRA and PC standard scores are summed to obtain a Reading Quotient (M = 100, SD = 15). The VOC raw score can be converted to the same set of derived scores as WRA and PC but does not enter into the Reading Quotient. Users should note that although the test's author provides appropriate cautions regarding the use of grade equivalents, the lack of precision of grade equivalent scores is quite marked for primary grade examinees. For example, for a child aged 7-6 in the 8th month of Grade 2, standard scores of 10 on PC, WRA, and VOC are associated with grade equivalents of 1.8, 2.0, and 1.8, respectively, that is, 8 months to a year below actual grade placement (2.8). Norms are in 6-month increments for ages 6-0 through 13-11 and 1-year increments for ages 14-0 through 14-11. Because children's reading problems are typically evaluated in terms of grade peer comparisons, grade norms should be added. An appendix in the manual provides a rationale for the Predictive Comprehension answers but offers no normative data, such as percent correct by grade level. The author also presents optional error analysis systems based on the percentage of four types of comprehension errors (factual, inferential, lexical, and predictive) and three types of word recognition "irregularities" (self-corrections, hesitations, and ignoring punctuation); a 3-point scale for rating word attack skills; and a reading behavior observation scale.

Interpretation

A case example of a third grader aged 7-10 is included to demonstrate how to complete the record booklet information, calculate and record scores, and evaluate score discrepancies. The manual provides tables with the differences in subtest scores for both forms required for statistical significance and clinical utility, the latter defined according to Reynolds's (1984–1985, 1990) formula. There is an error in the section in which the case example's scores are used to illustrate discrepancy analyses. Beginning on page 27, PC and WRA raw scores rather than standard scores (raw scores = 28 and 20 vs. SSs = 10 and 11) are used to compute the Reading Quotient (RQ), which results in an RQ of 64 instead of 103 and subtest raw score differences that meet the criteria for statistical and clinical significance, whereas the standard scores do not. The error is perpetuated in the discussion of procedures for evaluating differences between the SRI-2 and other tests, yielding a 41-point rather than a 2-point difference between the SRI-2 RQ and the General Mental Ability Quotient on the *Detroit Tests of Learning Aptitude–Fourth Edition* (Hammill, 1998). The author appropriately cautions that examiners should not draw conclusions from a single analysis and notes that miscue analysis for the SRI-2 is only designed to provide "clinical clues" for further assessment and instruction.

Technical Adequacy

Standardization

The SRI-2 was standardized between November 1996 and February 1998 on 1,099 children aged 6 to 14 residing in 28 states. Demographic characteristics of the sample are compared to 1997 U.S. census data in terms of age, geographic area, gender, race, residence, ethnicity, family income, educational attainment of parents, and disability status and are stratified by age for geographic area, gender, race, and residence. Although the norm group is generally representative of the U.S. school-age population, Northeastern and white examinees are slightly overrepresented, and African American and upper SES examinees are slightly underrepresented. Subgroup sizes for the early primary grade range vary from a low of 106 for age 6 to a high of 197 for age 8. Because norm group intervals are in 6-month blocks, this means that scores for 6-year-olds are based on only 53 examinees. Users should be especially cautious in interpreting SRI-2 results for African American 6-year-olds because only four African American children were included in the sample at that age.

Reliability Evidence

Coefficient alpha reliabilities for PC and VOC exceed .90 for the early primary grade range for both forms, whereas reliabilities for WRA range from .84 to .88 across forms. Reading Quotient (RQ) internal consistency estimates for both forms range from .91 to .94 across the early primary grade range. Coefficient alphas for nine subgroups in the normative sample are at or above .90 for the three subtests and RQ, with the exception of Form A WRA for African Americans ($r = .89$). For the original SRI, which contains the same reading passages as the SRI-2, alternate-form reliability for Levels 2, 3, and 4 PC and WRA for 30 third graders ranged from .80 to .84. Test–retest reliability (2-week interval) for the same sample ranged from .83 to .92 across the two forms, with coefficients somewhat higher for Form B. For the SRI-2, alternate-form reliability was evaluated by comparing the extent to which children obtained the same instructional and frustration reading levels on both forms, using all the students in the norm group who were considered to be reading on grade level (*ns* = 65 to 176 for levels preprimer through 3). Of those examinees, 70% to 82% obtained the same instructional and frustration reading level on Forms A and B, with slightly higher agreement for WRA. Stability for Form A VOC, based on 50 examinees (age and grade unspecified) who took it twice (2-week interval), was .95. Although means and standard deviations for Form A and B subtests for eight age intervals are listed in the validity section, correlation coefficients for the two forms are not reported by age. Correlations between subtests on the two forms range from a low of .88 for PC to a high of .97 for VOC. Evidence of form equivalence or score stability for the RQ for examinees of any age is lacking.

Interscorer reliability based on independent scoring of 30 completed protocols by the test's author and a colleague yielded 97% agreement for estimating instructional level for both PC and WRA (test form and examinee ages and grades not specified). Interscorer agreement based on the same examiners' independent recording and scoring responses for audiotaped test sessions of 20 randomly selected students (age and grade unspecified) from the standardization sample was 95% for Form A and 90% for Form B for PC agreement and 90% for both Forms A and B for WRA agreement. The author and publisher are to be commended for using this method for evaluating interscorer agreement, which provides much more accurate information about not only interscorer consistency but also examiner variance than estimates based on completed protocols.

Test Floors and Item Gradients

Floors for PC and WRA for both forms are inadequate below age 8-0, and floors for VOC are inadequate below age 9-0. A 6-year-old who obtains a raw score of 1 on VOC achieves a standard score of 8 (average range). Floors for the RQ are inadequate below age 7-6 for both forms. Although the SRI-2 displays no item gradient violations for early primary grade examinees, it is not sensitive to small differences among younger readers because of inadequate floors.

Validity Evidence

CONTENT VALIDITY EVIDENCE

SRI-2 story passages and comprehension questions are identical with those on the SRI. The test's author created graded word lists by compiling words typically introduced at preprimer through Grade 8 levels from five basal reading series. All of the series date from the late 1970s and early 1980s, and words considered "typical" may have changed in the last two decades. Two sets of passages were then written for each of the 10 levels, using words presented at that level in at least two reading series. The manual includes a table listing the number of words per passage, novel words, sentences, words per sentence, key words in two series, and key words in three or more series to demonstrate that the semantic and syntactic complexity of the passages increases with each level. Passage difficulty was not evaluated using readability formulae, however; nor were preestablished standards used to determine independent, instructional, and frustration levels (i.e., 90% accuracy and above = instructional level).

Instead, for a subgroup of examinees (number not specified) in the standardization sample who were identified by their teachers as reading on grade level, SRI passages from one level below instructional level, at instructional level, and one level above instructional level were used to compute means and standard deviations for oral reading. For each passage, instructional level was defined as a score falling at ±1 standard deviation from the mean, whereas independent level was defined as a score falling at 1 standard deviation above the mean, and frustration level was defined as a score more than 1 standard deviation below the mean. The same graded word list was used to develop the VOC subtest. VOC items were administered to the entire standardization sample, with final selection and ordering based on an item analysis. Median item difficulties for primary grade examinees are acceptable for PC but fall at the low end of the acceptable range for VOC at age 6 (.16 and .15 for Forms A and B, respectively). Item discrimination coefficients are at adequate levels across the entire age range. DIF analyses using the delta scores procedure were used to compare performance on VOC and PC items for three dichotomous groups (males vs. females, African Americans vs. non-African Americans, and Hispanic Americans vs. non-Hispanic Americans). Although correlations were .98 or above, suggesting little item bias, the delta scores approach is not recommended because it is sample-dependent (Camilli & Shepard, 1994).

CRITERION-RELATED VALIDITY EVIDENCE

The manual presents five criterion-related validity studies, at least three of which included primary grade examinees. For 50 students (no age or grade specified), SRI-2 Form A VOC was highly correlated (.76) with the Reading Vocabulary subtest of the *California Achievement Tests* (CTB/McGraw-Hill, 1985). Correlations were lower for the same sample between SRI-2 PC and WRA and *Gray Oral Reading Tests–3* (GORT-3) Word Recognition (.40 to .67 across both forms), which is surprising, considering the similarities in format between the two instruments. Unfortunately, correlations and mean standard scores for GORT-3 and SRI-2 Passage Comprehension are not reported, which would shed light on the influence of format on performance (e.g., being permitted to look back at the passages; a single oral reading vs. both oral and silent reading). Correlations between the SRI-2 RQ and the *Gray Silent Reading Tests* were higher (*r*s = .63 to .71) in a study with 91 children aged 7 to 15. For 48 children ages 7 through 16, SRI-2 WRA was moderately to highly correlated with most of the subtests and all of the composites on the *Comprehensive Test of Phonological Processing* (CTOPP), with the strongest relationships for the CTOPP Phonological Awareness and Memory composites (*r*s = .62 to .63). In contrast, only 4 of the 17 CTOPP subtests and composites were significantly correlated with the SRI-2 RQ (*r*s = .35 to .67), with the highest correlation for the Phonological Memory composite. For the same sample, correlations between the SRI-2 and subtest and composite scores on the *Test of Word Reading Efficiency* were high for WRA (.65 to .74) but low to moderate for the RQ (.33 to .57). No evidence of predictive validity is reported.

CONSTRUCT VALIDITY EVIDENCE

As expected, SRI-2 means increase with age, with the greatest gains in the primary years. For a sample of 60 students in Grades 4, 6, and 8, the total raw score on word recognition and the total number of correct comprehension answers on the original SRI were moderately correlated (.41 to .64) with scores on the *Otis–Lennon School Ability Test–Sixth Edition* (Otis & Lennon, 1989). The manual reports two studies of group differentiation, one with each version of the test. In a study with 40 eighth graders, of whom 20 were defined as poor readers and 20 as capable readers based on their *Stanford Achievement Test* scores, mean numbers of oral reading errors and comprehension errors at SRI Levels 7 and 9 significantly differentiated between the two groups for both forms. In a study comparing two groups of examinees with exceptionalities in the norm group to nondisabled students, learning-disabled examinees scored significantly lower than controls for all three subtests across both forms (SSs = 6–8 vs. 10–11, respectively), with the lowest scores on Form A PC. Mean subtest scores for students with speech–language disabilities were also significantly lower than mean scores for nondisabled students, with the exception of Form B PC (SSs = 8–9 vs. 10–11). Subtest intercorrelations reported for the entire normative sample range from .62 to .97, with a median of .64. No evidence is provided to support the claim that the SRI-2 can be used to monitor the progress of students receiving interventions.

Usability

The SRI-2 offers examiners a range of reading assessment options in a single, inexpensive, and portable instrument. The VOC subtest can be administered to groups of children but because of floor effects, it is not appropriate for children below the age of 9. Scoring is quite time-consuming, especially for the first few administrations and especially if the optional error analyses are conducted. The Predictive Comprehension subtest, which yields only raw scores, contributes little additional information for diagnosis or instructional planning.

Links to Intervention

The manual presents a brief section on additional assessment that refers to assessment textbooks, as well as a one-page discussion of instructional strategies for improving reading skills in five categories: word meaning, reading rate, word attack, comprehension of narrative text, and comprehension of expository text. The discussion is general in nature and consists primarily of citations of textbooks and research studies, many of which date from the 1980s.

Source and Cost

The SRI-2 is available from PRO-ED for $231.00.

Test Reviews

Solomon, A. (2001). Review of the Standardized Reading Inventory, Second Edition. In B. S. Plake & J. C. Impara (Eds.), *The fourteenth mental measurements yearbook* (pp. 1169–1170). Lincoln, NE: Buros Institute of Mental Measurements.

Stevens, B. A. (2001). Review of the Standardized Reading Inventory, Second Edition. In B. S. Plake & J. C. Impara (Eds.), *The fourteenth mental measurements yearbook* (pp. 1170–1172). Lincoln, NE: Buros Institute of Mental Measurements.

Summary

The *Standardized Reading Inventory–Second Edition* (SRI-2) is a set of silent and oral reading measures for children ages 6 through 14 with a format similar to that of an informal reading inventory. The SRI-2 yields both criterion- and norm-referenced results that are useful for analyzing reading strengths and weaknesses and for planning instructional interventions. Despite its assets, its utility in early reading assessments is limited by several factors. Inadequate floors preclude the identification of low-performing children at ages 6 and 7 for all subtests and up to age 9 for the Vocabulary in Context subtest. Moreover, no fluency measures have been included in this edition, despite a large body of research documenting the importance of automaticity in reading proficiency. Studies documenting grade-specific subtest and composite stability, form equivalence, and the efficacy of the SRI-2 in predicting reading achievement and documenting progress as the result of interventions are needed. Comparisons of the relative diagnostic and predictive utility of the SRI-2 and the *Gray Oral Reading Tests–4*, which uses a similar oral reading format but includes a rate measure, would be especially interesting.

Case Example

Name of student: Tobias N.
Age: 8 years, 3 months
Grade: Second grade
Date of assessment: April

Reason for referral: Tobias was referred for an early reading assessment by his second-grade teacher because he is making very poor academic progress, especially in reading and spelling. His decoding skills are weak, and he has trouble understanding what he has read. On the fall administration of the second-grade reading screening battery, his understanding of letter-sound correspondences was very limited, and his oral reading accuracy for first-grade material was rated at the frustration level.

Assessment results and interpretation: The *Standardized Reading Inventory–Second Edition (SRI-2), Form A* is designed to assess oral reading, word recognition, and comprehension skills. The SRI-2 includes several components: (1) a set of graded word lists, (2) a set of graded reading passages, and (3) a measure of silent reading vocabulary. All of the tasks are untimed. On the Words in Isolation Checklists, children read 20-item graded word lists that provide an estimate of word identification skills and indicate the entry level for passage reading (the highest level at which the child misses fewer than 4 words). Tobias's performance on the Words in Isolation Checklists is shown below.

Word List	Raw Score	Rating
Preprimer	19/20	Independent
Primer	18/20	Independent
Grade 1	15/20	Instructional
Grade 2	0/20	Frustration

Tobias's word recognition skills, as measured by single word reading, are rated at an independent level for preprimer and primer material (beginning of Grade 1 material), at an instructional level for Grade 1 material, and at a frustration level for Grade 2 material. He was unable to read any of the words on the Grade 2 word list.

To assess Tobias's contextual reading skills, the SRI-2 reading passages and the Vocabulary in Context subtest were administered. On the reading passages, the child reads grade-level stories aloud, rereads them silently, and then answers comprehension questions about what has been read. The examiner reads the questions aloud, and the student is not permitted to look at the passage when answering the question. Tobias's performance on the reading passage is shown below.

Reading Level	Word Recognition Accuracy	Comprehension
Independent	Preprimer	Not reached
Instructional	Preprimer	Preprimer
Frustration	Primer	Primer

Tobias made a good effort to read the passages, but he read very slowly and laboriously. His ability to recognize words without assistance (independent reading level) is rated at a preprimer level. Even on the preprimer selection, however, he was unable to answer all of the comprehension questions correctly (4/5 correct). His instructional levels for both word recognition accuracy and comprehension fall at the preprimer level. His ability to obtain meaning from text is severely limited by his decoding problems. On the primer reading passage, he was able to answer only two of the seven comprehension questions correctly because he could not decode many of the key content words. For example, for the title of the passage (*A Picture of My Rabbit*), he read, "A Piece of a Riddle." In his efforts to read unfamiliar words, he appeared to rely primarily on the initial consonant sound and on visual memory for word forms (e.g., *for* for *frog*, *what* for *white*).

The SRI-2 also provides norms for comparing children's reading performance with that of others their age. Average scores for a student Tobias's age are as follows: Reading Quotient (RQ) = 100, Subtest Standard Score = 10, Percentile Rank (PR) = 50, Age Equivalent (AE) = 8-3, Grade Equivalent (GE) = 2.8. His performance on the passages and the Vocabulary in Context subtest is reported below.

Composite/Subtest	Reading Quotient	Subtest Standard Score	Percentile Rank	Age Equivalent	Grade Equivalent
Reading Quotient (PC + WRA)	70	–	2	–	–
Passage Comprehension (PC)	–	5	5	<6-0	<K.5
Word Recognition Accuracy (WRA)	–	5	5	<6-0	<K.5
Vocabulary in Context (VOC)	–	7	16	6-9	1.0

Tobias's overall reading performance is rated as poor (RQ = 70) and falls at the 2nd percentile for his age. His ability to decode words accurately and his ability to understand what he has read are both rated below the midkindergarten level (GE = <K.5). On the Vocabulary in Context subtest, which requires the child to read short sentences silently and choose the one of four words closest in meaning to an underlined word, his performance falls at a beginning first-grade level (GE = 1.0). Although his performance on this multiple-choice task was somewhat higher than on the oral reading measures (PR = 16 vs. 5, respectively), he worked very quickly and often appeared to be answering randomly rather than trying to read the sentences and word choices.

WOODCOCK READING MASTERY TESTS—REVISED/NORMATIVE UPDATE

Overview

The *Woodcock Reading Mastery Tests–Revised/Normative Update* (WRMT-R/NU; Woodcock, 1987/1998) is an individually administered, norm-referenced set of reading measures for examinees from 5 to 75+ years of age. First published in 1973, the WRMT is now in its third revision. The 1998 test easels are identical to those in the 1987 version, but the norms have been updated with a new sample assessed in 1995 and 1996. Other changes include additions and updates to the manual and modifications to the test records, which include new instructional level profiles, part score tables, and diagnostic profiles. The WRMT-R/NU has two forms: Form H, which contains four tests, and Form G, which includes three additional measures. The WRMT-R/NU and its predecessors have been used in numerous reading research studies as diagnostic, progress monitoring, and outcome measures. Uses identified by the manual include (1) clinical assessment and diagnosis, (2) individual program planning, (3) instructional placement, (4) guidance, (5) progress monitoring, (6) program evaluation, and (7) research. Materials for each form include an examiner's manual, an easel-format test book, a pronunciation audiocassette for the Word Attack and Word Identification tests, a sample combined-form summary test record, a sample parent report, and 25 test records, all packed in a carrying bag.

Tests and Composites

Tests

Like the WJ III, the WRMT-R/NU uses the term "tests" for measures yielding a score and "subtests" for tasks within a measure not yielding a separate score. The printout from the software scoring program uses the term "subtest" for "test," however. The WRMT-R/NU includes a total of seven tests across the two forms. Both forms include the first four tests listed in Table 5.32, and Form G includes two additional tests assessing readiness skills and a supplementary criterion-referenced letter identification checklist.

Composites

The six core WRMT-R/NU tests can be combined to form five overlapping composites, called "clusters" (see Table 5.33).

Administration

Testing time for the entire WRMT-R/NU is about 30–45 minutes, depending on the age and skill level of the child. The Short Scale, consisting of Word Identification and Passage Comprehension, can be administered in about 10 minutes to early primary grade children. For Visual–Auditory Learning, testing continues until an error cutoff is reached. For the other tests, basal and ceiling criteria are six or more consecutive items either passed or failed. Examiners are advised to administer an entire testing page even if the child has reached the ceiling before the end of the page. Unlike many test records, the WRMT-R/NU record booklet provides ample room for noting error responses for all tests except Visual–Auditory Learning. Word Attack pronun-

TABLE 5.32. Description of the WRMT-R/NU Tests

Tests	Description
Word Identification	The child reads single words (5-second time limit per word).
Word Attack	The child pronounces pseudowords or very low-frequency words (approximately 5-second limit per word).
Word Comprehension	This test consists of three subtests. For *Antonyms* and *Synonyms*, the child reads a stimulus word aloud and supplies a word with the opposite or same meaning, respectively. For *Analogies*, the child reads a pair of words aloud, determines the relationship between them, reads a third word, and provides a word with the same relationship to the third word as that between the first pair of words.
Passage Comprehension	The child reads a sentence or short paragraph silently and supplies a key missing word.
Visual–Auditory Learning (Form G only)	In this controlled learning task, the child learns to identify symbols representing words and to "read" sequences of those symbols that have been connected to form sentences. This test is virtually identical to the *Woodcock–Johnson III* test of the same name, with minor variations in the cutoffs and number of phrases per "story."
Letter Identification (Form G only)	The child identifies uppercase and lowercase letters presented in a wide variety of type styles. The child may say the letter name or the most common sound.
Supplementary Letter Checklist (Form G only)	The child identifies the entire alphabet presented in the sans serif type style commonly used in primary grade reading materials. The examiner may use the checklist to assess knowledge of letter names, letter sounds, or a mixture, except for digraphs and diphthongs, which must be identified by sound.

Note. The supplemental subtest is shaded.

TABLE 5.33. Clusters on the WRMT-R/NU

Cluster	Tests
Readiness	Visual–Auditory Learning Letter Identification
Basic Skills	Word Identification Word Attack
Reading Comprehension	Word Comprehension Passage Comprehension
Total Reading–Short Scale	Word Identification Passage Comprehension
Total Reading–Full Scale	Word Identification Word Attack Word Comprehension Passage Comprehension

ciation guides are provided in the manual, on the audiocassette, in the test book, and on the test record to promote accurate scoring. The audiocassette also provides pronunciations for the more difficult Word Identification items for each form.

Scores

The Visual–Auditory Learning score is based on the number of errors. For all other tests, items are dichotomously scored. Raw scores are converted to *W* scores, from which age- and grade-based standard scores ($M = 100$, $SD = 15$), percentile ranks, age and grade equivalents, Relative Performance Index (RPI) scores, and instructional ranges can be derived. Only raw scores are available for the Supplementary Letter Checklist. Several of the scores yielded by the Rasch-model WRMT-R/NU are unique to the Woodcock family of tests and reflect an examinee's expected quality of performance versus relative standing in a group (see the *Woodcock–Johnson III* review for complete score descriptions). RPI scores indicate the percentage of mastery demonstrated by the examinee on tasks that average individuals at the examinee's age or grade are expected to perform with 90% mastery. Instructional ranges, which parallel the reading levels yielded by informal reading inventories, indicate the level of instruction that would be easy or difficult for the examinee. On the WRMT-R/NU, the instructional range extends from an easy level, where the examinee's relative mastery is 96% or higher (RPI = 96/90), to a difficult level, where the examinee's relative mastery is 75% or less (RPI = 75/90). The WRMT-R/NU also makes use of *extended age and grade equivalent scales* that can represent performance above or below the average at both ends of the traditional age or grade equivalent scale. For example, a grade equivalent of $K.0^{25}$ on Visual–Auditory Learning indicates that the child's raw score on that test is equivalent to scores at the 25th percentile for children entering kindergarten. Similarly, the WRMT-R/NU uses an *extended percentile rank scale* that provides scores down to a percentile rank of 0.1 and up to a percentile rank of 99.9.

Several additional scoring and interpretive options are available. Raw scores for Word Comprehension can be evaluated across four reading vocabularies (general reading, science-mathematics, social studies, and humanities) by summing the item scores on the test record and comparing the results with midyear average raw scores for eight grade and age levels (including kindergarten, Grade 1, and Grade 3). Examiners can also complete a Word Attack error inventory and up to three diagnostic profiles (readiness, basic skills, and comprehension) comparing WRMT-R/NU scores with scores on the *Goldman–Fristoe–Woodcock Auditory Skills Test Battery* (Goldman, Fristoe, & Woodcock, 1974) and the *Woodcock–Johnson Psycho-Educational Battery* (WJ; Woodcock & Johnson, 1977), based on equating studies with 600 examinees (age and grade not specified). The combined test record for Forms G and H includes the instructional level profile, percentile rank profile, Word Attack error inventory for both forms, summary of scores, and diagnostic profiles for Basic Skills and Reading Comprehension clusters. Hand scoring, which is both time consuming and vulnerable to errors, requires more than an hour if the full array of scores and interpretive options is desired.

Interpretation

The manual describes four levels of interpretation: (1) error analysis; (2) developmental level, including *W* scores and age and grade equivalents; (3) quality of performance, including instructional ranges and RPI scores; and (4) relative standing in a group, including standard scores and percentile ranks. Most of the chapter on interpretation focuses on the process of calculating scores and completing the diagnostic profiles. Instructions are also provided for evaluating test and cluster differences and for analyzing aptitude–achievement discrepancies. A table in the manual provides estimated aptitude–achievement correlations for use in discrepancy analysis for three types of aptitude tests. Estimates are derived from validation studies conducted in the 1970s and 1980s with the WJ and the WRMT and not only are outdated but are confined to two correlations per grade—one for the Basic Skills cluster or Short Scale and the other for the Reading Comprehension cluster or Full Scale. Chapter 4 of the manual, "Instructional Implications," presents seven case studies, including a complete scoring example for a seventh-grade girl, a diagnostic readiness profile for a kindergarten boy, and a Word Attack error inventory for a sixth-grade girl. Although the case examples include much useful information, the manual is poorly organized and formatted and makes for laborious reading.

Technical Adequacy

Standardization

Information on the updated norms and norming process is provided in the test manual and the software scoring program user's guide. Norms for the 1998 version are based on a sample of 3,184 students in kindergarten through Grade 12 and 245 examinees aged 18 to 22, who were tested in 1995 and 1996 in 40 states as part of a norming program that included three additional achievement batteries: the *KeyMath–Revised* (Connolly, 1988), the *Peabody Individual Achievement Test–Revised*, and the *Kaufman Test of Educational Achievement*. The sample was selected to approximate March 1994 U.S. census data and was stratified for four grade levels and one age interval by sex, parental education, race/ethnicity, geographic region, and educational placement. Students in six special education and gifted programs were included in appropriate proportions. The four batteries were normed from kindergarten through Grade 12 for grade norms and through age 22 for age norms. Practitioners should note that the WRMT-R norms have not been updated for Grades 13 through 16 and ages 23 through 75. Of the total sample, 721 randomly selected individuals took the entire WRMT-R/NU, and each examinee also took one or more tests to increase the size of the sample for the five achievement domains measured by the batteries or for individual tests not included in a domain. Thus the size of the sample for the WRMT-R/NU varies from test to test, with a low of 751 examinees for Word Attack to a high of 2,662 for Word Identification. Because characteristics for the sample taking the WRMT-R as the primary battery are reported by intervals (Grades K–2, 3–5, 6–8, and 9–12 and ages 18–22), the number of children taking the test at each grade cannot be determined. Normative data were analyzed using Rasch procedures across the complete sample. Because the Word Attack items were a poor fit with the overall Word Reading domain, that test was normed separately.

According to the publishers, performance levels based on WRMT-R/NU norms differ little from those based on WRMT-R norms for average and above average students but show a decline on most tests and clusters for below average elementary and middle grade students. In other words, the WRMT-R/NU will yield *higher* standard scores and percentiles for below average students in these grades in comparison with the WRMT-R, although age and grade equivalent scores will not display any significant changes. The manual provides a brief discussion of the changes (if any) in the level of performance for each test and cluster, but it refers only to the direction of the change and the grades involved, rather than describing the average number of standard score point differences at specific age or grade levels. Nor is there any discussion of factors that may have contributed to these performance changes.

Test Floors and Item Gradients

As with other Rasch-model tests, evaluating test floors and item gradients by direct inspection of raw score-standard score relationships is not possible because of the *W*-scale transformation. Examiners can get a sense of the adequacy of floors and gradients by reviewing Table 1.1 in the manual, which presents midyear WRMT-R/NU mean raw scores for selected grade and age levels, including kindergarten and Grade 1. Users can also enter raw scores of 1 into the software scoring program for specific examinee ages and grades, as described in Chapter 2 of this text. My own experience indicates that floors for Word Attack, Word Comprehension, Passage Comprehension, and the Reading Comprehension cluster are problematic for examinees in Grade 1 and below. In addition, Word Attack yields standard scores no lower than 70 throughout the entire primary grade age range for both age- and grade-based norms. Interpreting performance on those tests should focus on RPI scores, which reflect examinee proficiency and are much more sensitive to individual skill differences.

Reliability Evidence

Users should note that the reliability and validity evidence in the manual is based on the 1987 version of the test and is unchanged from the previous manual. The manual reports split-half reliability coefficients and standard errors of measurement in *W*-scale units for Forms G or H or G + H for selected groups (Grades 1, 3, 5, 8, and 11; college students; and adults). For Grade 1 (*ns* of 422 to 602), internal consistency coefficients are at or above .94, with Total Reading–Full Scale at .99 and Total Reading–Short Scale at .98. Because of the manner in which the coefficients are presented, it is not possible to determine from which form the estimates were derived. No evidence of alternate-form, test–retest, or interrater reliability information is presented.

Validity Evidence

CONTENT VALIDITY EVIDENCE

Items were designed to be comprehensive in content and difficulty and to use an open-ended format to parallel the requirements of reading in real-life situations. Classical item selection procedures were used in the early stages of item development, whereas Rasch-model procedures were employed in the later stages. Word Comprehension content area vocabulary items were selected based on correlations with the 1977 WJ and WRMT-R content vocabulary total scores. No other information is provided about item selection, and there is no evidence of sensitivity reviews or DIF analyses. Several WRMT-R reviewers (e.g., Cooter, 1989; Jaeger, 1989) have questioned the content validity of Letter Identification, which presents a total of 51 letters in a wide variety of fonts, including rare type styles likely to be unfamiliar even to adult readers. The predictive or diagnostic utility of this type of letter-name measure is highly questionable and is unsupported by any data in the manual. The non-normed Supplementary Letter Checklist presents uppercase *I* twice and lowercase *a*, *g*, and *q* twice, without a rationale provided for these repetitions. Many of the pictures accompanying Passage Comprehension items appear outdated and portray males and females in stereotypical activities. For instance, men are attired in business suits and boys hold sports equipment, whereas a woman wearing an apron interacts with a child in a kitchen and a girl picks flowers. The vast majority of individuals appear to be of European descent.

CRITERION-RELATED VALIDITY EVIDENCE

Criterion-related validity evidence consists of concurrent correlation coefficients between the WRMT-R and the 1977 WJ Reading tests for Grades 1, 3, 5, and 8. Correlations were moderate to high across the four grade levels, with Grade 1 (n = 85) correlations between tests with similar titles ranging from .64 for Word Attack to .88 for Total Reading. Correlations between the 1973 WRMT and several reading measures not in the Woodcock family of tests, all of which have been updated, ranged from .78 to .92 for Grades 3, 5, and 12. No predictive validity evidence is presented.

CONSTRUCT VALIDITY EVIDENCE

Construct validity evidence is limited to test and cluster intercorrelations for five grade and age groups. For Grade 1 (n = 602), correlations between individual tests and the Total Reading–Full Scale score ranged from .62 for Visual–Auditory Learning to .96 for Word Identification. The lower correlations for Visual–Auditory Learning suggest that it is measuring somewhat different skills than the other tests. Because the WRMT-R/NU is often used in assessments designed to determine initial or continuing eligibility for special education services, studies comparing the performance of students with reading disabilities and other clinical groups with that of matched controls are needed.

Usability

The WRMT-R/NU ranks high in usability in terms of portability and content coverage but low for expense and scoring complexity. The software scoring program must be purchased separately, and hand scoring is so time-consuming and prone to error that it is not a viable option. The user-friendly ASSIST software scoring program generates a narrative report, score summary, and grade equivalent and standard score/percentile rank profiles for grade- or age-based norms. An optional aptitude–achievement discrepancy analysis can also be produced for 14 aptitude tests or scales, including WISC-III Full Scale, Verbal, and Performance IQs, using aptitude–achievement correlations corresponding to that particular test or composite or for other tests for which examiners supply the correlation. Neither the manual nor the software scoring program provides information for evaluating statistically or clinically significant differences among cluster scores. Users should note that the correlations provided by the ASSIST program do not vary by age or grade, unlike those presented in the test manual, and there is no information regarding the studies from which they are derived. Moreover, identical correlations are used for Wechsler Verbal and Performance IQs, despite evidence that Performance IQ is much less strongly correlated with reading performance than Verbal IQ.

Links to Intervention

The manual includes a chapter on instructional implications by Nancy Mather and Elaine Barnes, with seven case studies ranging from kindergarten through age 22. These authors present a five-step process for analyzing test results: (1) evaluating cluster scores, (2) evaluating component test scores, (3) evaluating individual item responses, (4) evaluating results from supplementary testing, and (5) evaluating aptitude–achievement discrepancies. The analysis of test and cluster performance is thoughtfully done, but the suggested supplementary tests date from the 1970s, and the suggestions for remediation have not been updated to incorporate recent research on reading intervention. For example, users are instructed to use a whole-word approach to reading to address the kindergarten case example's auditory and blending weaknesses. The test kit includes a single sample of a four-page parent report that describes the tests and clusters, score types, and score interpretations and provides space for score entry and a summary of results and suggestions. The form has not been updated since 1987 and is not reproducible, nor are additional copies available by separate purchase. Moreover, the report discusses and provides space only for grade equivalent and percentile ranks rather than standard scores or normal curve equivalents.

Relevant Research

The WRMT and WRMT-R have been used in a very large number of studies to assess reading proficiency and monitor reading growth, especially the Word Identification and Word Attack tests (e.g., Catts et al., 2001; Olson, Wise, Conners, Rack, & Fulker, 1989; Torgesen, Wagner, & Rashotte, 1997). No investigations using the most recent version of the test could be located. In a study with 59 children in Grades 1 and 3, McGuinness (1997) identified four types of faulty decoding strategies on WRMT-R Word Identification: (1) whole word guessing (e.g., *press* for *piece*), (2) part word assembling (*pie-eck* for *piece*), (3) phonetic illegal decoding (*peek* for *piece*), and (4) phonetic legal decoding (*pice* for *piece*). The type of decoding strategy used in first grade was highly correlated with concurrent WRMT-R reading performance and predicted up to 37% of the variance in Word Identification scores at the end of first grade and at the beginning of third grade. Use of either type of phonetic decoding was a strong predictor of positive reading outcomes, whereas part word decoding was a negative predictor at third grade, and whole word decoding was a negative predictor at both first and third grade.

There is some evidence that learning-disabled students obtain lower scores on the WRMT-R compared with the *Wechsler Individual Achievement Test* (WIAT). In a study investigating the relationships among four achievement tests, Slate (1996) compared scores on the WRMT-R, the WIAT, the *KeyMath–Revised*, and the *Peabody Individual Achievement Test–Revised* (PIAT-R) for 202 students with learning disabilities (mean age = 11-4). Although WRMT-R reading cluster and subtest scores were significantly correlated with WIAT reading subtest scores (.48 to .77), WRMT-R and PIAT-R mean cluster and total test scores fell in the low range (SSs = 72.2 to 78.3), whereas

WIAT scores for comparable clusters were higher, falling in the below average range (SSs = 81.7 to 85.9), with significant differences between WRMT-R and WIAT mean Reading Comprehension scores (SS = 78.9 vs. 84.1, respectively).

Source and Cost

The WRMT-R/NU is available from AGS Publishing for $264.95 for Form G, $259.95 for Form H, and $386.95 for the combined kit. The ASSIST program for Macintosh and Windows on CD-ROM is available for $199.95. A combined G/H kit with the ASSIST program is $485.95.

Test Reviews

Crocker, L. (2001). Review of the Woodcock Reading Mastery Tests–Revised/Normative Update. In B. S. Plake & J. C. Impara (Eds.), *The fourteenth mental measurements yearbook* (pp. 1369–1371). Lincoln, NE: Buros Institute of Mental Measurements.

Murray-Ward, M. (2001). Review of the Woodcock Reading Mastery Tests–Revised/Normative Update. In B. S. Plake & J. C. Impara (Eds.), *The fourteenth mental measurements yearbook* (pp. 1371–1373). Lincoln, NE: Buros Institute of Mental Measurements.

Sutton, J. P. (1999). Woodcock Reading Mastery Tests–Revised/Normative Update (WRMT-R/NU). *Diagnostique, 24*, 299–316.

Summary

The *Woodcock Reading Mastery Tests–Revised/Normative Update* (WRMT-R/NU) is the latest version of an individually administered, norm-referenced set of reading measures for individuals from 5 to 75+ years of age. Like its predecessors, the WRMT-R/NU is distinguished by its portability, coverage of a variety of reading domains, and provision of proficiency level as well as norm-referenced scores. Although the norms have been updated, the test items and most of the manual are identical to the 1987 edition. Reliability and validity evidence is outdated and/or limited for tests and clusters, the stimulus pictures for Passage Comprehension are characterized by outdated and stereotypical depictions, and two of the tests of greatest interest to examiners assessing early primary grade students yield results that are difficult to interpret. The Letter Identification test samples letters more than once using a variety of unfamiliar and elaborate type styles and permits examinees to report either letter names or sounds, and the Supplementary Letter Identification checklist is not normed. There is also evidence that lower achieving examinees will obtain higher standard scores with the new norms, so that children previously identified as needing preventive or remedial services may no longer qualify for extra assistance. With the recent publication of the *Woodcock-Johnson III*, practitioners now have access to updated versions of the core WRMT-R/NU tests, and this venerable battery can enjoy a well-earned retirement.

Case Example

Name of student: Carmen F.
Age: 6 years, 7 months
Grade: First grade
Date of assessment: April

Reason for referral: Carmen was referred for an early reading assessment by her first-grade teacher. Carmen tries hard in class, but her word recognition and decoding skills are very weak compared with those of her classmates. She also received very low scores on the fall administration of the gradewide early literacy screening battery, especially on letter sound naming and word list reading. On the preprimer word list, she was able to read only 3 of the 20 words presented.

Assessment results and interpretation: The *Woodcock Reading Mastery Tests–Revised/Normative Update* (WRMT-R/NU) is a battery of tests measuring a variety of reading skills, including word recognition, decoding, and comprehension. Average scores for students at Carmen's grade level are as follows: Standard Score (SS) = 100, Percentile Rank (PR) = 50, Relative Performance Index (RPI) = 90/90, Grade Equivalent (GE) = 1.8. Carmen's performance on the WRMT-R/NU is described below.

Composite/Test	SS	PR	RPI	GE
Total Reading (WI + WA + WC + PC)	83	13	42/90	1.1
Readiness Cluster	88	20	68/90	K.9
Visual–Auditory Learning	83	13	63/90	K.7
Letter Identification	92	29	75/90	1.3
Basic Skills Cluster	84	15	47/90	1.2
Word Identification (WI)	81	11	21/90	1.2
Word Attack (WA)	90	26	77/90	1.3
Reading Comprehension Cluster	82	11	37/90	K.8
Word Comprehension (WC)	78	7	21/90	K.7
Passage Comprehension (PC)	87	20	58/90	1.1

Carmen's overall reading skills, including word identification, phonemic decoding, and word and passage comprehension skills, fall in the below average range (SS = 83) and are rated at a beginning first-grade level (GE = 1.1). Her Total Reading Relative Performance Index (RPI) of 42/90 indicates that when students at her grade level perform reading tasks with 90% mastery, she performs them with 42% mastery. Her reading readiness skills, including her ability to learn new vocabulary and letter identification skills, are rated at an end-of-kindergarten level (GE = K.9). In terms of basic skills, including sight word vocabulary and phonemic decoding, as measured by nonsense word reading, her performance is rated at a beginning first-grade level (GE = 1.2). Although her Word Attack score falls within the average range for her grade, it should be noted that she was able to read only 4 of the 18 nonsense words presented. She tended to guess based on the first letter rather than trying to decode the entire nonsense word (e.g., *pack* for *pog*). Her errors also reflect lack of knowledge of short vowels (*bem* for *bim*) and confusion between the *b* and *d* sounds (e.g., *bee* for *dee*). Her overall reading comprehension skills, including understanding of words and short passages, fall at an end-of-kindergarten level (GE = K.8). She was unable to answer any antonym and word analogy items and only one of the synonym items on the Word Comprehension test because she could read so few of the stimulus words. Her performance was somewhat better on a task requiring her to read sentences and short paragraphs and supply a missing word (GE = 1.1). She had particular trouble understanding sentences in which the missing word was not a noun (e.g., a verb or an adjective).

The Supplementary Letter Checklist was also administered to assess Carmen's knowledge of letter names and sounds. The checklist is not normed and provides only raw scores. Letter-name knowledge was assessed using both uppercase and lowercase letters, and letter-sound knowledge was assessed using lowercase letters. Several letters are assessed more than once per list, so the totals exceed 26. On the lowercase letter list, several digraphs and diphthongs are also assessed. Carmen's performance on the WRMT-R/NU Supplementary Letter Checklist is presented below.

Supplementary Letter Checklist	Raw Score	Errors
Uppercase Letter Names	25/27	I (twice)
Lowercase Letter Names	28/29	p for q
Lowercase Letter Sounds	29/36	e (/uh/), u (/yuh/), c (/s/), ch (/c-/h/), sh (/s-h/), oo (/ah/), oi (/a-o/)

On the Supplementary Letter Checklist, Carmen was able to identify all the uppercase letters except uppercase *I*. She was able to pronounce most letter sounds in isolation but had difficulty with short vowels /e/ and /u/. She does not understand the concept of digraphs and tried to pronounce the sounds separately.

Multisubject Batteries with Reading and Reading-Related Measures

This section reviews two multisubject assessment batteries that include reading and reading-related measures for early primary grade examinees: the *Wechsler Individual Achievement Test–II* and the *Woodcock–Johnson III.*

WECHSLER INDIVIDUAL ACHIEVEMENT TEST—SECOND EDITION

Overview

The *Wechsler Individual Achievement Test–Second Edition* (WIAT-II; Psychological Corporation, 2001a) is an individually administered, norm-referenced achievement test battery for individuals aged 4 through 85+ and for students in prekindergarten through college. Like its predecessor, the *Wechsler Individual Achievement Test* (WIAT; Psychological Corporation, 1992b), the WIAT-II consists of subtests designed to cover the seven areas of learning disability specified in the Individuals with Disabilities Education Act (IDEA, 1997). The WIAT-II is statistically linked with three Wechsler scales: the *Wechsler Individual Scale for Children–III* (WISC-III), the *Wechsler Preschool and Primary Scale of Intelligence–Revised* (WPPSI-R; Wechsler, 1989), and the *Wechsler Adult Intelligence Test–Third Edition* (WAIS-III; Wechsler, 1997). The WIAT-II is also linked to the *Process Assessment of the Learner: Test Battery for Reading and Writing* (PAL-RW), which is designed to assess the reading and writing processes underlying the academic skills measured by the WIAT-II. Changes in the WIAT-II include (1) extension of the age range from 5 through 19 years to 4 years through adulthood; (2) changes in the items and administration and scoring procedures of several subtests, especially in reading and language; (3) addition of a pseudoword reading subtest; (4) expansion of error analysis procedures for use in instructional and intervention planning; and (5) provision for ability–achievement discrepancy analyses using Wechsler Verbal IQ, Performance IQ, and factor scores in addition to Full Scale IQ. In addition, the WIAT Screener, which yielded a composite score based on three subtests, has been eliminated and is now a separate instrument that provides only subtest scores (*WIAT-II Abbreviated*; Psychological Corporation, 2001b). The test kit includes an examiner's manual, two scoring and normative supplemental manuals (one for prekindergarten through Grade 12 and one for college students and adults), two easel-format stimulus booklets, 25 record forms, 25 response booklets, a pseudoword card, a pseudoword pronunciation audiotape, and a word card, all packed in a nylon bag. Examiners must furnish blank paper for several subtests and eight pennies for examinees in kindergarten or Grade 1 for the Numerical Operations subtest.

Subtests and Composites

Subtests

The WIAT-II consists of nine subtests covering four broad achievement areas and the seven domains specified in IDEA, as shown in Table 5.34. Table 5.35 describes the subtests and the grades in which they are administered. The Alphabet Writing task on the Written Expression subtest and the Pseudoword Decoding subtest are identical to those measures on the PAL-RW.

Composites

The nine WIAT-II subtests can be combined to form up to four achievement composite scores and a total test composite (see Table 5.36), depending on age and grade. For children age 4 or in prekindergarten, only the Oral Language composite can be calculated. For children age 5 or in kindergarten, only the Oral Language and Mathematics composites can be calculated.

TABLE 5.34. IDEA Areas of Learning Disability and Corresponding WIAT-II Subtests

IDEA Areas of Learning Disability	WIAT-II subtests
Oral expression	Oral Expression
Listening comprehension	Listening Comprehension
Written expression	Written Expression Spelling
Basic reading	Word Reading Pseudoword Decoding
Reading comprehension	Reading Comprehension
Mathematics calculation	Numerical Operations
Mathematics reasoning	Math Reasoning

TABLE 5.35. Descriptions and Target Grades of the WIAT-II Subtests

Subtest	Description
Word Reading	Grades PreK–16. The examinee reads aloud from a stimulus book and word list. Early items assess letter naming, rhyming, beginning and ending sounds, and sound matching skills.
Numerical Operations	Grades K–16. The examinee identifies and writes numbers, counts, and solves written calculation problems and simple equations involving the four basic operations.
Reading Comprehension	Grades 1–16. The examinee reads sentences and short passages silently or aloud and answers questions asked by the examiner. Early items require matching words with pictures. The examinee also reads short sentences aloud and answers comprehension questions.
Spelling	Grades K–16. The examinee writes letters, letter blends, and words dictated by the examiner.
Pseudoword Decoding	Grades 1–16. The examinee reads pseudowords aloud from a list.
Math Reasoning	Grades PreK–16. The examinee counts, identifies geometric shapes, solves single-step and multistep word problems, interprets graphs, identifies math patterns, and solves problems related to statistics and probability.
Written Expression	This subtest has five grade-specific tasks. For *Alphabet Writing* (Grades PreK–2), the examinee prints lowercase letters in order from memory, and the score is the number of correctly sequenced letters written at 15 seconds. For *Word Fluency* (Grades 1–16), the examinee writes words matching a prescribed category, and the score is the number of correct words written in 60 seconds. For *Sentences*, the examinee combines multiple sentences into one meaningful sentence (Grades 1–6) or generates a sentence from visual or verbal cues (Grades 7–16). For *Paragraph* (Grades 3–6), the examinee produces a rough-draft paragraph in response to a prompt (10-minute time limit). For *Essay* (Grades 7–16), the examinee writes a persuasive essay in response to a prompt (15-minute time limit).
Listening Comprehension	Grades PreK–16. This subtest consists of three tasks. For *Receptive Vocabulary* and *Sentence Comprehension*, the examinee identifies the one of four pictures that matches a word or sentence read by the examiner. For *Expressive Vocabulary*, the examinee generates a single word that matches a picture and an oral description (10-second limit to begin responding for each task).
Oral Expression	This subtest includes four tasks. For *Sentence Repetition* (Grades PreK–3), the examinee repeats sentences read by the examiner. For *Word Fluency* (all grades), the examinee generates as many words as possible in a given category in 60 seconds. For *Visual Passage Recall* (all grades), the examinee retells a passage read by the examiner. For *Giving Directions* (all grades), the examinee provides directions for completing a task (10-second limit to begin responding).

TABLE 5.36. WIAT-II Composites and Subtests

Composites	Subtests
Reading	Word Reading Reading Comprehension Pseudoword Decoding
Mathematics	Numerical Operations Math Reasoning
Written Language	Spelling Written Expression
Oral Language	Listening Comprehension Oral Expression
Total	Sum of all subtest standard scores

Administration

Administration times are approximately 45 minutes for prekindergarten and kindergarten, 90 minutes for Grades 1–6, and 1½ to 2 hours for Grades 7–16. Eight of the nine subtests have grade-specific start points, whereas Pseudoword Decoding begins with Item 1 for all examinees in Grade 1 and up. Practice items should be provided for the Expressive Vocabulary task on the Listening Comprehension subtest. In my experience, young children often fail to understand that they must produce a one-word response to the picture and verbal prompt. Guidelines should also be provided for querying responses that do not conform to the one-word requirement. Directions for the Word Fluency task on the Written Expression subtest should also be clarified. The directions in the examiner's manual specify that examinees in Grades 3 through 6 take Item 2 on the Word Fluency task, but they do not indicate that examinees in Grades 1 and 2 also take Item 2, as shown on the record form and in the norms tables. In an appendix to the scoring supplement, instructions for scoring Written Expression indicate on page 23 that examinees in Grade 1 and 2 take Word Fluency, but the directions on page 28 state that examinees in Grades 3–6 take Item 2, with no mention of younger examinees. All subtests except Written Expression have a reverse rule, a discontinue rule, or both. The WIAT-II uses two types of reverse rules. The first type is the usual procedure for establishing a basal (i.e., proceeding backwards from the start point if necessary to obtain three consecutive correct responses). The second type of reverse rule applies only to Reading Comprehension and involves reversing to a lower set of items for examinees who are reading significantly below their current grade placement. All of the necessary information for administration is contained in the stimulus booklets and record forms, so that examiners do not need to refer to the manual during testing. For Reading Comprehension, examinees must read sentence items aloud, but they may read passages aloud or silently. Beginning at the Grade 3 start point, passages are timed to obtain Reading Speed and Reading Rate scores. If examinees read the passages silently, they must indicate when they have completed a passage. The authors note that reading rate should not be calculated if an examinee appears to be skimming the selection or obviously cannot read the passage—a problem that I have frequently encountered with early primary grade children.

Responses for Expressive Vocabulary items on the Listening Comprehension subtest and for Sentence Repetition, Word Fluency, Visual Passage Recall, and Giving Directions items on the Oral Expression subtest must be recorded verbatim. The record form contains checklists of qualitative observations of examinee performance for several subtests, including Word Reading, Reading Comprehension, and Spelling; these observations can yield useful information for report writing and instructional planning. For word items on Word Reading, examiners can compare reading automaticity to accuracy by marking response times that exceed 3 seconds to obtain the percentage of words read automatically.

Scores

For most subtests, items are scored 1 or 0. Spelling items are now reproduced on the record form to facilitate scoring and report preparation. Correct pronunciations for Pseudoword Decoding items are provided on an audiotape as well as in the record form. For Item 54 (*tufle*), another correct pronunciation should be added (see the PAL-RW review above). The scoring and normative supplement provides detailed scoring guidelines for subtests involving the most subjective judgment (Reading Comprehension, Written Expression, and Oral Expression). Compared with the WIAT, scoring procedures have been clarified considerably; however, scoring time has also increased because of the multitask composition of many subtests, the increased complexity of scoring for several measures, and, if hand scoring is used, the necessity of converting some task scores to weighted or quartile scores before calculating total raw score. The manual should provide guidelines for dealing with spelling errors on the Written Expression Word Fluency task.

Three supplemental quartile-based scores can be calculated for Reading Comprehension: (1) Target Words, based on the number of correctly read highlighted words on the Sentences task; (2) Reading Speed, based on the total elapsed reading time for all passages administered; and (3) Reading Rate, based on the relationship between Reading Speed and Reading Comprehension scores. To calculate Reading Rate, the examiner first converts Reading Speed and Reading Comprehension total raw scores to quartile-based scores and then places an × on the point corresponding to the intersection of those quartiles on a graph on the record form. The point on the graph thus expresses rate in terms of the relationship between reading comprehension (which the authors define as reading accuracy) and silent reading speed. The use of the terms "speed" and "rate" for two different measures is confusing, and neither score reflects the standard metric of words read correctly per minute (WCPM). Up to three supplemental quartile- or decile-based scores can be calculated for language tasks: Alphabet Writing and Word Fluency on the Written Expression subtest and Word Fluency on the Oral Expression subtest. The score on Alphabet Writing is based on the number of letters written within 15 seconds, but recognizability is not sufficient for credit; letters written in cursive or uppercase, reversed, out of order, or not conforming to the letter formation guidelines are scored 0. Although the scoring guide provides several credit and no-credit examples for each letter, some of the no-credit examples differ minimally from those awarded credit. For kindergarten and prekindergarten examinees only, Alphabet Writing raw scores can be converted to decile scores. For examinees in Grades 1 through 12, Alphabet Writing is not a supplemental score but is a raw score added to the other items in the subtest to calculate the Written Expression total raw score. Scoring rubrics are provided for the Written Expression Paragraph and Essay tasks and for four of the five Oral Expression tasks. Written Expression Paragraph and Essay tasks can also be scored using a holistic scoring system, but standard scores are available only for analytic scoring.

WIAT-II subtests and composites yield age- and grade-based standard scores (*M* = 100, *SD* = 15), age- and grade-based percentile ranks, age and grade equivalents, normal curve equivalents, stanines, quartiles, and decile scores. Age-based standard scores are in 4-month intervals for ages 4-0 through 13-11, 1-year intervals for ages 14-0 through 19-11, a 2-year interval for ages 17-0 through 19-11, and five age bands for adults (17–20, 21–25, 26–35, 36–50, and 51–85). Grade-based standard scores are reported for fall, winter, and spring for examinees in prekindergarten through Grade 8 and by year for examinees in Grades 9 through 16. Norms for Grades 13 through 16 are separated by grade for 2-year and 4-year colleges.

Interpretation

The manual provides both quantitative and qualitative guidelines and procedures for interpreting WIAT-II results. For quantitative interpretation, the emphasis is on evaluating score differences, including subtest and composite score differences, intersubtest scatter, and ability–achievement discrepancies when the WIAT-II is administered with one of the Wechsler ability scales. Tables in appendices in the scoring and normative supplement indicate the score differences required for statistical significance and cumulative percentages of the standardization linking sample obtaining those differences (i.e., base rates) for both the predicted-achievement and simple-difference methods of discrepancy analysis. Other tables permit examiners to evaluate differences among subtest and composite standard scores in terms of statistical and clinical significance and degree of intersubtest scatter.

Discrepancy Interpretation

New with the WIAT-II is the option to select from the full range of WISC-III IQ and Index scores for use in discrepancy analyses, based on research indicating that Index scores are better predictors of WIAT achievement (Konold, 1999) and that the Full Scale IQ may be misleading when significant discrepancies exist between Verbal and Performance IQs (Flanagan & Alfonso, 1993b). When only the WIAT-II is administered, examiners can analyze three types of score differences: (1) differences among composite standard scores, (2) differences between a single subtest standard score and the average of all the other subtest standard scores, and (3) differences among subtest standard scores. When the WIAT-II is used with one of the Wechsler ability scales, ability–achievement discrepancies can be calculated using one of two methods: (1) the predicted-achievement discrepancy procedure and (2) the simple-difference discrepancy procedure (see the *Woodcock–Johnson III* review below for a discussion of the differences between these approaches). Because the WPPSI-R and WISC-III were normed more than 10 years earlier than the WIAT-II (WPPSI-R norms are keyed to 1986 U.S. census data; WISC-III norms are keyed to 1988 census data), predicted-achievement scores are based on reanchored scores derived from the WPPSI-R and WISC-III linking samples. The authors recommend the predicted-achievement method and include a cogent discussion of the shortcomings of the simple-difference method and the limitations of ability–achievement discrepancy analyses. Two other cautions are in order. First, only age-based standard scores can be used for discrepancy analyses because the Wechsler ability scales yield only age-based scores. Second, the WPPSI-R linking sample for children aged 4-0 to 6-11 is much smaller than the WISC-III linking sample for children aged 6-0 to 16-11 (n = 199 vs. 775, respectively). Practitioners should also note that statistical significance levels vary from one set of analyses to another. Although .05 and .01 levels are used to evaluate the significance of ability–achievement score differences, .05 and .15 levels are used to evaluate subtest and composite score differences, including intratest scatter. The .05 and .01 levels should be used for both types of comparisons for the sake of consistency and also because the .15 level of significance is rarely used in clinical or research applications.

The manual also provides guidelines for qualitative analysis of performance in terms of the component skills measured by each subtest. The description of skills assessed on the reading and writing subtests and the implication of skill deficits for classroom performance in those areas is comprehensive, drawing on the research of Berninger and her colleagues (e.g., Berninger et al., 1992). The skills analysis section for the oral language subtests is briefer and less detailed. The manual includes tables of skills measured by Word Reading, Numerical Operations, Reading Comprehension, and Math Reasoning and a table with guidelines for analyzing spelling errors according to seven broad categories. The authors recommend that examinees who display deficits on any of the WIAT-II reading or writing subtests should take the PAL-RW to identify the specific processing deficits underlying the poor performance. The authors also present a useful eight-step process for interpreting WIAT-II performance, which assumes that a Wechsler ability score has been obtained. The emphasis is on analysis of score differences, and the authors refer the examiner to the necessary tables for each step of the process. Despite the overall high quality of the interpretation chapter, not a single case example is included to illustrate the application of the guidelines and procedures.

Technical Adequacy

Standardization

The WIAT-II was standardized on two overlapping samples (age-based and grade-based) that were tested during the 1999–2000 and 2000–2001 school years. The age-based sample consisted of 2,950 individuals aged 4-0 to 19-11, 2,171 of whom also participated in the grade-based sample. Subgroup age sizes are 300 for ages 4 and 5 and 200 for ages 6 through 14. Because scores are reported in 4-month intervals for children at these ages, this means that derived scores are based on as few as 50 children per interval. The grade-based standardization sample included a total of 3,600 individuals in prekindergarten through Grade 12, of which 2,900 were in prekindergarten through Grade 8. Grade sizes are 200 for prekindergarten and 300 for each of the other grades. Half of the sample data were collected in the fall and half in the spring (winter norms were interpolated). Grade- and age-based samples were stratified by sex, race/ethnicity, geographic region, and parent educational level. Students receiving special education services were not excluded, so that between 8% and 10% of the sample at each grade level consisted of children classified as having a learning disability, speech/language impairment, emotional disturbance, mild mental impairment, ADHD, or mild hearing impairment, and approximately 3% of the sample at each grade level consisted of children enrolled in gifted and talented programs. Overall, the match between U.S. population data and sample characteristics is remarkably close, with the North Central region slightly underrepresented in the age-based sample.

To create the linking samples, one of three Wechsler intelligence scales was administered to a subset of the normative group, as follows: 199 children aged 4-0 to 6-11 took the WPPSI-R; 775 examinees aged 6-0 to 16-11 took the WISC-III; and 95 high school students aged 16 to 19 and a subset of the college and adult sample (*ns* = 268 and 90, respectively) took the WAIS-III. Demographic characteristics of the WPPSI-R and WISC-III linking samples are reported by race/ethnicity, parent/self education level, and geographic region, but not by age and grade, so it is not possible to determine how many early primary grade children are included.

Reliability Evidence

The manual reports split-half reliability coefficients for age-based scores and for grade-based fall and spring scores for examinees ages 4 through 19. Coefficients for ages 4 and 5 for Oral Expression were estimated based on data from age 6 and Grade 1 examinees because of insufficient sample sizes. Test–retest reliabilities were computed for Written Expression and Oral Expression subtests because item content for some tasks consists of a single response. Across the early primary grade range, age-based reliabilities for the five composites range from .91 to .99. Subtest age-based internal consistency coefficients are at or above .90 for Word Reading, Reading Comprehension, Spelling, Pseudoword Decoding, Math Reasoning, and Numerical Operations at age 8. Coefficients fall in the .80s for Numerical Operations at ages 5, 6, and 7; for Listening Comprehension at ages 6, 7, and 8; and for Written Expression and Oral Expression across the early primary grades. The Listening Comprehension coefficient at age 5 falls below criterion level (.75). Grade-based reliability coefficients are slightly lower. Fall grade-based coefficients for the five composites are .90 or higher, with the exception of Mathematics at Grade 1 (.88). Fall grade-based coefficients are in the .90s for Word Reading, Spelling, Pseudoword Decoding, Math Reasoning, and Written Expression for Grades 1 and 2 and in the .80s for Numerical Operations for kindergarten, Reading Comprehension for Grade 1, Listening Comprehension for Grades 1 and 2, and Oral Expression across the early primary grades. Coefficients fall in the .70s for Numerical Operations at Grades 1 and 2 and for Listening Comprehension at kindergarten. Spring grade-based coefficients for the five composites are at .90 or higher, with the exceptions of Mathematics at Grade 1 (.89) and Oral Language at Grades 1 and 2 (89 and .88, respectively). Spring grade-based coefficients are in the .90s for Word Reading, Reading Comprehension, Spelling at kindergarten and Grade 2, Pseudoword Decoding, Math Reasoning, and Written Expression. Spring reliabilities fall in the .80s for Numerical Operations for kindergarten and Grade 2, Spelling for Grade 1, Math Reasoning for kindergarten, Listening Comprehension for Grade 1, and Oral Expression across the early primary grades. Coefficients fall in the .70s for Numerical Operations at Grade 1 and Listening Comprehension at kindergarten and Grade 2.

Stability coefficients, along with means and standard deviations, are reported for three age groups: 6–9, 10–12, and 13–19 (total n = 297; intervals of 7–45 days). Test–retest correlations for the 6- to 9-year-old sample (n = 123) were at or above .90 for all five composites and for the Word Reading, Numerical Operations, Reading Comprehension, Spelling, Pseudoword Decoding, and Math Reasoning subtests. Stability estimates were in the .80s for Written Expression, Listening Comprehension, and Oral Expression. Listening Comprehension displayed practice effects, with an increase of nearly 5 points from first to second testing. No stability estimates are provided for examinees younger than 6.

The manual reports the results of two studies of interscorer agreement for Reading Comprehension, Written Expression, and Oral Expression, based on independent scoring by two unidentified scorers of 2,180 responses, including approximately 190 from each age for examinees from 6 to 16 and 140 from each age in the 17–19 age range. Interscorer agreement between pairs of scores for Reading Comprehension passage items ranged from .94 to .98 across ages, with an overall reliability of .94. For Written Expression, intraclass correlations between pairs of scores for responses to Prompts 1 and 2 combined ranged from .71 to .94 across ages, with an average correlation of .85. Intraclass correlations between pairs of scores for Oral Expression ranged from .91 to .99 across ages, with an overall correlation of .96. Because interrater reliability coefficients are reported for the age range as a whole, however, users cannot evaluate scoring consistency for their particular population of examinees. Moreover, because correlations were presumably based on completed protocols, they provide no information about interexaminer consistency in the verbatim recording of examinee responses. Interrater reliability estimates based on simultaneous scoring during testing sessions for specific age/grade groups are needed for other subtests and tasks vulnerable to interexaminer and interscorer variance, including Pseudoword Decoding; Reading Speed; the Alphabet Writing, Word Fluency, and Sentences tasks on the Written Expression subtest; and the Word Fluency, Visual Passage Recall, and Giving Directions tasks on the Oral Expression subtest.

Test Floors and Item Gradients

The addition of easier items for young examinees has eliminated many but not all of the floor problems notable on the WIAT reading and language measures. For age-based standard scores, floors for the Reading composite are inadequate below age 6-4 and for the Written Language composite below age 7-0. Subtest floors for Word Reading are inadequate below 6-0; floors for Spelling are inadequate below 6-8; and floors for Written Expression are inadequate below 8-0. Floors for Pseudoword Decoding are inadequate throughout the entire early primary grade range and do not achieve the criterion level until age 9-8. For grade-based standard scores, all composite scores are adequate across the early primary grades. Grade-based floors for Word Reading are inadequate for fall of kindergarten, floors for Spelling are inadequate for the entire kindergarten year, and floors for Pseudoword Decoding are inadequate until winter of Grade 4. Floor effects are also evident for Alphabet Writing grade-based decile scores for all three kindergarten norming periods. For example, a child in the fall of kindergarten who writes one letter correctly obtains a decile score of 70. For age-based standard scores, item gradients are inadequate for Spelling for ages 5-0 through 6-3 and for Written Expression for ages 5-0 through 7-11. For grade-based standard scores, item gradient violations are evident for Spelling for the entire kindergarten year and for Written Expression for all of Grades 1 and 2.

Validity Evidence

CONTENT VALIDITY EVIDENCE

WIAT-II subtests were designed to represent a composite of typical national curriculum specifications within each of the domains specified by the IDEA Amendments of 1997. As noted above, reading and writing subtest task formats and item content are based on the long-term research program of Virginia Berninger and her colleagues. The two oral language subtests have been modified and expanded considerably, but the tasks included in Listening Comprehension do not all match the domain. The WIAT items that required examinees to answer questions in response to examiner-read passages have been eliminated, and a modified form of the WIAT Oral Expression expressive vocabulary task, including some of the same items, has been moved to Listening Comprehension. No rationale is provided in the manual for the shift of this task from the expressive to the receptive language domain or the use of single-word expressive vocabulary items to assess listening comprehension skills.

Following development of subtest specifications, curriculum experts reviewed subtest items and compared the design, format, and content with those on the PAL-RW subtests. Pilot testing with a sample of approximately 400 individuals in prekindergarten through Grade 16 was conducted during the spring semester of 1997, followed by a large-scale tryout with 1,900 students in the same grades. Conventional item analyses, including percent-correct statistics, item–total correlations, grade-to-grade progression of mean scores, and internal consistency reliability, were conducted, but no specific item statistics, such as item difficulty or discrimination indices, are presented. IRT methods were also used to examine item difficulty, determine item order, and assess goodness of fit. Items were evaluated for possible bias by a panel of reviewers and by means of IRT analyses, but no specific information is provided regarding this process; nor does the manual present standard score means on WIAT-II subtests and composites for various demographic subgroups within the standardization sample to demonstrate lack of bias.

CRITERION-RELATED VALIDITY EVIDENCE

The manual reports concurrent coefficients between the WIAT-II and other individually administered achievement tests for five criterion-related validity studies, four of which included early primary grade children. For 70 examinees aged 7–15 (mean age = 11 years), correlations between the WIAT and WIAT-II were high to very high for reading and mathematics subtests and composites (.76 to .91), and moderate to high for the written language subtests and composite (.45 to .86); however, they were only low to moderate for the oral language subtests and composite (.29 to .50), reflecting the numerous changes in the Oral Expression subtest. For 120 students in Grades K–6, WIAT-II reading subtests were generally moderately to highly correlated with the PAL-RW subtests measuring orthographic coding and rapid naming (–.35 to .89), but weakly to moderately correlated with PAL-RW phonological coding subtests (.21 to .61). WIAT-II written language subtests showed a similar pattern: moderate to high correlations with PAL-RW orthographic and rapid naming measures (–.39 to .81) and low to moderate correlations with PAL-RW phonological coding measures (.30 to .59). Correlations between the WIAT-II and selected subtests and composites from the *Differential Ability Scales* (Elliott, 1990) for 27 examinees aged 6–9 and 12–14 were moderate to high (.57 to .76) for written language measures but low for reading measures (.31 to .37), suggesting that the two batteries are assessing different kinds of reading skills. The sample is so small and the age range so broad, however, that the results provide little evidence of criterion-related validity for either test. For 64 children aged 4–7 years, correlations between the *Peabody Picture Vocabulary Test–III* and WIAT-II reading and language subtests ranged from a low of .44 for Listening Comprehension to a high of .75 for Pseudoword Decoding. The authors attribute the former moderate correlation to the fact that WIAT-II Listening Comprehension measures expressive vocabulary and sentence comprehension in addition to receptive vocabulary. (Note that in the sentence in the manual discussing this, the terms *receptive vocabulary* and *expressive vocabulary* are reversed [p. 122].)

Correlations between WIAT-II reading and written language measures and comparable measures on group-administered achievement tests—including the *Stanford Achievement Test–Ninth Edition* (Harcourt Educational Measurement, 1996; Grades 1–12; $n = 129$) and the *Metropolitan Achievement Tests–Eighth Edition* (Harcourt Educational Measurement, 1999; Grades 2–9; $n = 147$)—were high to very high for reading composite scores (.66 to .77) and spelling subtest scores (.78 to .86), and high for (written) language composite scores (.60 to .68). The manual presents evidence from two studies correlating WIAT-II scores with classroom-based measures, but the grade range of the samples is so broad that they provide little information about the relationship between WIAT-II performance and the criterion measures for early primary grade children. For 97 students in Grades 1–12 whose teachers rated them on the *Academic Competence Evaluation Scales* (ACES; DiPerna & Elliott, 2000), correlations were generally moderate for the ACES Reading/Language Arts Subscale and WIAT-II reading, written language, and oral language subtests and composites (.45 to .68). Correlations between teacher-assigned reading grades and WIAT-II reading measures for a sample of students in Grades 1–12 (*ns* = 219 to 309) were also moderate (.40 to .46), whereas the correlation between spelling grades and WIAT-II Spelling was lower (.39). Interestingly, WIAT-II oral and written language measures were better predictors of reading and spelling grades than were WIAT-II reading measures; again, however, the grade range of the sample is so broad that no firm conclusions can be reached for examinees in the early primary grade range or any other specific grade level.

CONSTRUCT VALIDITY EVIDENCE

Intercorrelations are reported by age for WIAT-II subtest and composite standard scores and Wechsler IQ scores. For ages 6 and 7, WIAT-II reading measures show lower correlations with WPPSI-R and WISC-III Full Scale and Verbal IQs than do WIAT-II mathematics and oral language measures. By age 8, however, all of the WIAT-II subtests and composites are strongly correlated with both Full Scale and Verbal IQs. Raw score means increase across ages and grades, including from fall to spring, with the largest differences at the younger ages and lower grades, as expected. In studies comparing age-based performance for matched controls with examinees in nine clinical groups (individuals in gifted programs and examinees with mental retardation, emotional disturbance, learning disabilities in reading, learning disabilities not specific to reading, ADHD, comorbid ADHD and learning disabilities, hearing impairments, and speech and/or language impairments), differences were in the predicted direction for all groups. Reading-disabled students scored significantly lower than matched controls on all subtests and composites, with differences of more than 20 standard score points for reading and written language composites. Examinees with learning disabilities not specific to reading also scored significantly lower than matched controls on all WIAT-II measures, especially reading and mathematics measures. Interestingly, a higher percentage of these examinees obtained standard scores at or below 70 on the Reading composite than did examinees in the reading-disabled group (26% vs. 19%, respectively).

Usability

Examiners familiar with the WIAT will benefit from some transfer of training effects, but the learning curve for administration and scoring is steep, especially for the Written Expression and Oral Expression subtests. One WIAT-II-only software scoring program and several programs designed to score the WIAT-II in combination with one or more Wechsler ability tests are available. The WIAT-II Scoring Assistant produces a summary report for either age- or grade-based norms that evaluates subtest and composite scores for statistically and clinically significant differences, with options for a parent/guardian report and error analyses. The WISC-III/WIAT-II Scoring Assistant produces a parent/guardian report and a summary report with age-based norms that also evaluates ability–achievement score differences. The WISC-III/WIAT-II Writer offers the same features as well as a variety of other report options, including a clinical review that provides a skills analysis of examinee performance and an interpretive report that generates a comprehensive list of recommendations in the academic domains assessed. Users should note that the entire WIAT-II must be administered to generate intersubtest score comparisons and that the WIAT-II Scoring Assistant is the only program that provides grade norms and supplemental quartile or decile scores. On the WISC-III/WIAT-II Writer program, the intervention programs cited for word reading and spelling domains are up to date and evidence-based. In contrast, the list of WISC-III index score combinations has not been updated. Some of the score combinations date to the 1960s and 1970s, many have little or no empirical support, and none include citations so that users can evaluate their validity for themselves. The format for the new generation of Psychological Corporation software differs from that of most assessment software scoring programs and also has a steep learning curve. The publisher is encouraged to develop software scoring program guides that include step-by-step directions, examples of each of the reports provided, and documentation of the origins of and evidence (if any) for the index score combinations.

Links to Intervention

Chapter 7 of the WIAT-II manual offers suggestions for interventions and instructional resources for the component skills assessed by each subtest within the four broad achievement domains. Recommended interventions and resources for reading and written language, which draw on the research of Berninger (e.g., Berninger et al., 1991, 1997), are specific, up-to-date, and evidence-based. Interventions based on the results of the oral language subtests are briefer and more general. The record form contains a detachable parent report that presents a description of each subtest, a brief description of the derived scores, and a graph for displaying examinee scores, including a space for recording Wechsler Full Scale IQs in terms of descriptive category. The section entitled "Understanding the WIAT-II Scores" includes the following sentence: "Intervention may be indicated in instances when the ability score is much higher than the WIAT-II achievement subtest scores," presumably referring to the ability–achievement discrepancy criterion in determining eligibility for services in the area of learning disabilities. Although an earlier paragraph states that below average WIAT-II scores indicate that intervention "might be required," the wording in the paragraph mentioning the ability score should be modified to remove any implication that intervention is *not* indicated for students whose ability and achievement scores are commensurate (i.e., nondiscrepant or garden-variety learners). In addition, the discussion should emphasize the interpretation of composite rather than subtest scores and should include percentile ranks as well as standard scores. The parent report on the WIAT-II Scoring Assistant includes the same set of scores and information and should also be modified.

Relevant Research

Although no research on the latest version of the test could be located, WIAT-II tasks derived from the PAL-RW (i.e., Alphabet Writing, Pseudoword Decoding, as well as the structure of the Written Expression tasks) are based on Berninger's decade-long program of reading and writing research (see Berninger, 1998b;

Berninger, Stage, et al., 2001). Most of the studies with the WIAT have focused on patterns of WISC-III/WIAT performance for use in diagnosing learning disabilities (e.g., Flanagan & Alfonso, 1993a, 1993b; Konold, 1999) or have examined the relationship between the WIAT and other achievement batteries in normal or clinical populations (e.g., Brown et al., 2000; Riccio, Boan, Staniszewski, & Hynd, 1997; Slate, 1996; Smith & Smith, 1998). Surprisingly few investigators (e.g., Badian, 1994) have used WIAT reading and spelling subtests as criterion measures in studies with early primary grade examinees, perhaps because of floor problems. There is some evidence that WIAT grade and age equivalents are problematic for some subtests at some grade levels. Using the WIAT normative sample (n = 4,252, ages 5–19), Hishinuma and Tadaki (1997) demonstrated that line functions derived from standard scores for WIAT Basic Reading for kindergarten through Grade 2.0 were substantially higher than line graphs based on grade or age equivalents, with differences of about one-quarter to one-half of a grade unit. For example, a beginning first grader with a Basic Reading standard score of 99 obtained a grade equivalent that was approximately one-half grade below actual grade placement.

Source and Cost

The WIAT-II test kit with carrying bag is available from The Psychological Corporation for $340.00. The *WIAT-II–Abbreviated* is priced at $138.00, including a carrying bag. Combination kits include the WIAT-II with the WIAT-II Scoring Assistant ($440.00) and the WIAT-II kit with the WISC-III/WIAT-II Scoring Assistant ($488.00). Software scoring programs (all on CD-ROM for Windows) include the WIAT-II Scoring Assistant ($125.00), WISC-III/WIAT-II Scoring Assistant ($199.00), and WISC-III/WIAT-II Writer for $398.00. An administration training video for the WIAT-II is available in CD-ROM or videotape format for $50.00.

Test Reviews

Doll, B. J. (2003). Review of the Wechsler Individual Achievement Test, Second Edition. In B. S. Plake, J. C. Impara, & R. A. Spies (Eds.), *The fifteenth mental measurements yearbook* (pp. 996–999). Lincoln, NE: Buros Institute of Mental Measurements.

Stavrou, E. (2002). Wechsler Individual Achievement Test–Second Edition (WIAT-II). *The School Psychologist, 56*, 24–25.

Tindal, G., & Nutter, M. (2003). Review of the Wechsler Individual Achievement Test, Second Edition. In B. S. Plake, J. C. Impara, & R. A. Spies (Eds.), *The fifteenth mental measurements yearbook* (pp. 999–1002). Lincoln, NE: Buros Institute of Mental Measurements.

Summary

The *Wechsler Individual Achievement Test–Second Edition* (WIAT-II) is an individually administered, norm-referenced battery of tests for individuals aged 4 through 80. Statistically linked with three Wechsler ability tests (the WISC-III, WPPSI-R, and WAIS-III) and the PAL-RW, the WIAT-II offers practitioners a wide range of assessment options. Although the linkages to the Wechsler ability tests permit ability–achievement discrepancy analyses for examinees across the life span, the WIAT-II/PAL-RW combination is likely to be of greater interest to practitioners conducting early reading assessments because of the potential for identifying the processing difficulties underlying the academic skill deficits identified by the WIAT-II. The new version of the WIAT-II is a considerable improvement over its predecessor in terms of linkages to empirically validated interventions, emphasis on skills analysis, and expanded content coverage, especially in reading and language arts; however, administration and scoring procedures are also more complex and time-consuming. Several assessment procedures are likely to yield unreliable results for younger and less proficient readers, including the use of a silent reading format for assessing oral reading fluency and a method for calculating reading rate based on the relationship between reading comprehension and silent reading speed rather than words read correctly per minute. Moreover, although subtest and composite floors have been improved, floors for several reading and written language subtests continue to be problematic for young examinees. Because of the floor effects identified above, users should follow up with additional assessments if deficits appear to be present in the domains covered by these measures.

Case Example

Name of student: Alesandra G.
Age: 6 years, 7 months
Grade: First grade
Date of assessment: January

Reason for referral: Alesandra was referred for an early reading assessment by her first-grade teacher. Alesandra recently transferred to the school and is struggling to keep up with the pace of classroom instruction. Her teacher indicates that she lacks effective decoding strategies and can read very little connected text. She also has trouble completing any work on her own because she cannot read the directions for classroom assignments.

Assessment results and interpretation: The reading and language subtests of the *Wechsler Individual Achievement Test–Second Edition* (WIAT-II) were administered to evaluate Alesandra's current level of achievement in those areas. Average scores for a student at her grade level are as follows: Subtest and Composite Standard Scores = 100, Percentile = 50, Age Equivalent = 6-7, and Grade Equivalent = 1.5. Her WIAT-II performance is discussed below.

Composite/Subtest	Standard Score	Percentile Rank	Age Equivalent	Grade Equivalent
Reading Composite	80	9	–	–
Word Reading	80	9	5-8	K.7
Reading Comprehension	87	19	<6-0	<1.0
Pseudoword Decoding	81	10	4-0	PreK 5.0
Written Language Composite	82	12	–	–
Spelling	77	6	5.8	K.6
Written Expression	90	25	5-8	K.8
Oral Language Composite	102	55	–	–
Listening Comprehension	111	77	8-0	2.8
Oral Expression	94	34	6-0	1.0

Supplemental Scores	Raw Score	Quartile
Reading		
Reading Comprehension	–	1
Target Words	7	1
Reading Speed	100 seconds	3
Written Expression		
Alphabet Writing	4	
Word Fluency	0	0
Oral Expression		
Word Fluency	24	4

On the WIAT-II, Alesandra's overall reading skills are in the low average range for her grade (SS = 80, PR = 9). Her skills in single word reading and reading comprehension are also low average (PRs = 9 and 19, respectively). On the Word Reading subtest, she was able to identify 23 of 26 letters (except *b*, *g*, and *v*), to answer several rhyming and sound matching items, and to identify letter blends, but she was able to read only three of the words presented. On the Reading Comprehension subtest, she was able to match words with pictures and read several words in sentences. On the reading passages, she appeared to be skimming the material rather than reading it carefully; however, because she chose to read the passages silently, it was not possible to observe or count decoding errors. Although her reading speed, based on her own report of the time required to read the passages, is rated as above average (Quartile = 3), this rating is unlikely to be reliable, especially as she was able to answer very few questions about what she had read. Alesandra's ability to read phonically regular pseudowords (e.g., *nan*), as measured by the Pseudoword Decoding subtest, is very limited at this point (PR = 10). It should be noted that although her performance is rated as low average for her grade (SS = 81), she obtained a raw score of 0 on this task. Even with additional examples and practice, she was unable to decode any of the pseudoword items, and her errors reveal her difficulty with letter-sound correspondences. For example, presented with *bim*, she responded, "didma."

Her written language skills are in the low average range (SS = 82, PR = 12), but her performance varied considerably across tasks. Her overall written expression skills fall at the low end of the average range for her grade (PR = 25). On the Alphabet Writing task, which requires writing the alphabet in order from memory, she was able to write only four letters in the time allotted. On the Word Fluency task, which requires writing words within a particular category (e.g., things that are round), she said plaintively, "I can't spell anything." Encouraged to try, she wrote *man* and *cat*, neither of which qualified for any points. She did not answer any items correctly on the Sentences task, which requires the examinee to combine simple sentences. Alesandra's spelling skills fall in the low range (SS = 77, PR = 6). She was able to write single letters and a few initial blends but only one of the dictated words. Her errors reveal her limited knowledge of sound–symbol relationships, especially vowels (*ees* for *is*).

In contrast to her generally low average reading and writing skills, Alesandra's overall oral language skills are average compared with those of her grade peers (SS = 102, PR = 55). Her listening comprehension skills, as measured by tasks requiring her to identify pictures, understand sentences, and generate words matching pictures, are rated as above average (PR = 77). Her oral expression skills, as measured by tasks requiring her to repeat sentences, produce words within a specific category, describe a series of scenes, and provide directions for performing tasks, are somewhat less well developed, although still in the average range (PR = 34).

WOODCOCK–JOHNSON III

Overview

The *Woodcock–Johnson III* (WJ III; Woodcock, McGrew, & Mather, 2001a) is a comprehensive assessment system consisting of individually administered, norm-referenced tests designed to measure general intellectual ability, specific cognitive abilities, oral language, and academic achievement throughout the life span. It consists of two conormed instruments: the *Woodcock–Johnson III Tests of Cognitive Abilities* (WJ III COG; Woodcock et al., 2001b) and the *Woodcock–Johnson III Tests of Achievement* (WJ III ACH; Woodcock et al., 2001c), each divided into a Standard Battery and an Extended Battery. The WJ III ACH has two parallel forms matched for content. Age-based norms (ages 2 to 90+ years) and grade-based norms (kindergarten through Grade 12, 2-year college, and 4-year college, including graduate school) are available for both the WJ III COG and ACH. First published in 1977 and revised in 1989, the WJ III is based on Cattell–Horn–Carroll (CHC) theory, a combination of the *Gf-Gc* (fluid and crystallized intelligence) theory (Cattell, 1941, 1943, 1950; Horn, 1965, 1988) on which the 1989 version was based and Carroll's (1993) three-stratum theory of the content and structure of human cognitive abilities. Major changes in this revision include (1) extensive renorming, (2) the addition of 15 new tests and 17 new clusters, (3) expanded discrepancy procedures, and (4) the elimination of hand scoring as an option. Purposes of the WJ III include (1) diagnosis, (2) determination of discrepancies, (3) educational programming, (4) individual program planning, (5) guidance in educational and clinical settings, (6) assessment of growth, (7) research and evaluation, and (8) psychometric training. Materials for each instrument consist of two easel test books; an examiner's manual; 25 test records; 25 subject response booklets; scoring templates for WJ III COG Visual Matching 2, Decision Speed, and Pair Cancellation and WJ III ACH Reading and Math Fluency; an audiocassette; a combined technical manual; the Compuscore and Profiles Program scoring software; and an optional leather carrying case. The WJ III COG also includes five Brief Intellectual Ability test records.

Woodcock–Johnson III Tests of Cognitive Abilities

The WJ III COG consists of 20 tests divided into two batteries: a Standard Battery (Tests 1–10) and an Extended Battery (Tests 11–20). A newly released Diagnostic Supplement includes 11 additional cognitive abilities tests designed to increase the coverage for several broad and narrow CHC abilities. Changes in the current version relevant to early reading assessment include (1) an overall ability score based on a differentially weighted combination of tests at each age and grade level; (2) the removal of the oral language tests to the WJ III ACH; (3) 8 new tests and 9 new clusters; and (4) 5 new clinical clusters, including two Phonemic Awareness clusters. In addition, cognitive factor cluster scores have been expanded to include two or three measures of different narrow aspects of each broad ability, and clusters and tests have been grouped into three broad cognitive areas: Verbal Ability, Thinking Ability, and Cognitive Efficiency.

WJ III COG Tests and Clusters

WJ III COG Tests

The WJ III uses the terms "test" and "cluster" rather than "subtest" and "test." The authors reserve the term "subtest" to refer to tasks within a test that do not yield a separate derived score. Tables 5.37 and 5.38 describe the WJ III COG tests in the Standard and Extended Batteries, respectively, in order of administration.

WJ III COG Clusters

The 20 WJ III COG tests can be combined to produce 24 overlapping clusters based on CHC theory: 3 Intellectual Ability clusters, 6 Cognitive Performance clusters, 7 Cognitive Factors clusters, and 5 clinical clusters. Two additional clusters may be obtained by administering certain WJ III ACH tests (see Figure 5.6). A second Phoneme Awareness cluster (Phoneme Awareness 3) can be obtained by administering WJ III ACH Sound Awareness along with WJ III COG Sound Blending and Incomplete

TABLE 5.37. Description of the WJ III COG Tests, Standard Battery

Test	Description
Verbal Comprehension	This test consists of four orally presented subtests. For *Picture Vocabulary*, the child points to or names pictures of objects. For *Synonyms* and *Antonyms*, the child listens to a word and provides a synonym or antonym. For *Verbal Analogies*, the child listens to three words of an analogy and completes it with a fourth word.
Visual–Auditory Learning	In this controlled-learning task, which simulates the process of learning to read, the child is first taught and then identifies pictographic representations of words (i.e., rebuses).
Spatial Relations	The child identifies from a set of shapes the two or three pieces needed to form a complete target shape.
Sound Blending	The child listens to a series of tape-recorded syllables or phonemes and blends the sounds to form a whole word.
Concept Formation	In this controlled-learning task, the child identifies and states what is different about drawings that are inside a box compared with those outside a box (1-minute time limit for Items 27–40).
Visual Matching	There are two versions of this test. For *Visual Matching 1* (for preschool and developmentally delayed children), the child points to the two identical shapes in a row of four to five shapes (2-minute time limit). For *Visual Matching 2* (for examinees above a 5-year-old developmental level), the child circles the two identical numbers in a row of six numbers (3-minute time limit).
Numbers Reversed	The child listens to increasingly long spans of numbers presented on an audiocassette and then repeats them in reversed order.
Incomplete Words	The child listens to a series of tape-recorded words with one or more phonemes missing and identifies the complete word.
Auditory Working Memory	The child listens to a mixed set of numbers and words presented on an audiocassette and reorders the information by repeating first the words and then the numbers in sequential order. For example, the child hears, "dog, 1, shoe, 8, 2, apple" and responds, "dog, shoe, apple, 1, 8, 2."
Visual–Auditory Learning—Delayed	The child recalls and relearns after a 30-minute to 8-day delay the pictographic representations of words presented on the Visual–Auditory Learning test.

TABLE 5.38. Description of the WJ III COG Tests, Extended Battery

Test	Description
General Information	This test consists of two orally presented subtests. For *Where*, the child identifies where objects are usually found. For *What*, the child identifies what people usually do with objects.
Retrieval Fluency	The child names as many examples as possible in a given category within 1 minute. The three categories consist of things to eat or drink, first names of people, and animals.
Picture Recognition	The child views a page of pictures for 5 seconds and then identifies a subset of the previously presented pictures within a larger set of pictures.
Auditory Attention	The child listens to a word while seeing four pictures and points to the picture representing the word. The words are presented on an audiocassette with increasingly difficult sound discrimination requirements and increasingly intense background noise. For example, the child hears "dog" with background noise, sees pictures of a dog, log, fog, and bog, and points to the picture of the dog.
Analysis–Synthesis	In this controlled-learning task, the child analyzes the components of an incomplete logic puzzle and uses a colored key at the top of the page to identify the missing components (1-minute time limit for Items 26 through 35).
Decision Speed	The child circles the two pictures that are most similar conceptually in a row of seven pictures (3-minute time limit). For example, presented with pictures of a barrel, tooth, spider, toothbrush, hat, airplane, and horn, the child circles the pictures of the tooth and toothbrush.
Memory for Words	The child listens to increasingly long lists of unrelated words presented on an audiocassette and repeats them in the identical sequence.
Rapid Picture Naming	The child names as rapidly as possibly pictured common objects arrayed in rows (2-minute time limit).
Planning	The child plans and executes a tracing route that covers as many segments of a pattern as possible without removing the pencil from the paper or retracing any lines.
Pair Cancellation	The child circles instances of a repeated pattern as quickly as possible (3-minute time limit).

Words, although none of the test materials indicate how the cluster is obtained. The WJ III COG also provides an overall ability score, the General Intellectual Ability (GIA), for both the Standard Battery and Extended Battery; this score represents the first principal component or single *g* (general intellectual ability) factor that accounts for the most variance in overall performance on the tests constituting the scale for each age level. For example, at age 6, Verbal Comprehension contributes 20% of the GIA, followed by Concept Formation (18%), Visual–Auditory Learning (16%), Numbers Reversed (15%), Sound Blending (11%), Visual Matching (10%), and Spatial Relations (9%). The use of a differentially *g*-weighted score is unique to the WJ III and contrasts with other cognitive ability tests in which the overall IQ score is the arithmetic average of the subtests composing it. The first seven tests in the Standard Battery must be administered in order to obtain the General Intellectual Ability–Standard (GIA–Std). The GIA–Extended is obtained by administering all of the tests constituting the GIA–Std, plus the first seven tests from the Extended Battery. A Brief Intellectual Ability (BIA) score, consisting of the arithmetic average of Verbal Comprehension, Concept Formation, and Visual Matching, may also be obtained as a brief measure of intelligence for screening or reevaluation purposes.

	Tests of Cognitive Abilities	Intellectual Ability			Cognitive Categories						CHC Factors							Clinical Clusters						
		General Intellectual Ability-Std	General Intellectual Ability-Ext	Brief Intellectual Ability	Verbal Ability-Std	Verbal Ability-Ext	Thinking Ability-Std	Thinking Ability-Ext	Cognitive Efficiency-Std	Cognitive Efficiency-Ext	Comprehension-Knowledge (Gc)	Long-Term Retrieval (Glr)	Visual-Spatial Thinking (Gv)	Auditory Processing (Ga)	Fluid Reasoning (Gf)	Processing Speed (Gs)	Short-Term Memory (Gsm)	Phonemic Awareness	Working Memory	Broad Attention	Cognitive Fluency	Executive Processes	Delayed Recall	Knowledge
Standard Battery	1. Verbal Comprehension	■	■	■	■	■					■													
	2. Visual-Auditory Learning	■	■				■	■				■												
	3. Spatial Relations	■	■				■	■					■											
	4. Sound Blending	■	■				■	■						■				■						
	5. Concept Formation	■	■	■			■	■							■							■		
	6. Visual Matching	■	■	■					■	■						■								
	7. Numbers Reversed	■	■						■	■							■		■	■				
	8. Incomplete Words																	■						
	9. Auditory Working Memory																		■	■				
	10. Visual-Auditory Learning–Delayed																						■[1]	
Extended Battery	11. General Information		■			■					■													■[2]
	12. Retrieval Fluency		■					■				■									■			
	13. Picture Recognition		■					■					■											
	14. Auditory Attention		■					■						■						■				
	15. Analysis-Synthesis		■					■							■									
	16. Decision Speed		■							■						■					■			
	17. Memory for Words		■							■							■							
	18. Rapid Picture Naming																				■			
	19. Planning																					■		
	20. Pair Cancellation																			■		■		

[1] Also includes Test 12: Story Recall–Delayed from the *WJ III Tests of Achievement.*

[2] Also includes Test 19: Academic Knowledge from the *WJ III Tests of Achievement.*

FIGURE 5.6. WJ III COG selective testing table. From *Examiner's Manual: Woodcock-Johnson III Tests of Cognitive Abililites* (p. 12) by N. Mather and R. W. Woodcock, 2001b, Itasca, IL: Riverside. Copyright 2001 by The Riverside Publishing Company. All rights reserved. Reprinted with permission.

Woodcock–Johnson III Tests of Achievement

Each form of the WJ III ACH consists of 22 tests measuring 5 curricular areas and grouped into 19 overlapping clusters. Two tests (Sound Awareness and Punctuation and Capitalization) are identical across both forms. Two auxiliary writing evaluation procedures are also available. Changes to the new edition relevant to early reading assessment include (1) the addition of seven new achievement tests, including Reading Fluency and a separate Spelling test, and two supplementary tests of phonological and orthographic coding (Sound Awareness and Spelling of Sounds); (2) the addition of eight new clusters, including a Phoneme/Grapheme Knowledge cluster; (3) three tests for each broad achievement cluster, consisting of basic skills, fluency, and application measures; (4) placement of the oral language tests in the achievement rather than the cognitive battery; (5) an option for using the Oral Language–Extended cluster as the ability score for ability–achievement discrepancy analysis; and (6) additional items on reading tests for beginning readers. Moreover, 7 of the 19 clusters are now aligned with the seven areas of learning disabilities defined by IDEA, with two WJ III ACH tests covering each IDEA area.

WJ III ACH Tests and Clusters

WJ III ACH Tests

The WJ III ACH Standard Battery consists of 12 tests, which are described in Table 5.39 in order of administration. Three additional procedures are available for evaluating handwriting and writing skill. The WJ III ACH examiner's manual includes two procedures: (1) the Handwriting Legibility Scale, which provides a norm-based evaluation of handwriting on Writing Samples or samples from other sources; and (2) the Writing Evaluation Scale, an analytic scoring procedure for assessing nine components of writing competence for one or more writing samples, such as a story written in class. The Handwriting Elements Checklist in the test record provides an informal evaluation of six handwriting elements.

TABLE 5.39. Description of the WJ III ACH Tests, Standard Battery

Test	Description
Letter–Word Identification	The child identifies isolated letters and words.
Reading Fluency	The child reads simple sentences silently, decides if a statement is true, and circles *Y* (yes) or *N* (no). For example, the child reads, *A bird can fly* and circles *Y* (3-minute time limit).
Story Recall	The child listens to increasingly complex passages presented on an audiocassette and recalls as many details as possible.
Understanding Directions	The child listens to an increasingly complex series of directions presented on an audiocassette and responds by pointing to objects in colored pictures.
Calculation	The child performs addition, subtraction, multiplication, division, and combinations of these basic operations, as well as some trigonometric, logarithmic, and calculus operations. Initial items require writing single numerals.
Math Fluency	The child performs simple addition, subtraction, and multiplication problems as rapidly as possible (3-minute time limit).
Spelling	The child writes letters and words presented by the examiner. Initial items require drawing lines and tracing letters.
Writing Fluency	Given a set of three words and a stimulus picture per item, the child formulates and writes as many simple sentences as possible (7-minute time limit).
Passage Comprehension	The child silently reads a short passage and supplies a missing key word. Initial items require matching rebuses with pictures of objects and pointing to pictures represented by phrases.
Applied Problems	The child analyzes and solves orally presented mathematical problems.
Writing Samples	The child writes sentences in response to a variety of demands. Early items include pictorial prompts.
Story Recall–Delayed	The child recalls elements of stories presented 30 minutes to 8 days earlier on the Story Recall test.

The Extended Battery includes an additional 10 tests, described in Table 5.40 below in order of administration.

WJ III ACH Clusters

The WJ ACH tests can be grouped into 19 clusters: 3 reading clusters, 4 oral language clusters, 3 math clusters, 3 written language clusters, 1 academic knowledge cluster, and 5 supplemental clusters, including an overall total achievement composite (see Figure 5.7).

Administration

The WJ III is designed as a "toolbox" from which examiners can select tests and interpretive options for specific assessment purposes, not as a battery to be administered in its entirety to every examinee. Depending on the age and skill of the examinee, individual tests require between 5 and 15 minutes to administer, with the exception of Writing Samples, which takes about 10–25 minutes. Administering the WJ III COG Standard Battery requires about 45–50 minutes; the Extended Battery takes from 1½ to 1¾ hours. Administering the WJ III ACH Standard Battery requires about 60–70 minutes. The WJ III ACH manual does not provide time guidelines for the ACH Extended Battery, which range from about 1 to 1½ hours for early primary

TABLE 5.40. Description of the WJ III ACH Tests, Extended Battery

Test	Description
Word Attack	The child pronounces phonically regular pseudowords or low-frequency words. Initial items require the child to pronounce sounds for single letters.
Picture Vocabulary	The child names pictured objects. Initial items require pointing responses.
Oral Comprehension	The child listens to a short tape-recorded passage and provides the missing final word.
Editing	The child orally identifies and corrects errors of punctuation, capitalization, word usage, or spelling in short written passages.
Reading Vocabulary	This test consists of three subtests. For *Synonyms* and *Antonyms*, the child reads a word aloud and provides a synonym or antonym. For *Analogies*, the child reads two words aloud, determines the relationship between them, and completes the analogy aloud with another word.
Quantitative Concepts	This test consists of two subtests. For *Concepts*, the child counts and identifies numbers, shapes, and sequences and demonstrates knowledge of math terms and formulae. For *Number Series*, the child provides the missing number in a series.
Academic Knowledge	This test consists of three subtests: *Science*, *Social Studies*, and *Humanities*. For each subtest, the child orally responds to items presented by the examiner. Initial items require pointing to pictured objects.
Punctuation and Capitalization	The child uses punctuation and capitalization in orally dictated words and phrases. Initial items require writing uppercase and lowercase letters.
Sound Awareness	This test consists of four subtests tapping phonological and phoneme awareness: *Rhyming*, *Deletion*, *Substitution*, and *Reversal*. Initial *Rhyming* items require a pointing rather than an oral response. All *Deletion* items, *Substitution* Samples C and D and Items 4 through 9, and *Reversal* Sample B are presented by audiocassette.

	Tests of Achievement	Reading			Oral Language				Math			Written Lang.			Other Clusters					
		Broad Reading	Basic Reading Skills	Reading Comprehension	Oral Language-Standard	Oral Language-Extended	Listening Comprehension	Oral Expression	Broad Math	Math Calculation Skills	Math Reasoning	Broad Written Language	Basic Writing Skills	Written Expression	Academic Knowledge	Phoneme/Grapheme Knowledge	Academic Skills	Academic Fluency	Academic Applications	Total Achievement
Standard Battery	Test 1: Letter-Word Identification	■	■														■			■
	Test 2: Reading Fluency	■																■		■
	Test 3: Story Recall				■	■		■												
	Test 4: Understanding Directions				■	■	■													
	Test 5: Calculation								■	■							■			■
	Test 6: Math Fluency								■	■								■		■
	Test 7: Spelling											■	■				■			■
	Test 8: Writing Fluency											■		■				■		■
	Test 9: Passage Comprehension	■		■															■	■
	Test 10: Applied Problems								■		■								■	■
	Test 11: Writing Samples											■		■					■	■
	Test 12: Story Recall–Delayed																			
Extended Battery	Test 13: Word Attack		■													■				
	Test 14: Picture Vocabulary					■		■												
	Test 15: Oral Comprehension					■	■													
	Test 16: Editing												■							
	Test 17: Reading Vocabulary			■																
	Test 18: Quantitative Concepts										■									
	Test 19: Academic Knowledge														■					
	Test 20: Spelling of Sounds															■				
	Test 21: Sound Awareness																			
	Test 22: Punctuation & Capitalization																			

FIGURE 5.7. WJ III ACH selective testing table. From *Examiner's Manual: Woodcock–Johnson® III Tests of Achievement* (p. 12) by N. Mather and R. W. Woodcock, 2001a, Itasca, IL: Riverside.

grade examinees in my experience. The Brief Intellectual Ability (BIA) scale takes about 10–15 minutes to administer. To reduce administration time, most tests include suggested starting points based on the examinee's estimated ability or achievement level, as well as basals and ceilings. Exceptions are timed tests, such as Reading Fluency, and tests requiring the administration of specific blocks of items, such as Writing Samples. Examiners should note that even if a child reaches a ceiling in the middle of a testing page, they should administer the remaining stimulus material because it is visible on the child's page. If the examinee answers at least one additional item correctly on that page, testing continues until another ceiling is reached.

Each test manual provides a comprehensive set of supports for administration, including a chapter on general administration and scoring procedures and a chapter on administering and scoring the various tests. The Examiner Training Workbook for each battery reviews item-level scoring and includes practice exercises, a reproducible test observations checklist, and a reproducible examiner training checklist. The Test Session Observations Checklist on the front of the test record permits examiners to document testing observations with a seven-category behavior rating scale, which is converted to statements in the software scoring report.

Scores

For most tests, scoring is dichotomous. Exceptions include tests for which the raw score is based on number of errors (e.g., Visual–Auditory Learning), multiple-point tests (e.g., Spelling of Sounds), and timed tests (e.g., Reading Fluency), for which the raw score is the number correct minus number incorrect. Examiners can obtain estimated age- and grade-equivalent scores immediately for most tests by consulting the scoring tables on that page in the test record. Examiners who wish to record incorrect responses for later error analysis on Letter–Word Identification and Word Attack, as suggested in the Examiner Training Workbook, have very little space to do so. A response line should be added beside each item for this purpose. Responses other than English are acceptable on several WJ III COG tests, including Verbal Comprehension, General Information, Retrieval Fluency, and Rapid Picture Naming.

Of all the tests reviewed in this text, the WJ III offers the largest number of score types, including standard scores ($M = 100$, $SD = 15$), percentile ranks, age and grade equivalents, Cognitive–Academic Language Proficiency (CALP) levels, Relative Proficiency Index (RPI) scores (termed "Relative Mastery Index" scores in the WJ-R), Developmental Zones (WJ III COG) or Instructional Zones (WJ III ACH), and discrepancy scores. The exception to this is the WJ III ACH Story Recall—Delayed test, which generates only a z score indicating the discrepancy between the examinee's predicted and obtained delayed recall score. Table 5.41 describes the score types that are unusual and/or unique to the WJ III.

As noted above, hand scoring is no longer an option for the WJ III. The Compuscore and Profiles Program included with each kit produces a full set of derived scores and discrepancies, with options for printing a summary report in either English or Spanish, age/grade percentile rank profiles, and standard score/percentile rank profiles. The Summary Report consists of a brief narrative report of examinee performance and incorporates observations from the Test Session Observation Checklist. Users should note that age and grade equivalents are identical regardless of whether age or grade norms are selected, whereas standard scores, percentile ranks, RPIs, and Instructional/Developmental Zones vary according to the type of norm group. The Report Writer for the WJ III (Schrank & Woodcock, 2002), which must be purchased separately, provides additional scoring and interpretative options (discussed below in the "Usability" section).

Interpretation

The WJ III COG and ACH examiner manuals provide information on interpreting derived scores, age/grade and standard score/percentile rank profiles, and test performance in terms of task complexity, CHC theory, and comparisons with performance on other WJ III tests (e.g., discrepancy analyses). The manual presents an interpretive framework based on four hierarchical levels of interpretation, each linked to different kinds of information obtained in testing and having different applications. Emphasis is placed on interpretation at the cluster level, especially for the WJ III COG. The WJ III COG examiner manual also presents information on interpreting the clinical clusters and offers two models for interpreting performance. The Cognitive Performance Model represents cognitive performance as a function of the joint effect of four categories of cognitive abilities (acquired knowledge, thinking

TABLE 5.41 Description of Selected WJ III Scores

Score	Description
W score	*W* scores involve a special transformation of the Rasch ability scale. For each test, the *W* scores constitute an equal-interval scale centered on a value of 500, which is set to approximate the average performance of 10-year-old examinees. All of the WJ III ACH cluster scores and most of the WJ III COG cluster scores, except the General Intellectual Ability (GIA) clusters, are the average *W* scores of the tests included in that cluster. GIA clusters are weighted because the abilities measured by those tests vary in relative importance with the developmental level of the examinee.
Cognitive–Academic Language Proficiency (CALP)	CALP levels range from 1 (Negligible English CALP) to 5 (Advanced English CALP) and provide an estimate of how easy or difficult the examinee will find the English language demands of instruction at that age or grade level. CALP levels can be reported for all WJ III COG and ACH tests measuring English language proficiency, including the WJ III ACH Broad Reading and Reading Comprehension clusters, by selecting that option in the software scoring program.
Relative Proficiency Index (RPI)	RPIs range from 0/90 to 100/90 and predict an examinee's percentage of success on tasks on which average individuals in the age or grade comparison group would have 90% success. For example, for a grade-based comparison group of 2.5, a Basic Reading RPI of 60/90 indicates that the examinee is predicted to demonstrate 60% success on basic reading tasks that average children in the fifth month of second grade perform with 90% proficiency. Interpretation guidelines are similar to informal reading inventory criteria: 96/90 or above = independent level, 90/90 to 95/90 = instructional level, 75/90 or below = frustration level.[a]
Instructional Zone/Developmental Zone	The WJ III ACH Instructional Zone and the WJ III COG Developmental Zone are based on the RPI and identify a range along a developmental scale from easy (equal to or greater than 96/90) to difficult (equal to or less than 75/90). Each zone extends 10 *W* points above and below the examinee's *W* score, with the width depending on the rate of change for that ability. Wide bands indicate abilities with a slow rate of change, whereas narrow bands indicate abilities that change rapidly over time. The lower and higher points of these zones are labeled as EASY and DIFF in the score printout.
Discrepancy Percentile Rank	The Discrepancy Percentile Rank (labeled DISCREPANCY PR in the score printout) indicates the percentage of the examinee's age or grade peers with the same ability score who obtained the same or greater discrepancy score. For example, a Broad Reading DISCREPANCY PR of 5 for an examinee in Grade 1.7 indicates that 5% of children in Grade 1.7 in the normative group with the same predicted Broad Reading standard score obtained a Broad Reading standard score as low or lower.
Discrepancy Standard Deviation	The Discrepancy Standard Deviation (labeled DISCREPANCY SD in the score printout) is a standardized *z* score that indicates the number of standard deviation units (labeled SEE in the printout) between the examinee's discrepancy score and the average discrepancy score for examinees in the norm group with the same ability score and at the same age or grade level. The scoring program evaluates the significance of the difference, using a criterion of ±1.50 SEE or another value selected by the examiner. For example, for an examinee in Grade 1.7, a Broad Reading DISCREPANCY SD of –1.61 indicates that the examinee's Broad Reading discrepancy score is 1.61 SEE units lower than the average Broad Reading discrepancy score for other individuals in Grade 1.7 in the norm group with the same ability score. This statistic will be designated with a "YES" in the significance column on the printout because it meets or exceeds the criterion of ±1.50.

[a]The WJ III manuals use only these three categories to describe RPI scores. A five-category interpretive framework is presented in Schrank, Flanagan, Woodcock, and Mascolo (2002), and a seven-category interpretive framework is presented in Mather and Jaffe (2002). The latter is used in the case example on page 538.

abilities, cognitive efficiency, and external and internal facilitators–inhibitors). The second, more elaborated model, the Information Processing Model, is an effort to represent the manner in which cognitive and noncognitive variables interact to produce cognitive test performance and forms the basis for a Diagnostic Worksheet designed to assist practitioners in evaluating WJ III COG performance. A reproducible copy of the Diagnostic Worksheet is included in an appendix to the manual. The Examiner Training Workbook for each instrument includes a case example—a fifth-grade girl (aged 12-3) for the WJ III COG and a fifth-grade boy (aged 10-2) for the WJ III ACH.

Discrepancy Interpretation

The WJ III is unsurpassed among assessment batteries in the range of options it offers for analyzing score differences. Not only are the WJ III COG and ACH conormed, but comparisons of ability and achievement scores are based on actual discrepancy norms rather than estimated discrepancies. Because of the importance of conorming in discrepancy analyses and the unique nature of the WJ III discrepancy norms, additional information about these topics follows, drawn primarily from McGrew (1994, 1999), Reynolds (1984–1985, 1990), and McGrew and Woodcock (2001).

CONORMING AND DISCREPANCY NORMS

Conorming refers to the process in which normative data for cognitive ability and academic achievement tests are derived from the same examinees in a single standardization sample. Conormed tests permit examiners to make comparisons among an examinee's ability and achievement scores that have greater precision and validity than comparisons of scores derived from separately normed instruments. When comparisons are made using separately normed tests, observed discrepancies may result not from actual differences in the examinee's ability and achievement but from differences in the two norming groups. Conorming procedures also take into account the phenomenon known as *regression to the mean*—the tendency of above or below average scores on one test to move toward the mean on a second test, with the amount of movement toward the mean depending on the degree of correlation between the two tests (in the .60s and .70s for ability and achievement tests). As a result, an examinee with a standard score of 130 on an ability test would not be predicted to obtain a standard score of 130 on an achievement test. Rather, the predicted score would be closer to the mean of 100 (about 121 to 123). Similarly, for an examinee with a standard score of 85 on an ability test, the expected achievement score would be higher (about 86 or 87).

When ability–achievement comparisons do not take regression effects into account, as when examiners subtract achievement from ability scores (the so-called *simple-difference-score model*), this procedure will overestimate discrepancies for examinees with above average ability and underestimate discrepancies for examinees with below average ability. Consequently, when discrepancy analyses are used in determining the presence of learning disabilities, examinees with higher ability scores will be overidentified and those with lower ability scores will be underidentified. In the *regression-based discrepancy model*, predicted achievement scores are calculated by using the correlation between the ability and achievement tests in a regression formula that corrects for regression effects. Although this procedure is preferable to the simple-difference-score model, ability–achievement correlations may be available for only a few age or grade levels, based on small samples in validity studies. Moreover, ability–achievement correlations vary as a function of the nature of the sample, age and grade level, and the academic domain.

Although conorming and software scoring programs with options for regression-based discrepancy procedures are becoming the standard for comprehensive assessment batteries, the WJ III is unique in providing actual discrepancy norms based on data from the standardization sample rather than estimated discrepancy scores derived from a formula that corrects for regression effects. To calculate WJ III ability–achievement discrepancies, predicted achievement standard scores for each achievement cluster were first derived for each examinee in the norm group, based on a regression formula that included each examinee's ability score as well as age or grade variables. Each examinee's actual achievement standard score was then subtracted from the predicted achievement standard score, creating a distribution of discrepancy scores in the norming sample. Finally, the standard deviation (called the *standard error of estimate*) of the resulting ability–achievement discrepancy distributions was calculated by age or grade. The identical procedure was followed for the three ability score combinations (General Intellectual Ability, Predicted Achievement, and Oral Language) and each achievement cluster. WJ III intracognitive, intra-achievement, and intraindividual discrepancy norms (see below) were derived using similar procedures, with the difference that an intraindividual average score from a specific set of cognitive and/or achievement tests was used as the predictor score. For example, the WJ III ACH Extended Battery intra-achievement discrepancy norms for the nine achievement clusters are based on a comparison of each cluster with a predicted score based on the average of the other eight cluster scores.

DISCREPANCY PROCEDURES

The WJ III provides two basic types of discrepancy procedures for two different purposes: (1) *intra-ability*, which are discrepancies among the various cognitive and academic abilities and are designed to provide diagnostic information; and (2) *ability–achievement*, which are discrepancies between a predictor score and academic performance and are designed to provide predictive information. There are three intra-ability discrepancy procedures and three ability–achievement discrepancy procedures, which are described in Table 5.42.

Technical Adequacy

Standardization

The WJ III was standardized on 8,818 individuals designed to represent the U.S. population in 2000, with the largest proportion of examinees (4,783) in kindergarten through 12th grade. Subjects were randomly selected within a stratified sampling design that controlled for 10 subject and community variables: sex, race, Hispanic ori-

TABLE 5.42. Discrepancy Procedures on the WJ III

Discrepancy procedure	Description
Intra-ability discrepancy procedures	Intra-ability discrepancy procedures are bidirectional comparisons that compare a measured ability to the average of all the other abilities and skills in the target areas. All three intra-ability discrepancy options are designed to provide diagnostic information.
Intraindividual	The intraindividual discrepancy compares each measured cognitive ability and academic achievement area to the average of all other abilities. It can be used to determine strengths and weaknesses and to define how these abilities relate to the examinee's learning problems. This procedure is especially appropriate for determining specific learning disabilities because it permits domain-specific achievement skills to be evaluated conjointly with the related cognitive abilities.
Intracognitive	The intracognitive discrepancy procedure compares each measured cognitive ability to the average of the other abilities and can be used to document a processing disorder for determining eligibility for learning disability services. When the WJ III COG Standard Battery is administered, the predictor measure for each of the three broad areas of cognitive performance (Verbal Ability, Thinking Ability, and Cognitive Efficiency) is the average score of the other two clusters. When the Extended Battery is administered, the predictor measure is the average of the other six *Gf-Gc* cognitive factors.
Intra-achievement	The intra-achievement discrepancy procedure compares each measured achievement area to the average of the other achievement areas and is designed to examine an examinee's strengths and weaknesses among academic areas. For the WJ III ACH Standard Battery, the predictor measure for the four broad achievement clusters (Broad Reading, Broad Math, Broad Written Language, and Oral Language) is the average performance on the other three clusters. For the Extended Battery, the predictor measure for each of the nine achievement clusters is the average score on the other eight clusters.
Ability–achievement discrepancy procedures	Ability–achievement discrepancy procedures are unidirectional comparisons that use certain cognitive abilities to predict achievement. Each of the three procedures uses a different score as the predictor.
General intellectual ability–achievement	The general intellectual ability–achievement procedure uses the General Intellectual Ability (GIA) score as the predictor. Each test constituting the GIA score is differentially weighted to provide the best estimate of *g* at the examinee's age level. This procedure is designed to assess the presence and severity of a discrepancy between overall intellectual ability and a particular area of achievement. Either the GIA–Standard or the GIA–Extended score can be used as the ability measure.
Predicted achievement–achievement	The predicted achievement–achievement procedure is designed to determine whether an examinee's performance in a particular academic area is commensurate with his or her current levels of the cognitive abilities associated with that academic domain. Each predicted achievement score is a weighted combination of the first seven WJ III COG tests, with weights varying by age to provide the best prediction for the target achievement area at a given point in development. Learning-disabled individuals may not show this type of discrepancy because their weak cognitive abilities are reflected in lower predicted achievement scores. Instead, a significant discrepancy between predicted and actual achievement suggests that poor performance is related to other cognitive abilities not included in the predicted clusters or to extrinsic factors, such as poor instruction, economic disadvantage, or low motivation, rather than to intrinsic factors (i.e., the measured cognitive abilities related to the achievement domain).
Oral language ability–achievement	The oral language ability–achievement procedure uses the Oral Language–Extended cluster score to predict achievement on any of the broad, basic, or applied cluster scores. This procedure is designed to help distinguish individuals with adequate oral language abilities but poor reading and writing achievement (i.e., those with specific reading disabilities) from those whose oral language abilities are commensurate with their reading and writing achievement (i.e., examinees who have oral language disorders or are garden-variety poor readers).

gin, region, community size, type of school, type of college/university, education (adults), occupational status (adults), and type of occupation (adults in the labor force). In addition to region and size, communities were selected on the basis of 13 SES variables, including three levels of education among the adult population, four levels of household income, three categories of labor force characteristics, and three types of occupations. Students with disabilities who were enrolled at least part-time in regular classes were included. Individual subject weights were then applied to obtain a distribution of data that matched the distribution in the U.S. population for all 10 norming variables. For the school-age sample, norms were gathered continuously from September 1996 through May 1999. Norm group sizes for early primary grade examinees are between 313 and 437 for ages 5 through 8 and between 304 and 365 for kindergarten through second grade. Age-based norms are in 1-month increments from 24 months through 90+ years. Grade-based norms are in 1-month increments from kindergarten through Grade 12, with special norms for 2- and 4-year college students and first-year graduate students. Because both age- and grade-based subgroup intervals are so small, derived scores are based on as few as 26 examinees in the early primary grade range.

Reliability Evidence

Reliabilities of speeded tests and tests with multiple-point scoring systems were calculated using Rasch analyses, whereas reliability statistics for all other tests were calculated using split-half procedures. Reliabilities are reported by 1-year interval for ages 2 through 19, and values reported below refer to the early primary grade range (ages 5-0 through 8-11). Reliabilities were not calculated for grade-based scores, but no rationale is provided for this omission. For WJ III COG clusters, internal consistency reliability coefficients are at or above .96 for the GIA–Standard and GIA–Extended and at or above .94 for the BIA. Internal consistency reliabilities are at or above .90 across the early primary grade range for 13 of 21 WJ III COG clusters and at or above .80 for 7 clusters, with 1 cluster (Visual–Spatial Thinking) falling in the .70s for ages 6 through 8. For WJ III COG tests, internal consistency coefficients are at or above .90 across the early primary grade range for 5 of the 20 tests and at or above .80 for 8 tests. Values for 5 tests (Spatial Relations, Incomplete Words, Retrieval Fluency, Memory for Words, and Pair Cancellation) fall in the .70s for some age groups, and values for 2 tests (Picture Recognition and Planning) are in the .60s and .70s throughout the early primary grade range.

For WJ III ACH clusters, internal consistency coefficients for Total Achievement are at or above .93 for ages 5 through 8. Internal consistency coefficients for 10 of the 17 additional ACH cluster scores are at or above .90 across the entire primary grade range, whereas values for 5 clusters fall in the .80s. Coefficients fall in the .70s for Oral Expression at age 6 and Written Expression at age 5. For WJ III ACH tests, internal consistency coefficients are at or above .90 for 5 of the 22 tests and in the .80s and .90s for 8 tests. For some of the target age groups, reliabilities fall in the .70s for Story Recall, Writing Fluency, Writing Samples, Picture Vocabulary, Oral Comprehension, and Spelling of Sounds; in the .60s for Math Fluency and Story Recall–Delayed; and in the .50s for Punctuation and Capitalization.

The technical manual reports three studies of stability, all of which included early primary grade examinees. In the first study with the eight WJ III speeded tests with three age-differentiated samples, test–retest correlations (1-day interval) for the

7- to 11-year-old sample (*ns* = 30 to 59) were at or above .90 for Reading Fluency and Math Fluency; in the .80s for Visual Matching, Decision Speed, Retrieval Fluency, and Pair Cancellation; but in the .70s for Rapid Picture Naming and Writing Fluency. In a second study (*n* = 1,196, ages 2 through 95) that evaluated the stability of 15 WJ III COG and ACH tests for four age groupings and three extended retest intervals (less than 1 year to 10 years), 15 of the 34 stability coefficients for the 6 ACH tests were at or above .90 for the 2- to 7-year-old and the 8- to 18-year-old groups (subsample sizes not specified). Sixteen coefficients were in the .80s, with 3 of the values for Synonyms/Antonyms and Passage Comprehension in the .70s or below. Values for the nine cognitive tests were lower, with none of the 49 coefficients at or above .90. Fourteen were in the .80s, 18 were in the .70s, and 17 were in the .60s or below, with some values falling as low as the .30s. In the third study (*n* = 457, ages 4 to 17, 1-year interval), which evaluated the stability of 17 WJ III ACH clusters and 12 tests, test–retest coefficients for the 4- to 7-year-old group (*ns* = 39 to 145) were at or above .90 for 8 of the 12 clusters and between .80 and .89 for 3 clusters. The Academic Fluency cluster was the least stable (.74). Stability estimates for 3 of the 17 achievement tests were at or above .90, 7 were in the .80s, and 7 fell in the .70s or below, with Word Attack, Math Fluency, Editing, and Academic Fluency in the .70s and Story Recall, Handwriting, and Reading Fluency demonstrating the least stability (.69, .67, and .59, respectively). For the 8- to 10-year-old group (*ns* = 101 to 145), stability estimates for 8 of 12 achievement clusters were at or above .90, whereas coefficients for 4 clusters were between .80 and .89. Test–retest coefficients for 9 of the 17 tests were in the .80s, whereas values for 5 tests fell in the .70s (Reading Fluency, Math Fluency, Writing Fluency, Reading Vocabulary, and Oral Comprehension). Writing Samples, Handwriting, and Story Recall were the least stable (.65, .69, and .53, respectively).

Results of interrater reliability studies conducted during WJ-R standardization for Writing Samples, Writing Fluency, and Handwriting, which have remained unchanged in the WJ III, are presented again in the technical manual. For 19 randomly selected Grade 2 completed Writing Samples protocols, the median correlation for six raters with prior experience or 2 hours of training was .93. Interrater reliability for 21 randomly selected Grade 3 Writing Samples records was .99 for agreement and 1.00 for pair-consensus ratings for six raters. For a set of Writing Samples protocols from 47 learning-disabled examinees (age and grade unspecified), the median correlation for four trained raters was .93. For a sample of 47 Grade 3 Writing Fluency records, median interrater reliability was .98 for three independent raters. The median correlation for the Handwriting measure for three trained raters for 35 Grade 3 examinees was below the acceptable level ($r = .75$). Interrater reliability estimates based on independent scoring of the same examinees during actual test sessions should be provided for tests requiring subjective judgment, such as Story Recall, for pseudoword reading and phoneme manipulation tests, such as Word Attack and Sound Awareness, and for Rapid Picture Naming, especially in light of the fact that scores are based on a single trial.

Evidence for the equivalence of WJ III ACH Forms A and B is limited. The technical manual presents a rationale for alternate form construction using a spiraling omnibus approach. Item assignment was designed to provide about 3 items per 10 *W* unit change in difficulty and an equal mix of content between the forms. In support of this item-banking approach, the manual includes a chart with item difficulties plotted for Form A and Form B Calculation items to demonstrate that the range and density of *W* ability being measured is similar for both forms, as well as standard errors of measurement (SEMs) by *W* ability levels for both forms of Calculation. Additional evidence of equivalence consists of item difficulty comparisons, raw score/*W* ability ogives, and SEM comparisons by *W* ability levels for Calculation and *W* score correlations for 11 age groups for Passage Comprehension (.96 and .92 for ages 5 and 7). No information on the equivalence of means or SEMs between the two forms for any of the ACH tests or clusters is presented.

Test Floors and Item Gradients

As with other Rasch-model tests, the adequacy of WJ III floors and item gradients cannot be evaluated by inspecting conversion tables. The examiner and technical manuals state that WJ III standard scores extend from 0 to 200, but, as noted below, this range does not apply to all tests and clusters across all ages and grades. According to Fredrick Schrank of Riverside Publishing (personal communication, April 17, 2001), subtests for a particular age level were constructed with the goal that a raw score of 1 would yield a standard score at least 1 standard deviation below the mean (SS ≤ 85) and preferably 2 standard deviations below the mean (SS ≤ 70). Although easy items have been added to several tests, examiners will find that some clusters and tests, especially on the WJ III ACH, do not meet either goal for early primary grade examinees in terms of age- or grade-based scores. For example, when raw scores of 1 on all cognitive and achievement tests, are entered into the Compuscore program for an examinee aged 6-6 and in the third month of first grade, both age-based and grade-based standard scores for the Math Calculation Skills, Written Expression, and Academic Fluency clusters and the Auditory Working Memory, Reading Fluency, Calculation, Math Fluency, Writing Fluency, Editing, and Reading Vocabulary tests do not yield a standard score of 69 or below. A raw score of 1 on Reading Vocabulary earns a grade-based standard score of 94. Floors for Writing Fluency, Reading Vocabulary, and Editing are inadequate throughout the entire early primary grade range for grade-based scores (i.e., through Grade 2.9) and for the latter two tests for age-based scores (i.e., through age 8-11).

According to the technical manual, item gradients were designed to provide about 3 items for each 10 *W* unit change in difficulty, with an increase of 4 or 5 items at the bottom and top of the difficulty scale if additional items were available. Users can derive rough estimates of item gradient steepness as well as test floor adequacy by inspecting the age and grade equivalent tables provided in the record form for all tests except for the delayed recall tests.

Validity Evidence

CONTENT VALIDITY EVIDENCE

Content validity, especially for the WJ III COG, was developed by specifying test and cluster content according to Carroll's (1993) three-stratum CHC theory, which proposes a model of narrow and broad abilities with a general intellectual ability factor (*g*) at the apex. Each WJ III test is intended to serve as a single measure of one of the narrow abilities, whereas clusters have been constructed to include two or more different narrow abilities. For example, the broad CHC factor Auditory Processing is measured in the WJ III COG Standard Battery by Sound Blending, a test of synthetic phonetic coding, and in the WJ III COG Extended Battery by Auditory Attention, a test of speech-sound discrimination. For the WJ III ACH, the technical manual states that content was designed to measure the major aspects of oral language and academic achievement, as well as curricular areas and domains specified in federal legislation. Items were selected to fit the Rasch model and, as noted above, to meet an item density criterion reflecting an average difference in difficulty of 3–4 *W*-scale points between items. The examiner manuals include descriptions of test and cluster content, but little content validity evidence is presented for the WJ III ACH, despite the numerous changes in that battery.

The authors present growth curves for ages 5 through 90 for seven major cognitive factors, nine achievement clusters, and six narrow abilities, including reading, as evidence of the distinctiveness of each primary factor, cluster, or narrow ability score. Possible item bias was evaluated during test development by means of sensitivity reviews, with nine reviewers examining each item with regard to possible issues regarding women, individuals with disabilities, and cultural or linguistic minorities. Rasch-based DIF analyses were conducted for three group comparisons (male vs. female, white vs. nonwhite, and Hispanic vs. non-Hispanic), focusing on items from domains most likely to be biased because of language and achievement influences. All correlations between item difficulty pairs were at or above .99, indicating little DIF. Four items for the Hispanic versus non-Hispanic comparison and one item for the white versus nonwhite comparison met the criteria for both practical and statistical significance. One of the items, which had been flagged by the bias review committee, was dropped, and the remaining four items were retained on the grounds that statistically significant findings could have resulted from inflated error rates associated with multiple comparisons.

CRITERION-RELATED VALIDITY EVIDENCE

The technical manual reports the results of 11 studies comparing performance on the WJ III with performance on other tests of ability, achievement, and attention/behavior, 4 of which included early primary grade examinees. Two of the studies are discussed here, and two are discussed below under "Construct Validity Evidence." For 52 students in Grades 1–8, scores on the WJ III ACH reading clusters were moderately to highly correlated with reading subtest and composite scores on the *Wechsler Individual Achievement Test* (WIAT; *r*s = .63 to .82) and the *Kaufman Test of Educational Achievement* (K-TEA; *r*s = .44 to .81). WJ III mean Broad Reading scores were between 8 and 10 points lower than WIAT and K-TEA mean Reading composite scores (SSs = 95.9 vs. 105.1 and 104.4, respectively). Correlations between WJ III ACH and WIAT written language measures were lower (.31 to .77). (Note that the K-TEA does not include written language measures.) Interestingly, the WJ III ACH Written Expression cluster correlated more highly with WIAT Reading Comprehension and Reading composite scores (both *r*s = .49) than with WIAT Written Expression (.31). Moreover, WJ III Written Expression mean scores were more than 10 points higher than WIAT Written Expression mean scores (SS = 114.8 vs. 103.6, respectively).

In a normal sample of 100 students in kindergarten through eighth grade, correlations between the WJ III COG Visual–Spatial Thinking and Fluid Reasoning clusters and other measures of nonverbal cognitive ability—including the *Universal Nonverbal Intelligence Test* (Bracken & McCallum, 1998), *Comprehensive Test of Nonverbal*

Intelligence, and subtests from the *Leiter International Performance Scale–Revised Edition* (Roid & Miller, 1997)—were generally moderate (.37 to .62). Correlations between the WJ III GIA and full-scale or composite scores from a variety of other cognitive tests were generally in the .70s, supporting the use of GIA first-principal component scores as measures of overall intellectual functioning. Correlations between the four WJ III ability predictor options and 14 WJ III achievement criterion clusters for five age groups indicate that the Predicted Achievement option provides the strongest prediction of reading, mathematics, written language, and academic knowledge across all developmental levels, followed by the GIA–Std and GIA–Ext clusters, with the Oral Language cluster the weakest predictor.

The manual also presents comparisons of the concurrent validity of the WJ III ability clusters and measures of achievement with that of other major intelligence batteries for preschool, school-age, and university samples. For the Grades 3–5 sample (*ns* = 147 to 150), WJ III GIA and Predicted Achievement scores were more strongly correlated with WJ III ACH clusters than were WISC-III Full Scale IQ scores across all achievement domains, except for Academic Knowledge and Oral Expression.

CONSTRUCT VALIDITY EVIDENCE

Intercorrelations for the WJ III COG and ACH clusters are reported for seven broad age levels. For the 4- to 5- and 6- to 8-year-old age groups, the Phonemic Awareness cluster, which includes Sound Blending and Incomplete Words, is only moderately correlated with GIA (.56 and .59, respectively), whereas the Phonemic Awareness 3 cluster, which also includes WJ III ACH Sound Awareness, is highly correlated with GIA (.71 and .73), probably reflecting the greater requirements for phonemic manipulation and phonological memory in the latter task. Results of two sets of confirmatory factor analyses conducted for examinees in five age groups are presented in support of the CHC model. Most of the WJ III COG tests load on a single factor, indicating that construct-irrelevant variance has been minimized, whereas many of the WJ III ACH tests load on more than one factor, reflecting the complexity of the skills being assessed. Factor analyses are not reported for ages 2 to 5.

In support of the diagnostic utility of the WJ III, the manual presents three studies with one or more clinical groups, two of which included early primary grade examinees. In a sample of 90 students in Grades 1–6 that included 29 examinees with learning disabilities and 30 examinees with ADHD, participants took 15 WJ III COG tests, 9 WJ III ACH tests, and two criterion measures of attention and behavior: the *Tests of Variables of Attention* (Greenberg, 1998) and the School Problems ratings scales on the *Behavior Assessment System for Children* (Reynolds & Kamphaus, 1992). Of the 26 correlations (–.01 to –.54), 8 were significant, with the highest correlations for WJ III ACH Broad Reading and WJ III COG Concept Formation and Visual Matching. In another study with students with ADHD (*n* = 48, ages 6 through 17), age-adjusted standard scores were significantly lower than standard scores for the normative sample for 1 of 17 WJ III COG tests (Auditory Attention) and 3 of 8 WJ III ACH tests (Oral Comprehension, Passage Comprehension, and Calculation). (Note that in the discussion of this study in the technical manual, there is an error on page 95 indicating that the Letter–Word Identification score rather than the Calculation score was significantly different.) Additional studies comparing the scores of other clinical samples, including examinees with mental retardation, reading disabilities, and gifted/talented placements, are needed to document the WJ III's diagnostic validity.

To determine whether WJ III tests measure the same constructs across different demographic groups, confirmatory factor analyses based on a WJ III COG seven-factor model were conducted for three contrast groups (males vs. females, whites vs. nonwhites, and Hispanics vs. non-Hispanics) drawn from the normative group (age 6 and older). The tests loaded on the same factors across groups, supporting the contention that the WJ III measures the same cognitive and achievement constructs across gender, racial, and ethnic groups. The manuals do not present mean scores for various demographic groups in the normative sample, however. Nor are any studies presented to demonstrate the relationship of the WJ-R to the WJ III in terms of either correlation coefficients or differences in means and standard deviations, even for tests that have remained the same across both versions.

Usability

Compared with the WJ-R, which was distinguished by its lack of portability as well as its psychometric soundness, the WJ III has a much higher usability quotient. The testing books are smaller and lighter, the carrying cases are less cumbersome, and each test kit includes the basic software scoring program. The WJ III's technical excellence, extensive content coverage, and numerous assessment options do not come cheaply, however. Because of the breadth and complexity of the battery, the WJ III also requires a major investment in time and effort to achieve competency in administration, scoring, and especially interpretation, given the number and diversity of scores and interpretive options that even a partial administration yields. The authors and publishers have taken pains to help practitioners master the art and science of the WJ III by including a variety of excellent supportive materials, many of which are provided in the test kit or are available on the Riverside Web site (http://www.riverpub.com). Materials posted on the Web site include a series of useful Assessment Service Bulletins on a variety of topics and frequently asked questions for several categories, including administration, scoring, interpretation, and the software scoring programs. Additional useful materials available from other publishers are listed below under "Print Resources."

The WJ III COG and ACH examiner manuals include identical sections with guidelines for accommodating seven categories of examinees: young children, English-language learners, individuals with learning and/or reading disabilities, individuals with attentional or behavioral difficulties, individuals with hearing impairments, individuals with visual impairments, and individuals with physical impairments. The manuals' authors are to be commended for making the critical distinction between accommodations and modifications in their discussion. The narrative report from the Compuscore program can be printed in either English or Spanish and exported to a word-processing application. Although there is some on-screen information in the Help file, the Compuscore user's manual is far too brief. The "Troubleshooting" section lists only three questions, and readers receive no help on managing data files, which is the most challenging aspect of the program in my own experience. Available at additional cost and highly recommended is the Report Writer for the WJ III. The Report Writer includes all of the features in the Compuscore program, along with a host of other options, including a procedure for comparing WJ III ACH scores to scores on other major intelligence batteries, 10 reproducible checklists and forms, and a variety of report addenda, including the Diagnostic Worksheet and a Test Definitions list. Moreover, whereas the vast majority of the software scoring programs reviewed in this text provide users with little or no assistance, the Report Writer includes a comprehensive (125-page) spiral-bound manual that includes a description of program content; procedures for using the program, including a section on troubleshooting; interpretive options; and supplemental materials. An appendix includes all 10 of the checklists and scales in the program in reproducible form.

Links to Intervention

Examiner and technical manuals do not provide any specific information on linking test results to interventions, although the Report Writer checklists and questionnaires yield useful information for generating home- and school-based interventions. Case examples with suggestions for intervention are included in all three of the books listed under "Print Resources" on the next page. Especially helpful is the Mather and Jaffe (2002) book, which is a mine of information for practitioners seeking to translate WJ III results into effective interventions.

Relevant Research

The literature on the WJ family of tests and the CHC theory underlying the WJ III COG is vast, although studies on the WJ III itself are only beginning to appear. Among the WJ-R studies, examiners assessing early primary grade children may be especially interested in the research of Kevin McGrew and his colleagues on the relationship between WJ-R cognitive clusters and achievement in reading and written language (e.g., McGrew, 1993, 1994; McGrew & Knopik, 1993). In a study using data from participants aged 6 to 19 years from the WJ III norm group (n = 4,338 for Basic Reading Skills and n = 3,303 for Reading Comprehension), Evans, Floyd, McGrew, and Leforgee (2001) examined the validity of WJ III COG cluster scores in predicting reading achievement, as measured by the WJ III ACH Basic Reading Skills and Reading Comprehension clusters. Comprehension–Knowledge was strongly related to both reading components across the entire period, whereas Short-Term Memory and Phonemic Awareness were moderately related throughout this period. Auditory Processing, Long-Term Retrieval, and Processing Speed were moderately related to Reading Comprehension scores from ages 6 to 9 or 10, whereas the clinical clusters of Phonemic Awareness and Working Memory were moderately to strongly related to both reading components during the early elementary school years. Fluid Reasoning and Visual–Spatial Thinking were not significant predictors of reading achievement during childhood and adolescence.

Source and Cost

Available from the Riverside Publishing Company, the WJ III Complete Battery with two carrying cases is $1157.00 ($995.00 without carrying cases). The WJ III COG is priced at $700.00 with a carrying case ($619.00 without the case). Form A or Form B of the WJ III ACH is $538.00 with the case ($457.50 without the case). The Report Writer for the WJ III in Windows or Macintosh version is available for $295.00. Audio CD-ROM versions of the WJ III COG and ACH administration audiocassettes are available for $20.50 each. Training videos are $31.50 each for the WJ III COG and ACH, and a self-study training package that covers both instruments is $86.00.

Test Reviews

Cizek, G. J. (2003). Review of the Woodcock-Johnson III. In B. S. Plake, J. C. Impara, & R. A. Spies (Eds.), *The fifteenth mental measurements yearbook* (pp. 1019–1024). Lincoln, NE: Buros Institute of Mental Measurements.

Sandoval, J. (2003). Review of the Woodcock-Johnson III. In B. S. Plake, J. C. Impara, & R. A. Spies (Eds.), *The fifteenth mental measurements yearbook* (pp. 1024–1028). Lincoln, NE: Buros Institute of Mental Measurements.

Summary

The *Woodcock–Johnson III* (WJ III) is an individually administered, norm-referenced comprehensive assessment system designed to measure general intellectual ability, specific cognitive abilities, oral language, and academic achievement for individuals aged 2 through 90+ years. Designed as a toolbox for a wide range of assessment purposes, the WJ III is unsurpassed for its theoretical grounding, psychometric soundness, breadth of coverage, range of score types, and wealth of interpretive options. Practitioners conducting early reading assessments will welcome the new options for domain-specific testing; expanded discrepancy procedures for predicting and diagnosing reading disabilities; and new tests for assessing reading precursors, such as phonological awareness and rapid naming, and reading subskills, such as fluency.

Despite its general technical excellence, the WJ III is not without shortcomings, including an absence of reliability evidence for grade-based scores, floor effects for numerous reading and written language tests, limited evidence of form equivalence and content validity for the WJ III ACH, and limited interrater reliability data. Moreover, as is true of any cradle-to-grave battery, the WJ III tests include only a few items at each age or grade level; practitioners will thus need to conduct follow-up assessments to provide sufficient information for instructional planning when deficits are identified. Although the WJ III includes a much wider variety of reading-related measures than the WJ-R, the format and content of Reading Fluency and Rapid Picture Naming differ significantly from those of the typical measures of these skills, reducing the interpretability of the results. Finally, additional studies with early primary grade samples are needed to document the diagnostic utility and predictive power of these new reading-related tests and clinical clusters. Practitioners can follow research on the WJ III and CHC theory by visiting Kevin McGrew's frequently updated Web site, the Institute for Applied Psychometrics (http://www.iapsych.com).

Print Resources

Mather, N., & Jaffe, L. E. (2002). *Woodcock–Johnson III: Reports, recommendations, and strategies.* New York: Wiley.

This comprehensive (516-page) handbook is designed to assist practitioners using the WJ III in clinical and educational settings in preparing recommendations and writing reports. The "Reports" section contains 31 diagnostic reports, including 7 for early primary grade children, and the "Recommendations" section offers many useful suggestions arranged by category. Another section provides summaries of methods and interventions mentioned in the "Reports" and "Recommendations" sections for use in teacher consultation.

Mather, N., Wendling, B. J., & Woodcock, R. W. (2001). *Essentials of WJ III Tests of Achievement assessment.* New York: Wiley.

Cowritten by two authors of the WJ III, this book provides guidelines to the achievement portion of the WJ III, including information on administration, scoring, and interpretation; strengths and weaknesses; clinical applications; and illustrative case reports. Two case studies with test reports are included: the first of a fifth-grade boy referred for reading and writing problems and the second of a seventh-grade boy referred because of organizational and written language problems.

Schrank, F. A., Flanagan, D. P., Woodcock, R. W., & Mascolo, J. T. (2002). *Essentials of WJ III Cognitive Abilities assessment.* New York: Wiley.

Cowritten by the senior author of the Report Writer for the WJ III as well as the senior author of the WJ III, this book provides guidelines to the cognitive portion of the WJ III, including information on theoretical foundations; administration, scoring, and interpretation; strengths and weaknesses; and clinical applications. Two case examples, including reports, are presented: a fourth-grade boy referred because of difficulty completing assignments and a sixth-grade girl referred because of concerns about academic performance, especially in mathematics and writing.

Case Example

Name of student: Jerell A.
Age: 7 years, 11 months
Grade: Second grade
Date of assessment: January

Reason for referral: Jerell was referred for an early reading assessment by his second-grade teacher. He presents as a bright, motivated student, but he has made little progress in reading, despite receiving individual tutoring help for 2 years. On the early literacy battery administered to all second graders in the fall, he scored very poorly on all tasks, including spelling, letter-sound knowledge, and word identification. Selected tests from the *Woodcock–Johnson III Tests of Cognitive Abilities* (WJ III COG) and *Tests of Achievement* (Form A; WJ III ACH) were administered to evaluate the nature of his reading problems and to provide information for instructional planning.

Assessment results and interpretation: The WJ III COG and WJ III ACH assess a variety of abilities and skills important to school success. Because these two batteries are conormed, direct comparisons can be made among cognitive and achievement scores to help determine strengths and weaknesses. Score abbreviations and average scores for a student at Jerell's grade level are as follows: GE = Grade Equivalent (2.4); RPI = Relative Proficiency Index (90/90); PR = Percentile Rank (50); SS = Standard Score (100). Jerell's WJ III performance is described below in relation to his grade peers. Italicized tests in the tables below are included in more than one cluster.

WJ III COG CLUSTER/Test	GE	RPI	PR	SS
GENERAL INTELLECTUAL ABILITY	1.8	84/90	32	93
VERBAL ABILITY	1.2	70/90	18	86
Verbal Comprehension	2.0	87/90	18	86
THINKING ABILITY	2.0	83/90	40	96
Visual–Auditory Learning	K.9	72/90	13	83
Spatial Relations	2.5	90/90	51	100
Sound Blending	1.0	78/90	24	90
Concept Formation	3.4	96/90	68	107
COGNITIVE EFFICIENCY	2.1	83/90	39	96
Visual Matching	1.8	73/90	27	91
Numbers Reversed	2.4	90/90	51	100
PHONEMIC AWARENESS	K.7	79/90	19	87
Incomplete Words	K.3	79/90	24	89
Sound Blending	1.0	78/90	24	90
WORKING MEMORY	2.6	92/90	57	102
Numbers Reversed	2.4	90/90	51	100
Auditory Working Memory	2.9	93/90	62	104

Cognitive Performance: On the WJ III COG, Jerell's overall general intellectual ability falls in the Average range for his grade (SS = 93, PR = 32). His thinking ability, as measured by tasks of intentional cognitive processing, is in the average range (PR = 40), but his performance varied considerably, depending on the type of task. His performance was Average on tasks of visual–spatial thinking and inductive logic (PRs = 51 and 68, respectively) but Low Average to Average on tasks of auditory processing and associative and meaningful memory (PRs = 13 and 24, respectively). His working memory, that is, the ability to hold information in immediate awareness while performing a mental operation on it, is rated as Average (PR = 57), suggesting that memory problems are not a major factor in his poor reading performance. His cognitive efficiency, or capacity to hold information in conscious awareness and perform automatic tasks rapidly, is also in the Average range (PR = 39). His verbal ability, including acquired knowledge and language comprehension, is less well developed (PR = 18, Low Average). His phonemic awareness, including the ability to analyze and synthesize speech sounds, is also rated as Low Average for his grade (PR = 19).

WJ III ACH CLUSTER/Test	GE	RPI	PR	SS
ORAL LANGUAGE	1.0	80/90	18	86
Story Recall	5.0	94/90	77	111
Understanding Directions	K.1	50/90	7	78
BROAD READING	1.1	6/90	2	70
Letter-Word Identification	1.5	7/90	7	78
Reading Fluency	<K.8	6/90	3	73
Passage Comprehension	K.9	4/90	4	74
BASIC READING SKILLS	1.2	3/90	1	67
Letter-Word Identification	1.5	7/90	7	78
Word Attack	1.0	2/90	2	69
READING COMPREHENSION	K.9	8/90	4	74
Passage Comprehension	K.9	4/90	4	74
Reading Vocabulary	K.9	13/90	6	76

(continued)

BROAD WRITTEN LANGUAGE	1.4	57/90	10	81
Spelling	K.7	51/90	18	86
Writing Fluency	1.6	73/90	19	87
Writing Samples	1.2	45/90	3	72
WRITTEN EXPRESSION	1.3	60/90	8	79
Writing Fluency	1.6	73/90	19	87
Writing Samples	1.2	45/90	3	72
PHONEME/GRAPHEME KNOWLEDGE	K.9	8 /90	1	67
Word Attack	1.0	2/90	2	69
Spelling of Sounds	K.2	29/90	3	71
Sound Awareness (supplemental)	1.4	72/90	23	89

Academic Achievement: On the WJ III ACH, Jerell's oral language and academic skills are highly variable, ranging from High Average to Very Low for his grade placement (PRs = 77 to 1). In this section, his performance is discussed in terms of Relative Performance Index (RPI) scores, which represent his level of proficiency relative to his grade peers.

Oral Language. Jerell's RPI of 80/90 on the Oral Language cluster indicates that when average grade mates have 90% success on oral language tasks, he will have 80% success. Although his overall oral language skills are rated as Limited to Average, his performance varied considerably, depending on the task requirements. On a task that required him to recall story elements and that taps both receptive and expressive language skills, his performance was Average (RPI = 94/90). In contrast, his performance was Limited (RPI = 50/90) on a receptive language task requiring him to listen to a sequence of instructions and respond by pointing to objects in a picture.

Reading. Jerell's Broad Reading skills, including single word reading, reading fluency, and comprehension for textual material, are rated as Very Limited for his grade (RPI = 6/90). His ability to read single letters and words is also Very Limited (RPI = 7/90). He was able to name all of the letters presented but had trouble identifying common sight words (*there* for *they*) and phonetically regular words (*mud* for *must*). On a task of reading fluency, which required him to read a series of statements quickly, decide whether they were correct, and circle *Y* (yes) or *N* (no), he worked quickly but made numerous errors (RPI = 6/90; Very Limited). His overall reading comprehension skills are also Very Limited (RPI = 8/90). On a task assessing reading comprehension and lexical knowledge, he was able to match words and pictures, but he was able to answer only one of the items requiring him to supply a missing word in a sentence (RPI = 4/90). His skills were also Very Limited (RPI = 13/90) on a task requiring him to supply synonyms, antonyms, or the final word in a three-word analogy. Although he made a good effort, he was able to answer only two of the items presented correctly because he could read so few of the stimulus words. His Basic Reading Skills, including single word reading and phonemic decoding, are especially weak (RPI = 2/90; Negligible). On a task requiring him to read phonically consistent nonsense words, he was able to point to or identify sounds for three consonants, but he was unable to decode any of the nonsense words (*nin* for *nan*, *ib* for *ep*).

Written Language. Jerell's Broad Written Language skills, including spelling ability, fluency of written production, and quality of written expression, are rated as Limited (RPI = 57/90). On a task requiring him to write dictated letters and words, he had difficulty representing long vowels and vowel teams (*hese* for *he*, *rian* for *rain*) and spelling sight words (*tado* for *table*) (RPI = 51/90; Limited). His ability to formulate and write simple sentences under time pressure falls in the Limited to Average range of proficiency (RPI = 73/90). Many of his errors reflected lack of knowledge of syntax (*I catch a ball can*) and perhaps also his difficulty in reading the stimulus words. His ability to produce sentences in response to a variety of task criteria is rated as Limited (RPI = 45/90). Because he tended to produce phrases rather than complete sentences, he did not earn credit for most of his answers. Moreover, although children are not penalized for spelling and punctuation mistakes on this test, his writing contained numerous errors in spelling, usage, and punctuation. For example, to describe a picture of a bird singing in a cage, he wrote, "they dir sig." When his written language skills are considered in terms of writing fluency and quality of expression, they are also rated as Limited (Broad Written Expression RPI = 60/90).

Phoneme/Grapheme Knowledge. Jerell's score of 8/90 on the Phoneme/Grapheme Knowledge cluster indicates that his ability to use sound-symbol correspondences in reading or spelling is Limited. His skills in writing letter sounds and spelling phonically regular nonsense words are Limited (RPI = 29/90). He was able to write letters to represent single sounds, but he had great difficulty writing nonsense words, especially in terms of representing vowel sounds (*aft* for *ift*) and vowel teams (*foheu* for *foy*). His phonological awareness skills–including his ability to identify or produce rhymes and his ability to perform sound deletion, substitution, and reversal tasks–are Limited to Average (72/90). He was able to perform most of the rhyming tasks and to delete initial or final sounds from several words, but he had trouble with more advanced sound manipulation tasks, including substituting a word, word ending, or sound to form a new word and reversing word parts or sounds to form new words.

Ability-Achievement Score Comparisons: When Jerell's General Intellectual Ability is compared with his achievement, his performance is significantly lower than predicted in the areas of Broad Reading, Basic Reading Skills, Reading Comprehension, and Written Expression. Specifically, when his General Intellectual Ability standard score (SS = 93) is compared with his cluster standard scores in Broad Reading (SS = 70), Basic Reading Skills (SS = 67), Reading Comprehension (SS = 74), and Written Expression (SS = 79), only 1%, 0.5%, 3%, and 6%, respectively, of his grade peers would obtain the same or a lower score.

appendix a

Test Publishers and Sources

Academic Therapy Publications
20 Commercial Boulevard
Novato, CA 94949
(800) 422-7249
http://www.academictherapy.com

AGS Publishing
4201 Woodland Road
Circle Pines, MN 55014-1796
(800) 328-2560
http://www.agsnet.com

Paul H. Brookes Publishing Company
P.O. Box 10624
Baltimore, MD 21285-0624
(800) 638-3775
http://www.brookespublishing.com

CTB/McGraw-Hill
20 Ryan Ranch Road
Monterey, CA 93940-5703
(800) 538-9547
http://www.ctb.com

Roland H. Good III, Ph.D.
School Psychology Program
College of Education
5208 University of Oregon
Eugene, OR 97403-5208
(541) 346-2415
http://dibels.uoregon.edu

The Guilford Press
72 Spring Street
New York, NY 10012
(800) 365-7006
http://www.guilford.com

Heinemann
P.O. Box 6926
Portsmouth, NH 03802-6926
(800) 793-2154
http://www.heinemann.com

LinguiSystems
3100 4th Avenue
East Moline, IL 61244-0747
(800) 776-4332
http://www.linguisystems.com

Marianne S. Meyer, MA
Section of Neuropsychology
Wake Forest University
Bowman Gray School of Medicine
Medical Center Boulevard
Winston-Salem, NC 27157-1043
(336) 716-2261
mmeyer@wfusmc.edu

Phonological Awareness Literacy Screening (PALS) Office
P.O. Box 800785
Charlottesville, VA 22908-8785
(888) 882-7257
http://pals.virginia.edu

To order PALS:
University of Virginia Bookstore
P.O. Box 400820
Charlottesville, VA 22904-4820
(800) 759-4667
(434) 924-1066

PRO-ED
8700 Shoal Creek Boulevard
Austin, TX 78757-6897
(800) 897-3203
http://www.proedinc.com

The Psychological Corporation
19500 Bulverde Road
San Antonio, TX 78259-3701
(800) 872-1726
http://www.psychcorp.com

The Riverside Publishing Company
425 Spring Lake Drive
Itasca, IL 60143-2079
(800) 323-9540
http://www.riverpub.com

Sopris West Educational Services
4093 Speciality Place
Longmont, CO 80504-5400
(800) 547-6747
http://www.sopriswest.com

Texas Education Agency
P.O. Box 13817
Austin, TX 78701-3817
(800) 463-9027
http://www.tea.state.tx.us

University of Texas at Houston
Center for Academic and Reading Skills
7000 Fannin, 24th Floor
Houston, TX 77030
(713) 500-3685
http://cars.uth.tmc.edu

To order the Texas Primary Reading Inventory:
Texas Reading Instruments
http://www.txreadinginstruments.com

appendix b

Selected Internet Resources for Early Reading Assessment

ASSESSMENT SITES

Buros Institute of Mental Measurements
http://www.unl.edu/buros

The Web site of the organization that publishes the *Mental Measurements Yearbooks* and *Tests in Print* provides information about Buros publications and numerous links to other major assessment sites. Users may access test reviews as they appear in the most current and forthcoming editions of the *Mental Measurements Yearbooks* for $25 per test title by fax (slightly more for surface mail) and $15 per test title for online access.

Center for Equity and Excellence in Education (CEEE) Test Database
http://ceee.gwu.edu/standards_assessments/sa.htm

The Standards and Assessments Focus Area of the CEEE's Region III Comprehensive Center at the George Washington University includes a database containing abstracts and descriptions of nearly 200 tests commonly used with students who have limited English proficiency. Users may search by diagnosis, language dominance, test name, standardization status, and other descriptors.

Educational Resources Information Center (ERIC) Clearinghouse on Assessment and Evaluation
http://www.ericae.net

The ERIC Web site, which averages more than 10,000 hits a day, offers a wealth of information on educational assessment, evaluation, and research methodology. The Test Locator service includes test descriptions, test publishers, and locations of test reviews, an online assessment journal, an assessment library with more than 400 full-text online books and articles, and a pathfinder to 40 categories of assessment-related links.

Institute for Applied Psychometrics
http://www.iapsych.com

Kevin McGrew's Web site focuses on the Cattell–Horn–Carroll (CHC) theory of cognitive abilities and CHC assessment information, notably the *Woodcock–Johnson III* (WJ III) family of tests. Among its many resources are a reference database, a section on bilingual/multicultural assessment research, and information on upcoming WJ III workshops.

National Center for Research on Evaluation, Standards, and Student Testing (CRESST)
http://www.cresst.org

A partnership of UCLA, the University of Colorado, Stanford University, RAND, the University of Pittsburgh, the University of Southern California, Educational Testing Service, and the University of Cambridge in the United Kingdom, CRESST conducts research on educational testing in Grades K–12. Among the many resources on the Web site are a library of downloadable reports, newsletters, and policy briefs, and a large database of alternative assessments.

READING RESEARCH AND RESOURCES SITES

Center for the Improvement of Early Reading Achievement (CIERA)
http://www.ciera.org

A consortium of educators at five universities (University of Michigan, University of Virginia, Michigan State University, University of Minnesota, and University of Southern California), CIERA is a national center for research on early reading. The site provides access to downloadable technical reports on reading instruction and acquisition, as well as to the CIERA Archive, a repository of publications for researchers and practitioners in early literacy.

National Assessment of Educational Progress (NAEP): The Nation's Report Card
http://nces.ed.gov/nationsreportcard

The Web site of the National Center for Education Statistics provides a variety of reports documenting NAEP results, including 2002 reading and writing results, and national trends in reading achievement.

National Institute of Child Health and Human Development (NICHD)
http://www.nichd.nih.gov/reading.htm

This page provides a summary of the America Reads Challenge and the key points of NICHD research on the teaching of reading.

National Right to Read Foundation (NRRF)
http://www.nrrf.org

NRRF's mission is to support schools in providing scientifically based reading research in the schools. The Web site includes research reports; news on federal and state reading-related actions; reading reform news; and frequently updated essays on reading instruction, teacher training, and other topics.

Northwest Regional Educational Laboratory (NWREL)
http://www.nwrel.org/sky

NWREL's "Library in the Sky" contains over 1,611 educational Web sites links to educational resources on the Internet. The Assessment Resource library (http://www.nwrel.org/

assessment/library) contains over 1,000 assessment tools and related items for students in Grades K–12.

Southern Educational Development Laboratory (SEDL)
http://www.sedl.org/reading/rad

The SEDL Web site includes a reading assessment database for Grades K–2 with over 125 tests assessing reading, oral language, and other academic areas in either Spanish or both Spanish and English. Also included is an instructional resources database searchable by cognitive element, reader types, and language.

PROFESSIONAL ORGANIZATION SITES

American Psychological Association (APA)
http://www.apa.org/science/testing.html

The Testing and Assessment Section of the APA's Science Directorate includes frequently asked questions about psychological tests, sources for locating information about tests, ordering information for the 1999 *Standards for Educational and Psychological Testing*, a summary of the changes in the new *Standards*, a Testing Information Clearinghouse, and links to other assessment-related sites.

International Dyslexia Association
http://www.interdys.org

The Web site of the nation's oldest learning disabilities organization provides a wide variety of resources on reading and reading disabilities for parents, educators, children, and adults.

International Reading Association (IRA)
http://www.readingonline.org

The IRA's electronic journal focuses on issues in literacy and the teaching of reading for Grades K–12 and includes complete articles and book reviews.

National Association of School Psychologists (NASP)
http://www.nasponline.org

NASP's award-winning Web site offers extensive resources for educators, including links to a wide range of assessment- and reading-related resources.

appendix c

Glossary of Reading Assessment and Reading-Related Terms

alphabet(ic) a writing system consisting of symbols that represent sounds, such as English, Spanish, and most modern languages; as opposed to *logographies* and *syllabaries*

alphabetic principle the systematic use of printed letters to represent the individual sounds of spoken words in reading and writing; or the understanding that spoken words are composed of phonemes and that printed letters represent the phonemes in spoken words

automaticity fluency in reading, writing, spelling, or some other skill without conscious attention

benchmark a minimum level of proficiency that a student must achieve in order to benefit from the next level of instruction; for example, a widely accepted benchmark for oral reading fluency for the end of Grade 1 is 40 words read correctly per minute

blend two or three adjacent consonants forming a sound that retains the identities of each individual letter (e.g., *st* in *stop*)

blending combining individual phonemes together in speech to form a single syllable or word (e.g., /m/-/a/-/t/ = *mat*)

cloze procedure a procedure for assessing reading comprehension that requires the examinee to fill in missing words that have been deleted from a sentence or passage; when multiple choices are provided for each blank or when only one key word is omitted from the sentence or short passage, the procedure is described as a *modified cloze task*

coarticulation the merging of individual sounds within a syllable during pronunciation such that the sounds overlap or are modified by each other; isolating phonemes is difficult because of coarticulation

coding the representation of stimulus information in memory

concept of word the awareness of the one-to-one correspondence between spoken and printed words, as demonstrated by the ability to point accurately to the words of a memorized text while reading

consonant a speech sound formed by the constriction or obstruction of air moving through the vocal tract during articulation

consonant, syllabic liquid (/l/, /r/) and nasal (/m/, /n/) consonants that can act as syllables (e.g., lett*er*, kitt*en*)

cutoff score the score on a screening measure used to categorize an examinee as being at risk for development of problems in that domain

decoding using knowledge of spelling–sound correspondences to identify written words

digraph two adjacent consonants or vowels that represent a single sound; there are both consonant and vowel digraphs, although the term is more commonly used to refer to consonant digraphs (e.g., vowel digraph = *ea* in *seat*; consonant digraph = *gh* in *tough*)

diphthong two adjacent vowels representing a complex sound that begins with one vowel sound and moves to another within a single syllable (e.g., *oy* in *toy*, *ou* in *loud*)

dyslexia a language-based disorder that usually represents an impairment in phonological processing ability

fluency the ability to read with sufficient speed and accuracy to permit attention to focus on the meaning of the text

grapheme a letter or letter combination that represents a single speech sound or phoneme; the majority of graphemes consist of more than one letter (e.g., *ph* = /f/)

homophone a word that is pronounced like another but has a different meaning and different spelling (e.g., *bear–bare*); also called *homonym*

invented spelling young children's efforts to spell, using their limited knowledge of sound–symbol relationships

lexical referring to the words or vocabulary of a language

lexical access the ability to locate and retrieve name codes in long-term memory

lexicon the representation of a individual's word knowledge in memory; often referred to as the *mental dictionary*

logography a writing system in which the written symbols themselves convey meaning, such as the Chinese writing system and the Japanese Kanji script

long vowel the sound produced for vowels by tensing the vocal chords; the linguistic term for the long vowel sound is *tense*

morpheme the smallest unit of meaning in a language; morphemes can be free (e.g., *sit*) or bound (*s* in *sits*); for example, *unyielding* has three morphemes–*un*, *yield*, and *ing*

morphology the study of the meaningful units and word formation patterns in a language

nonword a string of letters that cannot be pronounced by using letter–sound correspondences and that has no meaning (e.g., *kszti*); often used as synonym for *pseudoword*

onset–rime the two parts of a word or syllable; the *onset* is the initial phoneme or consonant cluster that precedes the vowel in a syllable, and the *rime* is the vowel and remaining set of phonemes (e.g., in the word *slink*, *sl* is the onset and *ink* is the rime)

orthography the writing system of a language; English orthography consists of letters, numerals, punctuation marks, and *diacritics* (marks added to letters to indicate a phonetic clue or distinguish words that are otherwise identical in written form)

orthographic awareness familiarity with the written symbols (i.e., letters) representing the speech sounds of language, including the ability to distinguish between correct and incorrect spellings of written words

orthographic processing a general term that refers to the use of orthographic information in processing oral or written language

phoneme the smallest unit of sound that distinguishes one word from another; for example, *cat* and *mat* are distinguished by the initial phoneme

phonemic awareness the conscious awareness that spoken words are composed of sequences of individual sounds and the ability to detect and identify those sounds; also called *phoneme awareness*

phonetics the study of the manner in which speech sounds are articulated; also, the identification and classification of the speech sounds in a language

phonics an approach to reading instruction that teaches the systematic relationships between speech sounds (*phonemes*) and the letters that represent them (*graphemes*) for the purpose of decoding words

phonogram a sequence of letters representing the same sound unit in different words (e.g., *igh* in *high, sigh,* and *thigh*)

phonological awareness the conscious awareness of the sound structure of words in oral language, as distinct from their meaning; types of phonological awareness include *nonphonemic awareness* (rhyme awareness, word awareness, and syllable awareness) and *phonemic awareness* (awareness of individual sounds).

phonological memory the ability to represent information in terms of its sound features for temporary storage in working or short-term memory; also called *phonological (re)coding in working memory*

phonological processing the use of the sound structure of language to process written or oral language, including the perception, storage, retrieval, manipulation, and interpretation of the sounds of language

phonological recoding translating oral or written language information into the sound-based system to determine the meaning of words stored in long-term memory

phonology the sound system of language; the rules governing the way in which speech sounds are sequenced and pronounced in a given language

pragmatics the set of rules and conventions governing the use of language for social communication

print awareness knowledge of the forms, conventions, and functions of written language; also called *concepts of print*

prosody the rhythmic and melodic features of spoken language; prosodic features are measured in reading expression and some kinds of reading fluency tasks

pseudohomophone a pseudoword that, when pronounced, sounds the same as a real word (e.g., *tite* for *tight*)

pseudoword a group of letters that conforms to English phonetic rules and can be pronounced by applying letter–sound correspondences but that does not constitute a real word (e.g., *gusp, tracle*); also called *nonsense word* and *nonword*

rapid naming fluency in naming familiar visual stimuli; also called *phonological (re)coding in lexical access* and *naming speed*

rime the part of a syllable that includes the vowel and any preceding consonant sounds; *word families* are words that share the same rime unit (e.g., *fan, man, ran*)

segmentation dividing a spoken or written word into parts by pausing between each part; segmentation tasks can involve stimuli at the word level (i.e., compound words), syllable level, onset–rime level, or phoneme level

semantics the study of meaning in language

short vowel the vowel sound produced when the vocal chords are relaxed; the linguistic term for short vowel sounds is *lax*

sight word a word that is recognized as a whole and that does not require sounding out for identification; the term refers to any word that is automatically recognized, regardless of whether it is phonetically regular or irregular

sublexical term used to refer to skills that involve units smaller than words, such as identifying alphabet letters or beginning sounds; also called *subword*

syllabary a written language that uses single symbols to represent syllable units

syllable a unit of pronunciation that contains a vowel

syntax the structure of language; the set of rules for arranging words into meaningful phrases, clauses, or sentences; for example, in English, adjectives are typically placed before nouns

trigraph a sequence of three letters that represents a single consonant, vowel, or diphthong (e.g., *eau* in *bureau*)

vowel a speech sound created by the unobstructed flow of air through the vocal cords and mouth

References

Aaron, P. G. (1991). Can reading disabilities be diagnosed without using intelligence tests? *Journal of Learning Disabilities, 24*, 178–186, 191.

Aaron, P. G., Joshi, M., & Williams, K. A. (1999). Not all reading disabilities are alike. *Journal of Learning Disabilities, 32*, 120–137.

Ackerman, P. T., & Dykman, R. A. (1993). Phonological processes, confrontation naming, and immediate memory in dyslexia. *Journal of Learning Disabilities, 26*, 597–609.

Ackerman, P. T., Dykman, R. A., & Gardner, M. Y. (1990). Counting rate, naming rate, phonological sensitivity, and memory span: Major factors in dyslexia. *Journal of Learning Disabilities, 23*, 319, 325–327.

Adams, M. J. (1990). *Beginning to read: Thinking and learning about print.* Cambridge, MA: MIT Press.

Adams, M. J., Foorman, B. R., Lundberg, I., & Beeler, T. (1998). *Phonemic awareness in young children: A classroom curriculum.* Baltimore: Brookes.

Adams, M. J., & Huggins, A. W. F. (1985). The growth of children's sight vocabulary: A quick test with educational and theoretical implications. *Reading Research Quarterly, 20*, 262–281.

Adams, M. J., Huggins, A. W. F., Starr, B. J., Rollins, A. M., Zuckerman, L. E., Stevens, K. N., et al. (1980). *A prototype test of decoding skills* (Contract No. NO1-HD-7-2836). Bethesda, MD: National Institute of Child Health and Human Development.

Aiken, L. R. (2000). *Psychological testing and assessment* (10th ed.). Needham Heights, MA: Allyn & Bacon.

Alexander, A. W., Andersen, H. G., Heilman, P.C., Voeller, K. K. S., & Torgesen, J. K. (1991). Phonological awareness training and remediation of analytic decoding deficits in a group of severe dyslexics. *Annals of Dyslexia, 41,* 193–206.

Alfonso, V. C., & Flanagan, D. P. (1999). Assessment of cognitive functioning in preschoolers. In E. V. Nuttall, I. Romero, & J. Kalesnik (Eds.), *Assessing and screening preschoolers: Psychological and educational dimensions* (2nd ed., pp. 186–217). Needham Heights, MA: Allyn & Bacon.

Allinder, R. M., Fuchs, L. S., & Fuchs, D. (1998). Curriculum-based measurement. In H. B. Vance (Ed.), *Psychological assessment of children: Best practices for school and clinical settings* (2nd ed., pp. 106–129). New York: Wiley.

Allington, R. L. (1983). The reading instruction provided readers of differing reading abilities. *Elementary School Journal, 83*, 548–559.

Allor, J. H., Fuchs, D., & Mathes, P. G. (2001). Do students with and without lexical retrieval weaknesses respond differently to instruction? *Journal of Learning Disabilities, 34,* 264–275.

American Educational Research Association (AERA), American Psychological Association (APA), & National Council on Measurement in Education (NCME). (1999). *Standards for educational and psychological testing.* Washington DC: AERA.

American Psychological Association (APA). (2000). *Report of the Task Force on Test User Qualifications.* Washington, DC: Author.

Anastasi, A. (1988). *Psychological testing* (6th ed.). New York: Macmillan.

Anastasi, A., & Urbina, S. (1997). *Psychological testing* (7th ed.). Upper Saddle River, NJ: Prentice-Hall.

Aram, D. M. (1997). Hyperlexia: Reading without meaning in young children. *Topics in Language Disorders, 17*(3), 1–13.

Aram, D. M., Ekelman, B. L., & Nation, J. E. (1984). Preschoolers with language disorders: 10 years later. *Journal of Speech and Hearing Research, 27,* 232–244.

Aram, D. M., & Healy, J. M. (1988). Hyperlexia: A review of extraordinary word recognition. In L. Obler & D. Fein (Eds.), *The exceptional brain: Neuropsychology of talent and special abilities* (pp. 70–102). New York: Guilford Press.

Askew, B. J., Fountas, I. C., Lyons, C. A., Pinnell, G. S., & Schmitt, M. C. (1998). *Reading Recovery review: Understanding outcomes and implications.* Columbus, OH: Reading Recovery Council of North America.

Athanasiou, M. S. (2000). Current nonverbal assessment instruments: A comparison of psychometric integrity and test fairness. *Journal of Psychoeducational Assessment, 18,* 211–229.

Badian, N. A. (1988). The prediction of good and poor reading before kindergarten entry: A nine-year follow-up. *Journal of Learning Disabilities, 21*(2), 98–103, 123.

Badian, N. A. (1993a). Phonemic awareness, naming, visual symbol processing, and reading. *Reading and Writing, 5,* 87–100.

Badian, N. A. (1993b). Predicting reading progress in children receiving special help. *Annals of Dyslexia, 43,* 90–109.

Badian, N. A. (1994). Preschool prediction: Orthographic and phonological skills, and reading. *Annals of Dyslexia, 44,* 3–25.

Badian, N. A. (1995). Predicting reading ability over the long term: The changing roles of letter naming, phonological awareness and orthographic processing. *Annals of Dyslexia, 45,* 79–96.

Badian, N. A. (1996). Dyslexia: A validation of the concept at two age levels. *Journal of Learning Disabilities, 29,* 102–112.

Badian, N. A. (1998). A validation of the role of preschool phonological and orthographic skills in the prediction of reading. *Journal of Learning Disabilities, 31,* 472–481.

Badian, N. A. (1999). Reading disability defined as a discrepancy between listening and reading comprehension: A longitudinal study of stability, gender differences, and prevalence. *Journal of Learning Disabilities, 32,* 138–148.

Badian, N. A. (2000). Do preschool orthographic skills contribute to prediction of reading? In N. A. Badian (Ed.), *Prediction and prevention of reading failure* (pp. 31–56). Baltimore: York Press.

Badian, N. A. (2001). Phonological and orthographic processing: Their roles in reading prediction. *Annals of Dyslexia, 51,* 179–202.

Badian, N. A., Duffy, F. H., Als, H., & McAnulty, G. B. (1991). Linguistic profiles of dyslexic and good readers. *Annals of Dyslexia, 41,* 221–245.

Badian, N. A., McAnulty, G. B., Duffy, F. H., & Als, H. (1990). Prediction of dyslexia in kindergarten boys. *Annals of Dyslexia, 40,* 152–169.

Bailet, L. L. (2001). Written language test reviews. In A. M. Bain, L. L. Bailet, & L. C. Moats

(Eds.), *Written language disorders: Theory into practice* (2nd ed., pp. 221–248). Austin, TX: PRO-ED.

Baker, S. K., & Good, R. (1995). Curriculum-based measurement of English reading with bilingual Hispanic students: A validation study with second-grade students. *School Psychology Review, 24,* 561–578.

Baker, S. K., Plasencia-Peinado, J., & Lezcano-Lytle, V. (1998). The use of curriculum-based measurement with language-minority children. In M. R. Shinn (Ed.), *Advanced applications of curriculum-based measurement* (pp. 175–213). New York: Guilford Press.

Ball, E. W., & Blachman, B. A. (1991). Does phoneme awareness training in kindergarten make a difference in early word recognition and developmental spelling? *Reading Research Quarterly, 26,* 49–66.

Bankson, N. W. (1990). *Bankson Language Test* (2nd ed.). Austin, TX: PRO-ED.

Barker, T. A., Torgesen, J. K., & Wagner, R. K. (1992). The role of orthographic processing skills on five different reading tasks. *Reading Research Quarterly, 27,* 335–345.

Barron, R. W. (1986). Word recognition in early reading: A review of the direct and indirect access hypotheses. *Cognition, 24,* 93–119.

Bear, D. R. (1991). Copying fluency and orthographic development. *Visible Language, 25,* 40–53.

Bear, D. R., Invernizzi, M., Templeton, S., & Johnston, F. (2000). *Words their way: Word study for phonics, vocabulary, and spelling instruction* (2nd ed). Upper Saddle River, NJ: Prentice-Hall.

Beaver, J. (1997). *Developmental Reading Assessment.* New York: Celebrations Press.

Beery, K. E. (1997). *Developmental Test of Visual–Motor Integration.* Cleveland, OH: Modern Curriculum Press.

Bell, P. F., Lentz, F. E., & Graden, J. L. (1992). Effects of curriculum–test overlap on standardized test scores: Identifying systematic confounds in educational decision making. *School Psychology Review, 21,* 644–655.

Berninger, V. W. (1986). Normal variation in reading acquisition. *Perceptual and Motor Skills, 62,* 691–716.

Berninger, V. W. (1994). Introduction to the varieties of orthographic knowledge II: Relationships to phonology, reading, and writing. In V. W. Berninger (Ed.), *The varieties of orthographic knowledge II: Relationships to phonology, reading, and writing* (pp. 1–22). Dordrecht, The Netherlands: Kluwer Academic.

Berninger, V. W. (1998a). *Process assessment of the learner: Guides for intervention–reading and writing.* San Antonio, TX: Psychological Corporation.

Berninger, V. W. (1998b). Specific reading and writing disabilities in young children: Assessment, prevention, and intervention. In B. Y. L. Wong (Ed.), *Learning about learning disabilities* (2nd ed., pp. 529–555). San Diego, CA: Academic Press.

Berninger, V. W. (2000). Development of language by hand and its connections with language by ear, mouth, and eye. *Topics in Language Disorders, 20*(4), 65–84.

Berninger, V. W. (2001). *Process Assessment of the Learner: Test Battery for Reading and Writing.* San Antonio, TX: Psychological Corporation.

Berninger, V. W., & Abbott, R. D. (1994a). Multiple orthographic and phonological codes in literacy acquisition: An evolving research program. In V. W. Berninger (Ed.), *The varieties of orthographic knowledge I: Theoretical and developmental issues* (pp. 277–317). Dordrecht, The Netherlands: Kluwer Academic.

Berninger, V. W., & Abbott, R. D. (1994b). Redefining learning disabilities: Moving beyond aptitude–achievement discrepancies to failure to respond to validated treatment protocols. In G. R. Lyon (Ed.), *Frames of reference for the assessment of learning disabilities: New views on measurement issues* (pp. 163–183). Baltimore: Brookes.

Berninger, V. W., Abbott, R. D., Abbott, S. P., Graham, S., & Richards, T. (2002). Writing and reading: Connections between language by hand and language by eye. *Journal of Learning Disabilities, 35,* 39–56.

Berninger, V. W., Abbott, R. D., Billingsley, F., & Nagy, W. (2001). Processes underlying timing and fluency of reading: Efficiency, automaticity, coordination, and morphological awareness. In M. Wolf (Ed.), *Dyslexia, fluency, and the brain* (pp. 383–414). Timonium, MD: York Press.

Berninger, V. W., Abbott, S. P., Greep, K., Reed, E., Sylvester, L., Hooven, C., et al. (1997). Directed reading and writing activities: Aiming instruction to working brain systems. In S. M. Clancy Dollinger & L. F. DiLalla (Eds.), *Assessment and intervention issues across the life span* (pp. 123–158). Mahwah, NJ: Erlbaum.

Berninger, V. W., Abbott, R., Rogan, L., Reed, L., Abbott, S., Brooks, A., et al. (1998). Teaching spelling to children with specific learning disabilities: The mind's ear and eye beats the computer or pencil. *Learning Disability Quarterly, 21*, 106–122.

Berninger, V. W., Abbott, R. D., Thomson, J. B., & Raskind, W. H. (2001). Language phenotype for reading and writing disability: A family approach. *Scientific Studies of Reading, 5*, 59–106.

Berninger, V. W., Abbott, R. D., Zook, D., Ogier, S., Lemos-Britton, Z., & Brooksher, R. (1999). Early intervention for reading disabilities: Teaching the alphabet principle in a connectionist framework. *Journal of Learning Disabilities, 32*, 491–503.

Berninger, V. W., & Graham, S. (1998). Language by hand: A synthesis of a decade of research on handwriting. *Handwriting Review, 12*, 11–25.

Berninger, V. W., Stage, S. A., Smith, D. R., & Hildebrand, D. (2001). Assessment for reading and writing intervention: A three-tier model for prevention and remediation. In J. J. W. Andrews, D. H. Saklofske, & J. L. Janzen (Eds.), *Handbook of psychoeducational assessment* (pp. 195–223). San Diego, CA: Academic Press.

Berninger, V. W., Thalberg, S. P., DeBruyn, I., & Smith, R. (1987). Preventing reading disabilities by assessing and remediating phonemic skills. *School Psychology Review, 16*, 554–565.

Berninger, V. W., Yates, C., Cartwright, A., Rutberg, J., Remy, E., & Abbott, R. (1992). Lower-level developmental skills in beginning writing. *Reading and Writing, 4*, 125–280.

Berninger, V. W., Yates, C., & Lester, K. (1991). Multiple orthographic codes in reading and writing acquisition. *Reading and Writing, 3*, 115–149.

Biemiller, A. (1977–1978). Relationships between oral reading rates for letters, words, and simple text in the development of reading achievement. *Reading Research Quarterly, 13*, 223–253.

Bishop, D. V. M., & Adams, C. (1990). A prospective study of the relationship between specific language impairment, phonological disorders and reading retardation. *Journal of Child Psychology and Psychiatry, 31*, 1027–1050.

Blachman, B. A. (1984). Relationship of rapid naming ability and language analysis skills to kindergarten and first-grade reading achievement. *Journal of Educational Psychology, 76*, 610–622.

Blachman, B. A. (1994a). Early literacy acquisition: The role of phonological awareness. In G. P. Wallach & K. G. Butler (Eds.), *Language learning disabilities in school-age children and adolescents: Some principles and applications* (pp. 253–274). New York: Merrill.

Blachman, B. A. (1994b). What we have learned from longitudinal studies of phonological processing and reading, *and* some unanswered questions: A response to Torgesen, Wagner, and Rashotte. *Journal of Learning Disabilities, 27*(5), 287–291.

Blachman, B. A. (1997). Early intervention and phonological awareness: A cautionary tale. In B. A. Blachman (Ed.), *Foundations of reading acquisition and dyslexia: Implications for early intervention* (pp. 409–430). Mahwah, NJ: Erlbaum.

Bodrova, E., Leong, D., & Semenov, D. (1999). *100 most frequent words in books for beginning readers* [Online]. Retrieved from http://www.mcrel.org/resources/literacy/road/100words

Bowers, P. G. (1995a). Text reading and rereading: Determinants of fluency beyond word recognition. *Journal of Reading Behavior, 25*, 133–153.

Bowers, P. G. (1995b). Tracing symbol naming speed's unique contributions to reading disabilities over time. *Reading and Writing, 7*, 189–216.

Bowers, P. G., Steffy, R., & Tate, E. (1988). Comparison of the effects of IQ control methods on memory and naming speed predictors of reading disability. *Reading Research Quarterly, 23*, 304–319.

Bowers, P. G., & Swanson, L. B. (1991). Naming speed deficits in reading disability: Multiple measures of a singular process. *Journal of Experimental Child Psychology, 51*, 195–219.

Bowers, P. G., & Wolf, M. (1993). Theoretical links among naming speed, precise timing mechanisms and orthographic skill in dyslexia. *Reading and Writing, 5*, 69–85.

Bowey, J. A. (1995). Socioeconomic status differences in preschool phonological sensitivity and first-grade reading achievement. *Journal of Educational Psychology, 87,* 476–487.

Bowey, J. A., & Francis, J. (1991). Phonological analysis as a function of age and exposure to reading instruction. *Applied Psycholinguistics, 12,* 91–121.

Bracken, B. A. (1984). *Bracken Basic Concepts Scale.* San Antonio, TX: Psychological Corporation.

Bracken, B. A. (1987). Limitations of preschool instruments and standards for minimal levels of technical adequacy. *Journal of Psychoeducational Assessment, 4,* 313–326.

Bracken, B. A. (1988). Ten psychometric reasons why similar tests produce dissimilar results. *Journal of School Psychology, 26,* 155–166.

Bracken, B. A. (2000). Maximizing construct relevant assessment: The optimal preschool testing situation. In B. A. Bracken (Ed.), *The psychoeducational assessment of preschool children* (3rd ed., pp. 33–44). Needham Heights, MA: Allyn & Bacon.

Bracken, B. A., Keith, L. K., & Walker, K. C. (1994). Assessment of preschool behavior and social-emotional functioning: A review of thirteen third-party instruments. *Assessment in Rehabilitation and Exceptionality, 1,* 331–346.

Bracken, B. A., & McCallum, R. S. (1998). *Universal Nonverbal Intelligence Test.* Itasca, IL: Riverside.

Bracken, B. A., & Walker, K. C. (1997). The utility of intelligence tests for preschool children. In D. P. Flanagan, J. L. Genshaft, & P. L. Harrison (Eds.), *Contemporary intellectual assessment: Theories, tests, and issues* (pp. 484–502). New York: Guilford Press.

Bradley-Klug, K. L., Shapiro, E. S., Lutz, J. G., & DuPaul, G. J. (1998). Evaluation of oral reading rate as a curriculum-based measure within literature-based curriculum. *Journal of School Psychology, 36,* 183–197.

Brady, S. A. (1997). Ability to encode phonological representations: An underlying difficulty of poor readers. In B. A. Blachman (Ed.), *Foundations of reading acquisition and dyslexia: Implications for early intervention* (pp. 21–47). Mahwah, NJ: Erlbaum.

Brennan, R. L. (1998). Misconceptions at the intersection of measurement theory and practice. *Educational Measurement: Issues and Practice, 17*(1), 5–9, 30.

Breen, M. J., & Drecktrah, M. (1990). Similarity among common measures of academic achievement: Implications for assessing disabled children. *Psychological Reports, 67,* 379–383.

Brown, I. S., & Felton, R. H. (1990). Effects of instruction on beginning reading skills in children at risk for reading disability. *Reading and Writing, 2,* 223–241.

Brown, L., Sherbenou, R., & Johnsen, S. (1997). *Test of Nonverbal Intelligence–Third Edition.* Austin, TX: PRO-ED.

Brown, M. B., Giandenoto, M. J., & Bolen, L. M. (2000). Diagnosing written language disabilities using the Woodcock Johnson Tests of Educational Achievement–Revised and the Wechsler Individual Achievement Test. *Psychological Reports, 87,* 197–204.

Brown, V. L., Hammill, D. D., & Wiederholt, J. L. (1995). *Test of Reading Comprehension–Third Edition.* Austin, TX: PRO-ED.

Bruck, M. (1988). The word recognition and spelling of dyslexic children. *Reading Research Quarterly, 23,* 51–69.

Bruck, M. (1990). Word-recognition skills of adults with childhood diagnoses of dyslexia. *Developmental Psychology, 26,* 439–454.

Bruck, M. (1992). Persistence of dyslexics' phonological awareness deficits. *Developmental Psychology, 28,* 874–886.

Bruck, M., & Genesee, F. (1995). Phonological awareness in young second language learners. *Journal of Child Language, 22*, 307–324.

Bryant, B. R., & Wiederholt, J. L. (1991). *Gray Oral Reading Tests–Diagnostic.* Austin, TX: PRO-ED.

Bryant, B. R., Wiederholt, J. L., & Bryant, D. (in press). *Gray Diagnostic Reading Tests–Second Edition.* Austin, TX: PRO-ED.

Bryant, P. E., MacLean, M., Bradley, L. L., & Crossland, J. (1990). Rhyme and alliteration, phoneme detection, and learning to read. *Developmental Psychology, 26*, 429–438.

Burns, G. L., & Kondrick, P. A. (1998). Psychological behaviorism's reading therapy program: Parents as reading therapists for their children's reading disability. *Journal of Learning Disabilities, 31*, 278–285.

Byrne, B., & Fielding-Barnsley, R. (1991). Evaluation of a program to teach phonemic awareness to young children. *Journal of Educational Psychology, 83*, 451–455.

Byrne, B., & Fielding-Barnsley, R. (1993). Evaluation of a program to teach phonemic awareness to young children: A 1-year follow-up. *Journal of Educational Psychology, 85*, 104–111.

Byrne, B., & Fielding-Barnsley, R. (1995). Evaluation of a program to teach phonemic awareness to young children: A 2- and 3-year follow-up and a new preschool trial. *Journal of Educational Psychology, 87*, 488–503.

Byrne, B., Fielding-Barnsley, R., Ashley, L., & Larsen, K. (1997). Assessing the child's and the environment's contribution to reading acquisition: What we know and what we don't know. In B. A. Blachman (Ed.), *Foundations of reading acquisition and dyslexia: Implications for early intervention* (pp. 265–285). Mahwah, NJ: Erlbaum.

Byrne, B., Freebody, P., & Gates, A. (1992). Longitudinal data on the relations of word-reading strategies to comprehension, reading time, and phonemic awareness. *Reading Research Quarterly, 27*, 141–151.

Calfee, R. C., Lindamood, P., & Lindamood, C. (1973). Acoustic–phonetic skills and reading—kindergarten through twelfth grade. *Journal of Educational Psychology, 64*(3), 293–298.

Camilli, G., & Shepard, L. A. (1994). *Methods for identifying biased test items.* Thousand Oaks, CA: Sage.

Carlisle, J. F., & Beeman, M. M. (2000). The effects of language of instruction on the reading and writing achievement of first-grade Hispanic children. *Scientific Studies of Reading, 4*, 331–353.

Carran, D. T., & Scott, K. G. (1992). Risk assessment in preschool children: Research implications for the early detection of educational handicaps. *Topics in Early Childhood Special Education, 12*(2), 196–211.

Carroll, J. B. (1972). Review of the Illinois Test of Psycholinguistic Abilities–Revised Edition. In O. K. Buros (Ed.), *The seventh mental measurements yearbook* (pp. 819–823). Highland Park, NJ: Gryphon Press.

Carroll, J. B., Davies, P., & Richman, B. (1971). *Word frequency book.* New York: American Heritage.

Carroll, J. B. (1993). *Human cognitive abilities: A survey of factor-analytic studies.* New York: Cambridge University Press.

Carrow-Woolfolk, E. (1985). *Test of Auditory Comprehension of Language–Revised.* Circle Pines, MN: American Guidance Service.

Carrow-Woolfolk, E. (1988). *Theory, assessment and intervention in language disorders: An integrative approach.* Philadelphia: Grune & Stratton.

Carrow-Woolfolk, E. (1995). *Oral and Written Language Scales.* Circle Pines, MN: American Guidance Service.

Carrow-Woolfolk, E., & Lynch, J. I. (1981). *An integrative approach to language disorders in children.* San Antonio, TX: Psychological Corporation.

Castles, A., & Coltheart, M. (1993). Varieties of developmental dyslexia. *Cognition, 47*, 149–180.

Castles, A., Datta, H., Gayan, J., & Olson, R. K. (1999). Varieties of developmental reading disorder: Genetic and environmental influences. *Journal of Experimental Child Psychology, 72*, 73–94.

Cattell, R. B. (1941). Some theoretical issues in adult intelligence testing. *Psychological Bulletin, 38*, 592.

Cattell, R. B. (1943). The measurement of adult intelligence. *Psychological Bulletin, 40*, 153–193.

Cattell, R. B. (1950). *Personality: A systematic theoretical and factoral study.* New York: McGraw-Hill.

Catts, H. W. (1991). Early identification of dyslexia: Evidence from a follow-up study of speech-language impaired children. *Annals of Dyslexia, 41*, 163–177.

Catts, H. W. (1993). The relationship between speech–language impairments and reading disabilities. *Journal of Speech and Hearing Research, 36*, 948–958.

Catts, H. W., Fey, M. E., Zhang, X., & Tomblin, J. B. (1999). Language basis of reading and reading disabilities: Evidence from a longitudinal investigation. *Scientific Studies of Reading, 3,* 331–361.

Catts, H. W., Fey, M. E., Zhang, X., & Tomblin, J. B. (2001). Estimating the risk of future reading difficulties in kindergarten children: A research-based model and its clinical implementation. *Language, Speech, and Hearing Services in Schools, 32,* 38–50.

Center for Academic Reading Skills (CARS) & Texas Institute for Measurement, Evaluation, and Statistics (TIMES). (2002). *Technical report: Texas Primary Reading Inventory (1998–1999 edition)* [Online]. Retrieved from http://www.tpri.org

Center, Y., Wheldall, K., Freeman, L., Outhred, L., & McNaught, M. (1995). An evaluation of Reading Recovery. *Reading Research Quarterly, 30*, 240–263.

Chall, J. (1983). *Stages of reading development.* New York: McGraw-Hill.

Chall, J. S., & Dale, E. (1995). *Readability revisited: The new Dale–Chall readability formula.* Cambridge, MA: Brookline.

Chapman, J. W., Tunmer, W. E., & Prochnow, J. E. (2001). Does success in the Reading Recovery program depend on developing proficiency in phonological-processing skills?: A longitudinal study in a whole language instructional context. *Annals of Dyslexia, 51*, 141–176.

Children's Educational Services. (1987). *Test of Reading Fluency.* Minneapolis, MN: Author.

Christensen, C. A. (2000). Preschool phonological awareness and success in reading. In N. A. Badian (Ed.), *Prediction and prevention of reading failure* (pp. 153–178). Timonium, MD: York Press.

Cipielewski, J., & Stanovich, K. E. (1992). Predicting growth in reading ability from children's exposure to print. *Journal of Experimental Child Psychology, 54*, 78–89.

Cisero, C. A., & Royer, J. M. (1995). The development and cross-language transfer of phonological awareness. *Contemporary Educational Psychology, 20*, 275–303.

Clay, M. M. (1966). *Emergent reading behaviour.* Unpublished doctoral dissertation, University of Auckland Library.

Clay, M. M. (1968). A syntactic analysis of reading errors. *Journal of Verbal Learning and Verbal Behavior, 7*, 434–438.

Clay, M. M. (1972). *Sand–The Concepts About Print Test.* Auckland, New Zealand: Heinemann.

Clay, M. M. (1979a). *The early detection of reading difficulties: A diagnostic survey with recovery procedures* (2nd ed.). Auckland, New Zealand: Heinemann.

Clay, M. M. (1979b). *Stones–The Concepts About Print Test.* Auckland, New Zealand: Heinemann.

Clay, M. M. (1985). *The early detection of reading difficulties.* Auckland, New Zealand: Heinemann.

Clay, M. M. (1993a). *An Observation Survey of Early Literacy Achievement* (2nd ed.). Portsmouth, NH: Heinemann.

Clay, M. M. (1993b). *Reading Recovery: A guidebook for teachers in training.* Portsmouth, NH: Heinemann.

Clay, M. M. (2000a). *Concepts about print: What have children learned about the way we print language?* Portsmouth, NH: Heinemann.

Clay, M. M. (2000b). *Follow me, moon–The Concepts About Print Test.* Portsmouth, NH: Heinemann.

Clay, M. M. (2000c). *No shoes–The Concepts About Print Test.* Portsmouth, NH: Heinemann.

Clay, M. M. (2002). *An Observation Survey of Early Literacy Achievement* (2nd ed.). Portsmouth, NH: Heinemann.

Cohen, J. (1960). A coefficient of agreement for nominal scales. *Educational and Psychological Measurement, 20,* 37–46.

Cole, J. C., Muenz, T. A., Ouchi, B. Y., Kaufman, N. L., & Kaufman, A. S. (1997). Item analysis of written expression scoring systems from the PIAT-R and WIAT. *Psychology in the Schools, 34,* 1–9.

Comeau, L., Cormier, P., Grandmaison, E., & Lacroix, D. (1999). A longitudinal study of phonological processing skills in children learning to read in a second language. *Journal of Educational Psychology, 91,* 29–43.

Connolly, A. J. (1988). *KeyMath Revised.* Circle Pines, MN: American Guidance Service.

Cooter, R. B. (1989). Review of the Woodcock Reading Mastery Tests–Revised. In J. C. Conoley & J. J. Kramer (Eds.), *The tenth mental measurements yearbook* (pp. 910–913). Lincoln, NE: Buros Institute of Mental Measurements.

Cornoldi, C., & Oakhill, J. (Eds.). (1996). *Reading comprehension difficulties: Processes and intervention.* Mahwah, NJ: Erlbaum.

Cornwall, A. (1992). The relationship of phonological awareness, rapid naming, and verbal memory to severe reading and spelling disability. *Journal of Learning Disabilities, 25,* 532–538.

Cronbach, L. J., Gleser, G. C., Nanda, H., & Rajaratnam, N. (1972). *The dependability of behavioral measurements: Theory of generalizability for scores and profiles.* New York: Wiley.

CTB/McGraw-Hill. (1973). *Comprehensive Tests of Basic Skills.* Monterey, CA: Author.

CTB/McGraw-Hill. (1985). *California Achievement Tests.* Monterey, CA: Author.

CTB/McGraw-Hill. (1989). *California Achievement Tests–Forms E and F.* Monterey, CA: Author.

CTB/McGraw-Hill. (1992). *California Achievement Tests–Fifth Edition.* Monterey, CA: Author.

CTB/McGraw-Hill. (1997). *TerraNova: Technical bulletin 1.* Monterey, CA: Author.

CTB/McGraw-Hill. (2000a). *Fox in a Box: An Adventure in Literacy.* Monterey, CA: Author.

CTB/McGraw-Hill. (2000b). *Why Fox in a Box?: A brief overview of the research and literature that influenced the development of literacy assessment for grades K–2.* Monterey, CA: Author.

CTB/McGraw-Hill. (2001). *Fox in a Box: Technical report 1.* Monterey, CA: Author.

CTB/McGraw-Hill. (2002). *Adventures in literacy: Classroom and home activities for early readers.* Monterey, CA: Author.

Culatta, B., Page, J. L., & Ellis, J. (1983). Story retelling as a communicative performance screening tool. *Language, Speech, and Hearing Services in Schools, 14,* 66–74.

Cunningham, A. E., Perry, K. E., & Stanovich, K. E. (2001). Converging evidence for the concept of orthographic processing. *Reading and Writing, 14,* 549–568.

Cunningham, A. E., & Stanovich, K. E. (1990). Assessing print exposure and orthographic processing skill in children: A quick measure of reading experience. *Journal of Educational Psychology, 82,* 733–740.

Cunningham, A. E., & Stanovich, K. E. (1991). Tracking the unique effects of print exposure in children: Associations with vocabulary, general knowledge, and spelling. *Journal of Educational Psychology, 83,* 264–274.

Cunningham, A. E., & Stanovich, K. E. (1993). Children's literacy environments and early word recognition subskills. *Reading and Writing, 5,* 193–204.

Cunningham, A. E., & Stanovich, K. E. (1997). Early reading acquisition and its relation to reading experience and ability 10 years later. *Developmental Psychology, 33,* 934–945.

Curtin, S., Manis, F. R., & Seidenberg, M. S. (2001). Parallels between the reading and spelling deficits of two subgroups of developmental dyslexia. *Reading and Writing, 14,* 515–547.

Cutting, L. E., & Denckla, M. B. (2001). The relationship of rapid serial naming and word reading in normally developing readers: An exploratory model. *Reading and Writing, 14,* 673–705.

Daly, E. J., Wright, J. A., Kelly, S. Q., & Martens, B. K. (1997). Measures of early academic skills: Reliability and validity with a first grade sample. *School Psychology Quarterly, 12,* 268–280.

Day, K. C., & Day, H. C. (1984). Kindergarten knowledge of print conventions and later school achievement: A five-year follow-up. *Psychology in the Schools, 21,* 393–396.

Day, K. C., & Day, H. C. (1991). The concurrent validity of four tests of metalinguistic awareness. *Reading Psychology: An International Quarterly, 12,* 1–11.

de Jong, P. F., & van der Leij, A. (2002). Effects of phonological abilities and linguistic comprehension on the development of reading. *Scientific Studies of Reading, 6,* 51–77.

Denckla, M. B., & Cutting, L. E. (1999). History and significance of rapid automatized naming. *Annals of Dyslexia, 49,* 29–42.

Denckla, M. B., & Rudel, R. (1974). Rapid "automatized" naming of pictured objects, colors, letters and numbers by normal children. *Cortex, 10,* 186–202.

Denckla, M. B., & Rudel, R. G. (1976a). Naming of object-drawings by dyslexic and other learning disabled children. *Brain and Language, 3,* 1–15.

Denckla, M. B., & Rudel, R. G. (1976b). Rapid "automatized" naming (R.A.N.): Dyslexia differentiated from other learning disabilities. *Neuropsychologia, 14,* 471–479.

Deno, S. L. (1985). Curriculum-based measurement: The emerging alternative. *Exceptional Children, 52,* 219–232.

Deno, S. L. (1989). Curriculum-based measurement and special education services: A fundamental and direct relationship. In M. R. Shinn (Ed.), *Curriculum-based measurement: Assessing special children* (pp. 1–17). New York: Guilford Press.

Derr, T. F., & Shapiro, E. S. (1989). A behavioral evaluation of curriculum-based assessment of reading. *Journal of Psychoeducational Assessment, 7,* 148–160.

Derr-Minneci, T. F., & Shapiro, E. S. (1992). Validating curriculum-based measurement in reading from a behavioral perspective. *School Psychology Quarterly, 7,* 2–16.

DiPerna, J. C., & Elliott, S. N. (2000). *Academic Competence Evaluation Scales–Manual K–12.* San Antonio, TX: Psychological Corporation.

Dowhower, S. L. (1991). Speaking of prosody: Fluency's unattended bedfellow. *Theory into Practice, 30,* 165–175.

Downing, J., Ayers, D., & Schaefer, B. (1983). *Linguistic Awareness in Reading Readiness Test.* Slough, UK: National Foundation for Educational Research–Nelson.

Dryer, R., Beale, I. L., & Lambert, A. J. (1999). The balance model of dyslexia and remedial training: An evaluative study. *Journal of Learning Disabilities, 32,* 174–186.

Duncan, L. G., & Seymour, P. H. K. (2000). Phonemes and rhyme in the development of reading and metaphonology: The Dundee longitudinal study. In N. A. Badian (Ed.), *Prediction and prevention of reading failure* (pp. 275–297). Baltimore: York Press.

Duncan, S., & McNaughton, S. (2001). Research note: Updating the Clay word test. *New Zealand Journal of Educational Studies, 2.*

Dunn, L. M., & Dunn, L. M. (1981). *Peabody Picture Vocabulary Test–Revised.* Circle Pines, MN: American Guidance Service.

Dunn, L. M., & Dunn, L. M. (1997). *Peabody Picture Vocabulary Test–Third Edition.* Circle Pines, MN: American Guidance Service.

Dunn, L. M., Lugo, E. E., Padilla, E. R., & Dunn, L. M. (1986). *Test de Vocabulario en Imágines Peabody.* Circle Pines, MN: American Guidance Service.

Durgunoĝlu, A. Y., Nagy, W. E., & Hancin-Bhatt, B. J. (1993). Cross-language transfer of phonological awareness. *Journal of Educational Psychology, 85,* 453–465.

EDL. (1997). *EDL core vocabularies in reading, mathematics, science, and social studies.* Orlando, FL: Steck-Vaughn.

Ehri, L. C. (1989). The development of spelling knowledge and its role in reading acquisition and reading disability. *Journal of Learning Disabilities, 22,* 356–365.

Ehri, L. C. (1991). Development of the ability to read words. In R. Barr, M. L. Kamil, P. B. Mosenthal, & P. D. Pearson (Eds.), *Handbook of reading research* (Vol. 2, pp. 383–417). Mahwah, NJ: Erlbaum.

Ehri, L. C. (1992). Reconceptualizing the development of sight word reading and its relationship to recoding. In P. B. Gough, L. C. Ehri, & R. Treiman (Eds.), *Reading acquisition* (pp. 107–143). Hillsdale, NJ: Erlbaum.

Ehri, L. C. (1995). Phases of development in learning to read words by sight. *Journal of Research in Reading, 18,* 116–125.

Ehri, L. C. (1998). Grapheme–phoneme knowledge is essential for learning to read words in English. In J. L. Metsala & L. C. Ehri (Eds.), *Word recognition in beginning literacy* (pp. 3–40). Mahwah, NJ: Erlbaum.

Ehri, L. C., & Saltmarsh, J. (1995). Beginning readers outperform older disabled readers in learning to read words by sight. *Reading and Writing, 7,* 295–326.

Ehri, L. C., & Sweet, J. (1991). Fingerpoint-reading of memorized text: What enables beginning readers to process the print? *Reading Research Quarterly, 26,* 442–462.

Elbro, C. (1996). Early linguistic abilities and reading development: A review and a hypothesis. *Reading and Writing, 8,* 453–485.

Elbro, C., Borstrom, I., & Petersen, D. K. (1998). Predicting dyslexia from kindergarten: The importance of distinctness of phonological representations of lexical items. *Reading Research Quarterly, 33,* 36–60.

Elbro, C., Nielsen, I., & Petersen, D. K. (1994). Dyslexia in adults: Evidence for deficits in nonword reading and in the phonological representation of lexical items. *Annals of Dyslexia, 44,* 205–226.

Elliott, C. D. (1990). *Differential Ability Scales.* San Antonio, TX: Psychological Corporation.

Elliott, C. D., Murray, D. J., & Pearson, L. S. (1983). *British Ability Scales.* Windsor, UK: National Foundation for Educational Research–Nelson.

Elliott, J., Lee, S. W., & Tollefson, N. (2001). A reliability and validity study of the Dynamic Indicators of Basic Early Literacy Skills—Modified. *School Psychology Review, 30,* 33–49.

Embretson, S. E., & Hershberger, S. L. (Eds.). (1999). *The new rules of measurement: What every psychologist and educator should know.* Mahwah, NJ: Erlbaum.

Embretson, S. E., & Reise, S. P. (2000). *Item response theory for psychologists.* Mahwah, NJ: Erlbaum.

Escamilla, K., Andrade, A. M., Basurto, A. G. M., Ruiz, O. A., & Clay, M. M. (1995). *Instrumento de observación de los logros de la lecto-escritura inicial.* Westport, CT: Heinemann.

Evans, J. E., Floyd, R. G., McGrew, K. S., & Leforgee, M. H. (2002). The relations between measures of Cattell–Horn–Carroll (CHC) cognitive abilities and reading achievement during childhood and adolescence. *School Psychology Review, 31,* 246–262.

Fawcett, A. J., & Nicolson, R. I. (1994). Naming speed in children with dyslexia. *Journal of Learning Disabilities, 27,* 641–646.

Fawcett, A. J., & Nicolson, R. I. (1996). *The Dyslexia Screening Test.* London: Psychological Corporation.

Fawcett, A. J., & Nicolson, R. I. (2000). Systematic screening and intervention for reading difficulty. In N. A. Badian (Ed.), *Prediction and prevention of reading failure* (pp. 57–85). Baltimore: York Press.

Fawcett, A. J., Nicolson, R. I., & Dean, P. (1996). Impaired performance of children with dyslexia on a range of cerebellar tasks. *Annals of Dyslexia, 46,* 259–283.

Fawcett, A. J., Singleton, C. H., & Peer, L. (1998). Advances in early years screening for dyslexia in the United Kingdom. *Annals of Dyslexia, 48,* 57–88.

Felton, R. H. (1992). Early identification of children at risk for reading disabilities. *Topics in Early Childhood Education, 12*(2), 212–229.

Felton, R. H. (1998). The development of reading skills in poor readers: Educational implications. In C. Hulme & R. M. Joshi (Eds.), *Reading and spelling: Development and disorders* (pp. 219–233). Mahwah, NJ: Erlbaum.

Felton, R. H., & Brown, I. S. (1990). Phonological processes as predictors of specific reading skills in children at risk for reading failure. *Reading and Writing, 2,* 39–59.

Felton, R. H., & Wood, R. B. (1989). Cognitive deficits in reading disability and attention deficit disorder. *Journal of Learning Disabilities, 22,* 3–13, 22.

Felton, R. H., & Wood, F. B. (1992). A reading level match study of nonword reading skills in poor readers with varying IQ. *Journal of Learning Disabilities, 25,* 318–326.

Felton, R. H., Wood, F. B., Brown, I. S., & Campbell, S. K. (1987). Separate verbal memory and naming deficits in attention deficit disorder and reading disability. *Brain and Language, 31,* 171–184.

Flanagan, D. P., & Alfonso, V. C. (1993a). Differences required for significance between WISC-III Verbal and Performance IQs and WIAT subtests and composites: The predicted-achievement method. *Psychology in the Schools, 30,* 125–132.

Flanagan, D. P., & Alfonso, V. C. (1993b). WIAT subtest and composite predicted-achievement values based on WISC-III Verbal and Performance IQs. *Psychology in the Schools, 30,* 310–320.

Flanagan, D. P., & Alfonso, V. C. (1995). A critical review of the technical characteristics of new and recently revised intelligence tests for preschool children. *Journal of Psychoeducational Assessment, 13,* 66–90.

Flanagan, D. P., Mascolo, J., & Genshart, J. L. (2000). A conceptual framework for interpreting preschool intelligence tests. In B. A. Bracken (Ed.), *The psychoeducational assessment of preschool children* (3rd ed., pp. 428–473). Needham Heights, MA: Allyn & Bacon.

Fletcher, J. M., Foorman, B. R., & Boudousquie, A. (2002). Assessment of reading and learning disabilities: A research-based intervention-oriented approach. *Journal of School Psychology, 40,* 27–63.

Fletcher, J. M., Francis, D. J., Shaywitz, S. E., Lyon, G. R., Foorman, B. R., Stuebing, K. K., et al. (1998). Intelligent testing and the discrepancy model for children with learning disabilities. *Learning Disabilities Research and Practice, 13,* 186–203.

Fletcher, J. M., Shaywitz, S. E., Shankweiler, D. P., Katz, L., Liberman, I. Y., Stuebing, K. K., et al. (1994). Cognitive profiles of reading disability: Comparisons of discrepancy and low achievement definitions. *Journal of Educational Psychology, 86,* 6–23.

Flynn, J. M. (2000). From identification to intervention: Improving kindergarten screening for risk of reading failure. In N. A. Badian (Ed.), *Prediction and prevention of reading failure* (pp. 133–152). Baltimore: York Press.

Flynn, J. (2001). *Predictive Reading Profile.* East Moline, IL: LinguiSystems.

Flynn, J. M., & Rahbar, M. H. (1998a). Improving teacher prediction of children at risk for reading failure. *Psychology in the Schools, 35,* 163–172.

Flynn, J., & Rahbar, M. H. (1998b). Kindergarten screening for risk of reading failure. *Journal of Psychoeducational Assessment, 16,* 15–35.

Flynn, J. R. (1987). Massive IQ gains in 14 nations: What IQ tests really measure. *Psychological Bulletin, 101,* 171–191.

Flynn, J. R. (1999). Searching for justice: The discovery of IQ gains over time. *American Psychologist, 54,* 5–20.

Foorman, B. R. (1994). Phonological and orthographic processing: Separate but equal? In V. W. Berninger (Ed.), *The varieties of orthographic knowledge: I. Theoretical and developmental issues* (pp. 321–357). Dordrecht, The Netherlands: Kluwer Academic.

Foorman, B. R., Fletcher, J. M., Francis, D. J., Carlson, C. D., Chen, D.-T., Mouzaki, A., et al. (2000). *Texas Primary Reading Inventory technical manual, 1998 edition* [Online]. Houston: Center for Academic and Reading Skills, University of Texas–Houston Health Science Center and University of Houston. Retrieved from http://cards.uth.tmc.edu/manualbody.htm

Foorman, B. R., Fletcher, J. M., Francis, D. J., Carlson, C. D., Chen, D.-T., Mouzaki, A., et al. (2002). *Texas Primary Reading Inventory–2002–2003.* Houston: Center for Academic and Reading Skills, University of Texas–Houston Health Science Center & University of Houston.

Foorman, B. R., & Francis, D. J. (1994). Exploring connections among reading, spelling, and phonemic segmentation during first grade. *Reading and Writing, 6,* 65–91.

Foorman, B. R., Francis, D. J., Fletcher, J. M., Schatschneider, C., & Mehta, P. (1998). The role of instruction in learning to read: Preventing reading failure in at-risk children. *Journal of Educational Psychology, 90,* 37–55.

Foorman, B. R., Francis, D. J., Fletcher, J. M., Winikates, D., Mehta, P., Schatschneider, C., et al. (1997). Early interventions for children with reading problems. *Scientific Studies of Reading, 1,* 255–276.

Foorman, B. R., Francis, D. J., Novy, D M., & Liberman, D. (1991). How letter–sound instruction mediates progress in first-grade reading and spelling. *Reading and Writing, 6,* 65–91.

Foorman, B. R., Francis, D. J., Shaywitz, S. E., Shaywitz, B. A., & Fletcher, J. M. (1997). The case for early reading intervention. In B. A. Blachman (Ed.), *Foundations of reading acquisition and dyslexia: Implications for early intervention* (pp. 243–264). Mahwah, NJ: Erlbaum.

Foorman, B. R., & Liberman, D. (1989). Visual and phonological processing of words: A comparison of good and poor readers. *Journal of Learning Disabilities, 22,* 349–355.

Forness, S. R., Kavale, K. A., Blum, I. H., & Lloyd, J. W. (1997). Mega-analysis of meta-analyses: What works in special education and related services. *Teaching Exceptional Children, 29*(6), 4–9.

Fowler, A. E. (1991). How early phonological development might set the stage for phoneme awareness. In S. A. Brady & D. P. Shankweiler (Eds.), *Phonological processes in literacy: A tribute to Isabelle Y. Liberman* (pp. 97–117). Hillsdale, NJ: Erlbaum.

Freebody, P., & Byrne, B. (1988). Word-reading strategies in elementary school children: Relations to comprehension, reading time, and phonemic awareness. *Reading Research Quarterly, 23,* 441–453.

Frith, U. (1985). Beneath the surface of developmental dyslexia. In K. E. Patterson, J. C. Marshall, & M. Coltheart (Eds.), *Surface dyslexia: Neuropsychological and cognitive studies of phonological reading* (pp. 301–330). Hillsdale: NJ: Erlbaum.

Fry, E. (1977). Fry's readability graph: Clarifications, validity and extension of level 17. *Journal of Reading, 21,* 242–252.

Fry, E. B., Kress, J. E., & Fountoukidis, D. L. (1993). *The reading teacher's book of lists.* Englewood Cliffs, NJ: Prentice-Hall.

Fuchs, L. S., & Deno, S. L. (1992). Effects of curriculum within curriculum-based measurement. *Exceptional Children, 58,* 232–243.

Fuchs, L. S., & Deno, S. L. (1994). Must instructionally useful performance assessment be based in the curriculum? *Exceptional Children, 61,* 15–24.

Fuchs, L. S., & Fuchs, D. (1999). Monitoring student progress toward the development of reading competence: A review of three forms of classroom-based assessment. *School Psychology Review, 28,* 659–671.

Fuchs, L. S., Fuchs, D., Hamlett, C. L., Walz, L., & Germann, G. (1993). Formative evaluation of academic progress: How much growth can we expect? *School Psychology Review, 22,* 27–48.

Fuchs, L. S., Fuchs, D., Hosp, M. K., & Jenkins, J. R. (2001). Oral reading fluency as an indicator of reading competence: A theoretical, empirical, and historical analysis. *Scientific Studies of Reading, 5,* 239–256.

Fuchs, L. S., Fuchs, D., & Maxwell, L. (1988). The validity of informal reading comprehension measures. *Remedial and Special Education, 9*(2), 20–28.

Fugate, M. H. (1997). Letter training and its effect on the development of beginning reading skills. *School Psychology Quarterly, 12,* 170–192.

Garcia, G. E. (2000). Bilingual children's reading. In M. L. Kamil, P. B. Mosenthal, P. D. Pearson, & R. Barr (Eds.), *Handbook of reading research* (Vol. 3, pp. 813–834). Mahwah, NJ: Erlbaum.

Gardill, M. C., & Jitendra, A. K. (1999). Advanced story map instruction: Effects on the reading comprehension of students with learning disabilities. *Journal of Special Education, 33,* 2–17, 28.

Gardner, E. F., Rudman, H. C., Karlsen, B., & Merwin, J. C. (1982). *Stanford Achievement Test–Seventh Edition.* San Antonio, TX: Psychological Corporation.

Gardner, J. (1985). *Receptive One-Word Picture Vocabulary Test.* Novato, CA: Academic Therapy.

Gardner, J. (1990). *Expressive One-Word Picture Vocabulary Test–Revised.* Novato, CA: Academic Therapy.

Gathercole, S. E. (1995). Is nonword repetition a test of phonological memory or lexical knowledge?: It all depends on the nonwords. *Memory and Cognition, 23,* 83–94.

Gathercole, S. E., & Baddeley, A. D. (1993a). Phonological working memory: A critical building block for reading development and vocabulary acquisition? *European Journal of Psychology of Education, 8,* 259–272.

Gathercole, S. E., & Baddeley, A. D. (1993b). *Working memory and language.* Hillsdale, NJ: Erlbaum.

Gathercole, S. E., Willis, C. S., Emslie, H., & Baddeley, A. D. (1992). Phonological memory and vocabulary development during the early school years: A longitudinal study. *Developmental Psychology, 28,* 887–898.

Geva, E., & Ryan, E. B. (1993). Linguistic and cognitive correlates of academic skills in first and second languages. *Language Learning, 43,* 5–42.

Geva, E., & Siegel, L. S. (2000). Orthographic and cognitive factors in the concurrent development of basic reading skills in two languages. *Reading and Writing, 12,* 1–30.

Geva, E., Wade-Woolley, L., & Shany, M. (1993). The concurrent development of spelling and decoding in two different orthographies. *Journal of Reading Behavior, 25,* 383–406.

Geva, E., Wade-Woolley, L., & Shany, M. (1997). The development of reading efficiency in first and second language. *Scientific Studies of Reading, 1,* 119–144.

Geva, E., Yaghoub-Zadeh, Z., & Schuster, B. (2000). Understanding individual differences in word recognition skills of ESL children. *Annals of Dyslexia, 50,* 123–154.

Gillam, R. B., Crofford, J. A., Gale, M. A., & Hoffman, L. M. (2001). Language change following computer-assisted language instruction with Fast ForWord or Laureate Learning Systems software. *American Journal of Speech–Language Pathology, 10,* 231–247.

Goldman, R., Fristoe, M., & Woodcock, R. W. (1974). *Goldman–Fristoe–Woodcock Auditory Skills Test Battery.* Circle Pines, MN: American Guidance Service.

Good, R. H., & Jefferson, G. (1998). Contemporary perspectives on curriculum-based measurement validity. In M. R. Shinn (Ed.), *Advanced applications of curriculum-based measurement* (pp. 61–88). New York: Guilford Press.

Good, R. H., & Kaminski, R. A. (1996). Assessment for instructional decisions: Toward a proactive/prevention model of decision-making for early literacy skills. *School Psychology Quarterly, 11,* 326–336.

Good, R. H., & Kaminski, R. A. (2002a). *DIBELS oral reading fluency passages for first through third grades* (Technical Report No. 10). Retrieved from http://dibels.uoregon.edu

Good, R. H., & Kaminski, R. A. (Eds.). (2002b). *Dynamic Indicators of Basic Early Literacy Skills–Sixth Edition* [Online]. Retrieved from http://dibels.uoregon.edu

Good, R. H., & Salvia, J. (1988). Curriculum bias in published, norm-referenced reading tests: Demonstrable effects. *School Psychology Review, 17,* 51–60.

Good, R. H., Simmons, D. C., & Kame'enui, E. J. (2001). The importance and decision-making utility of a continuum of fluency-based indicators of foundational reading skills for third-grade high-stakes outcomes. *Scientific Studies of Reading, 5,* 257–288.

Good, R. H., Simmons, D. C., & Smith, S. B. (1998). Effective academic interventions in the United States: Evaluating and enhancing the acquisition of early reading skills. *School Psychology Review, 27,* 45–56.

Good, R. H., Wallin, J., Simmons, D. C., Kame'enui, E. J., & Kaminski, R. A. (2002). *System-wide percentile ranks for DIBELS benchmark assessment* (Technical Report No. 9). Retrieved from http://dibels.uoregon.edu

Goodman, K. S. (1986). *What's whole in whole language: A parent–teacher guide.* Portsmouth, NH: Heinemann.

Goodwin, L. D., & Goodwin, W. L. (1991). Using generalizability theory in early childhood special education. *Journal of Early Intervention, 15,* 193–204.

Goodwin, W. L., & Goodwin, L. D. (1993). Young children and measurement: Standardized and nonstandardized instruments in early childhood education. In B. Spodek (Ed.), *Handbook of research on the education of young children* (pp. 441–463). New York: Macmillan.

Gottardo, A., Stanovich, K. E., & Siegel, L. S. (1996). The relationships between phonological sensitivity, syntactic processing, and verbal working memory in the reading performance of third-grade children. *Journal of Experimental Child Psychology, 63*, 563–582.

Gough, P. B. (1996). How children learn to read and why they fail. *Annals of Dyslexia, 46*, 3–20.

Gough, P. B., & Tunmer, W. E. (1986). Decoding, reading, and reading disability. *Remedial and Special Education, 7*(1), 6–10.

Graham, S., Berninger, V. W., Abbott, R. D., Abbott, S. P., & Whitaker, D. (1997). Role of mechanics in composing of elementary school students: A new methodological approach. *Journal of Educational Psychology, 89*, 170–182.

Gray, S., Plante, E., Vance, R., & Henrichsen, M. (1999). The diagnostic accuracy of four vocabulary tests administered to preschool-age children. *Language, Speech, and Hearing Services in Schools, 30*, 196–206.

Gray, W. S., & Robinson, H. (1963). *Gray Oral Reading Tests*. Austin, TX: PRO-ED.

Gray, W. S., & Robinson, H. (1967). *Gray Oral Reading Tests*. Austin, TX: PRO-ED.

Gredler, G. R. (1992). *School readiness: Assessment and educational issues*. Brandon, VT: Clinical Psychology.

Gredler, G. R. (1997). Issues in early childhood screening and assessment. *Psychology in the Schools, 34*, 99–106.

Gredler, G. R. (2000). Early childhood screening for developmental and educational problems. In B. A. Bracken (Ed.), *The psychoeducational assessment of preschool children* (3rd ed., pp. 399–411). Needham Heights, MA: Allyn & Bacon.

Greenberg, L. M. (1998). *Tests of Variables of Attention*. Los Alamitos, CA: Universal Attention Disorders.

Gresham, F. M. (2002). Responsiveness to intervention: An alternative approach to the identification of learning disabilities. In R. Bradley, L. Danielson, & D. P. Hallahan (Eds.), *The identification of learning disabilities: Research to practice* (pp. 467–519). Mahwah, NJ: Erlbaum.

Gunn, B., Biglan, A., Smolkowski, K., & Ary, D. (2000). The efficacy of supplemental instruction in decoding skills for Hispanic and non-Hispanic students in early elementary school. *Journal of Special Education, 34*, 90–103.

Gunning, T. G. (1998). *Assessing and correcting reading and writing difficulties*. Needham Heights, MA: Allyn & Bacon.

Haager, D., & Windmueller, M. P. (2001). Early reading intervention for English language learners at-risk for learning disabilities: Student and teacher outcomes in an urban school. *Learning Disability Quarterly, 24*, 235–250.

Habedank, L. (1995). Best practices in developing local norms for problem solving in the schools. In A. Thomas & J. Grimes (Eds.), *Best practices in school psychology III* (pp. 701–715). Washington, DC: National Association of School Psychologists.

Hambleton, R. K. (1996). Advances in assessment models, methods, and practices. In D. C. Berliner & R. C. Calfee (Eds.), *Handbook of educational psychology* (pp. 899–925). New York: Simon & Schuster Macmillan.

Hambleton, R. K., Swaminathan, H., & Rogers, H. J. (1991). *Fundamentals of item response theory*. Newbury Park, CA: Sage.

Hambleton, R. K., & Zaal, J. N. (Eds.). (1991). *Advances in educational and psychological testing: Theory and applications*. Boston: Kluwer Academic.

Hammill, D. D. (1998). *Detroit Tests of Learning Aptitude–Fourth Edition*. Austin, TX: PRO-ED.

Hammill, D. D., Brown, L., & Bryant, B. R. (1992). *A consumer's guide to tests in print* (2nd ed.). Austin, TX: PRO-ED.

Hammill, D. D., & Hresko, W. P. (1994). *Comprehensive Scales of Student Abilities*. Austin, TX: PRO-ED.

Hammill, D. D., Mather, N., Allen, E. A., & Roberts, R. (2002). Using semantics, grammar, phonology, and rapid naming tasks to predict word identification. *Journal of Learning Disabilities, 35*, 121–136.

Hammill, D. D., Mather, N., & Roberts, R. (2001). *Illinois Test of Psycholinguistic Abilities–Third Edition.* Austin, TX: PRO-ED.

Hammill, D. D., & Newcomer, P. L. (1997). *Test of Language Development–Intermediate: Third Edition.* Austin, TX: PRO-ED.

Hammill, D. D., Pearson, N. A., & Wiederholt, J. L. (1997). *Comprehensive Test of Nonverbal Intelligence.* Austin, TX: PRO-ED.

Harcourt, Brace & World. (1964). *Stanford Achievement Test.* New York: Author.

Harcourt Educational Measurement. (1996). *Stanford Achievement Test Series–Ninth Edition.* San Antonio, TX: Author.

Harcourt Educational Measurement. (1999). *Metropolitan Achievement Tests–Eighth Edition.* San Antonio, TX: Author.

Harris, A. J., & Jacobson, M. D. (1982). *Basic reading vocabularies.* New York: Macmillan.

Harris, A. J., & Sipay, E. (1985). *How to increase reading ability: A guide to developmental and remedial methods* (8th ed.) New York: Longman.

Harrison, P. L. (1990). *Early Screening Profiles.* Circle Pines, MN: American Guidance Service.

Hartley, D. N., & Quine, P. G. (1982). A critical appraisal of Marie Clay's "Concepts About Print test." *Reading, 16*, 109–112.

Hartman, J. M., & Fuller, M. L. (1997). The development of curriculum-based measurement norms in literature-based classrooms. *Journal of School Psychology, 35*, 351–375.

Hasbrouck, J. E., & Tindal, G. (1992). Curriculum-based oral reading fluency norms for students in grades 2 through 5. *Teaching Exceptional Children, 24*, 41–44.

Hatcher, P. J., & Hulme, C. (1999). Phonemes, rhymes, and intelligence as predictors of children's responsiveness to remedial reading instruction: Evidence from a longitudinal intervention study. *Journal of Experimental Child Psychology, 72*, 130–153.

Havey, J. M., Story, N., & Buker, K. (2002). Convergent and concurrent validity of two measures of phonological processing. *Psychology in the Schools, 39*, 507–514.

Hecht, S. A., Burgess, S. R., Torgesen, J. K., Wagner, R. K., & Rashotte, C. A. (2000). Explaining social class differences in growth of reading skills from beginning kindergarten through fourth-grade: The role of phonological awareness, rate of access, and print knowledge. *Reading and Writing, 12*, 99–127.

Hecht, S. A., & Greenfield, D. B. (2001). Comparing the predictive validity of first grade teacher ratings and reading-related tests on third grade levels of reading skills in young children exposed to poverty. *School Psychology Review, 30*, 50–69.

Henderson, E. H. (1990). *Teaching spelling* (2nd ed.). Boston: Houghton Mifflin.

Hessler, G. L. (1993). *Use and interpretation of the Woodcock–Johnson Psycho-Educational Battery–Revised.* Chicago: Riverside.

Hintze, J. M., Owen, S. V., Shapiro, E. S., & Daly, E. J. (2000). Generalizability of oral reading fluency measures: Application of G theory to curriculum-based measurement. *School Psychology Quarterly, 15*, 52–68.

Hintze, J. M., & Pettitte, H. A. P. (2001). The generalizability of CBM oral reading fluency measures across general and special education. *Journal of Psychoeducational Assessment, 19*, 158–170.

Hintze, J. M., Ryan, A. L., & Stoner, G. (2002). *Concurrent validity and diagnostic accuracy of the Dynamic Indicators of Basic Early Literacy Skills and the Comprehensive Test of Phonological Processing* [Online]. Retrieved from http://dibels.uoregon.edu

Hintze, J. M., & Shapiro, E. S. (1997). Curriculum-based measurement and literature-based reading: Is curriculum-based measurement meeting the needs of changing reading curricula? *Journal of School Psychology, 35*, 357–375.

Hintze, J. M., Shapiro, E. S., Conte, K. L., & Basile, I. M. (1997). Oral reading fluency and authentic reading material: Criterion validity of the technical features of CBM survey-level assessment. *School Psychology Review, 26*, 535–553.

Hintze, J. M., Shapiro, E. S., & Lutz, J. G. (1994). The effects of curriculum on the sensitivity of curriculum-based measurement in reading. *Journal of Special Education, 28*, 188–202.

Hishinuma, E. S., & Tadaki, S. (1997). The problem with grade and age equivalents: WIAT as a case in point. *Journal of Psychoeducational Assessment, 15*, 214–255.

Hoge, R. D., & Coladarci, T. (1989). Teacher-based judgments of academic achievement: A review of literature. *Review of Educational Research, 59*, 297–313.

Hohn, W. E., & Ehri, L. C. (1983). Do alphabet letters help prereaders acquire phonemic segmentation skills? *Journal of Educational Psychology, 75*, 752–762.

Hoien, T., Lundberg, I., Stanovich, K. E., & Bjaalid, I.-K. (1995). Components of phonological awareness. *Reading and Writing, 7*, 171–188.

Holland, P. W., & Wainer, H. (Eds.). (1993). *Differential item functioning*. Hillsdale, NJ: Erlbaum.

Honig, B., Diamond, L., & Gutlohn, L. (2000). *Teaching reading sourcebook*. Novato, CA: Arena Press.

Honig, B., Diamond, L., & Nathan, R. (1999). *Assessing reading: Multiple measures for kindergarten through eighth grade*. Novato, CA: Arena Press.

Hooper, S. R. (2002). The language of written language: An introduction to the special issue. *Journal of Learning Disabilities, 35*, 2–6.

Hooper, S. R., Montgomery, J., Swartz, C., Reed, M. S., Sandler, A. D., Levine, M. D., et al. (1994). Measurement of written language expression. In G. R. Lyon (Ed.), *Frames of reference for the assessment of learning disabilities: New views on measurement issues* (pp. 375–417). Baltimore: Brookes.

Hoover, H. D., Hieronymus, A. N., Frisbie, D. A., & Dunbar, S. B. (1996). *Iowa Tests of Basic Skills*. Chicago: Riverside.

Hoover, W. A., & Gough, P. B. (1990). The simple view of reading. *Reading and Writing, 2*, 127–160.

Horn, J. L. (1965). *Fluid and crystallized intelligence*. Unpublished doctoral dissertation, University of Illinois.

Horn, J. L. (1988). Thinking about human abilities. In J. R. Nesselroade & R. B. Cattell (Eds.), *Handbook of multivariate psychology* (2nd ed., pp. 645–865). New York: Academic Press.

Hoyt, W. T., & Melby, J. N. (1999). Dependability of measurement in counseling psychology: An introduction to generalizability theory. *The Counseling Psychologist, 27*, 325–352.

Hulme, C., & Roodenrys, S. (1995). Verbal working memory development and its disorders. *Journal of Child Psychology and Psychiatry, 36*, 373–398.

Hultquist, A. M., & Metzke, L. K. (1993). Potential effects of curriculum bias in individual norm-referenced reading and spelling achievement tests. *Journal of Psychoeducational Assessment, 11*, 337–344.

Hurford, D. P., Schauf, J. D., Bunce, L., Blaich, T., & Moore, K. (1994). Early identification of children at risk for reading disabilities. *Journal of Learning Disabilities, 27*, 371–382.

Hutcheson, L., Selig, H., & Young N. (1990). A success story: A large urban district offers a working model for implementing multisensory teaching into the resource and regular classroom. *Annals of Dyslexia, 40*, 79–96.

Hutton, J. B., Dubes, R., & Muir, S. (1992). Assessment practices of school psychologists: Ten years later. *School Psychology Review, 21*, 271–284.

Individuals with Disabilities Education Act, 20 U.S.C. Ch. 33, Sec 1400 (1997).

Invernizzi, M. (1992). The vowel and what follows: A phonological frame of orthographic analysis. In S. Templeton & D. Bear (Eds.), *Development of orthographic knowledge and the foundation of literacy* (pp. 105–136). Hillsdale, NJ: Erlbaum.

Invernizzi, M., & Meier, J. (2002a). *PALS 1-3: Phonological Awareness Literacy Screening 2002–2003*. Charlottesville: Curry School of Education, University of Virginia Press.

Invernizzi, M., & Meier, J. (2002b). *PALS 1-3: Phonological Awareness Literacy Screening 2002–2003 technical reference*. Charlottesville: Curry School of Education, University of Virginia Press.

Invernizzi, M., Meier, J., Swank, L., & Juel, C. (2002a). *PALS-K: Phonological Awareness Literacy Screening Fall 2002*. Charlottesville: Curry School of Education, University of Virginia Press.

Invernizzi, M., Meier, J., Swank, L., & Juel, C. (2002b). *PALS K: Phonological Awareness Literacy Screening 2002–2003 technical reference*. Charlottesville: Curry School of Education, University of Virginia Press.

Invernizzi, M., Robey, R. R., & Moon, T. R. (2000). *PALS: Phonological Awareness Literacy Screening 1998–1999 technical manual and report*. Charlottesville: Curry School of Education, University of Virginia Press.

Invernizzi, M., Rosemary, C., Juel, C., & Richards, H. C. (1997). At-risk readers and community volunteers: A 3-year perspective. *Scientific Studies of Reading 1*, 277–300.

Invernizzi, M., Sullivan, A., & Meier, J. (2002). *PALS-PreK: Phonological Awareness Literacy Screening for Preschool*. Charlottesville: Curry School of Education, University of Virginia Press.

Iversen, S., & Tunmer, W. E. (1993). Phonological processing skills and the Reading Recovery Program. *Journal of Educational Psychology, 85*, 112–126.

Jaeger, R. M. (1989). Review of the Woodcock Reading Mastery Tests–Revised. In J. C. Conoley & J. J. Kramer (Eds.), *The tenth mental measurements yearbook* (pp. 913–916). Lincoln, NE: Buros Institute of Mental Measurements.

Jastak, J. F., & Jastak, S. (1978). *Wide Range Achievement Test*. Wilmington, DE: Jastak Associates.

Jastak, S., & Wilkinson, G. S. (1984). *Wide Range Achievement Test–Revised*. Wilmington, DE: Jastak Associates.

Johns, J. L. (1980). First graders' concepts about print. *Reading Research Quarterly, 15*, 529–549.

Johnson, D. J. (1994). Measurement of listening and speaking. In G. R. Lyon (Ed.), *Frames of reference for the assessment of learning disabilities: New views on measurement issues* (pp. 203–227). Baltimore: Brookes.

Johnston, F. R., Invernizzi, M., & Juel, C. (1998). *Book buddies: Guidelines for volunteer tutors of emergent and early readers*. New York: Guilford Press.

Johnston, R. S. (1998). The role of letter learning in developing phonemic awareness skills in preschool children: Implications for explanations of reading disorders. In C. Hulme & R. M. Joshi (Eds.), *Reading and spelling: Development and disorders* (pp. 287–301). Mahwah, NJ: Erlbaum.

Jorm, A. F., & Share, D. L. (1983). Phonological recoding and reading acquisition. *Applied Psycholinguistics, 4*, 103–147.

Joshi, R. M. (1995). Assessing reading and spelling skills. *School Psychology Review, 24*, 361–375.

Joshi, R. M., Williams, K. A., & Wood, J. R. (1998). Predicting reading comprehension from listening comprehension: Is this the answer to the IQ debate? In C. Hulme & R. M. Joshi (Eds.), *Reading and spelling: Development and disorders* (pp. 319–327). Mahwah, NJ: Erlbaum.

Juel, C. (1988). Learning to read and write: A longitudinal study of 54 children from first through fourth grades. *Journal of Educational Psychology, 80*, 437–447.

Juel, C., Griffith, P. L., & Gough, P. B. (1986). Acquisition of literacy: A longitudinal study of children in first and second grade. *Journal of Educational Psychology, 78*, 243–255.

Kail, R., & Hall, L. K. (1994). Processing speed, naming speed, and reading. *Developmental Psychology, 30*, 949–954.

Kail, R., Hall, L. K., & Caskey, B. J. (1999). Processing speed, exposure to print, and naming speed. *Applied Psycholinguistics, 20*, 303–314.

Kame'enui, E. J. (2002). *Final report on the analysis of reading assessment instruments for K–3*. Eugene: Institute for the Development of Educational Achievement, College of Education, University of Oregon.

Kame'enui, E. J., & Simmons, D. C. (Eds.). (2001). The role of fluency in reading competence, assessment, and instruction: Fluency at the intersection of accuracy and speed [Special issue]. *Scientific Studies of Reading, 5*(1).

Kame'enui, E. J., Simmons, D. C., Good, R. H., & Harn, B. A. (2001). The use of fluency-based measures in early identification and evaluation of intervention efficacy in schools. In M. Wolf (Ed.), *Dyslexia, fluency, and the brain* (pp. 307–414). Timonium, MD: York Press.

Kamhi, A. G., & Catts, H. W. (1999). Reading development. In H. W. Catts & A. G. Kamhi (Eds.), *Language and reading disabilities* (pp. 25–49). Needham Heights, MA: Allyn & Bacon.

Kamhi, A. G., & Catts, H. W. (2002). The language basis of reading: Implications for classification and treatment of children with reading disabilities. In K. G. Butler & E. R. Silliman (Eds.), *Speaking, reading, and writing in children with language learning disabilities: New paradigms in research and practice* (pp. 45–72). Mahwah, NJ: Erlbaum.

Kaminski, R. A., & Good, R. H. (1996). Toward a technology for assessing basic early literacy skills. *School Psychology Review, 25*, 215–227.

Kaminski, R. A., & Good, R. H. (1998). Assessing early literacy skills in a problem-solving model: Dynamic Indicators of Basic Early Literacy Skills. In M. R. Shinn (Ed.), *Advanced applications of curriculum-based measurement* (pp. 113–142). New York: Guilford Press.

Kaplan, E., Goodglass, H., & Weintraub, S. (1983). *The Boston Naming Test.* Philadelphia: Lea & Febiger.

Karlsen, B., Madden, R., & Gardner, E. (1985). *Stanford Diagnostic Reading Test–Third Edition.* San Antonio, TX: Psychological Corporation.

Katz, R. B. (1986). Phonological deficiencies in children with reading disability: Evidence from an object-naming task. *Cognition, 22*, 225–257.

Katz, R. B. (1996). Phonological and semantic factors in the object-naming errors of skilled and less-skilled readers. *Annals of Dyslexia, 46*, 189–208.

Kaufman, A. S., & Kaufman, N. L. (1983). *Kaufman Assessment Battery for Children.* Circle Pines, MN: American Guidance Service.

Kaufman, A. S., & Kaufman, N. L. (1985a). *Kaufman Test of Educational Achievement: Brief Form.* Circle Pines, MN: American Guidance Service.

Kaufman, A. S., & Kaufman, N. L. (1985b). *Kaufman Test of Educational Achievement: Comprehensive Form.* Circle Pines, MN: American Guidance Service.

Kaufman, A. S., & Kaufman, N. L. (1990). *Kaufman Brief Intelligence Test.* Circle Pines, MN: American Guidance Service.

Kaufman, A. S., & Kaufman, N. L. (1993). *Kaufman Survey of Early Academic and Language Skills.* Circle Pines, MN: American Guidance Service.

Kavale, K. A., & Forness, S. R. (2000). Auditory and visual perception processes and reading ability: A quantitative reanalysis and historical reinterpretation. *Learning Disability Quarterly, 23*, 253–270.

Kenny, D. T., & Chekaluk, E. (1993). Early reading performance: A comparison of teacher-based and test-based assessments. *Journal of Learning Disabilities, 26*, 227–236.

Kincaid, J., & McDaniel, W. (1974). *An inexpensive way of calculating Flesch Reading Ease scores* (Patent Disclosure Document No. 0310350, 215). Washington, DC: U.S. Patent Office.

Kingslake, B. (1983). The predictive (in)accuracy of on-entry to school screening procedures when used to anticipate learning difficulties. *British Journal of Special Education, 1*, 23–26.

Kirk, S. A., McCarthy, J. J., & Kirk, W. D. (1968). *Illinois Test of Psycholinguistic Abilities–Revised Edition.* Urbana: University of Illinois Press.

Knoff, H. M., & Dean, K. R. (1994). Curriculum-based measurement of at-risk students' reading skills: A preliminary investigation of bias. *Psychological Reports, 75*, 1355–1360.

Konold, T. R. (1999). Evaluating discrepancy analyses with the WISC–III and WIAT. *Journal of Psychoeducational Assessment, 17*, 24–35.

Korhonen, T. T. (1991). Neuropsychological stability and prognosis of subgroups of children with learning disabilities. *Journal of Learning Disabilities, 24*, 48–57.

Koslin, B. L., Koslin, S., Zeno, S. M., & Ovens, S. H. (1989). *The Degrees of Reading Power Test: Primary and standard forms.* Brewster, NY: Touchstone Applied Science Associates.

Kranzler, J. H., Brownell, M. T., & Miller, M. D. (1998). The construct validity of curriculum-based measurement of reading: An empirical test of a plausible rival hypothesis. *Journal of School Psychology, 36*, 399–415.

Kranzler, J. H., Miller, M. D., & Jordan, L. (1999). An examination of racial/ethnic and gender bias on curriculum-based measurement of reading. *School Psychology Quarterly, 14*, 327–342.

Larrivee, L. S., & Catts, H. W. (1999). Early reading achievement in children with expressive phonological disorders. *American Journal of Speech–Language Pathology, 8*, 118–128.

Larsen, S. C., & Hammill, D. D. (1976). *Test of Written Spelling.* Austin, TX: PRO-ED.

Larsen, S. C., & Hammill, D. D. (1986). *Test of Written Spelling–Second Edition.* Austin, TX: PRO-ED.

Larsen, S. C., & Hammill, D. D. (1994). *Test of Written Spelling–Third Edition.* Austin, TX: PRO-ED.

Larsen, S. C., Hammill, D. D., & Moats, L. C. (1999). *Test of Written Spelling–Fourth Edition.* Austin, TX: PRO-ED.

Leather, C. V., & Henry, L. A. (1994). Working memory span and phonological awareness tasks as predictors of early reading ability. *Journal of Experimental Child Psychology, 58*, 88–111.

Lennon, J. E., & Slesinski, C. (1999). Early intervention in reading: Results of a screening and intervention program for kindergarten students. *School Psychology Review, 28*, 353–364.

Leslie, L., & Caldwell, J. (1995). *Qualitative Reading Inventory–II.* New York: HarperCollins.

Levin, B. E. (1990). Organizational deficits in dyslexia: Possible frontal lobe dysfunction. *Developmental Neuropsychology, 6*(2), 95–110.

Levy, B. A., Abello, B., & Lysynchuk, L. (1997). Transfer from word training to reading in context: Gains in reading fluency and comprehension. *Learning Disabilities Quarterly, 20*, 173–188.

Lewis, B. A., & Freebairn, L. (1992). Residual effects of preschool phonology disorders in grade school, adolescence, and adulthood. *Journal of Speech and Hearing Research, 35*, 819–831.

Lewis, B. A., Freebairn, L. A., & Taylor, H. G. (2000a). Academic outcomes in children with histories of speech sound disorders. *Journal of Communication Disorders, 33*, 11–30.

Lewis, B. A., Freebairn, L. A., & Taylor, H. G. (2000b). Follow-up of children with early expressive phonology disorders. *Journal of Learning Disabilities, 33*, 433–444.

Lewis, B.A., O'Donnell, B., Freebairn, L. A., & Taylor, H. G. (1998). Spoken language and written expression: Interplay of delays. *American Journal of Speech–Language Pathology, 7*, 77–84.

Lexile Framework. (2000). *Lexile system of readability* [Online]. Retrieved from http://www.lexile.com

Liberman, I. Y., & Shankweiler, D. (1985). Phonology and the problems of learning to read and write. *Remedial and Special Education, 6*(6), 8–17.

Limbos, M. M., & Geva, E. (2001). Accuracy of teacher assessments of second-language students at risk for reading disability. *Journal of Learning Disabilities, 34*, 136–151.

Lindamood, C. H., & Lindamood, P. C. (1971/1979). *Lindamood Auditory Conceptualization Test–Revised Edition.* Austin, TX: PRO-ED.

Lindamood, C. H., & Lindamood, P. C. (1998). *The Lindamood phoneme sequencing program for reading, spelling, and speech–Third Edition.* Austin, TX: PRO-ED.

Lindamood, P. C. (1994). Issues in researching the link between phonological awareness, learning disabilities, and spelling. In G. R. Lyon (Ed.), *Frames of reference for the assessment of learning disabilities* (pp. 351–373). Baltimore: Brookes.

Lindamood, P. C., Bell, N., & Lindamood, P. (1992). Issues in phonological awareness assessment. *Annals of Dyslexia, 42*, 242–259.

Lombardino, L. J., Morris, D., Mercado, L., DeFillipo, F., Sarisky, C., & Montgomery, A. (1999). The Early Reading Screening Instrument: A method for identifying kindergartners at risk for learning to read. *International Journal of Language and Communication Disorders, 34*, 135–150.

Lombardino, L. J., Riccio, C. A., Hynd, G. W., & Pinheiro, S. B. (1997). Linguistic deficits in children with reading disabilities. *American Journal of Speech–Language Pathology, 6*(3), 71–78.

Lonigan, C. J., Burgess, S. R., & Anthony, J. L. (2000). Development of emergent literacy and early reading skills in preschool children: Evidence from a latent-variable longitudinal study. *Developmental Psychology, 36*, 596–613.

Lovett, M., Steinbach, K. A., & Frijters, J. C. (2000). Remediating the core deficits of developmental reading disability: A double-deficit perspective. *Journal of Learning Disabilities, 33*, 334–358.

Lundberg, I. (1988). Preschool prevention of reading failure: Does training in phonological awareness work? In R. L. Masland & M. W. Masland (Eds.), *Prevention of reading failure* (pp. 163–176). Parkton, MD: York Press.

Lundberg, I., Frost, J., & Petersen, O.-P. (1988). Effects of an extensive program for stimulating phonological awareness in preschool children. *Reading Research Quarterly, 23*, 263–284.

Lyon, G. R. (1995). Toward a definition of dyslexia. *Annals of Dyslexia, 45*, 3–27.

Lyon, G. R. (1996a). Learning disabilities. *The Future of Children: Special Education for Students with Disabilities, 6*, 54–76.

Lyon, G. R. (1996b). The state of research. In S. C. Cramer & W. Ellis (Eds.), *Learning disabilities: Lifelong issues* (pp. 3–61). Baltimore: Brookes.

Lyon, G. R., Fletcher, J. M., Shaywitz, S. E., Shaywitz, B. A., Torgesen, J. K., Wood, F. B., et al. (2001). Rethinking learning disabilities. In C. E. Finn, Jr., A. J. Rotherham, & C. R. Hokanson, Jr. (Eds.), *Rethinking special education for a new century* (pp. 259–287). Washington, DC: Thomas B. Fordham Foundation.

MacDonald, G. W., & Cornwall, A. (1995). The relationship between phonological awareness and reading and spelling achievement eleven years later. *Journal of Learning Disabilities, 28*, 523–527.

MacGinitie, W. H., Kamons, J., Kowalski, R. L., MacGinitie, R. K., & MacKay, T. (1978). *Gates–MacGinitie Reading Test.* Chicago: Riverside.

Majsterek, D., & Ellenwood, A. (1996). Screening preschoolers for reading learning disabilities: Promising procedures. *LD Forum, 16*, 6–14.

Manis, F. R., Custodio, R., & Szeszulski, P. A. (1993). Development of phonological and orthographic skill: A 2-year longitudinal study of dyslexic children. *Journal of Experimental Child Psychology, 56*, 64–86.

Manis, F. R., Doi, L. M., & Bhadha, B. (2000). Naming speed, phonological awareness, and orthographic knowledge in second graders. *Journal of Learning Disabilities, 33*, 325–333, 374.

Manis, F. R., Seidenberg, M. S., & Doi, L. M. (1999). See Dick RAN: Rapid naming and the longitudinal prediction of reading subskills in first and second graders. *Scientific Studies of Reading, 3*, 129–157.

Manis, F. R., Seidenberg, M. S., Doi, L. M., McBride-Chang, C., & Peterson, A. (1996). On the basis of two subtypes of developmental dyslexia. *Cognition, 58*, 157–195.

Manis, F. R., Szeszulski, P. A., Holt, L. K., & Graves, K. (1988). A developmental perspective on dyslexic subtypes. *Annals of Dyslexia, 38*, 139–153.

Mann, V. A. (1993). Phoneme awareness and future reading ability. *Journal of Learning Disabilities, 26*, 259–269.

Mann, V. A., Cowin, E., & Schoenheimer, J. (1989). Phonological processing, language comprehension, and reading ability. *Journal of Learning Disabilities, 22*(2), 76–89.

Mann, V. A., & Ditunno, P. (1990). Phonological deficiencies: Effective predictors of future reading problems. In G. T. Pavlidis (Ed.), *Perspectives on dyslexia: Vol. 2. Cognition, language and treatment* (pp. 105–131). Chichester, UK: Wiley.

Mann, V. A., & Liberman, I. Y. (1984). Phonological awareness and short-term memory. *Journal of Learning Disabilities, 17*, 592–599.

Mann, V. A., Tobin, P., & Wilson, R. (1987). Measuring phonological awareness through the invented spellings of kindergarten children. *Merrill-Palmer Quarterly, 33*, 365–391.

Mantzicopoulos, P. Y., & Morrison, D. (1994). Early prediction of reading achievement: Exploring the relationship of cognitive and noncognitive measures to inaccurate classifications of at-risk status. *Remedial and Special Education, 15*(4), 244–251.

Mardell-Czudnowski, C. D., & Goldenberg, D. S. (1990). *Developmental Indicators for the Assessment of Learning–Revised.* Circle Pines, MN: American Guidance Service.

Margolese, S. K., & Kline, R. B. (1999). Prediction of basic reading skills among young children with diverse linguistic backgrounds. *Canadian Journal of Behavioural Science, 31*(4), 209–216.

Markell, M. A., & Deno, S. L. (1997). Effects of increasing oral reading: Generalization across reading tasks. *Journal of Special Education, 31*, 233–250.

Markwardt, F. C. (1989). *Peabody Individual Achievement Test–Revised.* Circle Pines, MN: American Guidance Service.

Marston, D. B. (1989). A curriculum-based measurement approach to assessing academic performance: What it is and why do it. In M. R. Shinn (Ed.), *Curriculum-based measurement: Assessing special children* (pp. 18–78). New York: Guilford Press.

Marston, D., & Magnusson, D. (1985). Implementing curriculum-based measurement in special and regular education settings. *Exceptional Children, 52*, 266–276.

Martens, B. K., Steele, E. S., Massie, D. R., & Diskin, M. T. (1995). Curriculum bias in standardized tests of reading decoding. *Journal of School Psychology, 33*, 287–296.

Mather, N., & Jaffe, L. E. (2002). *Woodcock–Johnson III: Reports, recommendations, and strategies.* New York: Wiley.

Mather, N., & Woodcock, R. W. (2001a). *Examiner's manual: Woodcock–Johnson III Tests of Achievement.* Itasca: IL: Riverside.

Mather, N., & Woodcock, R. W. (2001b). *Examiner's manual: Woodcock–Johnson III Tests of Cognitive Abilities.* Itasca: IL: Riverside.

Mathes, P. G., Torgesen, J. K., & Allor, J. H. (2001). The effects of peer-assisted literacy strategies for first-grade readers with and without additional computer-assisted instruction in phonological awareness. *American Educational Research Journal, 38*, 371–410.

McBride-Chang, C. (1995). What is phonological awareness? *Journal of Educational Psychology, 87*, 179–192.

McBride-Chang, C. (1998). The development of invented spelling. *Early Education and Development, 9*(2), 147–160.

McBride-Chang, C. (1999). The ABCs of the ABCs: The development of letter-name and letter-sound knowledge. *Merrill-Palmer Quarterly, 45*, 285–308.

McBride-Chang, C., & Manis, F. R. (1996). Structural invariance in the association of naming speed, phonological awareness, and verbal reasoning in good and poor readers: A test of the double deficit hypothesis. *Reading and Writing, 8*, 323–339.

McCabe, P. P., Margolis, H., & Barenbaum, E. (2001). A comparison of Woodcock-Johnson Psycho-Educational Battery–Revised and Qualitative Reading Inventory–II instructional reading levels. *Reading and Writing Quarterly: Overcoming Learning Difficulties, 17*, 279–289.

McCarthy, J. J., & Kirk, S. A. (1961). *Illinois Test of Psycholinguistic Abilities–Experimental Edition.* Urbana: University of Illinois, Institute for Research on Exceptional Children.

McDougall, S., Hulme, C., Ellis, A., & Monk, A. (1994). Learning to read: The role of short-term memory and phonological skills. *Journal of Experimental Child Psychology, 58*, 112–133.

McGrew, K. S. (1993). The relationship between the Woodcock–Johnson Psycho-Educational Battery–Revised *Gf-Gc* cognitive clusters and reading achievement across the life-span. *Journal of Psychoeducational Assessment* [Monograph Series], 39–53.

McGrew, K. S. (1994). *Clinical interpretation of the Woodcock–Johnson Tests of Cognitive Ability–Revised.* Needham Heights, MA: Allyn & Bacon.

McGrew, K. S. (1999). *Applied psychometrics 102: All ability–achievement discrepancy score procedures are not created equal: A hierarchy of discrepancy procedures* [Online]. Retrieved from http://www.iapsych.com/iaprr5.htm

McGrew, K. S., & Flanagan, D. P. (1998). *The intelligence test desk reference (ITDR): Gf-Gc cross-battery assessment.* Needham Heights, MA: Allyn & Bacon.

McGrew, K. S., & Knopik, S. N. (1993). The relationship between the WJ-R *Gf-Gc* cognitive clusters and writing achievement across the life span. *School Psychology Review, 22,* 687–695.

McGrew, K. S., & Woodcock, R. W. (2001). *Technical manual: Woodcock–Johnson III.* Itasca, IL: Riverside.

McGrew, K. S., Werder, J. K., & Woodcock, R. W. (1991). *WJ-R technical manual.* Allen, TX: DLM Teaching Resources.

McGuinness, D. (1997). Decoding strategies as predictors of reading skill: A follow-on study. *Annals of Dyslexia, 47,* 117–150.

McGuinness, D., McGuinness, C., & Donohue, J. (1995). Phonological training and the alphabet principle: Evidence for reciprocal causality. *Reading Research Quarterly, 30,* 830–852.

Mehrens, W. A., & Clarizio, H. F. (1993). Curriculum-based measurement: Conceptual and psychometric considerations. *Psychology in the Schools, 30,* 241–254.

Messick, S. (1989a). Meaning and values in test validation: The science and ethics of assessment. *Educational Researcher, 18,* 5–11.

Messick, S. (1989b). Validity. In R. L. Linn (Ed.), *Educational measurement* (3rd ed., pp. 13–103). New York: Macmillan.

Messick, S. (1995). Validity of psychological assessment: Validation of inferences from persons' responses and performances as scientific inquiry into score meaning. *American Psychologist, 50,* 741–749.

Meyer, M. S. (2000). The ability–achievement discrepancy: Does it contribute to an understanding of learning disabilities? *Educational Psychology Review, 12,* 315–337.

Meyer, M. S., & Felton, R. H. (1999). Repeated reading to enhance fluency: Old approaches and new directions. *Annals of Dyslexia, 49,* 283–306.

Meyer, M. S., Wood, F. B., Hart, L. A., & Felton, R. H. (1998a). Longitudinal course of rapid naming in disabled and nondisabled readers. *Annals of Dyslexia, 48,* 91–114.

Meyer, M. S., Wood, F. B., Hart, L. A., & Felton, R. H. (1998b). Selective predictive value of rapid automatized naming in poor readers. *Journal of Learning Disabilities, 31,* 106–117.

Moats, L. C. (1994). The missing foundation in teacher education: Knowledge of the structure of spoken and written language. *Annals of Dyslexia, 44,* 81–102.

Moats, L. C. (1995). *Spelling: Development, disability, and instruction.* Baltimore: York Press.

Moats, L. C. (1999, June). *Teaching reading is rocket science: What expert teachers of reading should know and be able to do* [Online]. Retrieved from http://www.aft.org/edissues/rocketscience.htm

Moats, L. C., & Lyon, G. R. (1996). Wanted: Teachers with knowledge of language. *Topics in Language Disorders, 16*(2), 73–86.

Mogliner, A. (1992). *Children's writer's word book.* Cincinnati, OH: Writer's Digest Books.

Morris, D. (1992a). Concept of word: A pivotal understanding in the learning-to-read process. In S. Templeton & D. R. Bear (Eds.), *Development of orthographic knowledge and the foundations of literacy: A memorial festschrift for Edmund H. Henderson* (pp. 53–77). Hillsdale, NJ: Erlbaum.

Morris, D. (1992b). What constitutes at-risk: Screening children for first grade reading intervention. In W. A. Secord & J. S. Damico (Eds.), *Best practices in school speech–language pathology: Vol. 2. Descriptive/nonstandardized language assessment* (pp. 43–51). San Antonio, TX: Psychological Corporation.

Morris, D. (1993). The relationship between children's concept of word in text and phoneme awareness in learning to read: A longitudinal study. *Research in the Teaching of English, 27,* 133–154.

Morris, D., & Perney, J. (1984). Developmental spelling as a predictor of first-grade reading achievement. *Elementary School Journal, 84*, 441–457.

Morris, R. D., Stuebing, K. K., Fletcher, J. M., Shaywitz, S. E., Lyon, G. R., Shankweiler, D. P., et al. (1998). Subtypes of reading disability: Variability around a phonological core. *Journal of Educational Psychology, 90*, 347–373.

Muehl, S., & Di Nello, M. C. (1976). Early first-grade skills related to subsequent reading performance: A seven year followup study. *Journal of Reading Behavior, 8*, 67–81.

Muenz, T. A., Ouchi, B. Y., & Cole, J. C. (1999). Item analysis of written expression scoring systems from the PIAT-R and WIAT. *Psychology in the Schools, 36*, 31–40.

Murphy, S. (1998). *Fragile evidence: A critique of reading assessment.* Mahwah, NJ: Erlbaum.

Muter, V. (1996). Predicting children's reading and spelling difficulties. In M. Snowling & J. Stackhouse (Eds.), *Dyslexia, speech and language: A practitioner's handbook* (pp. 31–44). San Diego, CA: Singular.

Muter, V. (2000). Screening for early reading failure. In N. A. Badian (Ed.), *Prediction and prevention of reading failure* (pp. 1–29). Baltimore: York Press.

Muter, V., Hulme, C., & Snowling, M. (1997). *Phonological Abilities Test.* London: Psychological Corporation.

Muter, V., Hulme, C., Snowling, M., & Taylor, S. (1998). Segmentation, not rhyming, predicts early progress in learning to read. *Journal of Experimental Child Psychology, 71*, 3–27.

Muter, V., & Snowling, M. (1998). Concurrent and longitudinal predictors of reading: The role of metalinguistic and short-term memory skills. *Reading Research Quarterly, 33*, 320–337.

Nathan, R. G., & Stanovich, K. E. (1991). The causes and consequences of differences in reading fluency. *Theory into Practice, 30*, 176–184.

Nation, K. (1999). Reading skills in hyperlexia: A developmental perspective. *Psychological Bulletin, 125*, 338–355.

Nation, K., & Snowling, M. (1997). Assessing reading difficulties: The validity and utility of current measures of reading skill. *British Journal of Educational Psychology, 67*, 359–370.

Nation, K., & Snowling, M. (1998a). Individual differences in contextual facilitation: Evidence from dyslexia and poor reading comprehension. *Child Development, 69*, 996–1011.

Nation, K., & Snowling, M. (1998b). Semantic processing and the development of word-recognition skills: Evidence from children with reading comprehension difficulties. *Journal of Memory and Language, 39*, 85–101.

National Association of School Psychologists. (2000). *Professional conduct manual* [Online]. Bethesda, MD: Author. Available at http://www.naspweb.org

National Center for Education Statistics. (1995). *Listening to children read aloud: Oral fluency, Vol. 1*(1). (NCES Publication No. 95-762). Washington, DC: U.S. Department of Education.

National Center for Education Statistics. (2002). *The nation's report card: Reading 2002* (NCES 2003-521) [Online]. Washington, DC: U.S. Department of Education. Available at http:/nces.ed.gov/nationsreportcard/reading

National Center for Education Statistics. (2003). *The nation's report card: Writing 2002* (NCES 2003-529) [Online]. Washington, DC: U.S. Department of Education. Available at http:/nces.ed.gov/nationsreportcard/writing

National Reading Panel. (2000). *Teaching children to read: An evidence-based assessment of the scientific research literature on reading and its implications for reading instruction.* Bethesda, MD: National Institute of Child Health and Human Development.

Neuhaus, G., Foorman, B. R., Francis, D. J., & Carlson, C. D. (2001). Measures of information processing in rapid automatized naming (RAN) and their relation to reading. *Journal of Experimental Child Psychology, 78*, 359–373.

Neuhaus, G. F., & Swank, P. R. (2002). Understanding the relations between RAN letter subtest components and word reading in first-grade students. *Journal of Learning Disabilities, 35*, 158–174.

Neuman, S. B. (1999). Books make a difference: A study of access to literacy. *Reading Research Quarterly, 34*, 286–311.

Newborg, J., Stock, J. R., Wnek, L., Guidubaldi, J., & Svinicki, J. (1984). *Battelle Developmental Inventory*. Allen, TX: DLM Teaching Resources.

Newcomer, P. L. (1986). *Standardized Reading Inventory*. Austin, TX: PRO-ED.

Newcomer, P. L. (1990). *Diagnostic Achievement Battery–2*. Austin, TX: PRO-ED.

Newcomer, P. L. (1999). *Standardized Reading Inventory–Second Edition.* Austin, TX: PRO-ED.

Newcomer, P. L., & Hammill, D. D. (1997). *Test of Language Development–Primary: Third Edition* Austin, TX: PRO-ED.

Nicolson, R. I., & Fawcett, A. J. (1994). Comparison of deficits in cognitive and motor skills among children with dyslexia. *Annals of Dyslexia, 44*, 147–164.

Nicolson, R. I., & Fawcett, A. J. (1996). *Dyslexia Early Screening Test.* London: Psychological Corporation.

Nicolson, R. I., & Fawcett, A. J. (1999). Developmental dyslexia: The role of the cerebellum. *Dyslexia: An International Journal of Research and Practice, 5*, 155–177.

Nicolson, R. I., & Fawcett, A. J. (2001). Dyslexia, learning and the cerebellum. In M. Wolf (Ed.), *Dyslexia, fluency, and the brain* (pp. 159–187). Timonium, MD: York Press.

Nicolson, R. I., Fawcett, A. J., Moss, H., & Nicolson, M. K. (1999). Early reading intervention can be effective and cost-effective. *British Journal of Educational Psychology, 69*, 47–62.

Nicolson, T. (1991). Do children read words better in context or in lists?: A classic study revisited. *Journal of Educational Psychology, 83*, 444–450.

Noell, G. H., Freeland, J. T., Witt, J. C., & Gansle, K. A. (2001). Using brief assessments to identify effective interventions for individual students. *Journal of School Psychology, 39*, 319–355.

Nurss, J. R., & McGauvran, M. E. (1976). *Metropolitan Readiness Tests–Fourth Edition.* San Antonio, TX: Psychological Corporation.

Nurss, J. R., & McGauvran, M. E. (1986). *Metropolitan Readiness Test–Fifth Edition.* San Antonio, TX: Psychological Corporation.

O'Connor, R. E., & Jenkins, J. R. (1999). Prediction of reading disabilities in kindergarten and first grade. *Scientific Studies of Reading, 3*, 159–197.

Olson, R., Forsberg, H., Wise, B., & Rack, J. (1994). Measurement of word recognition, orthographic, and phonological skills. In G. R. Lyon (Ed.), *Frames of reference for the assessment of learning disabilities: New views on measurement issues* (pp. 243–277). Baltimore: Brookes.

Olson, R., Wise, B., Conners, F., Rack, J., & Fulker, D. (1989). Specific deficits in component reading and language skills: Genetic and environmental influences. *Journal of Learning Disabilities*, 22, 339–348.

Osgood, C. E. (1957). A behavioristic analysis of perception and language as cognitive phenomena. In University of Colorado (Boulder Campus) Department of Psychology, *Contemporary approaches to cognition* (pp. 75–118). Cambridge, MA: Harvard University Press.

Osgood, C. E., & Miron, M. S. (1963). *Approaches to the study of aphasia*. Urbana: University of Illinois Press.

Otis, A. S., & Lennon, R. T. (1982). *Otis-Lennon School Ability Test–Fifth Edition.* San Antonio, TX: Psychological Corporation.

Otis, A. S., & Lennon, R. T. (1989). *Otis-Lennon School Ability Test–Sixth Edition.* New York: Harcourt Brace Jovanovich.

Otis, A. S., & Lennon, R. T. (1995). *Otis-Lennon School Ability Test–Seventh Edition.* San Antonio, TX: Harcourt Brace Educational Measurement.

Parker, R., Tindal, G., & Hasbrouck, J. (1991). Countable indices of writing quality: Their suitability for screening-eligibility decisions. *Exceptionality, 2*, 1–17.

Pena, E. D., & Quinn, R. (1997). Task familiarity: Effects on the test performance of Puerto Rican and African American children. *Language, Speech and Hearing Services in the Schools, 28*, 323–332.

Pennington, B. F., Van Orden, G., Kirson, D., & Haith, M. (1991). What is the causal relation between verbal STM problems and dyslexia? In S. Brady & D. Shankweiler (Eds.), *Phonological processes in literacy: A tribute to Isabelle Y. Liberman* (pp. 173–186). Hillsdale, NJ: Erlbaum.

Perney, J., Morris, D., & Carter, S. (1997). Factorial and predictive validity of first graders' scores on the Early Reading Screening Instrument. *Psychological Reports, 81*, 207–211.

Pinnell, G. S., McCarrier, A., & Button, K. (1990). *Constructing literacy in urban kindergartens: Progress report on the Kindergarten Early Literacy Project* (Report No. 10, MacArthur Foundation). Columbus: Ohio State University.

Plante, E., & Vance, R. (1994). Selection of preschool language tests: A data-based approach. *Language, Speech, and Hearing Services in Schools, 25*, 15–24.

Plante, E., & Vance, R. (1995). Diagnostic accuracy of two tests of preschool language. *American Journal of Speech–Language Pathology, 4*, 70–76.

Prescott, G. A., Balow, I. H., Hogan, T. P., & Farr, R. C. (1985). *Metropolitan Achievement Tests–Sixth Edition.* San Antonio, TX: Psychological Corporation.

Psychological Corporation. (1992a). *Metropolitan Achievement Tests–Sixth Edition.* San Antonio, TX: Author.

Psychological Corporation. (1992b). *Wechsler Individual Achievement Test.* San Antonio, TX: Author.

Psychological Corporation. (1993). *Wechsler Objective Reading Dimensions.* Sidcup, UK: Author.

Psychological Corporation. (2000). *Early Reading Diagnostic Assessment.* San Antonio, TX: Author.

Psychological Corporation. (2001a). *Wechsler Individual Achievement Test–Second Edition.* San Antonio, TX: Author.

Psychological Corporation. (2001b). *Wechsler Individual Achievement Test–Second Edition, Abbreviated.* San Antonio, TX: Author.

Psychological Corporation. (2002). *Early Reading Diagnostic Assessment–Revised.* San Antonio, TX: Author.

Purvis, K. L., & Tannock, R. (1997). Language abilities in children with attention deficit hyperactivity disorder, reading disabilities, and normal controls. *Journal of Abnormal Child Psychology, 25*, 133–144.

Quiroga, T., Lemos-Britton, Z., Mostafapour, E., Abbott, R. D., & Berninger, V. W. (2002). Phonological awareness and beginning reading in Spanish-speaking ESL first graders: Research into practice. *Journal of School Psychology, 40*, 85–111.

Raban, B. (1988). *The spoken vocabulary of five-year-old children.* Reading, UK: Reading and Language Information Centre, University of Reading.

Rack, J. P., Snowling, M. J., & Olson, R. K. (1992). The nonword reading deficit in developmental dyslexia: A review. *Reading Research Quarterly, 27*, 29–53.

Rapala, M. M., & Brady, S. (1990). Reading ability and short-term memory: The role of phonological processing. *Reading and Writing, 2*, 1–25.

Rasinski, T. V., & Padak, N. D. (2001). *From phonics to fluency.* New York: Addison Wesley Longman.

Rathvon, N. (1999). *Effective school interventions: Strategies for enhancing academic achievement and social competence.* New York: Guilford Press.

Raz, I. S., & Bryant, P. (1990). Social background, phonological awareness and children's reading. *British Journal of Developmental Psychology, 8*, 209–225.

Read, C. (1971). Pre-school children's knowledge of English phonology. *Harvard Educational Review, 41*(1), 1–34.

Read, C. (1986). *Children's creative spelling.* London: Routledge & Kegan Paul.

Reid, D. K., Hresko, W. P., & Hammill, D. D. (1989). *Test of Early Reading Ability–Second Edition.* Austin, TX: PRO-ED.

Reid, D. K., Hresko, W. P., & Hammill, D. D. (2001). *Test of Early Reading Ability–Third Edition.* Austin, TX: PRO-ED.

Reynolds, C. R. (1984–1985). Critical measurement issues in learning disabilities. *Journal of Special Education, 18*, 451–476.

Reynolds, C. R. (1990). Conceptual and technical problems in learning disability diagnosis. In C. R. Reynolds & R. W. Kamphaus (Eds.), *Handbook of psychological and educational assessment of children: Intelligence and achievement* (pp. 571–592). New York: Guilford Press.

Reynolds, C. R., & Kamphaus, R. W. (1992). *Behavior Assessment System for Children.* Circle Pines, MN: American Guidance Service.

Riccio, C. A., Boan, C. H., Staniszewski, D., & Hynd, G. W. (1997). Concurrent validity of standardized measures of written expression. *Diagnostique, 23*, 203–211.

Richardson, E., & DeBenedetto, B. (1985). *Decoding Skills Test.* Timonium, MD: York Press.

Richgels, D. J. (1995). Invented spelling ability and printed word learning in kindergarten. *Reading Research Quarterly, 30*, 96–109.

Riverside. (2000). *Gates–MacGinitie Reading Tests—Fourth Edition.* Itasca, IL: Author.

Riverside. (2002). *Basic Early Assessment of Reading.* Itasca, IL: Author.

Roberts, B. (1992). The evolution of the young child's concept of *word* as a unit of spoken and written language. *Reading Research Quarterly, 27*, 124–138.

Roberts, R., & Mather, N. (1997). Orthographic dyslexia: The neglected subtype. *Learning Disabilities Research and Practice, 12*, 236–250.

Robertson, C., & Salter, W. (1995). *Phonological Awareness Profile.* East Moline, IL: LinguiSystems.

Robertson, C., & Salter, W. (1997). *Phonological Awareness Test.* East Moline, IL: LinguiSystems.

Rodrigues, M., & Stieglitz, E. L. (1997). *Readability Master 2000* [Computer softerware]. Cambridge, MA: Brookline Books.

Roid, G. H., & Miller, L. J. (1997). *Leiter International Performance Scale–Revised Edition.* Wood Dale, IL: Stoelting.

Rosner, J. (1975/1979). *Test of Auditory Analysis Skills.* Novato, CA: Academic Therapy.

Rosner, J. (1993). *Helping children overcome learning difficulties* (3rd ed.). New York: Walker.

Rosner, J., & Simon, D. P. (1971). The Auditory Analysis Test: An initial report. *Journal of Learning Disabilities, 4*, 40–48.

Rudel, R. G., Denckla, M. B., & Broman, M. (1978). Rapid silent response to repeated target symbols by dyslexic and nondyslexic children. *Brain and Language, 6*, 52–62.

Rumelhart, D. E. (1977). Toward an interactive model of reading. In S. Dornic & P. Rabbitt (Eds.), *Attention and performance IV.* Hillsdale, NJ: Erlbaum.

Salvia, J., & Ysseldyke, J. E. (2001). *Assessment* (8th ed.). Boston: Houghton Mifflin.

Santa, C. M., & Hoien, T. (1999). An assessment of Early Steps: A program for early intervention of reading problems. *Reading Research Quarterly, 34*, 54–79.

Satz, P., & Fletcher, J. M. (1988). Early identification of learning disabled children: An old problem revisited. *Journal of Consulting and Clinical Psychology, 56*, 824–829.

Sawyer, D. J., Kim, J. K., & Lipa-Wade, S. (2000). Application of Frith's developmental phase model to the process of identifying at-risk beginning readers. In N. A. Badian (Ed.), *Prediction and prevention of reading failure* (pp. 87–103). Baltimore: York Press.

Scanlon, D. M., & Vellutino, F. R. (1996). Prerequisite skills, early instruction, and success in first-grade reading: Selected results from a longitudinal study. *Mental Retardation and Developmental Disabilities Research Reviews, 2*, 54–63.

Scanlon, D. M., & Vellutino, F. R. (1997). A comparison of the instructional backgrounds and cognitive profiles of poor, average, and good readers who were initially identified as at risk for reading failure. *Scientific Studies of Reading, 1*, 191–215.

Scarborough, H. S. (1990). Very early language deficits in dyslexic children. *Child Development, 61*, 1728–1743.

Scarborough, H. S. (1998a). Early identification of children at risk for reading disabilities: Phonological awareness and some other promising predictors. In B. K. Shapiro, P. J. Accardo, & A. J. Capute (Eds.), *Specific reading disability: A view of the spectrum* (pp. 75–120). Timonium, MD: York Press.

Scarborough, H. S. (1998b). Predicting the future achievement of second graders with reading disabilities: Contributions of phonemic awareness, verbal memory, rapid naming, and IQ. *Annals of Dyslexia, 48,* 115–136.

Scarborough, H. S., & Dobrich, W. (1990). Development of children with early language delay. *Journal of Speech and Hearing Research, 33,* 70–83.

Schatschneider, C., Carlson, C. D., Francis, D. J., Foorman, B. R., & Fletcher, J. M. (2002). Relationship of rapid automatized naming and phonological awareness in early reading development: Implications for the double-deficit hypothesis. *Journal of Learning Disabilities, 35,* 245–256.

Schatschneider, C., Francis, D. J., Foorman, B. R., Fletcher, J. M., & Mehta, P. (1999). The dimensionality of phonological awareness: An application of item response theory. *Journal of Educational Psychology, 91,* 439–449.

Schneider, W., Kuespert, P., Roth, E., & Vise, M. (1997). Short- and long-term effects of training phonological awareness in kindergarten: Evidence from two German studies. *Journal of Experimental Child Psychology, 66,* 311–340.

Schrank, F. A., Flanagan, D. P., Woodcock, R. W., & Mascolo, J. T. (2002). *Essentials of WJ III Cognitive Abilities assessment.* New York: Wiley.

Schrank, F. A., & Woodcock, R. W. (2002). *Report Writer for the WJ III* [Computer software]. Itasca, IL: Riverside.

Semel, E., Wiig, E. H., & Secord, W. A. (1995). *Clinical Evaluation of Language Fundamentals–Third Edition: Examiner's manual.* San Antonio, TX: Psychological Corporation.

Semrud-Clikeman, M., Guy, K., Griffin, J. D., & Hynd, G. W. (2000). Rapid naming deficits in children and adolescents with reading disabilities and attention deficit hyperactivity disorder. *Brain and Language, 74,* 70–83.

Sénéchal, J., LeFevre, J., Smith-Chant, B. L., & Colton, K. V. (2001). On refining theoretical models of emergent literacy: The role of empirical evidence. *Journal of School Psychology, 39,* 439–460.

Shankweiler, D., Crain, S., Katz, L., Fowler, A. E., Liberman, A. M., Brady, S. A., et al. (1995). Cognitive profiles of reading-disabled children: Comparison of language skills in phonology, morphology, and syntax. *Psychological Science, 6,* 149–156.

Shankweiler, D., Lundquist, E., Katz, L., Stuebing, K. K., Fletcher, J. M., Brady, S., et al. (1999). Comprehension and decoding: Patterns of associations in children with reading difficulties. *Scientific Studies of Reading, 3,* 69–94.

Shapiro, E. S. (1989). *Academic skills problems: Direct assessment and intervention.* New York: Guilford Press.

Shapiro, E. S. (1996). *Academic skills problems: Direct assessment and intervention* (2nd ed.). New York: Guilford Press.

Shapiro, E. S., & Derr, T. F. (1987). An examination of overlap between reading curricula and standardized achievement tests. *Journal of Special Education, 21*(2), 59–67.

Share, D. L. (1995). Phonological recoding and self-teaching: *Sine qua non* of reading acquisition. *Cognition, 55,* 151–218.

Share, D. L., Jorm, A. F., Maclean, R., & Matthews, R. (1984). Sources of individual differences in reading acquisition. *Journal of Educational Psychology, 76,* 1309–1324.

Share, D. L., & Stanovich, K. E. (1995). Cognitive processes in early reading development: Accommodating individual differences into a model of acquisition. *Issues in Education, 1,* 1–57.

Sharpley, C. F., & Stone, J. M. (1985). An exploratory investigation to detect cross-cultural differences on the PPVT–R. *Psychology in the Schools, 22,* 383–386.

Shavelson, R. J., & Webb, N. M. (1991). *Generalizability theory: A primer.* Newbury Park, CA: Sage.

Shaywitz, S. E., Escobar, M. D., Shaywitz, B. A., Fletcher, J. M., & Makuch, R. (1992). Evidence that dyslexia may represent the lower tail of a normal distribution of reading ability. *New England Journal of Medicine, 326,* 145–150.

Shaywitz, S. E., Fletcher, J. M., & Shaywitz, B. A. (1994). Issues in the definition and classification of attention deficit disorder. *Topics in Language Disorders, 14*(4), 1–25.

Shaywitz, S. E., Shaywitz, B. A., Fletcher, J. M., & Escobar, M. D. (1990). Prevalence of reading disability in boys and girls: Results of the Connecticut Longitudinal Study. *Journal of the American Medical Association, 264,* 998–1002.

Shinn, M. R. (Ed.). (1989). *Curriculum-based measurement: Assessing special children.* New York: Guilford Press.

Shinn, M. R. (1995). Best practices in curriculum-based measurement and its use in a problem-solving model. In A. Thomas & J. Grimes (Eds.), *Best practices in school psychology III* (pp. 547-567). Washington, DC: National Association of School Psychologists.

Shinn, M. R. (Ed.). (1998). *Advanced applications of curriculum-based measurement.* New York: Guilford Press.

Shinn, M. R., Good, R. H., Knutson, N., Tilly, W. D., & Collins, V. L. (1992). Curriculum-based measurement of oral reading fluency: A confirmatory analysis of its relation to reading. *School Psychology Review, 21,* 459–479.

Shinn, M. R., Good, R. H., & Stein, S. (1989). Summarizing trends in student achievement: A comparison of methods. *School Psychology Review, 18,* 356–370.

Short, E. J., & Ryan, E. B. (1984). Metacognitive differences between skilled and less skilled readers: Remediating deficits through story grammar and attribution training. *Journal of Educational Psychology, 76,* 225–235.

Shrout, P. E., & Fleiss, J. L. (1979). Intraclass correlations: Uses in assessing rater reliability. *Psychological Bulletin, 86,* 420–428.

Siegel, L. S. (1998). Phonological processing deficits and reading disabilities. In J. L. Metsala & L. C. Ehri (Eds.), *Word recognition in beginning literacy* (pp. 141–160). Mahwah, NJ: Erlbaum.

Siegel, L. S., & Ryan, E. B. (1988). Development of grammatical-sensitivity, phonological, and short-term memory skills in normally achieving and learning disabled children. *Developmental Psychology, 24,* 28–37.

Siegel, L. S., Share, D., & Geva, E. (1995). Evidence for superior orthographic skills in dyslexics. *Psychological Science, 6,* 250–254.

Slate, J. R. (1996). Interrelations of frequently administered achievement measures in the determination of specific learning disabilities. *Learning Disabilities Research and Practice, 11,* 86–89.

Smith, F. (1975). The role of prediction in reading. *Elementary English, 52,* 305-311.

Smith, F. (1979). *Reading without nonsense.* New York: Teachers College Press.

Smith, T. D., & Smith, B. L. (1998). Relationship between the Wide Range Achievement Test 3 and the Wechsler Individual Achievement Test. *Psychological Reports, 83,* 963–967.

Snow, C. E. (2002). *Reading for understanding: Toward a research and development program in reading comprehension* [Online]. Retrieved from http://www.rand.org/publications

Snow, C. E., Burns, M. S., & Griffin, P. (1998). *Preventing reading difficulties in young children.* Washington, DC: National Academy Press.

Snow, C. E., Tabors, P. O., Nicholson, P. A., & Kurland, B. F. (1995). SHELL: Oral language and early literacy skills in kindergarten and first-grade children. *Journal of Research in Childhood Education, 10,* 37–48.

Snowling, M. J. (1981). Phonemic deficits in developmental dyslexia. *Psychological Research, 43,* 219–234.

Snyder, L. S., & Downey, D. M. (1991). The language–reading relationship in normal and reading-disabled children. *Journal of Speech and Hearing Research, 34,* 129–140.

Snyder, L. S., & Downey, D. M. (1995). Serial rapid naming skills in children with reading disabilities. *Annals of Dyslexia, 45,* 31–49.

Southern California Comprehensive Assistance Center. (2002). *Taking a reading: A teacher's guide to reading assessment.* Los Angeles: Reading Success Network, Los Angeles County Office of Education.

Spector, J. E. (1992). Predicting progress in beginning reading: Dynamic assessment of phonemic awareness. *Journal of Educational Psychology, 84,* 353–363.

Speece, D. L., & Case, L. P. (2001). Classification in context: An alternative approach to identifying early reading disability. *Journal of Educational Psychology, 93,* 735–749.

Speer, O. B., & Lamb, G. S. (1976). First grade reading ability and fluency in naming verbal symbols. *The Reading Teacher, 29,* 572–576.

Spring, C., & Davis, J. M. (1988). Relations of digit naming speed with three components of reading. *Applied Psycholinguistics, 9,* 315–334.

Spring, C., & French, L. (1990). Identifying children with specific reading disabilities from listening and reading discrepancy scores. *Journal of Learning Disabilities, 23,* 53–58.

Stage, S. A., Abbott, R. D., Jenkins, J. R., & Berninger, V. W. (2003). Predicting response to early reading intervention from verbal IQ, reading-related language abilities, attention ratings, and verbal IQ–word reading discrepancy: Failure to validate discrepancy method. *Journal of Learning Disabiltiies, 36,* 24–33.

Stage, S. A., Sheppard, J., Davidson, M. M., & Browning, M. M. (2001). Prediction of first-graders' growth in oral reading fluency using kindergarten letter fluency. *Journal of School Psychology, 39,* 225–237.

Stage, S. A., & Wagner, R. K. (1992). Development of young children's phonological and orthographic knowledge as revealed by their spellings. *Developmental Psychology, 28,* 287–296.

Stahl, S. A., & Murray, B. A. (1994). Defining phonological awareness and its relationship to early reading. *Journal of Educational Psychology, 86,* 221–234.

Stanovich, K. E. (1981). Relationships between word decoding speed, general name-retrieval ability, and reading progress in first-grade children. *Journal of Educational Psychology,* 73, 809–815.

Stanovich, K. E. (1986). Matthew effects in reading: Some consequences of individual differences in the acquisition of literacy. *Reading Research Quarterly, 21,* 360–407.

Stanovich, K. E. (1991). Changing models of reading and reading acquisition. In L. Rieben & C. A. Perfetti (Eds.), *Learning to read: Basic research and its implications* (pp. 19–32). Hillsdale, NJ: Erlbaum.

Stanovich, K. E., Cunningham, A. E., & Cramer, B. B. (1984). Assessing phonological awareness in kindergarten children: Issues of task comparability. *Journal of Experimental Child Psychology, 38,* 175–190.

Stanovich, K. E., Cunningham, A. E., & Feeman, D. J. (1984). Relation between early reading acquisition and word decoding with and without context: A longitudinal study of first-grade children. *Journal of Educational Psychology, 76,* 668–677.

Stanovich, K. E., Cunningham, A. E., & West, R. F. (1981). A longitudinal study of the development of automatic recognition skills in first graders. *Journal of Reading Behavior, 13,* 57–74.

Stanovich, K. E., Feeman, D. J., & Cunningham, A. E. (1983). The development of the relation between letter-naming speed and reading ability. *Bulletin of the Psychonomic Society, 21,* 199–202.

Stanovich, K. E., Nathan, R. G., & Zolman, J. E. (1988). The developmental lag hypothesis in reading: Longitudinal and matched reading-level comparisons. *Child Development, 59,* 71–86.

Stanovich, K. E., & Siegel, L. S. (1994). Phenotypic performance profile of children with reading disabilities: A regression-based test of the phonological-core variable difference model. *Journal of Educational Psychology, 86,* 24–53.

Stanovich, K. E., Siegel, L. S., & Gottardo, A. (1997). Converging evidence for phonological and surface subtypes of reading disability. *Journal of Educational Psychology, 89,* 114–127.

Stanovich, K. E., & West, R. F. (1989). Exposure to print and orthographic processing. *Reading Research Quarterly, 24,* 402–433.

Stanovich, K. E., West, R. F., & Cunningham, A. E. (1991). Beyond phonological processes:

Print exposure and orthographic processing. In S. A. Brady & D. P. Shankweiler (Eds.), *Phonological processes in literacy: A tribute to Isabelle Y. Liberman* (pp. 219–235). Hillsdale, NJ: Erlbaum.

Stark, R. E., Bernstein, L. E., Condino, R., Bender, M., Tallal, P., & Catts, H. (1984). Four-year follow-up of language impaired children. *Annals of Dyslexia, 34*, 49–68.

Stemach, G., & Williams, W. B. (1988). *Word Express*. Novato, CA: Academic Therapy.

Sternberg, R. J., & Grigorenko, E. L. (2002). Difference scores in the identification of children with learning disabilities: It's time to use a different method. *Journal of School Psychology, 40*, 65–83.

Stevenson, H. W., & Newman, R. S. (1986). Long-term prediction of achievement and attitudes in mathematics and reading. *Child Development, 57*, 646–659.

Stinnett, T. A., Havey, J. M., & Oehler-Stinnett, J. (1994). Current test usage by practicing school psychologists: A national survey. *Journal of Psychoeducational Assessment, 12*, 331–350.

Stockman, I. J. (2000). The new Peabody Picture Vocabulary Test–III: An illusion of unbiased assessment? *Language, Speech, and Hearing Services in Schools, 31*, 340–353.

Stone, B., & Brady, S. (1995). Evidence for phonological processing deficits in less-skilled readers. *Annals of Dyslexia, 45*, 51–78.

Stothard, S. E., & Hulme, C. (1996). A comparison of reading comprehension and decoding difficulties in children. In C. Cornoldi & J. Oakhill (Eds.), *Reading comprehension difficulties: Processes and intervention* (pp. 93–112). Mahwah, NJ: Erlbaum.

Stuart, M. (1995). Prediction and qualitative assessment of five- and six-year-old children's reading: A longitudinal study. *British Journal of Educational Psychology, 65*, 287–296.

Suen, H. K. (1990). *Principles of test theories*. Hillsdale, NJ: Erlbaum.

Swan, D., & Goswami, U. (1997). Phonological awareness deficits in developmental dyslexia and the phonological representations hypothesis. *Journal of Experimental Child Psychology, 66*, 18–41.

Swank, L. K., & Catts, H. W. (1994). Phonological awareness and written word decoding. *Language, Speech, and Hearing Services in Schools, 25*, 9–14.

Tallal, P. (1984). Temporal or phonetic processing deficit in dyslexia?: That is the question. *Applied Psycholinguistics, 5*, 167–169.

Tan, A., & Nicholson, T. (1997). Flashcards revisited: Training poor readers to read words faster improves their comprehension of text. *Journal of Educational Psychology, 89*, 276–288.

Tangel, D. M., & Blachman, B. A. (1992). Effect of phoneme awareness instruction on kindergarten children's invented spelling. *Journal of Reading Behavior, 24*, 233–261.

Tangel, D. M., & Blachman, B. A. (1995). Effect of phoneme awareness instruction on the invented spelling of first-grade children: A one-year follow-up. *Journal of Reading Behavior, 27*, 153–185.

Taylor, H. G., Anselmo, M., Foreman, A. L., Schatschneider, C., & Angelopoulos, J. (2000). Utility of kindergarten teacher judgments in identifying early learning problems. *Journal of Learning Disabilities, 33*, 200–210.

Taylor, N. E., & Blum, I. H. (1980). *Written Language Awareness Test–Experimental Edition*. Washington, DC: Catholic University.

Taylor, S. E., Frackenpohl, H., White, C., Nieroroda, B., Browning, C., & Birsner, E. (1989). *EDL core vocabularies in reading, mathematics, science, and social studies* (7th ed.) Austin, TX: Steck-Vaughn.

Teisl, J. T., Mazzocco, M. M. M., & Myers, G. F. (2001). The utility of kindergarten teacher ratings for predicting low academic achievement in first grade. *Journal of Learning Disabilities, 34*, 286–293.

Templeton, S., & Bear, D. R. (Eds.). (1992). *Development of orthographic knowledge and the foundations of literacy: A memorial festschrift for Edmund H. Henderson*. Hillsdale, NJ: Erlbaum.

Texas Education Agency. (1991). *Norm-Referenced Assessment Program for Texas.* Itasca, IL: Riverside.

Texas Education Agency. (1992). *Texas Assessment of Academic Skills.* San Antonio, TX: Harcourt Brace.

Thorndike, E. L., & Lorge, I. (1963). *The teacher's word book of 30,000 words.* New York: Teachers College Press, Columbia University.

Thorndike, R. M., Hagen, E. P., & Sattler, J. M. (1986). *Stanford–Binet Intelligence Scale–Fourth Edition.* Chicago: Riverside.

Thorndike, R. M. (1999). IRT and intelligence testing: Past, present, and future. In S. E. Embretson & S. L. Hershberger (Eds.), *The new rules of measurement: What every psychologist and educator should know* (pp. 17–35). Mahwah, NJ: Erlbaum.

Tindal, G., & Hasbrouck, J. E. (1991). Analyzing student writing to develop instructional strategies. *Learning Disabilities Research and Practice, 6,* 237–245.

Tindal, G., Marston, D., & Deno, S. L. (1983). *The reliability of direct and repeated measurement* (Research Report No. 109). Minneapolis: University of Minnesota Institute for Research on Learning Disabilities.

Tomblin, J. B., Zhang, X., Buckwalter, P., & Catts, H. (2000). The association of reading disability, behavioral disorders, and language impairment among second-grade children. *Journal of Child Psychology and Psychiatry, 41,* 473–482.

Torgesen, J. K. (1996). A model of memory from an information processing perspective: The special case of phonological memory. In G. R. Lyon & N. A. Krasnegor (Eds.), *Attention, memory, and executive function* (pp. 157–184). Baltimore: Brookes.

Torgesen, J. K. (1998, Spring–Summer). Catch them before they fail. *American Educator,* pp. 32–39.

Torgesen, J. K. (1999). Assessment and instruction for phonemic awareness and word recognition skills. In H. W. Catts & A. G. Kamhi (Eds.), *Language and reading disabilities* (pp. 128–153). Needham Heights, MA: Allyn & Bacon.

Torgesen, J. K. (2000). Individual differences in response to early interventions in reading: The lingering problem of treatment resisters. *Learning Disabilities Research and Practice, 15,* 55–64.

Torgesen, J. K. (2002a). Empirical and theoretical support for direct diagnosis of learning disabilities by assessment of intrinsic processing weaknesses. In R. Bradley, L. Danielson, & D. P. Hallahan (Eds.), *The identification of learning disabilities: Research to practice* (pp. 565–613). Mahwah, NJ: Erlbaum.

Torgesen, J. K. (2002b). The prevention of reading difficulties. *Journal of School Psychology, 40,* 7–26.

Torgesen, J. K., Alexander, A. W., Wagner, R. K., Rashotte, C. A., Voeller, K. K. S., & Conway, T. (2001). Intensive remedial instruction for children with severe reading disabilities: Immediate and long-term outcomes from two instructional approaches. *Journal of Learning Disabilities, 34,* 33–58, 78.

Torgesen, J. K., & Bryant, B. R. (1994a). *Phonological awareness training for reading.* Austin, TX: PRO-ED.

Torgesen, J. K., & Bryant, B. R. (1994b). *Test of Phonological Awareness.* Austin, TX: PRO-ED.

Torgesen, J. K., & Burgess, S. R. (1998). Consistency of reading-related phonological processes throughout early childhood: Evidence from longitudinal–correlational and instructional studies. In J. L. Metsala & L. C. Ehri (Eds.), *Word recognition in beginning literacy* (pp. 161–188). Mahwah, NJ: Erlbaum.

Torgesen, J. K., & Davis, C. (1996). Individual difference variables that predict response to training in phonological awareness. *Journal of Experimental Child Psychology, 63,* 1–21.

Torgesen, J. K., & Houck, D. G. (1980). Processing deficiencies in learning-disabled children who perform poorly on the Digit Span task. *Journal of Educational Psychology, 72,* 141–160.

Torgesen, J. K., & Mathes, P. G. (2000). *A basic guide to understanding, assessing, and teaching phonological awareness.* Austin, TX: PRO-ED.

Torgesen, J. K., Morgan, S. T., & Davis, C. (1992). Effects of two types of phonological awareness training on word learning in kindergarten children. *Journal of Educational Psychology, 84*, 364–370.

Torgesen, J. K., Rashotte, C. A., & Alexander, A. W. (2001). Principles of fluency instruction in reading: Relationships with established empirical outcomes. In M. Wolf (Ed.), *Dyslexia, fluency, and the brain* (pp. 333–355). Timonium, MD: York Press.

Torgesen, J. K., & Wagner, R. K. (1998). Alternative diagnostic approaches for specific developmental reading disabilities. *Learning Disabilities Research and Practice, 13*, 220–232.

Torgesen, J. K., Wagner, R. K., & Rashotte, C. A. (1994). Longitudinal studies of phonological processing and reading. *Journal of Learning Disabilities, 27*, 276–286.

Torgesen, J. K., Wagner, R. K., & Rashotte, C. A. (1997). Prevention and remediation of severe reading disabilities: Keeping the end in mind. *Scientific Studies of Reading, 1*, 217–234.

Torgesen, J. K., Wagner, R. K., & Rashotte, C. A. (1999). *Test of Word Reading Efficiency*. Austin, TX: PRO-ED.

Torgesen, J. K., Wagner, R. K., Rashotte, C. A., Alexander, A. W., & Conway, T. (1997). Preventive and remedial interventions for children with severe reading disabilities. *Learning Disabilities: A Multidisciplinary Journal, 8*, 51–61.

Torgesen, J. K., Wagner, R. K., Rashotte, C. A., Burgess, S., & Hecht, S. (1997). Contributions of phonological awareness and rapid automatic naming ability to the growth of word-reading skills in second- to fifth-grade children. *Scientific Studies of Reading, 1*, 161–185.

Torgesen, J. K., Wagner, R. K., Rashotte, C. A., Rose, E., Lindamood, P., Conway, T., et al. (1999). Preventing reading failure in young children with phonological processing disabilities: Group and individual responses to instruction. *Journal of Educational Psychology, 91*, 579–593.

Torgesen, J. K., Wagner, R. K., Simmons, K., & Laughon, P. (1990). Identifying phonological coding problems in disabled readers: Naming, counting, or span measures? *Learning Disability Quarterly, 13*, 236–243.

Tracey, T. J. G., & Glidden-Tracey, C. E. (1999). Integration of theory, research design, measurement, and analysis: Toward a reasoned argument. *The Counseling Psychologist, 27*, 299–324.

Traub, R. E., & Rowley, G. L. (1991). Understanding reliability. *Educational Measurement: Issues and Practice, 10*, 37–45.

Trieman, R. (1997). Spelling in normal children and dyslexics. In B. A. Blachman (Ed.), *Foundations of reading acquisition and dyslexia: Implications for early intervention* (pp. 191–218). Mahwah, NJ: Erlbaum.

Treiman, R., & Broderick, V. (1998). What's in a name?: Children's knowledge about the letters in their own names. *Journal of Experimental Child Psychology, 70*, 97–116.

Treiman, R., Goswami, U., & Bruck, M. (1990). Not all nonwords are alike: Implications for reading development and theory. *Memory and Cognition, 18*, 559–567.

Treiman, R., & Rodriguez, K. (1999). Young children use letter names in learning to read words. *Psychological Science, 10*, 334–338.

Treiman, R., Sotak, L., & Bowman, M. (2001). The roles of letter names and letter sounds in connecting print and speech. *Memory and Cognition, 29*, 860–873.

Trieman, R., Tincoff, R., & Richmond-Welty, E. D. (1996). Letter names help children to connect print and speech. *Developmental Psychology, 32*, 505–514.

Treiman, R., Tincoff, R., Rodriguez, K., Mouzaki, A., & Francis, D. J. (1998). The foundations of literacy: Learning the sounds of letters. *Child Development, 69*, 1524–1540.

Tunmer, W. E. (1989). The role of language-related factors in reading disability. In D. P. Shankweiler & I. Y. Liberman (Eds.), *Phonology and reading disability: Solving the reading puzzle* (pp. 91–131). Ann Arbor: University of Michigan Press.

Tunmer, W. E., Herriman, M. L, & Nesdale, A. R. (1988). Metalinguistic abilities and beginning reading. *Reading Research Quarterly, 23*, 134–158.

Tunmer, W. E., & Hoover, W. A. (1992). Cognitive and linguistic factors in learning to read. In P. B. Gough, L. C. Ehri, & R. Treiman (Eds.), *Reading acquisition* (pp. 175–214). Hillsdale, NJ: Erlbaum.

Uhry, J. K., & Shepherd, M. J. (1997). Teaching phonological recoding to young children with phonological processing deficits: The effect on sight-vocabulary acquisition. *Learning Disability Quarterly, 20,* 104–125.

Ukrainetz, T. A., & Duncan, D. S. (2000). From old to new: Examining score increases on the Peabody Picture Vocabulary Test–III. *Language, Speech, and Hearing Services in Schools, 31,* 336–339.

Van Orden, G. C., Pennington, B. F., & Stone, G. O. (1990). Word identification in reading and the promise of subsymbolic psycholinguistics. *Psychological Review, 97,* 488–452.

Vellutino, F. R. (1979). *Dyslexia: Theory and research.* Cambridge, MA: MIT Press.

Vellutino, F. R., & Scanlon, D. M. (1987). Phonological coding, phonological awareness, and reading ability: Evidence from a longitudinal and experimental study. *Merrill–Palmer Quarterly, 33,* 321–363.

Vellutino, F. R., & Scanlon, D. M. (1991). The preeminence of phonologically based skills in learning to read. In S. A. Brady & D. P. Shankweiler (Eds.). *Phonological processes in literacy: A tribute to Isabelle Y. Liberman* (pp. 237–252). Hillsdale, NJ: Erlbaum.

Vellutino, F. R., Scanlon, D. M., & Chen, R. (1994). The increasingly inextricable relationship between orthographic and phonological coding in learning to read: Some reservations about current methods of operationalizing orthographic coding. In V. W. Berninger (Ed.), *The varieties of orthographic knowledge II: Relationships to phonology, reading, and writing* (pp. 47–111). Dordrecht, The Netherlands: Kluwer Academic.

Vellutino, F. R., Scanlon, D. M., & Lyon, G. R. (2000). Differentiating between difficult-to-remediate and readily remediated poor readers: More evidence against the IQ–achievement discrepancy definition of reading disability. *Journal of Learning Disabilities, 33,* 223–238.

Vellutino, F. R., Scanlon, D. M., Sipay, E. R., Small, S. G., Pratt, A., Chen, R., et al. (1996). Cognitive profiles of difficult-to-remediate and readily remediated poor readers: Early intervention as a vehicle for distinguishing between cognitive and experiential deficits as basic causes of specific reading disability. *Journal of Educational Psychology, 88,* 601–638.

Vellutino, F. R., Scanlon, D. M., & Sipay, E. R. (1997). Toward distinguishing between cognitive and experiential deficits as primary sources of difficulty in learning to read: The importance of early intervention in diagnosing specific reading disability. In B. A. Blachman (Ed.), *Foundations of reading acquisition and dyslexia: Implications for early intervention* (pp. 347–379). Mahwah, NJ: Erlbaum.

Vellutino, F. R., Scanlon, D. M., & Spearing, D. (1995). Semantic and phonological coding in poor and normal readers. *Journal of Experimental Child Psychology, 59,* 76–123.

Vellutino, F. R., Scanlon, D. M., & Tanzman, M. S. (1994). Components of reading ability: Issues and problems in operationalizing word identification, phonological coding, and orthographic coding. In G. R. Lyon (Ed.), *Frames of reference for the assessment of learning disabilities* (pp. 279–332). Baltimore: Brookes.

Vellutino, F. R., Scanlon, D. M., & Tanzman, M. S. (1998). The case for early intervention in diagnosing specific reading disabilities. *Journal of School Psychology, 36,* 367–397.

Verhoeven, L. (2000). Components in early second language reading and spelling. *Scientific Studies of Reading, 4,* 313–330.

Waber, D. P. (2001). Aberrations in timing in children with impaired reading: Cause, effect, or correlate? In M. Wolf (Ed.), *Dyslexia, fluency, and the brain* (pp. 103–125). Timonium, MD: York Press.

Waber, D., Wolff, P. H., Forbes, P. W., & Weiler, M. D. (2001). Rapid automatized naming in children referred for evaluation of heterogeneous learning problems: How specific are naming speed deficits to reading disability? *Child Neuropsychology, 6,* 251–261.

Wagner, R. K., Balthazor, M., Hurley, S., Morgan, S., Rashotte, C., Shaner, R., et al. (1987). The nature of prereaders' phonological processing abilities. *Cognitive Development, 2,* 355–373.

Wagner, R. K., & Barker, T. A. (1994). The development of orthographic processing ability. In V. W. Berninger (Ed.), *The varieties of orthographic knowledge I: Theoretical and developmental issues* (pp. 243–276). Dordrecht, The Netherlands: Kluwer Academic.

Wagner, R. K., & Torgesen, J. K. (1987). The nature of phonological processing and its causal role in the acquisition of reading skills. *Psychological Bulletin, 101,* 192–212.

Wagner, R. K., Torgesen, J. K., Laughon, P., Simmons, K., & Rashotte, C. A. (1993). Development of young readers' phonological processing abilities. *Journal of Educational Psychology, 85,* 83–103.

Wagner, R. K., Torgesen, J. K., & Rashotte, C. (1994). Development of reading-related phonological processing abilities: New evidence of bi-directional causality from a latent variable longitudinal study. *Developmental Psychology, 30,* 73–87.

Wagner, R. K., Torgesen, J. K., & Rashotte, C. A. (1999). *Comprehensive Test of Phonological Processing.* Austin, TX: PRO-ED.

Wagner, R. K., Torgesen, J. K., Rashotte, C. A., Hecht, S. A., Barker, T. A., Burgess, S. R., et al. (1997). Changing relations between phonological processing abilities and word-level reading as children develop from beginning to fluent readers: A 5-year longitudinal study. *Developmental Psychology, 33,* 468–479.

Walsh, D. J., Price, G. G., & Gillingham, M. G. (1988). The critical but transitory importance of letter naming. *Reading Research Quarterly, 23,* 108–122.

Washington, J. A., & Craig, H. K. (1992). Performances of low-income, African American preschool and kindergarten children on the Peabody Picture Vocabulary Test–Revised. *Language, Speech, and Hearing Services in Schools, 23,* 329–333.

Washington, J. A., & Craig, H. K. (1999). Performances of at-risk, African American preschoolers on the Peabody Picture Vocabulary Test–III. *Language, Speech, and Hearing Services in Schools, 30,* 75–82.

Watkinson, J. T., & Lee, S. W. (1992). Curriculum-based measures of written expression for learning-disabled and nondisabled students. *Psychology in the Schools, 29,* 184–191.

Webster, R. E., & Braswell, L. A. (1991). Curriculum bias and reading achievement test performance. *Psychology in the Schools, 28,* 193–199.

Wechsler, D. (1974). *Wechsler Intelligence Scale for Children–Revised.* San Antonio, TX: Psychological Corporation.

Wechsler, D. (1989). *Wechsler Preschool and Primary Scale of Intelligence–Revised.* San Antonio, TX: Psychological Corporation.

Wechsler, D. (1991). *Wechsler Intelligence Scale for Children–Third Edition.* San Antonio, TX: Psychological Corporation.

Wechsler, D. (1997). *Wechsler Adult Intelligence Scale–Third Edition.* San Antonio, TX: Psychological Corporation.

Whitehurst, G. J., & Lonigan, C. J. (1998). Child development and emergent literacy. *Child Development, 69,* 848–872.

Wickes, K., & Slate, J. R. (1999). Math and reading tests: Dissimilar scores provided by similar tests for African-American students. *Research in the Schools, 6,* 41–45.

Wiederholt, J. L. (1986). *Formal Reading Inventory.* Austin, TX: PRO-ED.

Wiederholt, J. L., & Blalock, G. (2000). *Gray Silent Reading Tests.* Austin, TX: PRO-ED.

Wiederholt, J. L., & Bryant, B. R. (1986). *Gray Oral Reading Tests–Revised.* Austin, TX: PRO-ED.

Wiederholt, J. L., & Bryant, B. R. (1992). *Gray Oral Reading Tests–Third Edition.* Austin, TX: PRO-ED.

Wiederholt, J. L., & Bryant, B. R. (2001). *Gray Oral Reading Tests–Fourth Edition.* Austin, TX: PRO-ED.

Williams, K. T. (1997). *Expressive Vocabulary Test.* Circle Pines, MN: American Guidance Service.

Williams, K. T. (1998). Peabody Picture Vocabulary Test–III: What is new and different? *Clinical Connection, 11*(3), 6–8.

Williams, K. T. (2002). *Group Reading Assessment and Diagnostic Evaluation.* Circle Pines, MN: American Guidance Service.

Williams, K. T., & Wang, J. (1997). *Technical references to the Peabody Picture Vocabulary Test–Third Edition (PPVT-III).* Circle Pines, MN: American Guidance Service.

Wilkinson, G. S. (1993). *Wide Range Achievement Test–Third Edition.* Wilmington, DE: Jastak Associates.

Wilson, M. S., & Reschly, D. J. (1996). Assessment in school psychology: Training and practice. *School Psychology Review, 25,* 9–23.

Wimmer, H. (1993). Characteristics of developmental dyslexia in a regular writing system. *Applied Psycholinguistics, 14,* 1–33.

Wise, B. W., Ring, J., & Olson, R. K. (1999). Training phonological awareness with and without explicit attention to articulation. *Journal of Experimental Child Psychology, 72,* 271–304.

Wolf, M. (1986). Rapid alternating stimulus naming in the developmental dyslexias. *Brain and Language,* 27, 360–379.

Wolf, M. (1991a). Naming speed and reading: The contribution of the cognitive neurosciences. *Reading Research Quarterly, 26,* 123–141.

Wolf, M. (1991b). The word-retrieval deficit hypothesis and developmental dyslexia. *Learning and Individual Differences. 3,* 205–223.

Wolf, M. (1999). What time may tell: Towards a new conceptualization of developmental dyslexia. *Annals of Dyslexia, 49,* 3–29.

Wolf, M. (Ed.). (2001). *Dyslexia, fluency, and the brain.* Timonium, MD: York Press.

Wolf, M., Bally, H., & Morris, R. (1986). Automaticity, retrieval processes, and reading: A longitudinal study in average and impaired readers. *Child Development, 57,* 988–1000.

Wolf, M., & Bowers, P. G. (1999). The double-deficit hypothesis for the developmental dyslexias. *Journal of Educational Psychology, 91,* 415–438.

Wolf, M., Bowers, P. G., & Biddle, K. (2000). Naming-speed processes, timing, and reading: A conceptual review. *Journal of Learning Disabilities, 33,* 387–407.

Wolf, M., & Katzir-Cohen, T. (2001). Reading fluency and its intervention. *Scientific Studies of Reading, 5,* 211–238.

Wood, F. B., & Felton, R. H. (1994). Separate linguistic and attentional factors in the development of reading. *Topics in Language Disorders, 14*(4), 42–57.

Woodcock, R. W. (1973). *Woodcock Reading Mastery Tests.* Circle Pines, MN: American Guidance Service.

Woodcock, R. W. (1987). *Woodcock Reading Mastery Tests–Revised.* Circle Pines, MN: American Guidance Service.

Woodcock, R. W. (1987/1998). *Woodcock Reading Mastery Tests–Revised/Normative Update.* Circle Pines, MN: American Guidance Service.

Woodcock, R. W. (1997). *Woodcock Diagnostic Reading Battery.* Itasca, IL: Riverside.

Woodcock, R. W., & Johnson, M. B. (1977). *Woodcock-Johnson Psycho-Educational Battery.* Allen, TX: DLM Teaching Resources.

Woodcock, R. W., & Johnson, M. B. (1989). *Woodcock-Johnson Psycho-Educational Battery–Revised.* Allen, TX: DLM Teaching Resources.

Woodcock, R. W., McGrew, K. S., & Mather, N. (2001a). *Woodcock-Johnson III.* Itasca, IL: Riverside.

Woodcock, R. W., McGrew, K. S., & Mather, N. (2001b). *Woodcock-Johnson III Tests of Achievement.* Itasca, IL: Riverside.

Woodcock, R. W., McGrew, K. S., & Mather, N. (2001c). *Woodcock-Johnson III Tests of Cognitive Abilities.* Itasca, IL: Riverside.

Worden, P. E., & Boettcher, W. (1990). Young children's acquisition of alphabet knowledge. *Journal of Reading Behavior, 22,* 277–295.

Wyatt, T. A., & Seymour, H. N. (1999). Assessing the speech and language skills of preschool children. In E. V. Nuttall, I. Romero, & J. Kalesnik (Eds.), *Assessing and screening preschoolers: Psychological and educational dimensions* (2nd ed., pp. 218–239). Needham Heights, MA: Allyn & Bacon.

Yopp, H. K. (1988). The validity and reliability of phonemic awareness tests. *Reading Research Quarterly, 23,* 159–177.

Yopp, H. K. (1992). Developing phonemic awareness in young children. *The Reading Teacher, 45,* 696–703.

Yopp, H. K. (1995a). Read-aloud books for developing phonemic awareness: An annotated bibliography. *The Reading Teacher, 48,* 538–542.

Yopp, H. K. (1995b). A test for assessing phonemic awareness in young children. *The Reading Teacher, 49,* 20–29.

Yopp, H. K., & Yopp, R. H. (1997). *Oo-pples and boo-noo-noos: Songs and activities for phonemic awareness.* Orlando, FL: Harcourt Brace.

Young, A., & Bowers, P. G. (1995). Individual difference and text difficulty determinants of reading fluency and expressiveness. *Journal of Experimental Child Psychology, 60,* 428–454.

Author Index

Subject Index

f indicates figure, *t* indicates table, boldface indicates test reviewed.